Proletarian Imagination

PROLETARIAN IMAGINATION

Self, Modernity, and the
Sacred in Russia, 1910–1925

MARK D. STEINBERG

Cornell University Press

ITHACA AND LONDON

First published 2002 by Cornell University Press
First printing, Cornell Paperbacks, 2002

Printed in the United States of America

Library of Congress Cataloging-in-Publication Data

Steinberg, Mark D., 1953–
    Proletarian imagination : self, modernity, and the sacred in Russia, 1910–1925 / Mark D. Steinberg.
        p.   cm.
Includes bibliographical references and index.
        ISBN 0-8014-4005-X (cloth : alk. paper)—ISBN 0-8014-8826-5 (pbk. : alk. paper)
    1. Russian literature—20th century—History and criticism.   2. Working class writings, Russian—History and criticism.   3. Self in literature.   4. Holy, The, in literature.   5. Working class authors—Soviet Union.   6. Working class authors—Russia.   7. Working class—Soviet Union—Intellectual life.   8. Working class—Russia—Intellectual life.   I. Title.
PG3026.L3 S74   2002
891.709'920623—dc21   2002003313

Cornell University Press strives to use environmentally responsible suppliers and materials to the fullest extent possible in the publishing of its books. Such materials include vegetable-based, low-VOC inks and acid-free papers that are recycled, totally chlorine-free, or partly composed of nonwood fibers. For further information, visit our website at www.cornellpress.cornell.edu.

Cloth printing   10 9 8 7 6 5 4 3 2 1

Paperback printing   10 9 8 7 6 5 4 3 2 1

For Jane and Sasha

Contents

Illustrations

Acknowledgments

I thank first my colleagues at the University of Illinois, who have offered me not only wise counsel and criticism of many of these chapters but an exceptionally stimulating intellectual environment in which to work. I have benefited especially from discussions with Diane Koenker and Peter Fritzsche (exemplary scholars as well as ideal colleagues and friends) and with participants in the history workshop, the Cultural Studies Group, the interdisciplinary faculty seminar on the "Stranger," the seminar of the Program for Cultural Values and Ethics, the seminar and conference on cities sponsored by the Illinois Program for Research in the Humanities (led by Michael Berubé), and the Russian and East European Center. I am also grateful to colleagues at Yale University, where this project began. Katerina Clark, one of the best cultural historians of modern Russia, read early drafts of a couple of these chapters, offering insightful comments. Vladimir Alexandrov, Ivo Banac, Paul Bushkovitch, Victor Erlich, Michael Holquist, Susan Larsen, John Merriman, Jaroslav Pelikan, and James C. Scott were responsible for many of the conversations that influenced this book. In addition, I have benefited greatly from comments on my work by Barbara Engel, Stephen Frank, Jane Hedges, Catriona Kelly, Anna Krylova, Bernice Glatzer Rosenthal, Barbara Walker, James von Geldern, the anonymous readers chosen by Cornell University Press, and the participants in numerous conferences and workshops: the St. Petersburg conference on workers and intelligentsia in 1995; the conference "Inventing the Soviet Union" in Bloomington, Indiana, in 1997; the conference "Revolution and the Making of Modern Identity" in Tel Aviv in 1999; the Midwest Russian History Workshop; the University of Chicago Russian Studies Workshop; and annual meetings of the American Association for the Advancement of Slavic Studies. For essential research assistance I am grateful to Marjorie Hilton, Greg Kveberg, and Susan Smith, as well as to Valerii Brun-Tsekhovoi and Larisa Brun-Tsekhovaia in Moscow. I also express my appreciation to the many students in my courses on Russian history and on comparative popular and lower-class cultures who have taught me much in energetic discussions about so many of the questions explored in this book. I must also thank those who first taught me Russian history and culture. Although it may seem long ago, their influence on this work can still be felt: John Ackerman, Peter Kenez, Victoria Bonnell, Grigory Freidin, Reginald Zelnik, Nicholas Riasanovsky, and Martin Malia. At Cornell University Press, I am very grateful to John Ackerman for his encouragement, blunt criticism, and advice. Barbara Salazar did much to improve the readability and clarity of this book with her exceptionally sensitive and intelligent editing. Ange Romeo-Hall contributed in many ways to helping this book on its path to print. Richard Miller prepared the index.

Essential support for research travel and academic leave time was provided by the National Endowment for the Humanities, the International Research and Exchanges Board, the University of Illinois Research Board, the College of Liberal Arts and Sciences of the University of Illinois, the Illinois Program for Research in the Humanities, the Program for the Study of Cultural Values and Ethics, the Yale Center for International and Area Studies, and Yale University. I could not have written this book without their help.

Finally, I am pleased to be able publicly to thank and dedicate this work to my family, Jane and Sasha, for their great forbearance and love.

Archives Cited in the Notes

Arkhiv A. M. Gor'kogo	Maxim Gorky Archive, Institute for World Literature, Moscow
GARF	Gosudarstvennyi arkhiv Rossiiskoi Federatsii (State Archive of the Russian Federation) (formerly TsGAOR), Moscow
RGALI	Rossiiskii gosudarstvennyi arkhiv literatury i isskustva (Russian State Archive of Literature and Art) (formerly TsGALI), Moscow
RGASPI	Rossiiskii gosudarstvennyi arkhiv sotsial'no-politicheskoi istorii (Russian State Archive of Social and Political History) (formerly TsPA IML), Moscow

Proletarian Imagination

Introduction

The imaginary . . . is constitutive of man, no less certainly than
everyday experience and practical activities.
—MIRCEA ELIADE

Self-consciousness . . . is the demon of the man of genius in our time
. . . providing so much of its cheerful and its mournful wisdom.
—JOHN STUART MILL

This is a book about particular, even odd, historical subjects: working-class Russians with little or no formal education who wrote poetry, fiction, and other creative texts.[1] These workers did more than just occasionally put down a few lines of poetry or prose. They wrote with a determination and persistence that justifies our calling them writers. And they wrote less to create "art" than to speak aloud about the world—about the everyday life around them and about the extraordinary, about the meaning of existence, and about themselves. Their world—Russia during the final years of the tsarist order and the first years of the Soviet era, but also the larger world of modern Europe as seen from its most unstable boundary—was one of enormous ferment and flux. The years in focus here, roughly 1910 to 1925, extend from a period of complex stasis after the revolutionary upheavals of 1905–7 and the establishment of a partially reformed political order, through a time of world war and revolution followed by bloody civil conflict, into the first unstable years of socialist experimentation and construction. These were whirlwind years in which very little seemed clear or certain, though a great deal seemed possible.

These individuals stood in a special relation to their times. As worker authors, even proletarian intellectuals—a hybridity full of the unease and power

---

[1] More precisely, I have focused on individuals who began writing before 1917, while still employed in wage-earning jobs, whose work found its way into print (even if much remained unpublished), and who lived and were active in the predominantly Russian regions of the empire.

we have come to associate with liminal social identities—they moved about on sensitive borders of social and cultural meaning. They inhabited, negotiated, and often challenged the unstable social and cultural boundaries between classes and categories: between manual and intellectual labor, between making things and creating ideas, between producing and possessing culture and consuming it. From this vantage point, their voices offer rare insights into many of the social dynamics and strains of the time. No less important, unlike most lower-class Russians, they had the ability and the determination to put their thoughts and feelings into writing, leaving us an exceptionally rich record of their efforts to make sense of their world and to define themselves. They did not approach these questions innocently, of course. Their thinking was constructed not only from everyday experiences but also from an available cultural language (found in old stories, modern literature, the daily press, and conversation) that brought to them usable symbols, images, ideas, and sentiments. In these complex dialogues with the surrounding culture and with their own social lives, these individuals offer a compelling and complex view of a society and individual lives in ferment.

These plebeian authors engaged many of the key cultural issues of their day—questions about how Russians interpreted their own lives that historians are still only beginning to explore in any depth. At the same time, as many of these worker writers themselves well understood, these were issues not just of their own time—or, for that matter, place. Worker writers grappled with the problem of culture—as a standard to define, a measurement and tool to deploy, and an ideal to which to aspire. Ethics and morals preoccupied them— as sweeping, even universal, standards of right and wrong that could be applied to all of political and social life, but also as a matter of personal behavior and individual choices. And power was never ignored—whether it was the cultural power to define truth (universal moral truth, for example) or the existential power to determine one's own fate and being. As they engaged these questions, particular themes loomed especially large. Three of these often troubling questions about existential meaning and purpose were especially preoccupying: the self, modernity, and the sacred. These themes have given this book its shape.

Self

Notwithstanding stereotypes about the essential collectivism of the Russian cultural mentality, concerns with the self and its social and moral meanings have a long history in Russian culture and pervaded Russia's flourishing civic life in the final decades of the old order and into the early Soviet years.[2] Ple-

---

[2] Some of the first sustained scholarly inquiries into this important theme were brought together in a conference and then a collection of essays on narratives of the self in Russian history and literature: Laura Engelstein and Stephanie Sandler, eds., *Self and Story in Russian History* (Ithaca, 2000). For a sophisticated if somewhat idiosyncratic discussion of the concept of self in

beian Russian authors were no less preoccupied with these questions. The idea of the self, in Russia as in much of the modern world, has been a potent category with which people have thought and acted, and which they have invoked as they grappled with such fundamental existential questions as identity, moral good, and truth. Conceptions of self, of course, are not universal. Shaped on the indeterminate terrain where the natural actions of the mind grapple with external worlds of experience and meaning (ranging from material life and political structures to cultural landscapes of language, imagery, and symbol), the self has been variously recognized, imagined, presented, and used. It is precisely this variability in the category of the self and of its dialogues with morality, identity, and ideas of truth that makes histories of this notion so revealing.

The idea of an interior and autonomous personhood, reflexively aware, actively self-fashioning, and by nature endowed with a universal humanity and dignity, is only one of a range of self concepts, though it is one that has had a powerful historical effect in shaping moral thinking and social and political reasoning in much of the modern world. While the introspective effort to know one's self is ancient, only in the last two or three centuries has the preoccupation with the self become characteristic and even popular; the nineteenth century in particular became, especially in the European world, "the age of introversion." This "century-long effort to map inner space," as Peter Gay has described it, nurtured art, literature, philosophy, and even science, and had important effects on the personal lives of individuals.[3] It also generated ethical conceptions that converted easily into political and social convictions. The notion of the inward self dignified by nature nurtured the very consequential view that every person possesses certain natural rights, not because of any particular status, situation, or role but simply by virtue of being human. We should not impute more cohesion or orderly progress to this particular history of self and morality than it had. It has been resisted even in its alleged Western European home by groups—early-modern villagers, for example—who refused to see the individual person as having any meaning apart from his or her connections to community and place or who saw the self as porous and changeable. Recent scholars have described other fractures in this supposedly coherent Western history of the self: ways, for example, in which culturally evolved notions of gender, of the nature and place of male and female, helped to construct different standards of selfhood and of the realized self. Some work has gone further and explored still more ambiguous and often quite dark histories of the self and self-awareness: in which selfhoods and ideas of self were profoundly shaped by feelings of anxiety, alienation, melancholy, and fear, and by the self's own leanings toward narcissism, deception, and irrational desire.[4]

Russian culture and practice, focused mainly on the Stalinist and later Soviet years, see Oleg Kharkhordin, *The Collective and the Individual in Russia: A Study of Practices* (Berkeley, 1999).

[3] Peter Gay, *The Naked Heart*, vol. 4 of *The Bourgeois Experience* (New York, 1995), 4.

[4] Influential studies in a variety of disciplines have explored varied self concepts and especially

The story I present here dwells on how the self has been imagined in Russian culture. I examine a plebeian version of a widespread discourse about human selfhood and human dignity, which helped worker writers (and many others) to articulate a moral challenge to subordination and exploitation. At the same time, these writers were often drawn to more elaborate and transcendent images of selfhood: images of the genius, the savior, the mythic hero, the Nietzschean superman. Even after the authoritative rise of an ideology of collectivism after 1917, we find persistent idealization of heroic individualities and persistent and often preoccupying concern with self-perfection and the inward emotional and moral world of the individual. No less apparent, however, was a darker narrative of self, highlighting the inescapability (but also suggesting the allure) of solitude, estrangement, suffering, and death—a vision of life's course and meaning as fundamentally tragic. These were often not competing perspectives or alternative choices. And as time passed—as individuals aged and the movements of history, especially the outcomes of the revolution, disappointed—the darker side tended to overshadow the transcendent. Often, though, the heroic and the tragic remained inseparable and ambiguously intertwined.

The ideas and images of the self in the writings of workers and former workers ask us to question our assumptions about what mattered to people in the past, especially common people. Among at least some Russian workers we find a rather subtle worldview that has less in common with the rigid categories of political ideology or even social history than with the concerns of moral philosophy. Though speaking from a very different time and place, Immanuel Kant came very close to describing the mentalities of many of these worker authors in his observations on the sublime. The sublime, in Kant's account, is an aesthetic and emotional view of the world that arises from a deep feeling of the beauty, dignity, and richness of human nature, of the human self, and blends a vision of great beauty with deep melancholy or even

---

the interrelations between the self, ideas about the self, and moral reasoning. Among works I have found most suggestive are (in order of publication) Jacques Rancière, *The Nights of Labor: The Workers' Dream in Nineteenth-Century France,* trans. John Drury (Philadelphia, 1989—originally published in French 1981); Clifford Geertz, "'From the Native's Point of View': On the Nature of Anthropological Understanding," in *Local Knowledge* (New York, 1983), 55–70; Natalie Zemon Davis, *The Return of Martin Guerre* (Cambridge, Mass., 1983); David Warren Sabean, *Power in the Blood: Popular Culture and Village Discourse in Early Modern Germany* (Cambridge, 1984); Michael Carrithers, Steven Collins, and Steven Lukes, eds., *The Category of the Person: Anthropology, Philosophy, History* (Cambridge, 1985); Charles Taylor, *Sources of the Self: The Making of Modern Identity* (Cambridge, Mass., 1989); Richard A. Shweder, *Thinking through Cultures: Expeditions in Cultural Psychology* (Cambridge Mass., 1991), 113–85; Roy Porter, ed., *Rewriting the Self: Histories from the Renaissance to the Present* (London, 1997). On gendered constructions of the self, see esp. Joan Scott, "Gender: A Useful Category of Historical Analysis," in her *Gender and the Politics of History* (New York, 1988), 28–50. Michel Foucault's work on the history of sexuality was focused strongly on the "constitution of the self" and the historical importance of ideas about the self in the "genealogy of ethics." See his *History of Sexuality,* esp. vol. 3, *The Care of the Self* (New York, 1986), and his interview in Hubert L. Dreyfus and Paul Rabinow, *Michel Foucault: Beyond Structuralism and Hermeneutics,* 2d ed. (Chicago, 1983), 229–52.

dread.[5] This was a mental and emotional orientation very familiar, sometimes painfully so, to many Russian worker writers.

Modernity

As city dwellers, proletarians, and often participants in revolution, worker writers felt the textures of modern life, as the expression had it, on their flesh. As we would expect, the physical and social life of the modern city and its industrial landscape of factories, machines, and wage labor helped give form to their thinking aloud about the modern. In doing this thinking and in inscribing thoughts in writing, however, they engaged not only the tangible realities of urban and industrial life but also an existing and ongoing public discourse about the meanings of the modern, especially of the characteristically modern spaces of city and industry. This cultural terrain heightened their sensitivity to the physical and social landscape even as the physical and the social continued to affect the way they thought about and used the ideas of others. Together, social and cultural experiences helped give their representations of the modern a distinct sensibility.

The city has long stood as one of the most potent symbols of human capacities and nature. As the largest and most enduring creation of human imagination and hands, and as the largest and most sustained locus of human association and interaction, the city has been seen as a marker of what humans are and of what they do. This signification has almost always been shaded with ambivalence. In old legends, epics, and utopias, cities (both actual and symbolic) appeared as places of exceptional but also contradictory meaning. Troy, Babel, Sodom, Babylon, and Rome were viewed as standing for human power, wisdom, creativity, and vision, but also for human presumption, perversion, and fated destruction. Images of the modern city restated this ambivalence with fresh intensity. Great modern cities such as London, Paris, Berlin, and New York have repeatedly been portrayed as sites of opportunity and peril, power and helplessness, vitality and decadence, creativity and perplexity. This contradictory face of the city has appeared so often in Western thought as to suggest an essential psychological and cultural anxiety about civilization and about its creators. Modernity, with its plenitude of human artifice and moral contradiction, poured salt on these wounds.

Modernity is an elusive category, not least because of its essential ambiguity. Only in part can modernity be defined by the processes and values of rationalistic and scientific modernization: by the modernizing project of administrative and aesthetic ordering of society and nature, by the driving will to modify and control the physical environment and social and economic re-

---

[5] Immanuel Kant, *Observations on the Feeling of the Beautiful and the Sublime,* trans. John T. Goldthwait (Berkeley, 1960), 47–67. Similarly, in writing about French worker philosophers in the mid–nineteenth century, Jacques Rancière wrote of those who felt the "melancholy of the infinite" (*Nights of Labor,* 109).

lationships with applied science and technology, by the vision of cities and machines as emblems of rationality, efficiency, and change.[6] Nor can modernity be defined solely by Charles Baudelaire's famous phrase "the ephemeral, the fugitive, the contingent,"[7] by the aesthetic and modernist vision of modernity as the cultural experience of disjuncture and ambiguity. Attempting to reconcile these contradictory aspects of the modern, Matei Calinescu, a literary theorist, has written of "two modernities." One modernity can be characterized by "the cult of reason," "the doctrine of progress, confidence in the beneficial possibilities of science and technology, [and] the concern with time." The other is an aesthetic modernity, repelled by the contemporary bourgeois applications of reason, science, and time and embracing instead a modernity of defiant rebellion, passion, and often an ambivalent and pessimistic vision of progress and the future.[8] The political theorist Marshall Berman has argued similarly that modernism in literature, art, and intellectual life embraced less the rationalizing and reordering drive of modernization than its dynamic disruption, chaos, and flux, though tempered by an essential, if sometimes faltering, faith that a new and better life (and beauty) would emerge from the maelstrom.[9]

Theorists of postmodernity have moved beyond these dualisms to recognize the multiple worlds of modernity: the pervasiveness of disjuncture and difference, shaped by, for example, gender, race, class, and locality; the centrality to the nature of modernity of the experiences of those on the bottom and at the margins; the varied rhythms of time, in which hybrid temporalities are marked not only by acceleration, newness, and innovation but also by continuity, repetition, and revival; and the variety of modernities over time and space.[10] Complicating the effort to define the modern, Zygmunt Bauman has emphasized the false and unsettling relation of modernity to its own contingency, flux, and uncertainty. Modernity, he argues, characteristically denied

[6] For an excellent discussion of the "high modernism" of the modern state, see James C. Scott, *Seeing like a State* (New Haven, 1998). Much of Michel Foucault's work describes the modernizing rise of systems and structures of power that subject individuals to ever greater surveillance and control. For a general discussion of Western models of modernity as modernization, see Michael Adas, *Machines as the Measure of Men: Science, Technology, and Ideologies of Western Dominance* (Ithaca, 1989), esp. 409–15. On the notion of "man as machine" in Western cultures since the Renaissance, see Bruce Mazlish, *The Fourth Discontinuity: The Co-evolution of Humans and Machines* (New Haven, 1993). See also Charles Beard's definition of the modern West as a "machine civilization": Charles Beard, ed., *Whither Mankind* (New York, 1928), 14–20.

[7] Charles Baudelaire, "The Painter of Modern Life" (1863), in *The Painter of Modern Life and Other Essays* (London, 1964), 13.

[8] Matei Calinescu, *Five Faces of Modernity* (Durham, 1987), esp. 10, 42, 48, 89, 90, 162. For discussion of Western models of modernization, see Adas, *Machines as the Measure of Men*, esp. 409–15.

[9] Marshall Berman, *All That Is Solid Melts into Air: The Experience of Modernity* (New York, 1982).

[10] Arjun Appadurai, *Modernity at Large* (Minneapolis, 1997); Paul Gilroy, *The Black Atlantic: Modernity and Double Consciousness* (Cambridge, Mass, 1993); Rita Felski, *The Gender of Modernity* (Cambridge, Mass, 1995) and *Doing Time: Feminist Theory and Postmodern Culture* (New York, 2000), chap. 2.

its own self and nature. Inherently critical, restless, and insatiable, modern culture paralleled a modern society that was in a constant state of upheaval, destruction, and instability. But it simultaneously struggled to overcome all these uncertainties: to disenchant the world by imposing the artifice of "meaning-legislating reason"; to embark on a never-ending flight from the natural wilderness; to struggle constantly for universality, homogeneity, and clarity, to "purge ambivalence." In a word, it was in the very nature of modernity to "live in and through self-deception," to engage in a constant denial—in the name of necessity, universality, scientific truth, certainty, and natural order—of the contingency, artifice, undecidability, provisionality, and ambivalence of its own making.[11] Modernity, I find, is most usefully defined by these contradictory and unstable dialogues, by the ambiguity (in the sense of unresolved contradiction) that stems from the interdependence of contingency and its denial, of positivist rationality and questioning iconoclasm, of disciplining repression and libidinal excess, of legibility and startling multiplicity, of faith in progress (even pleasure in change) and deep unease.

Modern cities exemplified the ambiguities of the modern. The rapid growth and industrial transformation of European and world cities since the eighteenth century provoked a flood of discourse in which modernity itself was at issue. By the middle of the nineteenth century, the most common and paradigmatic images of the city in European and American writing were deeply modern. The city was vital energy and constant flux ("moving chaos," in Baudelaire's phrase); a physical landscape of stone, cement, machines, and noise; a psychological terrain of loneliness and anxiety ("paved solitude," in Nathaniel Hawthorne's famous phrase); a site of mythic domination and existential alienation; a disorienting labyrinth where only fragments of the whole could ever be seen at one time.[12] These are modern images of the city, inspired by a modern way of seeing and apprehending the world as much as by the determinate forms and rhythms of that world. Historians of modern Europe have highlighted the ambiguities in these narratives of the modern: ambivalence about both unleashed individuality and the subordination of individualities; anxieties about the new roles women and others took on in the fluid

---

[11] Zygmunt Bauman, *Modernity and Ambivalence* (Ithaca, 1991) and *Intimations of Postmodernity* (London, 1992), esp. Introduction and chap. 9.

[12] For discussion of ideas and representations of the city in Western culture, see esp. Carl Schorske, "The Idea of the City in European Thought: Voltaire to Spengler," and Sylvia Thrupp, "The City as the Idea of Social Order," both in *The Historian and the City*, ed. Oscar Handlin and John Burchard (Cambridge, Mass., 1963), 95–114, 121–32; Lewis Mumford, "Utopia, the City, and the Machine," *Daedalus*, Spring 1965, 271–92; Philip Fisher, "City Matters: City Minds," in *The Worlds of Victorian Fiction*, ed. Jerome Buckley (Cambridge, Mass., 1975), 371–89; Burton Pike, *The Image of the City in Modern Literature* (Princeton, 1981); John H. Johnston, *The Poet and the City: A Study in Urban Perspectives* (Athens, Ga., 1984); David Harvey, *Consciousness and the Urban Experience: Studies in the History and Theory of Capitalist Urbanization* (Baltimore, 1985), esp. 180–206; Kristiaan Versluys, *The Poet in the City: Chapters in the Development of Urban Poetry in Europe and the United States (1800–1930)* (Tübingen, 1987); Graeme Gilloch, *Myth and Metropolis: Walter Benjamin and the City* (Cambridge, 1996); Susan Buck-Morss, *The Dialectics of Seeing: Walter Benjamin and the Arcades Project* (Cambridge, Mass., 1999).

public sphere of modern life; judgments of modern politics as both emancipatory and increasingly repressive; the allure of science and fears of science gone mad; and a new experience of time that simultaneously included faith in rapid progress, nostalgia, and an intensified vision of a coming end time. Of course, anxiety about change or about the human subject is neither new nor particularly modern. What is modern is the interdependence of these anxieties with contradictory feelings—with the simultaneous drive to rationalize and discipline, with delight in contingency and ambiguity—and the explicitness with which many people were conscious of all this contradiction.[13]

Russians shared deeply in these European experiences and visions of modernity, which were intensified by Russia's notorious and often obsessively self-aware "backwardness": by its lateness to embrace and experience industrialization, urbanization, and the contradictory drives of modern discipline and disorder. By the late nineteenth and early twentieth centuries, Russian literature and the Russian press were increasingly preoccupied by the fascinating vitality and sinister dangers of modern life; by, on the one hand, the lure of modernist simplification and scientific ordering of society, politics, and even the human personality and, on the other hand, the no less modernist allure of self-invention, subversion, and despair.[14]

Russian worker writers' encounters with the modern landscape were especially intimate and severe. Their necessarily indeterminate identities and experiences as simultaneously urban workers and creative writers gave their symbolic treatments of city, factory, and machine a particular shape and pathos. This was a sharply modern vision, especially in its ambiguity. City, factory, and machine remained stubbornly alien and malevolent even for those who vigorously embraced the industrial city's vitality, aesthetic beauty, and promise. Workers' writings combined a sense of freedom with feelings of regret and loss, self-discovery and self-fashioning with estrangement from one's own essential self, pleasure in the intoxicating rhythms and flux of urban industrial life with an often despairing sense of soulless cruelty. Some of these worker writers were quite explicit about the ambivalence of modernity as a place and time where "wonders grow into horrors and horrors into wonders," where "unexpected pains and joys . . . appear at every step."[15] Even the most intellectually subtle, however, did not find these contradictions anything but

---

[13] See esp. T. J. Clark, *The Painting of Modern Life* (Princeton, 1984); Judith Walkowitz, *City of Dreadful Delight: Narratives of Sexual Danger in Late Victorian London* (Chicago, 1992); Felski, *Gender of Modernity*; Peter Fritzsche, *Reading Berlin, 1900* (Cambridge, Mass., 1996).

[14] Only recently have historians begun to examine explicitly the complex culture of Russian modernity. See esp. Laura Engelstein, *The Keys to Happiness: Sex and the Search for Modernity in Fin-de-Siècle Russia* (Ithaca, 1992); Joan Neuberger, *Hooliganism: Crime, Culture, and Power in St. Petersburg, 1900–1914* (Berkeley, 1993); Roshanna Sylvester, "Crime, Masquerade, and Anxiety: The Public Creation of Middle-Class Identity in Pre-Revolutionary Odessa, 1912–1916," Ph.D. diss., Yale University, 1998. Literary studies of Russian modernism have been plentiful, though they have paid relatively little attention to the wider social and cultural settings. A major exception is Katerina Clark, *Petersburg, Crucible of Revolution* (Cambridge, Mass., 1995).

[15] N. Liashko, "O byte i literature perekhodnogo vremeni," *Kuznitsa*, no. 8 (April–September 1921), 29.

painful. This modernist frame of mind hesitated, alas, before a postmodern sensibility. These proletarian intellectuals took no pleasure in indeterminacy, paradox, or irony. They wanted to see the world with greater clarity, certainty, and faith. To their visible sorrow, they could not.

The Sacred

A feeling for the sacred—for the cultural field of images and stories that speak with a sense of awe and mystery of structures of meaning and power that reach beyond the known material world toward transcendent mythic qualities— was essential to these varied ways of making sense of modern life and of the inward self. In treating these themes, as in interpreting languages of self and modernity, we again face the challenge (this time with a vengeance) of trying to comprehend and describe clearly how people handled an elusive and ambiguous form of knowledge. But we cannot afford to neglect this knowledge and sensibility. A sense of the sacred in the world and in their own lives pervaded workers' writings.

Historians of modern Russia have begun to examine seriously the vital and complex place of religion, spirituality, and the sacred in Russian life, especially popular life. This subject, too long neglected for both political and methodological reasons, is now recognized as among the most important and compelling fields of study for understanding Russia's modern experience. During the decades before and after the turn of the century—including the early Soviet years—Russia experienced what has been called a religious renaissance, rich in variety and passion and full of complexity and contradiction. Many educated Russians, even on the political left, were attracted by religious idealism, Theosophy, Eastern religions, spirituality, mysticism, and the occult. Among the lower classes, too, though scholars have only begun to explore this history, one sees a renewed vigor and variety in religious life and spirituality.[16]

These studies have been influenced by research and theorizing about religion in other places, especially modern Western Europe, and other times. Par-

---

[16] Major works include Nicolas Zernov, *The Russian Religious Renaissance of the Twentieth Century* (New York, 1963); George L. Kline, *Religious and Anti-Religious Thought in Russia* (Chicago, 1968); Christopher Read, *Religion, Revolution and the Russian Intelligentsia, 1900–1912* (London, 1979); Maria Carlson, *"No Religion Higher than Truth": A History of the Theosophical Movement in Russia, 1875–1922* (Princeton, 1993); Vera Shevzov, "Popular Orthodoxy in Late Imperial Rural Russia," Ph.D. diss., Yale University, 1994; Catherine Evtukhov, *The Cross and the Sickle: Sergei Bulgakov and the Fate of Russian Religious Philosophy, 1890–1920* (Ithaca, 1997); Bernice Glatzer Rosenthal, ed., *The Occult in Russian and Soviet Culture* (Ithaca, 1997); Glennys Young, *Power and the Sacred in Revolutionary Russia: Religious Activists in the Village* (University Park, Pa., 1997); Daniel Peris, *Storming the Heavens: The Soviet League of the Militant Godless* (Ithaca, 1998); Heather Coleman, "The Most Dangerous Sect: Baptists in Tsarist and Soviet Russia, 1905–1929," Ph.D. diss., University of Illinois, 1998; Laura Engelstein, *Castration and the Heavenly Kingdom* (Ithaca, 1999); Christine Worobec, *Possessed: Women, Witches, and Demons in Imperial Russia* (DeKalb, Ill., 2001). Additional works are listed in Chapters 6 and 7.

ticularly important has been the shift away from a primary focus on institutions and formal theologies toward a view of religion as social and cultural practice, as a living process in which people create intellectual and emotional meaning. This shift echoes and parallels larger methodological changes in the study of history, but also new work by anthropologists and others on religion, magic, and the sacred. Challenging arguments about the progressive "secularization of the European mind" and about the presumed growing separation, as modernization advanced, of the sacred and the profane into separate spheres, histories of religion in early and late modern Europe have demonstrated the persistence and even periodic intensification of religion, spirituality, and the sacred. Religion, it is argued, is not an autonomous phenomenon but a body of meaningful symbols and rituals entwined with modern politics, social relations, gender, and community, without being reducible to any of them. Religious beliefs and practices, including forms not approved by clerical establishments, have served to define and assert identities, articulate ethical norms and values, and exercise and contest power. And sacred and transcendental visions of the world have remained powerful.[17]

Most writing on the history of religion has been better at elaborating the social and cultural functions of religion than at describing and theorizing its subjective power. Yet it is clear that religion provides needed emotional knowledge and expression. Religion answers human needs to see as orderly and comprehensible what otherwise would seem to be the meaningless chaos, evil, and suffering of everyday life and to exercise some power over the unknown (religion as nomos), but also to express feelings about the world as a place of mystery and awesome power (religion as ethos). Religion provides meaning and a measure of control, but it also gives form to imagination, to nostalgia for lost perfection, and to potent feelings of awe and the sublime.[18] The religious evocation of mood and meaning—and the extent to which feeling and meaning define each other—has been most evident in studies of such forms as death rituals, miraculous apparitions, possession, spiritualism, and devotion to saints, but also in research on less definable forms of sacred imagination such as symbol and metaphor, memory, and the gendering of

[17] For reviews of the scholarly literature and of some of the theoretical issues in the study of popular religion, see esp. Natalie Zemon Davis, "From 'Popular Religion' to Religious Cultures," in *Reformation Europe: A Guide to Research,* ed. Steven Ozment (St. Louis, 1982), 321–41; Ellen Badone, ed., *Religious Orthodoxy and Popular Faith in European Society* (Princeton, 1990), Introduction; Caroline Ford, "Religion and Popular Culture in Modern Europe," *Journal of Modern History* 65, no. 1 (March 1993): 152–75; and Daniel L. Pals, *Seven Theories of Religion* (Oxford, 1996).

[18] Although I am using these terms slightly differently, on religion as nomos, see Peter Berger, *The Sacred Canopy: Elements of a Sociological Theory of Religion* (New York, 1967), esp. 19–25. On religion as ethos, see esp. Clifford Geertz, "Religion as a Cultural System" and "Ethos, World View, and the Analysis of Sacred Symbols," both in *The Interpretation of Cultures* (New York, 1973), esp. 89–103, 126–41; and the works of Mircea Eliade, notably *The Sacred and the Profane: The Nature of Religion* (New York, 1959) and *Myths, Dreams, and Mysteries* (New York, 1960). A useful summary of Eliade's work may be found in Pals, *Seven Theories of Religion,* esp. 159–80.

piety.[19] Still, most historians have remained cautious before this difficult terrain, hesitating to look beyond the traditional focus on shaping contexts to consider deeper layers of motivation and meaning. Among these, it is essential that we recognize the persistent and ubiquitous power of aesthetic, mythic, and emotional forms of understanding as well as their connections to the social and the political.

Russian worker writers engaged these issues and contexts complexly. When these authors wrote in a religious idiom, as they often did, their writings were usually not religious in a literal sense—that is, in the sense of expressing faith in an ecclesiastical doctrine or belief in a stable, uniform, and "true" cultural system and ordering of a sacred cosmos.[20] Christian and other sacred terminologies, imageries, and narratives were invoked not primarily for their literal meaning in relation to Christian faith but rather for their metaphoric and symbolic power as a means of speaking about the sacred. These were stories, images, vocabularies, and symbols that—to paraphrase a common definition of the sacred—reached across boundaries of time and space to manifest the transcendent, to link the immediate and the visible to universal, even eternal, narratives and places.[21] When such epiphanic practices—in which the sacred is made manifest—do not insist on the literal truth of the stories evoked, as was typically the case in Russian workers' writings, this becomes a still more complex expression of the religious. Images—crucifixion and resurrection, for example—did not need to be literally true in order to exert imaginative and emotional power. The symbolic language of the sacred, as it most often does, helped read the disjointed fragments of everyday experience as part of a meaningful and purposeful narrative, a coherent conception of existence and time. This was also a discourse of affect and emotion, an effort to voice the imagination, to articulate things sublime and terrible.

Interpreting Cultural Practice

This book is a history of ideas (and of their elusive relatives: values and sentiments), but unlike traditional intellectual history, it focuses on ideas expressed by people who were relatively uneducated and, for much of their lives, subordinate. I treat these ideas not as a separate sphere but as entwined with social and political life. And unlike traditional social history, the focus here is less on collectivities and commonalities than on individuals and margins, less on ex-

---

[19] See, e.g., Caroline Ford, *Creating the Nation in Provincial France: Religion and Political Identity in Brittany* (Princeton, 1993); Ford, "Religion and Popular Culture," esp. 162–69; David Blackbourn, *Marpingen: Apparitions of the Virgin Mary in Nineteenth-Century Germany* (Oxford, 1993), 9, 12, 29, 32, 142; Sabean, *Power in the Blood*, 30, 32, 43, 103–12, 212.

[20] I am using a definition of "religion" as distinct from "the sacred" (though they never are fully distinct) similar to that in Geertz, "Religion as a Cultural System," 98–123, and Berger, *Sacred Canopy*, 26.

[21] Eliade, *Sacred and the Profane*, esp. Introduction and chap. 1, and his *Cosmos and History: The Myth of Eternal Return* (New York, 1959).

plicitly social and political ideas than on categories of thought better defined as philosophical. These are immodest purposes. With only texts to go on—notably such notoriously indeterminate texts as poetry— I am not so naive as to claim that I have fully described what these worker writers thought (much less felt) about Russian social and political life, not to mention self, modernity, and the sacred. I can read these writings again and again, listen carefully, consider what we know about the larger social and cultural context, and question my own assumptions, but I remain on the uncertain ground of interpretation. And while theoretical and comparative studies may offer suggestive hints toward constructing a plausible picture out of these fragments, they also increase the risks of misreading. These are the risks of cultural study, which, as an interpretive discipline in search of meaning, must remain "intrinsically incomplete."[22] For historians, the risk is worth it, I think, if our purpose is to understand not just why events happened but also (though this impinges on understanding causation) what events (and also the uneventful everyday) *meant* for people.

We necessarily have to sort out the ways people make and use cultural forms (language, symbols, rituals) and how their making and using have been shaped, constrained, and provoked by the harder surfaces of their lives (material conditions and objects, social location, relative power, the process of cultural practice itself). It is by now an interpretive commonplace to recognize the power of discourse to constitute meanings about the world, to rearrange the givens of experience, to shape vision and purpose. More persuasive theorizing, however, recognizes the persistent intersections and mutual invasions of structure and agency, the intertwining of the material and the cultural, the "dialogue" between the word and the world. Put more strongly, people's social and cultural lives involve an experiential, practical dynamic (theorists speak of "practice") in which the physical and social worlds retain power to shape, limit, and disrupt discourse, in which cultural meaning is inescapably "burdened with the world," as well as the reverse.[23] Russian worker writers drew upon and made use of an assortment of available ideas, vocabularies, and images, but they also necessarily reflected upon and were influenced by tangible forms of experience, including poverty, social sub-

---

[22] Geertz, *Interpretation of Cultures*, 5, 29.

[23] Marshall Sahlins, *Islands of History* (Chicago, 1985), 138. For influential theoretical discussions on the complex mutual interactions of culture and structure, see also Geertz, *Interpretation of Cultures;* Marshall Sahlins, *Culture in Practice: Selected Essays* (New York, 2000); Pierre Bourdieu, *Outline of a Theory of Practice* (Cambridge, 1977); Michel de Certeau, *The Practice of Everyday Life* (Berkeley, 1984) and *The Writing of History* (New York, 1988); William H. Sewell, Jr., "Toward a Post-materialist Rhetoric for Labor History," in his *Rethinking Labor History: Essays on Discourse and Class Analysis* (Urbana, 1993), 15–38; Alf Lüdtke, ed., *The History of Everyday Life* (Princeton, 1995); M. M. Bakhtin, *The Dialogic Imagination,* ed. Mikhail Holquist (Austin, 1996). For useful summaries and evaluations of many of these theoretical issues, see the Introduction to and articles by Sherry Ortner and Stuart Hall in *Culture/Power/History: A Reader in Contemporary Social Theory,* ed. Nicholas Dirks, Geoff Eley, and Sherry Ortner (Princeton, 1994); and Roger Chartier, "Intellectual History or Social-Cultural History? The French Trajectories," in *Modern European Intellectual History,* ed. Dominick LaCapra and Steven L. Kaplan (Ithaca, 1982).

ordination, new opportunities, war, and revolution. At the same time, the cultural practices being considered here were not merely responses to particular events or conditions. The historical time present in these practices was not only immediate and contingent. The world that "burdened" these worker writers was both present and remembered, visible and imagined, *événementiel* and essential.

Notions of the active subject are central to these arguments about cultural practice. Accounts of power, especially cultural power, that posit inescapable and totalizing hegemonies, or even the subjectless play of cultural fields of force, make for dramatic rhetorical accounts of the world but necessarily ignore or deny much of the real complexity of human agency and power relations. There is plenty of evidence that individuals and groups retain power and space to rework, subvert, and even misuse available cultural forms. We must recognize not only the controlling and debilitating forces surrounding the subject but also the ways people follow errant trajectories, seize moments and opportunities, and actively appropriate forms and meanings. Russian worker writers often understood all this, if in plainer terms. They believed themselves to be subjects in their own history. They knew that the world threw up obstacles at every turn. They refused to be deterred.

Minor Lives on the Margins

This book approaches questions of cultural meaning on a peculiar margin of Russian life (itself significantly at the margin of modern Europe)—at the edges of both popular culture and the culture of the educated, in an odd space where some of the literate poor embraced reading and writing with exceptional passion. This inquiry assumes (or rather insists) that there are important benefits to studying such small stories located so far from typicality—useful not just to fill gaps in our knowledge but as a way of viewing the whole picture differently, of rethinking the larger narrative. This is no longer a novel argument. The insight that odd stories and marginal histories reveal much beyond themselves and that liminal sites and individuals often exercise special power in a culture has produced important historical writing. Studies of coalescing and contested national boundaries, of the margins of cities, of the atypical life stories of women or workers, of individuals of all sorts creating selves on the frontiers of the everyday, have revealed much about the meanings of nation, the dynamics of urban life, and the pressures and possibilities of gender and class. These works have usefully undermined the assumption that truth lies in aggregates and that the past (or the present) is best understood by the stories that are most typical and representative.[24]

[24] See, e.g., Scott, *Gender and the Politics of History;* Rancière, *Nights of Labor;* Giovanni Levi, "On Microhistory," in *New Perspectives on Historical Writing,* ed. Peter Burke (Cambridge, 1991), 93–113; Carlo Ginzburg, *The Cheese and the Worms: The Cosmos of a Sixteenth-Century Miller,* trans. John and Anne Tedeschi (New York, 1982); Natalie Davis, *Women on the*

The group of Russians examined here is best described as "strange"; their identities, even in their own eyes, were suffused with otherness. Taking up pencil and pen to express ideas and feelings about the world around them and the world within, worker writers signaled and nurtured their strangeness as both workers and writers. This is a telling strangeness, for it occurred at some of Russia's most critical boundaries during its most troubled and tumultuous years. These were social boundaries: the edges of manual labor and intellectual creation, of popular culture and the literature and ideas of the educated, of everyday life in the working class and the exceptional lives of wanderers, dreamers, misfits, and leaders. No less important, these writers explored intellectual and sentimental boundaries: the spaces of contact and tension between collective identification and personal alienation, social criticism and literary imagination, the sacred and the profane, revolutionary enthusiasm and existential melancholy.

Even if the thoughts and feelings these worker writers articulated were only their own, they would still be compelling as passionate contemporary visions of an important time and place in modern history. Pure originality, of course, is impossible. These writers were inescapably working with experiences and ideas that were at hand. Their writings were part of a dialogue with the world and with culture. They were not "representative" or typical, but they were hardly anomalous. The repetition of themes in the writings of so many of these writers (the result more of common experiences and common reading than of mutual influence) is an important sign of patterns in their engagement with the world around them. At the very least, their writings suggest "horizons of possibility" within the larger culture, patterns of popular (and not only popular) thought whose traces would otherwise have been lost.[25]

These particular and even strange writings also remind us of the variety of what we call popular culture or working-class consciousness. Although these Russian worker writers were more strangers than comrades in their own class, they were also leaders and spokesmen, roles shaped by the same singular passions and revelations of a different world. For all their liminality, indeed because of it, their actions and words influenced others. No less important, their stories help us see past the usual stereotypes about what working-class consciousness was or could be—about, for example, how workers thought about class or socialism or their attitudes toward self, modernity, and the sacred. As will be seen, heterodox ideas were to be found among even supposedly "conscious workers." My aims are to shed light beyond familiar stories, but also to disturb them.

Margins: Three Seventeenth-Century Lives (Cambridge, Mass., 1995). More than historians, anthropologists have explored the category of liminality and the meaningful and often powerful lives of liminal individuals in a culture.

[25] See Ginzburg, *Cheese and the Worms*, 128.

Emotion, Subjectivity, Imagination

The question of emotion, especially its relation to meaning and morality, plays a significant role in my efforts to explore plebeian thought. Clearly this is a difficult subject for historical analysis. It is hard enough to determine and explicate the ideas and values of people long dead without asking questions about sentiment and mood. Yet for all the risks, we must recognize that emotion was a crucial part of the *meaning* of the past for those we are seeking to understand. It may be more prudent to resist trying to penetrate layers of consciousness that we can only infer from our sources. Yet such prudence does not change the still obvious fact that human experience and action are composed of emotion as well as rational perception, of moral sensibilities as well as ethical conviction, of what Russian worker writers themselves called "life feeling" (*zhizneoshchushchenie*) and the "emotional side of ideology." Ideas and emotions—meaning and feeling—are linked in a complex but potent dialogue.[26]

For many Europeans from the late eighteenth century on, the power and value of emotion were matters of principle, literally of selfhood, morality, and virtue—a view that was an essential component of the great intellectual upheaval that has been boiled down into the notion of Romanticism.[27] A large number of educated Europeans viewed truth, especially moral truth, as necessarily requiring attention to a voice that lay within the deep self and held that passions and sensations were the keys to unlock the deepest moral and universal truths. At the same time, as part of this pursuit of the inward self, sentiment and affective expression were prized in themselves. There were, of course, older traditions to draw upon—Christian ideas of soul and passion, and, still further back, ancient ideas about the centrality of emotion to rhetoric and ethics and about the sources and meaning of the sublime. With Romanticism, these notions became a far more elaborate and explicit body of ideas about emotion and much more strongly linked to questions of the inward self. The arts, in particular, acquired enormous importance as expressive forms, as means of communicating the creations of intertwined intellect and feelings of the inward self, as the "spontaneous overflow of powerful feelings" (William Wordsworth's famous definition of poetry).[28]

[26] The study of emotion as a social phenomenon has become increasingly widespread. See, e.g., Sabean, *Power in the Blood*, esp. 45–53, 94–112, 170–72; Gay, *Bourgeois Experience*; Theodore Zeldin, "Personal History and the History of Emotions," *Journal of Social History* 15 (1982): 339–48, and *An Intimate History of Humanity* (New York, 1994); William Reddy, *The Invisible Code: Honor and Sentiment in Postrevolutionary France, 1814–1848* (Berkeley, 1997).

[27] On the conceptual problems of defining Romanticism, see, e.g., Arthur O. Lovejoy, "On the Discrimination of Romanticisms," in his *Essays in the History of Ideas* (Baltimore, 1948); Lilian Furst, *Romanticism in Perspective* (New York, 1969), and idem, ed., *The Contours of European Romanticism* (London, 1979).

[28] See, e.g., M. H. Abrams, *The Mirror and the Lamp: Romantic Theory and the Critical Tradition* (New York, 1953), esp. 21–26, 54–55, 71–78 (quotation 21); Taylor, *Sources of the Self*, 368–90.

Imagination, especially the expressive inward power out of which emerge creative works of art (including, perhaps with particular force, poetry written by scarcely educated authors), is at the heart of this complex interplay of emotion, thought, and intellect. For Romantic theorists such as Wordsworth, Samuel Coleridge, and Friedrich Schelling, imagination is precisely the place where sentiment is combined with rationality, the external world with inner meaning, the infinite cosmos with the infinite self. Imagination, these theorists maintained, is the force that synthesizes images, thoughts, and feelings. It is the exercise of the imagination that makes images of the world not simply mimetic reflections of finite external objects but expressive articulations of both the inward self and eternal truth. Imagination resolves the contradiction between the conscious and the unconscious and hence functions as the truest and deepest thought.[29] Russian worker writers were probably ignorant of this Romantic tradition, though not of its strong elaborations in nineteenth-century Russian literature. In any case, whether we speak of influence or resonant similarities, we see a common spirit. My effort to reconstruct the "imagination" of Russian worker writers is directed precisely at this interplay of the external world and the inward self, at the intertwining of intellect, thought, and emotion.

A darker voice of Romanticism, especially the more skeptical post-Romantic elaborations of this expressive sensibility, was also echoed in the mentalities of Russian worker writers. In their writings, we encounter (surprisingly often for leftist workers in an age of revolution) expressions of pessimism, *toská* (a mixture of melancholy, sadness, anguish, depression, and longing), existentialist feelings of life's pointlessness, and a tragic view of life. Unexpected echoes of Arthur Schopenhauer, Friedrich Nietzsche, and Søren Kierkegaard abound. These philosophers were known in Russia, and their ideas about suffering, tragedy, melancholy, and the dark interior of the self resonated indirectly in the works of some Russian writers. We cannot easily assume influence, however, much less determine it. The reading experiences of worker authors were scattered and often unsophisticated. One can speak with certainty only of telling affinities. Yet we also see an important difference. Worker writers could not so easily share the sensibility of the many Romantic and post-Romantic writers who found something inspiring in tragedy and consoling and even pleasurable in melancholy—who found in the sufferings of the world and the self "reverie and voluptuous sadness."[30] The sense of tragedy and melancholy we find in workers' writings was more a bitter moral sensibility—a critical though sometimes unfocused protest against the injustice of the world—than a pleasurable aesthetic. They could not theorize their way to accept suffering: perhaps they were too unsophisticated; perhaps the hardships of daily life were too personal and overwhelming. Whatever the rea-

---

[29] Abrams, *Mirror and the Lamp*, 22, 54–55, 119, 130, 169, 210; Taylor, *Sources of the Self*, 371, 378–79, 512–13.

[30] Daniel Mornet, *Le Romantisme en France au XVIIIᵉ siècle* (Paris, 1912), quoted in Taylor, *Sources of the Self*, 296.

sons, their melancholy tended to lead less to consoling and voluptuous sadness than to either defiant engagement or (to appropriate a notion from later existentialist writing) philosophical and emotional nausea.

Ambivalence and Ambiguity

Complicating efforts to understand and describe clearly the thinking and feelings of worker writers about self, modernity, and the sacred is the problem of ambivalence and ambiguity. Briefly, I mean by "ambivalence" a form of thought, understanding, and feeling about the world that is unstable and even contradictory in meaning. Ambiguity is a way of expressing ambivalence, though also a perception less certain than ambivalence and a definition of the world itself, of the irresolvable contradictions that make ambivalence and uncertainty necessary and true. These are simplifications, however, of categories that by definition resist simplification.

Most commonly, and in its origins, the concept of ambiguity has been used as a linguistic and literary category. The classic definition of ambiguity is William Empson's: a "verbal nuance" that "gives room for alternative re-actions to the same piece of language."[31] More recently, literary scholars have written of ambiguity as language that calls for a choice between alternative meanings but provides no ground for making that choice.[32] Although these are primarily linguistic definitions, they hint at phenomenological ones, at interpretations of the external world that language and literature seek to depict, at a world beyond the text that is by its nature unstable and even contradictory in meaning.

It is telling that until the twentieth century, ambiguity had been viewed mainly as something harmful. It was seen as standing in the way of a clear understanding of a reality that was assumed to be coherent and knowable. The modernist drive to impose order and legibility is evident here, though the roots of this anxiety about ambiguity are much older. In the ancient world, Stoic philosophers criticized ambiguity as an obstacle to expressing clear reason and hence as opposed to truth.[33] It has been in the modern era, however, that critics and philosophers have been most vigilant in warning against ambiguity in expression, as a "vice or deformity in speech and writing,"[34] as an obstacle to truth—which, it was believed, had coherent and knowable order and purpose—or even worse, as a device for deliberate equivocation and obfuscation, and thus as morally and epistemologically dubious. Modern social thought has tended to share this general view of ambiguity. One of the defining char-

---

[31] William Empson, *Seven Types of Ambiguity*, 2d ed. (London, 1947), 1.

[32] Shlomith Rimmon, *The Concept of Ambiguity: The Example of James* (Chicago, 1977).

[33] Catherine Atherton, *The Stoics on Ambiguity* (Cambridge, 1993).

[34] George Puttenham, *The Art of English Poesie* (1589), quoted in Leonard Orr, *Dictionary of Cultural Theory* (New York, 1991), 34. This was approximately the time when, according to the *Oxford English Dictionary*, the term "ambiguity" began to be used in English.

acteristics of Western social theory (including the emerging social sciences) from the seventeenth century into the early twentieth was a "potent urge" to view human society "in strictly unambiguous terms."[35] Modern statecraft (including that of modern revolutionary movements) has also tended to share this refusal to accept ambiguity, pursuing instead a "high modernist" aesthetic of simplification, purity, and order, a driving compulsion to make society and nature "legible,"[36] and a determination to "purge ambivalence" in the name of "universality, homogeneity, and clarity."[37]

Modern life, of course, has never been so unambiguous, orderly, or legible. On the contrary, this ordering discourse emerged partly as an effort to control, even deny, the characteristic contingency, flux, and upheaval of modernity. And modern thought itself always contained a strong countercurrent to this denial of ambiguity. Renaissance humanists such as Michel de Montaigne, such connoisseurs of modern flux as Charles Baudelaire, and fin-de-siècle artists (including, notably, Russian Futurists and Symbolists) were all able to see and take pleasure in ambiguity, paradox, and uncertain meaning. By the twentieth century, against prevailing currents in the social sciences, interpretation in the humanities and the cultural sciences increasingly recognized the need to account for and understand ambivalence, ambiguity, and indeterminacy. Postmodernist and poststructuralist thought, in particular, has taken its philosophical stand largely on the disordered flux and uncertainty of modernity and has tended to abandon faith in the possibility of resolving ambiguity. Literary critics have tended to insist on the ultimate "indeterminacy" and interpretive undecidability of texts. As social interpretation, postmodernist and poststructuralist theory has similarly rejected the allegedly modern lure and deceit of a monistic, ordered, and unambiguous world, insisting on the inescapable presence in human thought, communication, and action of ambivalence, ambiguity, multivalence, indeterminacy, and paradox.[38] Many of these accounts echo definitions of modernity that emphasize the ephemeral and the contingent, noting the disorderliness of modern social "practice"—the pervasiveness of bricolage, plasticity, disruption, and chance—and how the complex and often subversive ways people use and appropriate culture and other structures introduce a pervasive ambiguity into social and cultural life.[39] Histori-

[35] Donald N. Levine, *The Flight from Ambiguity: Essays in Social and Cultural Theory* (Chicago, 1985).

[36] Scott, *Seeing like a State*. Michel Foucault made similar arguments in much of his work, though Scott focuses more on the impossibility and failure of the modern project of visibility and control.

[37] Bauman, *Modernity and Ambivalence* and *Intimations of Postmodernity*, esp. Introduction and chap. 9 (quotation 120).

[38] See the discussions in Timothy Bahti, "Ambiguity and Indeterminacy: The Juncture," *Comparative Literature* 38, no. 3 (Summer 1986): 211–23; Gerald Graff, "Determinacy/Indeterminacy," in *Critical Terms for Literary Study*, 2d ed., ed. Frank Lentricchia and Thomas McLaughlin (Chicago, 1995), 163–85; Dirks et al., *Culture/Power/History*, 17–22; Bauman, "Postmodernity, or Living with Ambivalence," in his *Modernity and Ambivalence*, 231–45; P. Kruse and M. Stadler, eds, *Ambiguity in Mind and Nature* (Berlin, 1995).

[39] See esp. Certeau, *Practice of Everyday Life*, xiii, xv–xvi.

cal studies have similarly shown a growing recognition of the importance of taking the measure of ambivalence and ambiguity in people's attitudes and cultural expressions, of the "indeterminate multiplicity" and "hybridity" of identity, of the "multivocality" of texts and other discourses, of the unstable meanings that people read onto their social landscapes. As historians seek to interpret such motivational and perceptual categories as morality, pleasure, desire, and fear, they are especially likely to recognize contradictory and unstable meanings.[40]

Russian and Soviet Marxists shared the high-modernist attraction to order and legibility, to purity and clarity, in aesthetics as in politics.[41] Many sought literally to "purge ambivalence" from the emerging socialist culture. Influential cultural officials repeatedly reminded worker writers that there could be no place in Soviet literature for "doubt" or "imprecision," that proletarian culture "requires clarity, precision, solidity, and a forged shape, not endless indeterminacy."[42] Quite simply, a leading Marxist literary critic declared (with visible dismay and impatience), worker writers "cannot and ought not to know ambivalence [*razdvoeniia*]."[43] From the Marxist perspective, an effective revolutionary movement requires a solid, stable, and clear foundation of images, values, and ways of communicating, a clear and inspiring set of myths and ideals, a confidence in the future. And worker writers, as leading cultural representatives of the proletariat, the ostensible new ruling class, bore a particular responsibility to speak correctly and clearly. Unfortunately, Marxist intellectuals had to admit, many proletarians displayed a great deal of "agonizing ambivalence" (*muchitel'naia razdvoennost'*),[44] especially about touchstone questions of life's meaning, purpose, and direction.

The proletarian imagination described in this book suggests a great deal of heterodoxy in both working-class and socialist culture. Plentiful here are acts of subversive appropriation and willful protest—against autocracy and capitalism, and sometimes against the new Communist order. But the story is not simply one of difference and resistance. Doubt, ambivalence, and unresolved

---

[40] See, e.g., Rancière, *Nights of Labor,* 73, 86, 175, 185, 271, 376; Davis, *Return of Martin Guerre,* 40–41, 47, 51; Walkowitz, *City of Dreadful Delight,* 10, 48–49, 56–57, 80, 85, 93, and passim; Lüdtke, *History of Everyday Life,* 9, 16–17. Prefiguring these arguments (and much closer to the subjects of this book), Mikhail Bakhtin developed an extensive argument about the persistent *raznorechivost'* (variously translated as heteroglossia, multivocality, and multilanguagedness) in all communication: the irresolvable "dialogue" within discourse and between discourse and the world: Bakhtin, *Dialogic Imagination;* Michael Holquist, *Dialogism: Bakhtin and His World* (London, 1990).

[41] For an insightful discussion of "purification" as the master narrative of the revolution—with strong echoes of Bauman's arguments about the modern "dream of purity" and Scott's arguments about "legibility"—see Clark, *Petersburg,* 3, 56–57, 60–62, 66, 69, 84, 209–11, 252, 290.

[42] V. Polianskii (Pavel Lebedev-Polianskii), review of *Gorn* in *Proletarskaia kul'tura,* no. 5 (November 1918), 42–43, and review of *Pereval* in *Rabochii zhurnal* 1925, no. 1–2: 262.

[43] S. Rodov, "Motivy tvorchestva M. Gerasimova," *Kuznitsa,* no. 1 (May 1920), 23.

[44] A. Voronskii, "O gruppe pisatel'ei 'Kuznitsa': Obshchaia kharakteristika," *Iskusstvo i zhizn': Sbornik statei* (Moscow and Petrograd, 1924), 136. See also P. I. M., review of Aleksandrovskii, "Shagi," *Rabochii zhurnal* 1925, no. 1–2: 277.

ambiguity play large parts in this history. And in this, as in much else, these odd writers on the margins turn out to be rather typical of their time. As an "intelligentsia of the people [*narodnaia intelligentsia*]," it was said, they represented "that part of the laboring population that lives a conscious life, that seeks truth and spiritual beauty in the world."[45] As proletarians, in the view of most contemporary radicals and Marxists, they should have found this truth and beauty to be a source of optimism and faith. They were not supposed to suffer from the angst and doubts so common among bourgeois intellectuals. But like many Russians (educated and not), they found this path hard to follow. The grand narrative of modern progress continually faded from their gaze and broke apart in their hands.

[45] A. Shvedskaia, letter to *Drug naroda,* no. 2 (31 Jan. 1915), 16.

I *Cultural Revolution: The Making of a Plebeian Intelligentsia*

> This circle seeks to unite . . . an intelligentsia that has emerged out of the depths of the people's life by the strength of its own spirit. . . . It is clear that only those who have experienced all the charms of a life without rights can weep the people's sufferings and rejoice the people's joys.
>
> —*Drug naroda* (Friend of the people), 1915

> The intellectual can still think for the young working class, but he cannot feel for it.
>
> —FEDOR KALININ, 1912

Culture was one of the most embattled terrains in Russian life during the vital and tortured years from the 1905 revolution into the first years of socialist revolution. The idea and meaning of culture were invariably entwined with much of both public and private life: with conceptions of self and community, definitions of personal and civic morality, visions of social betterment, and questions of rights and power. Many Russians—officials, cultural reformers, civic activists, educators, journalists, writers, and revolutionaries—pursued in various ways the common goal of making Russian life conform to their notions of culture, which was assumed to be not an object to construct at will but something intrinsic to be found, defined, and set before self and others as a measure of the good. Rhetoric and arguments about what culture was and meant changed over time. Before 1917 the talk tended to be mainly about advancing the "mental and moral development" of the country and the people. After the revolution, among the new public leaders and activists, more aggressive dreams of "cultural revolution" and more imaginative visions of developing and promoting a new world-transforming "proletarian culture" predominated. But a common assumption united these efforts: that culture mattered—that the admittedly elusive terrain of shared ways of knowledge, judgment, value, taste, and behavior was essential in the effort to alter (or to preserve) social and political structures and relationships.

Historians have explored these struggles over culture mainly by studying the attitudes and actions of activist elites. Less often, questions are asked about the impact of these efforts on ordinary Russians and about how the human objects of these efforts appropriated and altered the messages. But this entire story of culture building, contest, and revolution was greatly complicated by the active presence of individuals who questioned the very boundaries of elite culture bearer (or cultural revolutionary) and plebeian culture learner, of intellectual activist and culture-deficient commoner, of producer and consumer. They challenged also the representations of what lower-class Russians were said to think and feel, and especially of what they ought to think and feel. In the ongoing culture wars of these years—battles against the "darkness" of the people as well as over what sort of culture the people and the nation required—plebeian intellectuals questioned the terms of the debate. Their very existence undermined any simple narratives about who controlled and expressed culture. But they were also intensely self-conscious about their daring. Reflecting on the significance of their experiences and actions, of their reach across the boundaries of social class and cultural level, they offered their own arguments about the sources of knowledge and value and about the shape of culture as a measure of good and a means of transformation.

The remarkable growth of an "intelligentsia" comprising not educated elites but scarcely educated urban workers was remarked upon by contemporaries. The newness and strangeness of such a group was reflected in the proliferation of names for it: most often "worker intelligentsia" (*rabochaia intelligentsia*), the term preferred by Marxists, and "intelligentsia from the people" (*narodnaia intelligentsia*), preferred by populists and other non-Marxist socialists, but also "advanced workers," "thinking [*mysliashchie*] workers," "*intelligentnye* workers," and worker *intelligenty* (members of an intelligentsia). The frequent use of the term "intelligentsia" testified to the perceived momentousness of such a remarkable new presence, for this was one of the most laden categories in Russian cultural history, signifying, especially among opponents of the status quo, not so much the well educated as the intellectually awakened and morally committed, who would ultimately lead Russia out of its backwardness and lack of freedom. Populists and Marxists had noticed and begun talking about such workers as early as the 1870s and had often tried to understand, recruit, and educate them.[1] But their visibility was far greater after 1900 and especially in the years after the revolution of 1905. This visi-

---

[1] See esp. Georgii Plekhanov, *Russkii rabochii v revoliutsionnom dvizhenii*, 2d ed. (Geneva, 1902; first published in the Geneva paper *Sotsial-Demokrat* in 1892); Reginald Zelnik, "Populists and Workers: The First Encounter between Populist Students and Industrial Workers in St. Petersburg, 1871–1874," *Soviet Studies* 24, no. 2 (October 1972); idem, ed., *Workers and Intelligentsia in Late Imperial Russia* (Berkeley, 1999), passim.

bility was due in part simply to the growing numbers and public presence of such workers, especially as they established links to one another. Educated Russians also paid them more notice as activists on both left and right worried about the lower classes' dangerously low levels of culture and as cultural work, in the more repressive environment after early 1907, replaced open oppositional politics. Finally, these lower-class intellectuals were making themselves more visible by insisting on their right to be heard and on the uniqueness and necessity of their perspective and vision. The rise of this plebeian intelligentsia was, in its own way, a cultural revolution, and it complicated all others.

Defining a Worker Intelligentsia

In 1913, in the social-democratic journal *Sovremennyi mir* (The modern world), the Marxist critic Lev Kleinbort began a series of articles on what he called "workers' democracy," a term he used to speak of workers' public voices, especially in the growing labor press—voices he identified as belonging to a growing "worker intelligentsia," to an "intelligentsia from the people."[2] This group included political activists, trade unionists, participants in underground study circles, essayists, poets, and writers of fiction. Many of these worker *intelligenty* at some point in their lives were all of the above. Almost all wrote. Indeed, public writing was one of the defining characteristics of this plebeian intelligentsia. In the 1890s, Nikolai Rubakin, the leading investigator of popular reading in Russia, already noted a tendency among peasant and worker readers to take a more active relation to the written word and become "self-taught writers" (*pisateli-samouchki*).[3] Especially in the years after 1905, such writers, mostly writing poetry (the genre of verse was more familiar, accessible, and brief) became a sustained presence in Russian cultural life.

We do not know how many hundreds or thousands of Russian workers occasionally put down a few lines of poetry or sketched out a story, or even how many had works appear in any of the many publications around the country that published popular writing. We know that between 1891 and 1904 Rubakin personally collected writings of various types by more than a thousand workers and peasants.[4] We know that in the years from 1905 through

[2] L. M. Kleinbort, "Ocherki rabochei demokratii," *Sovremennyi mir,* March 1913, 22–45; May 1913, 151–72; August 1913, 175–98; October 1913, 150–76; November 1913, 168–90; December 1913, 148–68; January 1914, 212–35; April 1914, 28–52. These and a few other prerevolutionary articles (listed in the bibliography) were reprinted in the 1920s along with some new essays in L. M. Kleinbort, *Ocherki rabochei intelligentsii,* 2 vols. (Petrograd, 1923).

[3] N. A. Rubakin, *Etiudy o russkoi chitaiushchei publike* (St. Petersburg, 1895), 167–82, 202–14.

[4] N. A. Rubakin, "Bor'ba naroda za svoe prosveshchenie: Doklad, chitannyi na III s"ezde deiatelei po tekhnicheskomu i professional'nomu obrazovaniia, 4 ianvaria 1904 goda," in his *Chistaia publika i intelligentsiia iz naroda,* 2d ed. (St. Petersburg, 1906), 239.

1913, almost every issue of a trade union or socialist party newspaper included at least a couple of poems by self-identified workers, and that these papers received many more pieces of writing than they printed, some of them from scarcely literate workers.[5] We know that in the decades before 1917 Maxim Gorky, the most famous and most successful Russian "writer from the people," received letters from hundreds of self-taught beginning writers (*samouchki*) all over the country—most of them factory workers or peasants, but also artisans, sales clerks, cooks, maids, prostitutes, laundresses, and many others—appealing to him for criticism, advice, and help (and often for a few rubles to get by on or to purchase books).[6] When Gorky and his publisher advertised in 1913 for submissions to Gorky's first "anthology of proletarian writers," within three months they received 450 manuscripts from 94 authors.[7] During 1917, along with huge numbers of letters and appeals from lower-class Russians, hundreds of poems about the revolution were sent to the government, the Soviet, and other authorities.[8]

We know relatively little about most of the working-class Russians who expressed themselves creatively in prose and poetry (and even less about peasant writers). A substantial number of worker writers, however, were active, determined, and successful enough to have left more than a trace of their lives and works. My files contain the names of more than 150 regularly published working-class writers about whose personal histories we know at least something and 62 individuals on whom we have detailed biographical information.[9] The sample is selective. Part of the selectivity is mine. Because I seek to follow the experiences and thinking of a coherent group of people over time, I have focused on a particular group of worker writers: individuals who were already adults at the time of the revolution, who began writing before 1917 while employed in wage-earning jobs, who lived in the central regions of the empire, and who wrote in Russian. This sample, however, is also restricted by external circumstance: it is a collection of the remains of a much larger and richer picture, left in far from a random manner.[10] Still, these lives reveal much about the genealogies of worker intellectuals and about the cultural and social histories of their times. It is useful to pause over these life stories, for the

[5] E.g., see the unpublished manuscripts of poems sent to the Bolshevik paper *Pravda* on the eve of the First World War: RGASPI, f. 364 (*Pravda*), op. 1, d. 202, esp. l. 6–60b (a poem about bakery workers written in a labored hand and full of spelling errors).

[6] In Gorky's 1914 essay on self-taught writers, he described 348 individuals who wrote to him. These and many other letters are held in Arkhiv A. M. Gor'kogo, collection KG-NP (korrespondentsiia Gor'kogo—nachinaiushchim pisateliam).

[7] *I [Pervyi] sbornik proletarskikh pisatelei* (St. Petersburg, 1914), 3.

[8] See Mark D. Steinberg, *Voices of Revolution, 1917* (New Haven, 2001).

[9] The Selected Bibliography lists the main archival, periodical, and published sources on the basis of which these files were constructed.

[10] Workers whose writings found their way into print and especially those who left extensive records about their lives did so for reasons shaped by particular circumstances: interest shown in certain writers by journalists or other established writers, the efforts of Soviet cultural activists to promote and document proletarian writing, and their own will to write down their lives. These conditions shaped the selection of stories that remain and the way they were told and recorded.

lives of worker writers were at once exceptional and common. Sociologically, worker writers as a group were rather unremarkable. On average, they were somewhat more urbanized, mobile, literate, and politically active than most workers, but not dramatically so. Born in years of rapid industrial and urban growth, social and cultural change, and political turmoil, these individuals reflected the flux of their times, even as they stood out and often apart.

Like most Russian workers by the early years of the twentieth century, worker writers were likely to have been born as peasants, though a higher than average percentage were from urban backgrounds.[11] Slightly more than half of the worker writers about whom we have detailed biographical information (33 of 62) were born in the countryside. Of the rest, half came from small provincial towns and half from larger cities—the national capitals of St. Petersburg and Moscow (including their industrial suburbs) and provincial capitals such as Smolensk, Orel, Voronezh, Penza, Kharkov, Ekaterinoslav, Kazan, and Tomsk. Among those from rural backgrounds, most were not born in stereotypical "peasant" families, but this did not mark them as untypical. The economic and social changes that were transforming Russia in the years when they were born had already so altered rural life that the conventional image of the peasant as farmer was becoming increasingly an image from the past.[12] More than half of rural-born worker writers (20 of 33) were born to parents (or at least fathers) who no longer lived only or even mainly by agricultural work. The fathers of these writers included industrial workers who migrated back and forth between village and city (some eventually moved their families to the city), but also workers employed in wage jobs outside the cities: we find here bricklayers, railroad workers, bakers, a church guard, a carter, a stevedore, a gardener, a shoemaker, a weaver, a glassmaker, a leatherworker, a trader, and others. Other writers' fathers died when they were still children, forcing their mothers to leave the village to seek urban work to survive. It is likely that this relatively high degree of urban and industrial experience in their childhoods encouraged these individuals to reach still further beyond the traditions of peasant life. But these experiences were also no longer exceptional in Russia.

Worker writers covered much of the range of urban lower-class employment. Many worked in relatively skilled occupations, especially those who were born in a city or moved there as young children. Skilled metalworkers,

---

[11] Although precise aggregate data on the birthplaces of workers in Russia were not collected, the particular data collections that exist suggest a much smaller proportion of urban-born workers than in our sample of worker writers. See Victoria Bonnell, *Roots of Rebellion: Workers' Politics and Organizations in St. Petersburg and Moscow, 1900–1914* (Berkeley, 1983), chap. 1; *Rabochii klass Rossii ot zarozhdeniia do nachala XX v.,* 2d ed. (Moscow, 1989), 255–60, 286–93; A. G. Rashin, *Formirovanie rabochego klassa Rossii* (Moscow, 1958), 404–53.

[12] Christine Worobec, *Peasant Russia: Family and Community in the Post-Emancipation Period* (Princeton, 1991); Barbara Alpern Engel, *Between the Fields and the City: Women, Work, and Family in Russia, 1861–1914* (Cambridge, 1994); Jeffrey Burds, *Peasant Dreams and Market Politics: Labor Migration and the Russian Village, 1861–1905* (Pittsburgh, 1998); Stephen Frank, *Crime, Cultural Conflict, and Justice in Rural Russia, 1856–1914* (Berkeley, 1999).

especially fitters (*slesari*) and turners (*tokari*), were the most numerous: they accounted for 14 of the total 62 (about the same proportion of metalworkers as in the Petersburg labor force in 1902, though higher than in Moscow and other cities).[13] There were also a couple each of printers, shoemakers, woodworkers, and weavers, and a glassmaker. The majority of worker writers, however, like the majority of workers, were to be found in various semiskilled and unskilled jobs in manufacturing (leather, tobacco, matches, paper, boxes, bookbinding, wood, tin, metal, hats, candy, vinegar, and clothing), offices, stores (as shop assistants or helpers selling goods ranging from vegetables to books), bakeries, taverns, tearooms, and mines; on the railroads (in various skilled and unskilled jobs), barges, and merchant ships; and as laborers (*chernorabochie*), bricklayers, furnace stokers (*kochegari*), teamsters (*gruzchiki*), cab drivers, barbers, house painters, construction workers, porters (*dvorniki*), port workers, stevedores, barge haulers, gardeners, shepherds, farmworkers, and even itinerant musicians. Anyone young enough and male at the outbreak of war in 1914 was also likely to experience life as a soldier at the front.

It would be a mistake, however—one made by many labor historians—to reify these jobs into identities. Mobility and instability were distinguishing features of the employment careers of many of these worker writers, and they were not all that unusual among workers more broadly. Only a minority of these workers, mainly the most skilled, spent their whole adult lives at a single trade. The majority tended to change jobs often—sometimes when they were fired for participating in strikes and for political activities, but often for more personal reasons. Many spent a good deal of time without work at all, wandering the country in search of new employment and of variety in life, even of adventure. Some of them began their experiences of wandering as children, when their families left their ancestral villages in search of work, often after the fathers died.[14] A few of these writers, especially those with links to the socialist movement, worked abroad, in Western Europe. It is not possible to measure how common such occupational and residential instability was; this is a subject that needs greater study. But it was certainly not exceptional, especially in the years of Russia's industrial growth from the 1890s into the early 1900s. Studies of labor in the printing industry, for example, describe a high level of itinerancy, vagrancy, and vagabondage, especially among the highly skilled and literate type compositors.[15] Still, we can only wonder how typical their wanderings were. It may be that the high levels of evidently voluntary mobility among workers who wrote was a marker of personal distinctiveness, a sign of intangible qualities of individuality and personality that led

[13] Bonnell, *Roots of Rebellion*, 32–33.

[14] It is striking that of the seventeen most important worker writers, about whom we consequently know the most (and whose lives are briefly described in the Appendix), seven were left without fathers when they were still young (Aleksandrovskii, Eroshin, Gan'shin, Kalinin, Kirillov, Mashirov, and Oreshin).

[15] Mark Steinberg, *Moral Communities: The Culture of Class Relations in the Printing Industry, 1867–1907* (Berkeley, 1992), 85–86.

them to look beyond their everyday lives and identities and become writers. Yet such mobility was hardly unique to them. These life stories may be telling indications of what helped make workers into writers, but they also remind us of the larger ambiguities and instabilities of the markers we often use to speak of lower-class people in the past: urban, rural, skilled, unskilled, metal-worker, printer.

Another sign of difference, though one shared with many hundreds of lower-class Russians who did not become writers, was an inclination to become politically active—an evident concern with public matters that paralleled and was probably connected to their desire to have their words heard by others. Two-thirds (41 of 62) of the total number of worker writers about whom we have detailed biographical information claimed to have joined or become associated with left-wing political organizations before 1917, or at least participated in political demonstrations or strikes. The majority of the politically active claimed to be members of the Russian Social Democratic Workers' Party (RSDRP) before 1917 (both Mensheviks and Bolsheviks, though the latter seem to have been slightly predominant). There were also a few neo-populist Socialist Revolutionaries and anarchists. These data are obviously not without problems, considering the politicized conditions under which this information was originally preserved.[16] Still, it remains clear that many worker writers were politically active, though some could barely distinguish between the varied factions and parties (the distinctions appear much stronger in history writing than they did in the minds of many workers at the time). Nearly half of the politically active reported that they had suffered for their politics—been arrested, jailed, and often exiled from their hometowns. Yet only a small number (7 in this cohort of 62) were active in trade unions, perhaps reflecting the fact that most were not committed to any single trade and often worked in relatively nonunionized workplaces. At the same time, suggesting public identities connected more to cultural than social roles, about one-third of these worker writers were active in various prerevolutionary organizations that united "writers from the people" like themselves and a few became editors of magazines written for lower-class audiences. After 1917 nearly half of these writers joined the Proletcult, the semiofficial "proletarian cultural" movement, and most were able to become full-time writers. In many ways the revolution empowered them, endorsing proletarian self-assertion and cultural creativity as state policy and offering them politically and culturally influential roles in the new order—as editors of journals, leaders of local Proletcults and in the national organization, staff members at the Commissariat of Enlightenment, trade union activists, local party officials, and officers of writers' organizations.

---

[16] Since many of these biographical data were collected after 1917 from individuals still publicly active, the selection is necessarily skewed in favor of the more politically active and the more pro-Bolshevik. Also, the political environment after 1917 may have encouraged workers who had been less active or less Bolshevik, but who wished to play active public roles and to escape wage work for cultural employment, to represent their pasts more appropriately.

The attribute that most distinguished worker writers was their literacy. Literacy rates throughout the empire had increased impressively in the decades after the abolition of serfdom in 1861, though when worker writers were growing up, the vast majority of the country's population remained illiterate.[17] Aggregate data, however, obscure a deep if socially uneven rise in literacy even among the lower classes. This unevenness helped determine the milieux from which working-class writers emerged. Gender was a major distinction. Men were more than twice as likely as women to have had the opportunity to learn to read and write. According to Russia's first national census, in 1897, throughout the whole empire only 13 percent of women compared to 29 percent of men were literate, and in the European provinces of the Russian empire male literacy rates were even higher (33%), though the rate for women was scarcely different (13.6%).[18] Social class was also a major factor; urban workers were much more likely to read than peasants. In European Russia, only 17 percent of peasants could read in 1897 (25% of men and 10% of women) compared to 54 percent of industrial and commercial workers (58% of men and 28% of women).[19] Within the more literate working class, craft and skill further shaped these uneven literacy patterns. We see higher than average rates of literacy in certain professions, especially among printers (83% literate in 1897), sales workers (76%), and metalworkers (66%).[20] Likewise, trades within each profession, linked mainly to levels of skill, had different rates of literacy. In metalworking enterprises, for example, turners (*tokari*) and fitters (*slesari*) were much more likely to be literate than blacksmiths or laborers.[21]

Geographic place also influenced literacy. Closeness to the large urban and industrial centers of the empire greatly increased the likelihood of becoming literate. Thus, for example, while only 25 percent of all male peasants in European Russia overall could read in 1897, in Moscow province 49 percent of the male peasants were literate. Even if we consider only peasants living in the villages (as opposed to residents of cities and towns who were still legally designated as peasants, as many new workers were), we still find that more than 40 percent of male peasants in Moscow province were literate.[22] City dwellers, of course, were the most likely to be literate. In St. Petersburg, 74 percent of all male workers and 40 percent of female workers were literate

[17] Literacy nationwide had increased from approximately 6% in the 1860s to 21% in 1897 and to an estimated 28% by 1913: A. G. Rashin, *Naselenie Rossii za 100 let (1811–1913): Statisticheskii ocherk* (Moscow, 1956), 284–311, esp. 289, 291, 308, 311.

[18] *Obshchii svod po imperii rezul'tatov razrabotki dannykh pervykh vseobshchei perepisi naseleniia, proizvedennoi 28 ianvaria 1897 goda* (St. Petersburg, 1905), 39. See also Rashin, *Naselenie Rossii za 100 let*, 308.

[19] *Chislennost' i sostav rabochikh v Rossii na osnovanii dannykh pervoi vseobshchei perepisi naseleniia Rossiiskoi Imperii 1897 g.* (St. Petersburg, 1906), 1:10, table 3; A. G. Rashin, *Formirovanie rabochego klassa Rossii* (Moscow, 1958), 579, 584.

[20] *Chislennost' i sostav rabochikh v Rossii*, 1:10–17, table 3.

[21] Rashin, *Formirovanie rabochego klassa Rossii*, 590.

[22] *Pervaia vseobshchaia perepis' naseleniia Rossiiskoi Imperii 1897 g.*, vol. 24 (Moscow province) (St. Petersburg, 1905), 63.

in 1897.[23] Finally, reflecting the constant improvements over time, age made a difference. A teenage working-class boy in 1897 was more than one and a half times more likely to be literate than his father and more than twice as likely to read as his grandfather—and this calculation assumes, against the odds, that his parents and grandparents were workers not peasants. By the same measure, a working-class girl was almost four times as likely to read as her working-class mother or grandmother.[24] In the years that followed, all of these numbers continued to grow.[25]

Schooling followed similar patterns.[26] In 1856 official data list only about 8,000 primary schools in the Russian empire, enrolling 450,000 pupils (less than 1% of the population, whereas an estimated 9% were of school age); forty years later, in 1896, ten times this number of schools were enrolling more than eight times the number of students (3.8 million pupils—more than 3% of the population, and thus approximately a third of all school-age children). By 1911, 6.6 million children were in Russian schools (4% of the population, or nearly half of full enrollment). These aggregate numbers, however, like those for literacy, obscure important patterns of popular schooling. At the end of the nineteenth century, male youths living in cities or in industrial regions were the most likely to receive elementary education. In the central and northern industrial provinces, between 69 and 87 percent of school-aged children were enrolled by 1915, and the percentages were even higher for boys.[27] The length of stay in school also increased over time and varied by place, though the extent of schooling remained low overall. Even in the immediate prewar years, most students were leaving school—often pulled out by their parents— after only two or three years. Only a minority (about 11%) completed the full four grades of the standard Russian elementary school, and around 40 percent completed less than one year in school.[28] It is important to note that not all schooling in Russia was through the formal network of schools sponsored

[23] *Chislennost' i sostav rabochikh v Rossii,* 2:16, table 3, pt. 2; S. Bernshtein-Kogan, *Chislennost', sostav, i polozhenie Peterburgskikh rabochikh: Opyt statisticheskogo issledovaniia* (St. Petersburg, 1910), 64.

[24] Of workers throughout European Russia in 1897, 73% of males aged 15–16 were literate, compared to 58% of 20–39-year-olds, 43% of 40–59-year-olds, and 35% of those over 60. Among women workers, the rates for the same age cohorts were 47%, 22%, 12%, and 15%. *Chislennost' i sostav rabochikh v Rossii,* 1:10–11, table 3. See also Bernshtein-Kogan, *Chislennost', sostav, i polozhenie Peterburgskikh rabochikh,* 66, and Rashin, *Naselenie Rossii za 100 let,* 310.

[25] In addition to the sources above, see Bonnell, *Roots of Rebellion,* 57–58; *Rabochii klass Rossii ot zarozhdeniia do nachala XX v.,* 2d ed. (Moscow, 1989), 280–82; Jeffrey Brooks, *When Russia Learned to Read: Literacy and Popular Culture, 1861–1917* (Princeton, 1985), chap. 1.

[26] Ben Eklof, *Russian Peasant Schools* (Berkeley, 1986); Brooks, *When Russia Learned to Read,* chap. 2; *Entsiklopedicheskii slovar': Rossiia,* ed. F. A. Brokgauz and I. A. Efron (St. Petersburg, 1898), 400–409.

[27] Eklof, *Russian Peasant Schools,* 287, 293, 295, 310–11; Rashin, *Naselenie Rossii za 100 let,* 318; *Novyi entsiklopedicheskii slovar',* vol. 28 (Petrograd, 1916), 123–28 and tables following. Central and northern industrial provinces referred to comprise these provinces (from lowest to highest levels of schooling of children aged 8–11): Novgorod (69%), Iaroslavl, Tver, Vladimir, Kaluga, Petrograd, and Moscow (87%).

[28] Rashin, *Naselenie Rossii za 100 let,* 316–17; Eklof, *Russian Peasant Schools,* 294, 328–41.

by the national government, or even the variety of official, semiofficial, and private groups involved in promoting popular education. Many Russian peasants and workers were taught to read and write by parents or relatives, by tutors hired by families or communities, or by priests.[29] And many lower-class Russians continued their education by reading on their own or by studying together with other "self-taught" workers in study circles, workers' clubs, and adult education courses.

For all the many limitations on the breadth and depth of popular schooling and literacy, they influenced the lives of millions of lower-class Russians in the last decades of the old regime. To be sure, the impact was limited in many ways. As critics have argued, rote learning and the brevity of time spent in the classroom and at schoolwork restricted the impact of the school curriculum. And aggregate numbers of literates mask a great deal of difference in what "literacy" meant—from the rudimentary skill of being able to make out words and sign one's name to the more complex ability to read various sorts of texts and communicate ideas in writing. It is clear that for many lower-class Russians, schooling and literacy had primarily utilitarian value: to aid in one's work, function effectively in an urban environment, get a better job, handle everyday family or personal record keeping, improve the terms of military service, keep in touch with relatives, and perhaps to be amused and entertained. Nevertheless, it is also clear that for many ordinary Russians, literacy was a source of pride and self-esteem, of exposure to the world, and of moral ideas, all of which often had profound importance for the way they viewed themselves and the world.[30]

The biographies of worker writers echo the social characteristics that made a lower-class Russian likely to become schooled and literate. Most worker writers were male (among the more than 150 worker authors I have been able to identify who started writing before 1917, only 7 are women) and had been born either in cities or in the more industrialized central provinces of Russia. Many worked in trades where literacy was high. As for other literate lower-class Russians, their sources of literacy varied. Although some worker writers recalled a relative or some literate villager teaching them to read, the rapid spread of formal primary schooling had a strong impact. Almost all worker writers about whose educational histories we have information had some schooling, typically from one to four years (though many attended only during the winter, when they were not required to help with farmwork or other family needs). And the later they were born, the more likely they were to have attended school and to

[29] Rashin, *Formirovanie rabochego klassa*, 589; Ben Eklof, "Peasant Sloth Reconsidered: Strategies of Education and Learning in Rural Russia before the Revolution," *Journal of Social History* 14, no. 3 (Spring 1981): 367.

[30] Eklof, "Peasant Sloth Reconsidered," 370–77, and *Russian Peasant Schools*, chap. 9; Brooks, *When Russia Learned to Read*, chap. 1; Bonnell, *Roots of Rebellion*, 47–52; Reginald Zelnik, *A Radical Worker in Tsarist Russia: The Autobiography of Semen Ivanovich Kanatchikov* (Stanford, 1986), 19, 64; Steinberg, *Moral Communities*, 113–15; and Chapters 2 and 3 below. Scholarly debates on the impact of literacy on individuals are summarized by David Vincent in his *Literacy and Popular Culture: England, 1750–1914* (Cambridge, 1989), esp. 8–9.

have attended longer. Much of the huge variety of primary schools in Russia is evident in the schools they attended. Church parish schools, zemstvo schools (run by partially autonomous councils of local rural administration), and city and village schools under the Ministry of Education were the most common. But we also see a variety of special schools, such as agricultural, commercial, artisanal, factory, and railroad schools, which offered both basic education and special occupational training. A small but significant number of worker writers continued their elementary education with adult courses at Sunday schools, night schools, and "people's universities" (such as the very influential Shaniavskii People's University in Moscow). Their biographies reflect the history and achievements of popular education in Russia.

Most important, as these worker writers repeatedly testified in memoirs and stories about their own lives, they not only knew how to read but did read—often with a passion and drive that bordered on obsession. They wrote because they had a need to express themselves, to voice aloud their thoughts and feelings about their lives and the world. But the texts they created to embody what they had to say were inspired also by their encounters with other texts. These encounters were among the most important in their social lives. Their memoirs are filled with stories of losing (and finding) themselves in literature, of voracious reading, and of being inspired to write by some story or poem. Many do not identify what texts they read, speaking only of reading and books—perhaps because the act and pleasure of reading was as important as the particular author or style. (Besides, after 1917 some authors and genres of literature were viewed with disfavor and better left unmentioned.) But many do speak of the authors who influenced them.

The most frequently named authors, and the most likely to be described as inspirational, were almost all Russian poets of the early and middle nineteenth century: Nikolai Nekrasov (mentioned more often than any other author) and Ivan Nikitin, both mid-century poets who wrote with pathos and sympathy about the lives of the poor; the first famous "poets from the people," Aleksei Kol'tsov and Ivan Surikov; and the nearly iconic national poet Aleksandr Pushkin. The only living author mentioned so often as inspirational was Maxim Gorky, another "writer from the people" who drew on the same literary traditions to describe the harsh life of the common people but also to present lower-class heroes who were not unlike many worker authors as they saw themselves: strong and restless individuals, often living on the fringes of society, challenging both oppressive authorities and the slavish submissiveness of the masses. Beyond this first tier of influential authors were other recognized classical and contemporary writers. Among the Russian classics the most popular were the works of Mikhail Lermontov, Nikolai Gogol, and Lev Tolstoy, though some worker writers also read Ivan Turgenev, Fedor Dostoevsky, and the poets Semen Nadson, Fedor Tiutchev, Afanasii Fet, and (for Ukrainians) Taras Shevchenko. Among living authors, besides Gorky, were mentioned (though far less often than writers of the past) the lyrical and symbolic poets Konstantin Bal'mont, Aleksandr Blok, and Valerii Briusov; the realist prose writers Vladimir Korolenko, Leonid Andreev, Ivan Bunin, Aleksei Tolstoi, and Anton Chekhov; the Futurist poet Vladimir Maiakovskii; and finally, some of the better known proletarian authors, especially Mikhail Gerasimov, Vladimir Kirillov, and Vasilii Aleksandrovskii. Some foreign authors, read in translation, were also influential, especially the contemporary poets Walt Whitman and Emile Verhaeren and such European Romantic writers as Johann Goethe, Friedrich Schiller, George Byron, and Heinrich Heine, but also Edgar Allen Poe, Romain Rolland, Oscar Wilde, Rabindranath Tagore, William Shakespeare, and Homer. Among philosophers and thinkers mentioned as influential were such European-oriented socialists as Vissarion Belinskii, Nikolai Dobroliubov, and Dmitrii Pisarev; such Marxists as Georgii Plekhanov, Vladimir Lenin, and Aleksandr Bogdanov; but also Western thinkers as diverse as August Bebel, Friedrich Nietzsche, and Arthur Schopenhauer. Especially in their youths, the favorite reading of many worker writers included the popular boulevard press, with its romantic stories of bandits, heroes, adventure, and war, along with the Bible and lives of the saints. Finally, and tellingly, some worker writers insisted that they were influenced by no one.[31] Except perhaps for this last gesture of hubris, these lists of influential popular reading were much the same as those of other "conscious" and "cultured" workers—as can be seen, for example, in reports on workers' borrowing from trade union and workers' club libraries.[32]

These plebeian *intelligenty* frequently worried about the great "ocean of darkness" separating themselves from the masses of ordinary Russian workers.[33] And these critical worries echoed a chorus of public concern, heard steadily from the late imperial era into the early Soviet years, that the majority of the urban poor remained indifferent to learning and trapped in a cultural darkness of drunkenness, brutality, and passivity.[34] There is significant truth in this sense of great difference. But we should not take them literally at their word. These anxieties and estrangements were part of the lower-class *intelligenty*'s self-defining role, part of their own mythic self-image as individuals freed from the normal degradations of popular life and thus able to return and redeem the people. It is clear that they did not in fact emerge from a void or truly stand on the other side of a great sea of popular darkness. Certainly they were not "average" workers—in any case, a category both difficult to de-

[31] A particularly useful source was a questionnaire distributed to participants at the 1920 congress of proletarian writers. Question 32 asked, "Which writers had the most influence on you?" RGALI, f. 1638, op. 3, d. 4, ll. 1–62.

[32] I. D. Levin, *Rabochie kluby v dorevoliutsionnom Peterburge: Iz istorii rabochego dvizheniia, 1907–1914 gg.* (Moscow, 1926), 116; *Metallist*, no. 9 (26 Jan. 1912), 13; no. 10 (11 Feb. 1912), 4–5; *Zhizn' pekarei*, no. 2(5) (10 May 1914), 11.

[33] The phrase is from Ivan Kubikov, "Tragediia rabochei intelligentsii," *Rabochaia mysl'*, no. 1 (25 Aug. 1917), 6. See also Chapters 2 and 3 below.

[34] See Stephen Frank, "Confronting the Domestic Other: Rural Popular Culture and Its Enemies in Fin-de-Siècle Russia," in *Cultures in Flux: Lower-Class Values, Practices, and Resistance in Late Imperial Russia,* ed. Stephen Frank and Mark Steinberg (Princeton, 1994), chap. 4; Laura Engelstein, *The Keys to Happiness: Sex and the Search for Modernity in Fin-de-Siècle Russia* (Ithaca, 1992); Steinberg, *Moral Communities,* 56–61.

fine, given the data available, and of doubtful interpretive utility, given the enormous variety and flux in working-class life. Indeed, they were in many ways remarkable individuals. But their lives reflected a larger history: of urbanization and industrialization; of the movement of peasants to the city (and back and forth); of the spread and reception of education, texts, and new ideas among the lower classes; of the rising force of socialist politics; of the increase of working-class self-organization; of the definition and assertion of individualities; of the growing audibility and influence of all sorts of plebeian voices in public life; and, after 1917, of growing opportunities for upward mobility for talented individuals from the now ostensibly empowered working class. That their voices were stubbornly unorthodox, critical, and often deeply uncertain was also a sign of their times. Their later fates also echoed larger histories. Some of these writers fell into silence and oblivion in the face of the growing cultural uniformity imposed starting in the middle 1920s and especially in the 1930s. Some had successful careers as writers or cultural officials. Quite a few were arrested in the late 1930s and shot.[35]

It appears that in no other country, as Gorky claimed in 1914, were there so many worker and peasant writers as in Russia.[36] Perhaps the reason was that Russian workers had few alternative ways to express themselves; perhaps it was the intensity of the Russian experience in those years. In any case, it is not only the fact of widespread worker writing in Russia that is so striking, but also the passion and desire for creative self-expression we see among many working-class Russians. Some of these plebeian writers and poets no doubt viewed their experiments in creativity as ephemeral. Others, like many of those who wrote to Gorky, tried seriously to become writers but lacked the talent or will to persist in finding more than a handful of listeners and readers. A remarkable number of lower-class Russians, however, wrote with enough persistence and talent to attract publishers, and found themselves driven to improve their skills and to write as often as possible. The literary merit of most of this work, from the standpoint of contemporary standards of technique and form, was low. As even a sympathetic Marxist critic observed, most of the literary writing by workers that appeared in the press during these years was "naively childlike" in style and amounted to little more than "rhymed prose" or "doggerel."[37] Nevertheless, these writings reveal an enormous desire for self-expression, a key condition for the emergence of an "intelligentsia from the people." And these writings are often deeply expressive of a range of complex ideas and emotions.

[35] See the Appendix.

[36] Maksim Gor'kii, Introduction to *Pervyi sbornik proletarskikh pisatelei* (St. Petersburg, 1914), 7. On worker writers in Western Europe, see, e.g., Martha Vicinius, "Literary Voices of an Industrial Town: Manchester, 1810–1870," in *The Victorian City: Images and Realities,* ed. H. J. Dyos and Michael Wolff (London, 1973), 2:739–61; Jacques Rancière, "Ronds de fumée (Les Poètes ouvriers dans la France de Louis-Philippe)," *Revue des sciences humaines,* no. 190 (April–June 1983), 31–47.

[37] V. L. L'vov-Rogachevskii, *Ocherki proletarskoi literatury* (Moscow and Leningrad, 1927), 5, 25–27.

Although many educated elites admired and tried to help promote these advanced peasants and workers, the relations between the two groups were often, as historians of the Russian labor movement have noted, distant and distrustful. The years after 1905 were a time of heightened organizational possibility and diversity but also of frequent frustration with the failures of political radicalism and with the ideological bickering among the educated. Although worker *intelligenty* and educated elites continued to interact in various organizations and groups, especially the parties and the press, workers tended to prefer their own organizational space, if they sought organization at all. As Kleinbort, himself a Marxist intellectual, acknowledged, in workers' unions, cooperatives, and cultural organizations the intelligentsia was forced largely to the side as worker *intelligenty* moved to control things themselves.[38]

This proclivity pervaded workers' own evaluations of the shape and nature of Russia's emerging worker intelligentsia.[39] Unlike educational organizations run by elites for enlightenment of the common people, it was said, only workers' "self-education societies" were nurturing the "worldview" and "independent initiative" (*samodeiatel'nost'*) workers needed, and helping to give birth to a needed "worker intelligentsia."[40] In the view of the Menshevik worker critic Ivan Dement'ev, this intelligentsia first appeared in "the gravelike quiet" of the first years of the century but grew rapidly after 1905 as unions, clubs, and other workers' organizations nurtured advanced workers. As a result, he argued, by the eve of the war, "thinking and developed workers" had become a normal part of working-class life. And even though their numbers remained small, their significance was great, for they alone truly defended the "right" of workers to "self-organization" and they were the truest voice of workers' most developed ideas, feelings, and historical memories.[41] For the non-Marxist members of the Surikov Literature and Music Circle, established in Moscow in 1903 by "writers from the people," the same separatist values held even if their more populist language was different. The goal of the circle, it was declared in 1915, was to unite the "intelligentsia from the people" (*narodnaia intelligentsiia*), an intelligentsia that had "emerged out of the depths of the life of the people," not by the educational efforts of elites working among the people but by the efforts of plebeians alone, "by the strength of their own spirit."[42] The bakery shop assistant Mikhail Savin—a poet, an activist in the Moscow bakers' union, editor of the trade union paper *Bulochnik* (The baker) in 1906 and of the "people's journal" *Balalaika* in 1913, and a member of the Surikov Circle—made this point even more

---

[38] Kleinbort, *Ocherki rabochei intelligentsii*, 193.

[39] See also Kleinbort's account of these arguments in the workers' press, ibid., 175–79.

[40] "Rabochiia obshchestva samoobrazovanii," *Professional'ny vestnik*, no. 25 (18 Aug. 1909), 37.

[41] Kvadrat [Ivan Demen'tev, better known by his other pseudonym, Kubikov], "Rabochaia kul'tura," *Luch'*, no. 129 (7 Jan. 1913), 2.

[42] *Drug naroda* 1915, no. 1 (1 Jan.): 1; Ivan Kubikov, "Tragediia rabochei intelligentsii," *Rabochaia mysl'*, no. 1 (25 Aug. 1917), 4–7.

strongly in a 1915 essay on the people's intelligentsia. Who, he asked rhetorically, can bring light to the "dark masses" of the people? Only those who know the people's life: "Only those who have experienced all the charms of a life without rights can weep the people's sufferings and rejoice the people's joys."[43] Similarly, in 1917 the editors of the journal *Rabochaia mysl'* (Workers' thought), a paper "of a Menshevik tendency" representing and uniting the worker intelligentsia, argued that the worker intelligentsia is the "bearer" of workers' "class feelings" as well as the truest voice of working-class "consciousness."[44]

The emphasis on high consciousness and deep social feeling was entwined with the definition of "intelligentsia" in Russian culture. Until after 1917, when the term fell into disrepute as standing for a discredited part of the liberal bourgeoisie and was transformed into an occupational and educational category, "intelligentsia" was primarily a cultural, moral, and political category, not a social one. It designated not merely the well educated or the professional but people of any class (though some questioned this possibility) with an intellectual and moral commitment to knowledge as a force for emancipating human beings from conditions and attitudes that were seen to deny their natural dignity and rights. The precise qualities of mind and belief that earned this label remained endlessly contested—indeed, this contestation was also part of the term's definition.[45] The "worker intelligentsia" and the "intelligentsia from the people" were similarly defined as representing "that part of the laboring population that lives a conscious life, that seeks truth and spiritual beauty in the world" and "works for the good of [their] native people and of all humanity."[46] The same defining notions were applied to the related category of "people's writer," which also echoed nineteenth-century idealizations of the role and character of the writer. According to the worker writer Nikolai Liashko, the people's writer (*narodnyi pisatel'*) was not simply a writer for the people or even a writer from the people but a writer who, inspired by both commitment and life experience, "would show us the spirit of the people, bring to life their confused and troubled dreams, and spiritually take upon his shoulders all the people's burdens." This was not a position to which one could appoint oneself. One became a people's writer not by calling oneself one but when the people "feel themselves, their own soul, in his works."[47]

---

[43] Em.-Es. (I have identified the author as Savin from the initials as well as from his association with this journal and with such ideas), "Neskol'ko slov," *Drug naroda*, no. 5–7 (1915).

[44] "Ot redaktsii," *Rabochaia mysl'*, no. 1 (25 Aug. 1917), 1–2. Ivan Dement'ev (Kubikov) was one of the leading figures on this paper. See also Dement'ev's article on the "tragedy of the workers' intelligentsia" on pp. 4–7 and the appeal to readers in issue no. 4–5 (12 Nov. 1917), 2.

[45] Among contemporary efforts to define the intelligentsia, see esp. Ivanov-Razumnik [R. V. Ivanov], *Istoriia russkoi obshchestvennoi mysli*, vol. 1 (St. Petersburg, 1914), chap. 1.

[46] A. Shvedskaia, letter to *Drug naroda*, no. 2 (31 Jan. 1915), 16; [Mikhail Loginov], "Usnavaite po plodam," *Zvezda utrenniaia*, no. 17 (23 May 1912), 2.

[47] N. Nikolaev [Liashko], "O narodnom pisatelem, pisateliakh i 'pisateliakh,'" *Ogni*, no. 3 (January 1913), 26.

Building Popular "Culture"

The possibility of the emergence in late imperial Russia of a sizable group of lower-class Russians with the education, self-confidence, and personal freedom to make themselves into what observers would define as a new plebeian "intelligentsia" clearly depended on more than "the strength of their own spirit."[48] It depended on a variety of enabling social and cultural changes, not least the spread of literacy and education among the common people. But no less important was a widening of the sphere of public life where ideas could be nurtured, exchanged, and expressed aloud, and where like-minded individuals could associate. Many of these developments came from above, the work of worried or sympathetic elites, though even these efforts, however manipulative and controlling, offered important opportunities for commoners to think about and even transform their own lives. At the same time, the possibilities and practices of self-organization were steadily growing.

Urban growth and industrialization heightened state and public concern about the cultural and moral level of the common people and produced varied efforts to bring knowledge and civilizing culture to the masses, to reshape existing popular culture into proper culture for the people. Whether motivated by fear of a "dark" underclass or by a desire to spread enlightenment as a necessary moral good—or by the two in combination—many educated elites (including socialists and trade unionists) joined the state and the church in efforts to bring to Russian commoners, especially to the growing masses of urban workers, what they considered the civilizing essentials of "culture." Culture was defined, of course, as it was throughout Europe at the time, not as an open category of constructed meanings but as an absolute body of knowledge, thought, and behavior, which included, among other virtues, sobriety, rationality, self-respect, a sense of community, and a literate appreciation of improving cultural forms. This culturalist drive—known in Russian at the time as *kul'turnichestvo* (culturism) or *kul'turtregerstvo* (from the German *Kulturträger,* one who spreads civilization)—took many forms, including adult education, temperance organizations, movements for improving recreation, and publishing for the people. These structures often profoundly touched the lives of lower-class Russians, especially the emerging worker intelligentsia.[49]

From the perspective of culture-minded workers, these culturalist efforts

---

[48] *Drug naroda* 1915, no. 1 (1 Jan.): 1.

[49] For summary discussions of elite culturalist movements, see esp. Frank, "Confronting the Domestic Other"; Brooks, *When Russia Learned to Read,* 317–22; Joan Neuberger, *Hooliganism: Crime, Culture, and Power in St. Petersburg, 1900–1914* (Berkeley, 1993), 7–8 and passim; Joseph Bradley, "Voluntary Associations, Civic Culture, and *Obshchestvennost'* in Moscow," in *Between Tsar and People: Educated Society and the Quest for Public Identity in Late Imperial Russia,* ed. Edith Clowes, Samuel Kassow, and James West (Princeton, 1991), 141–47; Louise McReynolds and Cathy Popkin, "The Objective Eye and the Common Good," in *Constructing Russian Culture in the Age of Revolution: 1881–1940,* ed. Catriona Kelly and David Shepherd (Oxford, 1998), 57–81.

created greater opportunities to expand their rudimentary childhood learning and pursue greater knowledge and culture. The numbers of such aspiring workers is impressive. One educator, echoing many, spoke of a "great popular desire for knowledge" and noted with admiration (and a hint of condescending amusement) that when workers visiting adult education programs were asked what sort of lectures they most desired, their typical answer was "I want to know everything" (*Vse znat' khochu*).[50] Trade union leaders were similarly impressed. "The current striving for knowledge by workers," observed a union activist in 1907, "reminds one of the mid-nineties when the first mass awakening of the working class stimulated struggle not only for better working conditions but also toward the light of knowledge." But the difference between then and now was "enormous," he argued. Then it involved hundreds or thousands of workers, whereas now hundreds of thousands were involved. Then the level of intellectual demands was rather "primitive," and the leadership came almost entirely from intellectuals, whereas now workers themselves "direct and define" this movement.[51] No less important, it was argued, whereas the thin layer of the "intelligentsia from the people" was completely isolated from the masses of workers in the 1890s, now there was a whole spectrum of cultural development, so that one saw the growth of an "intermediary layer" of cultured workers who could link the "intellectual heights" of the working class with its "depths."[52]

The growth of publishing in Russia created one important public space where such culture-minded commoners could develop their cultural knowledge and abilities. Proliferating newspapers, magazines, pamphlets, and books were influential sources of news, ideas, and stories to think with: moral tales about the familiar hardships of daily life, often bizarre accounts revealing areas of life that could not be personally seen, images of worlds both familiar and exotic, news accounts documenting possibility and danger in modern life, and works of fiction and poetry, all provided an enlightening and disturbing catalogue of the world around. The huge growth in popular reading in the late 1800s and the early years of the new century was often commented on, and publishers responded to and tried to stimulate this demand with a flood of cheap publications aimed expressly at lower-class audiences. Their offerings ranged from cheap printings of Russian classics to popular religious pamphlets to commercial "boulevard literature" focusing on adventure, crime, and romance; from "lowbrow" (in the view of many contemporaries) mass-circulation penny newspapers such as *Gazeta-kopeika* (The kopeck newspaper) to magazines directed at the more culturally aspiring lower-class readers. Of course, some lower-class readers considered the idea of a separate literature for the people insulting; they should be able to read the same books and

---

[50] G. V. Zimin, "Shkola i fabrika," *Zavety* 1913, no. 4: 49–50.

[51] D. [probably Dmitrii Kol'tsov], "Kul'turno-prosvetitel'naia rabota v soiuzakh," *Professional'nyi vestnik*, no. 15 (26 Oct. 1907), 1.

[52] L. M. Kleinbort, "Ocherki rabochei demokratii," pt. 2, "Umstvennyi pod"em," *Sovremennyi mir*, May 1913, 151–52.

periodicals as anyone else; universality was part of their very definition of culture.[53]

Lower-class Russians living in cities faced a burgeoning public life, an increasingly large and diverse sphere of civic institutions that deliberately crafted spaces where individuals could associate to pursue their interests and desires even within a still relatively rigid political and social order.[54] For the urban lower classes in the first decade of the twentieth century, and especially after the 1905 revolution, which stimulated civic organization and forced the state to recognize it under law, the possibilities for voluntary association and continuing education proliferated. A worker might join a mutual aid society (especially among the skilled crafts), a trade union (legalized in 1906), a workers' club, or an underground political party (many of which became partly legal after 1905). Worker writers tended to do many of these things. But most important for the development of the intellectual and literary drives of such individuals were the increasing opportunities to continue their education informally: circles of like-minded (especially literary-minded) workers, underground socialist study groups (typically led by party intellectuals), public lectures organized by various organizations devoted to "improving" the common people, evening and Sunday courses at people's universities and similar institutions, workers' theaters, cultural and literary activities organized (after 1905) by trade unions, and organizations of working-class "self-education."

Adult education played a large role in the lives of many culturally aspiring lower-class Russians. Among the most extensive efforts were the people's universities (*narodnye universitety*), which began to appear in Russia in the 1890s, modeled on European experiments in workers' adult education as well as on the older Russian tradition of Sunday and evening courses for workers. In Moscow in 1893, a group of liberal intellectuals began to organize public lectures for lower-class audiences. In Kazan in 1894, a local professor organized a course of public lectures. In St. Petersburg in 1898, the Pedagogical Museum established a "department for assistance to self-education." A few other cities saw a similar development of programs of public lectures for commoners. Some of the leading liberal intellectuals of the day were among the speakers who offered series of two-hour talks on their areas of specialization, typically modern science, literature, and history.

---

[53] Rubakin, *Etiudy o russkoi chitaiushchei publike* and *Chistaia publika i intelligentsia iz naroda*, 2d ed. (St. Petersburg, 1906), esp. 236–55 (1904 speech on education); L. M. Kleinbort, "Novyi chitatel'," *Sovremennyi mir*, May 1916, 92–115, and *Ocherki rabochei intelligentsii*, chap. 2; Jeffrey Brooks, "Readers and Reading at the End of the Tsarist Era," in *Literature and Society in Imperial Russia, 1800–1914*, ed. William Mills Todd III (Stanford, 1978), esp. 119–50; idem, *When Russian Learned to Read*; idem, "Popular Philistinism and the Course of Russian Modernism," in *History and Literature: Theoretical Problems and Russian Case Studies*, ed. Gary Saul Morson (Stanford, 1986), 90–110; Louise McReynolds, *The News under Russia's Old Regime* (Princeton, 1991), 229–39; Daniel Brower, "The Penny Press and Its Readers," in Frank and Steinberg, *Cultures in Flux*, 147–67.

[54] For a selection of works on Russia's expanding public sphere, see Clowes et al., *Between Tsar and People*.

The revolution of 1905, and especially the law of 4 March 1906 "on associations [*obshchestva*] and unions,"[55] allowed this movement to grow and the schools to establish themselves more firmly as public voluntary institutions. During these years, people's universities were established in most large provincial capitals and in many smaller cities as well. Among the most successful were the Shaniavskii People's University in Moscow and the Association of People's Universities in St. Petersburg. In January 1908, in St. Petersburg, the First All-Russian Congress of Representatives of People's Universities and Other Enlightenment Institutions Established by Private Initiative brought together active representatives of evening courses, people's universities, trade union cultural organizations, and workers' clubs (mainly from the capital, despite the formal claim that this was a national congress). After a bitter debate over how much control workers should have over their own education, it was decided to allow students (called *sluzhateli,* or listeners) to vote for officers and have some influence over the curriculum. Despite continuing criticism of "bourgeois" domination of the people's universities and their curricula, some trade unions and workers' clubs in the years after 1905, especially in St. Petersburg, entered into agreements with the people's universities to organize joint low-cost lectures for workers. Forbidden by the government to allow talks on controversial political or social topics, the lecturers spoke mainly on such themes as law, ancient history and culture, Russian economic history, and literature.[56]

Similar to the people's universities, and similarly important in the lives of worker *intelligenty,* were the people's houses (*narodnye doma*), modeled partly on European people's houses, polytechnics, settlements, and university extensions, but also a natural evolution of the people's "auditoria" and theaters and "people's readings" (*narodnye chtenie*), public readings of books for illiterate and semiliterate audiences, organized in many cities in the 1880s and 1890s. Especially in the years after 1899, when the Pushkin centenary inspired widespread efforts to improve popular culture, people's houses (still often called people's auditoria) emerged in the two capitals and in several provincial cities (sometimes several in a larger city). The 1905 revolution gave further impetus to this movement. Organizers included city governments, zemstvos, literacy societies, temperance organizations, and private individuals who sought to raise cultural levels among the lower classes. The typical people's house included a free reading room and library; an auditorium, often equipped with a "magic

[55] "O vremennykh pravilakh ob obshchestvakh i soiuzakh," *Polnoe sobranie zakonov Rossiiskoi imperii,* sobranie 3, vol. 26, pt. 1 (St. Petersburg, 1906), 201–7.

[56] *Trudy pervogo vserossiiskogo s"ezda deiatelei obshchestv narodnykh universitetov i drugikh prosvetitelnykh uchrezhdenii chastnoi initsiativy (S-Peterburg 3–7 ianvaria 1908 g.)* (St. Petersburg, 1908); *Professional'nyi vestnik* (St. Petersburg central bureau of trade unions), no. 17–19 (12 Jan. 1908), 5–7; *Kuznets* (St. Petersburg blacksmiths' union), no. 5–6 (19 Jan. 1908), 6–10; *Golos portnogo* (St. Petersburg garment workers' union), no. 1–2 (10 May 1909), 4; *Zhizn' pekarei* (St. Petersburg bakers' union), no. 1(4) (10 Mar. 1914), 18; E. N. Medynskii, *Vneshkol'noe obrazovanie: Ego znachenie, organizatsiia i tekhnika* (St. Petersburg, 1913); Lynn Mally, *Culture of the Future: The Proletkult Movement in Russia* (Berkeley, 1990), 12–13.

lantern" and a film projector; a shop that sold books, magazines, and prints; a hall for theatrical performances; classroom and exhibition spaces; a legal aid office; and a tearoom. Programs included a variety of activities for the lower-class public, such as choirs, theater groups, orchestras, reading circles, sport circles, performances, lectures, exhibits, consumer cooperatives, courses (typically on science, history, and literature, but also on technical and professional topics), and "people's readings." One of the most successful people's houses in prerevolutionary Russia was the one organized by Countess Sofiia Panina on Ligovskaia Street in St. Petersburg. The countess took control of an older people's house in 1903 and, mainly with her own funds, greatly expanded its activities. Under her direction, the Ligovskii People's House (most often known simply as Panina's People's House) offered lectures, evening classes for men and women, a three-year course of artisanal classes, people's readings, children's gatherings, artistic and technical exhibits, a theater, legal aid, a savings bank, a tearoom, and a dining hall. Starting around 1912, Panina's People's House was also the home of a self-organized literary circle of worker writers, which published several "manuscript magazines" and two print editions of their works.[57] Socialists and union activists frequently complained about the limited and even "harmful" cultural offerings of the people's houses: "bad opera at high prices . . . , acrobats, clowns, magicians, balalaika pluckers [*balalaechniki*], singers, and cinemas with a preposterous repertoire."[58] At the same time, many worker *intelligenty* described the people's houses as appealing and necessary places of both enlightenment and refuge.[59]

Urban workers, especially in St. Petersburg and Moscow, encountered many other efforts by civic groups and individuals to provide them with "healthy" entertainment, recreation, and education. Civic reform groups such as the Society to Disseminate Useful Books, the Society to Organize Educational Public Amusements, and the Temperance Society joined local city councils and urban missionaries in organizing readings, lectures, concerts, magic lantern shows, meetings, and tearooms.[60] Urban secondary schools sometimes organized evening courses for adults, and semiautonomous civic institutions, such as the Cultural Commission on Technical Education of the Imperial Russian Technical Society, established evening courses for workers in several cities, notably the Prechistenskie Workers' Courses in Moscow, which were organized in 1897 and attracted thousands of workers over the years.[61] A variety of organizations established inexpensive popular theaters

[57] RGALI, f. 1821 (Samobytnik-Mashirov), op. 1, d. 1, l. 15–150b.

[58] Kvadrat [Ivan Dement'ev], in *Professional'nyi vestnik* (St. Petersburg), no. 26 (31 Oct. 1909), 8.

[59] For further information on the People's Houses, see "Narodnye doma," *Novyi entsiklopedicheskii slovar'*, vol. 27 (Petrograd, 1916), 946–49; P. Golubev, "Narodnye doma—dvortsy," *Russkoe bogatstvo*, 1901, vol. 12, pt. 2: 1–40; V. Ia. Danilevskii, *Narodnyi dom: Ego zadachi i obshchestvennoe znachenie* (Kharkov, 1915); Mally, *Culture of the Future*, 13–14.

[60] Bradley, "Voluntary Associations, Civic Culture, and *Obshchestvennost'* in Moscow," 131–48.

[61] Bonnell, *Roots of Rebellion*, 330; *Istoriia Moskvy*, vol. 5 (Moscow, 1955), 249; I. D. Levin,

starting in the 1870s and in later years helped urban workers establish theater groups.[62] Managers and owners of large private and state-owned factories organized courses of study, tearooms, choirs, orchestras, theaters, free libraries, lectures, and evenings of literature and music for their workers.[63] Cultural entrepreneurs established new public amusement parks (*uveselitel'nye sady*) in major cities.[64] Even foreigners joined in the effort at enlightenment; the American missionary John Stokes, for example, in 1900 established in St. Petersburg the Maiak (Lighthouse) Society for Aiding the Moral, Mental, and Physical Development of Young People; it lasted until about 1910 and counted a number of future trade union leaders among its members.[65] The central government not only supported many of these civic efforts but also established its own clubs and tearooms for workers under the auspices of the Okhrana (the political police) in the early years of the century.[66] Finally, one should mention the schools for workers established by émigré Russian socialists in Western Europe—the school organized by Bogdanov, Gorky, and Lunacharsky in 1909 at Gorky's home on the island of Capri (at which the most prominent student was the "worker philosopher" Fedor Kalinin), Bogdanov's school in Bologna (1910–11), Lenin's competing school near Paris, and especially, by 1912–13, Lunacharsky's Proletarian Culture circle (also known as the League of Proletarian Culture), where radicalized worker *intelligenty* (most of whom had some to Europe after fleeing exile in the Russian north or Siberia) met regularly to discuss literature and ideas, including their own literary creativity.[67]

Self-Organization and Self-Expression

The myth that the worker intelligentsia arose "by the strength of their own spirit" was part of a self-ideal, however fanciful, that created constant en-

---

Rabochie kluby v dorevoliutsionnom Peterburge: Iz istorii rabochego dvizheniia, 1907–1914 gg. (Moscow, 1926), 12.

[62] Golubev, "Narodnye doma," 3–8; Gary Thurston, "The Impact of Russian Popular Theater, 1886–1915," *Journal of Modern History* 55 (June 1983): 237–67; E. Anthony Swift, "Workers' Theater and 'Proletarian Culture' in Prerevolutionary Russia, 1905–1917," in *Workers and Intelligentsia in Late Imperial Russia*, ed. Reginald Zelnik (Berkeley, 1999), 260–91.

[63] See, e.g., Steinberg, *Moral Communities*, 57–61.

[64] Al'bin Konechnyi, "Shows for the People," in Frank and Steinberg, *Cultures in Flux*, chap. 6.

[65] Levin, *Rabochie kluby*, 7.

[66] Jeremiah Schneiderman, *Sergei Zubatov and Revolutionary Marxism* (Ithaca, 1976); Walter Sablinsky, *The Road to Bloody Sunday* (Princeton, 1977); Bonnell, *Roots of Rebellion*, 93; Gerald D. Surh, *1905 in St. Petersburg: Labor, Society, and Revolution* (Stanford, 1989), 99–153; Laura Engelstein, *Moscow, 1905: Working-Class Organization and Political Conflict* (Stanford, 1982), 59–65, 79–81.

[67] V. Kosarev, "Partiinaia shkola na ostrove Kapri," *Sibirskie ogni*, no. 2 (May–June 1922), 63–75; Mally, *Culture of the Future*, 6–7; Jutta Scherrer, "Les Ecoles du parti de Capri et de Bologne: La Formation de l'intelligentsia du parti," *Cahiers du monde russe et soviétique* 19, no. 3 (1978): 259–84, and "The Relationship between the Intelligentsia and Workers: The Case of the Party Schools in Capri and Bologna," in Zelnik, *Workers and Intelligentsia*, 172–85.

couragement for workers and workers' organizations to break away from the help and tutelage of others. The 1905 revolution encouraged this separatist inclination by stimulating lower-class activism and by legalizing, in the law of 4 March 1906, a wide range of nonprofit and nonpolitical associations. In the realm of culture, the law explicitly authorized trade unions (legalized in the same statute) to establish "libraries, trade schools, courses, and lectures" for workers.[68] As a result, trade union "cultural enlightenment" programs proliferated. But even more extensive were workers' clubs, typically known as "societies for self-education" (*obshchestva samoobrazovaniia*), which became major centers of cultural activity among urban workers, at least among an aspiring minority.[69]

The initiative to establish workers' educational and cultural societies came from socialist teachers at existing workers' courses (such as the Prechistenskie courses in Moscow and the Smolensk Evening Courses in St. Petersburg), individual socialist intellectuals (Mensheviks, Bolsheviks, Socialist Revolutionaries, and nonparty socialists), trade unionists, and activist workers. The development of such societies reached its height during the years 1907–11, when government repression against unions was effectively stifling social and political action. It was most extensive in the capital. During these years, twenty-one workers' "self-educational" associations appeared in St. Petersburg. Moscow had only a half dozen such clubs, and other cities had still fewer. A few clubs sought citywide membership, though most were based in particular neighborhoods or factories.

Like many nonworker organizations, these societies devoted themselves to the spread of "culture"—the recognized canon of cultural values and accomplishments, though embraced subversively to emancipate workers from their social otherness. They proclaimed their culturalist aspirations in such names as Znanie (Knowledge), Znanie-Svet (Knowledge is light), Prosveshchenie (Enlightenment), Nauka (Science), Nauka i zhizn' (Science and life), and Luch (Ray). Like other culturalist organizations working among the common people, these workers' clubs held lectures (typically at least once a week, often followed by discussion) and systematic courses. These programs covered such topics as arithmetic, history, health, language, literature, philosophy, psychology, science, social conditions, and spirituality. Clubs also established libraries, which held often large selections of books and current periodicals.

[68] "O vremennykh pravilakh ob obshchestvakh i soiuzov," 205.

[69] The following discussion of workers' self-education societies is based primarily on Levin, *Rabochie kluby*; Orlov, "Rabochie obshchestva samoobrazovaniia v S.-Peterburge;" *Professional'nyi vestnik*, no. 25 (18 Aug. 1909), 37–40; I. N. Kubikov (Ivan Dement'ev) "Rabochie kluby v Petrograde," *Vestnik kul'tury i svobody*, no. 1 (1918), 28–36; idem, "Literaturno-muzykal'nye vechera v rabochikh klubakh" and "Uchastie zhenshchin-rabotnits v klubakh," *Vestnik kul'tury i svobody*, no. 2 (1918), 32–34 and 34–37; Bonnell, *Roots of Rebellion*, 328–34; and reports in the trade union press: *Rabochii po metallu*, no. 21 (24 Sept. 1907), 16; *Nadezhda*, no. 1 (31 July 1908), 2–4, and no. 2 (26 Sept. 1908), 8–9; *Pechatnoe delo*, no. 3 (27 Jan. 1909), 12–13; no. 7 (20 May 1909), 15; no. 14 (16 Dec. 1909), 14–15; *Nash put'*, no. 4 (15 July 1910), 8–9; no. 7 (20 Sept. 1910), 8–9; no. 12 (14 Jan. 1911), 10–11; *Golos portnogo*, no. 6 (1 Mar. 1911), 5–6; *Novoe pechatnoe delo*, no. 11 (25 Nov. 1911), 2–7; *Trud* 1917, no. 1(7): 20–21.

And most organized public readings, literature discussion circles, literary-music evenings, choirs, balalaika orchestras, music circles, concerts, art classes (and, in at least one case in Moscow in 1913, an exhibition of workers' paintings),[70] excursions to museums and exhibits, country walks, dances, game nights, holiday parties, and shows for children and families (although many activists criticized dances, games, and other purely entertaining pursuits as not the proper task of self-education societies). In addition to these efforts by clubs, most of the larger trade unions and workers' cooperatives similarly offered programs of lectures, excursions, readings, concerts, and dances, organized theatrical and literary circles, and established their own often extensive libraries.

The world of clubs and organized self-education was overwhelmingly male. Contemporaries noted that few women attended the many activities of these organizations except the dances. This scarcity of women was due partly to the lower levels of female literacy and interest in self-education but also to deliberate exclusion—or at least women's justified sense that they were less welcome. Some male workers, in fact, were openly hostile to the attendance of their wives and other women at lectures and classes. "What would she do here?" was said to be the typical response when activists suggested that workers bring their wives. Even "advanced" workers, it seems, viewed the world of cultural development, which was so entwined with personal and civic notions of self and virtue, as decidedly male. Wishing to become "men" (though the preferred term, *chelovek,* is gender-neutral), these workers, like most of their male contemporaries, tended to treat this ideal as masculine. Some labor activists sought to challenge at least part of this assumption by establishing special women's clubs in both Moscow and Petersburg.

Even among men, the number of participants in workers' clubs was not huge—indeed, complaints about the disinterestedness of the majority were frequent—though neither was participation negligible. In St. Petersburg, almost every district had a club. Before the war, out of a working-class population of more than half a million workers, about 7,000 Petersburgers were club members. Lectures normally attracted audiences of between 50 and 150 and excursions to museums might attract about 100; evening dances tended to attract the largest crowds. The majority of members were young men between the ages of sixteen and thirty, from a wide range of occupations, though reports indicate that most worked in factories and were moderately skilled workers earning average wages and with average levels of education. The relatively low rates of participation in club life—the same problem plagued the lectures, cultural circles, and libraries established by trade unions—disturbed leaders and activists in these organizations, who often complained about the "passivity" of most workers and about the low cultural taste that led most workers to prefer dances to lectures. At the same time, others noticed

---

[70] L. K. Kleinbort, "Ocherki rabochei demokratii," pt. 8, "Rabochii—zritel' i artist," *Sovremennyi mir,* April 1914, 40.

that clubs and other cultural organizations were meccas for the minority of workers eager for self-improvement. This was a minority, to be sure, but a consequential one. Indeed, it was said to be precisely in these clubs that "that worker intelligentsia so essential to the modern labor movement took form."[71] And not surprisingly, their voices were the ones heard most often and most loudly chastising the common mass of workers for their cultural backwardness.

Although workers' clubs and trade union cultural programs were typically organized by intellectuals—especially activists of the various socialist parties—a strong workerist tendency animated the movement. The directing boards of most self-education societies, as a matter of principle, were formed through elections and in most cases limited to workers. And though self-education societies and union cultural committees regularly collaborated with people's universities, people's houses, and other civic and private initiatives to aid their cultural life, ideological differences over cultural power became a source of growing debate and conflict. A. V. Orlov, a representative of workers' clubs at the Congress of People's Universities in 1908, expressed the view of the typical worker activist when he declared, in an openly provocative speech filled with the language of class conflict, that "workers perfectly understand . . . that knowledge will become power in the hands of workers only when the work of setting up and organizing education is directed by the workers themselves."[72] This workerist separatism was a leitmotif in the history of workers' cultural movements in Russia.

Along with other worker *intelligenty,* worker writers took part in the activities of many institutions of popular education and self-education. A few were activists in them. But invariably, workers who were driven not simply to consume culture but to create it gravitated together to form organizations for their own particular needs and under their own control. As the numbers and visibility of self-taught writers (*samouchki* or, less often, *samorodki*) in urban areas grew, many were led to one another and to ideas of association for practical and artistic mutual support. During the winter of 1886–87, for example, the fourteen-year-old Maksim Leonov, whose peasant father had recently come to Moscow to set up a vegetable shop in which Maksim worked, organized a circle of young Moscow *samouchki,* who met regularly at a tavern to talk about poetry. Within two years, aided by the participation of some already accomplished lower-class poets, such as the tailor Ivan Belousov, the circle managed to publish the first of several anthologies of their own writings. Pride in their accomplishment and autonomy, a leitmotif in the lives of many worker writers, was visible in the book's opening pages, probably written by Belousov: "The authors of this anthology are all self-taught writers [*pisateli-samouchki*], who received no formal education, but by their own strength,

[71] *Professional'nyi vestnik,* no. 25 (18 Aug. 1909), 37.

[72] A. V. Orlov, "Rabochie obshchestva samoobrazovaniia v S.-Peterburge: Doklad," *Trudy pervogo vserossiiskogo s"ezda deiatelei obshchestv narodnykh universitetov,* 154. For discussion of debate around control at the congress, see Levin, *Rabochie kluby,* 125–33.

without any outside help, forced their way into the world."[73] Other small circles were formed about the same time, and often succeeded as well in publishing small anthologies of their work, though Leonov's remained the largest. In 1902 the Leonov circle adopted a more formal structure and named itself the Moscow Cooperative Circle of Writers from the People. Among its organizers were some of the most prominent worker writers in Moscow during these years: the shop assistant Fedor Shkulev, the itinerant and shop assistant Spiridon Drozhzhin, the woodworker Petr Travin, the bakery shop assistant Mikhail Savin, and the glassworker Egor Nechaev. Within a year the circle split as Leonov, Drozhzhin, Nechaev, Shkulev, Travin, and others left to establish the Surikov Literature and Music Circle, named in memory of Russia's then best known self-taught poet, Ivan Surikov, who, like many members of the Surikov Circle, had been born a peasant and worked for many years as a shop assistant in Moscow.

The Surikov Circle, which continued to be active until 1921, when most of its remaining members joined the new Union of Peasant Writers (the designation "peasant" being an ideological and thematic one identifying what they wrote less than a social one about who they were), was ultimately the most important of all these early circles. It helped *samouchki* improve their work and published large numbers of anthologies and magazines. Many worker writers, including many later associated with the Proletcult, were at one time members of the Surikov Circle. Although formally a Moscow organization, the circle sought and began to acquire a national role. In December 1905 Travin tried to organize an All-Russian Circle of Writers from the People. A conference was held, but no new organization resulted. By 1909, the Surikov Circle functioned as if it were a national organization. At the same time, however, other circles of "writers from the people" were forming, often on the model of the Surikov Circle, such as Nikolai Liashko's circle around the magazine *Ogni* (Firelights), established in Moscow in 1912.

The Surikov Circle, a strong presence in the world of lower-class writing, would be much criticized in Soviet writings for its "ideological weakness," for an alleged tendency toward pastoral Romanticism in works it published, and for a troubling "cult of melancholy." Such "unproletarian" perspectives were attributed to the large role played in the circle by writers born as peasants whose working lives were spent not in factories but in petty retail trade. Such ways of viewing the world, however, were common among even urban-born factory workers. Still, measured by the ideological sense that Marxists were beginning to give the category "proletarian" even before the revolution, the Surikov Circle failed the test. In 1915 the circle declared its goal to be to unite "writers from the people" with the larger "intelligentsia from the people" and with "the conscious peasant, the factory worker, the teacher, the sales employee, and all people sympathizing with the renaissance of the intelligentsia

---

[73] *Rodnye vesti: Sbornik stikhotvorenii pisatelei-samouchek* (Moscow, 1889), 1, quoted in Kleinbort, *Ocherki rabochei zhurnalistiki.*

from the people."[74] And though Surikov Circle leaders shared the Marxist dream of a society in which distinctions of class and even gender would vanish, they believed this happy world would come about not through class struggle but through recognition that all people are part of the same human family.[75] Whether we call this sort of generous and moralizing socialism populist, social democratic, or even liberal—and though this naming would matter a great deal to Bolsheviks, especially after 1917—it is clear that this outlook, and even the often melancholy mood of the Surikov poets, appealed to many worker writers, including those who called themselves Marxists and even Bolsheviks.[76]

During the years 1907–16, we see a remarkable intensification of self-organization among lower-class writers, and also a greater variety of individuals taking part. Whereas most of the leaders of the early circles were shop assistants or artisanal workers, we see not only far more factory workers involved but also more diversity of backgrounds and occupations. Circles proliferated, probably far beyond the traces left in the historical record (when they published a collection or a magazine or when their members became prominent enough that later recollections of their lives were deemed worthy of saving). We know of self-education circles of worker writers in Moscow, St. Petersburg, and a handful of provincial cities. One of the best known of these circles, since so many worker writers who later became prominent were involved in it, was a literary circle organized in 1912 among workers studying at Countess Panina's People's House in St. Petersburg. The circle met on Sunday afternoons and evenings for several hours, at which time members read and discussed the works of well-known writers, led by members who gave reports on authors they had been reading. The desire and need for a literature written by workers themselves were also discussed. With this aim in mind, a few manuscript magazines (*rukopisnye zhurnaly*) were put together. In 1913 members of the circle calling themselves Trudovaia Sem'ia (Labor Family) gathered together a collection of writings, chiefly by members of the circle, called *Nashi pesni: Sbornik stikhotvorenii: Poety-rabochie* (Our songs: An anthology of verses by worker poets), and had it printed in Moscow. It was immediately banned and confiscated by the police for its ideological tendentiousness. A second volume appeared in 1914. Significantly, these writers were explicit in identifying themselves in a new way as *worker* writers, as distinct from writers "from the people" or "self-taught" writers. In the introduction to the first volume they made it clear that this identity marked a degree of proud separation from intellectuals who claimed to speak for workers.

[74] *Drug naroda* 1915, no. 1 (1 Jan.), n.p. (inside front cover).

[75] *Drug naroda* 1916, no. 1 (October), 17.

[76] On these early circles, including the Leonov and Surikov circles, see L. Kleinbort, *Ocherki rabochei zhurnalistiki* (Petrograd, 1924), 7–9; L. M. Kleinbort, "Ocherki rabochei demokratii," pt. 5, *Sovremennyi mir*, November 1913, 168–69; *Russkie pisateli, 1800–1917: Biograficheskii slovar'*, 4 vols. to date (Moscow, 1992–), 1:224 (I. A. Belousov), 3:322–33 (M. L. Leonov); E. S. Kalmanovskii, *I. Z. Surikov i poety-surikovtsy* (Moscow, 1966); RGALI, f. 1068, op. 1, d. 30, l. 50b (autobiography of N. I. Volkov).

There is a truth about working-class life, they insisted, that cannot be heard until "workers write about themselves."[77] The "our" in "Our songs" was argumentative.[78]

Determined to "force their way into the world," to have their voices heard, worker writers turned to the press as the most important institution connecting them to others—their chief means of being heard and often a place to find others like themselves. Most worker writers sent their early works to local newspapers and magazines and especially to provincial papers, hoping to get into print and to be paid a few kopecks. But the greatest opportunities opened after 1905, when the trade union press, which thrived in the decade after the first Russian revolution, and especially the legal social-democratic press, which was allowed to exist during a period of relaxed censorship from 1912 to 1914, gave worker writers important means to reach a public. Trade union papers regularly published essays and commentaries by worker writers and occasionally printed workers' poetry and fiction. The socialist political press gave lower-class writers their largest arena. The Bolshevik *Pravda* (and its successive reincarnations during 1912–14 as the government shut it down but allowed reregistration under new names and new editors) and the Menshevik *Novaia rabochaia gazeta* (and its subsequent forms during these same years), as well as other publications more loosely affiliated with these parties, regularly featured the writings of working-class poets and story writers. Their presence in the party press by no means made workers' writing uniform or conformist, or even clearly political. Nor did worker writers, even those affiliated with political parties, feel the need to limit themselves to publishing in leftist publications.

Most important, lower-class writers were driven to find and create publications that were exclusively plebeian in content and control. Indeed, their words first began to proliferate in public through anthologies and periodicals identifying themselves as the productions of "self-taught writers from the people." During the years between 1877 (though mainly after 1900) and 1916, at least forty collections, anthologies, and almanacs devoted to works by lower-class writers appeared. Their orientation was advertised in their titles: *Rodnye zvuki* (Native sounds, 1889), *Nuzhdy* (Needs, 1893), *Malye velikim* (The small address the great, 1902), *Pesni truda* (Songs of labor, 1905), *Pesni mira* (Songs of the world, 1910), *Narodnye pesni: "Dolia moya"* (People's songs: "My burden," 1911).[79] Many of these collections were published by associations of lower-class authors such as the Surikov Circle and the St. Petersburg People's House circle, though one of the most successful collections,

[77] *Nashi pesni: Pervyi sbornik stikhotvorenii: Poety-rabochie*, vol. 1 (Moscow 1913), 5.

[78] Kleinbort, *Ocherki rabochei zhurnalistiki*, 12–13; Aleksei Mashirov, autobiographical essays in RGALI, f. 1821, op. 1, d. 1, ll. 1–13; Semen Rodov, ed., *Proletarskie pisateli: Antologiia proletarskoi literatury* (Moscow, 1925), 548–50; P. Ia. Zavolokin, ed., *Sovremennye raboche-krest'ianskie poety* (Ivanovo-Voznesensk, 1925), 26–28; *Nashi pesni*, vol. 2 (Moscow, 1914).

[79] A nearly complete bibliography of these publications appeared in the journal of the Surikov Circle, *Drug naroda* 1918, no. 1: 15.

combining the work of some of the best (and most political) worker writers of the time, the *First Anthology of Proletarian Writers* in 1914, was sponsored by Maxim Gorky.

An equally significant forum for worker writers in these years was the growing number of literary magazines that tried not only to appeal to culture-minded popular readers but to give lower-class writers their own publications. "Manuscript magazines" were a particularly eloquent form. Though they reached few readers, they testified to the desire among lower-class writers to create their own publications, even if they lacked the means to start a print magazine. Given the highly ephemeral nature of these works, it is likely that others existed of which we have no record. Lev Kleinbort, a contemporary Marxist journalist and cultural critic who collected handcrafted workers' magazines, came across several in St. Petersburg, Moscow, Kiev, Kherson, and provincial towns during the years after 1905. Written and illustrated by hand, reproduced by hectograph or individually copied out and passed from hand to hand (a samizdat before the name),[80] most manuscript magazines were created by informal workers' self-education circles and typically allowed no involvement by outsiders. These magazines bore such names as *Gusli-Mysli* (Gusli [a folk instrument] thoughts), *Golos niza* (A voice from below), *Volnaia dumka* (Free thought), *Zaria* (Dawn), and *Prosnuvshaiasia zhizn'* (Awakened life, produced in 1913 by the literary circle at the Ligovskii People's House in St. Petersburg). Among the longest lived (at least sixteen issues appeared) and best known of these manuscript magazines was *Gusli-Mysli,* the work of a self-education circle in St. Petersburg made up of several metalworkers (mostly fitters), electrical workers, and a tram driver.[81]

Printed people's magazines (*narodnye zhurnaly*) and newspapers appeared in impressive numbers during the years of cultural ferment after 1905. Aimed at popular audiences and produced and priced cheaply, they were usually edited and published by plebeian autodidacts (often by a group who pooled their money to get started) and featured writings by lower-class authors. Compared to the better-known (and more studied) magazines produced by educated intellectuals for culturally minded commoners, such as *Novyi zhurnal dlia vsekh* (The new magazine for everyone, 1908–17) and *Vestnik znaniia* (Herald of knowledge, 1903–8), which had circulations around 30,000–40,000,[82] these were small operations, often with about a thousand subscribers, though a few had circulations of several thousand.[83] These publica-

---

[80] Manuscript magazines also prefigured revolutionary and Soviet-era wall newspapers (*stengazety*) in workplaces, schools, and other institutions, though the wall newspapers' concerns tended to be less literary than political and social.

[81] L. Kleinbort, "Rukopisnye zhurnaly rabochikh," *Vestnik Evropy* 52, no. 7–8 (July–August 1917): 275–98; Kleinbort, *Ocherki rabochei zhurnalistiki,* 42–80; *Proletarskie poety,* vol. 2 (Leningrad, 1936), 278. I was not able to find copies of manuscript magazines in the archives; Kleinbort's archive was closed during my research.

[82] Brooks, "Popular Philistinism," 92.

[83] Kleinbort, *Ocherki rabochei zhurnalistiki,* 82, and "Pechatnye organy intelligentsii iz naroda," *Severnye zapiski* 1915, no. 7/8: 112–28; *Bibliografiia periodicheskikh izdanii Rossii, 1901–1916 gg.* (Leningrad, 1958).

tions were also generally brief and briefly lived; they failed for both financial and political reasons, though they often started afresh under a new name. Still, they were remarkably numerous. During the years from 1907 until the revolution, dozens of self-identified people's magazines or newspapers appeared, most of them in Moscow, where many were established by individuals associated with the Surikov Circle. In 1911, for example, fourteen people's magazines or newspapers were published in Moscow, including *Dolia bedniaka* (Poor man's burden), a "people's newspaper" edited by the woodworker Petr Travin; *Balalaika*, a "people's satirical and humor magazine," published and edited by the former garment worker Mariia Chernysheva (one of the handful of known women worker writers); *Dumy narodnye* (The people's thoughts), a weekly "people's literary magazine" under the editorship of Mikhail Loginov until his death in 1912; the Surikov Circle's *Narodnaia mysl'*, which advertised itself as featuring "writers from the people"; and *Rodnye vesti* (Native news), a "magazine of the laboring people" published and edited by the worker writer Sergei Stepanov (known as Stepan Bruskov), which featured the works of many people's writers. Important later publications include *Ogni*, a monthly magazine in 1912–13 established by the former metal turner Nikolai Liashko together with an association of worker writers he had organized, and the Surikov Circle's *Drug naroda* (Friend of the people), which appeared during the war. Among the smaller number of such papers published in other cities was the shoemaker Petr Zaitsev's "literary, satirical, and humorous magazine" *Kolotushka* (a peasant word meaning variously a wooden rattle, a windmill, and a whack), which appeared in Tver in 1911. Although none of these papers had very large readerships, most closed when they could not afford to pay a fine levied by the censor or when they were shut by the government rather than because of financial failure. Although a relatively marginal presence in Russian publishing, these people's magazines reflected a vital cultural space dominated by the growing and increasingly assertive "intelligentsia from the people."[84]

As expressions of a particular, or at least desired, place in Russia's expanding civic culture, the people's magazines articulated an encompassing, even universalistic notion of "the people," but also a distinctly moralist one. When the editors identified the sorts of voices to be heard on their pages, they generally avoided the narrow Marxist focus on the factory proletariat in favor of a typically neo-populist class vocabulary that spoke more generously of all working people—*trudiashchiesia, truzheniki, trudovoi sloi, trudiashchiisia klass, rabochii narod*. The Surikov Circle's magazine *Drug naroda*, as we have seen, declared itself to be a friend to the "intellectual from the people" (*intelligent-narodnik*), but also to peasants, workers, teachers, commercial employees, and "all who sympathize with the renaissance of the intelligentsia from the people."[85] Rejection of notions of class conflict was sometimes ex-

---

[84] Quotations are from editorial statements in the first issues. The Selected Bibliography lists all such publications.

[85] *Drug naroda*, no. 1 (1 Jan. 1915), inside cover. Although the term *narodnik* was traditionally used to describe members of the populist movement of the nineteenth century, it was used

plicit, as in the editorial statement opening the first issue of *Rodnye vesti* in 1910, which averred that "in this magazine will be found no shouting, no rude outbursts against this or that class."[86] Such statements reflected the neo-populist humanism of these groups, though they may also have been intended to appease the censor. In any case, even while eschewing Marxist ideas of class, the editors of such publications often made clear their social and ethical biases. *Rodnye vesti*, for example, told "working people" that it would be their words appearing in the paper, and that what mattered was not skill in writing ("don't be timid worrying about form") but that people were heard who "have been cheated by fate and oppressed by untruth and evil."[87] Other people's magazines similarly spoke of the commitment to voice the "words and feelings" of the Russian common people, to provide a place where "people who had been through the harsh school of a life of labor" could write about their "sorrows and needs and the domination of employers," to describe lives among the urban poor (most papers had a section of correspondence on factory conditions), to make known to the people those writers and poets who, without education but with "God's gift," "sing of their sorrows and joy," and to promote self-education and "spiritual self-development."[88]

The Proletarian Culture Movement

The fall of the autocracy and the coming to power of the Bolsheviks dramatically expanded the personal and social opportunities facing worker *intelligenty,* at least for those willing to accept the Bolsheviks' leadership of the revolution. As a cultural force, Bolshevism began its efforts to transform Russian life with a massive, if vaguely formulated and even contradictory, initiative to stimulate and shape proletarian culture and creativity. In an uneasy relationship, proletarians joined in with a great deal of initiative of their own. Starting almost immediately after the fall of the autocracy in February 1917 and continuing throughout the civil war years and into the early 1920s, worker writers and other worker *intelligenty* were faced with a proliferation of organizations to join and publications interested in printing their writings. At the center of this movement stood the Proletcult, which, as Lynn Mally has

---

here and in other people's magazines to identify a person both devoted to the cause of the people and personally from the people. See *Narodniki*, no. 1 (1912), 2.

[86] *Rodnye vesti*, no. 1 (1910) 2.

[87] Ibid. See also the editorial statement in *Rodnye vesti*, no. 2 (1911) 2. These words were most likely written by the editor, Sergei Stepanovich Stepanov (1873–1943), who often wrote under the pseudonym Stepan Bruskov. Born to a family of workers on the outskirts of Moscow, where he received two years of education in a rural primary school, he began work in a factory at the age of ten; he held many other jobs in later years. He joined the Leonov circle in the 1890s and later the Surikov circle.

[88] *Dumy narodnye*, no. 4 ([20 Feb.] 1910), 1–2; *Narodnaia mysl'*, no. 1 (January 1911), 3; *Narodniki*, no. 1 (1912), 2; *Ogni*, no. 1 (November 1912), 1, and no. 2 (1912), 8; *Zvezda utrenniaia*, no. 1 (25 Jan. 1912), 7; *Drug naroda*, no. 1 (1 Jan. 1915), inside cover.

shown, was less a coherent and centralized national organization than an open and contested site where diverse individuals and groups came together to promote culture among and by workers, though they were not in agreement over what this culture comprised.[89]

One week before the Bolsheviks took power in Russia, on 16 October 1917, nearly 200 representatives of workers' cultural-enlightenment societies, trade unions, factory committees, cooperatives, and members of the Social Democratic and Socialist Revolutionary parties in Petrograd gathered to establish a new cultural organization for workers. The idea of forming such a national organization of proletarian cultural-enlightenment organizations was raised and approved in mid-August 1917 at a conference of Petrograd factory committees, where Anatoly Lunacharsky forcefully argued against those who saw "cultural-enlightenment work" as simply "dessert," as icing on the cake of the labor and socialist movement. Cultural work, he insisted, was "as essential as other forms of the workers' movement."[90] The committees approved the idea of the conference, which was held in October and chaired by Lunacharsky, soon to be named the first People's Commissar of Enlightenment. Although initiative for this meeting came largely from Petrograd factory committees, leadership from the first fell to a group of intellectuals and worker *intelligenty* associated with Lunacharsky and with the other left-wing Bolsheviks who had been responsible for the workers' schools in Capri and Bologna. Two worker students from the schools, Fedor Kalinin and Pavel Bessal'ko, who had also been members of Lunacharsky's Proletarian Culture circle in Paris in 1912, played key roles in organizing the October conference, along with other Bolshevik intellectuals, some leading local worker writers, and factory committee activists. As a result of this meeting, by the middle of November 1917 emerged a loose alliance known as Proletarian Cultural-Enlightenment (*kul'turno-prosvetitel'nye*) Organizations, an awkward and vague title that was soon abbreviated to Proletcult (*Proletkul't*).[91]

With the support of the new Soviet government and the ruling Bolshevik (soon Communist) party, the Proletcult grew into a national network of cultural clubs and associations, though as an organization it remained rather diffuse. As the Proletcult expanded during 1918–19, Lynn Mally has shown, "local groups shaped their own agenda with little concern for national programs."[92] Proletcult expansion was rapid and chaotic as local Proletcults arose (and sometimes quickly collapsed) all over the country. Organizers included existing local cultural organizations, trade unions, factory committees, soviets, branches of the Commissariat of Enlightenment, local branches of the Bolshevik party, and individual activists. On some occasions, proletarian cultural organizations formed independently of the emerging Proletcult network.

---

[89] Mally, *Culture of the Future.*
[90] *Oktiabr'skaia revoliutsiia i fabzavkomy* (Moscow, 1927), 1:234.
[91] *Novaia zhizn'*, no. 155 (17 Oct. 1917), 3; *Rabochaia gazeta*, no. 188 (17 Oct. 1917), 4; Mally, *Culture of the Future*, 25–28.
[92] Mally, *Culture of the Future*, 50.

For example, a union of proletarian writers, poets, and artists, called Iskusstvo i Sotsializm (Art and Socialism), took shape in Petrograd in the spring of 1917, organizing lectures and literary evenings and publishing a literary magazine of worker writing called *Griadushchee* (The future). In 1918 the magazine and its sponsoring group became part of the Proletcult.[93] Because motives for organization varied among locales, so did organizational functions. Proletcults served variously as centers of local entertainment, schools for adult literacy, organizations for culturally and politically advanced workers, and (their chief intent in the eyes of the national leadership) organizing centers for workers' cultural education. Echoing the work of prerevolutionary workers' clubs, people's houses, and people's universities, a Proletcult organization was likely to include in its activities a lecture series, seminars, exhibitions, films, choirs, orchestras, drama circles and theater spaces, art and literature classes, sporting activities, libraries, and reading rooms.[94]

At the heart of the work of a Proletcult, especially for the most culture-minded and creative workers, were its "studios," workshops where members developed their creative skills in literature, music, theater, or art. Despite a theoretical preference among the national leadership for innovative forms of collective study, the studios were likely in practice to be run as conventional courses led by trained specialists, especially in Moscow and Petrograd. Indeed, in the literary studios of many Proletcults, workers could study writing with some of Russia's leading modern poets, including Andrei Belyi, Valerii Briusov, Nikolai Gumilev, and Vladislav Khodasevich. Beyond the studios, and often a function of them, one of the most important activities of the Proletcult for worker writers was publishing. Literary magazines, which featured much writing by worker members of the studios, and anthologies of proletarian writing were printed by local Proletcults in large numbers. Between 1918 and 1920, for example, amidst the difficult years of civil war and economic collapse, at least two dozen Proletcult magazines were published (in Petrograd, Moscow, Tver, Tula, Orel, Tambov, Voronezh, Samara, Orenburg, Odessa, and elsewhere), and about thirty anthologies.

The Proletcult was not alone in trying to nurture proletarian culture. An important role was also played by trade unions and clubs, which proliferated after the fall of the autocracy and during the early years of Soviet power. By August 1917, sixty workers' clubs existed in Petrograd alone, with more than 36,000 members. While some were direct heirs to prewar self-education societies (many of which, along with other workers' organizations, had been shut down by the government in the early years of the war), most were new organizations, established by political parties, cooperatives, trade unions, factory committees, and other groups.[95] Like the Proletcult, and sometimes in direct competition with it, were efforts to combine workers' clubs into a common

---

[93] V. K. (Kirillov), "Pis'ma o proletarskom tvorchestve," *Griadushchaia kul'tura*, no. 3 (January 1919), 12.

[94] Local and national Proletcult papers regularly reported these various activities. See the Selected Bibliography.

[95] *Trud: Zhurnal rabochei kooperatsii* 1917, no. 1 (August): 37–39.

movement. In 1918, in Petrograd, Maxim Gorky helped to establish, in implied opposition to the Bolshevik-led Proletcult and in explicit opposition to Bolshevik power, a short-lived society to be known as Culture and Freedom, which sought to unite the cultural-enlightenment work of workers' cooperatives, unions, and clubs.[96] Similarly in Moscow, and in stated opposition to the Proletcult, the Moscow Central Workers' Cooperative—whose slogan was "the emancipation of workers is the cause of the workers themselves"— formed a special cultural-enlightenment division in 1918 to establish new clubs and encourage cooperation between clubs.[97] Without hostility to the Proletcult but still separate from it were literary and culture clubs organized by Lunacharsky's People's Commissariat of Enlightenment (Narkompros).[98] But the largest role in organizing clubs was played by the trade unions. Moscow trade unions, for example, operated more than two hundred clubs in the region by 1920 and nearly as many libraries—a high priority for many unions—as well as a couple of hundred cultural circles.[99]

In these early Soviet years, especially starting in 1920, workers' clubs attracted official attention as important means for the new state to convey political and economic values to workers, including "cultured" manners and tastes. Like prerevolutionary clubs, with their emphasis on raising the levels of workers' culture and knowledge to empower them for the struggle for change in Russia, Soviet clubs offered workers a mixture of "improving" activities along with events aimed at getting workers to come to the clubs at all (as opposed to the local tavern). Clubs offered buffets, put on performances, showed movies, and held evening dances. They also offered lectures and literacy classes, held evening readings, organized orchestras and choirs, and hosted a variety of voluntary cultural circles to bring together workers interested in studying and creating their own literature, theater, music, and art. Activists established political education circles as well, but these groups attracted much less interest. As the mass movement they sought to be, clubs were a failure—organizers constantly complained, as they had done before 1917, of the passivity of the majority, and culturally high-minded critics complained that club organizers were to blame for low interest because they offered dirty surroundings, bad tea, and crass, petty-bourgeois entertainments. Still, again as before the revolution, these clubs provided important cultural opportunities to an active minority. And they provided an important audience for the already developed worker intelligentsia. Worker writers could often be found giving readings at club-organized evenings.[100]

---

[96] *Trud* 1918, no. 5–6 (May–June): 30–31.

[97] *Rabochii mir: Organ Moskovskogo Tsentral'nogo rabochego kooperativa*, no. 2 (14 Apr. 1918), 39–41.

[98] Narkompros had a special Department of Clubs, which published a journal, *Revoliutsionnye vskhody: Zhurnal proletarskikh klubov* (Petrograd, 1920).

[99] John B. Hatch, "The Formation of Working-Class Cultural Institutions during NEP: The Workers' Club Movement in Moscow, 1921–1923," Carl Beck Papers in Russian and East European Studies (Pittsburgh, 1990).

[100] V. F. Pletnev, *Rabochii klub: Printsipy i metody raboty* (Moscow, 1923), esp. 5–7; Hatch, "Formation of Working-Class Cultural Institutions" and "The Politics of Mass Culture: Work-

Some workers organized their own informal circles, reminding us again of the desire among many workers for self-education and self-organization but also of the inability of the new state, notwithstanding its preoccupation with proletarian culture, to control and direct these desires as it wished. In the residential barracks of the old Guzhon steel mill in Moscow (renamed the Hammer and Sickle), for example, an elderly worker *intelligent* at the factory organized his own "cultural circle" (*dukhovnyi kruzhok*). The circle put together a band to play at factory meetings and workers' funerals, debated the politics of the day, served as informal chroniclers of the life of the factory, studied together (especially philosophy and history), and united factory poets and writers. The circle's independence from party, union, and even factory committee was reduced after 1921, when the organizer died. The circle was then moved out of the barracks and into the building of the local Proletcult club and the agenda of the club was directed away from culture-building (*kul'turnichestvo*) to focus on such matters as improving production and ending hooliganism. Still, many circle members continued to meet in the old barracks, which had been evacuated as a residence, to discuss freely whatever most interested them.[101]

For worker writers a variety of organizations offered opportunities to work together to promote their art and their material interests, including the greater possibility after 1917 for proletarians to make a living as professional writers. The Proletcult offered worker writers not only a site of literary study but also occasional paid employment as activists. Some joined the literary section of the Union of Journalists, formed in 1918, which worked mainly to help writers find work and publishing opportunities.[102] Older noncommunist groups of worker writers such as the Surikov Circle continued in existence into the early 1920s, and new ones were formed, such as the Moscow Literature-Music-Art Circle of Independents in 1918 and the Krasnyi Gusliar (Red gusli player) Literary Circle, organized by the worker writer Ivan Eroshin in Moscow in 1923.[103]

By far the most important association of worker writers was Kuznitsa (The smithy). On 1 February 1920, amidst the devastating civil war, a group that included some of the most experienced and accomplished worker writers in Moscow met and sent a brief note to the Communist party newspaper *Pravda* declaring that they were quitting the Proletcult, which "for a whole series of reasons was hindering the expression of the creative capacities of proletarian

---

ers, Communists, and Mass Culture in the Development of Workers' Clubs, 1921–1925," *Russian History* 13, no. 2–3 (Summer–Fall 1986): 119–48; *Gorn*, no. 2–3 (1919), 43; Lynn Mally, *Revolutionary Acts: Amateur Theater and the Soviet State, 1917–1938* (Ithaca, 2000). Diane Koenker's forthcoming book on the politics and culture of labor in the 1920s explores many of these themes.

[101] GARF, f. R-7952, op. 3, d. 293, ll. 4–10 (a 1933 account of the club).

[102] RGALI, f. 1600, op. 1, d. 2, ll. 1–6.

[103] Sergei Gan'shin to Maksim Gor'kii, 7 Jan. 1918, in Arkhiv A. M. Gor'kogo, KG-NP/a, 7-11-3; Gan'shin to Zavolokin, August 1923, in RGALI, f. 1068, op. 1, d. 34, l. 8.

writers," to establish a special Proletarian Writers' Department under the auspices of the Literary Department of Lunacharsky's Commissariat of Enlightenment (LITO Narkomprosa), with which many leading worker writers had already become associated. The authors of the declaration included party members and independents. Worker writers predominated and took the lead, especially Mikhail Gerasimov (who had been a member of the Proletcult Central Committee), but also Grigorii Sannikov, Sergei Obradovich, Vasilii Kazin, and Vasilii Aleksandrovskii, all relatively established writers by 1920 who had been working together since 1918 editing and writing for the weekly magazine of the Moscow Proletcult literary studio, *Gudki* (Factory whistles). A single middle-class intellectual joined them, Semen Rodov, a left-wing Bolshevik committed to nurturing a new proletarian literature.[104] Soon other prominent worker writers joined them: Ivan Eroshin, Ivan Filipchenko, Nikolai Liashko, Egor Nechaev, Nikolai Poletaev, Aleksandr Pomorskii, Il'ia Sadof'ev, Mikhail Sivachev, Mikhail Volkov, and others. Two prominent worker writers from Petrograd, Vladimir Kirillov and Aleksei Mashirov (Samobytnik), joined the group, though both also retained their ties to the Petrograd Proletcult.[105]

Two large steps were taken in May 1920 to build this proletarian secession from the Proletcult into a national organization of worker writers devoted to removing obstacles to "creativity": the publication, also under the auspices of the Literary Department of Narkompros, of a journal named *Kuznitsa*—the point at which the group began to call itself by this name—and the organization of a national congress of proletarian writers. The literary and critical journal *Kuznitsa* lasted for nine issues, from 1920 until 1922. Many of Russia's most influential worker writers were involved as editors or contributors, together with a handful of ideologically "proletarian" writers who were not from worker backgrounds but shared *Kuznitsa*'s combination of political radicalism with insistence on creative freedom for workers and devotion to literary craftsmanship and professionalism. The First All-Russian Conference (*soveshchanie*) of Proletarian Writers was held in Moscow in May 1920 (it was meant to be a national congress, but poor organizational work kept many non-Muscovites from attending). Invited worker writers, representatives of such groups as the Proletcult and the Surikov Circle, and various nonproletarian guests (nonvoting, for this was designated a workers' meeting) met to discuss how to promote proletarian culture. Aleksandr Bogdanov, the most prominent Russian theorist of proletarian culture, was invited to give the opening report, but his arguments that proletarian culture must be accessible to common readers and focused intellectually on the life of the labor collective were subjected to a long debate and openly criticized by many of the

---

[104] *Pravda*, 5 Feb. 1920, 2.
[105] L'vov-Rogachevskii, *Ocherki*, 174–76; Edward J. Brown, *The Proletarian Episode in Russian Literature, 1928–1932* (New York, 1953), 10–11; Barbara Kernick, "Die Lyriker der 'Kuznica' (1920–1922)," in *Von der Revolution zum Schriftstellerkongress*, ed. G. Erler et al. (Berlin, 1979), 269; Mally, *Culture of the Future*, 154–55; *Literaturnaia entsiklopediia*, 5:703–4; Gottfried Kratz, *Die Geschichte der "Kuznica" (1920–1932)* (Giessen, 1979), 73–82.

worker organizers of the meeting. (In turn, in a review of the first issue of *Kuznitsa,* Bogdanov sharply disparaged the new journal as unproletarian in its preoccupation—which he overstated—with technique and form.)[106]

A new gathering, this time to be a truly national congress, was planned for the fall of 1920. This meeting, the First Congress of Proletarian Writers, was held in Moscow on 18–20 October. Like the preceding conference, the congress was deliberately led by its working-class majority. All of the presiding officers were well-known writers of worker backgrounds—Vladimir Kirillov, Mikhail Gerasimov, Il'ia Sadof'ev, and Sergei Obradovich—though many nonworkers also attended by invitation. On its final day, the congress voted to establish the All-Russian Union of Proletarian Writers (VSPP), which was shortly after renamed the All-Russian Association of Proletarian Writers (VAPP). The union, like the congress, was headed entirely by established writers of working-class origins. In addition to publishing a journal and facilitating the association of Soviet Russia's most experienced worker writers, Kuznitsa-VAPP organized public literary readings and lecture-discussions on proletarian culture in clubs, people's houses, hospitals, factories, and trade unions, especially in Moscow but also in other cities. Within only a couple of years of its founding, however, the Kuznitsa group began to disintegrate as many members grew disillusioned with the direction of the revolution—especially the New Economic Policy, a political retreat from radicalism begun after the end of the civil war—and fell out with one another or were alienated from public activism altogether, in the course of the increasingly acrimonious literary debates over the meaning and role of proletarian literature.[107]

The Meanings of Proletarian Culture

The meaning of "proletarian" was contested sharply after October, as was the shape of the sought-after "culture," proletarian or otherwise, that was so much a part of the idealism and rhetoric of those times, and as was the related notion, becoming increasingly explicit, of "cultural revolution."[108] The argu-

---

[106] *Proletarskaia kul'tura,* no. 15–16 (1920), 91–92.

[107] RGALI, f. 1638 (Kuznitsa), op. 3, dd. 1 and 4–5 (1920 congress); *Kuznitsa,* no. 1 (May 1920), 17–18; L'vov-Rogachevskii, *Ocherki,* 176–77; Brown, *Proletarian Episode,* 10–16; L. A. Skvortsova, "Zhurnaly 'Kuznitsy,'" in *Ocherki istorii russkoi sovetskoi zhurnalistiki, 1917–1932* (Moscow, 1966), 345–55.

[108] For discussion of the history and uses of the term "cultural revolution," see Michael David-Fox, "What Is Cultural Revolution?" *Russian Review* 58, no. 2 (April 1999): 181–201, and the critical comments by Sheila Fitzpatrick that follow. I agree with David-Fox on the need to broaden the concept beyond the familiar 1928–31 application, though without losing sight, as Fitzpatrick argues, of variations and specificities. But I also would emphasize more than David-Fox does the roots and continued evolution of thinking about cultural revolution outside of the Bolshevik party. The party did not merely "embrace" these other projects of transformation (187), it also had continually to contend with them. For a provocative discussion of the Marxist cultural construction of the "proletariat" and "proletarian," see Igal Halfin, *From Darkness to Light: Class, Consciousness, and Salvation in Revolutionary Russia* (Pittsburgh, 2000), chap. 2.

ments were not new in 1918. The essential issues had already emerged in debates during the first years after 1905 about how to define the worker intelligentsia. Worker intellectuals, as we have seen, responding partly to frustration in their dealings with the intelligentsia and partly to the growing self-confidence that came with reading, studying, and writing, had begun to insist on controlling their own cultural life. Independence, self-organization, "self-education" (*samoobrazovanie*), initiative (*samodeiatel' nost,* literally "self-activity," also often translated as "autonomy") were constantly spoken of as necessities and virtues. And these values were elaborated, even in the prewar years, into strong epistemological arguments about who possessed the sort of knowledge necessary to create the culture needed by workers or by the people more broadly. Repeatedly it was said that only individuals *from* the people could understand enough of that life to speak *for* the people. One of the most influential statements of this argument was an article that appeared in 1912 in the popular magazine *Novyi zhurnal dlia vsekh* (New magazine for everyone) in which Fedor Kalinin—a former woodworker, printer, and weaver, and a leading worker *intelligent*—insisted that a barrier of understanding stood between workers and nonworkers that the latter could never cross. "The intellectual can still *think* for the young [working] class," Kalinin declared in words that would often be quoted, "but he cannot *feel* for it." And since true knowledge of the world requires emotional understanding as well as scientific reason, the nonworker could never fully understand or represent workers.[109] These ideas were echoed (or paralleled) by worker writers from the St. Petersburg People's House who published their writings in the collection *Nashi pesni* in 1913. Until workers themselves begin writing about their own lives, they declared in the introduction to the collection, no "honest" and "true" portrayal of proletarian life could appear.[110] As we have already heard, it was said that only plebeians could "weep the people's sufferings and rejoice the people's joys," that only workers could share and speak workers' deepest "class feelings."

These workerist arguments, paradoxically perhaps, had long been nurtured and may well have been inspired by leftist intellectuals. The Marxist slogan "The emancipation of workers is the cause of the workers themselves" was widely used by socialist organizations and parties, especially the nonvanguardist Menshevik and Socialist Revolutionary parties. And workers often understood Marxist arguments about the determining influence of social being on social consciousness as grounding proletarian class consciousness in their own working-class experience. Many party intellectuals, especially among the Mensheviks, shared this assumption and worried about the dangers of intelligentsia control of the labor movement in Russia.[111]

[109] F. Kalinin, "Tip rabochego v literature," *Novyi zhurnal dlia vsekh* 1912, no. 9 (September): 96–97, 106.
[110] "Ot redaktsii," in *Nashi pesni* (Moscow, 1913), 4.
[111] See the discussion of the relations between workers and intelligentsia in Allan K. Wildman, *The Making of a Workers' Revolution: Russian Social Democracy, 1891–1903,* and essays in Zelnik, *Workers and Intelligentsia.*

Within the Bolshevik movement, such leftists as Aleksandr Bogdanov and Anatoly Lunacharsky played an influential role in encouraging such workerist ideas. Fedor Kalinin, along with many of the worker writers who would lead the Proletcult and later Kuznitsa, was directly linked to this so-called left Bolshevism. In 1908, Bogdanov, together with Lunacharsky, Maxim Gorky, and others, established the Vpered (Forward) group as an alternative to Lenin's version of Bolshevism. Although this move led to their expulsion from the Bolshevik party (which Bogdanov, unlike the others, never rejoined), their ideas remained a visible presence in Bolshevik intellectual life. The Vperedists viewed cultural work among the proletariat as their first priority, but were inspired by a conception of class and culture very different from Lenin's. In nurturing a proletarian vanguard, Lenin insisted on the need for intellectuals to bring to workers the developed ideas of socialist ideology, which could never arise out of the narrow perspectives of workers' everyday life experiences. Bogdanov and the Vperedists did not contest the need for intellectuals to bring culture to workers, but they remained skeptical about the possibility that nonworkers could ever fully express a truly working-class point of view. Such intellectuals, Bogdanov liked to say, were as rare as "white crows." Instead, he argued, intellectuals should help develop "independent ideologists from within the proletariat itself." The working class needed teaching, Bogdanov and the Vperedists argued ambivalently, but it also needed to be encouraged to "trust no one . . . , to verify everyone and everything in its own mind." Ultimately, Bogdanov argued, "the liberation of the working class—materially and culturally—will be the cause of the workers themselves," and at the head of this movement would stand a new "purely proletarian intelligentsia."[112] Such worker *intelligenty* would play not only a leading role in the labor movement but a creative one, generating a new "proletarian" culture—a new science, art, and literature—which could be a new universal, "all-human" culture.[113] This was the purpose of the schools Bogdanov and Lunacharsky organized in Capri and Bologna in the years 1909–11, and of Luncharsky's Proletarian Culture league in Paris in 1912 and 1913. Kalinin had been a student in Capri and a member of Lunacharsky's circle in Paris. The worker poet Mikhail Gerasimov, one of the leaders of the Moscow Proletcult and of the Kuznitsa secession, had also been a member of Lunacharsky's circle.

From the first days of the Proletcult, defining "proletarian culture" proved contentious. At the conference in October 1917 at which the Proletcult was organized, participants argued about whether nonproletarians could participate at all in the creation of proletarian culture—what role was there, it was asked, for nonworkers who embraced a working-class point of view—and

---

[112] Maksimov [A. Bogdanov], "Proletariat v bor'be za sotsializma," *Vpered: Sbornik statei po ocherednym voprosam*, no. 1 (July 1910), 4–5, 8; St. Krivtsov, "Pamiati A. A. Bogdanova," *Pod znamenem marksizma*, no. 4 (April 1928), 183; Zenovia Sochor, *Revolution and Culture: The Bogdanov-Lenin Controversy* (Ithaca, 1988), 37–38.

[113] For discussion of Bogdanov and *Vpered*, see esp. Sochor, *Revolution and Culture*, and Mally, *Culture of the Future*, 3–10.

about the relation of the emerging proletarian culture to the old bourgeois culture. These debates were intensified and made more political by the attitude of the Communist party leadership. Lenin and Trotsky viewed the Proletcult with great suspicion and brought increasing pressure to bear on its leaders to rein in talk about creating a new, purely proletarian culture in favor of a more conventional vision of cultural revolution and, no less important, to accept greater party guidance and control.[114] Within the Proletcult, compromise positions tended formally to prevail. In deciding the relation of the new culture to the old, the first conference resolved that while the proletariat would develop "its own independent forms" of art and science, it would also make use of the "fruits of the old culture," though it would approach this old culture critically, "not as a student, but rather as a builder who is called to erect bright new structures using bricks from the old ones."[115] But the debate continued into the 1920s as party leaders and some intellectuals active in the Proletcult regularly criticized those proletarian writers who continued to hold deviant notions about culture.

A source of even greater tension was the criticism, often repeated by party and Proletcult intellectuals, that many worker writers, in their efforts to create a distinctive and well-crafted proletarian culture, were neglecting their class duty to make their work accessible and uplifting for the masses. Proletarian writers were regularly criticized for their abstractness, Romanticism, and cosmic lack of interest in the everyday task of building a new society and educating Russia's still backward working class.[116] An especially heated conflict over these issues arose in 1924 when Lev Trotsky publicly criticized the worker writer and Proletcult leader Valerian Pletnev for disdaining cultural-enlightenment work among the masses, for his contempt for *kul'turnichestvo* and *kul'turtregerstvo* in favor of promoting the absurd notion of creating a new class culture. Pletnev replied testily that Trotsky failed to understand that there is no pure "culture" to be conveyed to people, only class culture, which must be treated in a revolutionary and critical way.[117] Many worker writers did not disagree with Trotsky. Indeed, this party critique of efforts to create a new proletarian culture was most strongly shared by more conservative worker writers, especially Mensheviks such as Ivan Dement'ev (Kubikov) and Nikolai Liashko.[118] More radical worker writers sometimes also shared this more traditional view of culture and cultural revolution. By the early 1920s,

---

[114] This conflict is described in Mally, *Culture of the Future.*

[115] *Rabochii put'*, 19 Oct. 1917, quoted in Mally, *Culture of the Future,* 30.

[116] E.g., "Protokoly pervogo Vserossiiskogo Soveshchaniia proletarskikh pisatelei," 10–12 May 1920), in RGALI, f. 1638, op. 3, d. 1, ll. 10b-2 (speech by Bogdanov); *Proletarskaia kul'tura,* no. 5 (November 1918), 42–45; no. 9–10 (June–July 1919), 66; no. 15–16 (April–July 1920), 91–92; *Kuznitsa,* no. 1 (May 1920), 23; A. Voronskii, "O gruppe pisatelei 'Kuznitsa': Obshchaia kharakteristika," in *Iskusstvo i zhizn': Sbornik statei* (Moscow and Petrograd, 1924), 136; *Rabochii zhurnal* 1925, no. 1–2, 262, 277.

[117] V. F. Pletnev, *Rabochii klub: Printsipy i metody raboty* (Moscow, 1923); *Prizyv,* no. 5 (August 1924), 18–19 (Trotsky's critique); V. Pletnev, *Prav li t. Trotskii* (Moscow, 1924).

[118] *Rabochaia mysl'*, no. 2 (23 Sept. 1917), 9–10; *Rabochii mir,* no. 15 (13 Oct. 1918), 28–31.

many writers associated with the Proletcult and Kuznitsa agreed, at least formally, that it was their responsibility to write "for the present, not the future," to direct their words to ordinary workers, to concern themselves with everyday life, and to devote their efforts to "mastering" established literary techniques for themselves and spreading elementary cultural knowledge and aesthetic taste to the masses of still quite ignorant and uncultured workers.[119]

The main issue that troubled worker writers was less their relation to the old culture or even to the masses of workers than their relation to the intelligentsia. At the founding Proletcult conference in October 1917, critical acceptance of the intelligentsia formally prevailed. Many of the organization's leaders came from educated elite backgrounds, such as Bogdanov, who served as an editor of the national Proletcult journal and was a member of the Proletcult central committee; Pavel Lebedev (known as Valerian Polianskii), who was chair of the national organization from 1918 to 1920; and the party intellectual Platon Kerzhentsev, also an officer of the national organization and on the editorial board of the journal *Proletarskaia kul'tura*. More radical ideas about the restricted place of the intellectual in the "workers' cause" had not died, however. Even these intelligentsia activists insisted that the Proletcult was "an organization of proletarian self-activity [*samodeiatel'nosti*]," and intellectuals had to be kept under close watch.[120] Bogdanov, however, warned workers against carrying this argument too far. He and other party and Proletcult leaders regularly reminded workers that being sociologically proletarian did not guarantee that one was ideologically proletarian. This was especially the case for proletarian writers. Hence he was able to argue in 1918 that "up to the present the poetry of workers is too often, indeed in most cases, not workers' poetry." The thing that decides what is proletarian, he bluntly averred, "is not the author but the point of view." A nonworker can write proletarian poetry, or, by the same logic, he implied, run the Proletcult. At the same time, adding to the persistent ambiguity of these arguments, Bogdanov admitted that outsiders were not likely to fill such roles often and that workers should avoid trusting or relying on them.[121]

Worker *intelligenty* were even less sanguine than Bogdanov about the role of nonworkers in creating the new culture or expressing proletarian thought and feeling. They were much less likely to accept party criticisms of proletarian autonomy and control. And most important, in resisting these criticisms, they questioned the underlying philosophical arguments about the sources of knowledge. Old arguments, once nurtured by the work of Bogdanov and Lunacharsky, that intellectuals might be able to think for the still young work-

---

[119] L'vov-Rogachevskii, *Ocherki*, 178; RGALI, f. 1638, op. 3, d. 1, ll. 3–4 (debates at May 1920 conference); d. 5, ll. 2–4 (Kirillov's report to 1920 conference and discussion); *Proletkul't*, no. 1–2 (April–May 1919), 27; Vasilii Kazin, "Esteticheskie vospitaniia mass," *Gudki*, no. 2 (April 1919), 13–14.

[120] V. Kerzhentsev, "'Proletkul't'—organizatsiia proletarskoi samodeiatel'nosti," *Proletarskaia kul'tura*, no. 1 (July 1918), 7–8; Mally, *Culture of the Future*, 106–7.

[121] A. Bogdanov, "Chto takoe proletarskaia poeziia," *Proletarskaia kul'tura*, no. 1 (July 1918), 20.

ing class but could certainly not feel for it, were heard again. Worker writers were even inclined to reject the argument that the idea of proletarian culture was the work of émigré intellectuals such as Bogdanov and Lunacharsky. Proletarian culture, Vladimir Kirillov argued in early 1919, was born in Russia in the years after 1905 among workers who were developing their own creative talents. If educated elites had a role to play, it was a negative one, as workers were encouraged to develop their own abilities by their growing disgust at the "passivity and detachment of the intelligentsia."[122] After 1917, the argument was mainly over interference and control. When many of the most experienced worker writers quit the Proletcult in early 1920, it will be recalled, they explained that the Proletcult was "hindering" their "creative capacities." At various gatherings and in the press, worker writers similarly voiced their resentment at being told, for example, that they should write simply and about everyday life in order to be more accessible to audiences of ordinary workers rather than in the complex, emotional, and abstract revolutionary styles many of them favored.[123] At issue in part, were class and power. Even when worker writers agreed that they must reach out in accessible language to ordinary workers, they still tended to insist that this writing was best done and workers' cultural life best led by "an intelligentsia formed among workers themselves."[124] Workers, they insisted again and again, were best enlightened and inspired by writers and artists who were "their own" not only in political ideology but in "life-feeling" (*zhizneoshchushchenie*).[125] But also at issue were questions of cultural truth and freedom. While party leaders insisted on the singularity of cultural truth—though they too argued over substance—many worker writers, at least implicitly, questioned whether there could, even in theory, be a unified and unambiguous culture of the proletariat. Tellingly, when the authors invited to the First Congress of Proletarian Writers in October 1920 were asked which "literary tendency" they sympathized with or belonged to, only a minority said "proletarian," "communist," or "Proletcultist." The majority gave a striking range of answers, among them realist, naturalist, Impressionist, Futurist, satirical, workerist, poetic, Romantic, artistic, lyric, Christian, Gorkyist, and Surikovist. And several pointedly answered that they followed no tendencies but their own.[126] Insistence on creative freedom, a leitmotif in both the arguments and the practices of working-class authors, expressed, it often seems, potentially dangerous philosophical doubts about the growing demands for cultural uniformity.

[122] V. K., "Pis'ma o proletarskom tvorchestve," *Griadushchaia kul'tura*, no. 3 (January 1919), 11.

[123] L'vov-Rogachevskii, *Ocherki*, 178; RGALI, f. 1638, op. 3, d. 1, ll. 1–3 (debates at May 1920 conference).

[124] *Griadushchee* 1918, no. 2 (May): 10.

[125] N. Liashko, "O zadachakh pisatelia-rabochego," *Kuznitsa*, no. 3 (July 1920), 26.

[126] RGALI, f. 1638, op. 3, d. 4 (1920 Congress of Proletarian Writers questionnaire).

2   *Knowledges of Self*

The world without us would be desolate except for the world within us.

—WALLACE STEVENS, *Opus Posthumous*

What the worker needs in order "to stand tall in the face of that which is ready to devour him" . . . is a knowledge of self that reveals to him a being dedicated to something else besides exploitation, a revelation of self that comes circuitously by way of the secret of others.

—JACQUES RANCIÈRE, *Nights of Labor*

. . . amidst the prose of everyday life . . . living in dreams, drunk with poetry and the thirst for light.

—MIKHAIL SAVIN, 1909

Plebeian Russian authors, like many of their contemporaries, were preoccupied with the question of selfhood and particularly with exploring and nurturing their own individual selves in the critical years between Russia's two revolutions. The nature, social place, and moral significance of the individual person was an obsession. Such keywords as *lichnost'* (person, personality, individual, self) and *chelovek* (the human person, man) saturate their writings, typically as grounding for moral or political appeals. One contemporary observer of prerevolutionary working-class attitudes saw a full-blown "cult of the self" (*kul't lichnosti*) and "cult of man" (*kul't cheloveka*) pervading the discourse of activist and outspoken workers in Russia.[1] This was a subversive

---

[1] L. M. Kleinbort, "Ocherki rabochei demokratii," pt. 1, *Sovremennyi mir,* March 1913, 32–44, and pt. 5, November 1913, 178–85 (the terms appear on 182 and 185). "Cult of the person" was earlier used by Emile Durkheim, whose work was known in Russia. See Durkheim's "L'Individualisme et les intellectuels" (1898), trans. Steven Lukes, *Political Studies* 17, no. 1 (March 1969): 19–30. Although Kleinbort employs "kul't cheloveka" in quotation marks, he mentions no source.

and dangerous discourse, even a revolutionary one, but it was also a troubled discourse, carrying hints of alienated self-absorption, pessimistic rage, and even philosophical despair.

Lichnost': The Self in Russia's Civic Culture

Notwithstanding the persistent stereotype of Russian political culture as antagonistic to the modern liberal notion of the autonomous individual endowed with natural rights and dignity, such ideas pervaded Russia's flourishing civic discourse in the final decades of the old order. This discourse about the self and its social and moral meanings provided an essential context for workers' articulation of notions of self and morality, and one to which they, in turn, contributed. Since the end of the eighteenth century, though mostly after the middle of the nineteenth, public discussions of ethics and social order in Russia—in journals, newspapers, and literary works and at meetings of all sorts—had focused increasingly (as in Western Europe, and often drawing on European sources) on the innate worth, freedom, and rights of the individual. The keyword in these reflections was *lichnost'*, a term that denoted not simply the individual or person but the person's inward nature and personality, the self, which made individuals naturally deserving of respect and freedom.[2]

These ideas were especially notable among Russia's intelligentsia, from liberals to most Marxists, among whom it had become an article of faith that the primary task of social change was to promote the freedom and dignity of the human person by removing the social, cultural, and political constraints that hindered the full development of the individual personality. As early as the late eighteenth century, such influential civic intellectuals as Nikolai Novikov and Aleksandr Radishchev and such sentimentalist writers as Nikolai Karamzin promoted a growing preoccupation with the inward personality and the moral significance of recognizing the inherent dignity and worth of the human self. By the middle of the nineteenth century, such values were elaborated into an increasingly influential body of social, political, and cultural criticism, echoing European intellectual traditions but reworked with a moral passion that was distinctly Russian. The concept of *lichnost'* was at the heart of all "Westernizing" liberal and socialist thought in the nineteenth century. Such influential nineteenth-century critics of the status quo as Vissarion Belinskii, Alexander Herzen, Dmitrii Pisarev, Nikolai Dobroliubov, Nikolai Chernyshevskii, and Petr Lavrov repeatedly and fervently voiced arguments typified by these comments by Belinskii in the early 1840s: "the human person" (*che-*

---

[2] For discussion of the meanings of *lichnost'* in Russian language and culture since its appearance in the mid–eighteenth century, see V. V. Vinogradov, *Istoriia slov* (Moscow, 1994), 271–309; Oleg Kharkhordin, *The Collective and the Individual in Russia* (Berkeley, 1999), 184–90; Derek Offord, "*Lichnost'*: Notions of Individual Identity," in *Constructing Russian Culture in the Age of Revolution: 1881–1940*, ed. Catriona Kelly and David Shepherd (Oxford, 1998), 13–25.

lovecheskaia lichnost') is the "idea and the thought of the age" and stands "higher than history, higher than society, higher than Humanity"; "the fate of the subject, the individual, the personality [*sud'ba sub"ekta, individuuma, lichnosti*] is more important than the fate of the whole world."[3] Contrary to the Orientalizing stereotype of Russia's essential collectivist culture and to the history of disregard and harsh oppression of the individual in Russia's social life, a strong countercurrent in Russian intellectual life continuously and vigorously asserted the prime importance of the individual and the self. It was even argued that the essential meaning of Russian history, after Russia's embrace of Christianity in the tenth century, was the liberation and advancement of the human individual, the progress of the "great and sacred significance . . . of human *lichnost'*," of the "unconditional dignity of man and personality."[4]

Although this ideal of the self was universalizing in its assumptions about human nature and the possibilities of rational change, it was not absolute. Russian Westernizing philosophers insisted on the social nature of their individualism—indeed, this social idea was central to what defined them as members of the intelligentsia. Most of Russia's influential socialist and liberal thinkers, from the mid–nineteenth century to the revolution, shared Lavrov's conviction that "individual dignity is maintained only by upholding the dignity of all."[5] Lavrov's idea of the "critically thinking individual," one of the central tropes of Russian radicalism, embodied this socialized individualism while expanding it to elucidate the active subject. Critically thinking individuals were expected, as Pisarev similarly wrote, to assert their "originality and autonomy" against both the conventional moralities of the established state and "the mob."[6] But the morally necessary purpose of their self-assertion, and what would make them historical actors, was to fight for social changes that would emancipate all. Socialists such as Herzen, reacting with moral disgust at the selfish, "philistine" individualism widespread in Western Europe, reasserted the equal value of the collective in defining the ethical place of the individual self. Some even questioned the capacity of the individual to achieve personal fulfillment and turned to various forms (political, artistic, spiritual) of the ideal of self-realization through self-abnegating union with others through, love, duty, and sacrifice.[7] In the 1890s and after, Nikolai Mikhailovskii and others linked this tradition explicitly to Nietzsche's ideal, increasingly influential in Russia, of the sacred and morally autonomous self reaching out beyond narrow individualism.[8] In a similar spir-

---

[3] V. G. Belinskii to V. P. Botkin, 4 Oct. 1840 and 1 Mar. 1841, in Belinskii, *Sobranie sochinenii,* vol. 9 (Moscow, 1982), 403, 442.

[4] K. D. Kavelin, in an essay in 1846, quoted in Vinogradov, *Istoriia slov,* 296. Belinskii and others also often spoke of Christian ethics as a foundation for their notion of human dignity.

[5] Petr Lavrov, *Historical Letters* [1868–69], trans. and ed. James P. Scanlan (Berkeley, 1967), 113.

[6] Quoted in George L. Kline, "Changing Attitudes toward the Individual," in *The Transformation of Russian Society,* ed. Cyril E. Black (Cambridge, 1960), 609.

[7] Offord, "*Lichnost',*" 20.

[8] See the discussions in Bernice Glatzer Rosenthal, ed., *Nietzsche in Russia* (Princeton, 1986).

it, some Marxists, especially Lunacharsky and Bogdanov, advocated what Lunacharsky called a "macropsychic individualism" in which the personal "I" is "identified with some broad and enduring 'we,'" and the vital and autonomous revolutionary hero strives not for wolfish private gain but for the progress of all humanity.[9] Further on the political and nationalist right, though the boundaries of such concepts never fit neatly into ideological spaces, such important writers as the Slavophile Konstantin Aksakov and Dostoevsky argued passionately that salvation lay in reintegrating the self into a moral and spiritual community.

Such ideas were part of a much wider civic discourse in late imperial Russia in which we see heightened awareness of the personal self, obsessive introspection, and a growing sense of the moral and social implications of acknowledging the self. In the late nineteenth century progressive jurists and lawmakers, influenced by their knowledge of Western European thought, began to reinterpret established notions of crime (a key terrain for defining subjecthood) to accord with liberal principles of personal dignity and individual autonomy and responsibility. Similarly, physicians, among them those in the increasingly prominent specialties of psychology and psychiatry, spoke more readily of drives and instincts, of psychological harm individuals suffered, of the problems of self-abasement and the need for self-esteem, of deformed and healthy personalities, and generally of the need both to protect and to control the inner self (the keyword in most cases being *lichnost'*). Other professions had similar concerns. Educators grew more attentive to nurturing the self-esteem and imaginations of children. Philosophers sought to understand and promote the knowing and active subject. Theater was transformed (under the notable influence of Konstantin Stanislavskii) by the desire to create performative personalities in ways that were truer to real inward emotions and character and drew upon the actors' own selves as inspiration. Finally, many educated Russians were driven to write about and often rewrite their lives in letters, diaries, and memoirs.[10]

This was a conflicted and often troubled discourse. Many openly contested the autonomy and moral valence of the individual self, insisting on the moral superiority of the social and the communal. Many resisted the challenge to sci-

On Mikhailovskii, see Ann Lane, "Nietzsche Comes to Russia: Popularization and Protest in the 1890s," ibid., 63–65.

[9] A. V. Lunacharskii, "Voprosy morali i M. Meterlink" (1904), quoted in Kline, "Changing Attitudes toward the Individual," 619. See also A. V. Lunacharskii, "Meshchanstvo i individualizm" (1909), in his *Meshchanstvo i individualizm: Sbornik statei* (Moscow and Petrograd, 1923), 5–136.

[10] Kline, "Changing Attitudes toward the Individual," 606–25; Laura Engelstein and Stephanie Sandler, eds., *Self and Story in Russian History* (Ithaca, 2000); Kelly and Shepherd, *Constructing Russian Culture*; David Joravsky, *Russian Psychology: A Critical History* (Oxford, 1989); Edith Clowes, Samuel Kassow, and James West, eds., *Between Tsar and People: Educated Society and the Quest for Public Identity in Late Imperial Russia* (Princeton, 1991); Laura Engelstein, *The Keys to Happiness: Sex and the Search for Modernity in Fin-de-Siècle Russia* (Ithaca, 1992); William G. Wagner, *Marriage, Property, and Law in Late Imperial Russia* (Oxford, 1994); Irina Paperno, *Suicide as a Cultural Institution in Dostoevsky's Russia* (Ithaca, 1997).

entific rationalism posed by the search for deeper human truths in inward subjectivities. Many openly doubted the accessibility of the self. And most im portant, we see a great deal of anxiety about the self. A growing number of writers, journalists, and others joined physicians in focusing attention on deformed personalities, irrational drives, deviance, and dangerous passions. Intensified by the deep political and social unease that arose in the wake of the upheavals of 1905, these doubts introduced more than a little ambivalence to implicitly liberal arguments about the worth and rights of the individual person. The centrality of the self was not displaced in these deliberations, though its nature was increasingly in doubt and contested.

Although even most literate workers were likely to have been only faintly aware of these discussions among the educated, many of them aired in professional journals and publications and at congresses and meetings, they encountered similar language and argument in more accessible and popular settings and texts. Newspapers, magazines, the cinema, and much popular fiction featured stories about individuals discovering and fashioning varieties of modern selves. The ethical weight of these narratives was often explicit. In particular, essays, reviews, and feuilletons in popular magazines and daily papers— exploring, for example, such preoccupying problems of modern social life as hooliganism, prostitution, and suicide—regularly spoke of "human dignity," "the rights of the person," "consciousness of the individual 'I,'" and "respect for the personality" (*lichnost'*). And they regularly chastised conditions that "degraded," "insulted," or harmed the personality.[11] When the noted public health physician Mariia Pokrovskaia criticized Russia's system of regulated prostitution in 1907 as evidence of "contempt for the human dignity of women" and argued that men and the law needed to "recognize women as people" rather than treat them as "commodities," she was making use of an established rhetoric—one, in fact, that was given a certain power precisely because of its familiarity as part of an increasingly accepted discourse about the self and its ethical value.[12]

Of particular importance for the more literate common readers were popular belles lettres. Such widely read Russian poets and writers as Nikolai

---

[11] Surveying news articles that appeared in the large Moscow and Petersburg dailies *Rech'*, *Novoe vremia,* and *Russkoe slovo* in 1913, I found repeated use of this vocabulary and its logic. In *Rech'*, e.g., see report on the Congress on Family Education, 3 Jan. 1913; E. Koltonovskaia, "O zhenshchine," 2 Dec. 1913; and "Khronika," 6 Dec. 1913. Even the leading encyclopedia of the day, *Entsiklopedicheskii slovar'*, ed. F. A. Brokgaus and I. A. Efron (St. Petersburg, 1890– 1907), features an entry on lichnost', framed in this way, written by the philosopher Vladimir Solov'ev (17:868). See also Louise McReynolds, *The News under Russia's Old Regime: The Development of a Mass Circulation Press* (Princeton, 1991); Joan Neuberger, *Hooliganism: Crime, Culture, and Power in St. Petersburg, 1900–1914* (Berkeley, 1993); Daniel Brower, "The Penny Press and Its Readers," in *Cultures in Flux: Lower-Class Values, Practices, and Resistance in Late Imperial Russia,* ed. Stephen Frank and Mark Steinberg (Princeton, 1994), 147–167; Roshanna Sylvester, "Crime, Masquerade, and Anxiety: The Public Creation of Middle-Class Identity in Pre-Revolutionary Odessa, 1912–1916," Ph.D. diss., Yale University, 1998; Engelstein and Sandler, *Self and Story in Russian History,* esp. chaps. 5, 6, 9.

[12] M. I. Pokrovskaia, "Prostitutsiia i bespravie zhenshchin," *Zhenskii vestnik* 1907, no. 10: 226.

Nekrasov, Vladimir Korolenko, Fedor Dostoevsky, Lev Tolstoy, Leonid Andreev, Anton Chekhov, and Maxim Gorky offered readers various incarnations of the ideal of the self as an essential moral category. These authors placed the individual and the self at the center of their attention, focusing, though with different purposes, on the development, sufferings, and assertions of their characters' inward and social beings. Starting in the 1890s, echoes of Nietzsche's idealization of the proud, striving, exuberant, and rebellious individual became influential among writers, including many whom lower-class Russians read, notably Gorky and Andreev.[13] Gorky's stories in particular were filled with vital, restless, freedom-seeking individuals—plebeian supermen—living and wandering on the fringes of society, challenging established moralities and authorities, and condemning the slavish submissiveness of the masses.[14] At the same time, many leading poets and prose writers, notably such "decadent" writers as Konstantin Bal'mont, Valerii Briusov, Fedor Sologub, and Zinaida Gippius, seemed to celebrate the darker, egoistic side of concern and care for the self. Combining aestheticism with amoralism, they worshiped both the creative personality and the all too human ego and id— the influences of Nietzsche and Freud were widely evident. In a complex psychological and philosophical frame influenced by European intellectual and literary trends and by a dramatic sense of the decline and failure of all established values and order, their writing explored human sensuality, lust, depravity, cruelty, and other irrational drives and passions.[15]

It is telling that worker writers themselves sometimes explicitly characterized Russian intellectual and literary history as fundamentally concerned with the self. While invariably criticizing decadent egoism, they interpreted the essence of Russia's literary heritage as the exploration and promotion of the human person. Nikolai Liashko, one of Russia's best-known worker authors, portrayed the entire corpus of classical Russian literature as fighting a heroic struggle "for the oppressed and humiliated, for truth and the dignity of the person."[16] Ivan Kubikov, a compositor turned literary critic and a union activist, writing in the paper of the Petersburg printers' union in 1909, likewise found the most important "teaching" in Nikolai Gogol's writings to be that "one must not forget one's human dignity."[17] Kubikov similarly viewed Belinskii as having taught chiefly "the dignity and social worth of man" and hav-

[13] See esp. the essays by Ann Lane, Mary Louise Loe, and Edith Clowes in Rosenthal, *Nietzsche in Russia*. Of course, Nietzsche was not the only source of "Nietzschean" ideas. Dostoevsky voiced quite similar ideas. See also the essay by Mihajlo Mihajlov in the same volume.

[14] For a discussion of Gorky's attitude toward the individual in the light of Nietzsche's ideas, see Mary Louise Loe, "Gorky and Nietzsche: The Quest for the Russian Superman," in Rosenthal, *Nietzsche in Russia*, 251–73. See also Mark D. Steinberg, Introduction to Maxim Gorky, *Untimely Thoughts* (New Haven, 1995).

[15] Evelyn Bristol, "Decadence," in *Handbook of Russian Literature*, ed. Victor Terras (New Haven, 1985), 94; Renato Poggioli, *The Poets of Russia, 1890–1930* (Cambridge, Mass., 1960), 79–115; S. A. Vengerov, "Etapy neo-romanticheskago dvizheniia," in *Russkaia literatura XX veka*, ed. Vengerov, 3 vols. (Moscow, 1914–16), 1:1–26.

[16] *Ogni*, no. 3 (January 1913), 27.

[17] I. Dement'ev [Kubikov], "N. V. Gogol'," *Pechatnoe delo*, no. 5 (21 Mar. 1909), 9.

ing shown how social conditions in Russia "hinder the development of the human person [*lichnost'*]."[18]

Workers did not need to have read Gogol or even Gorky, however, to be encouraged to think about the worth and importance of the self and the individual, or to have read Sologub or Gippius to be exposed to representations of the self's darker face. The popular commercial print media increasingly set before common readers images of the degradation and humiliation that individuals suffered in Russia and models of autonomous moral choice and individual achievement. As one type compositor observed in 1903, "the recognition of the human personality [*lichnost'*]" is a principle about which "we read and set type every day."[19] The best-selling author Anastasiia Verbitskaia—whose novel about personal and sexual exploration and independence, *Keys to Happiness* (1910–13), was immensely popular in prewar Russia—dedicated her 1908 autobiography to those who shared her devotion to "the affirmation and growth of the self [*lichnost'*]."[20] Similarly, popular tales of bandits and adventurers brought to a wide Russian audience positive images of "self-assertive and superior individuals," rebellious outsiders challenging authority and conventional restraints.[21]

Even if we question the argument that commercial publishers and writers necessarily accurately reflected popular values in order to sell their books and newspapers—after all, popular readers were perfectly capable of disregarding the message when the medium was sufficiently appealing, so the message need not necessarily have coincided with their actual views—it is clear that commercial literature exposed lower-class readers to a popularized version of the same idealizations of (and anxieties about) selfhood and individuality that so preoccupied educated readers and writers. Also, these themes engaged and reinforced a strain of individualism already present in lower-class culture, notwithstanding assumptions about the collectivist mentality of the Russian common folk. We see this strain in the images of heroic champions and ingenious peasant tricksters that proliferated in popular peasant folklore, and in the tales of saints, prophets, holy men, and visionaries common in popular religious narratives (and in religious ideas about the divine spark in each person). Most important, as popular culture evolved over time, attention to the individual and the inner person grew. The increasing attention to the personal needs of the individual in popular folk songs was among the signs of this developing culture of the individual and the self.[22]

---

[18] *Novoe pechatnoe delo*, no. 1 (16 June 1911), 3–6.

[19] *Naborshchik* 1, no. 52 (26 Oct. 1903): 796. See also no. 19 (9 Mar. 1903): 313.

[20] A. Verbitskaia, *Moemu chitatel'iu* (Moscow, 1908), quoted in Engelstein, *Keys to Happiness*, 401.

[21] Jeffrey Brooks, *When Russia Learned to Read: Literacy and Popular Culture, 1861–1917* (Princeton, 1985) and "Competing Modes of Popular Discourse: Individualism and Class Consciousness in the Russian Print Media," in *Culture et révolution*, ed. M. Ferro and S. Fitzpatrick (Paris, 1989), 71–81.

[22] Robert Rothstein, "Death of the Folk Song?" in Frank and Steinberg, *Cultures in Flux*, 108–20.

One must take care not to simplify this popular culture of the self in Russia. When such socialist worker critics as Liashko and Kubikov tendentiously embraced the confident ethical idea of the self in Russia's cultural traditions, they were clearly advancing an argument about the human personality and even about human existence altogether, one designed to discount widespread uncertainties and anxieties. The "boulevard press" and the popular cinema were producing their own decadent representations of the self in dozens of works issued between 1905 and 1917 by authors such as Mikhail Artsybashev, Anastasia Verbitskaia, Evdokiia Nagrodskaia, Mikhail Kuzmin, and (more modestly) Lidiia Charskaia, and in the films of Evgenii Bauer, which dwelled on secret, often sexual, passions and on personal and often sensual fulfillment; and these popular creative works framed these narratives, philosophically, in more or less explicit concern with the inner self, its needs, and its journey, often derailed, toward personal identity and self-fulfillment.[23] Similarly, ostensibly nonfictional reportage in the commercial press, especially the "boulevard press," dwelled constantly on irrational and inexplicable human behaviors and on the modern pervasiveness of death, suicide, and despair.[24] We see an even more complex picture of the popular culture of the self as we turn to the writings by lower-class Russians themselves.

The Proletarian "Cult of Man"

The modern ideal of the self as the inward source of identity, dignity, and rights shared by all human beings occupied a central place in the discourse of activist workers in Russia in the late nineteenth and early twentieth centuries. Historians of Russian labor have often noted workers' demands for "polite address" and, more generally, for treatment befitting their worth as "human beings."[25] These challenges to "humiliation and insult" (*unizhenie i oskorblenie*), however, were often much more than mere items on a list of demands.

---

[23] Brooks, *When Russia Learned to Read*, esp. 154–62; Engelstein, *Keys to Happiness*, chap. 10; Louise McReynolds, Introduction to Evdokia Nagrodskaia, *The Wrath of Dionysus*, trans. and ed. McReynolds (Bloomington, 1997), and "The Silent Movie Melodrama: Evgenii Bauer Fashions the Heroine's Self," in Engelstein and Sandler, *Self and Story*, chap. 5; and Susan Larsen, "Girl Talk: Lydia Charskaia and Her Readers," chap. 6 in the same volume.

[24] These themes were pervasive in *Gazeta-Kopeika* and *Peterburgskii listok* between 1907 and World War I. See the discussion in Neuberger, *Hooliganism*, and McReynolds, *News under Russia's Old Regime*.

[25] V. F. Shishkin, *Tak skladyvalas' revolutsionnaia moral': Istoricheskii ocherk* (Moscow, 1967); Reginald E. Zelnik, "Russian Bebels," *Russian Review* 35 (July 1976): 265, 272–77; Victoria E. Bonnell, *Roots of Rebellion: Workers' Politics and Organizations in St. Petersburg and Moscow, 1900–1914* (Berkeley, 1983), 43–72, 90, 102, 170–71, 183–84, 191, 264, 449, 452; Tim McDaniel, *Autocracy, Capitalism, and Revolution in Russia* (Berkeley, 1988), 161, 169–74, 194–95; Leopold H. Haimson, "The Problem of Social Identities in Early Twentieth Century Russia," *Slavic Review* 47, no. 1 (Spring 1988): esp. 2–8; Diane P. Koenker and William G. Rosenberg, *Strikes and Revolution in Russia, 1917* (Princeton, 1989), esp. 172–74, 231; Mark D. Steinberg, *Moral Communities: The Culture of Class Relations in the Russian Printing Industry, 1867–1907* (Berkeley, 1992), 235–36, 242–45.

They were at the heart of an ethical vision with which many workers judged the entirety of social and political life. At the core of this ethics was the belief in the inward self as the source of universal human identity, hence natural and equal worth, and hence the moral rights of the individual as a human being. The natural dignity of the person, not the particularistic interests of a class, became a foundation for social judgment and for imagining a just society.

Variations on these themes pervaded workers' critical writings in the years from 1905 to the revolution. When, writing on the eve of the First World War, Lev Kleinbort surveyed the Russian labor press of recent years, he found a fundamental, even obsessive, preoccupation with questions of "honor and conscience" (*chest' i sovest'*) and of insult and humiliation, and pervasive demands to be recognized as "human beings," not slaves, machines, or animals. Such language and argumentation was inescapable in the labor press. Hundreds of articles, essays, and letters by workers (encouraged and echoed by these papers' nonproletarian activists) repeatedly voiced moral outrage at the treatment of workers as "beasts of burden" (or "cattle," "machines," even "camels"), at conditions that forced workers to sell not only their labor but also their human dignity, at society's blindness to workers' "human personality" (*lichnost' chelovecheskaia* or *lichnost' cheloveka*) and "common human dignity" (*obshchechelovecheskoe dostoinstvo*), and at the refusal of the upper classes to recognize the "freedom" and "autonomy of the human person" or the simple fact that "a man is a man."[26]

In fiction and especially poetry, worker writers articulated and elaborated on these key ethical themes. The language of these "voices from the soul"—as the provincial glassworker Egor Nechaev titled a 1906 poem about the insulted dignity of workers—was filled with the key words and images of this discourse: the "pain," "insult," and "depersonalization" (*obezlichenie cheloveka*) of workers resulting from their lack of freedom to act according to their own will; the "spiteful" disdain of workers' "honor"; the degradation of workers into "literal automatons"; and the need for the world to see that "we are people, not animals, not cattle," and that "the soul of the worker is no different from that of the educated rulers of the world."[27] A telling illus-

---

[26] L. M. Kleinbort, "Ocherki rabochei demokratii," pt. 1, *Sovremennyi mir*, March 1913, 26–29; *Pechatnyi vestnik* 1905, no. 3 (23 June): 21–23; no. 9 (28 Aug.): 8; no. 11 (11 Sept.): 3, 7; *Vestnik pechatnikov* 1906, no. 3 (9 May): 4; no. 5 (20 May): 3, 5; no. 6 (28 May): 2–3; *Pechatnik* 1906, no. 3 (14 May): 12–13; no. 8 (23 July): 6–7; *Bulochnik*, no. 1 (19 Feb. 1906), 8; no. 3 (12 Mar. 1906), 39–40; *Pechatnoe delo*, no. 24 (11 Sept. 1910), 4; *Nash put'*, no. 10 (3 Dec. 1910), 6; *Chelovek*, no. 1 (13 Feb. 1911), 1; *Metallist*, no. 8 (13 Jan. 1912), 8. See further discussion in Mark Steinberg, "Worker-Authors and the Cult of the Person," in Frank and Steinberg, *Cultures in Flux*, 168–84.

[27] Nechaev, "Golos dushi," *Zhurnal dlia vsekh*, 1906, rpt. in *U istokov russkoi proletarskoi poezii* (Moscow and Leningrad, 1965), 88, and later in the 1914 collection of his poems, *Vecherniia pesni*; Ofitsiant [waiter] S. P., "Sovremennye kuplety," *Rodnye vesti* 1912, no. 4: 7; Kleinbort, "Ocherki rabochei demokratii," pt. 5, *Sovremennyi mir*, November 1913, 178; [Chechenets, a metalworker and leading poet of the St. Petersburg metalworkers' union], "Nevol'niki truda," *Nash put'* 1911, no. 17 (23 May): 8–9 (rpt. and author identified in *Proletarskie poety*, 3 vols.

tration of these ideas was offered by the metalworker Aleksei Bibik in his 1912 novel *K shirokoi doroge* (Toward the open road), the first novel written by a Russian worker to be published. In the midst of a passionate discussion with a comrade at his factory about questions of pride, envy, dignity, art, morality, doubt, and death, Ignat Pasterniak, the young worker who is the semi-auto-biographical hero of the novel, offers this moral fantasy:

> Imagine a huge hall. Before a crowd of thousands of self-important and conceited people, someone is playing the piano. Or a violin. It doesn't matter. His playing is so inspired that everyone is spellbound by his music. They don't even move. Then there is some whispering: who is this, who is he? So he stands up and throws off some sort of cloak he has been wearing and stands there in a simple, dirty blue shirt. He's a worker! . . . Imagine the picture. . . . Everyone would be amazed and he would say to them, "So you thought that under this dirty blue shirt was empti-ness? An animal? What gave you the right to think that? To think that we don't feel or understand beauty? What made you think that only you are the salt of the earth? You are pitiful! I can't bear to stay here with you anymore!"[28]

Ideas about labor, the existential practice that most defined workers socially (and, for socialists, also defined workers politically, morally, and historically), were entangled in all these discussions. The recognition that work and self-hood are interdependent is at least as old as the Hebrew Bible, with its argu-ment that we are doomed to labor because of the Fall (though complicated by the Scriptures' moral and spiritual valorization of labor over wealth). Among influential modern philosophies, socialism, especially its Marxist version, is notable for placing labor at the center of ideas about the self—and for the am-bivalence of this appreciation. Labor is viewed as essential if humans are to realize their nature—to "develop their slumbering powers," in Marx's phrase. Indeed, human beings come to see, name, and measure themselves by the things they make. Man, Marx wrote, "sees his own reflection in a world which he has constructed." In modern times, however, work is degraded: into a sell-able commodity in a system of production in which the producer feels alien-ated from his product and hence from himself. Such conditions, Marx judged, "mutilate the labourer into a fragment of a man, degrade him to the level of an appendage of a machine, destroy every remnant of charm in his work and turn it into a hated toil."[29] Out of this contradiction of work's meanings, it has been argued, has come much of the pain of modern working-class life and its potential explosiveness.

[Leningrad, 1935–39], 2:10–13); letter accompanying verses submitted to *Pravda* by the miner Aleksei Chizhikov, 4 Mar. 1914, 4, in RGASPI, f. 364, op. 1, d. 315, ll. 1–3.

[28] A. Bibik, *K shirokoi doroge (Ignat iz Novoselovki)* (St. Petersburg, 1914), 80. The novel was first published in 1912 in the leftist journal *Sovremennyi mir.*

[29] Karl Marx, *Capital: A Critique of Political Economy* (Chicago, 1906), 1:708. See the dis-cussion of Marx's ideas of work and alienation in Kai Erikson, "On Work and Alienation," in Kai Erikson and Steven Peter Vallas, *The Nature of Work: Sociological Perspectives* (New Haven, 1990), 19–35.

In the historical discourse of working people, similarly ambivalent attitudes toward labor were widespread. As we know from the autobiographies of many worker radicals, in Russia as elsewhere, pride in one's acquired skills and in the value of labor to society was for many workers a potent source of self-esteem and of a sense of moral injury and injustice.[30] Among Russian worker writers we see some recognition of the potentially enriching value of work for the self. "When labor is satisfying, life is good," the essayist Ivan Kubikov wrote, quoting Gorky. Labor, when it is "normal" rather than "enslaving," can "enrich the human being," G. D. Deev-Khomiakovskii wrote, "make him a man and a citizen," and allow each individual's "personality" (*lichnost'*) to flower forth. "Honest labor," some said, is a sacred thing, nurturing us like the sun. Labor was even compared to prayer.[31] Often, however, labor was appreciated more distantly and abstractly for what it did for others rather than for what it did for the self: for the things of value workers created, for the contribution of labor to "progress," for work's symbolic value as a representation of strength, bold determination, even eternity.[32]

Most often, however, worker writers dwelled on the harm and injuries labor inflicted on the self. This was an ambiguous condemnation of work. These writers tried to distinguish between labor in theory (that which can enrich life and create value and pleasure) and labor in practice: the real thing rather than the imagined idyll of peasant labor; the "forced drudgery" (*katorzhnyi trud*) of factory and artisanal work, which "cannot be a source of happiness and joy."[33] Only "slaves" could love such work, Aleksandr Shliapnikov wrote in a story about factory labor. Men with spirit hate it and flee it.[34] Often, however, while this framing logic may have been implicit, the explicit argument was more simply focused on the harmfulness and hatefulness of labor. "Life is but cursed toil / Thoughts of happiness a pathetic delusion."[35] Most workers, these writers averred, hated work (and we must remember that all of these worker authors were looking to escape from physical labor into another sort of creative work). "Our whole life is nothing but hard labor. The hell with it," a character in an Andrei Bibik story declares before heading off into the countryside and nature.[36] What do workers most

[30] See esp. Zelnik, "Russian Bebels"; Bonnell, *Roots of Rebellion*; McDaniel, *Autocracy, Capitalism, and Revolution*; Steinberg, *Moral Communities*.

[31] Kvadrat [I. Kubikov], "A. V. Kol'tsov," *Pechatnoe delo*, no. 12 (23 Oct. 1909), 6; G. D. Deev-Khomiakovskii, "I. Z. Surikov v pesniakh o zhenshchine i trude," *Drug naroda* 1916, no. 1 (October): 16; M. Savin, "Chestnyi trud," in *Gallereia sovremennykh poetov*, ed. A. A. Tiulenev (Moscow, 1909), 12; Samobytnik [Mashirov], "Vesennye grezy" (1916), *Voprosy strakhovaniia*, rpt. in *Proletarskie poety*, 3:26.

[32] Samobytnik [Mashirov], "Proletarii!" *Proletarskaia pravda*, 16 Jan. 1914; Krot, "Tiazhelaia tvoia dolia naborshchik," *Nashe pechatnoe delo*, 8 July 1915, rpt. *Proletarskie poety*, 3:64; Aksen-Achkasov [I. Sadof'ev], "Pred razsvetom," *Rabochii put'* [*Pravda*], 23 Oct. 1917.

[33] Kvadrat [I. Kubikov], "A. V. Kol'tsov," *Pechatnoe delo*, no. 12 (23 Oct. 1909), 6.

[34] A. Shliapnikov, "Na fabrike," in *Pervyi sbornik proletarskikh pisatelei* (St. Petersburg, 1914), 66–67.

[35] [Chechenets], "Nevol'niki truda," *Nash put'* 1911, no. 17 (23 May): 8–9.

[36] A. Bibik, "Bor obrechennoi," *Novaia rabochaia gazeta*, no. 56 (13 Oct. 1913), 2.

want? a coal miner and poet named Aleksei Chizhikov wrote in a letter to the Bolshevik paper *Pravda* in 1914: "More free time," which could be used "for productive uses, for one's own intellectual development."[37] Workers wrote of their laboring lives as an endless "chain of suffering."[38] Emancipation for many workers was to be found not in more deeply identifying with their work but in transcending the antihumanistic reduction of their identities to those of mere laborers.

The seemingly simple identification of the worker as a human being—that is to say, the very particular construction of all human beings as subjects possessing natural dignity and intrinsic rights—was in Russia as elsewhere in the modern world a potentially inspiring and explosive idea. It helped make sense of social structures and relationships, especially subordination and unequal exchange. Most essential in shaping these meanings were the perceived effects these relationships had on workers' inward selves—on their *lichnost'*. It mattered less that these were *unequal* relationships than that they "trampled in the dirt" workers' "feelings of human dignity"[39]—in other words, that they were relationships of insult and indignity. This was a powerful discourse. It was a force of great interpretive and discursive power for workers to be able to see and speak of capitalist social relationships not simply as subordination and unequal exchange but, as the worker-critic Ivan Kubikov did, as "moral oppression."[40]

The Moral Poetics of Suffering

> Unless suffering is the direct and immediate object of life, our existence must entirely fail of its aim.
>
> —ARTHUR SCHOPENHAUER, *Parerga*

> Кто живет без печали и гнева—
> Тот не любит отчизны своей.
> (One who lives without sorrow and anger
> Is one who loves not his own native land.)
> —NIKOLAI NEKRASOV (motto of *Rodnye vesti*
> [Native news: A journal of the laboring folk, 1911–12])

Suffering preoccupied Russian worker writers, for it was strongly intertwined with these ways of experiencing and valuing the self—and of deploying these notions critically. Suffering, it is worth emphasizing, is interpretation. Physical injury, disease, loss, and death are primarily material facts; suffering is a category through which people perceive, value, and represent such facts, as well as less tangible experiences such as oppression, insult, be-

---

[37] *Pravda*, 4 Mar. 1914, 4, in RGASPI, f. 364, op. 1, d. 315, ll. 1–3.
[38] N. Dodaev, "Trud," *Zhizn' pekarei* 1914, no. 1/4 (10 Mar.): 2.
[39] *Golos portnogo*, no. 1–2 (10 May 1910), 10.
[40] Kvadrat [Kubikov], "Vpechatleniia zhizni," *Pechatnoe delo*, no. 24 (11 Sept. 1910), 2.

trayal, and unfulfilled desire. The meanings of suffering are necessarily unstable and variable. Certainly the naming and explaining of suffering have been shown to vary among cultures and over time.[41] Literature, art, and song— from sacred liturgies to the songs of slaves and workers to modern philosophies—are filled with suffering named, explained, and valued in a wide variety of ways, and with discourses of suffering used to argue about (often against) the world. There is one constant. Ideas of suffering are almost always tied up with notions of self and with the moral and spiritual meanings attached to varied self-concepts. It matters, for example, whether physical suffering— illness, for example—is viewed as "immanent justice," as punishment for sin, or is blamed on social conditions, thus externalizing the moral fault. More subtly, it matters how suffering is treated emotionally, aesthetically, and spiritually: as proof of a warrior's manhood, for instance, or of a saint's humility, or of an oppressed people's nobility (applied to diasporic Africans or Jews, for example), as a devalued state of body and mind to be avoided, ignored, or cured (reflecting a definition of the good life, at least in part, as the absence of suffering), or as an edifying good, even a source of great soulfulness, beauty, and inspiring power, to be contemplated and retold, often with various moral lessons attached. These meanings are not mutually exclusive. Sorrow and suffering, like tears, can express contradictory and ambiguous meanings. But ideas about the self, however variant the category, seem persistently to occupy the center.

In Russia, suffering had tangible social form and history—a "sociopolitical causal ontology," in the rich but inelegant language of social science.[42] We know that the everyday lives of the urban poor in Russia were harsh: crowded and unsanitary living conditions, wide social and political inequalities, low wages and debilitating working conditions, limited social protections, and restricted civil rights. Yet the organization of these raw facts into a narrative of *suffering* introduced layers of meaning and intent that were not intrinsic. When lower-class Russian authors did interpret such experiences as suffering, they necessarily drew upon what was culturally and intellectually available to them. Frequent use of literary form gave them more scope to articulate and employ possible meanings of suffering—and more space to adapt and invent.

In emphasizing cultural context, one must be cautious in generalizing about the meaning of discourses of suffering in Russian culture. Efforts to demonstrate a persistent and deep-seated Russian cultural inclination toward self-injury, self-humiliation, and self-sacrifice—what one author has called "moral masochism"—tend toward cliché and stereotype, overgeneralize from scattered evidence, and reduce the deliberate rhetorics of contemporary cultural criticism to straightforward statements of fact from inside the culture.[43] To

---

[41] This is a major theme in Richard A. Shweder's collection of essays, *Thinking through Cultures: Expeditions in Cultural Psychology* (Cambridge, Mass., 1991), e.g. 313–31.

[42] Ibid., 313.

[43] Anna Feldman Leibovich, *The Russian Concept of Work: Suffering, Drama, and Tradition*

the extent that there was a "cult of suffering" in Russian culture, it was diverse, changing, and contradictory (and not uniquely Russian). Most important, it also contained the opposite of moral masochism: a self-elevating rejection of degrading and destructive humiliation. Orthodox Christianity viewed suffering not simply as the fate of sinful humanity but also as the elevating practice of the virtues of humility, emulation of Christ's Passion, and a way to transcendence, redemption, and salvation.

Russian literature, especially from the mid–nineteenth century, also devoted a great deal of energy to exploring the complex psychic and moral meanings of suffering. Even a brief review of common interpretations of some of the major writers in the Russian literary canon by the early 1900s conveys a clear enough idea of the centrality, and hence availability, of a complex poetics of suffering.[44] Critics have spoken of Lermontov's introspective and melancholy poetry, with its dominant motifs of sorrow, grief, and estrangement from the petty and sinful human world; Ivan Nikitin's "songs of sorrow, sadness, and bitterness";[45] Nekrasov's pathos-suffused portraits of peasant misery, grief, and death, written in a "sorrowing tone" that was still striking to mid-century contemporaries but would, critics noted, become familiar to readers of the many poets who following Nekrasov;[46] Dostoevsky's psychological and metaphysical explorations of humiliation, guilt, cruelty, madness, and death; the melancholy and pessimistic visions of evil and death in the writings of many fin-de-siècle symbolists and decadents; and Andreev's popular stories of torment, alienation, deceit, disease, nightmares, violence, demonic sexual drives, and death. Russian folk culture—in less baroque form and less influenced by European modernism (though by no means locked, as some have imagined, in an insular and unchanging tradition)—also provided workers with a rich body of treatments of suffering: the narratives of the lives of martyr-saints and passion-bearers (*strastoterptsa*); the evolving traditions of women's laments, especially the ritualized funeral laments, or *plachi*; the "sorrow songs" of workers, soldiers, and exiles; and the large body of folktales and epics about misery and misfortune (*gore* and *gore-zloschastie*).[47]

---

in Pre- and Post-Revolutionary Russia (Westport, Conn., 1995); Daniel Rancour-Laferriere, *The Slave Soul of Russia: Moral Masochism and the Cult of Suffering* (New York, 1995).

[44] Useful contemporary and later scholarly summaries of thematic trends in Russian literature can be found in D. N. Ovsianiko-Kulıkovskii, ed., *Istoriia russkoi literatury XIX v.*, 5 vols. (Moscow, 1908–11); Vengerov, *Russkaia literatura XX veka; Istoriia russkoi literatury*, 4 vols. (Leningrad, 1980–83); Poggioli, *Poets of Russia*; Terras, *Handbook of Russian Literature*; Evelyn Bristol, *A History of Russian Poetry* (New York, 1991).

[45] A phrase, often used in describing his writings, adapted from the opening lines of Nikitin, "Portnoi" (1860).

[46] Ovsianiko-Kulikovskii, *Istoriia*, 3:400.

[47] See Roberta Reeder, ed. and trans., *Russian Folk Lyrics* (Bloomington, 1992); *Pesni russkikh rabochikh* (Moscow and Leningrad, 1962); N. V. Os'makov, *Russkaia proletarskaia poeziia, 1896–1917* (Moscow, 1968), 50–51. For an eloquent contemporary description of the mournful spirit of Russian workers' songs, see Maxim Gorky's story "Twenty-six Men and a Girl"

All of these (and many other) images of suffering and sorrow expressed and evoked, often in uneasy combination, different meanings: a Romantic infatuation with the sorrowing self; an empathetic and often penitential sympathy for the downtrodden; a melancholy "philosophy of despair," which some contemporaries argued was typically Russian;[48] an appreciation of the transcendent spiritual significance of world suffering; a metaphysical faith in redemption and salvation through suffering; a complex sense of the uplifting experience of the tragic; moral outrage at humiliating social conditions (grief as grievance); recognition and elevation of the self as the experiential and moral site of suffering. All of these understandings of suffering were part of the cultural terrain on which worker writers tried to make sense of their social and personal experiences, articulate ideas about selfhood, and voice criticism.

Indeed, when literate Russian workers wrote about their lives—typically first in emotive lyric verse—their writings were saturated with a rich vocabulary of personal affliction: *grust', pechal'* (sadness), *unynie* (hopeless sadness, depression), *gore* (misery, grief), *skorb'* (sorrow), *muka, muchenie* (torment), *stradanie* (suffering), *slezy* (tears), *bol'* (pain), and, most frequently, *toska* (a mixture of melancholy, sadness, anguish, depression, and longing). The earliest literary writing by urban commoners—notably by the "self-taught poets from the people" associated with Moscow's Surikov Circle and similar plebeian literary gatherings—were focused almost entirely on the personal miseries of the poor. Ivan Surikov—a small shopkeeper who often signed his published verses "the peasant Ivan Surikov," typically blurring what we normally think of as boundaries of social identity—was a major influence. Writing about the tormented lives of peasants and of the urban poor, he sought to give voice to their anguish. But his preoccupations were more existential than social. His poems were filled with images of decay, death, burial, and graves, and suffused with tones of sadness, anguish, and despair, all set against a background of nostalgic thoughts of childhood and nature. Among the self-taught poets from the people whom Surikov organized and helped inspire, the sensibility remained the same and even intensified: the world about and the world within the individual soul were places of unending sorrow, bitterness, torment, tribulation, and weeping, framed by the partial comforts of faith, nature's beauty, and death.[49]

(1899). I borrow the term "sorrow songs" from W. E. B. Du Bois, *The Souls of Black Folk: Essays and Sketches* (Chicago, 1903), chap. 14. The Russian equivalent, *skorbnye pesni*, was the title of a 1915 collection of poems by the self-taught author L. Ia. Bystrov. See interview and discussion in N. Vlasov-Okskii, "Ogon'ki v stepi (Iz vstrech s pistateliami-samouchkami)," *Griadushchee* 1921, no. 1–3: 41–44. The anthropologist Nancy Ries has used the Russian term for misery, grief, and sorrow to describe this folk song tradition as *"gore* songs" in her *Russian Talk: Culture and Conversation during Perestroika* (Ithaca, 1997), 124–25.

[48] D. Ovsianiko-Kulikovskii, "Itogi russkoi khudozhestvennoi literatury XIX veka (prodolzhenie)," *Vestnik vospitaniia* 22, no. 6 (September 1911): 12, 22–24. See Maxim Gorky's praise of these observations (written in response to his story "Toska" [Melancholy]) in *Maksim Gorky: Selected Letters,* ed. Andrew Barratt and Barry Scherr (Oxford, 1997), 160.

[49] I. Z. *Surikov i poety-surikovtsy* (Moscow and Leningrad, 1965), and the introductory es-

Writers who were later called the first generation of *proletarian* poets—for, unlike the *Surikovtsy,* they typically worked in industrial enterprises and wrote mainly about the lives of urban workers—largely shared this sorrowing vision of life. Among the best known were the Moscow weaver Fedor Shkulev, the provincial glassworker Egor Nechaev, the Jewish itinerant M. Rozenfel'd, the Nikolaev metalworker Aleksei Gmyrev, and the Moscow sales clerk Mikhail Savin. Characteristically, after Savin had become a union activist and journalist for the Moscow baker's union, he looked back at his early writing with guilty regret that he had been unable to free it from the "motif of melancholy and sorrow" (*skuchnyi i tosklivyi motiv*).[50] He was hardly an exception. Nechaev, for example, who began to write verses as a young glassworker in the 1880s, wrote dozens of poems and stories describing the physical and psychic torments he experienced or witnessed at the factory: painful weariness, the sickly pallor of workers, insults and cruel beatings, sleeplessness and disturbed dreams, weeping, bitterness, despair, and the simultaneous dread and relief of death. The Marxist critic V. L. L'vov-Rogachevskii, with a note of impatient scorn, described Nechaev as "a typical poet-sufferer."[51]

The 1905 revolution, which involved many worker writers in strikes, meetings, trade unions, and political organization—and drew still more workers toward reading and writing—helped introduce a more optimistic tone to workers' prose and poetry. But it did not supplant constant attention to the suffering self. On the contrary, images of the suffering personality of the worker were more plentiful than ever, not only during the years of political repression and economic recession from 1907 to 1911 but during the subsequent years of "revolutionary advance" as well. The images and tales of suffering in poems, stories, and critical essays were diverse and imbued with an insistent critical pathos: childhoods ruined and lost;[52] sleepless nights yielding only to dreams "tortured by exhaustion";[53] the frustrated sexuality of

---

say by E. S. Kalmanovskii, "Surikov i poety-surikovtsy," 5–54. The most widely published poets of this group, besides Surikov, were Maksim Leonov and Spiridon Drozzhin. See also the discussion of the *Surikovtsy* in L. Kleinbort, *Ocherki rabochei zhurnalistiki* (Petrograd and Moscow, 1924), 22–23.

[50] Tiulenev, *Gallereia sovremennykh poetov,* 11. See discussions of these writers and selections from their writings ibid. and in V. M. Friche, *Proletarskaia poeziia,* 3d ed. (Moscow, 1919), 58– 83; I. N. Kubikov, *Rabochii klass v russkoi literature* (Ivanovo-Voznesensk, 1924), 185–88; I. N. Kubikov, "Egor Nechaev," Introduction to E. E. Nechaev, *Guta: Polnoe sobranie sochinenie v odnom tome* (Moscow, 1928); V. L. L'vov-Rogachevskii, *Ocherki proletarskoi literatury* (Moscow and Leningrad, 1927), 16–20; Valerian Polianskii (P. I. Lebedev), "Motivy rabochei poezii" (1918), in his *Na literaturnom fronte* (Moscow, 1924), 23–28; *U istokov.*

[51] *Poet-goremyka,* a slightly mocking term meaning something like poor, unfortunate wretch: L'vov-Rogachevskii, *Ocherki,* 17.

[52] Nechaev, "Moia pesnia" (1906), in *Vecherniia pesni: Stikhotvoreniia* (Moscow, 1914), 79 (also in *U istokov,* 92), and "Sirota," *Dolia bedniaka,* 19 July 1909 (the issue was confiscated because of this and another poem; see *U istokov,* 406); Mariia Chernysheva, "Ne prigliadite kartiny . . . ," *Balalaika* 1910, no. 18: 2.

[53] F. Gavrilov, "Son," in *Proletarskie poety,* 1:197–201; Nechaev, "V bessonitsu" (1906), *Vecherniia pesni,* 98; S. Obradovich, "Bezsonnoiu noch'iu," *Severnoe utro* (Archangelsk), no. 52 (6 Mar. 1913), 2 (a cutting in RGALI, f. 1874, op. 1, d. 2, l. 8); M. Gerasimov, "Zavodskii gudok," in *Pervyi sbornik proletarskikh pisatelei* (St. Petersburg, 1914), 91–92.

male workers from the villages who could not afford to keep their wives with them in the city;[54] the anguish of a mother watching her children starve,[55] drunkenness as a way to "obliterate this hell on earth;"[56] the beatings, work-related maiming, and death that often occurred in factories;[57] nature itself—especially damp, windy, and melancholy autumn—echoing and framing the harsh lives and dark moods of workers,[58] or the beauties of awakened nature made inaccessible by the "anguish, pain and bitterness / in my weary soul."[59] Above all, these writings were filled with constant assertions that "the life of a worker is a chain of suffering / A river of sweat, a sea of tears."[60]

The insults and injuries that women suffered, though still a relatively infrequent theme until after 1917, were treated with particular moral pathos. But images of women's suffering also complicate these arguments. Women's suffering was treated as exemplifying violation and injury not only to the universal ethical ideal of human dignity but also to the particular virtues associated with women's gender, with women's difference. Thus G. D. Deev-Khomiakovskii, a leader of the Moscow Surikov Circle, argued that women's "majestic" potential as "a force of love and good" was suppressed by the actual social and legal position of women in Russia.[61] Similar was a once well known poem by Aleksandr Pomorskii on the lives of women who worked in factories. Innocent and pure country girls were corrupted by their lives as urban workers. When they became factory workers, they were transformed visibly into "doomed sacrifices / pale, tired, darkened by sadness." Seeking to escape factory work, they fell further as they "sold" their "pure bodies."[62] This was a conventional and easily recognizable image: prostitutes as emblems of fallen innocence and debased purity, an image growing out of the larger convention of representing women as weaker but naturally purer creatures than men.[63]

Still, and most often, stories and images of degraded women were used to speak about the universal suffering human self. This ideal was explicit, in a

[54] Mark Bich [Savin], "Tsentrovoi (Prodolzhenie)," *Bulochnik*, no. 2 (26 Feb. 1906), 20–22.

[55] Stepan Bruskov [Stepanov] in *Rodnye vesti* 1911, no. 3 (4): 5–6.

[56] G. Deev-Khomiakovskii, "Sorok let kak odin den'," *Rodnye vesti* 1912, no. 3: 4–5.

[57] *Metallist* 1911, no. 4 (10 Nov.): 7–8; *Pechatnoe delo*, no. 24 (11 Sept. 1910), 3–4.

[58] V. Aleksandrovskii, "Osen'iu," *Novaia rabochaia gazeta*, no. 5 (13 Aug. 1913), 2; S. Gan'shin, "Ne prikhodi vesna," *Zhivoe slovo*, no. 10 (March 1913), 6; Il'ia Volodinskii, "Dumy naborshchika," *Nashe pechatnoe delo*, no. 18 (21 Feb. 1915), 5.

[59] Semen Popov, "Vesna," *Chelovek*, no. 4 (24 Apr. 1911), 32.

[60] N. E. Dodaev, "Trud," *Zhizn' pekarei* 1914, no. 1/4 (10 Mar.): 2.

[61] G. Deev-Khomiakovskii, "I. Z. Surikov v pesniakh o zhenshchine i trude," *Drug naroda* 1916, no. 1 (October): 13. See also L. Sergievskaia in *Drug naroda* 1915, no. 5–7: 4; and Chitatel' iz naroda [Reader from the people], in *Narodnaia sem'ia*, no. 5 (4 Mar 1912) 13–14.

[62] A. Pomorskii, "Zhertvam goroda," in *Nashi pesni: Pervyi sbornik* (St. Petersburg, 1913), 9, and *Metallist* 1913, no. 5/29 (19 July): 4.

[63] Engelstein, *Keys to Happiness*; Laurie Bernstein, *Sonia's Daughters: Prostitutes and Their Regulation in Imperial Russia* (Berkeley, 1995); Barbara Heldt, *Terrible Perfection: Women and Russian Literature* (Bloomington, 1987). See also discussions of comparable cultural usages in Judith Walkowitz, *Prostitution and Victorian Society: Women, Class, and the State* (New York, 1980) and *City of Dreadful Delight: Narratives of Sexual Danger in Late-Victorian London* (Chicago, 1992).

rather complex way, in Ivan Kubikov's argument that a "conscious worker," sensitive to the "human personality" of prostitutes, might have sex with a prostitute but could never free himself from doubt and guilt for having done so.[64] It was implicit in complaints about viewing women as mere "sex objects."[65] It was strongly evident in a story published in the 1914 anthology of proletarian writers. Called "The Death of Agasha," it told the story of a young woman who came to the city from the village to find work. Agasha was not completely frail and innocent; she coped well with the roughness of urban working-class life and as a waitress in a tearoom had learned to laugh off the degrading and insulting suggestions so often made by male customers. But when her employer raped her, the injury to her self was more than she could endure: she hanged herself—the ultimate answer to a moral (and, implicitly, mortal) assault on the self.[66]

In a growing number of workers' literary writings and in numerous essays in trade union publications, male workers insisted on the dignity of women, on their "honor" and "moral dignity" as human beings.[67] Attention to women's human selves was most explicit in the few women's voices we hear. Mariia Chernysheva, a seamstress and sales clerk who wrote under the name Baba Mar'ia, wrote exclusively about inner feelings—loss, sorrow, and tears—in exploring the hardships of her working-class life.[68] A young woman working in a St. Petersburg tailoring shop, in a letter to a trade union journal, even more directly linked her experiences as a worker and as a woman to the universalized moral ideal of the self. She spoke of the "humiliations" and "insults" suffered at the hands of foremen and employers by all of the female apprentices in her shop—"white slaves," she called them, using a term often used to describe young women forced into prostitution. And she condemned this treatment in the keywords of the moral discourse about the self: "their feelings of human dignity" were "trampled in the dirt."[69] These remain complex images. To some degree, especially in the writings of men, the self whose dignity and humiliation so passionately concerned worker writers was assumed to be male. Thus critiques of the neglect or denial of the equal dignity of women's selves were often voiced to remind *men* of what it meant to be fully human in relation to others. And images of the particular suffering of women

[64] Kvadrat [Kubikov], "Propoved' khuliganstva v russkoi literature," *Pechatnoe delo*, no. 33–34 (1 Apr. 1910), 3–4.

[65] Chitatel' iz naroda [Reader from the people], *Narodnaia sem'ia*, no. 5 (4 Mar. 1912), 13–14.

[66] Nikolai Ivanov, "Smert Agashi," in *Pervyi sbornik proletarskikh pisatelei*, 56–61.

[67] This was an early and common theme in the printers' union press after 1905. For some early examples, see *Vestnik Pechatnikov* 1906, no. 5 (20 May): 3; no. 6 (28 May): 2; no. 8 (11 June): 3; *Balda*, no. 2 (9 Jan. 1907), 1, 5–7. Similar articles, stories, and poems can be found throughout the labor press; e.g., *Golos portnogo*, no. 1–2 (10 May 1910), 10; *Metallist* 1913, no. 13/37 (14 Dec.): 2–3.

[68] Mariia Chernysheva, "Ne prigliadite kartiny . . . ," *Balalaika* 1910, no. 18: 2; "Zaveshchanie," *Dumy narodnye*, no. 7 ([13 Mar.] 1910), 5.

[69] *Golos portnogo*, no. 1–2 (10 May 1910), 10. See also ibid., 9; and An. Petrova, "Kul'tura i kooperatsiia," *Trud* 1916, no. 5 (October–November): 23.

often served as reminders of the need for men to protect and defend female purity and innocence. But no less often, the female self was thought to be beyond gender, its injury to be harm to that which made women human.

Death, among the many images of the suffering self in these writings, is perhaps the most important in illuminating meanings of this discourse on suffering. Images of premature death figured prominently in workers' writings. We see workers crushed by machines, dying of hunger and of disease associated with poverty, especially tuberculosis (and, adding further insult, being cruelly treated in the public clinics where they sought care), and dying young and innocent.[70] When they died, one poet suggested, black blood would flow from their mouths, a sign of lifelong suffering.[71] These were complex images. Death was often portrayed as an answer and an escape, a comfort and a way to freedom. Thus poems and stories repeatedly pondered or described suicide—a phenomenon also reported with shocking regularity in the daily press in the prewar years—or voiced prayers that death would come, bringing a long-sought "oblivion" and "rest."[72]

But intertwined with these traces of despondency was moral rage. And the suffering self was at the heart of this moral argument. For example, an "epidemic" of suicides around 1910 among garment workers was explained not by poverty and unemployment—since conditions were in fact relatively good—but by workers' feelings that life had become a "big, dark, empty and cold barn" in which there is "no one to whom they may tell of their insults."[73] Stories and images of suicide and death—especially of the young and innocent—were strong signs of how much the "spirit ached," of how deeply the self was wounded.[74] Death spoke loudly (as both discursive symbol and material proof) of the denial of the workers' "right to live as human beings."[75]

As may be noticed, this discourse of suffering held competing and ambiguous meanings. Marxist and Soviet critics saw mainly peasant traditions of stoic passivity and fatalism in workers' preoccupation with the suffering self. They were not altogether wrong. Like traditional peasant funeral songs (*plachi*), these poems and stories were partly cathartic laments, songs of suf-

---

[70] *Zvezda utrenniaia*, no. 21 (20 June 1912), 7. In addition to references below, [Chechenets], "Nevol'niki truda," *Nash put'* 1911, no. 17 (23 May): 8–9.

[71] Stepan Bruskov, "Smert' byvshago cheloveka," *Rodnye vesti* 1912, no. 3: 2–3.

[72] Mariia Chernysheva, "Zaveshchanie," *Dumy narodnye*, no. 7 ([13 Mar.] 1910), 5; Shkulev, "Pil'shchik," *Narodnaia mysl'*, no. 2 (February 1911), 107; Bruskov, "Smert' byvshago cheloveka," *Rodnye vesti* 1912, no. 3: 2–3; S. Obradovich, "Bezsonnoiu noch'iu," *Severnoe utro* (Arkhangel'sk), no. 52 (6 Mar. 1913), 2 (a cutting in RGALI, f. 1874, op. 1, d. 2, l. 8); E. Nechaev, "K ditiati," *Zhivoe slovo*, no. 20 (May 1913), 6.

[73] Syryi, "Pomnite o samoubiitsakh," *Golos portnogo*, no. 3 (10 July 1910), 3–4, 8.

[74] Petr Zaitsev (a shoemaker who briefly published and did most of the writing for this magazine for the common reader), "Ot chego" and "Umru ia," *Kolotushka* 1911, no. 1: 3; no. 2: 4; Semen Popov (a waiter), "Iz pesen goria i nuzhdy," *Chelovek*, no. 3 (27 Mar. 1911), 11; S. Obradovich, "Na zavode," *Rabochii den'* (Moscow), no. 8 (11 June 1912), 1 (a cutting in RGALI, f. 1874, op. 1, d. 2, l. 6); Samobytnik, "Zdes' . . . ," *Voprosy strakhovaniia* (October 1915), rpt. in *Proletarskie poety*, 3:25.

[75] For some early examples of this interpretive construction: *Pechatnyi vestnik* 1906, no. 1 (12 Feb.): 2; *Pechatnik* 1906, no. 1 (23 Apr.): 12; *Vestnik pechatnikov* 1906, no. 6 (28 May): 3.

fering that helped the writers and readers cope with hardship by voicing it. No doubt, too, these plebeian writers were influenced by familiar Christian teachings about the inevitability of human suffering in the sinful temporal world. As Mikhail Savin complained, for too long workers tended to see "fate" rather than the "boss's fist" as the cause of their misery.[76] Extending these arguments ideologically, Soviet critics insisted that the preoccupation with suffering was not truly "proletarian." Defining the proletarian world-view ideologically as expressing a certain view of life—bold, optimistic, and focused on collective experience and action—rather than sociologically as the views of actual workers, these critics could then more easily purge this grim aesthetic from the orthodox canon, or at least relegate such views and emotions to a backward stage in the development of a conscious working class. Preoccupation with suffering, this Marxist argument ran, was most common before the class awakening of the 1905 revolution and among workers of recent peasant background. When such themes persisted beyond these boundaries, as they undeniably did, they did so as false consciousness.[77] This political manipulation of the definition of proletarian perception partly reflected ideological clichés about what class consciousness should be. Worse, it spoke also of a blindness to the complexities of proletarian thought and emotion, in particular to the range of meanings evident in workers' attention to the sorrowing self.

Articulated sorrow could have a critical, transgressive, and inspiring power. Of course, the same may be said for larger cultural traditions: even traditional folk laments blended themes of discontent into resignation before fate.[78] Sometimes the fatalist argument was explicitly resisted (though such resistance, if the censor was alert, could block publication). For example, in Nechaev's poem "To Work" (written in 1881 but denied publication until 1919), a young worker tries to convince a comrade who has suggested collective suicide that such a thought is the voice of the devil, and he recalls the Christian teaching "We are doomed to suffer unto death / for the sins of our fathers." But he is rebuffed bitterly: this is a "fairy tale" and a priestly deceit.[79] A similar lesson was implied in a story that appeared in 1911 about a homeless man who finds it painful to be reminded of "the usual philosophy" that "life is an unbroken chain of suffering" and "harsh duty."[80] Of course, deny-

---

[76] Dedushka s Protivy [Savin], "Sovremennaia pesenka bulochnika," *Bulochnik,* no. 1 (19 Feb. 1906), 13.

[77] See, e.g., Valerian Polianskii (P. I. Lebedev), "Motivy rabochei poezii" (1918), in his *Na literaturnom fronte* (Moscow, 1924), 23–28; L'vov-Rogachevskii, *Ocherki,* 14; A. M. Bikhter, "U istokov proletarskoi poezii," in *U istokov,* 6, 8, 10, 13; Os'makov, *Russkaia proletarskaia poeziia,* 50–51, 69–70, 100; "Proletarskaia poeziia," in *Istoriia russkoi literatury* (Leningrad, 1983), 4:396–97.

[78] Christine Worobec, "Death Ritual among Russian and Ukrainian Peasants," in Frank and Steinberg, *Cultures in Flux,* 24.

[79] Nechaev, "Na raboty," in *U istokov,* 43. This argument was repeated in Nechaev's poem "Golos dushi," published in 1906 in *Zhurnal dlia vsekh* and in his 1914 collection *Vecherniia pesni.* See *U istokov,* 87–88.

[80] Mikhail Zaharov in *Rodnye vesti* 1911, no. 2/3: 5.

ing such comfort could make the suffering only harder to bear—suicide, after all, as the daily press made abundantly clear, was not only a trope. At the same time, religious teachings spoke not only of necessity and a passive relation to one's fate. In the Christian tradition suffering was also part of a positive valorization of saintly emulation of Christ's Passion and martyrdom and a reminder of Christ's promise of redemption. In Russia these traditions were complicated by the influence of another familiar cultural current upon which worker writers drew: the empathetic and socially critical tradition of Russian "civic poetry" and journalism, with its moving accounts of popular suffering. As an echo of this writing, plebeian songs of suffering evoked pity (even self-pity) as a critical device. Moreover, lower-class writers transformed this tradition by becoming, as it were, speaking subjects in this civic intellectual tradition—active citizens in this discourse rather than silent objects of attention and care.

It matters also that these writings were almost all *public* texts: written with audiences in mind and published in popular newspapers and in magazines aimed at lower-class readers. In the face of state censorship, simply chronicling the sufferings of the poor and the subordinate was an implicit challenge and protest. It is thus telling that so many of these authors took explicit pride in "singing of suffering," treating it as an act of moral witness to injustice and inequality and a reminder of the virtue of the poor. "Don't expect from me joyful tunes / Friend, I cannot comfort you / I learned to sing in sinister times / With sorrow in my soul and mind."[81] "I am a bard of the working masses / No one envies my song / I sing not of flowers or the sun / Of twilight I sing."[82] "Let others be joyful / And clink their glasses / . . . We are not capable of joy / . . . We are dying as we work / And suffering without a word."[83]

At the intellectual heart of the moral anger in these writings was the self and its ethical value, and, more precisely, the particular ideal of the self as the seat of emotions, creative genius, spiritual worth, and individual dignity, and hence as fundamental moral measure. These writers seem to have found in suffering evidence not just of the hard lot of the poor but of an inner spirit in the persons of the poor that made their hard lot constitute spiritual injury and moral wrong. To gaze at the self was to say that it mattered ontologically and ethically, that it was a key to understanding and valuing the world. Thus much of what workers wrote concerned the self and its social and spiritual journey. Typically, Sergei Obradovich wrote his first autobiography at the age of sixteen—though he had been thinking of such an act of remembering and self-reflection since he had learned to write.[84] To dwell on suffering, it has been

---

[81] Nechaev, "Mne khotelos' by pesniu svobodnuiu spet'" (1906), in *U istokov,* 89.

[82] A. Pomorskii, "Pesnia," *Metallist* 1913, no. 4/28 (3 July): 4. See also Neliudim [A. Solov'ev], "Grustny pesni tvoi, proletarskii baian . . ." (from *Sotsial Demokrat,* 24 Aug. 1917), in *Proletarskie poety,* 3:185.

[83] P. Zaitsev, in *Kolotushka,* no. 1 [1911], 2.

[84] Sergei Obradovich, "Minuvshee: Moi vospominaniia" (1908), in RGALI, f. 1874 (Obradovich), op. 1, d. 184, l. 2.

observed, was at once to "contract full intimacy with the Stranger within"[85] and to remind oneself and one's readers of the great evil of conditions that harm the self. In other words, by casting the everyday brutalities of lower-class life in a language of the injured self, these writers were helping to craft a potent and very usable *moral identity*. Suffering simultaneously defined workers and the poor by an essential common experience, valorized these sufferings as signs of the worthy interior lives of the poor, and condemned poverty and social hardship as harm to the self and hence as violations of a universal ethical truth.

In one regard, Soviet critics were right—the 1905 revolution was a turning point—not in the replacement of images of suffering by the mythic optimism of the "proletariat," but in the more explicit and systematic use of these images to condemn oppressive social conditions and relationships. Yet to categorize these usages as expressions of a heightened "class consciousness"—as critical awareness of the social inequalities of capitalism and of the progressive historical mission of the working class—tells us rather little. To be sure, most of these writers would have identified themselves as class conscious and understood class consciousness to mean a social critique of capitalist oppression of the working class. But for our purposes of understanding them, this identification is both too sweeping and too anemic to convey the full weight and reach of their critique. This critique was built upon ideas of moral right (a universal category of judgment) much more than on ideas about the class structure (a relative and historical category). And at the core of this moral critique was the category of the self. Social anger, even when it became more explicit in 1905 and after, remained persistently constructed around a core of inward suffering and moral regard for the inner life of the individual. Although the suffering of workers and the poor was (and was acknowledged to be) shared with others in a similar social position, the notion of the injured self was at the very heart of these writers' understanding of social oppression and inequality, and defined them as intolerable injustice. By the same token, this understanding fueled a moral rage that was far more emotionally convincing and rhetorically powerful than ideas about the historical development of capitalist class relations or the extraction of surplus value.

At the same time, we must not dismiss the importance of the idea of class in this language. As activist workers endeavored to make sense of their own lives and the lives of others, and to give public voice to their experiences, anger, and ideals, they reworked the various ideas, metaphors, and images that came to hand, including the ethical idealization of the human self. Paradoxically, viewed through the prism of their own and other workers' lives, the universalized ideal of the individual person also encouraged class identity and commitment to class action. Heightened feelings of self-awareness and self-worth

---

[85] Advice to beginning authors by Edward Young, *Conjectures in Original Composition* (1759), quoted in Stephen D. Cox, *"The Stranger within Thee": Concepts of the Self in Late-Eighteenth-Century Literature* (Pittsburgh, 1980), 3.

also stimulated workers to feel more intensely their *class* oppression. Indeed, the discovery of self may have been essential to the discovery of class. To become class conscious, workers did not need to be told that they were poor and exploited. This they already knew. What workers needed, as Jacques Rancière has described for nineteenth-century France, was "a knowledge of self" that revealed "a being dedicated to something else besides exploitation."[86]

Civilization and the Self

The moral anger fueled by these ideas about the human person was not limited to a critique of social inequities and oppressions; it was also directed against the weak or decayed selves of individuals. Just as the condition of the self was so central to the worker writers' critique of society, so the individual stood at the center of the solutions they envisioned to end the sufferings of the poor. This cultural critique reached beyond criticism of the structures of social inequality and even beyond the goal of overcoming capitalism. This critique also looked beyond "society's" humiliations of the selves of the poor to face workers' own failures to recognize, respect, and nurture their inward personalities and their autonomous wills. At the heart of these questions were ideas about culture as the key to recovering the self and nurturing its will.

Like many educated Russians of the time, worker authors were obsessed with the idea of culture as a universal moral ideal and goal. There was little debate over what it entailed—cultural relativism was still alien to their way of thinking—but there was much argument against violations of this norm. The parameters of culture were laid out in this negative critique of its transgression. They saw much to offend them: the "journalistic cretinism" of the boulevard press with its obsession with scandals, crime, sex, rape, murder, and suicide; the shallow pointlessness of the cinema; the growing popularity of horse racing, auto racing, and other diversions; the modern "epicureanism" of the rich, echoing ancient Rome's "sated, perverted, and debauched" elites who degraded ideals of nature and beauty into their purely "animal and physical" form; the spread of "pornographic" literature; and the "sexual hooliganism" of popular literary writing that preached unrestrained sexual expression and fulfillment.[87]

While echoes of Victorian ideals of "respectability" may be seen in these critiques of violations of morality and culture, most central were ideas about the inward self. As in many other rhetorics of respectability, at issue was not

---

[86] Jacques Rancière, *The Nights of Labor: The Workers' Dream in Nineteenth-Century France*, trans. John Drury (Philadelphia, 1989), 20.

[87] *Nadezhda*, no. 2 (26 Sept. 1908), 6; M. Volkov, "Obzor pechati," *Narodnaia sem'ia*, no. 4 (19 Feb. 1912), 12–14; Kvadrat [Kubikov], "Deshevaia gazeta i kinematograf," *Pechatnoe delo*, no. 11 (30 Sept. 1909), 4; M. Loginov in *Dumy narodnye*, no. 3 ([13 Feb.], 1913), 1–2; Mikhail Tikhoplesets [M. Loginov], "Epikuritsy," *Zvezda iasnaia* [*Zvezda utrenniaia*], no. 6 (29 Feb. 1912), 5–6; *Balalaika* 1910, no. 12: 1; *Metallist*, no. 10 (11 Feb. 1912), 4; Kvadrat [Kubikov], "Propoved' khuliganstva v russkoi literature," *Pechatnoe delo*, no. 33–34 (1 Apr. 1910), 3–7.

superficial propriety but the development of what might be called the cultural self—the maturation of the inner personality in accord with the highest cultural values. Thus simple self-indulgence and self-veneration were scorned as false ideals. Like many educated liberal and radical social critics, many of these lower-class writers denounced the selfishness, egotism, and crass indulgence they saw around them, in daily life as well as in much modern literature. Their ideal was a human being elevated above his ordinary self. Mikhail Sivachev, for example, inspired explicitly by Nietzsche's idea of self-overcoming, excoriated educated society for its false and regressive preoccupation with the self: a pervasive devotion to satisfying "individual desires and needs" that was leading society not toward a true knowledge of self that would elevate individuals into "real human beings" but only toward "the atrophy of the soul of man." For Sivachev, this was an effect of the very nature of modern life: "The highest value in modern culture is the cultivation of instincts of only the lowest order—the instincts of the 'I' alone. . . . Now little remains in humanity of the eternal values."[88] This sort of bitter critique was directed not only, or even mainly, at educated society.

Worker writers focused a steady stream of criticism against the weak, undeveloped, and "fallen" personalities of the majority of lower-class Russians, for which they blamed, at least in part, individuals themselves. A huge outpouring of published criticism targeted drunkenness, swearing, cruelty, and lowbrow cultural tastes. Such criticisms obviously echoed the "culturalist" arguments of many elite Russians worried about the dangerous backwardness of the poor.[89] The difference, though not absolute, was telling: when worker critics of popular culture talked of raising the culture of the poor and nurturing the self and the will, the logic was more defiant and transgressive than integrative. In other words, the goal was to make the poor more dangerous to an unequal social order, not less.

In essays, feuilletons, satirical writings, and other forms—in both Marxist-oriented trade union papers and the more populist papers of "writers from the people"—these writers tried persistently to shame their fellow workers away from behaviors and mentalities that were said to degrade the personality and weaken the will. This list was long: drunkenness, thievery, superstition, bigotry, fighting, crass tastes in entertainment, sexual harassment, prostitution, dishonesty, and passivity. The Russian vocabulary used was richly moralistic: *poshlost'* (self-satisfied crassness), *nravstvennaia padenie* (moral fall), *raznuzdannost'* (licentiousness), *razvrat* (debauchery), *nochestnost'* (dishonesty, dishonor), *durnye instinkty* (low instincts), *skandal* (scandalous behavior), *pakosti* (trash, depravities, obscenities).

---

[88] Mikhail Sivachev, *Na sud chitatelia: Zapiski literaturnago Makara* (Moscow, 1910), 1–14, and *Prokrustovo lozhe (Zapiski literaturnago Makara)*, 2 vols. (Moscow, 1911), 1:197. In the first lines of his introduction to *Na sud chitatelia*, Sivachev quotes Zarathustra's teachings on the superman and self overcoming.

[89] Stephen Frank, "Confronting the Domestic Other," in Frank and Steinberg, *Cultures in Flux*, 74–107; Brooks, *When Russia Learned to Read*, chap. 9.

Drunkenness was a particularly common target and was generally treated both as a sign and an aggravation of a weak self and as a practice that "defaces the image of man" (*obezlichivaet obraz cheloveka*) and leads to immorality and depravity.[90] But drunkenness was only the most obvious sin, only one piece of a larger story about the common people's degraded cultural selves. Mikhail Loginov, writing in the "people's" (*narodnye*) journals he edited, regularly wrote of the "darkness and chaos" he saw in the life of the common people: the fall in morals, breakdown of families, wasteful and harmful time spent in taverns and *café chantants*, inhuman crimes, cruelty, ignorance, superstition, and fatalism.[91] He described with disgust, for example, "laboring people" resting along the shore of the Volga near Moscow on summer evenings: "course swearing, arguments, and fights," "drunkenness, violence, and depravity."[92] The printer Ivan Kubikov similarly castigated the "tavern civilization" that threatened urban workers and complained, as others did, of workers escaping to the crass diversions of the movie house, the fair booth (*balagan*), or the gramophone.[93] A waiter complained that his fellows wasted their free time on nothing but degrading "buffoonery": "as soon as a few comrades get together, right away they start in with stupid witticisms, obscenities, card games, drunkenness, and other such trash [*pakosti*]."[94]

In hundreds of essays, stories, and poems, plebeian authors wrote of the "savage manners" and crass tastes of ordinary lower-class Russians, of workers' "moral and physical fall" and troubling "indifference" to "self-betterment," and of superstition and bigotry (especially anti-Semitic prejudice).[95] The Bolshevik miner and poet Aleksei Chizhikov wrote of the majority of "working folk" (*rabochii liud*) as only just beginning to wake up from a "long and heavy nightmarish sleep."[96] Others were less confident and wrote with undisguised contempt for "backward" workers who seemed not to care that they were living "the life of an animal."[97] Many wrote about popular reading tastes, especially the ill effects on the "nerves" and on the moral "taste"

[90] *Pechatnik* 1917, no. 2–3 (6 Aug.): 6. For a few other typical examples, see *Dumy narodnye*, no. 2 ([February] 1910), 1, 6–8; *Balalaika* 1910, no. 8: 6–7.

[91] *Dumy narodnye*, no. 2 ([February] 1910), 1; *Zvezda iasnaia* [*Zvezda utrenniaia*], no. 6 (29 Feb. 1912), 2–4; *Zvezda utrenniaia*, no. 17 (23 May 1912), 2.

[92] M. T-ts [M. Loginov], *Dumy narodnye*, no. 1 ([February] 1910), 2.

[93] Kvadrat [I. Kubikov], "Kul'tura i prosveshchenie," *Pechatnoe delo*, no. 8 (27 June 1909), 5, rpt. *Edinstvo*, no. 7 (10 July 1909), 7–8; Kvadrat, "Deshevaia gazeta i kinematograf," *Pechatnoe delo*, no. 11 (30 Sept. 1909), 4–6; Sinebluznik, "Gramofon i soiuz," *Nash put'*, no. 6 (30 Aug. 1910), 3; letter from a reader, Odinokii, "O razvlecheniiakh dlia rabochikh," *Edinstvo*, no. 15 (12 Mar. 1910), 11–12.

[94] I. Shch-v (probably I. I. Shcherbakov, a leader of the Waiters' Mutual Aid Society), "Budem rabotat'," *Chelovek*, no. 3 (27 Mar. 1911), 12.

[95] E.g., the writings by Savin and Chernysheva in *Balalaika*, 1910–11; Blizhnyi, "Prosvetimsia liudi," *Rodnye vesti* 1912, no. 4 [Easter]: 3; *Trud* 1916, no. 5 (October–November): 24–25.

[96] Aleksei Chizhikov, letter to *Pravda*, 4 Mar. 1914, 3, in RGASPI, f. 364, op. 1, d. 315, ll. 1–3.

[97] Kirill Babich (worker at the Nevskii textile factory), poem "Ostavshemu tovarishchu," sent May 1914 to *Pravda*, ibid., d. 324, l. 4.

of reading boulevard newspapers such as *Gazeta-Kopeika*. Long-term reading of such papers might, it was feared, cause a reader to grow so accustomed to "the smell of scandal and rowdy disorder [*deboshirstvo*]" that he would lose his natural "taste for that which is clean and bright."[98] Aleksei Bibik translated these perceptions and concerns into literary form in his novel of the popular life he grew up with, painting a hellish scene of a drunken father philosophizing about patience and endurance, a drunken mother who neglected her hungry and crying baby, and all around the sounds of swearing, weeping, crass arguing, and the baying of a dog.[99]

These writers saw weakness and disintegration deep in the very selves of most workers. An essay in the paper of the Petersburg metalworkers' union in 1908 gloomily noted the irony that just at the moment when employers' assaults on labor were reaching the most "crude and inhuman forms," workers exhibited a "growing shallowness [*izmel'chanie*] of proletarian thinking [and] the manifestation of base instincts."[100] A year later, Aleksei Gastev described the world of workers—harshly but not untypically—as the "realm of the unconscious, the realm of dark melancholy, impenetrable unbelief, stagnating inertia."[101] In 1910 the prominent worker leader of the metalworkers' union, Fedor Bulkin, wrote a stinging indictment of workers' "moral nonchalance" (*nravstennyi khalatnost'*), dishonesty, crass literary tastes (*Pinkertonovshchina*), and general "low instincts."[102] Similarly, the printer Ivan Kubikov complained of finding in many workplaces an "abyss of self-satisfied crassness [*poshlost'*] and apathy" and "philistine indolence."[103]

It is important to keep in mind how deeply rhetorical these accusations were. As these workers no doubt knew, and as historians of Russian labor have extensively documented,[104] the number of literate, cultured, and socially conscious workers was in fact greater than ever before; they could be found by the hundreds in trade unions, workers' clubs, religious movements, and other organizations that featured cultural programming for workers. So, just as we should not mistake the derogatory rhetoric of "culturalist" intellectuals, church missionaries, and temperance activists for simple factual reporting about the poor, we must also not misapprehend the testimonies of worker intellectuals. These too were pieces of rhetoric, though with their own distinctive and revealing logic.

Like other Marxists, Bulkin blamed society and especially the autocratic

---

[98] *Nadezhda*, no. 2 (26 Sept. 1908), 6

[99] A. Bibik, *K shirokoi doroge (Ignat iz Novoselovki)* (St. Petersburg: 1914), 23–28. The novel was first published in 1912 in the leftist journal *Sovremennyi mir*.

[100] Metallist, "K karakteristike nastroenii v rabochei srede," *Nadezhda*, no. 2 (26 Sept. 1908), 10.

[101] A. Zorin [Gastev], "Sredi tramvaishchikov (Nabrosok)," *Edinstvo*, no. 12 (21 Dec. 1909), 11.

[102] Bulkin, "Bol'noi vopros (upadok nravov v rabochei srede)," *Nash put'*, no. 11 (20 Dec. 1910), 7–8.

[103] Kvadrat [Kubikov], "Vpechatleniia zhizni," *Pechatnoe delo*, no. 24 (11 Sept. 1910), 6.

[104] E.g., Zelnik, "Russian Bebels"; Bonnell, *Roots of Rebellion*; McDaniel, *Autocracy, Capitalism, and Revolution;* Steinberg, *Moral Communities.*

state for "dehumanizing" workers.[105] Others similarly complained that workers were deliberately excluded from "real culture"—kept away from serious theater, decent entertainment, and healthy reading.[106] But most of these writers also argued that workers, and especially workers' leaders, must take responsibility for these effects. This was Bulkin's argument. Similarly, August Tens, a composer well known for his writings in trade union papers and for his years of leadership in the Petersburg printers' union, insisted that drunkenness could not be dismissed as simply a product of social conditions: "Drunkenness is a disease of the will, and the will depends on reason. It is necessary to develop reason. It is all about culture."[107] And, one might add—for this was implicit—it was about the self.

Drunkenness, indiscipline, crude manners, ignorance, and a general lack of culture were condemned partly as practical obstacles to workers' collective struggle, as making workers "passive," "apathetic," "undisciplined," and unable to "stand up for their interests."[108] Attention was paid to certain "moral" faults that had particular significance for class solidarity and militancy: groveling and deference before employers, stealing from other workers, selling jobs to the unemployed, fighting and beatings, overtime work, and strikebreaking.[109] Taking a longer but still largely practical view, some worker authors, such as Ivan Kubikov—writing in 1909, when he was chair of the Petersburg printers' union—insisted that workers needed to be culturally and morally prepared for their future historical role. Quoting Ferdinand Lassalle, Kubikov maintained that since workers were the "stone upon which the church of the future will be built," that foundation needed to be strong *and polished*. More immediately, Kubikov argued, echoing many activists, workers' "class consciousness" was closely connected with their "cultural consciousness": every lecture on science and every reading of a classic work of literature led workers to "understand the order of things."[110]

It is important to note the logical dependence of the collective on the individual in these arguments. Individual development was essential for effective class struggle. Sometimes the argument was mainly individualistic. As one essayist put it, we need to "worry about our own moral and intellectual condition," for in order to solve our problems, "we must rely on our own individ-

---

[105] Bulkin, "Bol'noi vopros (Upadok nravov v rabochei srede)," *Nash put'*, no. 11 (20 Dec. 1910), 7–8.

[106] Odinokii, "O razvlecheniiakh dlia rabochikh," *Edinstvo*, no. 15 (12 Mar. 1910), 11–12; K. T-ts, "Russkie rabochie," *Zvezda utenniaia*, no. 10 (4 Apr. 1910), 2.

[107] *Pechatnoe delo*, no. 13 (24 Nov. 1909), 10–11.

[108] *Pechatnik* 1906, no. 1 (23 Apr.): 11–12; *Pechatnoe delo*, no. 15 (9 Feb. 1907), 7; *Protokoly pervogo vserossiiskoi konferentsii soiuzov rabochikh pechatnogo dela* (St. Petersburg, 1907), 80, 82, 109.

[109] Bulkin, "Bol'noi vopros (upadok nravov v rabochei srede)," *Nash put'*, no. 11 (20 Dec. 1910), 7–8; Kvadrat [Kubikov], "Vpechatleniia zhizni," *Pechatnoe delo*, no. 24 (11 Sept. 1910), 3–4; Kleinbort, "Ocherki rabochei demokratii," pt. 1, *Sovremennyi mir*, March 1913, 35–38.

[110] Kvadrat [Kubikov], "Alkogolizm i usloviia bor'by s nim," *Professional'nyi vestnik*, no. 26 (31 Oct. 1909), 6–8. This essay also appeared in *Pechatnoe delo*, no. 13 (24 Nov. 1909), 4–5.

ual abilities."[111] Even when the focus was on class struggle, the individual stood at the logical center. Just as personal culture was seen to aid the class struggle, so was class struggle seen as serving the development of the individual self, of emancipating workers' human selves and creating a society, as it was so often said, where people could "live like human beings." Moral and cultural backwardness was denounced not only as evidence of social oppression or on the pragmatic grounds of the needs of the class struggle, but also as inherent evil, for the harm it inflicted on the individual self.

Strangers

> A secret wound, often unknown to himself, drives the foreigner to wandering. . . . He is a devotee of solitude, even in the midst of a crowd, because he is faithful to a shadow: bewitching secret . . . inaccessible ambition.
>
> —JULIA KRISTEVA, *Strangers to Ourselves*

Paradoxically, the inspiration driving most of these worker authors to articulate social activism was a profound sense of being strangers—outsiders and wanderers—in their own world. Estrangement strongly inflected their sense of themselves as individuals and their practices as self-proclaimed voices of popular feeling and will. In memoirs these writers often recalled feeling alienated from the crass everyday world around them, looking for truth and meaning in isolated reading, wandering, and thinking. Mikhail Savin, writing in 1909, claimed to have spent his youth feeling so out of place "amidst the prose of everyday life" that he preferred "living in dreams, drunk with poetry and the thirst for light."[112] We know that many of these worker writers in fact took to the road as wanderers and pilgrims: some went on religious pilgrimages; others "wandered" (*peredvizhit'*) and "tramped" (*brodiazhit'*) around the country (seeking happiness or truth, they would later often claim); a few even worked their way around Europe.[113] This sojourning and seeking was part of a familiar cultural tradition in Russia: tramping peasants and workers, wandering artists (*peredvizhniki*), literary wanderers such as Gorky and Tolstoy, roaming religious mystics (*stranniki*), lay preachers, holy fools (*iurodovye*), pilgrims, and, throughout popular literature and folk tales, questing heroes, sympathetic bandits, saints, and vagabonds.

In the lives and writings of these workers, wandering had particular meaning and pathos. Proletarian authors elaborated endlessly on feelings of cultural and moral isolation. Often feeling themselves to be more than simply

---

[111] Blizhnyi, "Prosvetimsia liudi," *Rodnye vesti* 1912, no. 4 [Easter]: 3.

[112] Tiulenev, *Gallereia sovremennykh poetov,* 11.

[113] See Appendix and the autobiographical sketches in P. Ia. Zavolokin, ed., *Sovremennye raboche-krest'ianskie poety* (Ivanovo-Voznesensk, 1925).

different, they tended to develop a sense of alienation that bordered on a sort of cultural and moral nausea. As we have seen, the labor press was filled with writings by workers voicing contempt for the ordinary sort of lower-class Russian. Many were quite explicit about the significance for their own selves of living in this environment. "Thinking workers," Ivan Kubikov wrote, find it a constant struggle to "defend their inner world from being spit upon," whether by bosses or by fellow workers. If anything, workers were worse, for the debased cultural personalities of workers increased the dangers that might pull a "thinking worker" back into the common corruption all around. In any case, the depravity of their fellow workers most disturbed "thinking workers": commenting on a recent story by Gorky, Kubikov observed, "How well Gorky portrays the thinking workers' feelings of being alone [*odinochestvo*] . . . amidst the gray and backward mass." Seeing "in what filth the soul of man is stewing," he feels like "an alien creature among these people."[114]

In the poetry and fiction of these writers—most of which, of course, had a strong autobiographical element—a major theme was the awakened and sensitive individual, estranged from the crass ordinary people all around them. They were, in the language of the time, "cultural loners" (*kul'turnye odinochki*),[115] and sometimes adopted noms de plume that reflected this spirit, such as Gastev's Odinokii (unique, peerless, solitary), Mashirov's Samobytnik (unique, self-made, autonomous), and Solov'ev's Neliudim (which may be loosely translated as "one who is not like ordinary people"). To borrow Savin's autobiographical remarks, these writers tended to dwell on the anguish of the "poetic" self mired in "the prose of everyday life." One fictionalized life story of a sensitive, high-minded, and lonely young worker described the hero's distaste for "the scarcely cultured or literate environment that surrounded him since childhood." As an adult, he had "always to hold himself apart from his co-workers, among whom he noticed many vices." This was not an easy stance. When he refused to join his fellow workers in stealing from the shop, he was ostracized.[116] Another author described the derisive laughter of workers against one who was obsessed with reading. He was repelled by the "fighting, swearing, and reproaches" of these fellow workers, who in turn dubbed him a "Pharisee."[117] This sort of conflict had become a cliché in writing by and about worker intellectuals, but one that was painfully true to life. At the same time, these authors occasionally suggested even more tragic results whenever such workers tried to fit it by joining their fel-

---

[114] Kvadrat [Kubikov], in *Novaia rabochaia gazeta*, no. 5 (13 Aug. 1913), 2. This is a review (begun in the preceding issue) of Gorky's story "The Boss: Pages from an Autobiography" (Khoziain: Stranitsy avtobiografii), published in *Sovremennik* 1913, nos. 3–5.

[115] G. Deev-Khomiakovskii, "Kul'turnye ugolki i kul'turnye odinochki," *Drug naroda* 1915, no. 2 (31 Jan.): 10–11.

[116] A-ch, "Ternistyi put'," *Samopomoshch'* 2, no. 1 (December 1911): 6.

[117] G. Deev-Khomiakovskii, "Prozrel," *Drug naroda* 1915, no. 1 (1 Jan.): 7–8.

lows in drink and revelry (and perhaps in beating their wives as well) and giving up the reading and search for truth that had set them painfully apart: one
such worker, briefly back in the mainstream, ended by throwing himself beneath the wheels of a train.[118] Sometimes this estrangement from the workers' milieu extended to an even more painful alienation from one's own social
self. Aleksei Chizhikov wrote in 1914 of the "worker's soul," no different in
essence from the soul of a tsar or a prince, "imprisoned in a rough worker's
hide" (*zakliuchena v grubuiu rabochuiu kozhu*).[119]

What did these stories of alienation mean? For some of these writers, the
image of the sensitive plebeian as stranger was an expression of a neo-
Romantic fascination with sensibility, an extension of the suffering self
into the stance of the "exquisitely depressed" stranger. Julia Kristeva (whose
phrase this is) has written eloquently of the stranger (though she had in
mind primarily the actual foreigner) as often nurturing a "precious exquisite pain," even a pleasurably bruised personality, as a proud but also anguished outsider.[120] A comparable ambivalent mix of pain and pleasure can
be seen in poems that appeared in journals created by and for "writers from
the people"—typically with such titles as "Mood" ("Nastroenie") and "Solitude" or "Loneliness" ("Odinochestvo"). Typical is Sergei Gan'shin's 1912
poem "Odinochestvo," placed on the first page of *Rodnye vesti* under a
drawing of a man who appears to be a homeless wanderer, leaning against an
old fence at the edge of a frozen road, his eyes downcast. "I stand alone / Heart
gnawed by anguish / Oppressed, tired, and troubled. / I glance to heaven,
where stars burn clearly / Bright stars of a faraway world."[121] Similarly, the
poems of L. Bystrov, published in 1915 (after his death in the war) in a collection called *Skorbnye pesni* (Songs of sorrow), were replete with images of
human weakness, of his alienation from human society ("I bear the heavy
cross of exile," he told an interviewer), and of suicide (especially of young
women).[122] Vladimir Aleksandrovskii, a young worker socialist, mused on
the ennui of solitude.[123] Even trade union papers featured such writings,
such as the waiter Semen Popov's lament, "I wander each night without
refuge / Having neither family nor friends."[124] Petr Zaitsev, long associated
with the Iaroslavl printers' union, frequently imagined dying alone, "forgotten by all," crushed by "sorrow and adversity," and disappointed by his

---

[118] D. I. Semenov (a metalworker on the railroad), "Kto vinovat," *Melitopol'skaia vedomosti*,
no. 83 (25 Dec. 1911), 2. The author sent this story, his first, to Gorky: Arkhiv A. M. Gor'kogo,
KG-NP/A, 22-4-2.

[119] Aleksei Chizhikov, letter accompanying verses submitted to *Pravda*, 4 Mar. 1914, in RGASPI,
f. 364, op. 1, d. 315, ll. 1–3 (quote on p. 4).

[120] Julia Kristeva, *Strangers to Ourselves* (New York, 1991), 5, 10, 21, 29, 38, 135–36.

[121] Gan'shin, "Odinochestvo," *Rodnye vesti* 1913, no. 3: 1.

[122] N. Vlasov-Okskii, "Ogon'ki v stepi (Iz vstrech s pistateliami-samouchkami)," *Griadushchee*
1921, no. 1–3: 41–44.

[123] V. Aleksandrovskii, "Odinochestvo," *Zhivoe slovo*, no. 30 (July 1913), 4.

[124] Semen Popov, "Iz pesen goria i nuzhdy," *Chelovek*, no. 3 (27 Mar. 1911), 11.

failure to find "light and truth," welcoming the peaceful oblivion of death.[125]

More common than these sentimental and pathetic images of the thinking worker as a stranger was a critically edged alienation: estrangement as an expression of the awakened and moral self, as part of a creative drive (widely discussed in Russian culture of the fin de siècle) to "transcend the banal self" and "make oneself other."[126] We see this aspiration in the many expressions of contempt for the common order of people in the world. In a lengthy morality tale written by the Petersburg seamstress Nadezhda Sanzhar', the long-suffering heroine concludes bitterly that "there are no human beings to be found among people" (*cheloveka net sredi liudi*).[127] Similarly, though with more disdain than distress, Dmitrii Odintsov took a God's-eye view of the earth and found it crawling with petty and care-worn "little men" (*chelovechki*).[128] Hope and pleasure for many were to be found elsewhere. Although Egor Nechaev felt as if the world around him were a "prison," filled with "the noise of machines and the talk of people" (barely differentiated), he found comfort in an inner fire—his "best friend"—calling him to an unknown future.[129] Odintsov wrote of reading in the lonely dark of night and of distracted thoughts amidst the noises of factory work as secret moments when he nurtured his inner fires.[130] Likewise, Aleksei Mashirov (Samobytnik) described a worker sitting alone in his cramped room after work, reading by the "pale light of a lamp," trying to ignore the "laughter and tears of carefree fellows" in an adjoining room.[131]

Although the point, as we have seen, was to enlighten one's fellows, ambivalence about them persisted even among the most politically committed. Radicalized workers such as Odintsov and Mashirov portray themselves as improving their minds in order to bring a message back to their fellow workers. Mashirov, for example, is reading about workers' hardships and struggles. And when he finally "gives in to his exhaustion," he "quietly lies down, full of thoughts and dreams," determined to "tell his friends all about them" the next day at work. As a socialist and as a worker *intelligent,* Mashirov resolved to share his enlightenment with others—at least with his "friends." But, as this last hesitancy may suggest, this was not a simple matter of a conscious worker committed to his backward class fellows. As an intellectually developed worker—an *intelligentnyi-rabochii*—he remained a cultural loner

---

[125] Petr Zaitsev, "Umru ia," *Kolotushka* 1911, no. 2: 4. See other poems by him in this and other issues of *Kolotushka*. See also Vladimir Korolev, *Lazurnye prakhi* (Yalta, 1912) and *Vsem skorbiashchim* (Iaroslavl, 1915).

[126] N. Evreinov, *Teatr kak takovoi* (St. Petersburg, 1913), 27, 29, 34–36, paraphrased and discussed in Katerina Clark, *Petersburg, Crucible of Cultural Revolution* (Cambridge, Mass., 1995), 105.

[127] Nadezhda Sanzhar', *Zapiski Anny* (St. Petersburg, 1910), 129.

[128] D. Odintsov, "Pod lunoi," in *Sbornik proletarskim pisatelem* (Petrograd, 1917), 7.

[129] Nechaev, "Moia pesnia," in *Vecherniia pesni,* 79–80.

[130] D. Odintsov, "Vpered," *Pravda,* 31 Oct. 1912, 2, and in *Pervyi sbornik proletarskikh pisatelei,* 166.

[131] Mashirov, "Posle raboty," *Pravda,* 8 Nov. 1912, and *Pervyi sbornik proletarskikh pisatelei,* 160.

(*kul'turnaia odinochka*) in everyday life, sitting alone in his room reading (even if partly for others), feeling himself a stranger to the laughter and tears "beyond the wall."[132]

Such ambivalence was common and "tragic," thought the Marxist literary critic L'vov-Rogachevskii, commenting on the writings of Aleksei Bibik, especially his popular 1912 autobiographical novel *Toward the Open Road*. For a person to be both a "proletarian" and "cut off from the masses" was wrong, though unfortunately all too common. This was surely the existential situation of Bibik's worker heroes. Once awakened to "culture" by reading and seeking answers, they were repelled by the smell of beer, herring, and tobacco in their working-class homes, by the passivity and drunkenness of ordinary workers (including their own parents), and by the hostility of other workers toward "worker philosophers."[133] The novel's two protagonists (a duality that represented some of the ambivalence in the minds of awakened workers, though much of the tension remained within each character) seek different paths from this degraded everyday to a higher truth and hope. They discuss these paths, toward the end of the novel, in a prison cell where both are awaiting likely sentences of exile for leadership of a strike. The more politicized and militant Artëm insists that one must go "among people . . . into humanity." But Ignat— the character closest to the author, the central figure in the novel and the most ambivalent—seeks truth more complexly. He looks to nature and to "the inner world" and proposes that they become wanderers. The phrase he uses is *idti v odinochku*—literally "to go into [a state of being] singular and alone," or, more loosely, to withdraw from society, to drop out. "You know what, Artëm, let's go into *odinochka*! Come on! It's not so terrible there. It's easier there to get into one's self, to sort things out." And if one must be among people, Ignat argues, Siberia is the place to go ("harsh semimythical Siberia," Bibik calls it): "There are real people there—strong, great souls!"[134]

As L'vov-Rogachevskii recognized, there was a certain tragedy in the painful ambivalence that so many worker intellectuals felt in being simultaneously class-conscious activists and alienated from "the masses." A vanguard mentality, dedicated to sharing thoughts and ideals with others, competed and often mixed with contempt for those others. Sentimental pride in the richness of soul that could feel exquisite torments of solitude competed and often mixed with anguish over lonely isolation.

The Poetics of Genius

When these worker writers felt confident that resistance to the injuries to the self was worth the effort—such confidence was most common in periods of social and political mobilization such as 1905–7 and 1912–17 and for a few

[132] Ibid.
[133] L'vov-Rogachevskii, *Ocherki*, 217–18; Bibik, *K shirokoi doroge*, 23–30, 39, 49, 74.
[134] Bibik, *K shirokoi doroge*, 104–5.

years thereafter—they penned vigorous protests and calls for struggle. But their focus was typically less on collective action than on the inner will and power of awakened individuals to challenge inequalities, lead others, and change society. Marxist and Soviet critics have argued, often convincingly, that this was not conventional individualism—that is, not "petty bourgeois," "philistine" individualism.[135] We see this distinctiveness in the ethical commitment to others articulated in the ideas of the dignity of *all* people and of the need to struggle against the social causes and the agents of humiliation and insult. In practice, many worker writers joined unions (and sometimes led them) and socialist parties and participated in strikes, demonstrations, and revolution. In writing, they made these distinctions between individualisms themselves. A few did so explicitly, criticizing, for example, "worker aristocrats" who believed that individual self-cultivation and virtue were means enough to change conditions.[136] More commonly they implied as much by writing, in the already well established language of socialist collectivism, of "we," "our sufferings," "workers," the "proletariat," and "humanity," and, though still very rarely, of a future when individuals would forget their selves, give up individual names, and "know only one objective, great, growing, thrillingly felt world of harmony."[137] Most commonly and most complexly, they resisted "philistine" individualism by articulating a more poetic and inspired individualism, built around Romantic ideals of inward genius and heroic will—especially their own.

Writing itself was seen as a heroic act, grounded in inward genius—in the Renaissance and Romantic senses of each person's unique inward personality and capacities, of an inward and perhaps divine guiding spirit. Invariably these writers portrayed their will to write as reflecting a deep personal need, even a sacred inspiration, and as marking them as special individuals with a special mission. Gorky, who corresponded with hundreds of beginning writers, reported in 1911 that many of the workers and peasants who wrote to him similarly described a higher or inner force driving them to read and write. One worker, a turner, told Gorky that he could not sleep nights because he was so tortured by the thoughts that were inside him, trying to get out. A metalworker claimed—and Gorky reported that such expressions were typical—that a "mysterious force" (*nevedomaia sila*) drove him to write.[138] Many spoke of "fires" burning within them.[139] Others spoke, more traditionally, of

[135] Kleinbort, "Ocherki," pt. 1, *Sovremennyi mir*, March 1913, 34, 40.

[136] E.g., Baikov, "Kakoi put' vernee (Zametki rabochii)," *Rabochii po metallu*, no. 18 (26 July 1907), 3–5.

[137] A. Zorin [A. Gastev], "Rabochii mir: Zavod i sindikat: I. Sila mashinizma," *Zhizn' dlia vsekh*, 1911, no. 3–4 (March–April), 395–96. Soviet collections of "proletarian poetry" tend to highlight the collectivist spirit; see esp. *Proletarskie poety*, vol. 2.

[138] Maksim Gor'kii, "O pisateliakh-samouchkakh" (1911), in A. M. Gor'kii, *Sobranie sochinenii*, vol. 24 (Moscow, 1953), 105–8. See also Arkhiv A. M. Gor'kogo, KG-NP/A, 22-4:1–2.

[139] See, e.g., Shkulev quoted in V. Friche, *Proletarskaia poeziia* (Moscow, 1919), 59; Savin, "Bor'ba," *Bulochnik*, no. 1 (19 Feb. 1906), 5; Nechaev, "Moia pesnia," *Vecherniia pesni*, 79.

"a divine spark."[140] Works of fiction similarly featured protagonists inexplicably driven to read and of moments of bright inspiration (like lightening or a meteor) while reading.[141] As we shall see, this theme was almost universal in the memoirs of worker writers written after 1917.

Workers typically viewed themselves not only as inspired to write but as sanctified as individuals by their sufferings in service to this calling. Many recalled being beaten when they were caught reading or writing at work or even by their parents at home.[142] The suffering continued for those who managed to persist in writing. They carried the "heavy cross" of "torturous poverty and oppressive labor." And they suffered from conditions that suppressed their creativity: "I think that everyone knows how shining thoughts and the tormenting and caressing sounds of the proletarian muse perish and consume the soul when they are unable to see the light."[143]

These autobiographical representations of inspired, striving, and suffering selves were mixtures of memory and conscious mythmaking. As acts of memory they remind us that these individuals were indeed different, that they were responding to a rare drive to create. But it is the elaboration of these memories into meaningful stories of self-awakening and self-expression that is the most revealing. While their stories were often framed by devotion to the common good, the heart of these tales was about striving and heroic individuals. The prevailing self-identities they described were of heroes and outsiders, agents inspired by an inward genius, not as common members of the popular community, proud working-class creators of material value, or even rank-and-file soldiers in the class struggle. We recognize in their life stories images refracted from literature: the self-assertive, superior, and rebellious individuals of bandit tales and adventure sagas;[144] Nietzschean rebels against convention and slavishness; even echoes of the lives of saints—often the first literature that workers encountered—with their inspiring accounts of exceptional individual suffering in the pursuit and in the service of truth.

This particular self-idealization was linked strongly to the glorification of the printed word and the writer in Russian civic culture. Since the nineteenth century it had become a familiar intellectual tradition for writers and critics to speak of writers as moral witnesses, prophets, and inspired voices of truth. Pushkin, Gogol, Dostoevsky, Tolstoy, and others were often spoken of in this way, and themselves often aspired to this role. Although by the early 1900s modernists were countering with the ideal of art and of the artist standing pure and apart from social and political life, this myth of the writer as civic hero

---

[140] G. Deev-Khomiakovskii on Surikov in *Drug naroda* 1915, no. 5–7: 2–3.

[141] E.g., A-ch, "Ternistyi put'," *Samopomoshch'* 2, no. 1 (18 Dec. 1911): 6; Bibik, *K shirokoi doroge*, 46–47.

[142] Gor'kii, "O pisateliakh-samouchkakh," 106, 108; G. Deev-Khomiakovskii on Surikov in *Drug naroda* 1915, no. 5–7: 3; Zavolokin, *Sovremennye raboche-krest'ianskie poety*, 53–54, 76, 107.

[143] S. Drozhzhin in *Drug naroda* 1915, no. 5–7: 13; Sergei Gremiacheskii, "K pisateliam iz naroda," ibid., no. 8–10 (October): 2.

[144] See Brooks, *When Russia Learned to Read*, esp. chap. 5.

was strongly felt in the self-perceptions of lower-class writers. Memoirs and letters that workers sent to political and trade union papers repeatedly expressed a reverence for the printed word and for those who wrote.[145] Nikolai Liashko, using a hyperbolic vocabulary that was not unusual, declared that "[our] national literature is our sanctum sanctorum—the only place where every one of us enters with reverence." Most important, in the face of oppression and passivity, it is literature that has struggled for change: "It has fought for faith and freedom, for the humiliated and the insulted, and for the rights and dignity of man. Like a nanny over a sleeping child, it has fought against all the monsters of the nightmarish night, because the life of the Russian common people . . . has been one continuous nightmare."[146]

Writers were the agents of this sacred cause. For Aleksei Mashirov, the "proud word 'poet'" evoked "the joy of the first breath, / the emergence in spring of the first growth." In particular, workers' poets were the "people's leader," arriving like "a peal of joyous thunder."[147] Poets, it was said, cared not about money or a full table: they loved only "the high ideal of thought," only the "sun of truth."[148] Others wrote similarly about the power of their songs to inspire others.[149] The Russian writer, it was argued, was "prophet and leader" and "rebel" against the evils of "bureaucratism, the bourgeoisie, and aristocratism."[150] The lower-class writer was especially honored. As Nikolai Liashko put it in 1913: "Is there a more brilliant name than the name of people's writer [*narodnyi pisatel'*]?"[151]

Indeed, plebeian authorship had particular symbolic power in the self-images of these writers and in their ideas about the individual. When subalterns write—especially when they write literature or criticism—they are performing an inherently transgressive act. Like slaves and former slaves in the Americas for whom writing stood as a complex "certificate of humanity," a political gesture that implicitly criticized the European social chain of being and their own low place on it by seizing hold of "Europe's fundamental sign of domination, the commodity of writing, the text and technology of reason,"[152] workers who wrote implicitly challenged their ascription as lower-class. When Russian workers wrote and published poems, stories, and essays, they violated the conventional divisions between manual and intellectual la-

---

[145] See Kleinbort, "Ocherki," pt. 5, *Sovremennyi mir*, November 1913, 184; Aleksei Chizhikov, letter to *Pravda*, 4 Mar. 1914, in RGASPI, f. 364, op. 1, d. 315, ll. 1–3.

[146] N. Nikolaev [Liashko], "O narodnom pisatele, pisateliakh, i 'pisateliakh,'" *Ogni*, no. 3 (January 1913), 27.

[147] Samobytnik [Mashirov], "Ne govori v zhivom priznan'e," in *Pervyi sbornik proletarskikh pisatelei*, 13. See also his "Ia ne odin, nas v mire mnogo," in *Nashi pesni*, 7.

[148] M. Savin in *Gallereia sovremennykh poetov*, 12.

[149] E.g., Nechaev, "Mne khotelos' by pesniu svobodnuiu spet'" (1906)," in *U istokov*, 89 (also see 20).

[150] M. Loginov, "Uznavaite po plodam," *Zvezda utranniaia*, no. 17 (23 May 1912), 2.

[151] N. Nikolaev [N. Liashko], "O narodnom pisatele, pisateliakh, i 'pisateliakh,'" *Ogni*, no. 3 (January 1913), 25.

[152] Henry Louis Gates, Jr., "Editor's Introduction: Writing 'Race' and the Difference It Makes," in *"Race," Writing, and Difference*, ed. Gates (Chicago, 1986), 12.

bor and between popular culture and the literary high culture. It was significant that Russian worker writers almost invariably adopted an established literary style rather than a folk or plebeian style. Instead of echoing the rhythms and vocabulary of peasant songs and rhymes, worker poets typically imitated popular established writers, notably Pushkin, Kol'tsov, Nekrasov, Nikitin, and Nadson, or such foreign writers as Whitman and Verhaeren, and occasionally, though rarely, contemporary poets such as Blok and Briusov. And instead of telling stories in the manner of the folk tale—a style often adopted by radical intellectuals who sought to appeal to the common people—worker writers were more likely to emulate Turgenev, Korolenko, Tolstoy, Gorky, or Chekhov. High literary style was an emblem of the culture from which workers were excluded. Thus, in Russia as elsewhere, "workers' poetry was not at first an echo of popular speech but an initiation into the sacred language, the forbidden and fascinating language of others."[153] Its fascination and power derived precisely from its sanctified position in the established culture. Its otherness made it a symbol of workers' subordination and exclusion, making cultural imitation also appropriation, a half-conscious act of self-assertion and social rebellion. Sometimes it was fully conscious and deliberate. The appearance in Russia of "people's writers," Liashko argued in 1913 (as one of them), was part of a "breaking down of centuries-old structures of popular life," of a "striving to change what not long ago seemed immovable," and of a "revaluation of cultural values" (*pereotsenki dukhovnykh tsennostei*). Most simply, it was an answer to "those who imagine the common people to be wild beasts."[154] This challenge defied boundaries that defined social groups, but it remained rooted in acts of individual will. Reading and writing remained individual acts even when cast as part of a scenario of social protest.

We return to the problem of sorting out the complex relationship in the thought of worker writers between the self and others—especially other workers. These writers mythologized their own individual inspiration and heroic role and sought to nurture their genius. At the same time—and fully in the tradition of the Russian intelligentsia—they sought to realize their selves by looking beyond themselves and attaching themselves to others. Thus, for Mikhail Loginov, a true *intelligent* is defined not by social rank or profession ("a blacksmith, plowman, teacher, clerk, student, writer, or even, though rarely, an aristocrat can be an *intelligent*") but by his "work for the well-being of his native people and for all humanity."[155] But it is the image of the inspired and heroic individual—stereotypically a heroic man—that remains most prominent and persistent. The pronoun "I" fills even the most militant poems of protest and struggle. Worker authors wrote of their refusal to "bow down" before anyone and of their dreams of imitating a heroic rebel such as

---

[153] Jacques Rancière, "Ronds de fumée (Les Poètes ouvriers dans la France de Louis-Philippe)," *Revue des sciences humaines,* no. 190 (April–June 1983), 33.

[154] N. Nikolaev [Liashko], "O narodnom pisatele, pisateliakh, i 'pisateliakh,'" *Ogni,* no. 3 (January 1913), 25.

[155] M. Loginov, "Uznavaite po plodam," *Zvezda utrenniaia,* no. 17 (23 May 1912), 2.

Spartacus or Stenka Razin, or the mighty heroism of legendary giants and warriors (*giganty, bogatyri*).[156] In the paper of the baker's union, Mikhail Savin offered this self-portrait:

> I go onto the road
> And meet evil.
> I am anger and vengeance!
> I am the terror of the enemy!
> Sacred honor
> Is my way.
> Where is darkness and lies?
> I am their scourge
> I am a sharp knife. . . .
> I am a warrior
> With a pen in my hand
> Fire in my breast
> Poetry on my lips.[157]

Others vividly imagined themselves appearing before the suffering people as saviors; sometimes relatively modestly, with words and verses starting "fires" in people's hearts,[158] sometimes not so modestly: though a Marxist, the young factory worker Vasilii Aleksandrovskii represented himself as a godlike savior: "I will be there, where backs are bent / Where labor is profaned and defiled / . . . I will be there, where children perish / I will give them new thoughts."[159]

Worker poets even envisioned themselves in flight, typically as eagles and falcons. For some, flight was an escape. A provincial metalworker wrote to Gorky that he wished he were a "free bird" and could escape his life and fly to Gorky on the island of Capri or that he could be an airplane pilot and soar away from the earth into the sky.[160] Mariia Chernysheva dreamed of "light, swift wings" with which she could fly "toward freedom, toward the expanse."[161] More politicized workers wished to use flight to serve others. Egor Nechaev and Sergei Gan'shin dreamed of being eagles or the sun, bringing happiness and freedom to the world.[162] Aleksei Mashirov portrayed intellectual-minded workers like himself as "free, proud birds / Curving their wings

---

[156] E.g., M. Zakharov, "Romans," *Rodnye vesti* 1912, no. 3: 5–6; Bibik, *K shirokoi doroge,* 36; Gerasimov in RGALI, f. 1374, op. 1, d. 6; Aleksei Chizhikov, letter to *Pravda,* 4 Mar. 1914, 5, in RGASPI, f. 364, op. 1, d. 315, ll. 1–3.

[157] M. Savin, "Bor'ba," *Bulochnik,* no. 1 (19 Feb. 1906), 5.

[158] Gorelyi, "Rabochemu-poetu," *Novoe pechatnoe delo,* 27 Feb. 1916, in *Proletarskie poety,* 3:71; Gan'shin, "V godinu bed," *Vpered!* no. 148 (2/15 Sept. 1917), 2.

[159] V. Aleksandrovskii, "Novye pesni," in *Nashi pesni,* 1:11.

[160] D. I. Semenov, "Moe zhelanie" and "K nebesam," sent to Gorky, 14 Nov. 1910, in Arkhiv A. M. Gor'kogo, KG-NP/A, 22-4-1.

[161] M. Chernysheva, "Daite mne kryl'ia!" *Dumy narodnye,* no. 3 (13 Feb. 1910), 5. See also the poem by V. E. Miliaev in *Narodnaia mysl',* no. 2 (February 1911), 126.

[162] Nechaev, "Pesnia nevol'nika," in *Vechernie pesni,* 151, and *U istokov,* 98–99. Gan'shin "Orel," a manuscript poem sent to Maxim Gorky, in Arkhiv A. M. Gor'kogo, RAV-PG 37-13-1.

against the black firmament," and coming to the people in sacrificial but inspiring flight as flashes of lightning or as a falling meteor.[163] In each case, these were heroic acts of inspired—indeed, transcendent—individuals, but acting not for themselves alone. In the tradition of the Russian intelligentsia, individualistic self-realization was linked to an identity and a purpose that went beyond self. Individual exaltation and devotion to the collective were said to be intertwined.

Activist worker writers made every effort to link the individual and the collective. In their minds, the linkage was partly philosophical: recognition of the equal worth of every person necessarily highlighted the discrimination against workers as a class. The linkage was also partly practical: class struggle would emancipate individuals from social and political constraints on their development, and the developed individual best served the common cause. However, the orderly logic of this identification of the individual with the collective did not remove the uncertainties and tensions in the self-identities and social identities of these workers.

Ambiguous Identities and Emotions

Ambivalence and ambiguity were endemic, pervading the stories of self that these writers presented. The savior was both selfless and an exalted self. Inspired and inspiring "flight" above the harsh and common world was a sign of both alienation and devotion to others, of both engagement and escape. The winged worker was a godlike fighter for others, but also simply godlike. The ethics these writers articulated was similarly ambivalent: the moral primacy given to workers' identity as human beings undermined class identity even as it provided a powerful sense of class injury and reason to fight as a class. After all, the ultimate purpose of the workers' movement was presumed to be not to build a "proletarian" social and cultural order but to demolish the barriers that kept workers separate, that identified them as anything other than human, and that restricted their individualities. Class struggle, in this conception, was aimed less against a different and dominant class than against class difference and domination itself. At least implicitly, this view echoed the Marxist dialectic that saw the particularistic class outlook of the proletariat negating the very idea of class, thereby giving to the working class a messianic historical role as a "universal class," destined not only to save itself but to deliver all humanity. But the tidy reasoning of this dialectic did not erase the ambiguity in the self-identities and self-images of many workers. At the heart of the self idea of most worker writers remained, at a minimum, the desire to be treated as human beings, and thus as individuals rather than as

---

[163] A. Mashirov (Samobytnik), "Zarnitsy," *Proletarskaia pravda*, 18 Sept. 1913, and "Moim sobrat'iam," *Prosnuvshaiasia zhizn'* [Rukopisnyi zhurnal], 1913, both rpt. in *Proletarskie poety*, 2:89–90.

workers. And this aspiration sometimes evolved into more radical ideals of individual genius and exaltation.

Recognizing and understanding these uncertainties and tensions in self-
identity require us to look beyond these logical constructions at the question
of emotional perception and judgment. Emotion was often on the minds of
worker writers and on the minds of educated critics of the proletarian imagination. Contemporary Marxist cultural critics and later Soviet literary historians repeatedly insisted on the boldly optimistic spirit defining the proletarian worldview. "Enthusiasm," "optimism," "bold confidence," and a generally "life-affirming" feeling were said to be the hallmarks of the proletarian
mood.[164] These arguments were tendentious—part of the politics of inventing a proletarian culture—but not without basis. The moral recognition that
all people are human beings with dignity and rights certainly helped inspire a
certain boldness and optimism. And the 1905 revolution, when the ideal of
natural human rights was openly and repeatedly deployed by various groups
against social and political inequalities, and resulted in the winning of important if limited legal guarantees for civil rights and democratic power, particularly stimulated this positive and militant mood. Almost every worker
writer, especially in the years from 1905, produced verses, stories, or essays
voicing such militant optimism. Fedor Gavrilov's 1905 "song of a workman" was typical in its ringing declarations of "boldness," "courage," and
faith in the coming victory over "darkness."[165] In subsequent years, even during the repressive years from 1907 through 1910, hundreds of writings used
a similar vocabulary of insistent and self-advertised optimism: "boldness"
(*bodrost'*), "hope," "enthusiasm," "mass heroism," "strength of spirit," feelings of "youthful life," "faith," and certainty that all obstacles would be overcome.[166] When suffering and tears were mentioned in such writings, it was to
insist that they be put aside: "This is not the time, friend, for us to sing of anguish [*toska*] and sadness."[167]

But this other voice was hard to silence, even within oneself. One needed
great faith in human goodness not to lose hope, Mikhail Loginov argued in
1910, and he admitted that it was difficult for many to sustain such faith and

---

[164] E.g., Gor'kii, "O pisateliakh-samouchkakh," 107; L. Kleinbort, "Rukopisnye zhurnaly
rabochikh," *Vestnik Evropy* 52, no. 7–8 (July–August 1917): 285; L'vov-Rogachevskii, *Ocherki*,
39–41; Bikhter, "U istokov," 13, 23.

[165] F. Gavrilov, "Iz pesen truzhenika," *Na zare* (Moscow, 1905), rpt. in *Proletarskie poety*,
1:194–95.

[166] Chechenets, "Pesnia rabov," *Rabochii po metallu*, no. 22 (10 Oct. 1907): 3; Zorin [Gas-
tev], in *Kuznets*, no. 7 (14 Feb. 1908), 4; Nik. R-tskii [Rybatskii], "Pesnia pariia," *Edinstvo*, no.
8 (10 Aug. 1909), 3; Kvadrat [Kubikov], "A. V. Kol'tsov," *Pechatnoe delo*, no. 12 (23 Oct. 1909),
6; Obradovich, "K svetu," *Ekho*, March 1912, 2 (a cutting in RGALI, f. 1874, op. 1, d. 2, l. 1);
Bibik, "Bor obrechennoi," *Novaia rabochaia gazeta*, no. 56 (13 Oct. 1913), 2; I. Cherdyntsev and
N. Dodaev in *Pervyi sbornik proletarskikh pisatelei*, 132, 143. Many examples can be found in
Soviet anthologies, such as the three volumes of *Proletarskie poety* and *Poeziia v bol'shevistskikh
izdaniiakh, 1901–1917* (Leningrad, 1967).

[167] Gorelyi, "Rabochemu-poetu," *Nashe pechatnoe delo*, no. 29 (27 Feb. 1916), 4. This poem
was addressed to a compositor-poet who had submitted a poem on misery (*gore*) to *Nashe pechatnoe delo*.

hope.[168] All too common was the mood Aleksei Gastev described among his fellow tram workers: "unenlightened melancholy [*bezprosvetnaia toska*], impenetrable skepticism, and stagnant inertia."[169] Much the same could be said of the mood among the most intellectually active workers. As we have seen, when these authors wrote of suffering, they tended most often to construct their accounts of misery around socially critical and even defiant narratives of inequality and oppression. But we must not ignore the moments (and there were many) when worker writers felt impelled to tell others about more intimate sorrows (and sometimes joys) that had more ambiguous social meanings. The printer poet Vladimir Korolev, for example, wrote of dying without ever finding love, tears of "blue longing" (*golubaia toska*), and the "hate in people's gaze."[170] Aleksei Gastev's first published work was an anguished tale of sexual passion, fear, and guilt. The hero of this tale is horrified by his own "elemental, animal passions," "weakening will," and "unhealthy and aroused imagination." When he succumbed to these drives, he experienced "a sensation of nausea and loathing, his hands seemed to be stained with blood—for several days he could not let them near food. His own self repelled him. . . . For a long time he could not even read his favorite authors."[171] Often such reflections expanded into more explicitly existential despair over life's meaning. Death alone seemed to hold an answer, if only that of "oblivion" and "rest."[172]

Yet there remained another, more positive answer, however ambiguously mixed with doubt. Even within these troubled thoughts, the importance and value of speaking aloud about the inner life of the self remained clear. As a great deal of modern social and political history makes evident, this discourse about the self had powerful critical and subversive potential. At the very least, even when despair lurked around the corner, there was a certain pleasure and pride—a "precious exquisite pain"—in the ability to feel and express one's inner torments. It demonstrated the sensitivity and hence worth of one's inner self and creative powers. In a society as profoundly unequal as prerevolutionary Russia, even this discourse was dangerous.

[168] *Dumy narodnye*, no. 2 ([February] 1910), 1.
[169] A. Zorin [Gastev], "Sredi tramvaishchikov (nabrosok)," *Edinstvo*, no. 12 (21 Dec. 1909), 11.
[170] Vladimir Korolev, *Vsem skorbiashchim* (Iaroslavl, 1915) (like many of Korolev's collections, this one was printed and distributed by the local printers' union).
[171] A. Odinokii [Gastev], *Prokliatyi vopros* (Geneva, 1904).
[172] Mariia Chernysheva, "Zaveshchanie," *Dumy narodnye*, no. 7 ([13 Mar.], 1910), 5; S. Obradovich, "Bezsonnoiu noch'iu," *Severnoe utro* (Arkhangel'sk), no. 52 (6 Mar. 1913), 2 (a cutting in RGALI, f. 1874, op. 1, d. 2, l. 8).

3 The Proletarian "I"

Пролеткульцы не говорят
Не про "Я",
Не про личность.
"Я",
Для пролеткульца
Все равно, что неприличность.

Proletcultists do not speak
About the "I"
Or about the self.
"I"
For the Proletcultist
Is utterly indecent.

   —VLADIMIR MAIAKOVSKII, "The Fifth International," 1922

The man of melancholy frame of mind cares little for what others
judge, what they consider good or true; he relies in this matter simply on his own insight. . . . Truthfulness is sublime and he hates lies
or dissimulation. He has a high feeling of the dignity of human nature.

   —IMMANUEL KANT, *Observations on the Feeling
of the Beautiful and the Sublime*

The revolutions of 1917 and the struggles for political survival and socialist
authority that followed helped nurture and spread in Russia's public intellectual life a forceful collectivist discourse about social class and human community. The Marxist theory of class and the leftist cultural battle cry, "We
stand fast on the rock of the word 'We' amidst a sea of catcalls and derision,"[1]

---

[1] From the Futurist manifesto, "Slap in the Face of Public Taste" (*Poshchechina obshchestvennomu vkusu,* 1912). In 1923 Maiakovskii, as leading former futurist and editor of the
journal *Lef,* argued that the proud isolation of that old stance, which he had helped to author,
was no longer necessary or healthy; now it was necessary only "to dissolve with joy the little

were now part of the reigning ideology. But these had always been unstable discourses, and they remained so. These philosophies and stances of collectivism had long been entwined in a complex relationship—sometimes a tidy dialectic, often a troubled dialogue—with ideas magnifying the individual and the inward self. After October 1917, "proletarian culture" became a centerpiece in this dialogue—as a source of the new culture, as an ideal to create, and as an actual body of contesting voices. Notably, actual proletarian voices were among the most troubled and ambivalent.

The Revolutionary Philosophy of Collectivism

To understand this difficult dialogue, it is important to recognize the radical sweep of the collectivist ideal that many Communists articulated in these years. Social class, though central to the narrative of the revolution's origins and to the political self-definition of the new society, was only an immediate ideal, and hence only a starting point for the revolutionary values that cultural radicals articulated. The larger aim and greater value—articulated in the first postrevolutionary decade, especially in its first years, by various ideologists, educators, psychologists, city planners, writers, and poets—was a more radical vision of human unity (of the "world commune"), of overcoming all difference, and even of the "dissolution of the individual human personality" (*rastvorenie lichnosti*) into a universal collective "we."[2] Before 1918, this Bolshevik "philosophy of collectivism" (as it was called in an influential collection of articles by left-wing Marxists published in 1909) had been nurtured mainly on the fringes of the party. Bogdanov, Lunacharsky, and Gorky—all of whom would play influential roles in shaping the emerging Soviet culture— were among those radical intellectuals who had been vigorously criticizing "bourgeois individualism," which, in Russia as elsewhere, increasingly placed the individual "I" at the center of ontological and moral judgment. Rejecting both sophisticated neo-Kantian ethics and what they saw as simply vulgar and selfish forms of bourgeois egoism, they espoused a collectivist philosophy of being and ethics in which the self exists meaningfully only as it is perceived and experienced by others (to the point where an individual may die physically but his or her self will survive in the life and experience of the collectivity) and in which the self is truly realized only through the "merging of individual lives into one vast whole."[3]

'we' of art into the huge 'we' of communism": *Lef: Zhurnal levogo fronta iskusstv*, no. 1 (March 1923), 9.

[2] See Richard Stites, *Revolutionary Dreams: Utopian Vision and Revolutionary Life in the Russian Revolution* (Oxford, 1989), esp. chaps. 6, 7, 9, 10; William G. Rosenberg, ed., *Bolshevik Visions: First Phase of the Cultural Revolution in Russia*, 2d ed., 2 vols. (Ann Arbor, 1990).

[3] *Ocherki filosofii kollektivizma* (St. Petersburg, 1909); A. A. Bogdanov, *Iz psikhologii obshchestva*, 2d ed. (St. Petersburg, 1906), 4–5 (quotation) and "Sobiranie cheloveka" (1904), in *O proletarskoi kul'ture, 1904–1924* (Leningrad and Moscow, 1924), 16–17; Robert C. Williams,

After October 1917, such ideas flourished as writers, social planners, and cultural activists promoted ideas of collective identification and active solidarity. In the arts especially, creators of the new culture, as a literary historian has observed, "did not merely vaunt social cohesiveness, they envisioned society as a collective body," and in a quite physical sense.[4] "Left" writers such as Maiakovskii imagined individuals melding their selves into this new unified national body. In the poem "150,000,000," for example, the ideal of the anonymous, impersonal mass is personified in "the unified Ivan" who feels and sings "the millions." The author himself is submerged in these millions, declaring "of this / my poem / no one is the author": "150,000,000 is the name of the creator of this poem ... / 150,000,000 speak with my lips."[5] These were more than metaphors. The argument that appeared in the national trade union journal in 1924, by the influential Soviet psychologist Aron Zalkind, was typical in its language and logic: "collective feeling" was replacing the "individualistic narcissism, self-satisfying 'morality,' [and] feeling of responsibility before one's own 'conscience'" that characterized "bourgeois ethics."[6] The Hungarian writer René Fülöp-Miller, an observer of Soviet cultural life in the early 1920s, described such talk as ubiquitous. He characterized Soviet political and artistic culture alike as driven by a pervasive striving toward "the complete absorption of all individuals in a million-headed impersonal mass," toward a new "collective man" who would be born when "the 'soul-encumbered individual man'" had been "mercilessly exterminated."[7] Evgenii Zamiatin, in his novel *We*, written in 1919–20, derided this collectivist ideology as a vision of a future in which "nobody is 'one' but is only 'one of,'" all life is social life, people have numbers, not names, and even the intimacy of sexual passion is rationally controlled and organized.[8] Zamiatin and Fülöp-Miller, of course, were responding as much to the depersonalizing effects of the emerging mass culture in the West as they were to the particular modernizing dreams of Soviet radicals. Still, these particular dreams were unusually evident and explicit, especially in discussions of proletarian consciousness and creativity.[9]

"Collective Immortality: The Syndicalist Origins of Proletarian Culture, 1905–1910," *Slavic Review* 39, no. 3 (September 1980): 389–402, and *The Other Bolsheviks: Lenin and His Critics, 1904–1914* (Bloomington, 1982), 38–39, 99–102, 146–49; Oleg Kharkhordin, *The Collective and the Individual in Russia* (Berkeley, 1999), esp. 78–80.

[4] Eric Naiman, *Sex in Public: The Incarnation of Early Soviet Ideology* (Princeton, 1997), 65; Kharkhordin, *Collective and the Individual*, 190–92.

[5] Vladimir Maiakovskii, "150,000,000" (1919–20), in his *Polnoe sobranie sochinenii*, 13 vols. (Moscow, 1955–61), 2:115.

[6] A. Zalkind, "Pionerskoe detskoe dvizhenie, kak forma kul'traboty sredi proletariata," *Vestnik truda* 1924, no. 3 (March): 108. This essay can be found in translation in Rosenberg, *Bolshevik Visions*, 2:84–91.

[7] René Fueloep-Miller, *The Mind and Face of Bolshevism: An Examination of Cultural Life in the Soviet Union* (1927; New York, 1965), 5, 7.

[8] Evgenii Zamiatin, *My: Roman*, in his *Sochineniia* (Moscow, 1988), 13.

[9] The noted Soviet literary historian Zinovyi Papernyi observed that during the first years after the Bolsheviks came to power the ideological "attack on the individual self [*gonenie na lich-*

Proletarian culture was said to be collectivist by nature, shaped by the socializing experiences of modern industrial labor. In 1918, in the first issue of the theoretical journal of the Proletcult, Aleksandr Bogdanov (a member of the Proletcult Central Committee and of the editorial board of the movement's national journal, *Proletarskaia kul'tura,* and, many have said, the movement's leading intellectual theoretician) asserted that "proletarian" poetry characteristically voiced "not the lyric of the personal 'I'" but the lyric of "comradeship," for the creating subject of proletariia poetry was not the "'I' of the poet" but the "real, most basic creator of this poetry—the collective."[10] In subsequent years, Bogdanov continued to elaborate and advocate ideas about the "collective-creative 'we'" as the hero and the theme of socialist art and the source of socialist creativity.[11] This idealized definition of proletarian culture was official Proletcult policy. Resolutions passed at the first national conference of proletarian cultural organizations, in September 1918, supported Bogdanov's call for a "class art" that was "collectivist" in both form and "spirit."[12] Numerous official Proletcult statements reiterated this ideal: "The proletariat needs to unfold before humanity the unbounded perspective of harmonious perfection . . . it needs to create its own morals and its own art in order to reveal the universal clear light where the rays of *individual* thought of the old world drown in the radiant dawn of *social* life."[13] And in a flood of critical essays about the new culture, Proletcult leaders pointed out and commended instances of proletarian creativity that exemplified the proletariat's natural aesthetic appreciation of the "beauty of collective happiness" and its natural ethical repugnance for such bourgeois ways of "feeling" as "petty-egoistic personal happiness."[14]

We must beware of stereotyping these views. Statements by Proletcult intellectuals were often paired with limiting clarifications, lest exaggerated forms of the philosophy of collectivism be allowed to grow unchecked. Bogdanov, for example, scrupulously denied that collectivism sought to obliterate the individual personality. This was a "stereotype" (*shablon*), he insisted. The collectivist aim was to allow individual personalities to flourish by creating social conditions in which people were truly free to realize their human selves.[15] Many advocates of collectivism also imagined and constructed the relation-

---

nost'] reached the most incredible extremes": *Poeticheskii obraz u Maiakovskogo* (Moscow, 1961), 70.

[10] A. Bogdanov, "Chto takoe proletarskia poeziia?" *Proletarskaia kul'tura,* no. 1 (July 1918), 12–22, esp. 20–21.

[11] This is a leitmotif in Bogdanov's collection of his own essays, *O proletarskoi kul'ture, 1904–1924* (Leningrad and Moscow, 1924).

[12] "Proletariat i iskusstvo," *Gorn,* no. 1 (1918), 31.

[13] "Ot Proletkul'ta," introduction to *Poeziia rabochego udara* (Petrograd, 1918), 3 (emphasis added). This was the first literary publication by the Proletcult. See also Lynn Mally, *Culture of the Future: The Proletkult Movement in Revolutionary Russia* (Berkeley, 1990), 93, 173.

[14] *Griadushchee* 1918, no. 3 (June): 4–5; A. Bogdanov, "Chto takoe proletarskaia poeziia?" *Proletarskaia kul'tura,* no. 1 (July 1918), 20–22.

[15] A. Bogdanov, "Ideal vospitaniia," *Proletarskaia kul'tura,* no. 2 (July 1918), 18. See also Zenovia A. Sochor, *Revolution and Culture: The Bogdanov-Lenin Controversy* (Ithaca, 1988), 137–38; Mally, *Culture of the Future,* 94.

ship between collective and self in more ambiguous ways than many of their own statements suggest. The example of Maiakovskii is illustrative. As scholars of his work have recognized, Maiakovskii struggled hard to maintain a consistent collectivist voice, but without success. His declarative clichés often barely masked contradictory attitudes and feelings. These contradictions were often visible in his writing: in changes he made, in antithetical and paradoxical emphases, in an unconvincing abstractness and declarativeness, in growing hostility to the Proletcultists' sneering at the individual, and in a subtle but steady return to his old lyrical and Romantic focus on his own self.[16] Maiakovskii's inconsistent and ambivalent embrace of the new collectivist culture may be emblematic: a truer reflection of the emerging Soviet cultural mentality than Zamiatin's or Fülöp-Miller's characterizations. Certainly most worker authors, including leftist writers associated with the Proletcult, cannot be easily cast (though they often have been in accounts of proletarian culture) as simplistic partisans of the great impersonal "We."

We: "The Feeling of One's 'I' in Others"

In the wake of October, enthusiastic collectivism quickly began to pervade the writings of politically leftist worker authors, especially of the younger generation who began to publish around the time of the revolution. But older authors were also inspired by the mood and values associated with the revolution, as Sergei Obradovich testified:

> When someone used to say "writer from the workers" or "poet-proletarian," I pictured a "loner" [*odinochka*] shut up in himself, languishing [*toskuiushchii*] with his "disordered Muse," alone with his fiery passion and insurgent song in some garret under the smoky sky or in some mildewed cellar. But then came the Revolution. The "loner" could be seen at meetings, lectures, clubs, proletarian schools, and in the Proletcults.[17]

Others similarly felt that the revolution was helping to tear down the wall that separated them from other workers.[18] Most important, the revolution was giving birth to a new collectivist society. In the numerous essays that appeared on culture and social ethics, especially on the new "proletarian culture," worker authors echoed (sometimes even more loudly) the arguments of left-Bolshevik intellectuals about the communal spirit of the coming new order, when "the interests of the collective push aside individual interests," individuals "experience the feeling of one's own 'I' in the Great Collective of la-

---

[16] See Papernyi, *Poeticheskii obraz u Maiakovskogo*, 68–111.

[17] R. O-ch [Sergei Obradovich], "Iz zhizni rabochikh pera," *Vestnik putei soobshcheniia*, no. 1 (1919), 18 (cutting in RGALI, f. 1874, op. 1 [Obradovich], d. 157, l. 1).

[18] E.g., R. Vitkovskaia, "V auditorii rabfaka" (1922), in RGALI, f. 1068, op. 1, d. 27, l. 5.

bor," and people's psychology all over the world becomes so "normalized" that millions are joined in a great "mechanized collectivism." [19]

Many of these writers also endorsed the insistence of Bogdanov and other Marxist theorists of culture that collectivism was endemic in the psychology of the proletariat, reflecting workers' experiences in modern industrial work. As the "proletarian philosopher" Fedor Kalinin expressed it, "Modern industrial capitalism brings to light every mark of impersonality, of socialization to the collective [obobshchestvlenie], and in this connection creates the collectivist psychology of the industrial proletariat. This form of organization in production, . . . where the workman is only a consciously disciplined link in the chain of the entire collective, must be carried over by the proletariat into ideological cultural work."[20] Valerian Pletnev, perhaps the most influential former worker to participate in the leadership of the Proletcult, similarly testified to the "collectivist psychology" of workers, which was born as workers learned from their industrial experiences that the strength of the individual lies in being a tiny part of something greater.[21] To be sure, he had to admit by 1921, this psychology was largely theoretical in respect to the majority of Soviet workers, whom the hardships of recent years had wearied of such visions. The consciousness of the working masses at the end of the civil war was limited mainly to "dreams of jam and cake." But this fact only pointed to the (admittedly paradoxical) mission for fully conscious proletarians to instruct the working masses in the very "cult of the collective" that grew naturally from their life and history.[22]

Worker essayists typically contrasted this proletarian collectivism to the bourgeois individualism of the intelligentsia. The poet Vladimir Kirillov, in a 1919 essay, recalled (echoing the familiar interpretation) that after the 1905 revolution most of the intelligentsia showed their true faces by abandoning the working-class movement and retreating into "philistine [obyvatel'skii] individualism or religious seeking."[23] Il'ia Sadof'ev, writing in 1920, portrayed with contempt even the behavior of radical intelligenty in tsarist prisons, where the "spiritual emptiness of the intelligentsia" was revealed in constant "quarrels, ugly scenes among the prisoners, and naked individualism."[24] This class-informed critique of individualism was also directed at the working

[19] Osen' bagrianaia: Sbornik literaturnogo otdela zavodskogo proletkul'ta pervykh Tul'skikh oruzheinykh zavodov, no. 1 (1921), viii; S. Obradovich, "Obraznoe myshlenie," Kuznitsa, no. 2 (June 1920), 20; A. Gastev, "O tendentsiiakh proletarskoi kul'tury," Proletarskaia kul'tura, no. 9–10 (June–July 1919), 44–45.

[20] F. Kalinin, "Ideologiia proizvodstva," Proletarskaia kul'tura, no. 5 (November 1918), 9.

[21] V. Pletnev, "O professionalizme," Proletarskaia kul'tura, no. 7–8 (April–May 1919), 35–36; idem, "O kolletivnom tvorchestve," Gorn, no. 5 (1920), 55–59; idem, "Chto takoe obyvatel'": Tesizy doklada, 12/XI/1923," in RGALI, f. 1230, op. 1, d. 468, l. 36.

[22] V. Pletnev, report to the Proletcult Central Committee, May 1921, Proletarskaia kul'tura, no. 20–21 (January–June 1921), 42–43.

[23] V. K. [Kirillov], "Pis'ma o proletarskom tvorchestve," Griadushchaia kul'tura, no. 3 (January 1919), 11.

[24] I. Sadof'ev, "P. K. Bessal'ko"(obituary), Griadushchee 1920, no. 3: 13–14.

class: at the many workers who failed to think as proletarians ought to think. But such ideological deviance only sharpened the need for conscious workers to reveal their destiny to the masses. Thus a trio of worker authors, writing collectively in 1918, echoed Bogdanov in calling on the Proletcult to "organize feelings and everyday relations in the spirit of collectivism" in order to increase the "spiritual strength" of the working class.[25]

The cult of the collective in critical essays by workers often took extreme and extravagant form. One Proletcult writer, Nikolai Torba, offered a rather more religious than class vision of proletarian collectivism, combining elements of Christian love with mystical notions of unbounded communal personhood. Human history, he maintained, is a process of development from an "animal-like" morality of egoistic "celebration of the individual self [*lichnost'*]" toward a "new spiritual state where the guiding sacred principle will be not personal egoism but love, that is to say, a feeling of one's own 'I' in others." The "heroes" of this new age, who will lead solely by the power of their personal example, will be distinguished not by physical strength or education or talent but by their "greater distance from animal-like egoism and greed." These heroes of the future socialist culture will be "people for whom 'the other' is the same as 'myself,' for whom 'others' grief' is 'my grief' and 'others' joy' is 'my joy.'" This new person will feel himself to be "not an isolated separate being but an entire ocean, embracing all of the souls that surround him."[26]

This apparent rejection of the very notion of an individual inner self—the notion that has been the essence, it has been argued, of identity and morality in modern Western cultures[27]—was repeated by many other worker writers in these early postrevolutionary years. Andrei Platonov came closest to explicitly identifying this revolutionary understanding of the self as a turn away from the European tradition. In one of the many essays he wrote during the civil war for Soviet and Communist papers in the provincial capital of Voronezh, Platonov argued pointedly that the Bolshevik revolution marked the start not of a Western European revolution but of the revolutionary rising of the East. Platonov's preoccupation with death in revolutionary struggle may partly have reflected this "Eastern" ideal, though it more certainly echoed the prerevolutionary musings on collective immortality of such Russian socialists as Bogdanov, Lunacharsky, and Gorky. Revolutionaries, Platonov contended, ought not tremble even in the face of their own individual deaths, for in dying they give "the best blood to the living heart of the revolution. Hail to

[25] Knizhnik, K. Ozol'-Prednek, and A. M., "God bor'by za proletarskuiu kul'turu," *Griadushchee* 1918, no. 8: 18. Karl Ozol'-Prednek was a Latvian worker poet. A. M. was most likely Aleksei Mashirov (Samobytnik). Both were among the leaders of the Proletkult recruited from the lower classes. The identity of Knizhnik is not known to me. See also the essay on proletarian art by Karl Ozol'-Prednek in *Proletkul't* (Tver), no. 1–2 (April–May 1919), 27.

[26] N. Torba, "Neravenstvo i nasilie," *Griadushchee* 1920, no. 5–6: 16–17.

[27] Charles Taylor, *Sources of the Self: The Making of Modern Identity* (Cambridge, 1989). David Sabean has demonstrated that this self-concept was not universal in the West: *Power in the Blood: Popular Culture and Village Discourse in Early Modern Germany* (Cambridge, 1984).

the dying and the dead! Hail to death, which gives birth to the new, higher life." Like other writers, Platonov described the birth out of the revolution of a new society in which individual selves would lose themselves in the sea of souls, in a "synthesis of selves in both body and character." "There will be a time, and it is near, when one person will say to another, 'I do not know you, nor do I know myself, I know all. I live when all live. Alone, I die. If you are struck, I feel pain. I have lost myself, but I have gained all.'"[28]

In creative writings after October, workers often elaborated on these notions of self and collective. As literary historians have often observed, "We" became a major leitmotif on the proletarian literary left. Some of these expressions were simply blunt statements of collectivist ideology put into rhymed and metered line, such as Leontii Kotomka's poem "My Idol Is the Collective."[29] Most writings tried to elaborate the contours of this idealized "We." A short story by "Groshik" (S. Kopeikin), published in a Proletcult journal in 1919, carefully laid out this ideal—and its relation to the cultural natures of different social classes—through the voice of an earnest, culture-minded metalworker active in his union. The young worker is interrupted in his reading by the intrusion of the physically and morally dissolute son of his landlady. An existential argument ensues. The visitor argues that a man has only two real choices in life: to "merge with the crowd, which will eventually swallow you up" and reduce you to an "ordinary commoner" (*obyvatel'*), or, like himself, to be a deliberate "cast-off from humanity," a "walking protest" (*khodiachii protest*). He admits only one other alternative: to be a "leader" (*vozhd'*), but this role is reserved only for "very strong people, able to master the minds of the masses." In response to this decadent Nietzscheanism, the worker activist proudly proclaims himself to be neither an *obyvatel'*, a *vozhd'*, nor a *khodiachii protest*: "I am completely satisfied to be an insignificant lever aiding the common work."[30]

More often, however, worker writers (especially poets) envisioned a more transcendent collectivism and tried to describe just how comprehensive this "We" really was. The proletarian "We" in Vladimir Kirillov's once well known poem of that name, first published in 1918 in the Petrograd Proletcult journal *Griadushchee* (The future), embodied "in itself Divinity, Judgment, and Law."[31] Mikhail Gerasimov's poem of the same name, published in 1918 in a collection from the Moscow Proletcult, embraced all time and space:

> We are Wagner, da Vinci, Titian. . . .
> We laid the stones of the Parthenon

[28] A. Platonov, "Vosstanie Vostoka," *Krasnaia derevnia*, 27 July 1920 (lead essay); "Tridtsat' krasnykh," *Krasnaia derevnia*, 6 July 1920; "Budushchii Oktiabr'," *Voronezhskaia kommuna*, 9 Nov. 1920; and "Lunacharskii," *Krasnaia derevnia*, 22 July 1920.
[29] L. Kotomka, "Moi kumir—kollektiv . . . ," *Zheleznyi put'* (Voronezh), no. 5 (1 Jan. 1919), 10.
[30] Groshik, "Roma," *Griadushchee* 1919, no. 2–3: 4–7.
[31] V. Kirillov, "My," *Griadushchee* 1918, no. 2 (May): 4.

And of the gigantic Pyramids.
For all the Sphinxes, temples, and Pantheons,
We hewed the ringing granite.

Was it not for us on Mount Sinai,
In the burning, unconsumed bush,
That the Red banner, glowing like the sun,
Appeared in wind and fire?[32]

Such cosmic revolutionary hubris was well received (judging by frequent readings and publications of these two poems) and not unusual. "We are lords, we are titans," sang Pavel Arskii.[33] "We are omnipotent," proclaimed Il'ia Sadof'ev, "and can do as we wish, / Destroy, achieve, / And we are growing stronger and multiplying."[34] Even in some writings focused formally on the narrative "I" (though ambiguities creep in here) the dominant logic could be the impersonal universality of the self, the absolute identification of the "I" and all humanity: "They call me Worker of the World. I am man and woman, old and young. . . . I am the eternal, unknown participant in Struggle and Victory. One of millions."[35]

Death in the revolutionary cause, the ultimate sign of the communion of the individual with the collective and the universal, was a common image. When Sadof'ev heard the news that V. Volodarskii (Moisei Gol'dshtein), a prominent Bolshevik and the commissar of press, propaganda, and agitation of the Petrograd Commune, had been shot through the heart by a counterrevolutionary, he responded in typical form: "We are immortal, and the murdered and fallen, / On the path to the goal, are eternal in us. / And living streams of burning blood / Weld together more firmly our formidable [*groznyi*] class."[36] More ecstatically, even mystically, Nikolai Rybatskii (Chirkov) wrote to his daughter about his own readiness for death as he was leaving for the front in the civil war—where, in fact, he would soon be killed: "I have for you only one testament / Be ruthless toward yourself! / Rise to the heavens, to god . . . / Gaze ahead with spirit. / And proudly and boldly. For a just cause / Do not tremble—die!"[37] After Rybatskii's death his friend Sadof'ev—they worked in the same factories and often discussed literature together—expressed his admiration for Rybatskii's readiness to sacrifice himself to "the cosmic movement of the proletarian revolution."[38]

[32] M. Gerasimov, "My," in *Zavod ognekrylyi* (Moscow, 1918), 19–20.

[33] P. Arskii, "Pesnia o molote," *Griadushchee* 1918, no. 9: 2.

[34] I. Sadof'ev, "Chto takoe proletkul't," *Mir i chelovek* (Kolpino), no. 1 (January 1919), 12. See also "My idem," in Sadof'ev's *Dinamo-Stikhi* (Petrograd, 1918), 5–6.

[35] I. Ivanov, "Mashinist," *Molot* (Orenburg), no. 1 (November 1920), 17. See also V. Aleksandrovskii, "Ia-Proletarii," *Pravda*, 10 Feb. 1922, rpt. in Vladimir Aleksandrovskii, *Zvon solntsa* (Moscow, 1923), 7.

[36] Aksen-Achkasov [Sadof'ev], "Venok: Pamiati V. Volodarskogo," *Griadushchee* 1918, no. 4: 12.

[37] N. Rybatskii, "Zaveshchanie," *Griadushchee* 1919, no. 3–4: 8.

[38] I. Sadof'ev, "Nikolai Rybatskii," *Griadushchee* 1920, no. 12–13: 16–17.

Images and stories of individual sacrifice and of readiness for death proliferated in these years. Some accounts were relatively prosaic, as in a tale Sadot'ev published in 1920, set in the midst of the October 1917 insurrection, in
which a wise old man counsels a frightened young worker, who fears that he
will never see his wife or son again if he joins in the revolutionary battle and
wonders what is the use of dying: they die not for themselves, the old man tells
him, but for their children, for all children.[39] Other accounts were more visionary and cosmic, as when Aleksei Kraiskii (Kuz'min) imagined the future
as an "iron giant" that workers feed with their own blood and bodies when
they run out of water and coal (an intimation of the Christian Eucharist). "We
are all one," he declared rapturously at this ultimate sacrifice.[40] The moral of
these stories of death and sacrifice was clear: the death of an individual was
only the death of the separate self and thus not final for those committed to
the common cause.

Communist literary critics were satisfied to hear worker authors echoing arguments of Bolshevik intellectuals about the self and the other and demon-
strating in their own writings the natural collectivism of the proletariat. They
insisted that this was the norm. V. Kremnev, for example, writing in 1920, cer-
tified that "an understanding of the collectivist first principle is the most characteristic feature of proletarian poetry. . . . The word We is a banner, a symbol of profound inner significance for all proletarian poets. It is the leitmotif
of the Great Poem of the Revolution."[41] Similarly, a report by Vasilii Ignatov,
one of the organizers of the Proletcult, on the festive May Day opening of a
Palace of Proletarian Culture in Petrograd in 1918, informed readers that the
audience was especially delighted to hear readings by such worker poets as
Vladimir Kirillov, Aleksandr Pomorskii, and Nikifor Tikhomirov, as "their
songs . . . revealed the beauty of collective happiness."[42] Insistence on the pre-
dominance of a correct collectivist consciousness in workers' creative writings
after 1917 was nearly universal among Soviet literary critics.[43]

But was all this really the proper collectivist thinking that it appears to be?
Stereotypes about Russia's "impersonal-collective" cultural traditions,[44] assumptions about communism extinguishing the individual, efforts by Soviet
ideologists and cultural critics to demonstrate the adhesion of the new proletarian culture to this ideal, and superficial or selective readings of what

---

[39] I. Sadot'ev, "Za detei," *Griadushchee* 1920, no. 11: 5–6. See also "Kak umirali nashi to-
varishchi," *Zheleznyi put'* (Voronezh), no. 3 (25 Nov. 1918), 8–9.

[40] A. Kraiskii, "Navstrechu griadushchemu," *Ponisov'e*, no. 5 (1922), 3–4 (first published in
1918 in *Tribuna Proletkul'ta*).

[41] V. Kremnev, "Poema Velikoi Revoliutsii," *Kuznitsa*, no. 5–6 (October–November 1920),
64–65.

[42] Vasilii Ignatov, "Otkrytie Dvortsa Proletarskoi Kul'tury," *Griadushchee* 1918, no. 3 (June):
5.

[43] E.g., Valerian Polianskii [P. Lebedev-Polianskii], "Motivy rabochei poezii" (1918), in his *Na
literaturnom fronte* (Moscow, 1924), 34; V. L. L'vov-Rogachevskii, *Ocherki proletarskoi literatury* (Moscow and Leningrad, 1927), 75, 136–37, 142, 147.

[44] Fueloep-Miller, *Mind and Face of Bolshevism*, 8.

workers actually wrote conspire to make it easy to believe that worker writers—at least those who associated themselves with Bolshevism and the proletarian culture movement—were proper proletarian collectivists. The true picture is much more subtle and complicated. In fact, some contemporary cultural critics recognized that something was amiss in all the revolutionary talk about "We" and about individuals yielding up their selfhood and even their bodies and blood to the proletarian mass. Aleksandr Voronskii, in the 1920s the editor of the influential journal *Krasnaia nov'* (Red virgin soil), stated his suspicions bluntly: "Revolutionary phraseology about the dissolution of the individual personality into the 'collective,' into the cosmos, cannot hide the true content of these ideas. Their roots are mystical and individualistic."[45]

Epic Heroes of the Collective

The collectivism most often expressed in the writings of workers in these years was at the very least paradoxical. In part it was what it claimed to be—a politically proper understanding of the practical, historical, and moral primacy of collective struggle and collective interests. But it was also a glorification of the self, especially the masculine self—an apotheosis of the individual man as inspired and heroic champion, as superman. Aleksei Gastev's famous poem "We Grow Out of Iron" (often reprinted and frequently declaimed after its first publication in December 1917) illustrates graphically the dialogue and tension between collectivism and individualism that was common in these writings. The poem begins and ends (from title to final word) with the symbolic word "We," and the hero of the poem speaks to his fellow workers as comrades. But at the verbal and visual center of the poem stands the revolutionary leader's transfigured (indeed, phallicized) and increasingly transcendent "I," as iron blood flows into his veins and his swelling body grows so tall and mighty that his head penetrates the roof of the factory, reaching the height of the smokestacks.[46]

Images of glorified, even transfigured individual heroes coming to lead the people and redeem humanity pervaded workers' revolutionary writing. Of course, the very notion of the hero contains an inherent ambiguity in its simultaneous emphasis on individual exploits and service, even sacrifice, for others. Appropriately (for we see there the same ambiguity about self and collective), echoes of Nietzsche's exaltation of titanic, promethean, godlike indi-

[45] A. Voronskii, "O gruppe pisatelei 'Kuznitsa': Obshchaia kharakteristika," in *Iskusstvo i zhizn': Sbornik statei* (Moscow and Petrograd, 1924), 140.

[46] Aleksei Gastev, "My rastem iz zheleza." The poem is the lead piece in all editions of Gastev's *Poeziia rabochego udara*. In his preface to the 5th ed. (1924), Gastev states that the poem was written in 1914. It was first published, under the pseudonym I. Dozorov, in *Metallist* 1917, no. 7 (16 Dec.): 4.

viduals were plentiful in workers' writings in early Soviet Russia. Sometimes, like Gastev's iron man or Mikhail Gerasimov's giant worker striding across villages and seas, holding aloft a factory smokestack as a beacon,[47] these were metaphoric images of heroic leadership. Sometimes they were even more abstract images of new socialist "god-men."[48] The Nietzschean term "superman"—Russified (and gendered neutral, at least linguistically) as *sverkhchelovek*—would also occasionally be heard: "Love to you, super-man [*sverkhchelovek*]," declared Aleksei Kraiskii (Kuz′min) in a poem published in a Proletcult journal in 1918, "Lord of the mountains, seas and rivers / Of earth and air. Creator / Of both God and miracles!"[49] Of course, the Nietzschean superman was only one of many available images of mythic heroes whose echoes can be recognized in portrayals of the new revolutionary hero: Russian folkloric *bogatyry;* gods and titans from classical and Russian myth; prophets and miracle workers of the Old Testament; Christ and the saints; the more secular pantheon of actual and fictional heroes of the revolutionary movements of Russia and Europe; adventurers and heroes from literary and popular fiction; even the Bolshevik ideal of the "professional revolutionary" and Bolshevik poster images of striding revolutionary giants. A complex and eclectic mixture of images—all possessing their own particular mixture of collectivist and individualist aspirations—influenced individual worker authors to imagine their own heroic leaders and saviors of the people.

Some of these individual heroes were named. In 1919 Vladimir Kirillov, a former sailor who once journeyed to America, lionized Christopher Columbus for his bold defiance of conventional thinking and of the hesitations of even courageous sailors: "Titan of indestructible faith . . . / With fire-winged faith / You overtook the unknown." Reaching your goal, "You stood like a great god / And those who grumbled in vain / Crawled in the dust at your feet."[50] This was hardly the image of an insignificant cog in the collective machine. Among living heroes, of course, Lenin stood out. Numerous panegyrists of the new order portrayed Lenin as a mixture of selfless saint, all-powerful and all-knowing leader, and Christlike embodiment of both the people and God.[51] Typically, though, Lenin's individuality was portrayed paradoxically. As described by Andrei Platonov, for example, Lenin was at once self-denying and exalted in his self. "Lenin is a rare, perhaps singular person in the world. Such people are created by nature only once in centuries." Lenin's originality was visible in both his "single superhuman [*sverkhchelovecheskaia*] will" and in his "uncommon, miraculous heart," burning with love for hu-

[47] M. Gerasimov, "Zavodskaia truba," *Tvorchestvo,* no. 32 (July 1918), 3.

[48] In *Griadushchee* 1918, V. Kirillov, "Gorodu," no. 2 (May): 6; P. Bessal′ko, "O poezii krest′ianskoi i proletarskoi," no. 7 (October): 14; Knizhnik et al., "God bor′by za proletarskuiu kul′turu," no. 8: 17. See discussions of the popularity of this image by V. Friche in *Tvorchestvo,* no. 2 (June 1918), 6, and by P. Lebedev-Polianskii in *Proletarskaia kul′tura,* no. 17–19 (August–December 1920), 93.

[49] A. Kraiskii, "Liudi i solntse," *Griadushchee* 1918, no. 7 (October): 2.

[50] V. Kirillov, "Kolumb," *Mir i chelovek* (Kolpino), no. 1 (January 1919), 8.

[51] Nina Tumarkin, *Lenin Lives! The Lenin Cult in Soviet Russia* (Cambridge, Mass., 1983).

manity.[52] A typical commentary by a worker author published immediately after Lenin's death in 1924 represented Lenin's paradoxical individuality: a modest man, willing to sleep in cemeteries and in poor workers' apartments in order to serve the people, but also possessing "superhuman" (*nechelove-cheskie*—literally "nonhuman") powers. Omniscient, he could hear all the sufferings and voices of the past and foresee the future. Like a god, he had the "hurricane of strength needed to turn the wheel of the machines that change the face of the planet and the face of man himself."[53]

More commonly, heroes were neither metaphors nor actual great men but ideal-type images of the "Red heroes" of the new age. Amidst all the talk about individuals dissolving their particularities in the mass, there was as much public talk (often by the same people) about extraordinary individuals leading and saving the masses or embodying their spirit and mission. In his essays for the Voronezh press in 1920, Andrei Platonov repeatedly returned to the need for "heroes and leaders [*vozhdi*]" of the people. Although these heroes could be ordinary workmen whose whole lives were focused on their work and their families—one of Platonov's illustrations was his own father, Platon Klimentov—they were nonetheless invariably men of "will," with spirits of "iron," "endurance," and "manly courage" (*muzhestvo*).[54] Responding to those who reminded him, in the cliché of the time, that "we are all heroes now," Platonov replied that it was still necessary to glorify individual heroes—if we are all heroes, than there are "heroes among heroes."[55] With similar argument, Platonov's fiction of these years often portrayed willful, courageous individuals, such as the worker Markun or the engineer Vogulov, industrial Prometheuses striving to build machines to harness unprecedented amounts of concentrated energy.[56] Markun expresses unbounded faith in individual human will and power. He rhetorically addresses Archimedes, the Greek mathematician who is said to have emphasized the potential power of the lever by saying (in a bit of cosmic imagery that writers such as Platonov could well appreciate), "Give me a point to stand on and I can move the world." Markun declares that he found that place: "The most forceful force, the best lever, the most pointed point is inside me, in man. If you were to have moved the world, Archimedes, it would not have been a lever that would have done it, but you."[57]

[52] A. Platonov, "Lenin," *Krasnaia derevnia*, 11 Apr. 1920. See also Rabochii [Worker] A. Rumiantsev, "V. I. Leninu," *Tvorchestvo*, no. 7 (November 1918), 22.

[53] I. Filipchenko, "Lenin," *Rabochii zhurnal* 1924, no. 1: 56–73. See also G. Sannikov, "Leniniada," ibid., 8–12, and no. 2: 76–80; 1925, no. 1–2: 126–30; S. Obradovich, "Vozhd'," *Prozhektor* 1924, no. 2; idem, "Leninmai," *Pravda*, 1 May 1924; idem, "Mavzolei," *Pravda*, 31 Aug. 1924.

[54] A. Platonov, "Krasnye vozhdi," *Krasnaia derevnia*, 16 June 1920; idem, "Gosudarstvo—Eto my," *Voronezhskaia kommuna*, 7 Nov. 1920; idem, "Geroi truda." *Voronezhskaia kommuna*, 7 Nov. 1920.

[55] A. Platonov, "K chestvovaniiu geroev truda," *Voronezhskaia kommuna*, 12 Dec. 1920.

[56] A. Platonov, "Markun," *Kuznitsa*, no. 7 (December 1920–March 1921), 18–22 (rpt. in his *Sobranie sochinenii v trekh tomakh* [Moscow, 1984], 1:25–31); A. Platonov, "Satana mysli (Fantaziia)," *Put' kommunizma* (Krasnodar), no. 2 (March–April 1922), 32–37.

[57] A. Platonov, "Markun," *Kuznitsa*, no. 7 (December 1920–March 1921), 18–22.

As can be seen, this heroic ideal was explicitly gendered, rooted in what was assumed to be the essentially masculine attribute of forceful will. Recent scholarship has underscored the extent to which the early Soviet "new man" was constructed according to traditional masculine values of personality and sociability, indeed that much of postrevolutionary Soviet culture was pervaded with normative assertions of fraternal comradeship and heroic selfhood paired with a desire to purge from the new culture the disturbing forces of femininity and heterosexual eros.[58] Among worker writers, Platonov was most explicit in this gendered vision of progress. Socialists may talk about the equality of men and women, he wrote, but this is merely "a noble gesture . . . it is not the truth and never will be true." Woman is the "embodiment of the sexual" (*voploshchenie pola*), of the virtues of self-sacrifice and embracing love. Man is the embodiment of different virtues: courage and will. Human progress depends on this male spirit. In Platonov's words, "humankind is manly courage" (*chelovechestvo—eto muzhestvo*). Communism will emerge from the same source. Thus, Platonov declared, "communist society is chiefly a society of men."[59] The argument, of course, was figurative, even metaphorical, not literal. But it still expressed quite clearly a particular vision of the ideal self. As we have seen and will see again, many worker writers in these years continued to see the traditionally assumed forms of the female gender as representing a different sort of selfhood.

Bold communist heroes populated the imaginations of worker writers. Although these new model people served others, they were anything but insignificant "cogs" or "levers." Many poems written by workers imagined the arrival of saviors—sometimes Christlike healers and wise men, but more often powerful and willful heroes—to break the people's chains and lead the masses to the millennium. It was not just in the literary imaginations of workers that we see images of heroic selves. Worker authors often envisioned *themselves* as heroes and saviors—partly in their roles as public activists but especially in their roles as writers. Although Marxist intellectuals criticized the "bourgeois notion" of the writer as "prophet and leader,"[60] this familiar value was still strongly felt among lower-class writers, intensified by the fact that their talents seem to have come more from nature than from education and by their special stature in revolutionary Russia as creators of the new culture. While there is some evidence that this self-idealization as writers (or at least its public profession) was fading by the mid-1920s,[61] it was very strong in the first years after 1917, especially during the civil war. Pavel Bessal'ko, a metalworker with a long career in the Social Democratic underground and in exile, and also a prose writer and cultural critic, acknowledged the mystical,

---

[58] Eliot Borenstein, *Men without Women: Masculinity and Revolution in Russian Fiction, 1917–1929* (Durham, 2000).

[59] A. Platonov, "Budushchii oktiabr'," *Voronezhskaia kommuna*, 9 Nov. 1920.

[60] P. Lebedev-Polianskii, "Samodeiatel'nost ili v putiakh burzhuaznoi kul'tury," *Proletarskaia kul'tura*, no. 15–16 (April–July 1920), 44.

[61] In a 1923 letter to P. Ia. Zavolokin, who was publishing a collection on worker writers, Eroshin complained that some Proletcult poets had forgotten that "to be a poet is a Godly thing": RGALI, f. 1068, op. 1, d. 56, l. 220b.

even "messianic" romanticism with which worker writers (especially poets) tended to view their calling.[62] Even Bolshevik worker writers who voiced explicit support for the official collectivist myth frequently presented their own selves, as writers, in heroic and often mystical roles—not as dissolving into the mass but exalted above the mass. Vladimir Kirillov's poem "Brat'iam" (To my brothers), for example, is clearly addressed to the collective, but it is entirely about a glorified "I":

> I transform into the smiles of roses
> All of the pain, all of the horrors of your life.
> I collect in an imperishable chalice
> The crystal of precious tears.
> I transform your harsh daily labor
> Into a magnificent holiday. . . .
> I am the echo of your rebellious soul.
> I am the rays of future beauty.[63]

Other worker writers described the poet (especially the worker poet) as a "messiah," a "bright genius," a fire-breathing, sun-bearing bard "dancing in the heavenly firmament," a "winged god" bringing inspiration and wisdom to the people.[64] In a skit performed at a workers' club in 1924, even a modest "worker-peasant correspondent" (*rabkor*) became an immortal prophet— or at least a mythic hero, for he was named Hercules—invulnerable to every attempt to murder him by those whose failings he exposed.[65]

Complicating any simple reading of such heroic individualism, the heroic figures described in workers' writings were almost always paradoxical individualities, who magnified themselves by serving others, humbled themselves in order to elevate their selves. Nikolai Torba's "new heroes" were typical. Like Christian saints or legendary populist revolutionaries (Nikolai Chernyshevskii's fictional Rakhmetov being the most influential archetype), these new heroes were ascetics, chastening their flesh in order to elevate their souls, to raise their inner selves above the everyday and the ordinary. "For them, what the animal body values—the pleasures of food, reproduction, sexual satisfaction, security, domination over others—has little essential value." This asceticism, this self-abasement, was ultimately elevating, however; it was a means to and a mark of their greatness. No less important, these heroes remained different from others in order to be able to lead or save them. They

[62] P. Bessal'ko, "Proletarskie poety," *Griadushchee* 1919, no. 1: 12.

[63] V. Kirillov, "Bratiam," *Zhizn' iskusstva* (Kologriv) 1918, no. 1: 1; rpt. by Petrograd Proletcult in Vladimir Kirillov, *Stikhotvoreniia, 1914–1918* (Petersburg [sic], 1918), 17. For an even more explicit focus on his own poetic genius, see his "Drugu-kritiku," *Kuznitsa*, no. 9 (1922), 17–18.

[64] See, e.g., I. Tachalov, "Dva mira (Poema)," *Ponizov'e* (Samara), no. 5 (1922), 7–11; P. Bessal'ko, "Proletarskie poety," *Griadushchee* 1919, no. 1: 12; N. Degterev, "Moia dusha," *Proletkul'tovets* (Moscow province), no. 1 (October 1920), 1.

[65] *Rabochii klub* 1924, no. 3–4 (March–April): 63–64.

possessed "consciousness and wisdom" and for this others would follow them, rewarding them with "faith and love." This was not equality or the dissolution of individual difference, Torba acknowledged, but "a new form of inequality and compulsion," needed so that humanity might continue along the road to "perfection."[66] Similarly, Andrei Platonov, in an essay he wrote for the Voronezh railway workers' journal in 1919, elaborated the rebirth on a higher plane of the individual self through love of others. In the bourgeois epoch, he argued, everything was focused on oneself, on animal-like physical needs and drives. Under socialism, "in place of this pitiful corporeal personality [*telesnaia lichnost'*], which any big dog could have fulfilled in 'the tender arms of Abraham,' arises a great, spiritual, social personality, which sees itself in others and therefore loves others as one loves oneself."[67]

In sacrificial death, too, the individual could be elevated and glorified. While death in struggle, as we have seen, was sometimes presented as the ultimate sacrifice of individuality, it was also often seen as the ultimate glorification of the heroic individual. When Il'ia Sadof'ev tells a comrade, as they face death during the civil war, "You and I will be eternal,"[68] there is a sense of individual transcendence and immortality as well as of readiness for sacrifice for the collective. The same may be said of the many references to the resurrection and immortality of dead revolutionary fighters. As it was said to be for Christ—and the analogy is not inappropriate when we consider the self-identities of many worker writers—in supreme sacrifice lay the greatest personal glory, the ultimate elevation of the self.

The conclusion to Platonov's tale about the energy-harnessing worker Markun reveals such a mystical and paradoxical transfiguration of the individual. In a dream inspired by a "flame," Markun is led to look beyond the physical limitations of his own self (a lesson reinforced symbolically when his machine explodes because it generates more energy than its physical structure can bear). The dream-flame "left in his soul" an idea that "changed him": the realization that "to man was given everything, but that he has taken only a little." To take it all, Markun "destroys" his separate self and "dissolves" it in the world.[69] But was this simple or proper collectivism? We certainly see a discontented view of the individual, a protest against its limitations. But this remains, typically, a paradoxical denial of self. Markun "dissolves" his self into the world in order to further his self, to "win the world." In opposition to the narrow, philistine individualism of the bourgeoisie, one might say, this was a new cosmic individualism. Frequent criticism by Marxist critics of the pervasiveness of the abstract and the mythic in so much proletarian writing partly reflected a recognition that ideological errors were often hidden behind the face of radical collectivism. Voronskii was not alone in seeing a "mystical

---

[66] N. Torba, "Neravenstvo i nasilie," *Griadushchee* 1920, no. 5–6: 16–17.

[67] A. Platonov, "K nachinaiushchim proletarskim poetam i pisateliam," *Zheleznyi put'* (Voronezh), no. 9 (April 1919), 25.

[68] I. Sadof'ev, "Sil'nye smerti," *Griadushchee* 1921, no. 1–3: 27.

[69] A. Platonov, "Markun," *Kuznitsa*, no. 7 (December 1920–March 1921), 18–22.

and individualistic" inspiration for much revolutionary discourse about the dissolution of the individual into the collective. In a sharply critical review of the first issue of the Samara Proletcult journal, *Zarevo zavodov* (The glow of the factories, 1919), Pavel Lebedev-Polianskii, then national chairman of the Proletcult, observed the "un-Marxist fashion" in which too many proletarian authors romanticized "genius" and "heroes."[70] He expanded on this idea a couple of months later in reviewing, with a good deal of sarcasm, the whole flood of poetry emerging out of provincial Proletcult organizations:

> All of the authors are imbued with deep love for the proletariat. It could not be otherwise. But not one of them is capable of presenting the figure of a real living worker, either from the past or from our present revolutionary period. We see either idealists, fighters for "the great holy truth," or titans and geniuses who "create fire out of ice crystals." We see either workers cursing their fate, cursing their "coerced labor," or "a mighty force—elemental power, a hurricane."[71]

The often described cultural shift in the 1930s to the romantic and mythic heroism of socialist realism, to the "cult of the *extra* ordinary" promethean hero,[72] may well be traced back to the very beginnings of Soviet culture. As a narrative of pure collectivism, however, it remained, at least at its origins, paradoxically individualistic and self-absorbed.

Self-Realization

The persistence and elaboration among worker intellectuals of the prerevolutionary humanistic "cult of man" (*kul't cheloveka, kul't lichnosti*) also continued to encourage a preoccupation with the individual self and personality. One continued to hear the familiar prerevolutionary discourse about the "dignity of man,"[73] the sacredness of all human beings, and the natural equality and rights that ensued from it: "We too are people / We need the sun / Within us is an immortal spirit / Within us is the spark of heaven."[74] Sometimes, especially in the first months after October, the moral claim to universal human dignity and rights and the moral challenge to social relations and structures that humiliated and degraded workers' human selves were directed against Bolshevik abuses. Petr Oreshin, who had been associated in 1917 with the Socialist Revolutionary party, told a story of the emotional and moral cri-

---

[70] *Proletarskaia kul'tura*, no. 6 (February 1919), 47.

[71] V. Polianskii [P. Lebedev-Polianskii], "Poeziia sovetskoi provintsii," *Proletarskaia kul'tura*, no. 7–8 (April–May 1919), 49.

[72] See Katerina Clark, "Utopian Anthropology as a Context for Stalinist Literature," in *Stalinism: Essays in Historical Interpretation*, ed. Robert C. Tucker (New York, 1977), esp. 183–92, and *The Soviet Novel: History as Ritual* (Chicago, 1981).

[73] V. Kirillov, "Griadushchee," *Pravda*, 13 Nov. 1917; also in Kirillov, *Stikhotvoreniia, 1914–1918*, 15–17.

[74] S. Potekhin, "Somknemsia druzhno . . . ," in *V bure i plameni* (Iaroslavl, 1918), 53.

sis of a peasant who kills a man during the revolution (a story with strong echoes of the moral quandary about murder that Dostoevsky explored in *The Brothers Karamazov*). The peasant kills a local landowner, known for his brutality, in defense of another peasant whom the rich man was beating. He meditates on possible justifications for this act: the landowner was cruel; he was assaulting a man; these things happen in revolution. But he concludes that these are excuses, not moral justifications. They cannot free him from his guilt for having killed another human being. Only by denying his own human self could he be absolved of this sin. But if he denied his humanness, he would be nothing—and neither, he implied, would the revolution.[75] In early 1918, Ivan Kubikov, still an active Menshevik, deployed such humanistic ethics even more directly against the Bolsheviks. In much the same language and with the same logic as Gorky was then using in his columns in *Novaia zhizn'* (New life),[76] Kubikov chastised the Bolsheviks for trying to legitimize "lynching and animal-like brutality" as acts of "class struggle"—which Kubikov understood in its humanistic sense as a struggle for humanity and hence as tied to all-human moral values. Such behaviors reflect the "mentality of slaves," not the "spiritual nobility" of human beings.[77]

Among most worker writers who supported the revolution, however, this humanistic ideal was focused less on immediate moral questions than on a more sweeping spiritual identification of the individual with all humanity. These writings were filled with idealized images of "man" (*chelovek* and *chelovechestvo)* and with talk about the all-human (*obshchechelovecheskii* or *vsechelovecheskii*) nature of the revolution and of the emerging proletarian culture.[78] The conscious proletarian was said to be one with all of human life. The classic humanist maxim "Nihil humani a me alienum puto"[79] was repeated constantly. The leaders of a factory Proletcult in Tula, for example, writing just after the end of the civil war, declared that "the proletarian is not only a fighter but also a human being, and nothing human is alien to him."[80] Valerian Pletnev even officially defined the Proletcult's cultural tasks as emerging from this embracing proletarian spirit: "Nothing human is alien to the proletariat."[81]

---

[75] P. Oreshin, "Koriavyi," *Rabochii mir*, no. 14 (1 Oct. 1918), 4–8.

[76] Maxim Gorky, *Untimely Thoughts: Essays on Revolution, Culture, and the Bolsheviks, 1917–1918* (New Haven, 1995).

[77] I. Kubikov, "Klassovaia bor'ba i zhestokost'," *Rabochaia mysl'*, no. 2–3 (7–8), 16 Mar. (3 Mar.) 1918, 11–12.

[78] In addition to examples below, see A. Smirnov, "Uragan," in *V bure i plameni*, 58; appeal from Association of Proletarian Writers (Cosmist) in *Pereval*, no. 1 [1922].

[79] The old credo "Nothing human is alien to me," attributed to the Roman playwright (and former slave) Terence, was long a favorite of humanists, from Montaigne to Marx. Marx told his daughter Laura that this was his "favorite maxim": from a manuscript rpt. in Erich Fromm, *Marx's Conception of Man* (New York, 1966), 257.

[80] *Osen' bagrianaia*, vi–viii.

[81] V. Pletnev, "Sovremennyi moment i zadachi proletkul'ta: K chitatel'iam-rabochim," *Gorn*, no. 6 (1922), 27. See also Platonov's remark that for the truly "alive" everything has beauty and "nothing is shocking" (*dlia zhivogo net bezobraziia*): Andrei Platonov, *Golubaia glubina* (Krasnodar, 1922), viii.

Such talk about the proletariat being one with humanity was pervasive in worker writers' discussions of socialism and socialist culture. Andrei Platonov, in his newspaper essays for Voronezh peasants and workers, portrayed the revolution as replacing all classes and nations with "one humanity," building "a shining and joyous temple of humanity," inaugurating the "reign of man," specifically of humanity empowered by science and technology, and promoting an intellectual and spiritual power that would enable man to transform nature itself.[82] Drawing on the Marxist dialectic, Platonov explained how out of the most violent and cruel class struggle the most radiant and humane new order would emerge: after "burning the corpse of the bourgeoisie in the fires of the revolution," the proletariat is bringing to the world the "epoch of the renaissance of the human spirit." Unlike the culture of the rich, which was merely "handmaid and apologist for restaurant and stock-exchange orgies," the culture of the victorious proletariat is the "bearer of everything eternal in humanity."[83]

The embracive collectivism of this ethical vision, however, still led worker writers to a preoccupation with the individual self, though the emphasis was shifting. When worker writers, especially those associated with the Proletcult, elaborated on the ideals of human dignity and rights after 1917, they turned increasingly from exploring the ethical imperatives for society of the sanctity of the person to exploring the heightened possibilities for individual self-realization now that the repressive old order had been overthrown. Indeed, this was said to be a central promise of the revolution and its most immediate task. "The revolution has turned inward," declared an editorial in the Proletcult journal *Griadushchee* (The future).[84] Or, as a female garment worker, employing a favorite metaphor of the day, put it in a letter to a Proletcult journal in 1919, "Now, to each one of us is given the possibility of gazing at the light."[85]

The message that the revolution had broken the fetters restricting personal self-realization was often reiterated in publications directed at workers. The leaders of the Proletcult in the industrial town of Kolpino, for example, called their journal *Mir i chelovek* (The world and man) to emphasize their goal of helping workers "feel themselves to be human beings in the most noble and proud meaning of that concept."[86] Leaders of a Proletcult established in an arms factory in Tula in 1921 similarly asserted that socialism, especially now that the civil war was over, was about living "with all the fullness of life."[87] People of the lower classes had been denied this natural right under the old

[82] A. Platonov, "Dva mira," *Krasnaia derevnia*, 8 June 1920; "Lenin," ibid., 11 Apr. 1920; A. P. [Platonov], "Chto takoe elektrifikatsiia," ibid., 13 Oct. 1920 (see also "O nauke," ibid., 25 June 1920); A. Platonov, "Proletarskaia poeziia," *Kuznitsa*, no. 9 (1922), 30.

[83] A. Platonov, "K nachinaiushchim proletarskim poetam i pisateliam," *Zheleznyi put'* (Voronezh), no. 9 (April 1919), 25–26.

[84] *Griadushchee* 1919, no. 7–8: 1.

[85] A. I. Andrievskaia, letter to *Gorn*, no. 2–3 (1919), 108.

[86] *Mir i chelovek*, no. 1 (January 1919), 1.

[87] *Osen' bagrianaia*, vi–viii.

order. As Andrei Platonov explained in responding to criticism of his poetry by a well-educated and socially elite literary critic, "For you it is a matter of habit to be a human being. But for me it is a rarity and a festival."[88]

Especially toward the end of the civil war and into the early 1920s, worker writers regularly explored the possibilities and meanings of human self-realization and self-fulfillment. A terminology of self-development became much more in evidence as plebeian authors wrote of pursuing "self-perfection" (*samosovershestvovanie*), of becoming a "new person," of developing "the 'spiritual,' psychic essence of the human person," of "being born again" to a new world of beauty, of "creating a new man—a beautiful, bright, dignified ruler of nature," of "creating a harmoniously beautiful person [*garmonichno prekrasnyi chelovek*]."[89] Inner transformation was seen as essential to progress. As Platonov put it, over the course of a series of essays on the subject written during the early 1920s, "For the world to become new" every person must "feel that he is not now what he was before." He must become more human, "more perfect." His "essence" must become different. "His very inward center must move."[90]

In portrayals by worker writers, this "new person" (a key ideal in early Soviet culture that has often been described schematically and stereotypically) was rarely merely one of the mass but almost always an extraordinary, often heroic figure. The new person was said to have individuality and character, to be strong in self-confidence and will, and to rise above the common man. Valerian Pletnev, then head of the Proletcult, contrasted the "individualism" of the *obyvatel'*, of the ordinary, everyday person, to the spirit of proletarian individuality. The obyvatel' faces life with fear and a lack of will; in illustration he quotes the folk saying "Den' proshel i slava Bogu" (The day is done and thank God for that). He has narrow mental horizons, is fetishistically attached to habitual ways of thinking and acting, is always a "slave of the strong," and fears standing up for his own opinions. The model proletarian is none of these things.[91] Like Nietzsche, these writers despised the slave mentality as the greatest insult to human possibility: "There is no greater shame than to be a slave," Platonov wrote.[92]

Even to be common and ordinary was seen as pitiable. Hence, as before 1917, though often now with a more radical pathos fed by a revolution that called for proletarian consciousness and heroism, these writers tended to feel

---

[88] Letter quoted in the introduction to Platonov, *Golubaia glubina,* viii.

[89] A. Sh., "L. N. Tol'stoi," *Revoliutsionnye vskhody,* no. 7–8 (December 1920), 10; A. Platonov, "Vospitanie kommunistov," *Krasnaia derevnia,* 30 July 1920, and "Kul'tura proletariata," *Voronezhskaia kommuna,* 20 Oct. 1920; Rabochii [Worker] Porokhovik, in *Griadushchaia kul'tura,* no. 3 (January 1919), 13; Grishkin (a "peasant" member of a proletarian club's literary circle), *Revoliutsionnye vskhody,* no. 3–4 (October 1920), 4; statement by Kuznitsa group, *Kuznitsa,* no. 7 (December 1920–March 1921), 2.

[90] A. Platonov, "Vospitanie kommunistov," *Krasnaia derevnia,* 30 July 1920; "O nauke," *Krasnaia derevnia,* 25 June 1920; "Proletarskaia poeziia," *Kuznitsa,* no. 9 (1922), 28.

[91] V. Pletnev, "Chto takoe obyvatel': Tesizy doklada, 12/XI-1923," RGALI, f. 1230, op. 1, d. 468, l. 36–36ob.

[92] A. Platonov, "Poslednii vrag," *Krasnaia derevnia,* 3 June 1920.

contempt for the common order of human beings. Worker writers continued to voice their painful alienation from the ordinary workers around them. According to Aleksei Mashirov, the "hardest years" of his life were his early years as a worker, when he first encountered the "drunkenness, debauchery, and crudity" of workmen and supervisors alike. This initiation into the moral life of his own class left in his memory, he wrote, "dark traces."[93] This was a common theme in autobiographies—a genre that proliferated after October, often at the request of Communist intellectuals interested in promoting proletarian creativity and recording narratives of working-class awakening. Many of these worker autobiographers recalled something like Pavel Druzhinin's appalled recognition (as a rural factory worker, an unskilled laborer in Moscow, and a tramp wandering the country) of the pervasive human degradation among Russia's ordinary folk: "low, dark instincts and repulsive passions," animating "bitter people" who had lost "all semblance of being alive and every sign of their individuality."[94] Gorky's stories of the everyday and pervasive ignorance, egoism, and brutishness of lower-class Russians had, of course, made such stories and their moral lessons familiar to many literate Russians. But worker authors could also easily draw on their own experiences in the social world and their own ambitions to be elevated above the world of their origins.

As such life stories begin to suggest, the new person was often viewed as marked by essential inward difference. Thus, when these workers narrated their own stories of awakening to consciousness or told tales about formally fictional workers awakened to the possibilities of a changed world, they tended to describe uncommon life experiences and uncommon personal capacities. The discovery of their offended human dignity was only the first step. Since these were individuals who went on to write poetry or fiction, almost all of them spoke, in trying to explain this avocation, of an "inner voice" or of an "inner need to express" themselves, or even of natural "sparks of creativity" in their "souls."[95] This obvious echo of the Romantic ideal of the self as expressive of nature was derided by the Proletcult chairman Lebedev-Polianskii as reflecting the old "bourgeois" notion of the writer as a person of a "higher essence, derived from God," revealing truths to the "crowd and rabble."[96]

It is striking how rarely we see the classic Marxist narrative of awakening: workers becoming conscious through pride in labor or in daily toil and shoulder-to-shoulder struggle beside their class comrades. Instead, the path to

---

[93] S. A. Rodov, ed., *Proletarskie pisateli* (Moscow, 1925), 548–49.

[94] P. Ia. Zavolokin, ed., *Sovremennye raboche-krest'ianskie poety* (Ivanovo-Voznesensk, 1925), 237; RGALI, f. 1068, op. 1, d. 54, l. 1.

[95] Rodov, *Proletarskie pisateli*, 434 (Nechaev); RGALI, f. 1068, op. 1, d. 56, l. 5 (Eroshin); Zavolokin, *Sovremennye raboche-krest'ianskie poety*, 15, 62, 128; V. Korolev, "Tvorets-Proletarii," in *V bure i plameni*, 3.

[96] P. Lebedev-Polianskii, "Samodeiatel'nost ili v putiakh burzhuaznoi kul'tury," *Proletarskaia kul'tura*, no. 15–16 (April–July 1920), 44–45. Ivan Golikov uses almost these exact words in describing his own youthful view of writers as "special people, endowed with a divine spark": RGALI, f. 1068, op. 1, d. 41, l. 3.

consciousness was typically described as a way of strangeness and wandering—of isolated reading and thinking, of alienation from the everyday world around them, and of inward searching and transformation. For Aleksei Mashirov, amidst the "drunkenness, debauchery, and crudity" all around him, the only "bright spots" were the few "conscious workers" who introduced him to the ideas of socialism.[97] This awakening was often, as before the revolution, more lonely: Ivan Ustinov described a worker sitting up late at night in his damp and cockroach-infested cellar apartment, reading while card players reveled in the room next door.[98] After the revolution as before, conscious and cultured workers often felt their alienation from the unchanged masses.[99] We see this intellectual and moral trajectory in a story by a member of a Petrograd workers' club. The tale's hero is a young shoemaker who inhabits a harrowing world of noise, shouts, demands, and the daily "wild dance of anger, vain cries and tears, and uncontrollable silent sobbing." He suddenly thinks, "Where is the true meaning of life? Where? Why do I feel this weight here in my chest? I long for something strong and good! What does life give me? What does it give me and what do I give to it?" He imagines himself screaming or running away from this life as "images and thoughts move and swirl in his head." Finally his feverish reverie is shattered by the shouts of his boss: "Iashka! Iashka! What the hell are you doing!? If you want to work, then work, don't think. . . . I don't pay you for nothing!" When Iashka goes home, his wife, who has heard about his scolding, also berates him for working badly. The author reflects: "No one knows and no one wants to know his thoughts, yet they are bursting within him, tugging at him, bubbling up inside, beckoning to him. How to live? What to do? 'Life is repugnant to me,' a voice within him speaks. When will it end?" The author has no real answer other than the clichéd conclusion that this was night—a portrayal of the prerevolutionary past—and dawn was surely coming.[100]

Wandering—as escape, searching, and self-assertion—was a leitmotif in most of these stories. Echoing familiar cultural stories of pilgrims, vagabonds, literary explorers, and the like, these writers typically described their own histories of individual wandering as a moral and existential journey in search of "the meaning of human life."[101] And by uprooting themselves they also turned wandering into a test of will and mettle and a means of exposing themselves to the world in order to find themselves and their place in it. Ivan Nazarov, for example, recalled that he was so disgusted with the crass everyday world of workers and bosses in his native Suzdal that he fled to a monastery and became a monk. When he did not find the answers he was seeking and became bored with the monk's life, he went into the world and began

---

[97] Rodov, *Proletarskie pisateli,* 548–49.

[98] I. Ustinov, "Noch'iu," *Tvorchestvo,* no. 6 (October 1918), 20.

[99] Rabochii [Worker] Porokhovik, in *Griadushchaia kul'tura,* no. 3 (January 1919), 13.

[100] Rabochii [Worker] F. B., "Pered rassvetom (Iz proshlogo)," *Revoliutsionnye vskhody,* no. 5–6 (November 1920), 12–13.

[101] Mikhail Kiriushkin, autobiography, in RGALI, f. 1068, op. 1, d. 72, l. 1.

"wandering" (*peredvizhenie*).[102] Aleksandr Golovin, who also became a religious pilgrim and then an itinerant laborer, recalls that at the age of thirteen, he and a group of friends, bored by everyday life and their minds filled with the popular adventure stories by Mayne Reid and the tales of the detective Nat Pinkerton, set out on foot for Africa (from Vilna they managed to get only as far as Grodno).[103] Aleksei Solov'ev, a construction worker, similarly told of "fleeing" the "petty and monotonous" life of the urban working class—inspired, he admitted, partly by popular stories he had read about bandits, heroes, and adventurers—to "tramp around old Rus'" (*brodiazhit' po Rusi*). But he soon discovered that he preferred the phantoms of literature to real people. Among real bandits he found no "beauty and heroism," only "disgrace [*merzost'*], conceit, and pettiness." As for ordinary working folk, after wandering throughout the country, he admitted to having met "few good people," though he had read many "good books."[104] Other worker writers similarly voiced a greater closeness, as one did in a letter to Gorky, to the "beloved volumes" in his "poor worker's library" than to people.[105]

A characteristic tale of alienation, wandering, and transcendence was Nikolai Liashko's 1919 story "S otaroi" (With the flock). The hero and narrator, a literate and cultured worker, is forced to work as a common shepherd. His employer makes jokes about his going into the field with books instead of a switch. And the locals wonder who and what is this literate shepherd who refuses bribes, does not drink, and on holidays "goes off somewhere, looking everywhere, seeking something." Faced with his individuality and his restless searching, the local community (the other "flock" in this story) decides that he must be a thief—the archetypal image in village legal culture of an individual living beyond community norms.[106] At the story's end, the hero is left gazing into the sky. Others took to the sky even more dramatically. Ivan Eroshin told the story of a working-class child obsessed with birds, for he desperately wanted to fly himself.[107] Some succeeded in their imaginative writing. Mikhail Gerasimov depicted himself flying with "frail wings" above mountains, seas, Scandinavian fjords, and native fields, finding beauty, mystery, and inspiration, until (with echoes of Icarus's flight) his "soul garbed in spring," in radiant "cascades of light," he soars so high he burns.[108] Petr Oreshin became one with the moon and joined it in flight above the earth.[109]

[102] RGALI, f. 1068, op. 1, d. 106, ll. 23–24.

[103] A. Golovin, "Zhizn' (Rasskaz rabochego)," *Tvorchestvo*, no. 3 (June 1918), 7–8. Grodno is about a hundred miles southwest of Vilna, in the northwestern region of the Russian empire.

[104] Zavolokin, *Sovremennye raboche-krest'ianskie poety*, 214.

[105] Rabochii [Worker] V. Sparskii, open letter to M. Gor'kii, *Sotsial-demokrat*, 25 Nov. (8 Dec.) 1917. See also Zavolokin, *Sovremennye raboche-krest'ianskie poety*, 237; RGALI, f. 1068, op. 1, d. 54, l. 1 (P. D. Druzhinin); and comments by Ivan Eroshin on the impact of "wandering" on his mental world, RGALI, f. 1068, op. 1, d. 56, l. 5.

[106] N. Liashko, "S otaroi," *Rabochii mir*, no. 2–3 (February 1919), 6–11. On thieves and the village community, see Stephen Frank, "Popular Justice, Community, and Culture among the Russian Peasantry, 1870–1900," *Russian Review* 46, no. 3 (1987): 239–65.

[107] I. Eroshin, "Detstvo (Rasskaz rabochego)," *Tvorchestvo*, no. 4 (August 1918), 10–11.

[108] M. Gerasimov, "Vzlet," in *Zavod vesennii* (Moscow, 1919), 47.

[109] P. Oreshin, "Mesiatsu sinemu," *Rabochii mir*, no. 8 (7 July 1918), 3.

Culture, especially books, was often central to these portrayals of self-realization. Fedor Kalinin quoted Nietzsche on the power of books to "burn thought into oneself" and to teach the proletariat to "think for themselves."[110] And to almost all of these writers, the essential and proper purpose of literature was, as Nikolai Liashko put it, the "spiritual" development of the personality. This was the reason that worker intellectuals such as Liashko were so hostile to the boulevard fiction and crass entertainment that continued to predominate in Russian popular culture. As he argued in an extensive critique, publishers of cheap, sensationalist commercial fiction (which Liashko grouped under the contemptuous label "Pinkertonovshchina," after the popular genre of stories about the American detective Nat Pinkerton) distort readers' psychology, encouraging them "to seek in books not ideas or images, but simply horrible facts." If such literature—created only to make money, thus shamefully turning "the word" into a mere "commodity"—teaches readers anything about the self, it is only to encourage "narrow egoism." Liashko similarly chastised much of the rest of popular commercial culture (especially "pornographic" literature and the cinema) for ruining the tastes and values of the masses rather than inspiring healthy feelings and facilitating "spiritual growth."[111] Other writers extended the critique even to the "entertainment" programs of workers' clubs and soviets, with their dances, masquerades, and "philistine theatricals."[112]

In this spirit, almost every memoir written in these years identified books (and occasionally the periodical press) as catalysts that awakened them to their own dignity, their capacity for self-improvement, their inner genius, and the need to fight against insult. The glassworker Egor Nechaev, for example, recalled that one day when he was seventeen years old his mother, a domestic, brought home leftovers from her employer's dinner wrapped in the pages of an old magazine that happened to contain the autobiography, portrait, and verses of the self-taught shopkeeper-poet Ivan Surikov. Nechaev was already an inspired reader of boulevard literature (he recalled such works as *The Living Dead, Eruslan Lazarevich,* and *Ataman Bear Paw*), which, he said, first "awoke" him to awareness that the oppressed can stand up. Now his encounter with this new sort of text, which he read "feverishly," evoked still higher thoughts: an "inner voice" told him that he too could become a writer.[113] Nikolai Kuznetsov, whose parents were textile workers near Moscow, recalled that as a child left to wander the streets he found himself uncontrollably drawn to book kiosks, where he would stand and stare at the books behind the windows, even before he had learned to read.[114] As a boy,

---

[110] F. Kalinin, "O kul'turno-prosvetitel'naia rabota proletariata," *Metallist,* no. 7 (16 Dec. 1917), 7–8.

[111] N. Liashko, "Dukhovnye iady," *Rabochii mir,* no. 15 (13 Oct. 1918), 28–29.

[112] I. Kubikov, "Kul'tura i tipografskie rabochie," *Pechatnoe delo,* no. 24 (13 July 1918), 3–4.

[113] Nechaev, autobiography written in 1921, in Rodov, *Proletarskie pisateli,* 434. Aleksei Sokolov describes a similarly inspiring encounter with Kol'tsov, in Zavolokin, *Sovremennye rabochekrest'ianskie poety,* 62.

[114] Zavolokin, *Sovremennye raboche-krest'ianskie poety,* 128.

Il'ia Sadof'ev wrote, he thought books were written not by ordinary people living on earth but by "winged angels."[115]

Numerous worker writers recalled voraciously and passionately reading everything they came upon: from Pinkerton to Pushkin, Jules Verne to Nikolai Nekrasov, the lives of the saints to Gorky, boulevard newspapers to "moral-spiritual" tracts and the Bible. The phrase "I read everything that I could lay my hands on" was repeated word for word in many of these memoirs. In these diverse texts, these workers tell us, they discovered new worlds of possibility and fantasy—places to which they might escape and find companions, places to nurture inward feelings and find ideas and new knowledge, images of the "true human being," stories of adventure and defiance, and the inspiring idea that they themselves might write.[116] As before 1917, some of these workers also took a certain pride in the particular sufferings this pursuit of knowledge and self cost them. Il'ia Sadof'ev, for example, wrote that at the age of ten he was given an "exemplary thrashing" by his father for "the shame of wanting to be a scribbler," a beating so severe that he was confined to bed for two weeks. Sergei Obradovich recalls being repeatedly tormented by his foreman for writing poems on scraps of paper. Some workers even claimed to torture themselves out of devotion—denying themselves food, for example, in order to save money to buy books.[117]

Other cultural forms were sometimes identified as sources of personal "spiritual" growth as well—art museums, for example, which elevated Mashirov's "soul" into a "winged bird."[118] Or music: Ivan Eroshin was inspired by the religious songs he sang in the church choir as a boy.[119] One beginning worker writer—a young woman who was a member of the workers' club of the Kostroma Proletcult—told an elaborate story of awakening inspired while she was listening to her fellow club member Vladimir Zafran playing the piano. As she listened, a painful memory was awakened, but one that now had new, more positive meaning. Once, while walking by the home of a wealthy family, she had stopped to listen to the music being played inside on a piano. Even after the music stopped, she remained on the spot, evidently still captivated by the sounds. The "rich lady" (*baryshnia*) who had been playing came to the window. When she "saw the figure of a poorly dressed girl lurking like a thief beside the window, she indolently laughed."[120] While possibly a true story, it was told as an obvious moral allegory of an emerging

---

[115] Ibid., 54.

[116] Ibid., 15 (Shkulev), 37 (Arskii), 53 (Sadof'ev), 62 (Sokolov), 115 (Alekseevskii), 180 (Golikov), 213 (Solov'ev), 237 (Druzhinin); RGALI, f. 1068, op. 1, d. 27, l. 2 (Vitkovskaia, who, in her manuscript autobiography, writes the names of her favorite authors with particular care and flourish); d. 30, l. 4–4ob. (Volkov); d. 41, ll. 3–4 (Golikov); d. 54, ll. 1–2 (Druzhinin, unpublished 1918 version of his autobiography); d. 56, l. 5 (Eroshin); d. 72, l. 1 (Kiriushkin); d. 152, ll. 2–3 (Sokolov); d. 193, l. 6 (Sannikov).

[117] Zavolokin, *Sovremennye raboche-krest'ianskie poety,* 53–54, 76.

[118] Samobytnik [A. Mashirov], "V muzee," *Griadushchee* 1920, no. 1–2:22.

[119] RGALI, f. 1068, op. 1, d. 56, l. 5.

[120] *Sbornik Kostromskogo proletkul'ta,* no. 1 (1919), 37.

inner self facing the self-satisfied mockery of those who stood beyond the social walls and windows that kept the poor outside and apart. In the Proletcult club, with a worker at the piano, she was now on the inside where her imaginative and emotional self would be encouraged, not mocked.

Stories of women's journeys of self-discovery and self-fulfillment were beginning to be included more regularly in this discourse. And even more than before 1917, emphasis was placed on the violation of women's dignity as human beings, as opposed to the violation of their particular innocence and virtue as women. In 1920, for example, Sergei Obradovich published a story describing the personal emancipation of a young working woman he called Ol'ga. She had suffered horribly as a child, including being sexually abused by her father. But exposure to books and to talk about new ideas awakened in her a sense of self-respect and autonomy. And as she is transformed within, she becomes more graceful and beautiful without. Ultimately she decides to leave her lover, a radical worker who taught her most of these new ideas and is also the father of her child. In a climactic scene, while nursing this baby, Ol'ga explains her decision:

> I began to live with him after the strike, do you remember? At first we lived fine, we got along. He patiently taught me things, lectured me about equal rights and the equality of women, and we studied Bebel. But after half a year, I became for him merely a thing, a piece of property. . . . What happened in my consciousness led me to what was real. When my own "I" could no longer reconcile itself to the everyday grind [*obydenshchina*], I mentioned living on my own and I began to put into life what he taught me. Our paths went different ways. We fought. After one crude and bitter fight, during which he criticized me, reproached me about my past, I left him.[121]

In many ways this tale was clearly a product of the post-1917 period: its heightened attention to women's self-discovery and assertion; the greater explicitness of the language of self-awakening (the vocabulary of "consciousness" and of nurturing one's "own 'I'"), and especially the readiness to apply this vocabulary to women. And the emphasis was now more than ever on the practical assertion of self. But the core value remained recognizably that of an older but still powerful discourse: the self as the ultimate source of identity, moral meaning, and life purpose.

The Intimate Self

One notes also a persistent, even growing, attention to the inward and personal self as the key to forming a new person and a new society. No less than before the revolution, though now with more problematic political significance, plebeian authors were preoccupied with the inner emotional and moral

---

121 S. Obradovich, "Perevorot," *Kuznitsa,* no. 4 (August–September 1920), 29.

world of the individual, and especially of their own selves. At one of the regular "Sunday conversations" at the Literary Studio of the Moscow Proletcult in the spring of 1919, some writers praised Obradovich for showing the personal and subjective inner life of the worker poet in his "Stikh o sebe" (Verse about myself)—though one person thought he recognized the baneful influence of the Acmeist poet Anna Akhmatova.[122] In fact, we see increasing efforts to, in the eighteenth-century phrase, "contract full intimacy with the Stranger within."[123] This pursuit was familiar, echoing older Romantic and sentimentalist literature but especially (as some critics recognized with dismay) the work of Russia's modernist poets, artists, and philosophers, including those who remained in Soviet Russia as uncomfortable allies, at best, of the new order. Such writers as Anna Akhmatova, Nikolai Gumilev, and Osip Mandel'shtam continued to cultivate inwardness, explore the personal and psychological, and elaborate on the philosophical meanings of the self and of its feelings and expressions. Lower-class writers, notwithstanding stereotypes about proletarian culture, often shared this preoccupation. As Ivan Eroshin (who was one of those who praised Obradovich at the Proletcult Sunday conversation) put it in a poem also published by the Moscow Proletcult, "I lift the dark cover off myself / And gaze trembling into my garden, my soul."[124] These concerns necessarily complicate any simple images we may have constructed of proletarian writing as expressing a consistent masculine ethos and self-ideal. The noticed specter of Akhmatova, in whose art the intimate self and especially love were defining themes, is suggestive. The traditional topos of femininity—tenderness, inwardness, emotion, sensuality, and even echoes of the religious and intellectual tradition of the "eternal feminine" as the embodiment of wisdom—pervade these writings, alongside and complexly entwined with the "masculine" attributes of bold courage and devotion to the cause.[125]

In the most literal sense, the inward gaze was expressed in the widespread early Soviet-era obsession with autobiography. In one of several large memoir projects directed at workers during the first years after 1917, P. Ia. Zavolokin appealed to almost every major worker and peasant poet in Russia to

[122] *Gudki*, no.5 (May 1919), 30. In 1920 Obradovich published "O sebe," probably a revised version of the poem read at this gathering, which was not published, in *Griadushchee* 1920, no. 9–10: 1.

[123] Edward Young, *Conjectures in Original Composition* (1759), quoted in Stephen D. Cox, *"The Stranger within Thee": Concepts of the Self in Late-Eighteenth-Century Literature* (Pittsburgh, 1980), 3.

[124] I. Eroshin, "Podnimu s sebia . . . ," *Gudki*, no. 2 (April 1919), 8.

[125] On the larger discourse in Russia during the 1920s about the assumed essential differences between men and women and their ideological and cultural significance, see Naiman, *Sex in Public*, Borenstein, *Men without Women*, and Igal Halfin, *From Darkness to Light: Class, Consciousness, and Salvation in Revolutionary Russia* (Pittsburgh, 2000), 121–46. On the traditional topos of femininity and its relation to the masculine, see also Barbara Heldt, *Terrible Perfection: Women and Russian Literature* (Bloomington, 1987); Joanna Hubbs, *Mother Russia: The Feminine Myth in Russian Culture* (Bloomington, 1988); and Mikhail Epstein, "Daniil Andreev and the Mysticism of Femininity," in *The Occult in Russian and Soviet Culture*, ed. Bernice Glatzer Rosenthal (Ithaca, 1997), esp. 332–35.

submit an autobiographical essay and a few sample poems for publication.[126] Most authors willingly responded, indeed relished telling their personal life stories, although they did not consider the genre of autobiographical sketch the place to talk about personal life. A few went further and suggested that it was wrong to write about themselves. Aleksandr Pomorskii was one of these. A Bolshevik party member since 1908, he was also the most socially marginal of leading worker authors in his claim to a working-class identity—his father was an impoverished writer and he himself briefly attended a gymnasium before leaving school for factory work and professional party work. Pomorskii attached an apology to his autobiographical sketch: "I am little interested in my own person [*svoei lichnost'iu*]. I see happiness and the goal of my life in creating humane living conditions for society, for the collective. I have to say that writing my autobiography involved the greatest difficulties for me."[127] Whether this self-effacement reflected Pomorskii's political understanding of the proper centrality of the collective over the individual or a more complex personal anxiety in writing about himself—influenced in part, perhaps, by the ambiguity of his claim to being a worker poet—his apology remains unusual. Another rare example of such hesitation points to the potential importance of deep anxieties about writing about the self, though in this case, such a denial of self prefigured a tragic outcome. In answering Zavolokin's request for an autobiography, Nikolai Kuznetsov began by rejecting the genre: "My life is exactly like the lives of hundreds and thousands of working-class people." As a youth, he insisted, he was "in no way different from all the other street lads." As an adult, though his father wanted him to become a clerk, "I wanted to be a simple worker." Barely a year after writing these autobiographical notes, on 20 September 1924, Kuznetsov hanged himself.[128] We know that he was regularly writing poems and joining proletarian literary groups in these years, but that he was not very successful in getting published and often went hungry. In an obituary, however, a friend wrote that it was not hunger that led him to suicide—he had been much hungrier in 1919–20. He despaired out of a constant longing to escape the cold urban life around him and a painful lack of faith in himself.[129] His denials of interest in his self, it would seem, reflected not a new positive identification with the collective but a fatal extinguishing of self.

As worker writers gazed within for understanding and truth, and most did, emotion became a major concern. Mindfulness of emotion was becoming a philosophical and political principle. Even before 1917 a few worker intellec-

---

[126] This effort resulted in the publication of Zavolokin, *Sovremennye raboche-krest'ianskie poety*. The collected materials for this project—including unpublished drafts, submissions not included in the final collection, and correspondence—are located in RGALI, f. 1068.

[127] RGALI, f. 1068, op. 1, d. 25, l. 6 (Pomorskii).

[128] Ibid., d. 83, ll. 1–5 (Kuznetzov autobiography dated 14 Mar. 1923).

[129] A. Kosterin, in *Rabochii zhurnal* 1925, no. 1–2: 232, 235. By contrast, Sergei Gan'shin, in a letter to Zavolokin, voiced contempt for Kuznetsov's "pitiable spirit." In the "bad old days," he recalled, "we were thrown out of publishing offices on our necks, but all the same we didn't hang ourselves": 7 Oct. 1924, in RGALI, f. 1068, op. 1, d. 34, l. 9.

tuals (notably those associated with Aleksandr Bogdanov, who had written explicitly about socialist art as the organizer of social feeling) began to argue about the importance of emotion in defining culture and especially its class constitution. Fedor Kalinin, who had studied at Bogdanov's party school for workers in Italy, argued, as we have heard, that "the intellectual can still *think* for the young [working] class, but he cannot *feel* for it." Emotions, he insisted, derive not from logical analysis of the "external facts and phenomena" of "political economy," which the intelligentsia may be best equipped to undertake, but from experience. Convinced that true knowledge of the world required both reason and intuition—external science and inward feeling—Kalinin maintained that proletarian ideology must be constructed out of both analytic and emotional knowledge, implying a sort of philosophical syndicalism that reclaimed for workers at least part of the intellectual leadership of the labor and socialist movement and of the creation of proletarian culture.[130] Soon after 1917, recognizing the heterodoxy of his argument, Kalinin returned to reason and logic as the touchstones of proletarian philosophy and condemned arguments emphasizing intuitive understanding as reflecting the decadent final stage of bourgeois thought.[131] Other leading proletarian intellectuals similarly took pains to argue against unscientific epistemologies. Andrei Platonov, writing in 1922, insisted that progress meant learning to "trample on our dreams" and replace them with "reality," to "bury" the "soul of the present human being, which is only the sum of his instincts, intuitions, and sensations," and replace it with the "soul of the future human being," which is composed of "consciousness and intellect."[132]

Still, belief in the centrality of emotion persisted and even thrived. Platonov paired his repudiation of "dreams" with a recognition that "consciousness is a symphony of emotions." He distinguished between the false fantasies of "imagination" and "sensation" (*predstavlenie* and *oshchushchenie*), which draw only upon the inward self, and the truth (*istina*) of emotional knowledge (*chuvstva*), which is entwined with the real natural world of things.[133] More concretely, there was the sense that an emotional knowledge that nonworkers could not fathom was precisely what led most worker writers to take up the pen. In autobiographies, we have seen, worker writers regularly spoke of being driven to write by a welling up of feelings that had to be expressed. Nikolai Liashko elaborated this idea into a political epistemology. After the revolution especially, he insisted, workers felt a need for artists who were "their

---

[130] F. Kalinin, "Tip rabochego v literature," *Novyi zhurnal dlia vsekh* 1912, no. 9 (September): 96–97, 106 (emphasis in original).

[131] F. Kalinin, "Put' proletarskoi kul'tury i kul'tury burzhuazii," *Gorn*, no. 1 (1918), esp. 27–28. Ironically, at a meeting in 1920, Lebedev-Polianskii echoed Kalinin's words that only workers can express "proletarian feeling": *Kuznitsa*, no. 2 (June 1920), 28. Much of the time, however, as a leading Proletcult intellectual and later head Soviet censor, he tried to direct these "feelings" into politically correct channels.

[132] A. Platonov, "Proletarskaia poeziia," *Kuznitsa*, no. 9 (1922), 28–29.

[133] Ibid.

own" not only in political ideology but especially in "life-feeling" (*zhizneo-shchushchenie*).[134]

In dwelling on emotion, worker writers treated certain feelings as particularly valuable and meaningful. One was love. In 1918 Liashko criticized the still widespread "pornography" for dwelling on feelings of physical excitement, which tended to overshadow and degrade the truly important feelings of "love."[135] In a story published in a workers' cooperative journal the same year he explored the platonic affection found by a lonely man and the lonely prostitute with whom he goes home on Christmas Eve.[136] Sexual love, almost never spoken of in workers' writings before 1917, was now admired as long as it was emotionally inspiring and enriching. Many worker writers in these years created romantic poems about a long-awaited tryst, the fragrance of a lover's hair, gentle embraces, kissing a beloved's eyes and lips, and the erotic mystery of women's laughter.[137] One writer, a long-time member of a circle of "writers from the people" in Simbirsk, even proposed that a local House of People's Creativity (Dom narodnogo tvorchestva) include in its program "moral perfection through sexual love."[138]

Notwithstanding ideological insistence that proletarian culture went beyond "petty-egoistic personal happiness" and an increasingly dominating cultural ethos that sought to purge both tender sentimentality and erotic desire,[139] worker writers found important human values in personal and even sensual love. Sergei Obradovich identified love (along with struggle, with which love was often said to stand in contradiction) as fundamental to all human life and history.[140] Some writers elaborated these ideas into a sweeping cultural ideal about the revolutionary power of sensual love. This was often a gendered ideal, part of the still familiar distinction between essential male and female selves; but it was also an ideal in which the joining of these differences was seen as necessary to emotional (and hence human) wholeness. Writing in a provincial Communist newspaper in 1920, and contradicting some of his own arguments about the need to eradicate heterosexual desire

---

[134] N. Liashko, "O zadachakh pisatelia-rabochego," *Kuznitsa*, no. 3 (July 1920), 26.

[135] N. Liashko, "Dukhovnye iady," *Rabochii mir,* no. 15 (13 Oct. 1918), 28–29.

[136] N. Liashko, "Kholod," *Rabochii mir,* no. 8 (7 July 1918), 4–7.

[137] See, e.g., V. Aleksandrovskii, "Rozhdestvennskie mechti," *Sotsial-demokrat,* 30 Dec. (12 Jan.) 1917; idem, "Bogine," *Gudki,* no. 1 (March 1919), 3–6; and many of the poems in Aleksandrovskii, *Zvon solntsa;* N. Poletaev, "Vorobei i roza," *Kuznitsa,* no. 9 (1922), 17; Mikhail Gerasimov, *Doroga: Poemy* (Moscow, 1924); Vladimir Kirillov, *Vesennyi svet: Stikhotvoreniia kniga 1: 1913–1922,* 2d ed. (Moscow, 1928) (esp. poems in the final section, "Sokrovennye pesni"); M. Gerasimov, "Tvoi vzgliad morskoi . . . ," *Kuznitsa,* no. 7 (December–March 1921), 10; Vlad. Korolev, *Povozka* (Buguruslan, 1921).

[138] Letters from Nikolai I'lin to Maksim Gor'kii, Arkhiv A. M. Gor'kogo, KG-NP/A, 11-46-6.

[139] *Griadushchee* 1918, no. 3 (June): 4–5; A. Bogdanov, "Chto takoe proletarskaia poeziia?" *Proletarskaia kul'tura,* no. 1 (July 1918), 20–22; and see Borenstein, *Men without Women,* and Naiman, *Sex in Public.*

[140] Sergei Obradovich, *Vintovka i liubov'* (Moscow, 1924). See review in *Rabochii zhurnal* 1925, no. 3: 153–55.

from the new Communist culture,[141] Andrei Platonov declared the sensual attraction of a man (for him, the thinking subject was by definition male) to a woman to be an essential though subversive assertion of the human spirit.

> The passion of the body that draws a man toward a woman . . . not only is a matter of pleasure but also is a prayer, a mysterious true labor of life in the name of hope and renaissance, . . . in the name of the victory of humanity. Open tenderness, living close to a woman—this is a rupture in the stone wall of the world's inertia and animosity. This is the majestic moment when all the black serpents of the earth are covered by the ice of death.[142]

The mixture of transgressive, prayerful, and tender images in these lines deliberately presents a complex image of a man's sexual passion for a woman, for the argument was about the need to unite the sexual with the emotional. To suppress the "black serpents" required awakening and unleashing feelings that existed outside the conventional bounds of masculinity. This formulation echoed the most familiar mystique of femininity—the differentiation and idealization of women's selves as both inspiring objects of passion and icons of virtue. More complexly, it hinted at mystical ideas of the "eternal feminine" and at ideals of androgynous wisdom. And it paralleled a widening Soviet discourse (especially by the early 1920s) about sexual difference and sexuality.[143] But the most essential issue here was the drive to lay claim to the central value of emotional love. Love was still often conventionally attached to ideals of the feminine, but even then the goal was to bring its power into men's lives and hence into the larger sphere. This was an increasingly evident theme in proletarian writing. Thus Mashirov's "Woman," who addresses a group of boisterous male workers with a speech about class sufferings and dreams, silences and inspires them less with her words than with her shadowy paleness, her smile, and the "gestures of her beautiful arms."[144] Vasilii Aleksandrovskii told of being dazzled by the beauty, laughter, and secrets of an unknown woman disembarking from a ship.[145] And Mikhail Gerasimov, in his famous 1918 poem "Mona Lisa," wrote of the "bewitching and intoxicating" power of a ubiquitous feminine smile.[146]

Politically, positive emotions were most valued. We have already seen the importance of insistent and self-advertised confidence and optimism in prerevolutionary worker writing—the language of "boldness," "hope," "enthusiasm," "strength of spirit," "faith," and the like. After 1917, this mood was

---

[141] See esp. A. Platonov, "Budushchii Oktiabr'," *Voronezhskaia kommuna*, 9 Nov. 1920, and the discussion of this essay in Borenstein, *Men without Women*, 210–17.

[142] A. Platonov, "Dusha mira," *Krasnaia derevnia*, 18 July 1920.

[143] See Heldt, *Terrible Perfection*; Naiman, *Sex in Public*; and Borenstein, *Men without Women*.

[144] Samobytnik [A. Mashirov], "Zhenshchina," *Griadushchee* 1918, no. 5 (July): 7.

[145] V. Aleksandrovskii, "Pri razruzke," *Kuznitsa*, no. 4 (August–September 1920), 6. See the similar image in V. Kamshitskii, "Son," *Griadushchee* 1918, no. 5 (July): 9–10.

[146] M. Gerasimov, "Monna Liza," *Gorn*, no. 1 (1918), 11–16.

increasingly canonical for revolutionaries. It was especially in evidence among the young generation of peasants and workers who began to write after 1917. Especially among the Komsomol (Communist Youth League) writers of the early 1920s, who had come of age in the struggles of 1917–21, we see the most unalloyed examples of what L'vov-Rogachevskii called the spirit of "winged youth mad with courage and drunk with joy," inspired by a burning "faith without doubts, without vacillation, without reflection, without looking back."[147] Soviet-era anthologies of early postrevolutionary "proletarian poetry" endeavored to show that this mood was universal.[148] The evidence could certainly be found easily. All proletarian writers penned such poems. Many insisted on their superiority. Sergei Obradovich, in a typical gesture, claimed that by 1920 he could no longer even "comprehend" the once familiar "humility and sadness" of a Russian song.[149] And, like other authors, he demonstrated the preferred "new song" with writings expressing the bold moods of collective struggle, joyous labor, and confidence in the future. Vladimir Kirillov's description of the spirit and mood of the proletarian "We" was typical: "We love life, are drunk with its wild rapture."[150] The phraseology, narratives, and images for such writing were long familiar from socialist and radical writing (throughout Europe as well), echoed here in the endless repetition of cries of "forward," "be bold," "we are the joy of Free Labor," and the like.[151] The revolution and Soviet power gave this language new plausibility and meaning, generating an often hyperbolic pathos about emerging from darkness into "a new life," "being like an eagle," the joyful heroism of "sacred struggle," the "blossoming of a Great Universal Springtime," or the flight of the "soul with beating wings."[152]

These writers continued to write also in a quite different key, however, as before 1917, but with a new poignancy (and political significance) against the background of the heightened spirit of youthful boldness and joyfulness after October and the growing identification of this mood as a sign of political and social belonging. As these writers incessantly looked into their selves and pondered emotional values and expression, they dwelled often on anguish, alienation, melancholy, and sadness. Almost all the worker writers of these years offered elaborate explorations of inward suffering. Vasilii Aleksandrovskii, a

---

[147] L'vov-Rogachevskii, *Ocherki*, 183.

[148] The most authoritative example is *Proletarskie poety pervykh let sovetskoi epokhi* (Leningrad, 1959), part of the noted series Biblioteka poeta (bol'shaia seriia; vtoroe izdanie).

[149] S. Obradovich, "Na Vorob'evykh gorakh," *Obshchee delo*, no. 3 (10 May 1920) (cutting in RGALI, f. 1874, op. 1, d. 7, l. 20).

[150] V. Kirillov, "My," *Griadushchee 1918*, no. 2 (May): 4.

[151] See poems throughout *Proletarskie poety pervykh let*.

[152] S. Obradovich, "K novoi zhizni," *Nasha zhizn'* (Orel), no. 11–12 (15 Nov.–1 Dec. 1918), 1 (cutting in RGALI, f. 1874, op. 1, d. 2, l. 17); V. Kirillov, "Gremiat miatezhennye raskaty," *Pravda*, 10 Feb. (28 Jan.) 1918; Kirillov, "Poetam revoliutsii," *Znamia truda* 8 (21) February 1918, rpt. in Kirillov, *Stikhotvoreniia, 1914–1918 gg.*, 11; E. Nechaev, "Privet proletarskim ptentsam," *Tvorchestvo*, no. 7 (November 1918), 12; Groshik (S. Kopeikin), "Prival'noe," *Mir i chelovek*, no. 1 (January 1919), 2; V. Aleksandrovskii, "Molodezhi" (1922), rpt. in *Proletarskie poety pervykh let*, 107.

young Marxist worker (and thus, according to the stereotype, the least inclined to write in this vein), wrote scores of quite somber poems about anguish and longing. In a poem published in 1918 in the journal of the Moscow Proletcult he explored the emotions of an "outcast": "anguish impudent as a prostitute," the experience of "insults multiplying insanely," and "suffering beyond all measure." In the end, the inevitable occurs: "When, like a thief, the dawn stealthily / Breaks into the room of torment / Death covers the dilated eyes / With eternal mystery."[153] Repeatedly, side by side with poems of heroism and hope, Aleksandrovskii, like many others, was drawn to explore feelings of anguish, sorrow, and despair.[154]

Solitude and loneliness were the subjects of a number of poems and stories. In a poem published in 1918 in the journal of the Petrograd Proletkult, Aleksei Mashirov (Samobytnik) described the feelings of a lonely young man and woman, both workers, both seeking personal happiness, but never meeting; instead they must listen, with embarrassment, through the thin walls of their rooms, to the pleasures of other people.[155] Similarly, Vladimir Kirillov described the loneliness and alienation that led him, vainly, to offer flowers to an unknown young woman.[156] Aleksandr Smirnov went further in exploring human solitude, in this case his own, and drew up a list of "friends" in which no people appeared—only places and memories (forests, the sky, flying cranes), emotions (love, melancholy), and, most important, for they tied all the rest together, "My friends, my sufferings."[157]

As before the revolution, reflections on feelings of *toska* (a mix of melancholy, sadness, anguish, depression, and longing) continued to appear frequently in proletarian publications. In a lengthy essay addressed to beginning proletarian writers in 1919, Andrei Platonov argued that the "primitive art" of folk songs, tales, legends, and religious myths, unlike the "artificial art" written later for elites or for the artist alone, was "the highest expression of the deepest feelings"—in particular, of "sorrow and dull *toska*"—and was thus "the cradle and source of truly human art," and therefore the true ancestor of proletarian art.[158] The word *toska* itself was used often as writers described feelings of loneliness, exhausted searching, autumnal sadness, and hearts weighed down with melancholy; it was even reified into a sort of natural phenomenon, as in Platonov's image of "*toska* frozen in the sky."[159] A member of a Petrograd

[153] V. Aleksandrovskii, "Otverzhennyi," *Gorn*, no. 1 (1918), 10.

[154] V. Aleksandrovskii, "Iz tsikla 'V tumane,'" *Gudki*, no. 6 (June 1919), 3–4; "U zhertvennika," *Tvori*, no. 2 (1921), 4.

[155] Samobytnik [A. Mashirov], "Liubov'," *Griadushchee* 1918, no. 2: 6.

[156] V. Kirillov, "Stolichnoe," *Krasnaia gazeta*, 25 June 1918 (evening ed.), rpt. in Kirillov, *Stikhotvoreniia, 1914–1918*, 24.

[157] A. Smirnov, "Moi druz'ia," in *V bure i plameni*, 58. Among other accounts of loneliness, see N. Poletaev, "Sem'ia," *Gudki*, no. 2 (April 1919), 9–11.

[158] A. Platonov, "K nachinaiushchim proletarskim poetam i pisateliam." *Zheleznyi put'*, no. 9 (April 1919), 25.

[159] A. Platonov, "Nad golubymi ozerami . . . ," *Krasnaia derevnia*, 5 May 1920, and "Toska," *Zheleznyi put'* 1919, no. 9 (April), 13; V. Aleksandrovskii, "U zhertvennika," *Tvori*, no. 2 (1921), 4; V. Korolev, *Povozka*; and many of the writings in the journal *Kuznitsa*; e.g., the poems by Po-

workers' club explored the gloomy thoughts and feelings that autumn aroused in a young woman—thoughts of sentient nature, sexual love, loss of innocence, death, suicide, and survival.[160] For many worker writers, even spring did not always bring happiness. Thus for Nikolai Poletaev the running waters, thick fog, mud, and feeble breezes of spring angered and depressed him. In the sleepless night his mournful "sobs" merged with the "noise, the high waters, the frenzy" of springtime.[161] Death, of course, was a common object of such emotional reflection. Vladimir Zafran, a little-known worker who was active as organizer, writer, and pianist in a Kostroma workers' club (he wrote that he played piano partly to express the "sorrows" of his "soul"), also pondered death and what lay beyond: "the darkness of eternity," the grave, "grief," and "tears."[162] Suicide was not an uncommon image, especially as a response to what one writer described as the impossibility of living a "human life" in this world.[163]

Marxist intellectuals, examining the emerging proletarian literary culture after 1917, were often troubled by the frequency with which proletarians wrote in such a sorrowful tone; one critic bluntly called it "bourgeois individualistic pessimism."[164] By the beginning of the 1920s, as the heroic and desperate struggles of the civil war gave way to political moderation and the return of many old social forms under the New Economic Policy, critics discovered such attitudes and moods to be more widespread than ever. Aleksandr Voronskii—reviewing the publications of writers associated with the journal *Kuznitsa,* a group that included such leading worker authors as Gerasimov, Kirillov, Obradovich, and Aleksandrovskii—observed that very often in the postrevolutionary writings of these authors, as in works written before the revolution, one saw a startling amount of "melancholy [*toska*], sorrow, solitariness, a tendency to dreaminess, to phantasms, to reveries and daydreams, to contemplativeness."[165] The exasperated tone of such complaints highlighted the continuing problem: even certifiably Bolshevik worker writers persisted in seeking the meaning of the revolution (and of life) in the murky reaches of the individual personality, in the inward spirit, and typically in their own selves. To be sure, as we have seen, these writers also continued to pen boldly joyous and heroic poems. But the resulting dissonance only underscored the presence and appeal of another language—the language, in Voronskii's phrase, of "the intimate and the individual,"[166] and often the sorrowful.

letaev and Kirillov in no. 7 (December–March 1921) and Poletaev's "Vorobei i roza" in no. 9 (1922), 17. A poem by Proskurin titled "Toska" was discussed at one of the Sunday conversations at the Moscow Proletcult Literary Studio in 1919: *Gudki,* no. 5 (May 1919), 30.

[160] Rognev, "Klenovye list'ia," *Revoliutsionnye vskhody,* no. 3–4 (October 1920), 8–9.

[161] N. Poletaev, "Noch'," *Kuznitsa,* no. 3 (July 1920), 12.

[162] V. Zafran, "U roialia," *Sbornik Kostromskogo proletkul'ta,* no. 1 (1919), 42, and "Boi," ibid., 41.

[163] A. Veselov (Sasha Veselyi), in *V bure i plameni,* 17. Also, in the same publication of "proletarian creation" by the Yaroslavl printers' union, N. Kustov, "Zhelanie" (1909), 51.

[164] S. Kluben', in *Griadushchaia kul'tura* (Tambov), no. 2 (December 1918), 24.

[165] Voronskii, "O gruppe pisatelei 'Kuznitsa,'" 126.

[166] Ibid., 135.

A Tragic Sense

As before 1917, songs of sorrow and suffering expressed not only Romantic attention to inward emotions and sensibilities but also meaningful if pathos-filled argument. This was in part a critical and political argument. A good deal of post-1917 writing about suffering was an explicitly retrospective critique of the overthrown capitalist society for the harm it inflicted on the human self: for crushing the souls and bodies of working-class children, for crippling the poor with "hard labor" (*katorzhnyi trud*), for the "moral suffocation of the human personality [*lichnost'*] of the worker."[167] Ivan Filipchenko's portrait of the degradation of peasants who came to the capitalist cities, in an essayistic prose poem written in 1924, was typical. Able only to gaze at the fantastic but untouchable luxury and wealth that surrounds them, these migrating workers roam the cities "in dirt and dust, sick, with mournful eyes, homeless, barefoot, in torn and stinking rags," with "the same constant moans, and the wailing of children, and the cries of desperation." They degrade themselves to survive: "Mothers with tears in their eyes" send their sons to beg and their daughters into the streets to sell their bodies, and starving men send their wives and even their future brides. Death awaits them at every turn, even if they are fortunate enough to find work in factories. In the end, "they lie in vacant lots and go out of their minds. They lie in railway stations and take their own lives, throwing themselves under trains. They fill the prisons and they fill the madhouses. And they fill the factories and shops."[168] The ostensible message of this characteristically melodramatic portrait was that these conditions represented the past, which was being overcome. Aleksandrovskii described "two Russias": one filled with "sorrow and pain," drunkenness, monotony, suffering, and suicide, and the "new country," born in suffering, filled with burning fire and ringing tocsins.[169]

This attention to social causes, shared suffering, and transforming teleologies was not absolute. Indeed, some critics worried that these writers were so focused on the *sufferings* of the people that they neglected the more important historical process by which suffering led to revolution.[170] The error was understandable and did indeed suggest differences in judging what was most important and essential. To be sure, material conditions in the present helped keep worker writers focused on suffering. The devastation of the civil war of 1918–20, in the wake of the protracted World War of 1914–18, meant that there was still no end to everyday hunger, cold, hardship, pain, and exhaustion. Treatment of these themes in creative writing was partly a relatively

[167] E. Nechaev, "Privet proletarskim ptentsam," *Tvorchestvo*, no. 7 (November 1918), 1; P. Bessal'ko, in *Griadushchee* 1918, no. 3 (June 1918), 12; I. Kubikov, introduction to Nechaev, *Guta*, 16.

[168] I. Filipchenko, "Lenin," *Rabochii zhurnal* 1924, no. 1: 57–58.

[169] V. Aleksandrovskii, "Dve Rossii" (written November–December 1920), *Kuznitsa*, no. 7 (December–March 1921), 3–6.

[170] V. Polianskii [P. Lebedev-Polianskii], "Poeziia sovetskoi provintsii," *Proletarskaia kul'tura*, no. 7–8 (April–May 1919), 47.

straightforward mimesis of reality.[171] But more important, I believe, these writers continued to dwell on suffering because they found something deeply meaningful and illuminating—at an existential as much as a historical level—in this pervasive experience. Most essential was the personal experience of suffering.

This perspective shaped their judgments of the past and its legacies. When they examined capitalist society, these writers tended to show more concern with its moral logic than with its dialectic, for its moral logic touched what mattered most: the self. This concern is evident in their autobiographical writings. When worker authors recalled their own poverty and physical suffering, they tended to focus not on causes or structures but on the inward experience of suffering, often on painful crises of self-worth that led to thoughts of suicide, the ultimate expression of a ruined self. Sergei Obradovich recalled being so depressed in his teens—with a sick mother, a gloomy father, and a hateful apprenticeship in a print shop—that he prepared to hang himself.[172] Tellingly, when he rewrote his autobiography in the once-again heroic (and intellectually more restrictive) early 1930s, Obradovich omitted this discussion of depression and suicide.[173] In an autobiography written in 1922, Ruta Vitkovskaia recalled her sufferings as a young worker and as a Jew: the drunken owner of a hat factory who "taunted" and "in every way humiliated" his female workers; the constant abuse and insults at the hands of everyone with authority over her; the "cold, sneering 'we don't need your sort here'" that often met her applications for jobs; the hungry nights in the "noisy streets" of the city; the beckoning lure of prostitution as an escape from hunger, though not from degrading treatment. At the age of thirteen, Vitkovskaia tells us, she "firmly decided to throw herself under a trolley car."[174]

Most often and most important, these writers treated suffering as part of an essentially philosophical vision: a tragic view of life's meaning. The tragic imagination, in the sense elaborated by philosophers from Aristotle to Nietzsche, views suffering as inescapable and inevitable but also as elevating the human spirit, deepening the soul, and even pointing toward transcendence. One can identify specific potential influences for such an understanding among Russian workers, though they were often indirect and almost always recast. Ideas about the sublime benefits of contemplating tragedy can be found in the Russian Orthodox liturgy and throughout the writings of Dostoevsky, Tolstoy, and other leading Russian authors. Possible Western European influences were also evident. Schopenhauer, whose works were widely read by Russian intellectuals and writers in the nineteenth century and after, forcefully argued for recognizing and accepting the tragic nature of the world and existence—"the unspeakable pain, the wail of humanity, the triumph of evil, the scornful mastery of chance, and the irretrievable fall of the just and inno-

---

[171] See I. Pchelintsev, "Zametki o proletarskoi belletristike," *Tvori!* no. 2 (1921), 23–24.
[172] Zavolokin, *Sovremennye raboche-krest'ianskie poety*, 76.
[173] RGALI, f. 1874, op. 1, d. 183, ll. 1–2 (autobiography dated 20 Aug. 1932).
[174] RGALI, f. 1068, op. 1, d. 27, l. 1.

cent."[175] Nietzsche's views on tragedy, which even more strongly linked recognition of inevitable suffering to affirmation of the vital power of life, were even more influential, notably among some of the intellectuals and writers who would become Soviet Russia's cultural leaders, such as Gorky, Maiakovskii, and Lunacharsky. For Nietzsche, tragedy enabled people to see "something sublime and significant" in their "struggles, strivings, and failures," "to take delight in the rhythm of grand passion and its victims," in order ultimately to know, especially in the face of the modern knowledge that we are all ultimately destined for extinction, that "the individual must be consecrated to something higher than himself."[176] Whatever the particular sources, influences, and dynamics of their understanding and use, it is clear that this general philosophy of the tragic was widely available in Russian cultural life as proletarian writers were trying to voice their understandings of the world. But it is equally important to keep in mind—especially for worker authors whose reading experiences were still scattered and often unsophisticated—that these were efforts to *express* views of the world. We must speak of affinities as much as influences. These intellectual traditions of defining the tragic may be less sources, therefore, than signs pointing to a tragic imagination with its own roots and history.

As before 1917, proletarian writers indicated their belief in the value of contemplated suffering. At the very least, the recall of personal suffering provided needed emotional catharsis. Thus when Aleksei Mashirov described the catalyzing appearance in a circle of partying workers of an unknown woman worker, "pale like a shadow / rage barely concealed in [her] smile," it was of suffering she spoke: "Of the indignation of youthful feelings / Of undeserved insult / . . . Of their age-old suffering." And her words evoked "tears of delight and sadness."[177] More significant, for many worker writers suffering remained a moral signature of their class experience, at once a mark of special identity and worth and a source of knowledge and will. In such valuations, the importance of the collective is again often visible, as the self finds its fulfillment in consecration to something higher than itself. Thus, for example, Aleksandr Smirnov identified the knowledge and historical purpose of the working class as defined by the sufferings they endured "in body and soul"—workers "drank to the very bottom the bitter cup of truth."[178] Similarly, the Iaroslavl poet Vladimir Korolev viewed suffering (especially the

[175] Arthur Schopenhauer, *The World as Will and Representation*, bk. III, sec. 51, in *Schopenhauer: Selections*, ed. DeWitt H. Parker (New York, 1928), 172. On Schopenhauer's influence on Russian writers, see "Shopengauer" in *Entsiklopedicheskii slovar'*, ed. F. A. Brokgaus and I. A. Efron (St. Petersburg 1890–1907), and Victor Terras, *A History of Russian Literature* (New Haven, 1991), 313–14, 382, 392, 400–401, 407.

[176] Friedrich Nietzsche, *Richard Wagner in Bayreuth* (1876), quoted in Laurence Lampert, *Nietzsche and Modern Times* (New Haven, 1993), 295–97, 417. For the influence of Nietzsche, esp. of his *Birth of Tragedy*, see Bernice Glatzer Rosenthal, ed., *Nietzsche in Russia* (Princeton, 1986), and *Nietzsche and Soviet Culture* (Cambridge, 1994). For an early and influential discussion of affinity more than influence, see Lev Shestov, "Dostoevsky and Nietzsche: The Philosophy of Tragedy" (1903), in Shestov, *Dostoevsky, Tolstoy, and Nietzsche* (Athens, Ohio, 1969).

[177] Samobytnik [A. Mashirov], "Zhenshchina," *Griadushchee* 1918, no. 5 (July): 7.

[178] A. Smirnov, "Dumy proletarii," in *V bure i plameni*, 57.

suffering of worker writers, who suffered more deeply than "other oppressed working people") as the chief source of proletarian creativity and greatness: out of the "oppression of their spirits and the slavelike yoke of poverty" comes the worker's particular vision, will, and artistic genius. Indeed, "the proletarian creator is made majestic in his suffering."[179] Marxist critics warned that it was not correct to emphasize suffering in the definition of the proletarian worldview, though they recognized that many worker writers did just that. Indeed, according to a dismayed critic, one poet went so far in this dangerous direction as to represent the hammer and sickle as the emblem not of proud labor but of "millions of torments and sufferings," and to describe the coming of socialism as "adorning the world with flowers of unheard-of suffering."[180]

Andrei Platonov expanded the inspiring effects of suffering to embrace the whole of human experience: "Despair, torment, and death—these are the true reasons for heroic human action and the most powerful motors of history. We must feel torment, millions must die, must fall from inexhaustible love, in order to obtain in ourselves the capacity to work. True work is the soothing of our eternal sorrow." These were not abstract reflections. Platonov was writing in the early fall of 1921, when millions of peasants, especially in the Volga region around Voronezh, where he lived, were starving to death. But the meaning of such devastation was to be understood, Platonov asserted, only as it passed through a person's inner spiritual self. "What is the meaning of hunger?" he asked. "What is happening now in the Volga region?" He answered indirectly: "Great visions, the truth about this world, we see only in dreams . . . when the sober nervous centers of the mind are held back."[181] Aleksei Gastev went even further and defined "catastrophe"—especially the succession of striving and failure—as essential to the emergence of the new psychology of proletarianized humanity.[182]

As some critics recognized, many proletarian writers also harbored a more everyday feeling of the tragic—a despondent pessimism that was far from cathartic or uplifting. This feeling was especially noticeable in writings of the early 1920s, during the first years of the New Economic Policy (NEP), when the feverish struggles with armed enemies and radical efforts to remake society (the pathos of "war communism") was giving way to a more modest and pluralistic—but also more ambiguous—approach to transforming a backward and devastated society into a modern socialist one. In this less clear terrain, despite (perhaps because of) the improvements in everyday material life, many radicals, including a large number of the best-known worker writers, felt increasingly dismayed and depressed. More than ever, dark images and de-

[179] V. Korolev, "Tvorets-Proletarii," in *V bure i plameni*, 3–4.

[180] Rabochii [Worker] Porokhovik, in *Proletarskaia kul'tura*, no. 20–21 (January–June 1921), 55.

[181] A. Platonov, "Zhizn' do kontsa," *Voronezhskaia kommuna*, 25 Aug. 1921.

[182] A. Gastev, "O tendentsiiakh proletarskoi kul'tury," *Proletarskaia kul'tura*, no. 9–10 (June–July 1919), 44; "Bashnia," *Metallist*, 1917, no. 4 (18 October): 4–6; and *Griadushchee* 1918, no. 2 (May): 11–12.

spairing tones appeared in their writings, and they retreated into an increasingly personal world of private emotion. Some spoke out against the retreat from radicalism. Some of the most direct poetic denunciations of the NEP social order appeared in the final issue of *Kuznitsa* in 1922. In the poem "Chernaia pena" (Black foam)—the title contains "NEP" in reverse—Mikhail Gerasimov (one of the most prominent worker poets and one with a long history in both industry and the revolutionary movement) chastised the NEP order with its "white ladies and prostitutes" strolling along Strastnyi Boulevard, "hungry men with leaden faces" living under the Moscow River bridge, and the horrible rich in the theaters ("white globs piling up in the parterre"). At the center of this poem stands the poet and his feelings. Railing against the bourgeoisie—especially the new "Sovbourgeois"—the poet bares his anguished "soul," out of which "bubbles black foam."[183] In the same issue of *Kuznitsa*, Vasilii Aleksandrovskii addressed "simple words on simple things" to readers who still had soul and character left, "not to those whose hearts are stone / Or to those who wither beneath the sun." He spoke of a "life that was so mangy" that it makes you as depressed (*tosklivo*) as "a dog in an inclement February." "Oh, cursed, shameful fate! / How one wants to smash one's head against granite."[184] Other works similarly spoke for the rebellion of the idealistic soul against the crass realities of NEP.

But more than NEP society was being judged in these works. Gerasimov's poem was unusually explicit in targeting NEP and the reemerging bourgeoisie; few others were so clearly focused. It was not, I believe, censorship that kept their focus more general; many direct criticisms of NEP appeared in the press. Rather, it was that more was at stake for these writers: not simply NEP society or even capitalism in general (though the effects of these social arrangements on people's lives troubled them and they said so) but the human personality and human fate more generally. In a review published in 1925 of a recent collection of poems by Vladimir Kirillov, Sergei Obradovich found troubling echoes of the "elegiac sadness of Nadson and the lilac-colored melancholy [*melankholichnost'*] of Blok." Especially worrisome were the poems Kirillov had written since 1921, in which Obradovich saw far too much "sarcasm," "irony," "contradictory philosophy," "confusion," and "self-torment."[185] Kirillov's mood and tone, however, were to be found in the writings of many other proletarians, including Obradovich himself, who wrote of wanting to escape and forget the "painful noise and weight of the everyday."[186] These writers had long been preoccupied with the inward self. Now, changing external circumstances and their own growing literary skill and in-

---

[183] M. Gerasimov, "Chernaia pena," *Kuznitsa*, no. 9 (1922), 6–8.

[184] V. Aleksandrovskii, "Budni," *Kuznitsa*, no. 9 (1922), 8–9. See also his "Golgofa" (1922), in *Zvon solntsa* (Moscow, 1923), 129–35.

[185] S. Obradovich, review of Kirillov, *Stikhotvoreniia* (Moscow, 1924), in *Rabochii zhurnal* 1925, no. 4: 156–58.

[186] S. Obradovich, "Pokinutaia lad'ia . . . ," *Kuznitsa*, no. 9 (1922), 14. See also his "Koshmar," *Pravda*, 18 Feb. 1922.

tellectual sophistication helped sustain and intensify this gaze at the human personality—at the "I," at *lichnost'*. And the harder they looked, the more troubled they became.

"Not Our Language"

Marxist critics frequently warned worker writers to beware of mistaken moods, language, and values. Pavel Lebedev-Polianskii, whose voice carried considerable political weight—he was national chairman of the Proletcult from 1918 to 1920, served as commissar for literature and publishing in the People's Commissariat of Enlightenment from the October revolution to 1919, and as head of the Main Administration on Literature and Publishing (Glavlit) was Soviet Russia's chief censor from 1921 to 1930—continually reminded misdirected worker writers that certain ways of expressing themselves were "not our language."[187] He had to admit, however, as other critics also did, that these other languages were still present (and potent) in the early years after the revolution.[188] Among these false discourses, the most troubling, in the words of Lebedev-Polianskii, came when these authors forgot that "in the place of the heroic, critically thinking individual, socialism has put the class, the collective above all." In too many poems purporting to be "proletarian," Lebedev-Polianskii complained, there was "only I, I, and I." He did not blame worker writers themselves for this error—they had simply not been taught properly to understand what socialism was all about.[189] Such arguments only half understood the problem. These Bolshevik intellectuals got the symptoms right, but their diagnosis was too narrow. What appeared to Lebedev-Polianskii, Bogdanov, and others as workers' simple misunderstanding of socialism may more accurately be seen as workers' different understanding of socialism. The stubborn "I, I, and I" was more than an error born of old habits and inadequate political education. It was key to the way even most leftist worker writers interpreted and valued the socialist revolution and the world in which they lived. In this sense, the intellectual guardians of "proletarian culture" may have underestimated the extent of heresy.

But what sort of heresy was this? Lebedev-Polianskii thought he recognized, hiding behind "proletarian terminology," the "all-embracing civic motifs of the liberal individualistic intelligentsia."[190] But ideas about the intrinsic worth, dignity, and rights of the human person were not merely "liberal" ideas. They were fully a part of the socialist tradition, too, in Russia as in West-

---

[187] V. Polianskii [P. Lebedev-Polianskii], review of *Gorn*, in *Proletarskaia kul'tura*, no. 5 (November 1918), 42.

[188] See also A. Bogdanov, "Chto takoe proletarskaia poeziia?" *Proletarskaia kul'tura*, no. 1 (July 1918), 20.

[189] V. Polianskii [P. Lebedev-Polianskii], in *Proletarskaia kul'tura*, no. 6 (February 1919), 37.

[190] V. Polianskii, "Poeziia sovetskoi provintsii," *Proletarskaia kul'tura*, no. 7–8 (April–May 1919), 43.

ern Europe. From Belinskii to Gorky, generations of Russian socialists spoke of the need to create social conditions under which individual capacities could flourish. Occasionally socialist intellectuals in Russia thought it necessary to remind workers of this tradition, as when, during a public debate about "proletarian art" held at the Tambov Proletcult in 1919, the prominent Marxist philosopher Liubov' Akselrod (a long-time revolutionary and former leader of the Menshevik party, whose party pseudonym had been Orthodox), declared that "socialist art should not drown the individual personality [*lichnost'*] in the collective, for socialism in no way seeks to negate the individual personality."[191] Even the leading intellectual proponent of the new culture, Bogdanov, as we have already noted, carefully denied that collectivism sought to obliterate the individual personality, attributing this "stereotype" (*shablon*) to enemies of real collectivism who were in fact trying to defend old-fashioned individualism. To make this argument, Bogdanov distinguished between the "individualism" of bourgeois society, in which individuals were arrayed against one another and their individual personalities restricted, and the "individuality" (*individual'nost'*) that would flourish only under socialism as individuals, as social beings, were freed to truly realize their human selves.[192] In various formulations, the same was said by most other leading Soviet intellectuals whose voices helped shape early Soviet culture: Maxim Gorky, Alexandra Kollontai, Anatoly Lunacharsky, Nikolai Bukharin, Nadezhda Krupskaia, Lev Trotsky, and others.[193] To be sure, there were Bolshevik intellectuals who warned workers to beware of the error of confusing socialism with "general democratic" ideals of "civil rights" and "freedom."[194] But others argued no less insistently that the proletarian revolution was not ultimately about emancipating a single class but about "emancipating all of humanity."[195]

Most worker writers needed no convincing. They wrote often about the "reign of man," about realizing and fulfilling one's full human potentiality, about living life to its fullest. This humanistic vision had inspired and been used by many workers to legitimate struggles before 1917 against the old order, against the social and cultural barriers that degraded workers and kept them apart and subordinate. It remained essential to the way most worker writers—and many other lower-class Russians[196]—viewed the revolution and socialism. Their view was filled with images of self-awareness and self-assertion, with ideas about what Platonov described as the personal "festival" of

---

[191] *Griadushchaia kul'tura* (Tambov), no. 4–5 (February–March 1919), 24.

[192] A. Bogdanov, "Ideal vospitanie," *Proletarskaia kul'tura*, no. 2 (July 1918), 18.

[193] Mark D. Steinberg, Introduction to Gorky, *Untimely Thoughts*, xvii–xx; essays by Kollontai, Trotsky, P. Stuchka, and others in Rosenberg, *Bolshevik Visions*, 2:61–94, 160, 230–35.

[194] E.g., P. Lebedev-Polianskii, in *Proletarskaia kul'tura*, no. 6 (February 1919), 41–42; no. 7–8 (April–May 1919), 43–44. On the other hand, he found it unhelpful for S. Spasskii to harp on the "general democratic" rather than "class proletarian" character of so much workers' writing: ibid., no. 5 (November 1918), 42.

[195] I. Trainin, "Proletarskaia kul'tura," *Zarevo zavodov* (Samara), no. 1 (January 1919), 33.

[196] See Mark D. Steinberg, *Voices of Revolution, 1917* (New Haven, 2001).

being allowed to live as a human being. Trotsky noted in 1924 that participation in workers' clubs was often motivated by the "fantasy" that everyday life could be transformed simply through individual self-perfection, through "individual moralization."[197]

But often more was involved in these workers' "fantasies" than traditions of socialist or even liberal humanism. More fundamental philosophical matters were at issue. Whereas before 1917, workers focused mainly on the oppression of the self, revolutionary-era worker writers experimented more in their imaginations with what the self might achieve now that the fetters were off, imagining various images of a triumphant, realized self: individuals expanding their consciousness to bind with the infinite, titanic supermen and messianic saviors, wanderers in search of truth, the genius of artistic intuition and creativity, self-fulfillment in art and love. Extreme and fantastic images of human will and individual genius appeared frequently—in Lebedev-Polianskii's insightful sarcasm, titans and geniuses who "create fire out of ice."[198]

One recognizes in these arguments between worker writers and their party-intelligentsia critics an essential philosophical dispute over the nature of human existence and mind. As in a great deal of modern argumentation about the human self—an argument that has been at the heart of much modern thought—we see a fundamental clash between what has been called, for simplicity, Enlightenment and Romantic views of the world. It mattered greatly to those concerned with mobilizing individuals to create a revolutionary society and culture in Soviet Russia whether the individual human self was understood as a point of rational and orderly understanding of scientifically knowable truths about the world or as an agent of individual inspiration and genius.[199] In artistic terms, this argument has been partly between mimetic and expressive views of creativity, between efforts to mirror nature's visible truth and efforts to reveal what could be seen only through the inspired imagination and awakened emotions of the creative mind.[200] The difference, as such critics as Lebedev-Polianskii understood, had practical political significance—especially if we accept the tenet, as Soviet cultural leaders certainly did, that knowledge is power, that the correct understanding of the world gave one the capacity to control and change it. In fact, however, the revolutionary culture of Bolshevism had not resolved this difference within itself. In these early years such political intellectuals as Lebedev-Polianskii still represented only part of the totality of Soviet or even Bolshevik culture, however powerful they were becoming. Notwithstanding their vigorous efforts to make proletarian culture choose society over self, rationality over inspiration, and ra-

[197] L. Trotskii, "Leninizm i rabochie kluby," *Prizyv*, no. 5 (August 1924), 13.
[198] V. Polianskii [P. Lebedev-Polianskii], "Poeziia sovetskoi provintsii," *Proletarskaia kul'tura*, no. 7–8 (April–May 1919), 49.
[199] These different interpretations are discussed at length in Taylor, *Sources of the Self*, chaps. 18–22.
[200] See M. H. Abrams, *The Mirror and the Lamp: Romantic Theory and the Critical Tradition* (Oxford, 1953).

tionalist mimesis over Romantic expressivity, the passions of the revolution kept most culture-minded proletarians on another—at least, less decided— path.

As these worker writers probed ever more deeply into the emotional and psychological self for existential and moral meaning, what they found was often disturbing. Different interpretations can be offered to make sense of this evidence. Contemporary critics affixed a variety of labels: "skepticism," "bourgeois individualistic pessimism," "philistine-Menshevik world-feeling-ness" [*obyvatel'sko-menshevistskoe mirooshchushchenitse*], or an unproletarian tendency to "melancholy [*toska*] . . . , dreaminess, phantasms, reveries."[201] More sympathetically—and closer to their own proclaimed views of what they were doing—we might speak of a search for meaning (of the revolution, of life) in the human self, an empathy for the oppressed, a desire to honor and free the suffering self, a sensitivity toward the "emotional side of ideology," and a recognition of the uplifting and sublime power of contemplated tragedy. But we must also recognize a maturing existential despair—a discovery in the self (shared with many modern thinkers) of a "heart of darkness."

Aleksandr Voronskii, the most sensitive and undogmatic of early Soviet Marxist literary critics, suggested that we might recognize in all this proletarian writing about the self echoes of the history of the Russian intelligentsia.[202] Indeed, many of the themes that preoccupied these worker writers were echoes and elaborations of questions about the human person (*lichnost'*) and about human will, freedom, and responsibility that the Russian intelligentsia had been struggling with for a century. Closer at hand, we also hear echoes of thinkers and writers often assumed to be alien to the proletarian imagination: such writers as Dostoevsky, such philosophers as Vladimir Solov'ev, and such modernist poets as Aleksandr Blok and even Konstantin Bal'mont. Many proletarians were as deeply concerned as they with the ontological and moral meaning of the self and with questions of individual responsibility, will, and fate. They, too, found meaning (often sublime meaning) in the contemplation of suffering. And they often shared with them a pessimistic sense that high ideals (beauty, morality, truth) were smashing against the crass and limited possibilities of the ordinary, everyday world. Not least, we see this intelligentsia mentality also in the growing weight of ambivalence and ambiguity in these writings. Self and other, rational conviction and emotion, enthusiasm and despair, and the inspirations of faith and of tragedy were in constant and unresolved dialogue. And, contrary to the wishes of leading Communist in-

---

[201] P. Lebedev-Polianskii, review of new writings by V. Aleksandrovskii in *Proletarskaia kul'tura*, no. 9–10 (June–July 1919), 65–66; S. Rodov, "Motivy tvorchestva M. Gerasimova," *Kuznitsa*, no. 1 (May 1920), 23; Semen Kluben', in *Griadushchaia kul'tura* (Tambov), no. 2 (December 1918), 24; Bogdanov quoting a review of the first issue of *Kuznitsa* in *Kommunisticheskii trud* (1920, no. 50), *Proletarskaia kul'tura*, no. 15–16 (April–July 1920), 91; Voronskii, "O gruppe pisatelei 'Kuznitsa,'" 126, 135.

[202] Voronskii, "O gruppe pisatelei 'Kuznitsa,'" 126.

tellectuals, these uncertainties were not signs of a transition from false consciousness to true. They appear to have been an inescapable and troubled state of mind.

Epilogue: A Fantasy

A story Andrei Platonov published in a provincial Communist journal in 1922 may serve as an archetype of such complexly ambivalent worker writing about the individual and the human condition. Titled "Satana mysli (Fantaziia)" (The Satan of thought: A fantasy), it is a strange work combining elements of utopian science fiction with the cosmic and mystical hyperboles typical of much civil war poetry. It is a story of world-transforming individual genius and heroism and of dreams of creating a world in which individuals can realize all their human capacities and live life to the fullest. But it is also a dark as well as inspiring allegory about love and genius, about a brilliant and deformed personality, about inspired hatred of human limitations, and about the power and destructiveness of the human will. The hero of this tale is equally its antihero, an evil genius, a moral and intellectual superman (in the Nietzschean sense) whom the author finds both attractive and repellent.

Like Platonov's Markun, the hero of this tale, the engineer Vogulov, is a modern Prometheus obsessed with finding a means of harnessing energy in order to liberate humanity. He has a formal assignment from the World Conference of Working Masses to develop and organize the "reconstruction of the earth." But his promethean ambition is motivated also by personal emotions. The seed of Vogulov's genius, Platonov tells us, is unfulfilled and hence sublimated love for a young woman who died soon after their first kiss. The energy force of that love poured from his heart into his brain, burst his skull, and created a brain of impossible, unimaginable power. That love became thought, and that thought became hatred for the present limited world, "where the only thing a person needs is the soul of another person." Vogulov is now determined to break the boundaries of what Nietzsche called this "all too human" world.

Vogulov's plan is to blow up mountain ranges and build giant canals in order to equalize climactic zones. He invents for this purpose an exceedingly explosive energy force he calls "ultralight" (*ultra-svet*)—an anticipation, it would seem, of nuclear energy. After the work of reconstructing the earth has been successfully completed—in only one year—Vogulov turns next, on his own initiative, to the whole universe. Discovering the universe to be a closed circle, confining as a "prison cell," he decides to blow it up with ultralight and "create a new superenergy formation, a different universe." He calculates that it will take three years to prepare enough ultralight. When this work goes too slowly, he introduces into the earth's atmosphere "microbes of energy." The effect is fantastic:

A person died working, he wrote books of incredible beauty, loved like Dante, and lived not years but days, but did not regret this. . . . Humanity lived as if in a hurricane. Each day was like millennia in the production of value. The rapid whirlwind succession of the generations created a new, perfected type of human being of ferocious energy and illumined genius. The microbe of energy made eternity unnecessary. Only a brief moment was necessary to drink of life to the fullest satisfaction.

The story ends as Vogulov is preparing to finish the job and obliterate the existing universe.[203]

I have found no record of how worker writers reacted to this story. But it is likely that they shared Platonov's enthusiasms as well as his evident ambivalence, his sense of existential tragedy. Here, vividly imagined, was their dream of human glorification and self-realization, and in the most modern dress. Here was the triumph of proletarian individuality over bourgeois individualism. Here was their vision of cosmic apocalypse out of which a new world would come. But also, as realized in Platonov's imaginative perception, here was their paradoxical and tragic sensibility—in this case, a tragic view of the victory of individual human genius and potential leading to the extinguishing of all human life in the name of transcending it.

[203] A. Platonov, "Satana mysli (Fantaziia)," *Put' kommunizma* (Krasnodar), no. 2 (March–April 1922), 32–37.

4 *The Moral Landscape*
of the Modern City

Swarming city, city full of dreams,
where ghosts by daylight accost the passer-by.
Mystery runs like sap in the narrow canals,
in the veins of this awesome Colossus. . . .
Foul yellow mist had filled the whole of space.
I roamed, steeling my nerves like a hero,
And argued with my flagging soul,
through back streets shaken by each lumbering cart.
—CHARLES BAUDELAIRE, *Les Fleurs du mal,* 1857

For Baudelaire, the ultimate hero of modernity is the figure who
seeks to give voice to its paradoxes and illusions . . . who is both
scornful and complicitous.
—GRAHAM GILLOCH, *Myth and Metropolis*

The modern city has often been viewed as embodying the ambiguity of modernity. In literary and interpretive writings about the city, which have proliferated in modern Europe and beyond, the urban terrain, especially the modern capitalist city, has often appeared as an exemplar of the contradictoriness of the modern: of the interdependence and inextricability of rationality and disorder, opportunity and peril, imagination and perversion, community and solitude, positive faith and existential unease. Russia shared deeply in these experiences and visions of modernity—the more deeply because it was so late to embrace and experience economic and social modernization and the contradictory drives of modern discipline and disorder. By the turn of the twentieth century, Russian literature and the press were visibly fascinated by the vitality and dangers of modern life (embodied especially in images of the city), with the lure of the modernist project of legibly seeing and ordering

147

society, politics, and the human person, and the no less modernist allure of self-invention, iconoclasm, decadence, ambiguity, and despair.

For Russians, the meaningfulness of the city was complicated and intensified by the particular and mythic weight of the "two capitals" in the Russian cultural imagination: the old capital, Moscow, long viewed as Russia's sacred center and the heir to "true" Christianity (the "Third Rome," inheriting the mantle of debased Rome and fallen Byzantium), and St. Petersburg, Peter the Great's deliberately designed and forcibly built symbol of rational order imposed on nature's chaos, "the most abstract and intentional city in the whole world," as Dostoevsky called it.[1] Even before the age of industrialization in Russia, which began with particular strength in the second half of the nineteenth century (urged by the state as well), St. Petersburg came to represent a characteristic urban modernity, a dynamic and rationally ordered but also chaotic and ephemeral place. Other Russian cities began to echo these features as rapid industrialization and urban development transformed the built environments of towns and cities throughout the empire and brought hundreds of thousands of peasants and others to St. Petersburg, Moscow, Warsaw, Odessa, Riga, Kiev, Kharkov, and other growing industrial and commercial centers. These cities became dynamic sites of social, cultural, and civic change, places where Russians encountered and participated in new social roles and relationships, new forms of work and pleasure, new ideas and images and objects, and new sources of opportunity, inspiration, adversity, anxiety, and fear.

Many of Russia's best-known writers were preoccupied with the modern city, especially St. Petersburg, and its significance. Gogol (in his St. Petersburg tales), Dostoevsky (in his feuilletons and other journalistic writings, in his early stories and novellas, and in *Crime and Punishment*), Gorky (in his writings about the urban lower classes), and Belyi (in his famous modernist novel *Petersburg*) created for Russian literature a poetics of the city that was rich in modern images and in a sense of the contradictoriness of the modern urban landscape. These influential works reflected an emerging reality but also helped catalyze the way many Russians saw and thought about the city and modernity. In these writings, the modern city appeared as a simultaneously vital and sinister place, a place of interwoven virtue and vice, of the fantastic and grotesque beside the orderly and rational, of bright lights and furtive shadows, of artistic creativity and smug vulgarity, of awakening and bewilderment, of transient beauty, and of vibrant possibility beside fragmented, fugitive, and fictive lives. In Gogol and Dostoevsky the city had already become a strangely fractured place in which, instead of whole human beings, only disembodied and disoriented mustaches, noses, sideburns, buttons, coats, hats, and specters are often to be seen, and the city itself becomes a maelstrom of windows, lamps, facades, staircases, noise, smoke, and fog. Beside the city's fascinating vitality was placed ubiquitous dirt, coldness, alienation, greed,

---

[1] Fedor Dostoevsky, *Notes from the Underground,* chap. 2.

cruelty, alcoholism, prostitution, crime, senselessness, misery, disease, moral transgression, madness, and death.[2]

Dostoevsky in particular intertwined hatred and admiration in his ambivalent fascination with the city. Part *flâneur* (privileged stroller and spectator across the boundaries of the urban terrain) and partly one of the struggling urban commoners he observed and reconstructed in writing, Dostoevsky stalked city streets and corners in search of images, sensations, and meanings. His influential portrait of the city was an ambivalent but mainly devastating critique of modernity. The *modern* character of the city, especially St. Petersburg, was explicit: "Here [in Petersburg] one cannot take a step without seeing, hearing, and feeling the contemporary moment and the idea of the present moment. . . . Everything is life and movement." For Dostoevsky, however, as for Gogol and Belyi, this vitality, though alluring, was deeply sinister. Petersburg, according to Dostoevsky, was a "dismal, foul, and stinking" place, filled with "big, black, sooty buildings" and "cold filthy streets," "the embodiment of some blank and dead spirit." And human life in the "vast city" was "senseless and abnormal," filled with "dull egoism, clashing interests, and gloomy vice." Still, Dostoevsky acknowledged (through the voices of such protagonists as Raskol'nikov in *Crime and Punishment* and the "underground man") that there was also a certain satisfaction and allure in the "pale, green, sickly faces" of passers-by, in the "sullen anxiety" that marks the physiognomies of city dwellers, even in one's own "nausea" as one walks through the city.[3]

The periodical press similarly dwelled often on the ambiguous delights and dangers of the city. Daily newspapers, of course, were characteristically modern phenomena: in their commercial concern with the market (with news as a commodity), in their use of modern communications technologies, but also in their way of seeing—in their immediate and fragmented reportage of urban life and in the ambiguities of their vision. No less important in articulating and shaping the way educated Russians thought about the city were the many literary and intellectual journals, professional publications, and ephemeral magazines. Writers in these newspapers and magazines discursively wandered over the new urban terrain, taking their readers on a tour of the modern metropolis, of both the familiar and the unfamiliar, the reassuring and the alarming. Mass-circulation newspapers, in particular, in Russia as elsewhere, made *flânerie*, "the modern urban spectatorship that emphasizes mobility and fluid subjectivity," into "a cultural activity for the generalized . . . public," providing what amounted to "a printed digest of the flâneur's roving eye, helping to

---

[2] The only major work on images of the city in Russian literature is Donald Fanger, *Dostoevsky and Romantic Realism: A Study of Dostoevsky in Relation to Balzac, Dickens, and Gogol* (Cambridge, Mass., 1967). Some Russian literary treatments of the city are also discussed in Burton Pike, *The Image of the City in Modern Literature* (Princeton, 1981), 89–99, and Marshall Berman, *All That Is Solid Melts into Air: The Experience of Modernity* (New York, 1982), 173–286.

[3] Quoted in Fanger, *Dostoevsky and Romantic Realism*, 143, 156, 172, 174, 184, 191, 198, 202.

constitute a new and distinctly modern public."[4] The stance of these writers on the city was often positive and confident: they documented and commended the spread of scientific knowledge and technical know-how; entrepreneurial success and opportunities for upward mobility; the increasing role of cultural institutions (museums, schools, libraries, exhibitions, theaters); the growth of civic organizations (scientific, technical, philanthropic); and the civilizing effects of the constructed beauty and ordered space of city streets and buildings. At the same time, these writers described and decried the city's tendency to esteem mainly material values (especially "vulgar" ones) over spiritual values; the egoistic and predatory practices of the many "capitalists"; the growth of social unrest (though it could not be openly discussed in the censored press); frightening attacks on respectable citizens and civic order by "hooligans"; criminal underworlds of thieves, con men, burglars, and pickpockets; sexual licentiousness and debauchery; prostitution, rape, murder, and suicide; widespread drunkenness (even among women); abandoned children, many of whom turned to vice; spreading morbidity, especially diseases such as syphilis, which resulted from immoral behavior assumed to be associated mainly with city life, and cholera, which seemed to be nurtured by the city's congestion and poor sanitation; the growing presence in the city of harmful aliens (foreigners, gypsies, and Jews, but also lower-class "invaders" from the outskirts of the city); the hazards posed by men and women masquerading as respectable citizens but motivated by lustful or predatory purpose; and the popularity of crass and "uncultured" entertainments such as *cafés chantants,* nightclubs, music halls, "pleasure gardens," cinemas, car races, and wrestling matches.[5]

Marxist intellectuals, in Russia as elsewhere, tried to resolve these contradictions in a dialectic that rationalized the brutal costs of modern progress as

[4] Vanessa Schwartz, *Spectacular Realities: Early Mass Culture in Fin-de-Siècle Paris* (Berkeley, 1999), 10.

[5] Although there has been no systematic study of ideas about the city in Russia, much useful evidence and discussion can be found in studies of late-imperial Russian society and culture, many of which have highlighted responses to problems of urban life and the quest for modernity. See esp. Reginald Zelnik, *Labor and Society in Tsarist Russia: The Factory Workers of St. Petersburg, 1855–1870* (Stanford, 1971); Joseph Bradley, *Muzhik and Muscovite: Urbanization in Late Imperial Russia* (Berkeley, 1985); Michael F. Hamm, ed., *The City in Late-Imperial Russia* (Bloomington, 1986); Daniel Brower, *The Russian City between Tradition and Modernity, 1850–1900* (Berkeley, 1990); Louise McReynolds, *The News under Russia's Old Regime: The Development of a Mass Circulation Press* (Princeton, 1991); Laura Engelstein, *The Keys to Happiness: Sex and the Search for Modernity in Fin-de-Siècle Russia* (Ithaca, 1992); Joan Neuberger, *Hooliganism: Crime, Culture, and Power in St. Petersburg, 1900–1914* (Berkeley, 1993); Stephen Frank and Mark Steinberg, eds., *Cultures in Flux: Lower-Class Values, Practices, and Resistance in Late Imperial Russia* (Princeton, 1994); Laurie Bernstein, *Sonia's Daughters: Prostitutes and Their Regulation in Imperial Russia* (Berkeley, 1995); Katerina Clark, *Petersburg, Crucible of Revolution* (Cambridge, Mass., 1995); Irina Paperno, *Suicide as a Cultural Institution in Dostoevsky's Russia* (Ithaca, 1997); Roshanna Sylvester, "Crime, Masquerade, and Anxiety: The Public Creation of Middle-Class Identity in Pre-Revolutionary Odessa, 1912–1916," Ph.D. diss., Yale University, 1998. My summary of treatments of the modern city also draws on my own survey of articles that appeared in the large Moscow and Petersburg dailies *Gazeta-Kopeika* and *Peterburgskaia gazeta* in 1909–10 and *Rech', Novoe vremia,* and *Russkoe slovo* in 1913.

part of a historical process in which the very horrors of modern life lead logically to a happy transcendence. Often this stance translated as an insistent embrace of the modern industrial city as a place of dynamic change, scientific enlightenment, and social struggle—in contrast to the dark, tradition-bound, and passive countryside. Most important for our concerns here, they presented this vision as the "proletarian" view of the modern city. As the unique product of modern industrial civilization and the primary source of the emerging socialist future, the proletariat was said to be best equipped to understand the full worth of the modern urban world. "Conscious proletarians," by definition, were supposed to have understood the positive values of the city, and to feel at home, as no other group before them ever could feel, in the modern landscape of streets, factories, machines, urban flux, and social conflict. Proletarian writers, as creative voices of this socially and ideologically determined class perspective, were said to have felt a particularly strong and natural love for the vitality of the industrial city, to be attracted to the city as a source of power and knowledge and as a terrain of struggle and hope, and to understand the dialectical historical meaning of the contradictions of modern life. As one Marxist literary critic stated confidently in 1914, in reviewing the newly published *Pervyi sbornik proletarskikh pisatelei* (First anthology of proletarian writers), proletarian writers "clearly see and understand that the modern city is an arena of struggle, the seething center where the liberating armies gather, struggling for a new world."[6] And within the city, it was precisely the most modern features of its landscape—factories and machines—that conscious proletarians, especially proletarian writers, were said to understand and love best. Inspired by the historical optimism of the proletarian outlook, it was said, worker writers felt great "love" for factories and machines. And any anger worker writers voiced against modern industry, in the words of a Bolshevik reviewer of the 1914 anthology of proletarian writers, was "directed not against factories and machines, but against the whole social order. The factory itself appears to the proletarian as something close and familial."[7] "Conscious" proletarians, it was said, understood "that in the whirl and noise of spinning wheels was born a new life, new thoughts, and a host of strong fighters for a bright life."[8]

[6] M. Kalinin [A. Karinian] in *Rabochii* [*Pravda*], 23 June 1914, rpt. in *Dooktiabr'skaia "Pravda" ob iskusstve i literature* (Moscow, 1937), 39. See also V. M. Friche, *Proletarskaia poeziia*, 3d ed. (Moscow, 1919), 68–69, 78; P. Bessal'ko, "Proletarskie poety," *Griadushchee* 1919, no. 1: 15.

[7] Friche, *Proletarskaia poeziia*, 88; V. L. L'vov-Rogachevskii, introduction to A. Bibik, *K shirokoi doroge (Ignat iz Novoselovki)* (St. Petersburg, 1914), iii–iv; M. Kalinin [A. Karinian] in *Rabochii* [*Pravda*], 23 June 1914, rpt. in *Dooktiabr'skaia "Pravda" ob iskusstve i literature*, 44. See also L. M. Kleinbort, "Ocherki rabochei demokratii: Fabrichnye-zavodskie poety," *Sovremennyi mir*, November 1913, 175–76, and "Ocherki rabochei demokratii: Belletristy-sotsiology," *Sovremennyi mir*, December 1913, 167. This view of "proletarian" literature became increasingly canonical in Soviet literary histories. See, e.g., L. I. Shishkina, "Proletarskaia poeziia," in *Istoriia russkoi literatury v chetyrekh tomakh*, 4 vols.(Leningrad, 1983), 4: esp. 398.

[8] V. Polianskii [P. Lebedev-Polianskii], "Motivy rabochei poezii," *Proletarskaia kul'tura*, no. 3 (August 1918), 5.

The modern city did indeed fascinate worker writers, but few ever succeeded in seeing the city as clearly and unambivalently as educated Marxists
thought they did or wished them to. Few, if any, ever managed to feel entirely
at home in the city—though not for want of trying. Notwithstanding arguments, which they embraced, about the historical and aesthetic values of modern urban life, the city and the factory remained stubbornly alien and even
malevolent in the minds of even conscious proletarian writers. Part of the
problem lay in the paradoxical nature of the Marxist vision of modernity.
Marxists simultaneously recognized the brutalities of urban industrial modernity—the oppression, the disenchantment of the world, the decadence, the
painful disorder—and celebrated its dynamic energy, productive power, and
emancipating change. Most important, they framed their radical critique of
modern industrial society in a theoretical promise of dialectical transcendence:
the certainty that the brutalities of capitalist modernity would result, precisely
out of its contradictions, in the creation of a society in which all human beings could live to their full potential and pleasure. As Marshall Berman has
encapsulated the essential paradox, Marx hoped "to heal the wounds of
modernity through a fuller and deeper modernity."[9] The paradox pervaded
Marxism, but it was not always comfortably resolved—least of all for urban
workers, for whom the harshness of modern life was particularly immediate
and tangible.

Workers' judgments about city life and machine industry were influenced
by their everyday experiences: by the opportunities and stimulation the city
and factory afforded them as well as by their intimacy with the harsh conditions and perils of urban life and work. Subjective experiences also shaped
their views of the urban landscape: traditions of peasant anti-urbanism; discourse in the popular press about modern city life; literary images of city, factory, and machine they encountered as they became more literate and well
read; and ideological values they acquired as they became politicized. But
workers' views of the city were not simply shaped by various influences. Workers also deliberately manipulated the images of the city, factory, and machine
to express ideas, values, and sentiments. The industrial city was both the physical place where workers lived and labored and a usable image, a symbolic
landscape with which they could express feelings and judgments about many
other things: about the social order, human relationships, and the whole of
their lives. The modern industrial city was both a real landscape demanding
their attention and shaping their perceptions and a means of intellectual expression. In these perceptions and expressions, ethics and aesthetics were central. If the modern city was both oppressive and liberating, both malevolent
and vital, these were as much physical as social facts, but also as much questions of beauty and moral feeling as of class or history.

[9] Berman, *All That Is Solid*, 98.

"The Beautiful City-Beast"

Some of the more politicized worker writers, armed with the modernist aesthetics and dialectics of Marxism, made every effort to voice an appreciative urbanism. And they looked to the modern city not only intellectually, as the setting for the dialectical dawning of a better future, but emotionally and aesthetically, as a place to be loved and admired, to be appreciated according to new values and standards of beauty. Among the poems and stories selected by the Marxist (and mainly Bolshevik) publishers of the first anthology of proletarian writers in 1914, many described the vital impression the city made.[10] Stories portrayed the migration of peasants to St. Petersburg and other industrial cities as sad—so many young people have left for the city, an old woodcutter muses, that "no songs are now heard in the village"—but as necessary, for the city is the place where the future lies. "It's not for nothing that all the boys and girls have left," the woodcutter admits.[11] Once in the city, young peasant-workers recognized its greater vitality: the shouting and swearing of the crowds at a bazaar, the noise of the streets, the singing of a young worker, the glow of lamps, the sounds of factory whistles, the power of labor and struggle.[12] In a second anthology of proletarian writers, edited and published by Gorky in 1917, Ivan Loginov, a Bolshevik metalworker, offered a nearly canonical view of the city. The author called on his readers to look beyond the "poverty-stricken villages / And decrepit peasant huts," beyond the "hopeless plains" of the past, and recognize that "away from sorrow / there is only one path: / Toward the great city-giant." For only in the city is there the possibility of "movement and struggle." Only in the city, in the "noisy and harsh . . . realm of factories and machines," can one escape the "plains of fate" and find "the embryo of a new life."[13]

These writers seem to have found in urban and industrial landscapes a new modern identity: a vision of self and self-fulfillment that was rooted in the artifice, vitality, and flux of city life. Many found the modern city emotionally compelling as well, as a place where life "seethes, dazzling and intoxicating."[14] But they invariably hesitated before this choice—contradicted it, tried

[10] *Pervyi sbornik proletarskikh pisatelei* (St. Petersburg, 1914). The publishers selected the works of 13 of the 94 authors who submitted writings. The collection, which featured an introduction by Gorky, was published by the Priboi publishing house, which had been established in St. Petersburg in 1912, under the liberalized censorship conditions, as a legal Marxist publishing house, and was run by Bolsheviks or individuals close to the Bolshevik Party. Lenin recognized Priboi as the official Bolshevik press: *Knigovedenie: Entsiklopedicheskii slovar'* (Moscow, 1981), 426.

[11] V. Torskii, "Na porubke," in *Pervyi sbornik*, 24.

[12] E.g., P. Strelkov, "Na zarabotke"; M. Gerasimov, "V gorode"; A. Pomorskii, "Fonarshchik"; and M. Artamonov, "Zabastovka," all in *Pervyi sbornik*, 32, 51, 52, 91, 93.

[13] I. Loginov, "V gorode," in *Sbornik proletarskii pisatalei*, ed. M. Gor'kii, A. Serebrov, and A. Chapygin (Petrograd, 1917), 174. The collection was published by Gorky's publishing venture, Parus (The sail).

[14] M. Artamonov, "Taet," *Metallist* 1914, no. 4/41 (1 Apr.): 5–6.

to flee from it, doubted their own faith. Typical was the poem "V gorode" (In the city) by Mikhail Gerasimov, probably the best-known and most accomplished Marxist worker poet at that time. The poem begins (and these are the lines most often quoted by Soviet literary historians) by subverting the conventional pastoral imagery that pervaded nineteenth-century poetry:

> Into gardens of iron and granite,
> Into parkways of stone,
> I went entwined with spring
> To the festive call of factory whistles.

But as the poem develops, Gerasimov speaks of hesitation and doubt, of a sense of regret, loss, and estrangement:

> I broke my friendship with the wind of freedom,
> And forgot the unbounded expanse,
> The quiet of broad native lands,
> The earth softened with flowers.
>
> I exchanged for the silk of gently singing grass
> Harsh stone.
> I fell in love with the flash of bright colors,
> And the noise of street pleasures.
>
> Caught up in the city's swift torrents,
> I became foreign to my own self [*ia stal dushe svoei chuzhei*],
> And former days among the fields
> Became like a distant dream.[15]

Two voices vie in this proletarian song of the city. Gerasimov was determined to see the city as a Marxist and a worker should, to suppress sentiment with will and rationality. But he also admitted the existential pain this effort caused: the sense of becoming a stranger to himself.

Such ambivalence is to be found in writings by many worker writers. A writer associated with the Surikov Circle of "writers from the people" described his migration from village to city as a pilgrimage, a journey "to the mountains [the Russian words for "city" and "mountain," *gorod* and *gora*, are phonetically close], to their snowy and pure heights . . . to find wisdom among the people there, to find truth there." He was disappointed—city people turned out to be cold, superficial, and vulgar.[16] The leader of the Surikov Circle, Grigorii Deev-Khomiakovskii, published a similar tale of a peasant migrant's ambivalent encounter with urban working-class life. The story was titled "Prozrel" (a verb indicating the gaining of sight and understanding). The tale begins as a young peasant boy is handed over by his parents to a mer-

---

[15] M. Gerasimov, "V gorode," in *Pervyi sbornik*, 51.
[16] S. Kashkarev, "Durak," *Drug naroda* 1915, no. 2 (31 Jan.): 9.

chant, who will take the boy to the city to work as a sales clerk. His reactions pass through stages of comprehension. His first response to the city, even before he leaves the country, is "envy," inspired by the sight of wealthy city people visiting country estates: their clothes, watches, cigarettes, and "white faces" convince him that all city people are "beautiful" and live lives that are "pure and good." This belief is shared, readers are told, by all the young people of the village, who therefore "dream of going to the city." Thus "tempted," the peasant lad leaves his village with excitement and anticipation. More complex feelings appear after he arrives in the city. "Stunned" by the noise of city streets, he is no longer certain where or even who he is, and he is frightened by the tall buildings, which seem to threaten to fall and crush him at any moment. And there are other dangers and fears: he might be run over by a tram, a cab, or a speeding automobile. Soon, however, he enters a new stage in seeing and understanding the city: fascination with its newness and beauty. Now he is "ready to spend all day gazing at the moving crowds, the rushing automobiles, the dressed-up ladies." After he begins to work and live among city people, this way of seeing and understanding is replaced by another: by the discovery that urbanites, especially the poor, are cruel, mean, vulgar, and violent. The city begins to disgust him. He begins to "despise his surroundings." He escapes first into books. And then, after he is fired from his job for striking back at a supervisor who was beating him, he returns to the countryside. "I do not want to live in this hell," he declares, "in this whirlpool of debauchery and ambition [*omut razvrata i chestoliubiia*]."[17]

For populist-inclined writers such as these, such a resolution may have seemed reasonable and possible. But for most worker writers, influenced by Marxism and democratic liberalism, rejecting the city was hopelessly retrograde and irrational. The city was necessary and progressive—and in any case inescapable. But this recognition made conflicted feelings about the city harder to resolve. We see this difficulty in Gerasimov's "In the City" and in many other writings by workers. For example, the Menshevik metalworker Aleksei Bibik, in his novel *K shirokoi doroge* (Toward the open road), has the politically and socially conscious Artem rebuke his wavering comrade Ignat (the more autobiographical protagonist) for not loving the city enough, for still feeling the lure of the woods and dreaming of a pastoral springtime filled with the songs of nightingales and orioles.[18] The argument, like the many dialogues in the book between these two worker friends, should be seen less as representing the efforts of conscious workers to correct the false consciousness of others than as dialogues within the consciousness of many individual workers. In theory, these two voices could be reconciled; the argument, as it were, could be won. Workers could deliberately *learn* to love the city by acquiring sufficient ideological knowledge to understand the historical dialectic of ur-

[17] G. Deev-Khomiakovskii, "Prozrel," *Drug naroda* 1915, no. 1 (1 Jan.): 4–9.
[18] A. Bibik, *K shirokoi doroge (Ignat iz Novoselovki)* (St. Petersburg, 1914), 59–60. The novel was first published in 1912 in the leftist journal *Sovremennyi mir*.

ban life. As a character states in a sketch by Bibik published in 1913 in a Menshevik newspaper: "I know that my life has been thoroughly poisoned by this vampire, which perpetually destroys life and then recreates it in new and ever more majestic forms. It is an oven in which we working people are burned up. But as we burn, we are creating steam engines, bridges, telegraphs, etc. We are creating new forms of human life—forms that will, in the end, give us our freedom!"[19]

Vasilii Aleksandrovskii similarly resolved contradictory feelings about the city—the subject and title of a poem published in September 1917—by recognizing the progressive teleology of history:

> It is greedy with hunger.
> And always merciless toward the weak.
> It poisons youthful dreams. . . .
> Bloody,
> It seeks more and more glory
> From timid, weak slaves.
> It laughs loudly
> At those who don't want
> Its deathly chains. . . .
> On awakening, like a beast, it is stern,
> Sowing seeds of enmity.
> But the time will come
> When it will forget
> Force, and cruelty, and blood.
> And, with awe,
> Grasp joy and humor, too,
> A new life and love.[20]

The Marxist historical dialectic allowed workers, in theory, to glorify the city without romanticizing its present realities, without denying the obvious horrors of city life. This ability to see—unlike Deev-Khomiakovskii's claim for true "vision" based on accumulated experience, which led to rejecting the city—depended on learned knowledge and deliberate reason, as well as faith in the promises of modernity and socialist change. Appropriately, some workers echoed the scriptural distinction between sinful earthly cities and the coming City of God in portraying the struggling proletariat marching through the present "gloom and fog" toward a "radiant new city."[21]

These deliberate acts of intellectual will and faith, however, did not efface conflicting ideas and feelings. Indeed, notwithstanding the encouragements of ideology, the brutalities of city life remained too palpable for workers to ignore. The ideological vision of progress and modernity offered still too faint a picture to conceal effectively what workers saw around them using ordinary

[19] A. Bibik, "Bor obrechennyi," *Novaia rabochaia gazeta*, 13 Oct. 1913.
[20] V. Aleksandrovskii, "Gorod," *Vpered!* 13 (26) September 1917.
[21] Koshennyi, "Na novyi god," *Nash put'*, no. 12 (14 Jan. 1911), 9.

sight. To be sure, worker writers sometimes emphasized the *particular* sufferings of the poor in the city, suggesting a class perspective on the evils of urban life. Thus, as we have seen, Aleksandrovskii portrayed the city as a devouring "beast" preying on "timid, weak slaves" (though there may have been as much Nietzsche here as Marx). More concretely, many described the particular sufferings of peasants who came to the city to work. Mikhail Loginov (himself a peasant turned urban worker who was dying of tuberculosis, the archetypal urban disease), described the peasant who comes to Moscow in search of work as finding the city to be a "web and a spider" that snare the poor "proletarian."[22] Peasants who came to the city to escape from poverty, like the peasant girl in Aleksandrovskii's story who sought work as a seamstress, were often shown finding only new suffering: a damp basement room, cockroaches, the heavy smell of kerosene, and sleepless nights worrying about feeding her son.[23] A story in one of the magazines that featured the works of "writers from the people" tells the tragic (and melodramatic) tale of a young worker, eagerly looking forward to a holiday when he will return to his native village, who is run over and killed by a speeding automobile—driven by rich theatergoers preoccupied with discussing art.[24] In one of the stories that appeared in the 1914 anthology of proletarian writers, the city drives a starving peasant migrant first to crime and then to a madness that causes him, even after he has fled the city, to leap into a fire to his death.[25] The "happy life of the city" may have existed, Petr Zaitsev wrote, but it was "not for us."[26]

Worker writers, however, did not confine themselves to viewing the city as the setting of class inequality and oppression. The harm of the city was seen to be not only social, and thus correctable by social reform or revolution, but also aesthetic and moral, and thus intrinsic to the nature of the modern city. The physical and visual spaces of the city were seen to reflect its alien spirit. The city was portrayed as a place of diminished light and restricted vision. Numerous workers described city streets as "stone corridors" that blocked out the warmth and light of the sun, city buildings as "high, cold, and gloomy" or as "blind, many-eyed boxes," and the "damp stone basements" in which workers lived as "in prison."[27] In a story by Mikhail Artamonov, which appeared in the journal of the Petersburg metalworkers' union, a metalworker feels a painful sense of confinement amidst the city's high walls and restricted views. After a day confined in his factory, he returns to his "apartment with its one window, a window that does not look out onto fields or the broad ex-

[22] M. T-ts [Tikhoplesets = M. A. Loginov], "Gorodskiia kvartiry," *Zvezda iasnaia* [*Zvezda utrenniaia*], no. 6 (29 Feb. 1912), 2.

[23] V. Aleksandrovskii, "Portnikha," *Luch: Rabochaia gazeta,* 31 May 1913.

[24] M. Buianov, "Sviatoe Iskusstvo," *Narodnaia sem'ia,* no. 5 (4 Mar. 1912), 8–9.

[25] P. Strelkov, "Na zarabotke," in *Pervyi sbornik,* 27–38.

[26] P. Zaitsev, "Sapozhnik ia," *Kolotushka,* no. 4 (Easter 1911), 2.

[27] M. T-ts [M. A. Loginov], "Gorodskiia kvartiry," *Zvezda iasnaia* [*Zvezda utrenniaia*], no. 6 (29 Feb. 1912), 2; Sergei Gan'shin, "Ia syn stepei," *Zhivoe slovo,* no. 18 (May 1913), 6; A. Bibik, "Bor obrechennyi," *Novaia rabochaia gazeta,* 13 Oct. 1913; P. Zaitsev, "Sapozhnik ia," *Kolotushka,* no. 4 (Easter 1911), 2.

panses of the Volga, but comes up against a brick wall."[28] Similarly, Petr Zaitsev, in a eulogy to a dead comrade, blamed the city for suffocating this fellow "worker and peasant" literally to death: "You perished in captivity, the stifling city destroyed you."[29] Even the dynamic physical growth of the city seemed fearsome: "Moscow grows, but it grows not like a fairy-tale hero [*skazochnyi bogatyr*], but like a horrible monster."[30]

The city, of course, was judged not only as a physical site but also as a human space. The city, it was said, was a "tedious" and "cursed" place, dominated by a "gloomy, soulless, and haughty crowd."[31] It was a place filled with "human hatred," "enmity" (even among the poor, wandering from town to town in search of work), the "cruelty" of people, even working people, to one another, and the loneliness of individuals unconnected to one another.[32] The soul of the city, it was said, was as cold as its face: "The whole city is built of stone, and the people in it live just as coldly, just as smooth as the stones from which buildings are made."[33] Even Vladimir Kirillov, writing amidst the 1917 revolution as a political activist publishing in a Bolshevik anthology, wrote of the cold terrors of the city, in this case at evening, when, "With shadows sinister and sullen / Fear creeps into the city, / And the restless noises fall silent / On streets gloomy and severe."[34] The coldness of urban life was a pervasive image—and, as it was applied to workers and the poor as much as to other classes, it tended to clash with the Marxist ideal of the city as uniting the proletariat in common awakening, sympathy, and purpose.

The city was also seen as alien in its moral character. Among the varied worker critiques of modern city life, the pervading moral depravity of the city drew the most attention. In numerous essays, stories, and poems, workers denounced the city's "crass vulgarity" (*poshlost'*), "dissoluteness" (*raspushennost'*), and "debauchery" (*razvrat*). Ivan Kubikov regularly warned workers against the dangers of the "'tavern civilization' of the city centers, with its chateaux-bars, open-stage musical comedies, cinemas, alehouses, gramophones, etc.," and generally against the crass commercial culture of the modern city.[35] The populist M. A. Loginov similarly warned against the decadent "epicureanism" of urban society and the "dissoluteness" (*raspushennost'*) of

---

[28] M. Artamonov, "Taet," *Metallist* 1914, no. 4/41 (1 Apr.), 4. See also M. Tsarev [V. Torskii], "V kazarme" (1916), in *Proletarskie poety*, 3 vols. (Leningrad, 1935–39), 3:137.

[29] P. Zaitsev, "Na mogile K. A. Molchanova," *Kolotushka* 1911, no. 2: 3.

[30] M. T-ts [M. A. Loginov], "Gorodskiia kvartiry," *Zvezda iasnaia* [*Zvezda utrenniaia*], no. 6 (29 Feb. 1912), 2.

[31] S. Gan'shin, "Ia syn stepei," *Zhivoe slovo*, no. 18 (May 1913), 6; *Vpered!* 21 July 1917.

[32] P. Zaitsev, "Sapozhnik ia," *Kolotushka*, no. 4 (Easter 1911), 2; A. Dikii, "Bezrabotnye," *Edinstvo*, no. 6 (15 June 1909), 3; D. Gordeev, "Noch'iu: Ocherki goroda," in *Pervyi sbornik*, 40–50.

[33] S. Kashkarev, "Durak," *Drug naroda* 1915, no. 2 (31 Jan.): 9.

[34] Vladimir Kirillov, "Trevozhnyi vecher," *Pod znamenem pravdy: Pervyi sbornik obshchestva proletarskikh iskusstv* (Petersburg [sic], 1917), 15–16. Also rpt. in V. Kirillov, *Stikhotvoreniia, 1914–1918* (Petersburg [sic], 1918), 23.

[35] Kvadrat [I. Kubikov], "Kul'tura i prosveshcheniia," *Pechatnoe delo*, no. 8 (27 June 1909), 5, and "Deshevaia gazeta i kinematograf," *Pechatnoe delo*, no. 11 (30 Sept. 1909), 2–6.

even the children of the city's poor.[36] Others wrote with disgust of pornography as "filth," "contagion," and "poison," and of commercial newspapers as filled with stories of prostitution, brothels, drunkenness, and "nothing but scandal and more scandal owing to drunkenness, 'heavenly nights,' and other abominations."[37] In poetry and fiction, worker writers (including social democrats writing in publications affiliated with Marxist parties) similarly condemned the "vulgarity of everyday life in the city" (*poshlosti dnei goroda*) and the moral dangers of the city, where, amidst "complacent, vulgar [*poshlyi*] laughter / The boulevard with a serpent's head / Calls you to terrible sin."[38]

The moral dangers of the city were seen to be especially hazardous for women—for, as we have seen, their fall was easily and conventionally understood to symbolize the fate of natural innocence, beauty, and weakness in the city. Stories of young peasant women falling into prostitution were especially potent moral tales. Like much of the public discussion of prostitution in Russia, as in other countries, workers' stories of "fallen women" tended to reflect a traditional but rhetorically powerful image of women as weak innocents and symbols of purity whose fall revealed the captivating evils of modern urban life.[39] The best-known and most influential example of this theme was the Bolshevik worker poet Aleksandr Pomorskii's 1913 poem "Zhertvam goroda" (For the victims of the city).

> Girls from the factory, doomed sacrifices,
> Pale, tired, darkened by sadness. . . .
>
> Lithe and youthful, rural treasures,
> You came to the beautiful city-beast [*gorod-chudovishche*]. . . .
>
> It enticed you, girls, with its golden colors,
> Lulled you with sounds and burning stories. . . .
>
> And you entered the factories, cramped prisons,
> Unknown girls, you sold your strength.
>
> In the morning, only the sun rises in the sky
> In your blood, the factory greedily bathes. . . .
>
> You could not endure the oppression—your patience ran out!
> And you fell into the cruel abyss, into autumnal dusk.

---

[36] Mikhail Tikhoplesets [M. Loginov], "Epikuritsy," *Zvezda iasnaia* [*Zvezda utrenniaia*], no. 6 (29 Feb. 1912), 5–6, and "Shirokiia natury," *Dumy narodnye*, no. 5 (27 Feb. 1910), 2.

[37] *Balalaika*, 1910, no. 12, 1; M. Volkov, "Obzor pechati," *Narodnaia sem'ia*, no. 4 (19 Feb. 1912), 12–14.

[38] S. Gan'shin, "Krest'ianka," *Zhivoe slovo*, no. 20 (May 1913); M. Gerasimov, "U vitriny," *Prosveshchenie* 1914, no. 1 (January), 6, rpt. in *Poeziia v bol'shevistskikh izdaniiakh, 1901–1917* (Leningrad, 1967), 285, and in *Privolzhskaia pravda*, 2 Sept. 1917.

[39] See Engelstein, *Keys to Happiness*; Bernstein, *Sonia's Daughters*; Barbara Heldt, *Terrible Perfection: Women and Russian Literature* (Bloomington, 1987); Judith Walkowitz, *Prostitution and Victorian Society: Women, Class, and the State* (New York, 1980) and *City of Dreadful Delight: Narratives of Sexual Danger in Late-Victorian London* (Chicago, 1992).

To the city you sold your pure body,
You cast your soul into the turbulent whirlpool.

And went out into the foggy evening streets.
Timid, afraid, long awaited by the beast.

He fell asleep, the monster, tired from roaring.
In the blue-clothed distance are concealed fragments of laughter.

The morning colors cast faint crimson—
Extinguishing terrible dreams, stories of drunken lives.

Despised girls, driven by the city,
Daughters no more beloved by nature.[40]

Like Mikhail Gerasimov's image of a prostitute—in a poem published in the summer of 1917 in a provincial Bolshevik paper—as an "injured, wingless seagull" (an apparent reference to Anton Chekhov's symbol of female innocence victimized by men),[41] whom "the city has nailed up," who throws herself into one of St. Petersburg's "rusty canals,"[42] these are images of women that evoke a moral lesson: the harm inflicted by city life and the ultimate deceit and cruelty of the city's charms and allure.

Machine Hymns

Machine industry was at the heart of the city's character as a modern terrain, especially in the minds of workers. In thinking and writing about factory and machine, as about the city, worker writers drew upon and deployed a mixture of political, social, and especially moral and aesthetic values. Like the city, factories and machines have long figured prominently in literary meditations on human civilization, especially on modernity, which has been driven by the will to modify both the physical environment and social and economic relationships with applied technology. Factories and machines—and the associated values of power, rationality, efficiency, and change—have been hallmarks, and hence symbols, of this modern spirit. In all of these treatments, factories and machines have simultaneously been seen as tangible realities and manipulable symbols:

---

[40] A. Pomorskii, "Zhertvam goroda," *Metallist* 1913, no. 5/29 (July 19), 4. The poem was also printed, with some small changes, in the anthology of writings by worker poets associated with Countess Panina's People's House (Narodnyi dom) in St. Petersburg, *Nashi pesni: Pervyi sbornik* (St. Petersburg, 1913), 9.

[41] In Chekhov's play *The Seagull* a male character explains to the aspiring actress Nina Zarechnyi the meaning of his killing of a seagull as "an idea for a plot": "A young girl like you has lived her life by a lake. Like a seagull, she loves the lake, and she's happy and free like a seagull. But a man happens to come along and wrecks her life for the want of anything better to do. As happened to this seagull": *The Oxford Chekhov*, trans. and ed. Ronald Hingley, vol. 2 (London, 1967), 257.

[42] M. Gerasimov, "Chaiki," *Privolzhskaia Pravda*, 25 Aug. 1917, rpt. in *Poeziia v bol'shevistskikh izdaniiakh*, 365–66.

emblems of human inventiveness and power, and even of new and better social relationships, but also as signs of the erosion of a once natural and organic human existence.[43] On the eve of World War I the Flemish writer Emile Verhaeren was one of the most popular poets in Europe—even in Russia, where his visit in the winter of 1913 was widely celebrated and extensively reported in the daily press. Like many progressive-minded Russians and Europeans, Verhaeren occasionally wrote of the "beauty of the modern" and voiced "enthusiasm" (a favorite term) for industrial and scientific progress—for factories and machines, industrial workers, street advertisements, the stock exchange. This modernist enthusiasm, however, was compromised (and as such made more "modern" in the fullest sense of the term) by a persistent anxiety, ambivalence, pessimism, and even regret in the face of the aggressiveness and destructiveness of the whole modern effort, the power of the "octopus cities" ("Les Villes tentaculaires"—translated into Russian as "Goroda-spruty"—was one of his best-known works) to destroy nature and draw men into their degrading clutches, the "formidable and criminal arms of hyperbolic machines," and the dehumanizing mechanization of life, work, and leisure.[44] Russian worker writers expressed the same anxieties and doubts. Even the few who claimed to admire the spirit of factory and machine could not silence contrary themes and ambiguity. More often, and more simply, worker writers placed machine industry at the heart of the city's physical ugliness and moral malevolence.

Workers who embraced industrial modernity did so partly for ideological reasons, as part of the Marxist faith in the beneficial march of industrial modernity, and this faith was reflected in the abstract and symbolic nature of most of their writing. According to an essay in 1907 in the journal of the Petersburg metalworkers' union (probably by an intellectual activist in this socialist-led union), factories and machinery represented the "power" man can potentially exercise over nature. A time will come, it was said, when, by means of cities, factories, machines, ships, trains, tall buildings, and the telegraph, man will have "subdued for himself land and sea, subjugated to himself wind and air, and conquered space." As a result, poverty, hunger, and cold will be vanquished and all people will live happy and creative lives filled with poetry, science, and art.[45] It was with such a vision that one of the leading worker po-

---

[43] See Arthur O. Lewis, Jr., ed., *Of Men and Machines* (New York, 1963); Leo Marx, *The Machine in the Garden: Technology and the Pastoral Ideal in America* (New York, 1964); Michael Adas, *Machines as the Measure of Men: Science, Technology, and Ideologies of Western Dominance* (Ithaca, 1989); Bruce Mazlish, *The Fourth Discontinuity: The Co-evolution of Humans and Machines* (New Haven, 1993).

[44] For a useful summary of Verhaeren's work, see P. Mansell Jones, *Verhaeren* (New Haven, 1957), esp. 33–34. For a contemporary Russian view, see the article on Verhaeren by Valerii Briusov (who translated many of Verhaeren's poems) in *Novyi entsiklopedicheskii slovar'* (St. Petersburg, 1911–16), 10:264–67. Verhaeren's works, in translation, appeared widely in Russian anthologies and journals as well as in individual volumes in the early 1900s. On Verhaeren's visit to Russia, see *Russkoe slovo*, 26, 28, and 30 Nov. and 4 and 6 Dec. 1913; *Novoe vremia*, 28 Nov. and 2 Dec.1913; *Rech'*, 13 Dec. 1913.

[45] I. Sm., "Zhizn' cheloveka v raznykh vremenakh," *Rabochii po metallu*, no. 23 (25 Oct. 1907), 4–6.

ets of the union, a metalworker who called himself Chechenets (Chechen), identified factories as symbols of "hope."[46] This rhetoric became noticeably more common among worker writers during the revolutionary upheavals of 1917. According to Vasilii Aleksandrovskii, who was politically close to the Mensheviks, the factory was where ideas of struggle were nurtured among workers.[47] Bolshevik writers in 1917 were even more insistent on the benefits of modern industry, though these assertions also tended to be the most abstract and symbolic. For Il'ia Sadof'ev, factories (especially the symbolic "smithy") were places where "strong" and "bold" workers forged their "happiness."[48] For Mikhail Gerasimov, the flames in the factory furnace were a symbolic force that workers would seize as they rose up in rebellion.[49] And "the noise of the factories," in the symbolic image offered by the Bolshevik metalworker Ivan Loginov, was "the might of the world's peoples."[50]

Sometimes these writings went beyond abstraction and symbolism toward a more fantastic image of factories and machines coming alive to voice similar arguments. A well-known worker writer who called himself Andrei Dikii, and who often published in the Petersburg metalworkers' paper, envisioned machines as living beings speaking to workers, telling them of "the need to seize happiness through struggle."[51] In answer, as it were, the author addressed himself to factories and machines to reassure them (implicitly against evidence to the contrary) that conscious workers felt no personal enmity toward them. Conscious workers love factories, Dikii argued, because workers feel their power over machines. But the relationship went beyond this equation of domination and love. Factories, Dikii wrote, "understand [workers'] miseries intimately," as is evident in the groans and cries of the machinery "during the hard and melancholy days of labor." Most important, factories and machines hold the promise of ending this suffering and bringing the new proletarian age: "Wheels sing with love / Of the new days that are to come. / In union with fire and metal / Creating, we fuse into one."[52]

An *aesthetic* love of machines and factories, a feel for the power, vitality, and inspiring sounds and rhythms of machines and factories, wove through many of these writings (foreshadowing what became a large part of the allure and power of these ideas after 1917). Typically, this was a gendered vision, a view of machine industry in conventionally masculine terms—as hard, strong, bold, and aggressive—and factories as places where men bond together. An early example of this aesthetic love of modern industry was a poem in the

---

[46] Chechenets, "Pesnia rabov," *Rabochii po metallu*, no. 22 (10 Oct. 1907), 3. The pseudonym was probably a romantic gesture of identification with the myth of the northern Caucasus rather than a reference to the author's ethnicity.

[47] V. Aleksandrovskii, "Na zavode," *Vpered!* no. 72 (3 June 1917), 3.

[48] Aksen-Achkasov [I. Sadof'ev], "Pred razsvetom," *Rabochii put'* [*Pravda*], 23 Oct. 1917.

[49] M. Gerasimov, "Na zavode," *Privolzhskaia pravda*, 18 Aug. 1917, rpt. in *Poeziia v bol'shevistskikh izdaniiakh*, 363–64.

[50] *Proletarskie poety*, 3:107.

[51] A. Dikii, "Za rabotoi," *Edinstvo*, no. 14 (16 Feb. 1910), 6.

[52] Andrei Dikii, "Mashinam," in *Pervyi sbornik*, 76. According to some sources, Dikii was Afanasii M. Gmyrev, the brother of the well-known Bolshevik worker poet Aleksei Gmyrev, who died in prison in 1911.

newspaper of the Petersburg metalworkers' union in 1907, which waxed enthusiastic about the vitality and living movement of the spinning gears, turning belts, and striking hammers.[53] We do not in fact know who wrote this poem—it is quite possible that the author was not a worker. And until after the October Revolution, this aesthetic remained rare and mainly Bolshevik: Bolshevik publications were virtually the only places such writings appeared, and most of the writers who favored such imagery (notably Chechenets, Dikii, Gerasimov, and Loginov) were associated with the party. Still, even for the few writers who occasionally explored the beauty (or at least necessity) of modern industry, a darker aesthetic view of industrial modernity remained present and often dominant.

It is telling that among worker writers before 1918 none embraced so fully the love of machines and factories as Aleksei Gastev. Having entered the proletarian world of factories and machines after being expelled for political activities from a teachers' institute, he had an exceptional relation to industry from the first. As early as 1910, Gastev wrote of his fascination with the forward-moving speed, power, and thrust of the machinery he operated as the driver of an electric streetcar in St. Petersburg.[54] Like other Marxist authors, he wrote of machines as symbols of "new hope"[55] and of the historically transformative force of industrial modernity. He wrote, for example, of a "marvelous" future when "the modern force of machinism" would create a "great, growing, thrillingly felt world of harmony."[56] But the attraction was as much aesthetic and physical (even sexual) as social or moral. Especially as Gastev turned from prose to poetry, which he began to do on the eve of the war, he gave his imagination freer reign and expressed a growing passion for the sensual power, bold sounds, and unifying and creative rhythms of lathes, cranes, gears, belts, engines, railroads, iron, and steel.[57]

> I fell in love with you, iron roar,
> With festive sound of steel and stone,
> With lava—the restless, insurgent fire
> Of machine hymns, and their daring, brilliant tone.
> I fell in love with your mighty whirlwind,
> With the stormy sea of shafts and wheels,
> Peals of thunder, melodious rhythms,
> Awesome stories, wordless tales.[58]

[53] A. Zakharov, "Na rabote," *Rabochii po metallu*, no. 18 (26 July 1907), 3.

[54] A. Zorin [Gastev], "Rabochii mir: Iz dnevnika tramvaishchika," *Zhizn' dlia vsekh* 1910, no. 10 (October): 68–70.

[55] I. Dozorov [Gastev], "Duma rabotnitsy," *Za pravdu*, 12 Nov. 1913.

[56] A. Zorin [Gastev], "Rabochii mir: Zavod i sindikat: I. Sila mashinizma," *Zhizn' dlia vsekh* 1911, no. 3–4 (March–April): 395–96.

[57] In addition to examples cited below, see I. Dozorov, "Zvony," *Pravda*, 11 June 1913; "Rel'sy: Dumy na paravoze," *Pravda truda*, 19 Sept. 1911; "My posiagnuli," *Sbornik proletarskikh pisatalei* [1917], 111–13.

[58] I. Dozorov [A. Gastev], "Ia poliubil tebia, rokot zheleznyi . . . ," *Metallist* 1917, no. 4 (18 Oct.): 4.

Most famously, as we have seen, writing in 1914 while employed in the Siemens-Halske metal works in St. Petersburg, Gastev imagined "new iron blood" flowing into his veins, causing him to grow into a superhuman metal giant, a bionic Bolshevik, leading the masses forward.[59] Before 1918, however, no other worker writer so romanticized factories, machines, and metal. In fact, few had anything at all positive to say about modern industry. And when they did, it was often undermined by hesitation and doubt.

Modern Hell

Most worker writers expressed a deep though complex anxiety about industrial modernity. Partly, this was social and historical: a revulsion before the particular social conditions of capitalism, and thus a plausible confidence that social change or revolution would correct these evils. As in their judgments of the city, however, workers' animosity toward factories and other industrial workplaces was also essential and moral. Capitalism may have been implied, but the focus was on more intrinsic features. Much attention, therefore, was focused on physical features—machines, smokestacks, factory buildings, dirt—for these things pointed beyond social relationships toward more permanent and essential aspects of modern industry. Indeed, at the heart of the factory's malevolence, as portrayed by these workers, was less the capitalist social structure than the modern machine.

Hell, an image in which the physical and the moral were by definition intertwined, was the most common metaphor for factories and other industrial workplaces. Chechenets, the metalworker and metal union poet, even while declaring the factory a symbol of hope for the future, wrote of the actual factory as a place marked by "hellish thunder," where "all around is / motion, movement, turning / as if it wants to collapse / like old Sodom."[60] Many other worker writers similarly compared the physical environment of the modern workplace to hell, especially because of the "hellish noise" of the machinery and the air thickened with burning fumes and stifling smoke.[61] They wrote of "the squealing and hissing of the drive belts, hellish thunder / And the unceasing roar of engines and machinery."[62] They described how, "like demons in hell, we are surrounded by gas and smoke."[63] Even when the metaphor was not explicit, worker writers dwelled on the horrible physical envi-

---

[59] Gastev, "My rastem iz zheleza." The 1914 date of authorship is given in Gastev's preface to the 5th ed. of his *Poeziia rabochego udara* (Moscow, 1924). The poem was first published, under the pseudonym I. Dozorov, in *Metallist* 1917, no. 7 (16 Dec.): 4.

[60] Chechenets, "Pesnia rabov," *Rabochii po metallu*, no. 22 (10 Oct. 1907), 3.

[61] In addition to examples following, V. Shibaev, "Razsvet," *Bulochnik*, no. 1 (19 Feb. 1906), 2–3; Starodub Starodubskii [M. Savin], "Sud v adu," *Bulochnik*, no. 1 (19 Feb. 1906), 14; G. D. Deev-Khomiakovskii, "Sorok let kak odin den'," *Rodnye vesti* 1912, no. 3: 4–5; V. Gorshkov, "Na fabrike," *Rodnye vesti* 1912, no. 6: 1; N. Dodaev, "Trud," *Zhizn' pekarei*, no. 1(4) (10 Mar. 1914), 2; Andrei Noskov, "Pesnia bulochnika," *Zhizn' pekarei*, no. 1/4 (10 Mar. 1914). 5.

[62] S. Obradovich, "Na zavode," *Rabochii den'*, no. 8 (11 June 1912), 1 (clipping in RGALI, f. 1874, op. 1, d. 2, l. 6).

[63] N. Afanas'ev, "Na zavode," *Drug naroda* 1915, no. 5–7: 20.

ronment in industry. Sometimes they targeted individual industries (especially in trade union publications). An essay that appeared in the metalworkers' union paper in 1913 described coal mines as scenes filled with endless toil, shouting overseers, belching smokestacks, "darkness, stifling air, and stench. Water oozes from below as if the earth itself were weeping over such a picture."[64] Bakers, Mikhail Savin wrote, labored in "dark crypts."[65] Women garment workers, it was said, were tormented by the endless "stuk, stuk, stuk" of their sewing machines.[66] And darkness, horrible filth, and stifling air were said to plague labor in a sausage plant.[67]

Most often, the subject of attention was a more generic factory—hence a more symbolic site, but one that was undeniably modern in its large size and mechanization. These workplaces were almost invariably described as places of "thunderous noise and whistles," deafening roars, stifling fumes and smoke, dirt and dust, unceasing rhythms, and death.[68] "The machines droned, the wheels shrieked / In the factory thunder and whistles, / And iron heaps and steel bands were all entangled."[69] To Chechenets, the deafening "banging and roaring," the "whistling of steam and clamor of machinery," and the numbing rhythms of the factory were turning workers into "automatons,"[70] or simply, as Mikhail Gerasimov wrote, crushing their spirits: "I bang shut the creaking door / And walk to the factory, where again / In mute anguish [*v glukhoi toske*], in pain, in turmoil / I will suffer all day."[71] For most workers, Andrei Dikii wrote, the factory meant not "life" but only "torment" (*muchen'ia*) and death.[72] The factory also contaminated everything around it: "Spring. In the factory settlement / The usual smoke, fumes, and coal vapors."[73] Sergei Obradovich's poem "Life" was typical in its images: a dimly lit factory, "suffocating walls," a pervading mood of "gloom and sullenness" among people worn out by tedious cares, the deafening noise of machines, and "the never silent clamor" of rumbling drive belts.[74] Some of these authors voiced hope, typically in their final lines, for a "bright future"—a cliché of so-

[64] A. Buiko, "Na shakhtakh: nabrosok iz zhizni sibirskikh rabochikh," *Metallist* 1913, no. 4/28 (3 July): 4–5.

[65] M. Savin, "Novyi pekar'," *Bulochnik*, no. 2 (26 Feb. 1906), 2. See also Pekar', "Mokritsa i tarakan: Basnia," *Zhizn' pekarei*, no. 2 (29 June 1913), 9.

[66] V. Papin, "Shveia," *Proletarskii igly*, no. 2–3 (24 May 1914), 4.

[67] Kol'basnik, "Zhizn' kol'basnika," manuscript sent to *Pravda*, received 18 June 1914, in RGASPI, f. 364, op. 1, d. 200, l. 5.

[68] In addition to examples below, N. R-tskii, "Chego zhaleet ego?" *Edinstvo*, no. 8 (10 Aug. 1909), 3; A. Buiko, "Na shakhtakh," *Metallist* 1913, no. 4/28 (3 July): 4–5; Aksen-Achkasov [I. Sadof'ev], "U stanka," *Pravda*, 3 July (20 June) 1917.

[69] N. Dodaev, "Poet-metallist," *Metallist* 1913, no. 11/35 (16 November): 9.

[70] [Chechenets], "Nevol'niki truda," *Nash put'* 1911, no. 17 (23 May): 8–9; rpt. and author identified in *Proletarskie poety*, 2:10–13.

[71] M. Gerasimov, "Zavodskii gudok," in *Pervyi sbornik*, 91–92; first published in *Prosveshchenie* 1913, no. 12 (December).

[72] A. Dikii, "Za rabotoi," *Edinstvo*, no. 14 (16 Feb. 1910), 6.

[73] M. Gerasimov, "Vesna," *Put' pravdy*, 17 Apr. 1914. This poem was republished in 1917, also in Bolshevik publications, in slightly revised form: *Sbornik proletarskikh pisatelei*, 115–16, and *Privolzhskaia pravda*, 17 Aug. 1917 (rpt. in *Poeziia v bol'shevistkikh izdaniiakh*, 362–63).

[74] S. Obradovich, "Zhizn'," *Sever Rossii* (Arkhangelsk), 23 Aug. 1913 (clipping in RGALI, f. 1874, op. 1, d. 2, l. 10).

cialist and especially later Soviet discourse whose rhetorical power, at least for worker writers, has to be understood against the literal as well as figurative darkness that surrounded them in their workplaces and homes. In a poem printed in the Bolshevik newspaper *Pravda* and later placed as the final entry in the first anthology of proletarian writers, Dmitrii Odintsov described himself, after a night of reading, carrying "burning thoughts" and "winged dreams" into the "dust, darkness, and bitter smoke" of the factory, and nurturing in his soul this "living fire" amidst the "roar of the whistle and the thunder of steel."[75] Many worker writers, however, as we shall see, saw no escape or transcendence.

The physical features of factory and machine were seen as expressions of their inner moral nature. For some, this nature was cold and soulless. Young sons of poor families, it was said, driven by hunger, were "sacrificed" and then "chained" to "the soulless machine" of modern industry.[76] The machine cared for no one: "The wheel turns, hearing nothing, having no mercy / If only it would die—cursed revolving / If only it would die—but it drones on and on and on."[77] The metalworker Ignat Pasterniak, the semi-autobiographical hero of Aleksei Bibik's novel of industrial life, similarly saw "in the soulless din of the factory . . . inward indifference and even insolent unbelief. It seemed to him that there was something here that was strange and needless. And he waited for it to die." At the very least, Bibik suggested, the factory conveyed a spirit of doom: "The workshop thundered like a huge cauldron filled with thousands of sounds, poured together into an unbroken howl—not celebratory but anguished [*tosklivyi*] and hopeless."[78]

More often, and even more complexly, these writers felt that the factory was not soulless at all, but possessed a vital spirit—one that was malevolent, even maniacal. Bibik began his 1912 novel with a harrowing image of an anthropomorphized factory growling and howling at a new worker seeing the factory for the first time.

> Ignat took hold of the door's handle and stepped across the high threshold. At that moment a wave of roaring and wild howling surged toward him.
>
> "There he is! There he is! Ignat from [the village of] Novoselovki," the drive belts beneath the ceiling squealed and banged and laughed like madmen.
>
> "A-a-urr, A-a-urr," droned and growled from somewhere the low bass of a monster [*chudovishche*].
>
> "Trrakh-takh-ta-a, Trrakh-takh-ta-a."
>
> "Vzzz!" nagged the air with a high falsetto.

[75] D. Odintsov, "Vpered," in *Pervyi sbornik*, 166. An earlier version of this poem appeared in *Pravda*, 31 Oct. 1912.

[76] I. Sm., "Zhizn' cheloveka v raznykh vremena," *Rabochii po metallu*, no. 24 (14 Nov. 1907), 4. Gastev used almost identical words: A. Zorin [Gastev], "Rabochii mir: S parizhskogo zavoda," *Zhizn' dlia vsekh* 1910, no. 7 (July): 144.

[77] I. Sm., "Zhizn' cheloveka v raznykh vremenakh," *Rabochii po metallu*, no. 24 (14 Nov. 1907), 3.

[78] Bibik, *K shirokoi doroge*, 30, 33.

In time, like many actual workers,[79] Ignat became fascinated with the power and might of the factory ("the dancing spirit of machines and motors, belts and wheels") and he considered his own mastering of machine skills a matter of personal pride. But even after he was fully "cooked in the factory kettle" (as Russian workers termed socialization to the urban and factory milieu), the factory and its machines continued to evoke in him, we are told, feelings of sadness, melancholy, coldness, apathy, and hopelessness. This ambivalence toward the spirit of modern machine industry is poignantly evident in Bibik's account of workers' thoughts and feelings as they gaze at the factory's machinery when it was shut down during a strike: "It was as if there was a deep wound in the enormous body of a roaring monster, paralyzing its iron limbs. These silent machines evoked an incomprehensible sort of terror. One either shunned them or approached them as one would approach corpses."[80] Similarly—and less ambivalently—Mikhail Artamonov, a factory worker from Ivanovo-Voznesensk, described the joy striking workers first feel after shutting down their factory as less the exhilaration of class solidarity and militant protest against the employer than the startling discovery that the relentless and thunderous factory could be silenced. More than anything else, it is the quiet of the machines that elates striking workers and gives them a sense of real power and satisfaction.[81]

Worker writers often viewed the spirit of factories and machines as not only menacing but aggressively hostile and evil. Its vitality, in this view, became something monstrous. Thus the factory was a "vampire" sucking workers' blood. The noise of industry was "cruel, hellish laughter." Factory smokestacks were seen to "gaze mockingly" at workers' "downcast shoulders." Machines were said to "suck the life" out of workers. Drive belts "whispered maliciously" and the "cursed factory whistle" was the cry of a "hungry beast."[82] In Mikhail Gerasimov's often-reprinted poem "Vesna"(Spring) machines were said to "howl and snarl like wolves."[83] As here, worker poets very often portrayed factories and machines as roaring "monsters" (*chudovishcha*) devouring workers in altogether hellish scenes filled with "horrible squeals," black smoke, grinding noise, and death.[84]

---

[79] See Reginald E. Zelnik, ed., *A Radical Worker in Tsarist Russia: The Autobiography of Semen Ivanovich Kanatchikov* (Stanford, 1986), 7, 65.

[80] Bibik, *K shiroke doroge*, 16, 30, 33, 89.

[81] M. Artamonov, "Zabastovka," in *Pervyi sbornik*, 93. Even Aleksei Gastev understood the pleasure of seeing the morning light in a "dead"—i.e., struck and silenced—factory: Dozorov, "Utrenniaia smena," ibid., 80–89.

[82] Chechenets, in *Rabochii po metallu*, no. 13 (26 Apr. 1907), 3; A. Pomorskii, "Zhertvam goroda," *Metallist* 1913, no. 5/29 (July 19): 4; N. Dodaev, "Trud," *Zhizn' pekarei*, no. 1/4 (10 Mar. 1914). 2; M. Gerasimov, "Zavodskii gudok," in *Pervyi sbornik*, 92; V. Aleksandrovskii, "Novye pesni," in *Nashi pesni*, 12; S. Obradovich, "Zhizn'," *Sever Rossii* (Arkhangelsk), 23 Aug. 1913 (clipping in RGALI, f. 1874, op. 1, d. 2, l. 10); Chechenets, in *Rabochii po metallu*, no. 13 (26 Apr. 1907), 3.

[83] M. Gerasimov, "Vesna," *Put' pravdy*, 17 Apr. 1914, and *Sbornik proletarskikh pisatelei*, 115–16.

[84] See also Aksen-Achkasov [I. Sadof'ev], "U stanka," *Pravda*, 3 July (20 June) 1917; and Po-

Even prophets of the new aesthetic of factory and machine like Andrei Dikii and Aleksei Gastev recognized the dark spirit of industrial modernity. Dikii wrote of machines as "cruel monsters" and of the factory as a "beast, grinding its teeth."[85] And Gastev, especially in his early portrayals of factory work, dreaded the factory even as he admired it. In 1912, reflecting on his experiences working in modern factories in France, where he was in political exile, Gastev wrote of workers "cowed into submission by the bulk and thunder" of the factory and the "oppressive hypnosis created by the eternal movement" of wheels and transmission belts, toiling "like automatons," like "flies" stuck to a "cooled stream of steel lava." Although he admired the organizational rationality, physical cleanliness, and technological modernity of large French factories (the Apollonian face of modernity, as it were), Gastev still found a hellish spirit to be no less part of the nature of modern industry: "as soon as one enters a factory, amidst these soulless machines and people shackled to them, black Mephistopheles rises up with his cynical laughter and bellowing." So oppressive was this atmosphere that the sufferers in this industrial hell had grown dumb: "No shouts of pain, no mention of justice—only force, cruelty, death."[86]

"Conscious" workers, we assume, knew theoretically that all these torments were the result of particular social relationships and a particular stage in social history. Some, like Gastev, made this understanding explicit: he blamed "the cruel tyrant of the age, soulless like steel, merciless like death, always malicious like a demon, always hungry—bloodthirsty capital."[87] But intellectually and emotionally, to judge by what most worker authors wrote most of the time about the conditions of modern industry, these writers found a more essential fault in modern life, an intrinsic spirit that was menacing and evil. We might expect such attitudes from recent peasant migrants to the factory or workers with a populist ideology. But this antagonism toward factories and machines was most strongly expressed by worker writers with long urban experience and often the Marxist's supposed ideological appreciation of modernity and progress. Ideological hostility to capitalist society contributed to these perceptions and judgments. But it is clear that what troubled them most was the essential spirit of factories and machines, especially their aesthetic and moral spirit.

A certain ambivalence remained evident in these judgments, however. For at least some of these writers, the factory was at once dreadful and alluring in its vitality and power. Writings that contemplated the horrors of the factory

---

lianskii [Lebedev-Polianskii], "Motivy rabochei poezii," *Proletarskaia kul'tura*, no. 3 (August 1918), 4–6.

[85] A. Dikii, "V rabochei slobodke," *Nash put'*, no. 13 (10 Feb. 1911), 4; "Smena," in *Pervyi sbornik*, 78–79.

[86] A. Zorin [Gastev], "Rabochii mir: Stariki (Otryvok iz dnevnika)," *Zhizn' dlia vsekh* 1912, no. 1 (January): 81, and "Rabochii mir: S parizhskogo zavoda," ibid., 1910, no. 7 (July): 146.

[87] A. Zorin [Gastev], "Rabochii mir: S parizhskogo zavoda," *Zhizn' dlia vsekh* 1910, no. 7 (July): 144.

might conclude, if only briefly, with a call to struggle and hope (especially writings produced by the more politicized workers during more optimistic years of political liberalization and mobilization—1905–7, 1912–14, 1917). Likewise, writers who found some value (if only for the future) and even beauty in factories, machines, and metal wrote also (and more often) of peril and ugliness. Sometimes these contrary themes intertwined in the familiar dialectical manner. In a poem published in the Bolshevik *Pravda* in 1914, Aleksei Mashirov recognized that the "whirl of turning wheels" and the "furious dance of drive belts" within the "stone colossus" of the factory terrified workers, especially new workers, but he argued that this same fearful power must be the force that welds workers together.[88] More often, the relationship between these contrary themes was less easily resolved: horror and wonder coexisted—undialectical, unreconcilable. We can see this ambivalence in the language with which worker writers described the threatening vitality of factories and machines: as *zveri* (beasts but also other living things) and especially as *chudovishcha* (monsters, but in the ambiguous sense that could evoke both fantastic might and enormous evil and cruelty). And the noises these creatures made similarly could evoke terror but also wonder and awe: they cried, moaned, growled, snarled, squealed, hissed, droned, guffawed, thundered, roared with laughter, wailed, howled, bellowed, and banged (*zaorali, stonali, rychali, vizzhali, shipeli, gudeli, khokhotali, grokhali, reveli, voiali, khlopali*). The noise of modern times, like its textures and relationships, inspired feelings that sometimes could not be made anything but ambivalent.

Nostalgia for Nature

Unspoiled and gentle nature was a familiar and appealing counterpoint to the artificial and brutal city of modernity. It was also, in just these terms, a way of articulating alternative values. Apparent nostalgia for a lost rural idyll pervaded workers' creative writings. No doubt there was genuine longing for the countryside where most had spent their childhoods. There was also actual return. Many Russian workers, as we know from studies of the social history of Russian labor, returned to the village periodically or permanently in infirmity or old age and occasionally simply quit work and the city (especially in the summertime) to roam for a time about the country, perhaps working at odd jobs, as vagabonds, itinerants, or pilgrims. But it was the imagined countryside that these writers were most attentive to. The natural landscape into which these workers wrote of escaping was less a physical space than a place in memory and imagination, and perhaps even more in rhetoric. It served purposes beyond what the real countryside could. The natural world of the imagination was a refuge to which workers could flee in an instant, a terrain in the mind where beauty reigned and the spirit was healed. Speaking of nature was

---

[88] Samobytnik [A. Mashirov], "Novomu tovarishchu," *Proletarskia pravda,* 17 Jan. 1914.

also a deliberate and critical discourse, a symbolic terrain against which workers could measure the very tangible realities of urban industrial life, a way of counterposing an aesthetic and moral alternative to the modern industrial city. With images of nature, worker writers could speak in a familiar language of feelings and desires, of moral and aesthetic values, of hope for change, and also of the fear that nothing would change. Metaphor as much as memory shaped this pastoral nostalgia.

Nostalgia for the lost countryside was sometimes explicit. Some worker writers portrayed themselves or other workers—typically while laboring at noisy machines or sitting in cramped and stuffy apartments, and often while gazing out a window—as longing for the village they left behind, for parents and family, for country pleasures, for the beauties of nature. Some wept as they remembered the smells of fields and rivers and the joy of springtime in the country, and regretted having ever left the village to work in the city, and having ever imagined that life there would be better.[89] These were sentimental memories, filled with rosy tinting and large erasures. Peasant poverty, hunger, and cruelty were absent. Hard labor in the fields was left in the darkness of what was best forgotten. And it was never winter. Like Vasilii Gorshkov, in a 1912 poem called "In the Factory," they preferred to remember the "untroubled calm" of their native villages, to recall "the happiness of days past," to bring to mind moments when one "reclined in a lazy pose, listening drowsily / As the Kama River lapped at one's feet."[90] Even Marxist workers writing for "proletarian" anthologies and periodicals offered memories of bucolic peasant life at one with the beauties of nature and of open spaces, filled with youthful happiness, dance, and song.[91]

Worker writers were often quite aware of the silences in these portraits. Even some who recalled the pastoral pleasures of their youths wrote bitterly about the dark sides of peasant life: the violence and cruelty of peasant community justice (*samosud*), the tenacity of "superstitious" rituals such as nighttime plowing of furrows around villages to halt animal epidemics (*opakhivan'ia*), and the pervasiveness of suffering and "slavelike" fatalism.[92] Occasionally the rough realities of peasant life were allowed symbolically to intrude on the prevailing nostalgia in workers' writings about the countryside. In Aleksei Bibik's novel *K shirokoi doroge* (Toward the open road) Ignat Pasterniak's reveries in a small village church are shattered when "two peasant men

[89] F. Gavrilov, "Son" (1905), in *Proletarskie poety*, 1:197–201; Mytar', "Dumy rabochego," *Balalaika* 1910, no. 20: 4; P. Zaitsev, "Na mogilu K. A. Molchanova," *Kolotushka*, no. 2 (1911), 3; V. Miliaev, in *Narodnaia mysl'*, no. 1 (January 1911), 51; Bibik, *K shirokoi doroge*, 98, 116; A. Shliapnikov, "Na fabriku," in *Pervyi sbornik*, 66–67; G. Deev-Khomiakovskii, in *Drug naroda* 1915, no. 5–7: 2.
[90] V. Gorshkov, "Na fabrike," *Rodnye vesti* 1912, no. 6: 1.
[91] S. Malyshev, "Utro v derevne," in *Pervyi sbornik*, 15–19; M. Artamonov, "Taet," *Metallist* 1914, no. 4/41 (1 Apr.): 4–7.
[92] E.g., M. L[oginov], "Narodnaia t'ma," *Zvezda iasnaia* [*Zvezda utrenniaia*], no. 6 (29 Feb. 1912), 2–4; *Zvezda utrenniaia*, no. 21 (20 June 1912), 2; Aksen-Achkasov [I. Sadof'ev], "Na pashne," *Pravda*, 10 July (27 June) 1917. See also the comments by Lev Kleinbort, "Rukopisnye zhurnaly rabochikh," *Vestnik Evropy* 52, no. 7–8 (July–August 1917): 285.

abruptly and noisily throw open the door and walk up to the altar, loudly stomping their boots."[93]

The essential point about pastoral memories, however, is not what worker writers actually remembered (we can never know, and in any case, the evidence suggests that they were not blind to the contradictions of peasant life) but what they wished to say. Pastoral nostalgia reflected, among other things, an awareness that they could not go home, perhaps even that such a "home" did not truly exist. But worker writers also typically "remembered" lost nature as part of a deliberate commentary on the aesthetic and ethical meanings of modern industrial life. Worker writers continually contrasted the beautiful, harmonious, and liberating world of nature with the ugly, discordant, and confining world of modern industry and the modern city. Even the most urbanized and politicized workers found something valuable and eloquent in this opposition. Writing in the midst of the 1917 revolution, Il'ia Sadof'ev— an experienced metalworker, Bolshevik, and deputy to the Petrograd Soviet— counterposed nature and the factory:

> Outside the window: spring, the radiant sun, beauty,
> Here, the "fetching" glance of filth and darkness.
> There, the caressing sounds of winged choirs,
> Here, the roaring talk of machine-monsters. . . .
> There, trees and the aromas of flowers,
> Here, unending steel, iron, smoke, and stench.[94]

This dichotomy was a familiar trope in workers' writing by 1917. Numerous poems and stories contrasted the noises and smells of machinery to whispering leaves and fragrant woods, opposed workers' dark and filthy urban homes to the brightness and open spaces of the countryside, and suggested that the rushing waters of spring might be able to "disturb the iron tongue of machines."[95] And the significance of these contrasts was clear. Most workers identified the place where one heard "factory whistles instead of bird songs"[96] as aesthetically and spiritually inferior.

Escape from the city was frequently imagined, but almost invariably as flight into an idealized rural landscape. This was a natural countryside largely separate from human society. If people appeared, they were almost never rough and ignorant muzhiks but typically lovely, innocent village girls. And the natural landscape they imagined was not the harsh and cruel nature that

[93] Bibik, *K shirokoi doroge*, 62.

[94] Aksen-Achkasov [Il'ia Sadof'ev], "U stanka," *Pravda*, 3 July (20 June) 1917.

[95] Samobytnik [A. Mashirov], "Grezy," *Pravda truda*, 19 Sept. 1913; also in *Pervyi sbornik*, 140–41, and in *Poeziia v bol'shevistskikh izdaniiakh*, 238–39; Samobytnik [A. Mashirov], "Vesennye grezy" (1916), *Voprosy strakhovaniia*, rpt. in *Proletarskie poety*, 3:26; M. Tsarev [V. Torskii], "V kazarme" (1916), rpt. in *Proletarskie poety*, 3:37.

[96] M. Gerasimov, "Vesna," in *Sbornik proletarskikh pisatelei*, 115–16, and *Privolzhskaia pravda*, 17 Aug. 1917, rpt. in *Poeziia v bol'shevistskikh izdaniiakh*, 362–63. This line did not appear in the first publication of the poem, *Put' pravdy*, 17 Apr. 1914.

peasants knew well, or even an untamed wilderness, but an Edenic garden. The imagined destination was most often a place of quiet refuge, open space, and freedom, where the air was cool and fresh, birds sang, the sun shone, flowers bloomed, and it was always spring. Mikhail Gerasimov, who would later become known as Soviet Russia's proletarian "poet of iron," wrote a typical piece in 1913:

> How good it is in the piney woods
> Far from streets and people.
> To toss handfuls of acorns
> Into a scarf of pale blue fog. . . .
> Such quiet,
> Such calm!
> How far I see from the hilltop! . . .
> Reddish outcroppings
> Mix with pine and ash
> And glisten over the web of fields.
> And above in the sky a line of cranes
> Extends a milky stream
> Above the calming land.[97]

In a number of poems and stories, workers described abandoning the city and the factory, especially when enticed by spring, to return to a village home or, more often, to wander the countryside.[98] Most often, however, the escape was more abstract and imaginary—flight (often in daydreams while at work) to woods and forests, to rivers and mountains, to the steppe or Siberia, or to "the open road."[99]

Whether these were dreams of returning home or of escape into a pastoral imaginary, the destination was always a place of superior beauty and spiritual value: a place of "eternal mystery" where the air shimmers with "tender evening harmonies" and "peace, clarity, and boundlessness" reign; where the woods and the steppe "smell of roses"; where listening to the echo of one's voice and romping like a "forest sprite" (*leshii*) can "fill one's empty soul"; where "there is no doubt in one's soul"; and where one can escape from the turbulent and oppressive city into "the peace of forgetting and happiness of

[97] M. Gerasimov, "Kak khorosho v lesu dubovom . . ." (1913), in his *Stikhotvoreniia* (Moscow, 1959), 29–30.

[98] Bibik, *K shirokoi doroge*, 21–23, 48–49, 104–5, and "Bor obrechennyi," *Novaia rabochaia gazeta*, 13 Oct. 1913; Kvadrat [I. Kubikov], "Novaia povest' M. Gor'kogo," *Novaia rabochaia gazeta*, 13 Aug. 1913; V. Torskii, "V poliakh" and "Selo," in *Nashi pesni*, 14–15; G. Deev-Khomiakovskii, "Prozrel," *Drug naroda* 1915, no. 1 (1 Jan.): 9.

[99] In addition to references in the preceding note and notes to the following paragraph, see I. Pechal'nyi, "Dumy rabochego," *Zvezda utrenniaia*, no. 14 (2 May 1912), 7; M. Zakharov, "Romans," *Rodnye vesti* 1912, no. 3: 5–6; V. Gorshkov, "Na fabrike," *Rodnye vesti* 1912, no. 6: 1; M. Artamonov, "Taet," *Metallist* 1914, no. 4/41 (1 Apr.): 4–7; B. Zylev, "V nabornoi letom," *Nashe pechatnoe delo*, no. 23 (26 Sept. 1915), 5.

the moment."[100] Marxist ideology did not deter workers from writing in this mode. Many of these sentiments were expressed by workers associated with the Bolshevik and Menshevik parties. Vasilii Aleksandrovskii, for example, wrote numerous poems about the majesty, mystery, and beauty of nature.[101] Aleksandr Pomorskii described his pursuit of "beauty in the golden, burning Heavens," of "beauty in the angry emerald Sea."[102] And Aleksei Mashirov even portrayed a conspiratorial gathering of workers in a pine forest—a typical locale where Russian workers planned strikes, exchanged illegal political literature, and secretly celebrated May Day with speeches and songs—as made meaningful not only by the "songs of freedom" they sang but equally by the presence of nature:

> Let the everyday noise of our lives
> Be silenced for the moment by the unfettered woodland.
> Walk with unaccustomed footsteps
> On the mossy velvet carpet. . . .
> Let the city in its murky gloom
> Notice with pain:
> We return with secret and cherished sounds
> Toward the melancholy furnaces and machines.[103]

Nature offered an aesthetic and sentimental alternative to city, factory, and machine. Beauty was seen to have emotional and even political value and force.

Natural Truths

Nature had rhetorical value and force also as a source of critical symbols. Worker writers made plentiful use of familiar symbols drawn from nature. The seasons were often invoked emblematically. Autumn appeared as an embodiment of workers' sufferings. Sullen skies, gray fog, pervasive dust and dirt, and cold bitter winds echoed workers' melancholy (*toska*), sorrow, sickness, and death, and personified the fading of beauty and the menace of worse times to come.[104] Winter similarly echoed and symbolized the harshness and

---

[100] M. Chernysheva, "Daite mne kryl'ia!" *Dumy narodnye*, no. 3 (13 Feb. 1910), 5; M. Gerasimov, "Zimnyi vecher," in *Pervyi sbornik*, 164; A. Dikii, "Na svidanie," in *Pervyi sbornik*, 63 (and see 62, 64); Bibik, *K shirokoi doroge*, 60–61; M. Zakharov, "Nastroenie," *Rodnye vesti* 1911, no. 3 (4): 7; V. Aleksandrovskii, "Dali," *Luch*, 15 June 1913 (rpt. in *Zhivoe slovo* 1914, no. 3 [January]: 37).

[101] V. Aleksandrovskii, "Dali," *Luch*, 15 June 1913; "Pered grozoi," *Luch*, 14 June 1913; "Zapushchennyi sad," *Zhivoe slovo* 1913, no. 4 (14 July): 2. Many similar poems by Aleksandrovskii appeared in these journals and in *Novaia rabochaia gazeta*, all Menshevik publications.

[102] A. Pomorskii, "Krasota," *Novaia rabochaia gazeta*, 11 Sept. 1913.

[103] Samobytnik [A. Mashirov], "V lesu," in *Nashi pesni*, 13.

[104] E. Nechaev, "Osen'," in *U istokov russkoi proletar'skoi poezii* (Moscow, 1965), 44–45;

terrors of workers' lives—misery, cold, death, though it could also cover the sorrowing earth with a "white shroud" of pleasing snow, stand as a source of inspiring strength, or, more ambiguously, represent "peace, clarity, boundlessness / and both joy and sadness."[105]

Spring was the favorite season symbolically, for it so obviously represented nature's promise of a new and better life. "Aromatic and clear," the smells of spring were the most antithetical to the modern city and factory.[106] Spring, it was repeatedly said, brought awakening, hope and faith, a changing life, and the end of hardship.[107] For Aleksei Mashirov, for example, springtime—the rays of the sun, the melodies of returned songbirds, a sudden spring rain, the laughter of children in the streets, strolling girls with lilacs in their hands— awoke life, inspired dreams of change, and brought to workers confidence and joy. From his stuffy room with mildew growing on its walls, the author opened his window wide to "heartily greet the free spring."[108] Similarly, Mikhail Gerasimov repeatedly invoked spring, and especially flowers—miraculous ruby flowers appearing in a dream, poppies like red flags covering a field, roses blooming in gloomy fields—as symbols of conscious awakening, optimism, and readiness for struggle.[109]

Springtime often stood as a symbolic challenge to city and factory. In many stories and poems, workers reversed the conventional "trope of the interrupted idyll";[110] instead of the noise of machines shattering pastoral reveries, nature invades the terrain of industry. In Ivan Korobov's 1912 poem, for example, "Breaking through slabs of asphalt / Pressing against a stone wall / Young grass laughs / And sun and spring laugh." The poem elaborates on the

---

Levitskii in *Rabochii po metallu*, no. 20 (5 Sept. 1907), 2; V. Aleksandrovskii, "Osen'iu," *Novaia rabochaia gazeta*, 13 Aug. 1913; M. Gerasimov, "Osen'," in *Pervyi sbornik*, 39; Matritsa, "Nasha osen'," *Nashe pechatnoe delo*, no. 25 (17 Nov. 1915), 4; M. Gerasimov, personal notebook, 1915–16, in RGALI, f. 1374, op. 1, d. 3, l. 23, and unpublished verses (probably from 1915–16), d. 6, l. 12; I. Morozov, "Iz osennikh motivov," in *Sbornik proletarskikh pisatelei*, 116–17.

[105] Levitskii in *Rabochii po metallu*, no. 20 (5 Sept. 1907), 2, and M. Bezymiannaia, "Zimnye dumy," *Kuznets*, no. 5–6 (19 Jan. 1908), 2; M. Chernysheva, in *Balalaika* 1910, no. 20: 5; M. Gerasimov, "Zimnyi vecher," in *Pervyi sbornik*, 164.

[106] E. Nechaev, "Na rabote," in *U istokov*, 1; Chechenets, "Sestre," *Rabochii po metallu*, no. 15 (13 June 1907), 3.

[107] In addition to examples following, N. Kustov, "Zhelanie" (1909), in *V bure i plameni* (Iaroslavl, 1918), 51; P. Zaitsev, "Vesna idet," *Kolotushka* 1911, no. 4 (Easter issue): 2; S. Popov, "Vesna," *Chelovek*, no. 4 (24 Apr. 1911), 32; ; A. Buiko, "Na shakhtakh," *Metallist* 1913, no. 4/28 (3 July): 4–5; A. Chizhikov (a miner), "Prikhod vesna," RGASPI, f. 364, op. 1, d. 315, ll. 1–3; Matritsa, "Nasha osen'," *Nashe pechatnoe delo*, no. 25 (17 Nov. 1915), 4.

[108] Samobytnik [A. Mashirov], "Na razsvete vesennei zari . . . ," *Pravda*, 28 Apr. 1912; "Vesennii dozhd'," *Voprosy strakhovaniia* (16 Mar. 1916), rpt. in *Poeziia v bol'shevistskikh izdaniiakh*, 304; "Vesennye grezy," *Voprosy strakhovaniia*, 1916, rpt. in *Proletarskie poety* 3:26; "V vesennii den'," *Voprosy strakhovaniia*, 5 Feb. 1917, rpt. in *Proletarskie poety*, 3:159.

[109] M. Gerasimov, "Rabochemu," *Prosveshchenie* 1913, no. 12 (December): 13, rpt. in *Poeziia v bol'shevistskikh izdaniiakh*, 283; "U vitriny," *Prosveshchenie* 1914, no. 1 (January): 6, rpt. in *Poeziia v bol'shevistskikh izdaniiakh*, 284–85; "Vesennee" and "V gorode," in *Pervyi sbornik*, 20, 51; "Vesna tak slavno dubovom . . . ," in his *Stikhotvoreniia*, 31–32.

[110] Marx, *Machine in the Garden*, 27.

intended symbolism: the young grass represents people striving for "truth and light" against the "lies" and "evil" of asphalt and stone.[111] Similarly, in 1914 an unskilled worker mailed to *Pravda* a poem describing his image of what it meant for a worker to become conscious and to be able to overcome the overwhelming "longing and grief" (*toska i grust'*) that pervaded working-class existence: a "small flower" grows in a forgotten corner of the factory amidst discarded "scraps of unneeded iron waste," amidst "melancholy and sorrow."[112] In 1910 Aleksei Gastev used a nearly identical image of a spring flower emerging in a "damp, stuffy basement" to symbolize human "striving for the light of the ideal."[113]

The sun (associated with spring as the time of its return to prominence) was a symbolic center in many of these writings. The gesture of looking out from factory or apartment windows (often so darkened that they have to be pushed open to be seen through or, even more symbolically, that allowed vision only through broken panes) to "see the sun" was a favorite symbol of struggle through darkness to the light of true consciousness or hope for change.[114] The sun could bring happiness and rid the earth of evil.[115] Some fantasized about becoming the sun or flying to it on mighty wings.[116] Especially at dawn or when its rays broke through dark clouds, the sun stood clearly for enlightenment and the coming of a new age.[117] Other images drawn from nature were similarly used to represent knowledge, hope, struggle, and change: wind blowing away clouds of evil; the bright light of Halley's comet (which appeared in 1910) frightening the ignorant; the brilliant if momentary light of a meteor; flashes of summer lightening breaking through the darkness to "write" with light in the sky.[118]

Freedom was a central value in this nature writing. Open fields, country roads, boundless forests, the expanses of the steppe, the flowing Volga, and

[111] Ivan Korobov, "Plity asfal'ta probivaia . . . ," in *Pervyi sbornik,* 153 (originally in *Nevskaia zvezda,* 28 May 1912, according to *Proletarskie poety,* 2:273).

[112] P. Treidub (he identified himself as an unskilled worker [*chernorabochii*] in a railroad machine shop), "Zavodskii tsvetok," RGASPI, f. 364, op. 1, d. 203, l. 30b.

[113] P. Zorin (Gastev), "Tsvetok," *Zhizn' dlia vsekh* 1910, no. 5 (May): 3.

[114] M. Savin, "V pekarne," *Bulochnik,* no. 1 (19 Feb. 1906), 2; Matritsa, "Nasha osen'," *Nashe pechatnoe delo,* no. 25 (17 Nov. 1915), 4.

[115] E. Nechaev, "Pesnia nevol'nika" (1907), in *U istokov,* 98–99; A. Chizhikov (a miner), "Prikhod vesna," RGASPI, f. 364, op. 1, d. 315, ll. 1–3.

[116] E. Nechaev, "Pesnia nevol'nika" (1907), in *U istokov,* 98–99; M. Chernysheva, "Daite mne kryl'ia!" *Dumy narodnye,* no. 3 (13 Feb. 1910), 5.

[117] Baikov, "Kakoi put' vernee?" *Rabochii po metallu,* no. 18 (26 July 1907), 3–5; V. Torskii, "Vidish li ty . . . ," in *Nashi pesni,* 8; V. Aleksandrovskii, "Novye pesni," in *Nashi pesni,* 11; Tikhoplesets [M. Loginov], "Dukhovnoe rabstvo" (essay), *Zvezda utrenniaia,* no. 16 (16 May 1912), 2; V. Aleksandrovskii, "Ne spitsia . . . ," *Novaia rabochaia gazeta,* 13 Sept. 1913; A. Dikii, "Smena," in *Pervyi sbornik,* 78–79; Neliudim [A. Solov'ev], "Grustnye pesni tvoi, proletarskii baian . . ." (from *Sotsial-demokrat,* 24 Aug. 1917), in *Proletarskie poety,* 3:185.

[118] Samobytnik [A. Mashirov], "Tuchi," *Pravda truda,* 29 Sept. 1913; [M. Loginov], lead essay in *Dumy narodnye,* no. 9 ([30 Mar.], 1910), 1–2; Bibik, *K shirokoi doroge,* 49; Samobytnik [A. Mashirov], "Zarnitsy," *Proletarskaia pravda,* 18 Sept. 1913, rpt. in *Proletarskie poety,* 2:90; S. Gan'shin, "Ia syn stepei," *Zhivoe slovo,* no. 18 (May 1913), 6; Samobytnik [A. Mashirov], "Zarnitsy," *Proletarskaia pravda,* 18 Sept. 1913, rpt. in *Proletarskie poety,* 2:90.

vast Siberia were often invoked as symbols of freedom from constraint.[119] Typical was a poem by Mikhail Zakharov ("Romance") on the libertarian pleasures of the open road: "The road stretches out before me . . . / And, again, filled with delight / I declaim madly, bowing to no one," and become "like a naive child."[120] We might expect such Romantic images of individual liberty from Zakharov, a frequently unemployed tavern employee who published his writings in and helped edit populist journals aimed at lower-class readers. But we hear the same from purer "proletarians"—factory workers publishing in Marxist journals and collections. Aleksei Bibik, for example, described metalworkers, intoxicated by the spirit of spring, suddenly quitting work and "heading off somewhere; they themselves did not even know where, simply that way, following the spring clouds."[121] These were not only symbols, of course. Memoirs by many Russian workers make it clear that workers did in fact sometimes quit their jobs (especially in the warm weather) to roam about the countryside. But worker writers inscribed these stories in fiction and poetry not simply to record facts. As always, they recorded aspects of everyday life to give them larger meaning and to deploy them in critical argument. Freedom was one of these arguments.

Natural symbols of liberty pervaded workers' creative writings: the free songs of birds heard outside a factory window, the flight of "free, proud birds" against a black sky (even workers imagined *as* birds flying freely);[122] the rushing waters of a mountain stream (created, appropriately, when the sun melted winter ice) cutting through a massive boulder in its path to rush in freedom to the sea;[123] the awaited "sun of freedom;"[124] and the momentary "song of freedom" of a "meteor falling into the deep abyss."[125] In Bibik's novel of searching and discovery, "Toward the Open Road," Ignat Pasterniak repeatedly looks for "truth" in the sky, the stars, the woods, and inward and external nature. He even tries to convince the members of his conspiratorial workers' study circle that what was most essential was "to define not only the relation of labor to capital, but also the relation of man to nature."[126]

---

[119] In addition to examples below, see E. Nechaev, "Rodina" (1907), in *U istokov,* 100–101; Samobytnik [A. Mashirov], "V lesu," in *Nashi pesni,* 13, and "V vesennyi den'," *Voprosy strakhovaniia,* 5 Feb. 1917, rpt. in *Proletarskie poety,* 3:159; M. Gerasimov, "Step'," in *Pervyi sbornik,* 26; M. Tsarev [V. Torskii], "V lesu" (1915), in *Proletarskie poety,* 3:36–37; M. Gerasimov, "Mechty v dymu," *Privolzhskaia pravda,* 17 Aug. 1917, rpt. in *Poeziia v bol'shevistkikh izdaniiakh,* 364–65.

[120] M. Zakharov, "Romans," *Rodnye vesti* 1912, no. 3: 5–6.

[121] Bibik, *K shirokoi doroge,* 49.

[122] M. Savin, "V pekarne," *Bulochnik,* no. 1 (19 Feb. 1906), 2; Chechenets, "Sestre," *Rabochii po metallu,* no. 15 (13 June 1907), 3; M. Chernysheva, "Daite mne kryl'ia!" *Dumy narodnye,* no. 3 (13 Feb. 1910), 5; Samobytnik [A. Mashirov], "Na razsvete vesennei zari . . . ," *Pravda,* 28 Apr. 1912, and "Zarnitsy," *Proletarskaia pravda,* 18 Sept. 1913; Gan'shin, "Orel," manuscript poem sent to Gorky, 1914, in Arkhiv A. M. Gor'kogo, RAV-PG, 37-13-1.

[123] Samobytnik [A. Mashirov] "Ruch'i," *Pravda,* 26 Apr. 1912, and "Gornye ruch'i," *Rabotnitsa* 1914, no. 6 (24 May): 2.

[124] Levitskii in *Rabochii po metallu,* no. 20 (5 September 1907): 2.

[125] Samobytnik [A. Mashirov], "Zarnitsy," *Proletarskaia pravda,* 18 Sept. 1913, rpt. in *Proletarskie poety,* 2:90.

[126] Bibik, *K shirokoi doroge,* 15, 39, 60–61, 82, 104, 109–10.

Many of these images—and the libertarian drive that inspired them—are visible in Sergei Gan'shin's poetic declaration of a self-ideal:

> I am a son of the steppes, born in the field,
> I am a meteor in human darkness,
> I am the lapping of ocean waves,
> I am a prisoner of city life. . . .
> It is tedious for me in the dismal,
> Soulless and haughty crowd,
> In its cursed city. . . .
> My father is the wind, my mother a winter storm,
> How can I, ruler of nature and free will,
> Endure the soulless city.[127]

Such an apotheosis of the individual struggling to be free was common in workers' writings. And, worker writers (including those who had embraced Marxist ideology) typically envisioned such free worker heroes with images drawn from nature or in a natural setting, as in Mikhail Gerasimov's 1914 poem of self-transfiguration, in which he felt himself transformed for the struggle after running at twilight about the rolling hills and woods of the steppe:

> At that moment, like an ancient champion,
> I look with blazing eyes
> At the wretched countryside
> And at my broad native lands.
> In the valor of the steppes I wrap
> My weakened chest
> And, my blood frothing like intoxicating home brew,
> I go again onto the distant path.[128]

The use of natural imagery was, at least implicitly, essential to the arguments workers were making—arguments about the need to end workers' sufferings, about the need for a satisfying and "beautiful" life, about the necessity of individual freedom. These were "truths" that were intrinsic and self-evident, rooted in nature itself. Such arguments seem to echo European philosophies of Enlightenment and Romantic naturalism, which viewed nature as the ultimate source of moral truth. To discover this truth we had only to overcome our estrangement from nature and learn to hear and heed nature's voice within ourselves. For such philosophers as Rousseau, Kant, Hegel, and Schiller—all of whom had profound influence among Russian intellectuals—nature was fundamentally good and spoke unambiguously of the dignity and rights of the individual, the value of imagination and feeling, and the

---

[127] S. Gan'shin, "Ia syn stepei," *Zhivoe slovo*, no. 18 (May 1913), 6, and *Vpered!* 21 July 1917.

[128] M. Gerasimov, "Step'," in *Pervyi sbornik*, 26.

necessity of freedom.[129] We cannot say for certain how much or by what avenues workers were influenced by these intellectual traditions. We can say that they shared these values of self, inward feeling, beauty, and liberty, and that, like so many other writers, they used nature to voice these ideals.

No Exit

For many of these writers, however, perceptions had become complicated and troubled. Worker writers' use of natural images was never simply symbolic, never only a way of representing ideas. Nostalgia and dreams of return—even if only to an imagined place—were real and always subtly present. This was often a characteristic nostalgia though: a painful sense not simply of home-sickness but of irrevocable loss, of permanent estrangement from "home," the "melancholy feeling of dispossession" that has been so characteristic of the modern age.[130] Most of these writers recognized that they could not escape the iron cage of city and industry and return to nature. Like childhood, with which this natural home was sometimes paired, this natural world was less a place than a memory—and often a sentimentally falsified or largely imagined one at that.

A few writers tried to embrace this alienation and proclaimed their repudiation of sentimentalized nature. The glassworker Egor Nechaev, known mainly for his many verses about the beauties of nature, in a 1910 poem appealed to poets to

> Leave flowers in peace,
> And not sing about golden dawns. . . .
> About the beauty of the boundless steppes,
> Be silent, until better days.
> Don't lull to sleep with gentle sounds
> The hearts of troubled people. . . .
> Don't you see how much grief and tears
> Remain in your native land?[131]

In similar poems, workers insisted that springtime could not cheer those oppressed by "hard and evil fate" and that it was pointless for worker poets to sing of flowers, sunshine, and all the other emblems of happiness.[132] "Spring, don't come here," Sergei Gan'shin wrote, "flowers are not for me / nor the

---

[129] See Charles Taylor, *Sources of the Self: The Making of Modern Identity* (Cambridge, Mass., 1989), 355–90.

[130] Peter Fritzsche, "Specters of History: On Nostalgia, Exile, and Modernity," *American Historical Review* 106 (Dec. 2001): 1588. See also Svetlana Boym, *The Future of Nostalgia* (New York, 2001).

[131] E. Nechaev, "Pevtsu" (1910), in *U istokov*, 107.

[132] S. Popov, "Vesna," *Chelovek*, no. 4 (24 Apr. 1911), 32; A. Pomorskii, "Pesnia," *Metallist* 1913, no. 4/28 (3 July): 4; N. Temnyi, "Uznik," *Proletarii igly*, no. 1 (22 Apr. 1914), 4.

songs of nightingales / when my life is broken and my dreams dissolved."[133] It is possible that these workers were groping toward a new proletarian aesthetic, toward an appreciation of the modern beauty and promise of the industrial landscape. The evidence, however, points more toward another meaning to this "denial" of nature: bitter and critical irony. By pointing to their utter estrangement from the gentle nature of the old poets, these writings underscored the extent of workers' degradation and exclusion, the alienated unnaturalness of workers' situation. This was, I would argue, a critical and ironic use of familiar aesthetics and values, not the articulation of a new modernist aesthetic. But this is still too simple.

Most of these writers, especially those associated with Marxist parties, made a point of noting the inaccessibility of idealized nature, and the argument tended to be more existential than ideological, more pessimistic than political. It reflected an evident skepticism about the possibilities of a happy life more than ideological conviction that modern progress was necessary and even desirable. In varied ways, these writers made it clear that there was no exit from the modern condition. Aleksei Mashirov, for example, in a poem that appeared in the Bolshevik *Pravda* in 1913, described a worker standing by his machine daydreaming of summer slopes radiant with wild blueberries, sparkling streams, whispering leaves, and the smell of mint and pine along a wooded path. Suddenly the "iron rumbling" of the factory "frightens away" his "free dreams." This yet conventional interrupted idyll deteriorates into a more hellish scene, typical, as we have seen, of worker's writing on modern industry. The factory comes demonically alive and taunts the worker for his pastoral dreams, reminding him that the only sounds and smells he will ever find here are industrial ones:

> You [*ty*] are captive in our prison
> Only we are around you
> We quiver with a rumbling of steel
> We breathe with the roar of machines. . . .
> You think you hear the rustling of leaves?
> That is the hissing and sliding of belts
> And it is the mad wind of wheels
> That carries to you sounds of the woods![134]

Other writers similarly told of nature interrupted by the rude sounds of machinery.[135] And when the sun, the heart of the natural world and a symbol of life and hope, appeared in these writings, it was often obscured by smoke belching from factory chimneys and by soot and grime darkening workplace

---

[133] S. Gan'shin, "Ne prikhodi vesna," *Zhivoe slovo*, no. 10 (March 1913), 6 (a manuscript version may be found in Arkhiv Gor'kogo, RAV-PG 37-13-1); Neliudim [A. Solov'ev], "Grustnye pesni tvoi, proletarskii baian . . . ," *Sotsial-demokrat*, 24 Aug. 1917, rpt. in *Proletarskie poety*, 3:185.

[134] Samobytnik [A. Mashirov], "Grezy," *Pravda truda*, 19 Sept. 1913; also in *Pervyi sbornik*, 140–41.

[135] E.g., V. Gorshkov, "Na fabrike," *Rodnye vesti* 1912, no. 6: 1.

windows.[136] Perhaps even more disturbing, nature could refuse the desired communion with it. When Aleksandr Pomorskii sought "beauty" in sky and sea, "the Great Heavens were wordless and mute / safeguarding their answer," and the "Mighty Sea was regal and silent."[137]

Again and again worker writers expressed awareness that there was no escape. Fedor Gavrilov, for instance, described the dream of a peasant-worker. He is back home, behind the plow, his own master, the beauties of nature all around him, and religious faith and personal pleasure plentifully intact. Then suddenly there is fire and destruction all around. He awakes in a cold sweat, nearly late for the factory, facing a mournful present and a dark future.[138] Others offered the same warning: your dreams of a happy life in the village are "only dreams"—there is no such happy village—and "from this dreary life / Be assured you will never get away."[139] Dreams of nature must yield to sadness and tears.[140] "Dreams of childhood" are vanity—one can never return.[141] At best, one may weep over the "fairy tales" of the past, but they cannot be recovered. There is the future, but at best it lives "only in faith."[142]

For some, this harsh demystification was part of preparing oneself and others to look only forward, only toward the new. In this spirit, Aleksei Gastev imagined some synthesis of old and new values and aesthetics (as many would do after 1917). In a poem published in *Pravda* in 1913, Aleksei Gastev told of a woman factory worker (the choice of gender is significant—women, as we have seen, were often viewed as symbols of nature and beauty) who is able to stop longing for her earlier life in the country and begin to feel the vitality of the factory. She expresses this new appreciation by trying to unite the two: decorating the factory's machines with freshly picked flowers.[143] When other worker poets wrote of flowers in the factory, sometimes pushing through asphalt and stone, they were offering a different message: a reminder of values and beauty other than those of city, factory, and machine. These were often symbols of some hope—of "faith" in a future that was the only hope for escape that remained. For many, however, at least much of the time, even this faith was elusive (at least, little mentioned), leaving only the tragic certainty that one was a "prisoner of city life."

The landscapes of urban and industrial modernity appeared in Russian workers' prerevolutionary imagination again and again as an ugly and dark

---

[136] M. Savin, "V pekarne," *Bulochnik*, no. 1 (19 Feb. 1906), 2; A. Dikii, "V rabochei slobodke," *Nash put'*, no. 13 (10 Feb. 1911), 4; M. Gerasimov, "Vesna," *Put' pravdy*, 17 Apr. 1914, and *Sbornik proletarskikh pisatelei*, 115–16.

[137] A. Pomorskii, "Krasota," *Novaia rabochaia gazeta*, 11 Sept. 1913.

[138] F. Gavrilov, "Son" (1905), in *Proletarskie poety*, 1:197–201.

[139] Mytar', "Dumy rabochego," *Balalaika* 1910, no. 20: 4.

[140] M. Zakharov, "Nastroenie," *Rodnye vesti* 1911, no. 3/4: 7. See also P. Zaitsev, "Na mogile K. A. Molchanova," *Kolotushka* 1911, no. 2: 3.

[141] Samobytnik [A. Mashirov], "Proletarii," *Proletarskaia pravda*, 16 Jan. 1914.

[142] A. Bibik, "Bor obrechennyi," *Novaia rabochaia gazeta*, 13 Oct. 1913.

[143] I. Dozorov [Gastev], "Duma rabotnitsy," *Za pravdu*, 12 Nov. 1913.

force, a mechanism frightful to look at and cruel to those caught in its works. At the root of this failure to embrace the modern industrial city was a larger "failure" to think as proletarians were supposed to think. Skepticism about the modern city (and perhaps about modernity in general) reflected a challenge to industrial capitalism, but one that was more concerned with essential aesthetic and moral values than with contingent social and historical values. Seeking the meaning of life and the path to a good life, these worker writers tended to focus on sentimental matters (beauty and pleasure) and moral values (especially liberty and happiness). They also tended to keep their gaze focused on the individual, on the modern self. While worker writers had much to say about class oppression and class struggle, they continually returned to the fate and will of the individual in modernity. They were preoccupied with the ways city and factory crushed the spirit and dignity of the human person: severed individuals from their families, corrupted the innocent, exploited the weak, wounded and destroyed individual bodies, deprived spirits of needed rest and liberty and of communion with nature, and generally turned living people into automatons. Echoing and reshaping ideals and anxieties found throughout Western culture, and especially in modernizing Russia, these worker writers articulated a radical critique of the society around them that was remarkably skeptical of the moral and aesthetic benefits of modernity. Marxism helped many of them see through this picture toward an appreciation of the productive power and energy of industrial modernity and even of the dialectical necessity of its cruelties. But this dialectic remained paradoxical, asking people to accept the benefits of modern progress even as it revealed its malevolence and brutality with exceptional clarity. This paradoxical vision was resolved only theoretically in an abstract and futuristic doctrine. Least of all did it satisfy urban workers, whose lives and bodies were at the vortex of these whirling contradictions.

Vasilii Aleksandrovskii
(1897–1934)

Mikhail Gerasimov
(1889–1939)

Vladimir Kirillov
(1890–1943)

Nikolai Liashchenko (Liashko)
(1884–1953)

leksei Mashirov (Samobytnik)
(1884–1943)

Egor Nechaev
(1859–1925)

Sergei Obradovich
(1892–1956)

Il'ia Sadof'ev
(1889–1965)

Andrei Klimentov (Platonov)
(1899–1951)

5　Revolutionary Modernity and Its Discontents

Others . . . relished the feeling that the modern world was heading toward catastrophe. Most . . . were artists, conscious promoters of an aesthetic modernity that was, in spite of all its ambiguities, radically opposed to the other, essentially bourgeois, modernity, with its promises of indefinite progress, democracy, generalized sharing of the "comforts of civilization," etc. Such promises appeared to these "decadent" artists as so many demagogical diversions from the terrible reality of increasing spiritual alienation and dehumanization.

—Matei Calinescu

The idea of modernity was a compelling presence in revolutionary Russia's political culture, though divided and unstable: an ideological model with pretensions to hegemony, but also a marker of difference, ambivalence, and even resistance. The revolutionary project of making a new world and new selves provided powerful metaphors and trajectories, shaping how people tried to understand the world and act in it. But this rhetoric also produced—as frustrated Bolshevik cultural leaders of the time complained—its own misappropriations, ambiguities, and subversions. Among working-class Russians, these departures were signs of difference and deviation behind the facade of a discourse that claimed to be the "proletarian" point of view. They were also signs of encounters with the recalcitrantly material world of modern structures and relationships that discourses had to make plausible sense of. Not least, they were signs of deep subjectivities: of the specific gravities of sentiment, emotion, and imagination.

The Bolshevik revolutionary ideal, we are accustomed to think, pushed aside the widespread ambivalence about urban modernity in Russia's intellectual culture. In place of a view of the modern city as at best a simultaneously vital and sinister place of interwoven virtue and vice, creativity and vulgarity, awakening and alienation—an ambiguous symbol of the possibilities and hazards of modern progress—Bolsheviks and their sympathizers are said to have embraced a fully confident "high modernism" in which city, factory, and machine were extolled as the womb and soul of the new society and the possibilities of rational organization and social refashioning were thought to be unlimited. The capitalist factory and city, for all their horrors (indeed, dialectically because of them), were lauded as the setting for the technical progress and heroic class struggle that would beget revolutionary progress. And the future communist civilization was imagined as the epitome of an urbanized, technologically empowered, and culturally advanced modernity. The metropolis—indeed, the cosmopolis, the "universal city"—became the imagined landscape of communism. Cities, factories, and machines were admired as practical means for overcoming Russia's desperate economic backwardness and the more recent wartime breakdown, as cultural devices for conveying modern sensibilities, and as illustrative and tutelary signs pointing citizens toward these goals. There is a stereotypical quality to this picture of single-minded devotion to modernization. In fact, diverse modernist visions identified themselves with the revolution and communism after 1917. Even Bolshevik modernism was not monolithic, nor could it be in the chaotic early years after October 1917. Even less could it mask the anxieties many Bolsheviks felt about the actual landscapes—physical, social, and moral—of modern life. Still, though the unambiguous embrace of the modern city and factory was a crude stereotype of the revolutionary mentality, it was one that had enormous political authority in Soviet Russia.

This positive modernism was especially visible in the first years after 1917, as state leaders, journalists, social activists, writers, and artists spoke constantly of the values of urban and industrial modernization. Bolshevism, heir to the Marxist idea that its ideology was modern and "scientific," unleashed and nurtured a spirit of urban and industrial modernism that was shaping the emerging new culture. The press featured stories on world developments in science and technology. Lenin and other Communist leaders regularly argued for the economic and cultural benefits of mechanization, rationalization, and, in Lenin's famous slogan, "electrification of the whole country." Lenin frequently and bluntly insisted that, in social life and politics as in war, "those who have the best technology, organization, and discipline and the best machines will gain the upper hand. . . . Without machines, without discipline, it is impossible to live in modern society. One must master the highest technology or be crushed."[1] The machine, one cultural historian has written, became "the dominant cultural symbol" in early Soviet Russia, standing for the official virtues of efficient rationality, relentless drive, iron discipline, and soli-

---

[1] V. Lenin, "Zakliuchitel'naia rech', 15 marta, Chetvertyi s"ezd sovetov," *Pravda*, 19 (6) Mar 1918, rpt. in V. I. Lenin, *Polnoe sobranie sochinenii*, 5th ed., vol. 36 (Moscow, 1962), 116.

darity.[2] The hammer and sickle were merely a political emblem representing a temporary social alliance. City, factory, and machine were the more important cultural symbols of the new society.

This spirit—with its dilemmas—was particularly evident in the creative work of leftist writers and artists. In the immediate prewar years, elaborating on similar Western European trends, Russian Futurists had begun championing a radical modernism that rejected past cultural values in the name of a new modern aesthetics. "We alone are the face of our Time," the Moscow Futurists declared in their famous 1912 manifesto. "The past suffocates us. . . . Throw Pushkin, Dostoevsky, Tolstoy, etc., etc. overboard from the Ship of Modernity. . . . From the heights of skyscrapers we gaze at their nothingness."[3] Paintings incorporated images and physical fragments of the modern material world: newspapers, trains, machines, glass, metal. And literature celebrated the fragmentary life of the city and the modern artifice and constructedness of all things—including language. After the revolution, these and other leftist artists placed themselves in the avant-garde of revolutionary modernism. Vladimir Maiakovskii, in his widely reproduced verses, invoked electricity, radios, telephones, airplanes, bridges, trains, and skyscrapers. Aleksandr Rodchenko, Gustav Klutsis, and other "Productivist" and "Constructivist" artists built sculptures ("constructions") using modern material objects (especially steel and glass) and montages of images (often cut from photographs or newspapers) of modern buildings, airplanes, electric pylons, city streets, and factories. Vladimir Tatlin designed a massive tower with a spiral iron frame and revolving glass rooms, incorporating a wide range of mechanical and electrical technologies, as the headquarters for the Third International. The sculptor-architect Anton Lavinskii sketched out a project for a mechanically elevated glass city of the future. Other "left artists" imagined the future similarly and filled the present with images of material modernity. Bolshevism, certain that it was a modern ideology grounded in science—viewing communism and the human transformations that were a necessary part of it as the outcomes of economic and technological progress, not moral fervor—unleashed and nurtured a spirit of urban and industrial modernism that was shaping the emerging new culture. This was, however, a particular modernism in its relation to the actual modern world. Little of the real hardships of contemporary urban and industrial life were visible. On the contrary, these were purified modern spaces, clean and orderly. Modern objects were displayed more as appealing fragments than as parts of a whole reality. Indeed, the everyday present was often invisible, as this appealing modernity was displaced into an imagined future. As suggested by the growing dismay and despair among former Futurist artists during the 1920s in the face of everyday life (*byt*), radical modernism sought not only to reject the past but also to deny the troubling present.

---

[2] Katerina Clark, *The Soviet Novel: History as Ritual,* 2d ed. (Chicago, 1985), 94.
[3] From the Futurist manifesto, "Slap in the Face of Public Taste" (1912), in *Poshchechina obshchestvennomu vkusu* (Moscow, [1912]), 3–4.

This emerging revolutionary culture was marked by ambivalence and the growing desire to overcome it. Marxism, with its notions of the explosive but fruitful contradictions of modern capitalism and its ideas of dialectical progress, nurtured a political-economic and historical version of the modernist embrace of vital disruption and disorder as part of a conception of progress that would overcome contingency and uncertainty. Modernist art, in an aesthetic rather than social or political manner, was also inclined toward a vision of iconoclasm and disorder pointing to transcendence. After October, however, with revolutionaries in power, the emphasis in both ideology and art was increasingly on the force of overcoming, on resolving contradictions, on moving beyond the modernist spirit of disruption. Increasingly, Soviet political thinking placed its emphasis on the modernism of scientific rationalism and progress and left less and less space for the modernism that stood in defiance of the materialism and ordering rationalism of bourgeois modernity, much less for the modernism that questioned progress, order, and the cult of science and reason. Soviet modernity, to borrow Zygmunt Bauman's phrase, struggled constantly to "purge ambivalence."[4] But Soviet cultural life could not escape it. Thoroughly modern, it was torn by contradictory and unstable dialogues (and sometimes struggles) between positivist rationality and questioning iconoclasm, disciplining repression and libidinal excess, legibility and startling multiplicity, faith in progress and deep unease.[5]

Working-class writers, especially the radical poets and authors associated with the proletarian culture movement, were generally said to have been imbued with a happy urbanist and industrial imagination, indeed, to have exemplified it. In his study of the proletarian poets of the early Soviet years, George Patrick stated this plainly: "The proletarian bards are turning all their affections to the tumultuous and roaring city. . . . They contemplate it with feelings that are bound up with their own life, their own energy, and they are impressed by its power and its utility."[6] Contemporary Soviet literary critics had been arguing the same. Pavel Lebedev-Polianskii, one of the most powerful figures on the early Soviet cultural scene, declared repeatedly that after October the worker writer had finally awakened to the progressive values of urban modernity and recognized the apparent evils of city life to be necessary contradictions in an unfolding historical dialectic.

[4] Zygmunt Bauman, *Intimations of Postmodernity* (London, 1992), 120.

[5] For evidence of these divergent modernisms in early Soviet culture and ideology, see Clark, *Soviet Novel*, 93–97; Richard Stites, *Revolutionary Dreams: Utopian Vision and Experimental Life in the Russian Revolution* (New York, 1989), esp. chap. 7; René Fueloep-Miller, *The Mind and Face of Bolshevism* (New York, 1927); Jeffrey Brooks, "The Press and Its Message: Images of America in the 1920s and 1930s," in *Russia in the Era of NEP*, ed. Sheila Fitzpatrick, Alexander Rabinowitch, and Richard Stites (Bloomington, 1991), 239–42; John Milner, *Vladimir Tatlin and the Russian Avant-Garde* (New Haven, 1983); Christina Lodder, *Russian Constructivism* (New Haven, 1983); Margarita Tupitsyn, *The Soviet Photograph, 1924–1937* (New Haven, 1996), chap. 1. Work that appeared in Maiakovskii's journal *Lef: Zhurnal levogo fronta iskusstv* was typical. See, e.g., *Lef*, no. 1 (March 1923), 61–64, 69, 105–8, 172–79; no. 2 (April–May 1923), 65–68; no. 4 (August–December 1924), 40–44, 58–62, 89–108.

[6] George Z. Patrick, *Popular Poetry in Soviet Russia* (Berkeley, 1929), 143–44.

If previously the city was portrayed as an octopus, and the worker's muse saw in it the celebration of gluttony beside want, of the blinding gleam of shop windows, fancy restaurants, and advertisements beside the lopsided hovels of the workers' neighborhoods, of flamboyantly chic ladies and idle fops of the bourgeoisie beside the prostitute and the unemployed—now [in 1918] the city seems quite different. The worker loves it.[7]

Now, Lebedev-Polianskii implied, workers understood that these were meaningful and necessary contradictions. Likewise, he claimed, worker writers looked in a new (and more correct) way at the features that made the city modern: machines, factories, smokestacks, sirens, and even the "sweat, blood, and tears of the working class." Now, Lebedev-Polianskii boldly asserted, "the worker poet loves the factory" as a great force for production and progress.[8] Other Marxist intellectuals writing on proletarian culture similarly insisted on the positive urbanist and industrial consciousness of worker writers, especially younger, urban-reared ones. Worker writers, they argued, quoting appropriate examples, renounce nostalgia for the country and celebrate iron and steel, sing of the tractor as the symbol of the technological victory of the city over the country, contrast the "insurgent city" with "rural stagnation," infuse their writings with the rhythms and objects of the city, and voice "the pathos of a poetry of iron and steel, the pathos of a poetry glorifying the iron and concrete city, love . . . of things and products and factories."[9]

This was a troubled modernism, however. To be sure, the revolutionary experience of 1917 and after, the proclaimed visions and values of those holding political power after October, and the promotional efforts of new cultural leaders and institutions no doubt stimulated real enthusiasm among many lower-class writers for the progressive landscapes of urban and industrial modernity. But George Patrick was partly right: these writers contemplated the city "with feelings that are bound up with their own life." The effect, however, was far from simply an upwelling of "affection" for the modern city. Marxist cultural leaders admitted that sometimes even revolutionary-minded workers failed to understand properly the modern landscape of city, factory, and machine. Least surprisingly, critics noted, writers born and raised in villages or provincial towns frequently failed to "feel love for the city with its eternal movement, with its factories and machines."[10] But even young, urban-

---

[7] V. Polianskii [P. Lebedev-Polianskii], "Motivy rabochei poezii," *Proletarskaia kul'tura*, no. 3 (August 1918), 9.

[8] V. Polianskii, "Dve poezii," *Proletarskaia kul'tura*, no. 13–14 (January–March 1920), 47.

[9] V. L. L'vov-Rogachevskii, *Ocherki proletarskoi literatury* (Moscow and Leningrad, 1927), 110–11; A. Voronskii, "O gruppe pisatelei 'Kuznitsa,'" in his *Iskusstvo i zhizn': Sbornik statei* (Moscow and Petrograd, 1924), 128–32 (originally published in *Krasnaia nov'*, no. 13 [1923]). For similar statements, see S. Rodov in *Kuznitsa*, no. 1 (May 1920), 24–25; P. Bessal'ko in *Griadushchee* 1919, no. 1: 15; S. Rodov in *Gorn*, no. 6 (1922), 118–19; I. Pchelintsev in *Rabochii zhurnal* 1924, no. 3–4: 211; L. Kleinbort, *Ocherki narodnoi literatury (1880–1923 gg.)* (Leningrad, 1924), 266–85.

[10] V. A-skii, review of M. Artamonov, *Zemlia rodnaia* (1919), in *Kuznitsa*, no. 1 (May 1920), 26–27; V. Polianskii, "Poeziia sovetskoi provintsii," *Proletarskaia kul'tura*, no. 7–8 (April–May 1919), 46.

born worker writers, they had to admit, could and did feel a painful ambivalence about city life, the factory, and, by extension, modernity itself.[11] These admissions, however, barely reveal the depth and scope of the problem. Like many more educated writers in Russia and other countries, some worker writers continued, after 1917 as before, to see aesthetic and moral decline in the growth of modern industrial cities. The Bolshevik revolution complicated this vision, inspiring most of these writers to embrace modernity with a passion rarely seen before 1918. More than ever, worker writers became advocates of the modern. But their vision also had much in common with the "other modernism": theirs was an aesthetic and moral vision that looked at the everyday forms of modern civilization with disgust, sustained a skepticism about the benefits of scientific and industrial progress, and viewed the present and often the future with a bitter sense of alienation, dehumanization, and looming catastrophe.

"Iron Flowers"

It is appropriate that the most canonically flawless portrayal of city life to appear in a proletarian publication in these early Soviet years was by a non-worker intellectual, the critic and cultural activist Semen Kluben' (Evgenov). In a story published in 1919 in the journal of the Tambov Proletcult, of which he was a leader, Kluben' described a young peasant lad coming to the city to work and growing infatuated with the urban environment. Even when he first journeys to the city he is filled with anticipation and excitement, having already heard "wonders" about urban life from earlier migrants to the town. He finds work in a huge metal factory—the politically correct choice, since metalworkers were conventionally viewed as the most proletarianized and conscious of workers and metal works as the most modern of factories. After a brief moment of longing for the country (even Kluben' cannot entirely ignore or deny this common sentiment) he learns to love the city. It becomes, as the title of the story also tells us, his "new native land." He loves the city partly because he can look at it with collectivist pride: "We created this!" But he also feels an aesthetic appreciation of the urban landscape. "I love the city. I love its tall buildings that reach practically up to the sky. With pleasure I hear the rattle of cars and the roar of trucks. . . . I listen to the clang of the streetcars. I watch as they clumsily creep along, rocking their fat red bodies, and I feel happy." The warm glow of city lights and the leaping sparks on overhead streetcar wires fill him with the same distinctly urban aesthetic joy.[12]

Similar appreciation of the modern industrial city was increasingly visible

[11] S. Rodov, "Motivy tvorchestva M. Gerasimova," *Kuznitsa*, no. 1 (May 1920), 23; Voronskii, "O gruppe pisatelei 'Kuznitsa,'" 136; L'vov-Rogachevskii, *Ocherki*, 104, 119–24; A. Kosterin on Nikolai Kuznetsov, in *Rabochii zhurnal* 1925, no. 1–2: 232; P. I. M., review of Aleksandrovskii, *Shagi*, in *Rabochii zhurnal* 1925, no. 1–2: 277–78.

[12] S. K. [Semen Kluben' (Evgenov)], "Novaia rodina," *Griadushchaia kul'tura*, no. 3 (January 1919), 1–3.

after the October revolution, especially among the politicized majority of worker writers, many of whom were or became party members and almost all of whom joined—and often helped organize—local Proletcults. Nearly every major worker writer after 1917 wrote about the city and its significance. Most wrote at least one major poem focusing explicitly on the city and, to emphasize the universality of their arguments, usually titled them simply "Gorod" (The City) or "Gorodu" (To the city). A few were named after a particular city, but most often it was Moscow or St. Petersburg/Petrograd, both cities that had long been viewed as symbols as much as actual places. Many of these writings, especially during the revolutionary-romantic years from 1918 to 1921, describe the enchanting physical beauty of the city: its street corners, squares, sidewalks, posters, rooftops, electric lights, noise, factories, granite, and steel.[13] Of course, these writers often claimed to take special pride—class pride—that all this was made by workers' hands.[14] These everyday charms, however, paled in their imagination before more hyperbolic images of the physical city. Increasingly the city appeared as an animate but supernatural hero: "a fire-faced Colossus," a "great iron-stone giant," a striding and talking creature made "entirely of steel and fire . . . breathing out cascades of light."[15] When in the mood, as they had rarely been before October, these writers could revere the physical city with sensual passion. In May 1918, in the journal of the Petrograd Proletcult, Vladimir Kirillov published a prose poem in which he spoke directly to "the great city," offering up fervent declarations of love for its "feverish and intense life," its struggles, its electric lights, and its promise for the future.[16] Vasilii Aleksandrovskii even more tersely professed his urbanist love: "Ach, I love you, I love your stones."[17]

Such declarations of love for the physical city were, for all their passion, still relatively rare, however. More common was a rather more theoretical love—a dialectical, historical love. This point of view allowed one to admit the ugliness, evil, and cruelty of the actual city, but to interpret them as required to produce a higher good—as part of a necessary dialectic of self-transcendence. Influenced by Marxist ideology, worker writers wrote of the city as the foundation of historical progress, in particular as the center of class struggle—the "cradle of the commune," as Il'ia Sadof'ev put it.[18] But the city was also, more

[13] P. Eroshin, "V derevne," *Zavod ognekrylyi* (Moscow, 1918), 69; I. Sadof'ev, "Ritm granita (Posviashchaiu Krasnomu Piteru)," *Griadushchee* 1919, no. 4: 1–3; N. Poletaev, "Chadilo chertova kadilo . . . ," *Gorn*, nos. 2–3 (1919), 4; S. Obradovich, "Gorod (Poema)" (1919–20), *Kuznitsa*, no. 5–6 (October–November 1920), 17–23; Ia. Berdnikov, "Gorod," *Griadushchee* 1920, no. 12–13: 1; V. Aleksandrovskii, "Iz tsikla 'Moskva,'" *Tvori!* no. 1 (December 1920), 4, and "V granite," *Kuznitsa*, no. 4 (August–September 1920), 8–9.

[14] E.g., S. Obradovich, "Gorod," *Kuznitsa*, no. 5–6 (October–November 1920), 17.

[15] V. Aleksandrovskii, "Iz tsikla 'Moskva,'" *Tvori!* no. 1 (December 1920), 4; V. Kirillov, "Gorodu," *Griadushchee* 1918, no. 2 (May): 6; Ia. Berdnikov, "Gorod," *Griadushchee* 1920, no. 12–13: 1.

[16] V. Kirillov, "Gorodu," *Griadushchee* 1918, no. 2 (May): 6.

[17] V. Aleksandrovskii, "Iz tsikla 'Moskva,'" *Tvori!* no. 1 (December 1920), 4.

[18] I. Sadof'ev, "Ritm ganita (Posviashchaiu Krasnomu Piteru)," *Griadushchee* 1919, no. 4: 3. See also Sadof'ev, "Petrogradu," in *Dinamo-stikhi* (Petrograd, 1918), 38. For a couple of other examples of this theme, see Eroshin, "V derevne," *Zavod ognekrylyi*, 69; and V. Aleksandrovskii, "Putnik," *Gorn*, no. 1 (1918), 10.

generally, the foundation of human civilization and progress: "In the city, science and art develop, dreams and thoughts mature. . . . Everything bright and profound, everything that leads people to the heights, with which the world is seen, was born, in the majority of cases, within city walls."[19] Pavel Bessal'ko insisted that "we love the city because it united us, because it taught us to protest, because it beat the prejudices of the peasant out of us."[20] Vladimir Kirillov expressed this same idea more ecstatically when he declared, "I love you, city, for you are the great bridge to the liberation and exaltation of man."[21]

More abstractly still, the city was appreciated as a symbol and promise of a better future, of a different and purified city. As in much utopian literature— from the biblical millenarian vision of a "Holy City, the new Jerusalem, coming down out of heaven from God,"[22] through Renaissance architectural and philosophical treatises on the *città felice* to Marxist futurology[23]—the future appeared in the imaginations of these worker writers often as an urban utopia. This might be a city to be found and reached: "a bright city along an untraveled pathway."[24] But more often it was a city to be built: "In the fire of delight we uplift our hammers, / We destroy mountains in our path. / Upon the earth's deserts we build a New City, / In the stone nets, machines begin to sing."[25] Unlike the city of the present—but much like the utopian cities of Revelation and the Renaissance and echoing the growing preoccupation with purifying lives and landscapes[26]—the Communist New City of the Future would be "gracefully elegant and crystalline in cleanliness."[27]

Whether viewed in the present or in the future, the idealized city was properly imagined, from the conventional Marxist perspective, as a modern city, a city of factories and machines. Marxist cultural intellectuals pointed with satisfaction to the evidence that worker writers—especially those associated with such groups as the Proletcult and the association of proletarian writers around the journal *Kuznitsa*—saw the factory as a positive force and symbol, and even felt a special "love and passion"[28] for the factory: as a source of useful products made by workers' hands, as a means of overcoming the country's backwardness (the "cradle of the new Russia"), as the social environment

[19] N. Liashko, "Dukhovnye iady goroda i kooperatsiia," *Rabochii mir* 1918, no. 7 (June 23): 24.

[20] P. Bessal'ko, "O poezii krest'ianskoi i proletarskoi," *Griadushchee* 1918, no. 7 (October): 13.

[21] V. Kirillov, "Gorodu," *Griadushchee* 1918, no. 2 (May): 6.

[22] Rev. 21:2. See also Rev. 3:12 and all of chap. 21; also Psalms 46:4 (45:5 in the Russian Orthodox Bible), which sees God living in a divine "city" (*grad*).

[23] See Frank E. Manuel and Fritzie P. Manuel, *Utopian Thought in the Western World* (Cambridge, Mass., 1979).

[24] I. Eroshin, "Po doroge," *Tvorchestvo*, no. 5 (September 1918), 19.

[25] A. Platonov, "Mai" (1920), in *Golubaia glubina: Kniga stikhov* (Krasnodar, 1922), 16.

[26] See Katerina Clark, *Petersburg, Crucible of Revolution* (Cambridge, Mass., 1995), esp. 3, 84, 141, 209–11, 252. For a discussion of the "dream of purity" as characteristic of modernity, see Zygmunt Bauman, *Postmodernity and Its Discontents* (New York, 1997), chap. 1.

[27] I. Filipchenko, "Lenin," *Rabochii zhurnal* 1924, no. 1: 65.

[28] V. Kremnev, "Poema Velikoi Revoliutsii," *Kuznitsa*, no. 5–6 (October–November 1920), 65.

where solidarity and striving and struggle are nurtured and sustained, as a spiritual force that replaced sadness and longing with struggle and overcoming, as the herald of the future, and as a symbol of everything alive, dynamic, and creative in life.[29] To illustrate this canonical proletarian perspective, the Proletcult leader Semen Kluben', in the story already mentioned (written in the first person as if a memoir, though the author had never been a peasant or a worker), describes a young peasant lad falling in love with factories and machinery. From the very first, the appearance of the train that will take this boy to the city fills him with "an inexplicable, deep feeling of sympathy" for this huge hissing machine, "a sort of strange love mixed with reverence." Once he starts work in a factory, he extends this passion (which is not without hints of eros, though the object remains, typically, male) to the machinery there: "Machines—steel, glistening, supple, like the body of a youth; dark and powerful like old sages, giants." Reversing values in the conventional contrast between the artificial city and the natural countryside, Kluben''s ideal-typical proletarian sees the splendor of the city precisely in its modern artifice: In the open steppe "there is merely the sun. . . . Here we created our own electric sun . . . brighter and warmer than their sun."[30]

There is no doubt that the revolution and the establishment of organizations devoted to promoting a new proletarian culture stimulated many worker writers, if not ordinary workers themselves, to see the factory and machines in new, more positive ways. Giving voice to their political convictions, worker writers mobilized a metaphoric language in which objects from industrial life were emblems of the revolution. Thus, for example, the factory smokestack was envisioned as the spire of a "temple" exhaling "incense to the new god-man," as a great torch casting sparks of light into the hearts of workers and peasants, and as a scepter of power in the "iron fist" of a worker giant.[31] Airplanes were described as "proud iron machines" that could fly along "solar traces" and "intersect the vortices of orbits," and that "sing our victory," or, in a rare literary contribution by Aleksandr Shliapnikov (the trade unionist and leader of the Workers' Opposition), as a means of enabling an aspiring worker to transcend the everyday grind.[32] Revolutionaries were viewed as "mechanics" making a new modern world, the revolution as standing for "the power of machines," and Soviet Russia as a giant with "machine muscles."[33]

[29] V. Polianskii, "Dve poezii," 47–51; S. Rodov in *Gorn*, no. 6 (1922), 116–20; Voronskii, "O gruppe pisatelei 'Kuznitsa,'" 130–35.

[30] S. K. [Semen Kluben'], "Novaia rodina," *Griadushchaia kul'tura*, no. 3 (January 1919), 1–3.

[31] V. Kirillov, "Gorody," *Griadushchee* 1918, no. 2 (May): 6; M. Gerasimov, "Zavodskaia truba," *Tvorchestvo*, no. 3 (July 1918), 3. Ivan Eroshin also portrayed the factory as a "temple" in "Iz tsikla 'Pesni truda,'" in *Zavod ognekrylyi*, 48.

[32] M. Gerasimov, "Letim," in *Zavod ognekrylyi*, 17; A. Shliapnikov, "Aviatory," *Proletarskaia kul'tura*, no. 7–8 (April–May 1919), 59–62. See also S. Obradovich, "Vzlet" (1922), in RGALI, f. 1874, op. 1, d. 7, l. 66.

[33] I. Sadof'ev, "Ritm granita," *Griadushchee* 1919, no. 4: 1–3; Iv. Ivanov, "Mashinist," *Molot*, no. 1 (November 1920), 16–17; V. Aleksandrovskii, "Krylia," *Gorn*, no. 5 (1920), 7–9; M. Gerasimov, "Iz poema 'Oktiabria,'" *Kuznitsa*, no. 3 (July 1920), 10–11.

That this appreciation of machines was often only abstract, purified, and symbolic was noticed, and it worried some critics. Workers' poems and stories were undoubtedly filled with "traditional" images of industry—furnaces, hammers, sparks, iron, and smokestacks—but, as some critics noted with concern, workers should have featured images of actual *modern* industrial technique: finely calibrated lathes, for example, or the quiet hum of an electric motor.[34] Indeed, the most common images of labor and industry were the least modern: the "blacksmith" (*kuznets*) and the "foundry" (*kuznitsa*). These images, of course, were in accord with an emerging Bolshevik iconography of work. But they also remind us of the abstract and ideological nature of these songs of industry. Like other Bolshevik artists, worker writers employed images of the blacksmith and his workshop, not as realistic pictures of modern industry, much less of their own work experience (none had been hot metal workers), but as increasingly canonical and abstract images representing the struggle to "forge" a new life.[35] The titles of Proletcult journals and anthologies were similarly industrial tropes meant to express the ideal of deliberate creation of a new society and culture: *Chugunnyi ulei* (The cast-iron beehive), *Gornilo* (The crucible), *Gudki* (Factory whistles), *Kuznitsa* (The smithy), *Molot* (The hammer), *Nash gorn* (Our furnace), *Sirena* (The siren), *Zarevo zavodov* (Glow of the factories), and *Zavod ognekrylyi* (Fire-winged factory).

Intellectually and emotionally, however, factories and machines often represented more than abstract metaphors for social transformation. Worker writers also found here, as in the city, a certain alluring beauty. Writers, especially those associated with the Proletcult movement—encouraged by Soviet cultural officials and critics[36]—deliberately and insistently proclaimed a revolution in aesthetic values. As one literary critic described it in the Petrograd Proletcult journal *Griadushchee* (The future), in contemporary Russian literature two class perspectives were in conflict: the antiquated bourgeois "poetry of gold and ornament" and the new proletarian "poetry of iron."[37] And even more than in the past, this was a strongly gendered aesthetic, a view of machine industry as a male terrain marked by what were assumed to be masculine qualities: iron hardness, bold assertiveness, thrusting power.[38]

Vladimir Kirillov's early and influential postrevolutionary manifesto in verse,

---

[34] For such criticism, see S. Grigor'ev, "Novaia fabrika," *Gorn*, no. 6 (1922), 113–16.

[35] E.g., V. Aleksandrovskii, "Kuznets," in *Zavod ognekrylyi*, 35; M. Gerasimov, "Zarevo zavodov," *Zarevo zavodov*, no. 1 (January 1919), 8–10. On the iconographic importance and significance of the blacksmith in Bolshevik culture, see Victoria E. Bonnell, *Iconography of Power: Soviet Political Posters under Lenin and Stalin* (Berkeley, 1997), chap. 1.

[36] See, e.g., A. Lunacharskii, "Nachalo proletarskoi estetiki," *Proletarskaia kul'tura*, no. 11–12 (December 1919), 8–10.

[37] E. Bogdat'eva, "Poeziia zolota i poeziia zheleza," *Griadushchee* 1918, no. 3 (June): 13.

[38] For discussion of the wider tendency in early Soviet culture to envision the social world in sexual and gendered terms, see Eric Naiman, *Sex in Public: The Incarnation of Early Soviet Ideology* (Princeton, 1997); Eliot Borenstein, *Men without Women: Masculinity and Revolution in Russian Fiction, 1917–1929* (Durham, 2000); and Igal Halfin, *From Darkness to Light: Class, Consciousness, and Salvation in Revolutionary Russia* (Pittsburgh, 2000), 130-41.

"We," was characteristic of this emerging genre and characteristically insistent that the proletariat was engaged in an aesthetic rebellion.

> Let them shout, "You are butchering beauty,"
> In the name of our Tomorrow, we will burn Raphael,
> Destroy museums, and trample the flowers of art. . . .
> In the bright kingdom of the Future
> Maidens will be more lovely than the Venus de Milo.
> Tears dry in our eyes and tenderness is crushed.
> We have forgotten the fragrance of grass and spring flowers.
> We have come to love the strength of steam and the might of dynamite,
> The song of sirens and the whirl of wheels and shafts. . . .
> Oh, poet-aesthetes, curse the Great Ham,
> Kiss the wreckage of the past under our heels,
> Bathe in tears the ruins of smashed temples. . . .
> We breathe a different beauty.[39]

Other worker authors joined this aesthetic revolution. In 1918 Mikhail Gerasimov, in one of his most famous verses, wrote of "iron flowers" forged in the factory, a bouquet made in the firestorm of the furnace.[40] Aleksei Mashirov (Samobytnik) counterposed to the conventional "gentle whispering" about a promised paradise of flowers, sun, and the scent of dew an aesthetically defiant "machine heaven" with birds of steel and iron that glistened like diamonds.[41]

For most of these social and cultural proletarians, a new sense of beauty was wrapped up with a new emotional orientation to the modern world—a great love and even a sensual passion. Numerous worker writers, especially those associated with the Proletcult, declared a passionate "love" for electricity, railroads, airplanes, dynamos, smokestacks, iron, steel, and the songs and dances of pulleys, belts, and machines.[42] For some, this was an intellectual

---

[39] V. Kirillov, "My," *Griadushchee* 1918, no. 2 (May): 4. The reference to "poet-aesthetes" who "curse the Great Ham" refers most obviously to Dmitrii Merezhkovskii, "The Coming Ham" (1906), in which Merezhkovskii condemned the dead positivism of the autocratic state, of petty-bourgeois philistinism, and of the lumpenproletariat as the "coming Ham," who can be defeated only by Christ. More generally—and this is implied also in Merezhkovskii's imagery—Kirillov's reference is to the Bible's Ham, one of Noah sons, whose name came to stand for rough boorishness (*khamstvo* can be translated as such). Because Ham revealed his father's drunkenness and nakedness, thus provoking Noah to put a curse on him and his descendants, causing them to live lives of servitude (Gen. 9:21–27), Ham is also associated with filial disrespect and rebellion. Reversing the usual values associated with Ham, Kirillov voices a type of defiant plebeian pride and a suggestion that worker poets were telling the naked truth about their own literary and social elders. By further extension, he associated this aesthetic rebellion with the greater "Hamism" of the poor (rebellious slaves) against the rich. Dmitrii Merezhkovskii, "Griadushchii Kham," in *Polnoe sobranie sochinenii Dmitriia Sergeevicha Merezhkovskago*, vol. 14 (Moscow, 1914), esp. 37–39.

[40] M. Gerasimov, "Zheleznye tsvety," in *Zavod ognekrylyi*, 16.

[41] Samobytnik [A. Mashirov], "Mashinnyi rai," *Griadushchee* 1920, no. 1–2: 1. See also N. Poletaev in *Gudki*, no. 6 (June 1919), 12–13.

[42] In addition to the examples below, see Pavel Bezsal'ko in *Griadushchee* 1918, no. 7 (October): 13.

and political passion. Sadof'ev, for example, declared that the revolution helped him to see and hear the "carnival" beauty and truth of the factory: in the "peals and roars" and in the "joyful, drunken dance of pulleys" he discovered "striving," "liberty," the "secrets of the world," the "Wisdom of the Word," and "Inspiration." Now, to be in the factory every day, "to understand this Iron tongue, to hear the mystery of the revelation," is "ecstasy."[43] But most often this passion was both more abstract (less tied to specific political ideas) and more physical. Thus Aleksei Gastev—whom a contemporary critic identified as the model "iron poet"—found in cranes, girders, molten metal, factory whistles, hammer blows, and the noise and "whirl of fire and machines" a "soul" and even an "alluring passion."[44] Others were similarly entranced by the beautiful "singing of steel" as it was hammered and worked, by the "wild choir" of screaming chisels, droning saws, and turning nuts and bolts, by the "dance of maidens" in the movements of pulleys and cranes, and even by the inspiring "growl of boilers."[45]

For some worker writers this passion for iron and machines was not simply aesthetic and emotional or ideological but part of a mythic psychocultural (and stereotypically masculine) identity in which proletarians merged with machines. Most famously, in his poem "We Grow Out of Iron," which was often reprinted after 1917, Aleksei Gastev wrote of the revolutionary worker growing into a mythic giant, reaching the height of smokestacks, as iron blood flows into his veins.[46] Into the early 1920s, Gastev continued to write about fusing man and machine, though he began to inscribe this ideal less in poetry than in advocacy of a new engineering. In a series of writings published in 1918 and 1919[47]—which drew explicitly, if eclectically, on Frederick W. Taylor's "scientific management," on the new field of industrial psychology or

[43] I. Sadof'ev, "V zavode," in *Dinamo-stikhi,* 44–45. Sadof'ev wrote many similar poems.

[44] A. Gastev, "Zeleznye pul'sy," in *Poeziia rabochego udara* (Petrograd, 1918), 116, 123 (this was the first publication of this story); "Kran," *Vooruzhennyi narod,* 6 Sept. 1918; "Rel'sy," *Zheleznyi put'* (Voronezh), no. 1 (1918), 11; and other writings in *Poeziia rabochego udara.* See also the discussion of Gastev's writings by Kurt Johansson, *Aleksej Gastev: Proletarian Bard of the Machine Age* (Stockholm, 1983); Stites, *Revolutionary Dreams,* 149–55; and (emphasizing the sexual and esp. phallic dimensions) Naiman, *Sex in Public,* 65–66, 68–69.

[45] I. Ustinov, "Pevuchaia stal'," *Tvorchestvo,* no. 3 (August 1918), 12; RGALI, f. 1641, op. 1, d. 36 (I. G. Ustinov); M. Gerasimov, "Vesennee utro," *Zarevo zavodov,* no. 2 (1919), 8; A. Sh. (a female member of a proletarian literary circle), review of N. Tikhomirov, *Krasnyi most: Stikhi, 1914–18* (Petrograd, 1919), in *Revoliutsionnye vskhody,* no. 3–4 (October 1920), 10; Fekuz, "Liub'vi rabochego," *Rabochee tvorchestvo* (writings by "worker correspondents" in Nizhnyi Novgorod), no. 1 (December 1923), 35; *Rabochee tvorchestvo,* no. 8 (November 1924), 13.

[46] I. Dozorov [A. Gastev], "My rastem iz zheleza," *Metallist* 1917, no. 7 (Dec. 16): 4.

[47] Aleksei Gastev, *Industrial'nyi mir* (Kharkov, 1919); idem, "Novaia industriia," *Vestnik metallista* 1918, no. 2: 5–27; idem, "O tendentsiiakh proletarskoi kul'tury," *Proletarskaia kul'tura,* no. 9–10 (June–July 1919), 35–45. The book *Industrial'nyi mir* (Industrial world) was published in 1919 by the All-Ukrainian Arts Department, a branch of the People's Commissariat of Enlightenment, which Gastev then headed. As the citations indicate, parts of the book were published in 1918 in the newspaper of the metalworkers' union in Petrograd, and the concluding sections, which described the emerging "culture" and "psychology" of the proletariat that modern industrial life was producing, appeared also as a "discussion piece" in the national journal of the Proletcult.

"psychotechnique," and on Marxist theories of imperialism and class struggle—Gastev predicted a "new industrial order" based on the growing unity of man and machine. Order and discipline would be maintained not by human directives but by the inner logic of the production process and the rhythms of the machines—a "great anonymity" in which the "will of machinism and the will of human consciousness" would be "unbreakably conjoined," and "machines move from being managed to being managers." In time, these self-regulating factories would evolve into "gigantic machines" and these factory-machines would fuse into "machine cities." As the power of this machinism grew, Gastev imagined, in a voice less of scientific manager than of modernist seer, the mentality and culture of the proletariat would also be transformed. The emerging proletariat would come to work, think, react, and gesture identically throughout the world. The result, the apex of proletarian culture, would be a "mechanized collectivism" in which "there are no individual features" but "a face without expression, a soul devoid of lyricism, and emotions measured not by screams or laughter but by manometer and taximeter."[48]

Although Gastev was unique among worker authors in his practical devotion to promoting economic and psychocultural "machinism"—as he was in his student-turned-worker social biography—other worker writers were similarly inspired by the ideal of a new iron and machine personality. In 1918, for example, Kirillov declared, "We have grown close to metal and fused our souls with machines."[49] Aleksandrovskii predicted that the new people would be "like machines."[50] And Gerasimov described himself as such a new, modern man:

> I am not a tender, hothouse type.
> You don't need to caress me.
> My mother gave birth to me in a clamorous factory,
> Beneath a machine. . . .
> I greedily sucked an electric pacifier,
> I was rocked in a steel cradle,
> And the bold factory whistle sang my lullabies.[51]

This proletarian personality, Gerasimov maintained, needed to be extended to all Russians, especially peasants, who would be saved only when each shepherd carried an "iron lash," farmers were awakened by a "bronze rooster," electric lights overcame the darkness of peasant huts, and the very "soul" of the peasant was "electrified."[52]

---

[48] Gastev, *Industrial'nyi mir*, 50–55, 68, 70, 74–77; "Novaia industriia," *Vestnik metallista* 1918, no. 2, cited in Johansson, *Aleksej Gastev*, 62; "O tendentsiiakh proletarskoi kul'tury," 42, 44–45.

[49] V. Kirillov, "My," *Griadushchee* 1918, no. 2 (May): 4.

[50] V. Aleksandrovskii, "Moi muskuly—Pruzhiny," in *Zavod ognekrylyi*, 36.

[51] M. Gerasimov, "Ia ne nezhnyi . . . ," *Tvori!* no. 2 (1921), 3. Similar themes and phrases appeared in 1918 in "Zheleznye tsvety," in *Zavod ognekrylyi*, 16.

[52] M. Gerasimov, "Derevnia," *Griadushchee* 1920, no. 11: 4; reused as the opening stanzas of "Elektrifikatsiia," in *Elektrifikatsiia* (Petersburg [sic], 1922), 3–5.

Amidst all this symbolic, aesthetic, sentimental, and psychological romanticism about factory and machine we find little argument for the practical uses of modern technology. Mikhail Volkov's story expressing hope that Lenin's modernizing plan of "electrification of the whole country" would eradicate rural backwardness and ignorance and an occasional literary use of the cliché of electricity bringing light to the countryside stand out for their rarity among workers' writing.[53]

Light and Shadows

This poetry of city, factory, and machine is largely what we might expect from proletarian writers after October 1917—though the greater weight of pathos than politics points suggestively to a more emotional than rationalist modernism. But the deviance ran still deeper. As the idealization and purification of modern landscapes and the tendency to focus on future time suggest, worker writers hesitated before actual, everyday modernity. Indeed, a closer and more balanced look at their writings—I have been deliberately selective—reveals currents of anxiety and ambivalence that persistently undermined whatever ideological enthusiasms led these writers to view city, factory, and machine as the aesthetic, social, and psychological cradle of the future. There is no doubt that increasing numbers of worker writers, especially those who proclaimed their ideological identity as "proletarians," embraced with increasing intensity the modern urban and industrial world and even came to appreciate, in the modernist fashion, the instability, upheavals, and contradictions of modern life by seeing through this flux to an unfolding new life. But, like many other modernists and Marxists—who, in Russia as elsewhere, tossed back and forth between "the most radiant joy and the bleakest despair"[54]—they found their faith in the benefits of modernity difficult to sustain. Frequently they admitted to feeling neither at home in the modern flux nor certain that there was any way out.

Worker writers were warned against such ambivalence in the face of modernity. Influential Communist critics repeatedly reminded writers who claimed to be proletarian in mentality as well as in social origin that workers, when contemplating the central Marxist values of city, factory, and machine, "cannot and must not know ambivalence [*razdvoeniia*]."[55] With various degrees of dismay, however, Marxist intellectuals admitted to finding precisely such ambivalence among proletarians, especially in writings about the touchstone question of city and factory.[56] The expectation that worker writers, as

---

[53] M. Volkov, "Letropikatsiia" (allegedly a peasant's mispronunciation of *eletrifikatsiia*), *Kuznitsa*, no. 8 (April–September 1921), 22–28; M. Gerasimov, "Iz poemy 'Elektrifikatsiia,'" *Griadushchee* 1921, no. 1–3: 6, and *Elektrifikatsiia*.

[54] Marshall Berman, *All That Is Solid Melts into Air: The Experience of Modernity* (New York, 1982), 102.

[55] S. Rodov, "Motivy tvorchestva M. Gerasimova," *Kuznitsa*, no. 1 (May 1920), 23. See also V. Polianskii [P. Lebedev-Polianskii], review of *Pereval*, in *Rabochii zhurnal* 1925, no. 1–2: 262, and his review of *Gorn* in *Proletarskaia kul'tura*, no. 5 (November 1918), 42–43.

[56] A. Voronskii, "O gruppe pisatelei 'Kuznitsa': Obshchaia kharakteristika," in *Iskusstvo i*

the leading cultural representatives of the new ruling class, bore a particular responsibility to be confidently single-minded and joyous in pondering the landscapes of urban modernity reflected not only a political effort to shape cultural expressions into more usable forms but also a crude sort of Marxism, one that seemed to resist, even deny, its own paradoxical vision of modernity as containing oppression, brutality, decadence, and painful disorder along with energy, productive power, and liberating dynamism. Such ideological simplifications were not universal, however, among those in power. Well into the 1920s and beyond, some of Soviet Russia's most prominent intellectual leaders, notably Anatoly Lunacharsky and Nikolai Bukharin, retained feelings of doubt and anxiety about the human and ethical costs of building a modern industrial society.

Worker writers felt this ambivalence doubly: both as writers pondering difficult questions of existence and morality and as workers (at least, former workers) who knew well the harshness of modern urban and industrial life. Some worker writers themselves emphasized the empirical truth of an ambivalent perspective on modern life. The trouble with so many educated Communist critics of real proletarian literature, Vladimir Kirillov commented in 1921 (in a widely read essay that provoked much controversy), was that they had plenty of Marxist theory and dialectical method but had never "tasted factory air." Ironically, Kirillov continued, these "theoreticians" tended to blame errors in workers' attitudes on "bourgeois influence" and inadequate "cooking in the factory boiler." In fact, "as in former times, the theoretician sits upon his high throne in Olympus" while the proletarian poet "remains below in the gloom of Hell." Such critics, though they may be "the very best Marxists," cannot "understand deeply and multifacetedly the nature of the artistic creativity of the proletarian writer."[57]

Other articulate worker intellectuals similarly warned—and defended themselves—against the false simplicities of the increasingly official paradigm of revered modernity. In recent years, complained Nikolai Liashko in 1920, a "falseness" and "forced intentionality" (*narochitost'*) had crept into proletarian writing under the effective pressure of demands by intelligentsia leaders that a "true worker writer" write only about "the life of iron, furnaces, cranes" and sing only about how "they are in iron, made of iron, made of steel." This stance is a lie, Liashko argued. It is a lie partly because it is so at odds with the reality of the present: collapsed industry, silent factories. But the main error of this "metal theme" runs deeper, Liashko insisted, for it clashes with the more subtle understanding that "true" worker writers have of reality and even with how they imagine the future. It is false and dangerous "to reduce the whole gamut of life to one or two chords." Truth, Liashko implied,

zhizn': *Sbornik statei* (Moscow and Petrograd, 1924), 136; P. I. M., review of Aleksandrovskii, "Shagi," *Rabochii zhurnal* 1925, no. 1–2, 277.

[57] V. Kirillov, "O proletarskoi poezii," *Kuznitsa*, no. 7 (December 1920–March 1921), 23–24.

is always what Mikhail Bakhtin would call *raznorechivyi* (heteroglossic, poly-phonic). To deny this complexity not only is coercive but in the long term threatens "to atrophy perception." The canonical "metal theme" is false be-cause workers cannot forget that cities of iron and smoke are "hells for work-ing people." But most important, workers' judgments and dreams are more complex: "Hatred of the stagnant countryside and irresistible love for it, en-mity toward the machine, which drains their strength, and tender feelings to-ward it exist side by side in the soul of the worker. A great spaciousness opens up before the worker writer: all of the heterogeneity of life, its light and its shadows." This complex perception went well beyond any simply dialectical appreciation of progress emerging from contradictions. At stake, Liashko im-plied, were questions of the sources and nature of knowledge and truth. Ra-tionality alone does not suffice: perception is simplified and one-dimensional when writers "stop consciousness at what is often born only in the head." But workers cannot stop here: "too much lies in the heart of the worker writer."[58] No Olympian theory of the dialectical unity of opposites, much less single-minded love of the modern city and factory, could satisfy.

"The Many-Headed, Bright-Eyed Dragon"

Proletarians, many worker writers acknowledged, had to struggle to appreci-ate the city. In a poem published by the Moscow Proletcult in 1919, Nikolai Poletaev described the daily urban ugliness workers had to endure and ad-mitted his own difficulty in learning to love such a city:

> I could not understand at first
> The dusky life of the capital,
> Where pale green figures,
> Shadowy blotches, streak by.
> But gradually, bewitched
> By its potent, shadowy beauty,
> I have become now forever welded
> To you, my dusky city.[59]

Poletaev here praised the city and depicted his conversion in tellingly dis-cordant language. He comes to love the city because it bewitches him with a beauty that is literally lethal and ghostly (*postepenno okoldovan/smertel'no prizrachnoi krasoi*). As a result, he has become "welded" (*prikovan*) to the city—a term that in all its normal meanings implies force.

Ivan Eroshin similarly tells us that he tried to flee urban life, but was inex-orably drawn back to the city. In the end, he professes an urbanist love, but

---

[58] N. Liashko, "O zadachakh pisatelia-rabochego (Zametka)," *Kuznitsa*, no. 3 (July 1920), 27–29.

[59] N. Poletaev, "Chadilo chertova kadilo . . . ," *Gorn*, nos. 2–3 (1919), 4.

cannot conceal his ambivalence: "I am your captive [*toboiu ia plenen*] / . . . again I strive toward you, now more strongly, more in love, / Into your furious jaws!!!"[60] Vasilii Aleksandrovskii also described a weary wanderer in the countryside inescapably forced toward the city, "beyond the peace of the steppe." This city was a compelling but painful place—a place of suffering and of struggle, of "victims" who felt at home only there.[61] The metaphors and modifiers these worker writers often chose to describe the city embodied their ambivalence. For Aleksandrovskii, the city was a "fire-faced" "city-giant."[62] Others similarly expressed admiration mixed with implicit dread in describing the city as a "sleepless iron-stone dragon," a "captivating-commanding" giant (*plenitel'no-vlastnyi*), an "unwearying, proud and wrathful protestant," a "many-headed, bright-eyed dragon."[63] Many of these writers evidently agreed that the city was "mighty, filthy, drunken," alien to the "beloved forests," but also that it had a beauty of its own.[64]

Although most of these workers shared the Marxist conviction that the contradictions of the city were theoretically resolved in a teleological dialectic in which the city was necessarily a contradictory place of suffering and salvation, they dwelled more on the suffering (which they were certain of) than on the salvation (which remained theoretical). The printer Sergei Obradovich, for example, offered the metaphor of two cities: the "sorrowing" city of today, which had "blood in every stone," and the coming new city, whose "stone legs" could already be heard "thundering in the distance," and which would replace the city of today with a city of marble streets and glistening palaces of labor.[65] Less confidently, Aleksandrovskii suggested that the blood and suffering of urban life held the promise of redemption: "We have been crucified by you, city," but "suffering is always holy / Love is always in blood."[66]

When worker writers dwelled on the dark side of urban modernity—as they did no less often than before 1917—the physical face of the city disturbed them not merely aesthetically but spiritually as well. Indeed, they were much more likely than before 1917 to view the city's physical ugliness as the outward sign of a dark and menacing sentience. Kirillov wrote of the "gloomy stones of the capital," Poletaev of "malicious" smoke from factory chimneys that, in Aleksandrovskii's words, "with the guile of Cain / hurries to fill the tears in black clouds," and Obradovich of the city's "coiled snakelike body"

[60] I. Eroshin, "V derevne," in *Zavod ognekrylyi*, 69.

[61] V. Aleksandrovskii, "Putnik," *Gorn*, no. 1 (1918) 10.

[62] Ibid.

[63] Quoted, along with similar statements, in P. Bessal'ko, "O poezii krest'ianskoi i proletarskoi," *Griadushchee* 1918, no. 7 (October): 13; I. Sadof'ev, "Ritm Granita (Posviashchaiu Krasnomy Piteru)," *Griadushchee* 1919, no. 4: 1.

[64] A. Sh., review of N. Tikhomirov, *Krasnyi most*, in *Revoliutsionnye vskhody*, no. 3–4 (October 1920), 9–10.

[65] S. Obradovich, "Griadushchee," in RGALI, f. 1874, op. 1, d. 7, l. 38 (this item is marked as a clipping from *Pravda*, 6 Dec. 1921, though I did not find it there).

[66] V. Aleksandrovskii, "Toboi my raspiaty, gorod" (1918), in his *Zvon solntsa* (Moscow, 1923), 19–20.

and its "satiated laugh and triumphant howl."[67] Most attention, however, was devoted to the human life of the city. The city's social relationships and its effects on the human personality continued to promote a deep moral skepticism about urban life. Sometimes, to be sure, descriptions of city life make it clear that these authors were describing a capitalist city and that the critique was a class one. Narratives often end, for example, with the outbreak of class struggle or revolution.[68] Most often, however, the social nature of the city, its particular structure of class relations, was secondary if it was indicated at all. The scores of poems titled simply "The City" provided few markers to suggest that these writers had in mind only the prerevolutionary capitalist city. Nor was there much reason to make such a distinction. After all, before the 1930s the Bolsheviks did not, except briefly and ineffectively during the civil war, uproot capitalism in Russia. Least of all did they do much deliberately to remake the face of the city, except in their imaginations. If anything, the revolution, by stimulating a millenarian desire to transform the world, may also have intensified moral dismay with the persistent realities of modern urban life.

In 1918 Nikolai Liashko published a series of essays on "the spiritual poisons of the city," in which he examined a range of urban evils: charlatanism, deceit, harmful "surrogates" for real art and knowledge, and commercial advertisements, which he branded "the most repulsive device for exploiting the ignorant city masses." The spread of these poisons, Liashko argued, was a pathological and distinctly urban phenomenon: "The cleanliness of streets in many cities conceals backyards where every second millions of germs are born in heaps of filth, spreading disease. So too high collars, hats, newspapers, books, concerts, balls, and everything that is worn rather than lived, to which many residents of cities dedicate their leisure, conceal darkness and spiritual narrow-mindedness." Urban civilization as much as capitalism—which, it is important to note, Liashko never specifically mentions—was the target of this criticism.[69]

This critique, of course, like many others by worker writers, was part of a long familiar complaint among educated Russians about the decadence and impurity of the modern city. The Bolsheviks inherited and intensified these concerns with urban vice and cultural impurity: vulgar commercialism, hooligan insolence and violence, sexual licentiousness, disease, drunkenness, and the crass entertainments of the *cafés chantants* (which Katerina Clark has described as a "cipher for Western decadence," though in the mid-1920s they were gradually displaced as symbols by the fox-trot.)[70] Worker writers, whose

---

[67] V. Kirillov, "Vesna v stolitse," *Stikhotvorenie* (St. Petersburg, 1918), 25; N. Poletaev, "Chadilo chertova kadilo . . . ," *Gorn*, nos. 2–3 (1919), 4; V. Aleksandrovskii, "Okraina," in *Zavod ognekrylyi*, 73; S. Obradovich, "Gorod," *Kuznitsa*, no. 5–6 (October–November 1920), 18.

[68] E.g., V. Aleksandrovskii, "Okraina," in *Zavod ognekrylyi*, 73–74; S. Obradovich, "Gorod," *Kuznitsa*, no. 5–6 (October–November 1920), 19–21.

[69] N. Liashko, "Dukhovnye iady goroda i kooperatsiia," *Rabochii mir* 1918, no. 7 (June 23): 24–25.

[70] Clark, *Petersburg*, 162.

lives were far more deeply embedded in the profane everyday urban realities than those of most educated Russians, shared this abhorrence of the moral face of urban modernity.

While many of these writers were explicit in condemning the capitalist city, their critique remained focused on the spiritual and moral harm capitalism caused. In a 1924 essay, for example, the poet Ivan Filipchenko described the capitalist city—presumably also the Soviet city of the NEP period—as a type of hell: a place of constant "wailing, weeping of little children, cries of despair"; where the poor lie about "on sidewalks, in vacant lots, in railway stations, exhausted, feverish, with typhoid"; a place of widespread drunkenness, family violence, and prostitution; and where death everywhere waits to claim more victims. The horrors of this life deformed people morally but also literally, producing epileptics, hysterics, syphilitics, and idiots.[71]

In creative writings, especially poetry, these workers crafted similar images of the life of the city, with even more pathos and less social or historical specificity. Attention was focused on human suffering in the modern industrial city, and little mention was made of the particular structure of class relations that, any Marxist would insist, generated these wrongs. The city, as portrayed by Vladimir Kirillov in his 1918 contribution to the genre of poems titled "The City," was a cold, alienating place:

> Oh, how many unknown people,
> And how many uncomprehending gazes!
> They go, they hurry, they run,
> They all wear masks on their souls. . . .
> Here is a look shining with mad torment,
> And that one, so vainly happy,
> Might not meet a new day. . . .
> And all pass by without a trace.[72]

Later he predicted fatalistically that such a life—now symbolized by the sexual parading of "cocks and hens" (*samtsy i samki*) beneath the gaze of "melancholy Pushkin"—would be just the same a thousand years hence.[73]

Sergei Obradovich, in his poem "The City," published in *Kuznitsa* in 1920 and reprinted several times during the 1920s as part of his cycle of poems about the city, is filled with images of moral decadence: the mad "café chantant crowd," the mass genuflecting before the gods of money, "the lending trade in wretched souls," the "bawling" of advertising and of the "bazaar," the depressing sight of prostitutes in the night gloom, and the sight and smells of the "crowd, stinking and drunken." The poem begins with declarations of love for the City (always capitalized): as a place "of great Beginnings and

---

[71] I. Filipchenko, "Lenin," *Rabochii zhurnal* 1924, no. 1: 58.

[72] V. Kirillov, "Gorod," in *Stikhotvoreniia, 1914–1918*, 26 (not previously published).

[73] V. Kirillov, "Byl vecher, kak vecher," *Kuznitsa*, no. 7 (December 1920–March 1921), 9. Aleksandrovskii was similarly disturbed by posters along the streets that addressed sexual questions: V. Aleksandrovskii, "Budni," *Kuznitsa*, no. 9 (1922), 8.

Journeys," and, slightly more ambivalently, as a place workers made and grew up with, whose "iron and stones we strengthened / with the cement of our sweat and tears." The poem concludes with a vision of salvation through struggle and revolution. But the message is far from consistent. Like so many proletarians, Obradovich found it difficult to reconcile his political certainties with his emotional and moral perceptions. The horrors of the city, like the "moans" of his suffering working-class father, Obradovich would "remember [his] whole life."[74]

The young factory poet Nikolai Kuznetsov tried to describe his own ambivalent perception when he said that he lived with his "mind in the city but the country in his heart."[75] I would emphasize and generalize the point. An unresolved argument was constant in the writings (and presumably in the minds) of these worker intellectuals. Just as it would be a mistake to conclude that these accounts were a social critique of the capitalist city alone, it would also be too simple to speak only of an absolute antiurbanism. A discordant ambiguity remained persistent. Antiurban and antimodern perceptions, values, and feelings intertwined and often clashed with formal and rational notions (though sometimes also different emotions) about the positive value of city and factory. Concerns with the immediacy of moral and spiritual problems intertwined with awareness of dialectical teleologies and intellectual abstractions. Indeed, it may be that this dialogue between rationalized ideas and emotional and moral perceptions was precisely the intellectual practice that most nurtured ambivalence. In this unstable and unresolved interplay between reason (willful cognition) and sensibility, ambiguity and heteroglossia thrived.

Urban Madonnas

The appearance of women in these imaginative commentaries on the city underscores the personal, sentimental, and moral nature of these writers' anxieties about modern landscapes, especially about a landscape traditionally interpreted as deeply masculine. To be sure, as in prerevolutionary writings, women were often represented as innocents cast into the pit of urban temptation and degradation. Poets still described the "sadness and longing" of innocent and beautiful young women from the countryside who came to the cities to work.[76] And women's fall into prostitution—a traditional image of urban debasement—was still most often viewed as a crime *against* women, not as willful acts *by* women, for which they could be blamed morally. Filipchenko's description was typical, indeed clichéd, in its hyperbole and tone

---

[74] S. Obradovich, "Gorod," *Kuznitsa*, no. 5–6 (October–November 1920), 17–19. Similar themes may be found in P. Oreshin, "Gorod," *Krasnyi zvon: Sbornik stikhov* (Petrograd, 1918): 69–70.

[75] A. Kosterin, "Nikolai Kuznetsov," *Rabochii zhurnal* 1925, no. 1–2: 232.

[76] P. Arskii, "Devushka, prishedshaia v gorod," *Griadushchee* 1920, no. 7–8: 1.

of outrage: "Mothers with tears of pain and shame in their eyes send their daughters into the streets to sell their bodies. Mothers, driven mad with hunger, sell themselves. Husbands send out their wives. Fiancés—their brides-to-be."[77]

In the hands of some worker writers, however, images of women in the city were becoming more complex. Femininity, as symbol and as existential value, was increasingly treated as a necessary positive ideal. Women in the factories continued to stand for beauty, gentleness, and innocence in a harsh setting, but they were also increasingly admired, as in Poletaev's poem to a woman weaver (a traditionally male skill in prewar Russian industry), for the particular skill and beauty of their labors: "Oh, how the golden threads scurry and play." Women's longing for more natural beauty and pleasure outside the factory was also recognized, and with a sensual sympathy that was rare in prerevolutionary poems by workers: "Go out into the golden sun. / With the ardor of spring fire / Let its rays penetrate your body."[78] The most telling figure in these worker writings, however, was the changing image of the prostitute.

A number of worker writers now voiced a kinship with the city's "fallen women," both as human beings and as symbols of certain "feminine" values, especially love.[79] Thus it was with a mixture of pity, irony, and a new sympathy that Kirillov acknowledged that amidst the cold crowds of the city, "Only prostitutes here and there / Openly proffer tenderness." They also shared his urban loneliness.[80] Aleksandrovskii, in his 1920 ode to Moscow, even more explicitly treated the prostitute as a sign of both the city's evil and its allure. The poem explores familiar themes of nostalgia for a rural childhood and anguish at the ugliness, hardships, and decadence of city life. In a central moment in this evidently autobiographical poem, Aleksandrovskii yields to the immoral pleasures of the city:

> I plunge my body into shame.
> I toss out the last scraps of decency,
> And wait like a proper husband,
> In the leer of boulevard puddles,
> For painted Beatrice.
> I don't know which pain is greater—

---

[77] I. Filipchenko, "Lenin," *Rabochii zhurnal* 1924, no. 1: 58.

[78] N. Poletaev, "Tkachikha," *Kuznitsa*, no. 2 (June 1920), 8. Aleksandrovskii also wrote a poem to a "girl weaver" with whose "sorrow" and "delightful dreams" he sympathized: "Devushke-tkachikhe," in *Zavod ognekrylyi*, 51. And in another poem he identified, as "brother" and "fiancé," with a "red-haired" factory "poetess" and her alienation from city and factory: "V zakate," *Gorn*, no. 2–3 (1919), 10–11.

[79] Incidentally, Baudelaire regarded the urban poet as spiritual cousin to the urban prostitute in their common identification with "all the professions, rejoicings, miseries" that confront them. Quoted in Carl Schorske, "The Idea of the City in European Thought: Voltaire to Spengler," in *The Historian and the City,* ed. Oscar Handlin and John Burchard (Cambridge, Mass., 1963), 110.

[80] V. Kirillov, "Gorod," in *Stikhotvoreniia, 1914–1918,* 26; "Stolichnoe," ibid., 24 (first published in *Krasnaia gazeta,* 25 June 1918).

The sores on the body of my lover,
Or that I became a man in that fire,
In the inescapable longing of night.

The ambivalence with which Aleksandrovskii viewed this encounter with a city prostitute—pleasure and anguish, self-degradation and self-becoming—paralleled his view of the city itself:

Moscow!
Oh, let me, let me
Kiss
Your swarthy street hands
For the sake of deep, secret torments,
For the sake of great, sweet pain.[81]

There is no simple moral formula here. Aleksandrovskii remained on the uneasy ground of ambivalence.

These writers were not alone among postrevolutionary authors, of course, in writing about women in the city or in treating their image uncertainly. The image of the woman was a major presence in early Soviet literature and journalism and served as a means of exploring diverse ideas, ideals, and anxieties. Women in the city appeared in these writings as inspiring and troubling objects of passion, as icons of virtue and tenderness as well as of sexual depravity and danger, as signs of purity and pollution, as figures representing backwardness but also emancipation and freedom, as markers of natural equality and of essential physical and spiritual difference.[82] Worker writers shared this deepening ambivalence in thinking about women—and by extension about men—in the city.

With particular complexity and ambiguity, Mikhail Gerasimov meditated on women and city life in his 1918 poem, "Mona Lisa" (a poem that Aleksandr Bogdanov, in the opening speech to the first All-Russian Conference of Proletarian Writers in May 1920, criticized as a disturbing example of the "too foggy" manner in which worker poets wrote).[83] At the heart of the poem are three female figures. The first two are familiar tropes: factory girl and city prostitute. The first, to whom the poem is dedicated and partly addressed, is a young woman "who came to us at our factory," a weapons factory, filled with the joy and laughter of innocence. But her spirit was inevitably crushed:

[81] V. Aleksandrovskii, "Moskva (Otryvki iz poemy)," *Kuznitsa*, no. 5 (October–November 1920), 12–16.

[82] See Richard Stites, *The Women's Liberation Movement in Russia* (Princeton, 1978), chaps. 10–11; Wendy Z. Goldman, *Women, the State, and Revolution* (Cambridge, 1993); Catriona Kelly, *A History of Russian Women's Writing, 1820–1992* (Oxford, 1994), chap. 9; Elizabeth Waters, "The Female Form in Soviet Political Iconography, 1917–1932," in *Russia's Women*, ed. Barbara Clements, Barbara Engel, and Christine Worobec (Berkeley, 1991), 225–42; Naiman, *Sex in Public*; Bonnell, *Iconography of Power*, chap. 2; Borenstein, *Men without Women*.

[83] "Protokoly pervogo Vserossiiskogo Soveshchaniia proletarskikh pisatelei," 10–12 (May 1920), in RGALI, f. 1638, op. 3, d. 1, ll. 10b–2.

"You, like all of us, have bound your wings / And covered your sorrowing eyes / With the dust of gunpowder." Prostitutes are portrayed as "wingless seagulls."[84] Staring into the Ekaterininskii Canal in Petrograd, the narrator ponders the reflections of prostitutes standing nearby. Thoughts of suicide, sexuality, injury, and sacred purity intertwine.

> One longs to pour out one's soul,
> There in the sparkling depths,
> Where rouged faces
> Fracture in the lifeless waves.
> And a whisper splashes: "Sweety, sweety!"
> A hoarse voice called pitifully—
> And the injured, wingless seagull
> Slides into the rusty canal.
> To me, you are sinless Madonnas.
> I loved the deprived ones,
> By the Alexander Column
> The city has nailed you up too. . . .
> The night sky is reddish blue,
> The soul is in the embrace of beauty,
> And you in the Petrograd muck
> Are poison-yellow flowers.

The third and most important figure is another "Madonna"—Leonardo da Vinci's Mona Lisa and especially her sad, enigmatic, "secret," and "bewitching" smile, which appears on all the surfaces of city life: in smoke pouring from factory chimneys, in factory windows, in the reflections of machines, on workers' blue shirts, in the "granite of my prison," in the factories' "iron fires," on the upturned dirty faces of workers, on graves.

> Crowned in the glow of dusk,
> The face of the Gioconda shines,
> A garland of roses and a garland of thorns,
> Borne on her clear brow.[85]

In this deliberately ambiguous and enigmatic poem, Gerasimov drew a complex picture of women (and male feelings about women and about their own gendered selves) in the city. The cliché of the innocent country girl whose vitality and dignity wither in the city and factory combines with ambivalent sympathy and revulsion before prostitutes, with sensual desire and fears of pollution, and, most complexly, with images of a transcendent universal feminine—hints of which are in each portrayed figure. Indeed, this poem is pervaded with echoes of mystical ideas of the Eternal Feminine as the embodi-

---

[84] Gerasimov also used this metaphor, an apparent reference to Chekhov's symbol of female innocence victimized by men, in his 1917 poem "Chaiki." Indeed, this part of "Mona Lisa" is an adaptation of those earlier verses (discussed in Chapter 4).

[85] M. Gerasimov, "Monna Liza: Poema," *Gorn*, no. 1 (1918), 11–16.

ment of both spiritual wisdom and sensuality, as well as of the related religious idea of the purity, loving-kindness, and suffering of the Mother of God.[86] Here, as in other reworkings of the image of the urban woman, long a touchstone for judging the moral meaning of city and factory life, meanings, as Bogdanov complained, were ambivalent.

"The Roar of Iron"

As these images indicate, it was the modern city that so disturbed and alienated these workers just as it was the modern city that so enraptured them. Factories and machines were at the heart of this troubling modernity. In 1922 Valerian Pletnev, then national leader of the Proletcult, described a certain "psychological Luddism" in the Russian working class.[87] Conversely, Nikolai Liashko spoke of the "solitude of those who sing of iron."[88] But this was a solitude not limited to a conscious vanguard among the backward masses. Such "backwardness" remained strongly evident even among radicalized proletarian writers. Persistently judging the world in mainly aesthetic and ethical terms, these writers tended still to see industry as an infernal place animated by a malevolent spirit. The revolution intensified these perceptions as these writers raised their voices ever more resoundingly against the evils of the old world. But this way of seeing and valuing also intensified their ambivalence about the new: embracing the now official ideology of scientific and rational progress, they continued to worry about its alienating, dehumanizing, and destructive effects.

The most outright and old-fashioned hostility to factories and machines is to be found in the writings of older workers such as Egor Nechaev, ideological antiurbanists such as Petr Oreshin, and beginning worker writers, especially from provincial cities.[89] We see this, for example, in the collective story written by thirteen students in the literary studio of the Samara Proletcult

---

[86] In Russian culture, adaptation of the Christian mystical ideal of Sophia, Divine Wisdom, as an Eternal Feminine was most closely associated with the philosopher Vladimir Solov'ev, whose influence was still strong among the literary intelligentsia, including some, such as Andrei Belyi and Aleksandr Blok, who initially embraced the Bolshevik revolution. Gerasimov knew these circles and had been playing with these ideas since at least 1914, when he had dedicated a poem to Blok, describing his own vision of a universal woman whose "insanely" beautiful face appeared wherever he looked or journeyed: "A. Bloku," in RGALI, f. 1374, op. 1, d. 6, l. 16. The poem was published in *Sovremennaia zhenshchina* (Warsaw) 1914, no. 3: 52. Gerasimov was also probably familiar with the appearance of Mona Lisa in the second volume of Dmitrii Merezhkovskii's trilogy *Christ and Antichrist* (1901). Merezhkovskii presents Mona Lisa herself and her emerging image in Leonardo's hands as a specifically "feminine" figure of wisdom and of spiritual and moral depth: Dmitrii Merezhkovskii, "Voskresshie bogi (Leonardo da Vinchi)," vol. 2 of *Khristos i Antikhrist*, in *Polnoe sobranie sochinenii Dmitriia Sergeevicha Merezhkovskago*, 3 vols. (Moscow, 1914), bk. 14 ("Mona Lisa Dzhiokonda"), esp. 199–201, 219.

[87] V. Pletnev, "Sovremennyi moment i zadachi proletkul'ta," *Gorn*, no. 6 (1922), 23.

[88] N. Liashko, "Solntse, plechi, i gruz" (1920–22), in *Rabochie rasskazy* (Moscow, 1924), 95.

[89] In addition to citations below, see, e.g., I. Doronin, "Na rabotu," in *Rabochaia vesna* (Moscow, 1923), 2:24–26; S. Khaibulin (a fifteen-year-old member of a "children's Proletcult"), "K 25-mu Oktiabria," *Detskii proletkul't*, no. 1 (7 Nov. 1919), 3.

(most of them workers and party members), which was published in 1920. The story was titled *Glukhar'*, factory slang for the worker who hammers bolts from within a factory steam boiler, a process that leaves him temporarily deaf (*glukhoi*, meaning "deaf" but also suggesting a dark, remote, and forsaken place). This symbolic figure was the chosen hero of the story. The tale takes place in a huge metal plant, portrayed as frightening and hellish: amidst a "purple haze" the machines roar and the walls shake and the windows stare "rapaciously" from the sooty walls. From working in such an environment, the boilermaker-*glukhar'* suffers agonizing pain in his head and ears. As he falls asleep at the end of the day, he deliriously imagines an army of "dirty-faced, unknown boilermakers, arising suddenly from under the ground," who begin to "rumble with their hammers and chaotically work on the boiler, laughing and winking" at the exhausted worker, and prepare, "with whistles and hellish knocks," to drop the boiler upon him.[90] Like these new writers, Egor Nechaev continued to write and publish poems pondering the harsh meanings of the "roar and rumble" of the factory and of workers' sweat and tears.[91] Petr Oreshin, the leading populist worker poet, similarly admitted that "factory smoke depressed my heart and soul" and "the roar of iron" felt "heavy like chains."[92]

These motifs were also to be found, however, in the writings of the most prominent Proletcult and Communist writers with worker backgrounds living in the capital cities. These authors continued to sympathize with the terror felt by a young worker (whether fresh from the countryside or from a working-class home) as he faces the fearsome appearance of the factory, the machines "knocking, screeching, and whistling all around," the drive belts slithering overhead like snakes, while even the factory air "buzzed and rang."[93] This image of the factory as hell continued to fascinate worker writers, including almost all of the leading Proletcultists. In a poem titled "In the Factory," published in 1918 in the journal of the Petrograd Proletcult, Aleksei Mashirov (Samobytnik) portrayed the factory as a place where "labor thunders and groans like a demon," where workers gaze with "emaciated dull looks," and every movement of their exhausted muscles is torment, while the furnace blazes and the metal gleams.[94] Mikhail Gerasimov imagined the factory as a "machine hell," where "even the black stones [of the factory] wept" and whose "poisonous smoke" was "eating away at the stars' golden lashes."[95] For Vasilii Aleksandrovskii, the factory was a "malicious devil."[96]

---

[90] *Glukhar': Rasskaz* (Samara, 1920), 3, 5–7.

[91] E. Nechaev, "Iz pesen' o zavode (Proshloe)," *Kuznitsa*, no. 1 (May 1920), 7.

[92] P. Oreshin, "Smychka," *Zheleznyi put'* 1923, no. 7: 1.

[93] Samobytnik [Mashirov], "Siluety iz zhizny rabochikh (Etiud)," *Griadushchee* 1918, no. 1 (January): 6; Ivan Eroshin, "Detstvo (Rasskaz rabochego)," *Tvorchestvo*, no. 4 (August 1918), 13–14.

[94] Samobytnik [Mashirov], "V zavode," *Griadushchee* 1918, no. 3: 11.

[95] M. Gerasimov, "My," *Zarevo zavodov*, no. 2 (1919), 9, and "Kochegar" and "Zavodu," in *Zavod ognekryly*, 43, 54.

[96] V. Aleksandrovskii, "Okraina," in *Zavod ognekryly*, 73–74. In "My" Gerasimov also described the factory as a satanic giant with great iron horns.

And Aleksei Gastev described a place of groans and prayers where even the screams of death could not be heard, but "where everything human was drowned in the thick lava of the iron roar, and the whole factory seemed to thunder apathetically over man perishing in toil."[97] Death and torment were ever present in these visions, as in Sergei Obradovich's sense that the smoke of the factories was a "black mourning dress" worn by a suffocating city.[98]

These images did more than contradict quite different portraits by the same authors: they were part of a pervasively and sometimes explicitly multivocal discourse on factories, machines, and metal as emblems of modernity. In a 1921 essay in *Kuznitsa* Nikolai Liashko defined modernity with an industrial metaphor, but one that evoked not cold rationality and order but vital (and frightening) chaos, flux, and upheaval.

> Modernity [*sovremennost'*] is a factory boiler trembling at full steam. There is not a moment's rest: it whistles, wheezes, and shudders. Many are afraid: the deposits inside the boiler are eating away at its walls, boiling lava surges forth and flows over the stokers and machinists—and with them perish both crew and helmsman. It seems to many that this is just what is happening. Bang!—the abyss. For some it is heaven in the abyss, for others hell. But no one is indifferent. Everyone trembles, listens, looks about. All seems quiet. But then appear new operators running the geographic map, new claimants to throne, knout, and barge. Into the furnace are cast anew tons of terrible passions [*strastei*] and blood, and again the boiler trembles, whistles, and wheezes. And in the midst of its roaring occurs only displacement and change and the opening up only of dizzying perspectives! Wonders grow into horrors and horrors into wonders. To enumerate the changes would fill thousands of pages, and to describe them would fill millions of pages. Unexpected pains and joys . . . appear at every step.[99]

In the face of the "contradictoriness and complexity" of modern times, Liashko argued, worker writers, who "stand close to life," necessarily view this life complexly and critically. Least of all could they write as some thought they did or wished they would: "factories, factories, and nothing else."[100] Mikhail Gerasimov, perhaps Soviet Russia's most renowned "poet of iron," similarly viewed the key symbols of industrial modernity as indeterminate. In his important "Poem on Iron," which appeared in 1918 in the national journal of the Proletcult, Gerasimov insisted on iron's many voices: "groans / the cry of fetters / the wail of the guillotine blade," and shrapnel, but also movement, "purity," "light," "the trill of a flute," tenderness, love, and power.[101] Likewise, the factory appeared as both an alluring and painful place—a place

---

[97] A. Gastev, "Vesna v rabochem gorodke," *Griadushchee* 1919, no. 7–8: 8.

[98] S. Obradovich, "Gorod," *Kuznitsa*, no. 5–6 (October–November 1920), 18.

[99] N. Liashko, "O byte i literature perekhodnogo vremeni," *Kuznitsa*, no. 8 (April–September 1921), 29.

[100] Ibid., 34.

[101] M. Gerasimov, "Stikhi o zheleze," *Proletarskaia kul'tura*, no. 4 (September 1918), 31 (30 in another printing).

where factory stoves "expose their hellish mouth / Burning and crudely caressing the body."[102]

Often, as in portrayals of the city, ambivalence about factories and machines was part of a dialectical vision of transcendence, of a perception of the necessary linkage between present sufferings and coming salvation. Images of sacrifice and suffering for the sake of the future were common. These writers described workers as "crucified" on an "iron cross" or buried in the "factory crypt" but certain to be "resurrected."[103] Aleksei Kraiskii imagined the future itself as a roaring and whistling "iron giant" crashing through cold fields and darkness, fueled by blood and bodies of workers willing to sacrifice themselves for the cause of progress.[104] A better life would arrive, most of these writers seemed to believe, but its coming was certain to be filled with suffering.

Aleksei Gastev went even further and defined "catastrophe" as essential to the very nature of modern life and progress.[105] He illustrated his theory of catastrophe in a prose poem of 1917, "Bashnia" (The tower), often reprinted and publicly declaimed after October. Like other real and legendary towers, from the Tower of Babel to the Eiffel Tower to Soviet Russia's own imagined headquarters for the Communist International, Gastev's "iron tower" built by workers' hands was a symbol of aspiration and achievement: "The iron tower was crowned with a forged bright polished steel spire, all aspiring to the future heights." But, for all its beauty and idealism, the tower was not an unambiguously joyous achievement. The builders suffered "desperate torments" and death. As it rose, workers fell into the pit and perished—eventually too many to count or even remember. As the heavy tower of cement and iron rose, groans from their graves accompanied the tower's ascent, though so did joyous iron music. And the growing tower itself, unlike its glistening steel spire, was a dark sight. Iron, Gastev also recognized, was a complex symbol: "Against the bright sky, the tower appears black, for iron knows no smiles: there is more misery in it than happiness, thinking more than laughing. Iron, covered with the rust of time, is the most serious thought, the gloomy thought of the age and epoch." But this was not the darkest aspect of the story. The tower soon collapses to the ground, brought down by workers' doubts, though workers return to begin building it again. And the disaster strengthens their will. Suffering, for Gastev, was not misfortune but essential to progress. Indeed, proletarians should revel in their sufferings.

Let there be still more catastrophes.
Ahead are still more graves, still more collapses!

[102] M. Gerasimov, "Zavodskoe," *Sbornik proletarskikh pisatelei* (Petrograd [1917]), 4.

[103] N. Liashko, "Zheleznoe tishina," *Kuznitsa*, no. 2 (June 1920), 16; M. Gerasimov, "Krest" and "Letim," in *Zavod ognekryly*, 17, 47. Images of sacred suffering and transcendence are documented and discussed in Chapter 7.

[104] A. Kraiskii, "Navstrechu griadushchemu," *Ponizov'e*, no. 5 (1922), 3–4.

[105] A. Gastev, "O tendentsiiakh proletarskoi kul'tury," *Proletarskaia kul'tura*, no. 9–10 (June–July 1919), 44.

So be it!
Again heavy concrete will rain down on all of the graves beneath the tower,
and all of the underground crypts will be entangled with iron, and to the
underground city of death you must fearlessly hurry,
And go,
And burn,
Try to raise your spire to the heights,
You, our insolently towering world![106]

Ambivalence shading into despair was especially characteristic of Andrei
Platonov's writings on factory and machines during these years. In pondering
the forces and landscapes of modernity, Platonov interwove ideas about human mastery over nature with skepticism about triumphant human consciousness and will and a sentimental and even erotic love of physical things
with a fear and attendant abhorrence of matter.[107] Platonov viewed the world,
it has been said, as embodying at the same time the opposing principles of
spirit and matter, reason and emotion, nature and machine.[108] Such "ambivalence" in Platonov, according to a contemporary critic, M. Iunger, was a "historical" characteristic of the "Russian worker in general," caught between a
partial mastery of the new life of city and factory and a persistent "longing"
for his rural heritage.[109] In an autobiographical letter to Iunger, Platonov
spoke of this divided sentiment in himself: "I forgot to mention that besides
fields, the country, mothers, and the tolling of bells, I also love (and the longer
I live the more I love) engines, machines, wailing factory whistles, and sweaty
labor."[110] The tension went much deeper, however, than these simple di-
chotomies—though Platonov's parenthetical "I forgot to mention" already in-
dicates a certain complicating imbalance.

In Platonov's journalism, stories, and poetry of 1918–22, factories, machines, and technology appear as both enticing and dreadful. Platonov admired workers he knew in the railroad shops, such as the smelter Fedor An-
drianov, who so "loved and knew" metal that he could identify varieties "by
color and even smell."[111] His first story, published in the Voronezh railway
workers' journal in 1918, was set in a smelting shop in a large metal plant,
which the narrator, a new worker, enters "almost joyfully." Platonov describes
the factory in ambivalent terms. He admires the "obedient machines" and

[106] A. Gastev, "Bashnia," *Metallist* 1917, no. 4 (October 18): 4–6; also in *Griadushchee* 1918,
no. 2 (May): 11–12, and in editions of Gastev's *Poeziia rabochego udara*. The poem was often
declaimed by soldiers in the civil war and at urban poetry readings and Proletcult theatrical events.
See the discussion in Johansson, *Aleksej Gastev*, 83–88.

[107] See Thomas Seifrid, *Andrei Platonov: Uncertainties of Spirit* (Cambridge, 1992), chap. 1;
V. V. Eidinova, "K tvorcheskoi biografii A. Platonova," *Voprosy literatury* 3 (1978): 213–28;
Thomas Langerak, "Andrei Platonov v Voronezhe," *Russian Literature*, no. 23–24 (1988), 437–
68.

[108] Eidinova, "K tvorcheskoi biografii A. Platonova," 222.

[109] M. Iunger, "Predislovie," in Platonov, *Golubaia glubina*, v.

[110] A. Platonov, *Golubaia glubina*, vi.

[111] A. Platonov, "Geroi truda," *Voronezhskaia kommuna*, 7 Nov. 1920.

flowing metal for their "mighty pulse" and metallic "song." But his descriptions continually imply something evil and dangerous in this might: the "rafters shudder," the "engine whirs derisively and inexorably," the "endless drive belts crack treacherously," and somewhere in the factory "something whistles and smiles," something "locked up, strong, and cruelly ruthless" that "wants its freedom, but cannot tear itself loose, and so wails and squeals, and furiously pounds and whirls in solitude and ceaseless rancor. It begs and threatens, and again shakes, with tireless muscles, the cunningly interwoven body of stone, iron, and copper." In this setting, workers toiled "happily" and "time passed unnoticed" until this innocent and vain joy was shattered by an inevitable accident: a "whip" of burning metal tears itself free and kills a young worker. No less inevitably, after a period of silence and some shedding of tears, the machines are back in motion.[112]

Persistently, Platonov treated modern technology with, in Thomas Seifrid's words, "an ambivalent mixture of ecstasy and terror."[113] In his work in the 1920s as a Soviet engineer and advocate of economic development, Platonov championed the cause of "machinism" and "electrification." But his inspiration was not love for machines and technologies per se. Unlike Gastev, who desperately sought to merge men and machines, Platonov was in many respects antimachine. His aim was to turn industry over to machines in order to "transfer man from the realm of material production to a higher sphere of life." Thus in Platonov's vision of the coming "golden age"—the "new October"—machines are both enemy and savior. Modern technologies, Platonov asserted paradoxically (though echoing a paradox characteristic of Marxism), would enable humanity to be "freed from the oppression of matter."[114]

Platonov's literary writings of these years even more complexly blended admiration and dread of machines and of modern technologies. His stories often portrayed engineers and workers filled with self-confidence in their ability to control matter through will and consciousness and with faith in modern technique and science. Two early stories in which Platonov described the efforts of the worker Markun and the engineer Vogulov to build machines that could harness vast amounts of energy both conclude with mighty and even appealing catastrophes. When Markun, standing before his mighty turbine, slips into a thoughtless rapture, his machine races to a higher and higher speed and then explodes, sending pieces flying destructively. Even more dramatically, as we have seen, the engineer Vogulov creates a high-energy power—"ultralight" (*ultra-svet*)—that is used to remake the world's natural landscape for human use, to help individuals overcome the normal physical limitations of ordinary life, and then to remake the whole universe. But the ultimate victory of technology over matter is paradoxical: ultralight obliterates the entire physical

---

[112] A. Platonov, "Ocherednoi," *Zheleznyi put'*, no. 2 (5 Oct. 1918), 16–17.

[113] Seifrid, *Andrei Platonov*, 53.

[114] A. Platonov, "Budushchii oktiabr' (Diskussionnaia)," *Voronezhskaia kommuna*, 9 Nov. 1920; idem, "Chto takoe eletrifikatsiia," *Krasnaia derevnia*, 13 Oct. 1920; idem, "Zolotoi vek, sdelannyi iz elektrichestva," *Voronezhskaia kommuna*, 13 Feb. 1921.

universe.[115] In a poem published in 1922, Platonov similarly envisioned the current earth and universe being "murdered by machines" and "killed by iron," to be replaced by a "new iron universe" in which "we transgress all boundaries and laws."[116] As in many proletarian writings, ecstasy and terror, good and evil, death and salvation are combined in these images of modern factories and machines and of modern change and progress.

Proletarian Pastorale

For most of these writers, the natural landscape still represented a meaningful topos: a place to imagine, an image to deploy, a symbol, a value. Communist intellectuals acknowledged with some dismay that most worker writers, even the most urbanized, felt a stubborn, even growing "longing" for "the charms of the countryside, of fields and trees." They explained this longing, comfortingly, as "nostalgia" for their rural origins.[117] As in prerevolutionary writings, however, this was a more complex nostalgia than these critics had in mind—constructed of memories that were more imagined than real, deployed rhetorically in aesthetic and moral argument, and often felt to reflect the tragedy of being trapped in the alien world of modernity. And to the extent that nature was viewed conventionally as feminine, it also raised doubts about the masculinist ideal of industrial modernity.

Remembrances of times past played only a small part, if any, in writing about nature and the countryside. While some of these workers had real memories of rural childhoods or at least of holidays spent out of the city, many were city born and bred. In any case, even when such memories were available, they do not sufficiently explain the ways these workers thought about nature and the countryside. The rural landscape provided images to use and manipulate as well as to recall, metaphors as well as memories. Trying to explain in 1918 this persisting metaphoric use of nature by proletarian poets, Bogdanov observed that nature was the "foundational metaphor" of all literature. But he also insisted that it represented a cultural past that would be transcended as true proletarian culture emerged. Nature writing, he argued (and warned), remained pervasive in proletarian literature only as a vestige of an older culture.[118] But matters were not so simple.

Even more than before the revolution, it was not the village that called to worker writers but romanticized nature. The human population of the coun-

---

[115] A. Platonov, "Markun," *Kuznitsa*, no. 7 (December 1920–March 1921), 18–22; A. Platonov, "Satana mysli (Fantaziia)," *Put' kommunizma*, no. 2 (March–April 1922), 32–37.

[116] A. Platonov, "Vecher mira," in *Golubaia glubina*, 17.

[117] Voronskii, "O gruppe pisatelei 'Kuznitsa,'" 128, 136; L'vov-Rogachevskii, in his *Ocherki*, 102–6; Rodov, "Motivy tvorchestva M. Gerasimova," *Kuznitsa*, no. 1 (May 1920), 21–23; M. Stoliarov on Volkov, in *Tvori!* no. 2 (1921), 32–33. See also V. A-skii in *Kuznitsa*, no. 1 (May 1920), 26–27.

[118] A. Bogdanov, "Chto takoe proletarskaia poeziia," *Proletarskaia kul'tura*, no. 1 (July 1918), 13.

tryside remained largely invisible in these portraits of rural life or appeared only as emblems of backwardness. In many of Nikolai Liashko's stories, for example, against a background of appealing nature, the village appears as a filthy and foul-smelling place and the people who live there as cruel, ignorant, blindly selfish, crude, drunken, primitive, even animalistic.[119] Other writers similarly deplored the "sleepy immobility" of the village and even peasants' lack of real appreciation of nature.[120] In one poem from 1920, Sergei Obradovich describes himself at the Sparrow Hills, on the rural outskirts of Moscow, hearing a traditional Russian song and finding it full of "submissiveness and sadness" and even "incomprehensible."[121] Fully in accord with most urban workers and Communists, these writers generally despised peasants. Petr Oreshin's explicitly populist admiration of the peasantry as a revolutionary force—the author was closely associated with the Socialist Revolutionary Party—was the exception that proved the rule.[122] Most often, though, the village and the peasantry were simply ignored as irrelevant to what these writers valued in the countryside. Nature is what mattered. One author expressed a sentiment many appear to have shared: "people spoil life"—nature is preferable.[123]

As before the revolution, worker authors wrote of escape into nature from factory and city. The former metal turner Aleksei Bibik, in an autobiography written sometime in the 1920s, described an "irrepressible, painful yearning for the forest and the river." This was not, typically, nostalgia for a lost rural childhood: Bibik was born to a family of workers in the city of Kharkov. In his youth, however, he was already fleeing to nearby woods and riverbanks. This yearning and flight, he tells us, were central to his emerging identity: "The forest and the river have remained for my entire life a source of absolution [*proshchenie*] and joy."[124] He was not alone. Petr Oreshin described himself dreaming of quitting the oppressive brick and iron of the factory and the city—a place where people symbolically "forget how to write poetry"—to return to the countryside (he speaks of return although he was born in the city), where in place of the "dirty-faced factory," brick walls, and the forge's sparks would be stars, hills, forests, and the freedom of the steppe.[125] Emphasizing

[119] E.g., N. Liashko, "S otaroi," *Rabochii mir*, no. 2–3 (February 1919), 6–11; "V stepi" and "Los'," in his *Rabochie rasskazy* (Moscow, 1924), 40–49, 68–80. See also discussion by Voronskii, "O gruppe pisatelei 'Kuznitsa,'" 129–30, and by I. Pchelintsev, "Zametki o proletarskoi belletristike," *Tvori!* no. 2 (1921), 23–24.

[120] Aleksandrovskii, "V glushe," *Tvori!* no. 1 (December 1920), 4 (see also his "Ia stikhami po gorlo syt," in *Shagi* [Moscow, 1924], 9); V. Pletnev, "Vesenniaia pesnia," *Gorn*, no. 5 (1920), 11

[121] S. Obradovich, "Na Vorob'evykh gorakh," *Gorn*, no. 5 (1920), 3.

[122] See Oreshin's poems in *Krasnyi zvon: Sbornik stikhov* (Petrograd, 1918).

[123] N. Vlasov-Okskii, "Ogon'ki v stepi (iz vstrech s pisateliami-samouchkami)," *Griadushchee* 1921, no. 1–3: 41.

[124] A. Bibik, unpublished autobiography in RGALI, f. 1849, op. 1, d. 1, l. 7.

[125] P. Oreshin, "Poimite, poimite: sovsem razuchilsia . . . ," *Zheleznyi put'* 1923, no. 2: 6; "Smychka," ibid., no. 7: 1. See also "Na prostore," in *Krasnyi zvon*, 59, and "Brodiaga," *Zheleznyi put'* 1923, no. 11: 2.

the feminine values nature represented, Ivan Eroshin, writing in a major Proletcult literary collection, described himself quitting the city and throwing himself upon the soil, which was like a smiling and inviting maiden, though at the same time a mother welcoming him home, and music, and love.[126] Others—among them Gerasimov and Platonov—meditated on workers escaping, if only briefly, into nearby gardens, into the warming rays of the spring sun, and into the dark of a starry and tender night after work had ended.[127] For the workers who crafted the collective story *Glukhar'*, the greatest victory of a strike came in bringing workers "rest" and escape. The hero of the tale, a worker named Uglov, relishes above all the freedom and joy of warming himself in the sun and listening to the silver river and the gentle sounds of music and nature.[128]

It is striking how often these worker writers imagined being in nature—always, of course, a gentle nature of great beauty and spiritual value. Such writings were especially pervasive among the postrevolutionary writings of the older generation of "writers from the people" as well as among those who were inclined, often because of populist political convictions, to classify themselves after 1917 as "folk" or "peasant writers." These authors were particularly likely to declare their "passionate love for nature" and to create in their writings idyllic pastoral romances filled with "sighs" and "aromas" wafting in from fields and groves, the innocent joys of running along forest paths and swimming in rivers, and the beauties of nature.[129] However, most urbanized worker writers associated with the Proletcult, Kuznitsa, and other "proletarian" cultural movements also regularly grew lyrical about fields and forests, dawn and storms, twinkling stars, fires along the Volga, the open steppe, the bright sun, and the music of the wind.[130] Even the most prominent Communist worker writers, including those with strong reputations as bards of city and factory, voiced a passion for nature. As Pavel Bessal'ko (a former metalworker) put it, "few suspect how passionately, even to the point of pain, 'people with steel muscles and iron blood' love nature."[131] Aleksei Mashirov, for

---

[126] I. Eroshin, "Vnov' idet k nam vesna blagodatnaia . . . ," in *Zavod ognekrylyi*, 63.

[127] M. Gerasimov, "Vesennee," *Zarevo zavodov*, no. 1 (January 1919), 12; A. Platonov, "Vecher posle truda," *Zheleznyi put'* 1919, no. 1 (Jan. 31): 11; N. Poletaev, "Tkachikha," *Kuznitsa*, no. 2 (June 1920), 8.

[128] *Glukhar': Rasskaz* (Samara, 1920), 8–9.

[129] E.g., the autobiographies of Vasilii Gorshkov in RGALI, f. 1641, op. 1, d. 12, l. 1, and I. V. Shuvalov, ibid., f. 1068, op. 1, d. 10, l. 7; E. Nechaev, "Kartinka," *Kuznitsa*, no. 3 (July 1920), 13; L. Kotomka [Zelenskii], "Prostye slova," *Griadushchee* 1918, no. 4 (June): 5. See esp. the work of Petr Oreshin, such as his "Poimite, poimite: Sovsem razuchilsia . . . ," *Zheleznyi put'* 1923, no. 2: 6; "Smychka," *Zheleznyi put'* 1923, no. 7: 1; "Na prostore," *Krasnyi zvon*, 59; and "Brodiaga," *Zheleznyi put'* 1923, no. 11: 2.

[130] Besides examples below, see A. Smirnov, "Moi druz'ia," in *V bure i plameni* (Iaroslavl, 1918), 58; I. Eroshin, "Veter" and other poems in *Zavod ognekrylyi*, 62–63, 65, 66, 68; also poems Eroshin submitted with his autobiography (1919) in RGALI, f. 1068, op. 1, d. 56, ll. 5–6; F. Groshik [Kopeikin], "Vesenniaia preliudiia," *Griadushchee* 1918, no. 2 (May): 13; Mikhail Artamonov, *Zemlia rodnaia* (Moscow, 1919) and reviews of his work in *Kuznitsa*, no. 1 (May 1920), 26–27; and L'vov-Rogachevskii, *Ocherki*, 101–2.

[131] P. Bessal'ko, "Proletarskie poety," *Griadushchee* 1919, no. 1: 13.

example, described by Bessal'ko as "one of the most conscious poets of the working class," wrote numerous lyrical passages about lilacs, "warm and tender spring winds," the warm rays of the sun, and the like.[132] Such pastoral lyricism, typically linked to a narrative of a (male) factory worker longing for (feminine) nature, was very common among "conscious" worker authors. We see it, for example, in Gerasimov's and Kirillov's civil war–era songs of spring, in Platonov's lyrical poems on night, rivers, and nature, and in the NEP–era worker correspondent Kavkazskii's poems about the beauties of flowers and trees and the aromas of the open field.[133] For some worker writers, a pastoral mood grew as time passed. As one critic noted of Vladimir Kirillov's writings of the early 1920s, "more and more strongly do we notice the smell of flowers and fields."[134] This pastoral mood persisted and deepened, for it made emotional and intellectual sense. As had long been the case, nature writing expressed sentiments rooted less in actual memories or longing for the past than in emotional and intellectual responses to the present. It offered an imaginary refuge and an argument.

Nature also continued to serve to express symbolically alternative ideals, values, and desires. Most of these symbolic uses—the images themselves and the meanings signaled—remained conventional. But evident was a new passion and intensity, an ardor for the revolution's promise of dramatic change. Images such as springtime and flowers continued to represent hope and coming happiness. May Day was said to be a "holiday of freedom, spring, and flowers," a festival of "sun and love."[135] Workers' coming redemption, it was said, will occur when the "pain and horrors" of their lives are transformed into "the smiles of roses."[136] Springtime, in particular, remained a favorite emblem: the freedom workers longed for while toiling under capitalism, the coming of revolution, the "renaissance of the nation" (the first flower among the dim pines), a new world of freedom and brotherhood ("The Great World Spring"), and a "winged" source of faith in the new.[137] Similarly, the sun appeared as a symbol of hope and coming happiness, as comforting "friend, brother, and sister," as "sun-mother" giving love to all, or as a comrade fighting on "the front of Labor."[138] In some cases, the vocabulary of nature liter-

---

[132] Ibid., 13–14. E.g., Samobytnik [Mashirov], "Krasnye svety," *Griadushchee* 1918, no. 1 (January): 7, and "Detstvo," ibid., no. 9: 3.

[133] M. Gerasimov, "Vesna," "Vzlet," and others, esp. in the section titled "Lirika," in his *Zavod vesennyi* (Moscow, 1919); V. Kirillov, "Vesna v stolitse," in *Stikhotvoreniia, 1914–1918*, 25; A. Platonov, "Noch'," "U reki," "Mart," *Zheleznyi put'* 1919, no. 7 (February): 10; no. 8 (March): 9, 12; idem, *Golubaia glubina*; materials on Kavkazskii in *Rabochee tvorchestvo*, no. 8 (November 1924), 13.

[134] L'vov-Rogachevskii, *Ocherki*, 110.

[135] V. K. [Vladimir Kirillov?], "Pervomaiskii gimn," *Griadushchee* 1918, no. 2 (May): 1; P. Arskii, "Prazdnik Maia," ibid., 1919, no. 4: 1.

[136] V. Kirillov, "Brat'iam," in *Stikhotvoreniia, 1914–1918*, 17 (first published in *Zhizn' iskusstv* 1918, no. 1: 1).

[137] Samobytnik [Mashirov], "V vesennyi den'," *Griadushchee* 1918, no. 1 (January): 10–11 and "Vesennee," ibid., 1919, no. 4: 1; V. Kirillov, "Gremiat miatezhnye raskaty . . . ," in *Stikhotvoreniia, 1914–1918*, 8–9; V. Aleksandrovskii, "Rabochii prazdnik," *Ponizov'e*, no. 5 (1922), 5.

[138] V. Pletnev, "Vesenniaia pesnia," *Gorn*, no. 5 (1920), 11; I. Filipchenko, "Lenin," *Rabochii*

ally was a source of pleasure: "People would be happier," according to Pletnev, "if they knew how to listen to and understand the language of nature."[139]

Beside these familiar and obvious symbolic statements we see—especially during the early years of revolutionary vision and enthusiasm—increasingly impassioned, imaginative, even spiritual uses of symbolic nature.[140] In the collective tale *Glukhar'*, at the moment when a prerevolutionary worker becomes conscious of the need to fight for freedom—inspired by an orator with blowing hair and burning eyes—he suddenly sees a vision of rivers, fields, sunshine, and gathering berries. Tears come to his eyes. Back in the factory, he feels that nature is calling to him so strongly that he must flee. He communes with nature. The next morning, he awakens with newly shining eyes.[141] In still more elevated tones, Gerasimov told of first seeing the ubiquitous smile of Mona Lisa (with all of this image's allusions to a transcendent universal feminine) in "the golden shadows of maple trees," in the "songs of falling leaves," and in a monastery garden.[142] In many works, the sun (occasionally the moon)[143] became an object of devotion and a subject of nearly mystical force. When Kirillov considered smashing his head against the stones of the city, he was saved when the sun "literally spoke" to him, reminding him of the joys of life and struggle. Now he could endure the city by focusing his gaze on "the sunny distance."[144] In other poems, worker authors imagined building a road to the sun or flying to it.[145] They "pray to the sun of the new Lord" or to the "new sun" placed in the heavens by the "Iron Messiah" or by a proletarian Prometheus.[146] For some the sun was a mystical force "shining above us and within us," or upon whose "ark" workers sailed into the future along the "solar path" toward the "mute horizon, the realm of sunny days, the world of imagination and dreams."[147]

---

zhurnal 1924, no. 1: 62–63, 65–66; A. Platonov, "Poslednii shag," *Voronezhskaia kommuna*, no. 15 (January 1921); V. Kirillov, "Etu pesn' zari griadushchei," in *Stikhotvoreniia, 1914–1918*, 15–17 (originally in *Pravda*, 13 Nov. 1917); M. Gerasimov, "Na front Truda," *Kuznitsa*, no. 1 (May 1920), 10–11.

[139] V. Pletnev, "Vesenniaia pesnia," *Gorn*, no. 5 (1920), 11.

[140] Voronskii spoke of "pantheism" and "cosmism" among the Kuznitsa poets, who included most of the best-known worker authors: "O gruppe pisatelei 'Kuznitsa,'" 137.

[141] *Glukhar'*, 10–14.

[142] M. Gerasimov, "Monna Liza: Poema," *Gorn*, no. 1 (1918), 11–12.

[143] P. Oreshin, "Mesiatsu sinemu," *Rabochii mir* 1918, no. 8 (7 July): 3.

[144] V. Kirillov, "Zov zhizni," in *Stikhotvoreniia, 1914–1918*, 28–29.

[145] N. Tikhomirov, "Starik," *Griadushchee* 1918, no. 9: 3; M. Gerasimov, "Kak v chernykh ranakh"and "Letim," both in *Zavod ognekrylyi*, 37, 17.

[146] I. Eroshin, "Iz tsikla 'Pesni truda,'" in *Zavod ognekrylyi*, 48; I. Eroshin, "Zemlia i Solntse," *Tvorchestvo*, no. 1 (May 1918), 17; V. Kirillov, "Zheleznyi messiia," *Griadushchee* 1918, no. 4 (June): 3; V. Aleksandrovskii, "Ia" (1922), in *Zvon solntsa* (Moscow, 1923): 7.

[147] A. Platonov, "Mysli," *Voronezhskaia kommuna*, 7 Oct. 1920 (also in *Golubaia glubina*, 13); V. Aleksandrovskii, "S luchama solntsa v dushi nashi . . . ," *Kuznitsa*, no. 1 (May 1920), 5; N. Vlasov-Okskii, quotations from his work in a review in *Krestianin i rabochii*, 2 Apr. 1919, in RGALI, f. 1068, op. 1, d. 28, l. 5. See also V. Kirillov, "Proletariatu," *Griadushchee* 1918, no. 1 (January): 3, and Mikhail Gerasimov, Sergei Esenin, and Sergei Klychkov, "Kantata," *Zarevo zavodov*, no. 1 (January 1919), 24–25.

In these aesthetic, intellectual, emotional, and symbolic uses of nature, ambivalence was also more intense and more openly acknowledged. Il'ia Sadof'ev described "two voices" calling to workers: the gentle aromas of the woods in spring and the warm light of the sun versus the "steam, steel, and fire" of factory and city. This was a normative choice: city and factory represented the future, and workers must learn to love them.[148] Most of these proletarians insisted that they were able to make this choice.[149] In Kirillov's words, "we have forgotten the fragrance of grass and of spring flowers."[150] Some even claimed now to recall joyfully the sounds of machines as they walked in the woods—the literary trope of the interrupted idyll, but here given positive value.[151] Deliberate insistence on these claims was part of their logic—loving the city was an act of will that overcame emotion and memory. And, it may be suggested, this was a masculine act, a defining assertion of gendered values and a gendered self, or at least of a certain type of gendered desire: a willful embrace of the ethos of urban toughness, iron muscles, and forceful machinery as opposed to the "feminine" (as they saw it) aesthetic and ethic of gentle nature, comforting warmth, and reviving "sighs" and "aromas."

Aleksandrovskii, who came to Moscow as an eleven-year-old peasant, admitted to hesitating before this choice and regretting that the city had lured him away from what "sacred memory preserved: / the ringing blue of the woods / the golden bast of fields."[152] When Aleksandrovskii was out in the countryside, the city seemed "far away and not ours," though he recognized that this escape was only a "mirage" that "motors" would soon "crudely scatter."[153] On other occasions, however, he admitted to feeling mournfully oppressed by the "stupefaction" and "flaccid, sunny immobility" of rural life, which made him long for the "fire-winged city."[154] One solution, at least for Aleksandrovskii, was to find in *winter* a better proletarian pastoral aesthetic. In the harsh winter of the far north Aleksandrovskii found a natural landscape with the intensity, violence, and necessity of struggle that suited the proper spirit of the working class. But this did not prevent him from also longing for spring and for the south—for the gentle warmth of the sun, which "loves as tenderly as a girl."[155] In a long poem written a couple of years later, Alek-

---

[148] I. Sadof'ev, "U stanka," *Griadushchee* 1918, no. 7 (October): 1.

[149] Besides examples below, see S. Obradovich, "Polustanok," *Tvori!* no. 1 (December 1920), 3, and "Rozhdennomu, kak ty, v granite . . . ," *Kuznitsa*, no. 4 (August–September 1920), 11; N. Poletaev, "Chadilo chertova kadilo . . . ," *Gorn*, no. 2–3 (1919), 4.

[150] V. Kirillov, "My," *Griadushchee* 1918, no. 2 (May): 4.

[151] Ia. Berdnikov, "V kosmakh belostvol'noi dali," *Griadushchee* 1920, no. 12–13: 1. On the "trope of the interrupted idyll," see Leo Marx, *The Machine in the Garden: Technology and the Pastoral Ideal in America* (New York, 1964).

[152] V. Aleksandrovskii, "Moskva," *Kuznitsa*, no. 5–6 (October–November 1920), 12.

[153] V. Aleksandrovskii, "V zakate," *Gorn*, no. 2–3 (1919), 10–11.

[154] V. Aleksandrovskii, "V glushe," *Tvori!* no. 1 (December 1920), 4.

[155] V. Aleksandrovskii, "Sever," *Gorn*, no. 4 (1919), 5–6 (also poems on winter, 7). Gerasimov also saw struggle in nature—e.g., the Neva River in Petrograd, moving between its granite walls, as the common people move forward: "Noch'iu," in *Zavod ognekrylyi*, 18.

sandrovskii openly despaired of what winter represented—monotony, harshness, suffering, death—and imagined "a Russia without snowstorms, melancholy, taverns," a Russia transformed by fire and spring.[156]

One attempted solution to these contradictions between nature and city was to imagine a synthesis, a new aesthetic environment in which nature entered into the factory and the boundaries between the natural and the artificial blurred. Mikhail Gerasimov, for example, wrote many poems (and they were among his best-known and most often reprinted writings of the post-October years) exploring a new relationship between city and country, nature and machine. In one 1918 poem (reprinted frequently into the 1920s) a spring day comes down to earth "like a hero," so that the "gloomy iron factory / blossoms with a pearl rainbow," and the factory "prison" is

> Suddenly transformed
> Into a melodious, happy temple.
> Steel leaves, like icons,
> Shine in golden fires. . . .
> The fiery hearths boil
> Like cups of red wine,
> And the smokestack, black with encrusted soot,
> Is filled with intoxicating juices. . . .
> And even the brick furnaces
> Bloom with a luxurious flower.[157]

In many poems of these years Gerasimov blended the language of nature into the language of industry—and the language of masculinity with that of the feminine—creating dozens of metaphoric correspondences: hardened slag and "clusters of pink coral," flames and "gold-red feathers," steel and trees, sparks in the furnace and stars in the sky, motors and swimming swans, fire and roses.[158] The androgynous union of gendered opposites was often explicit. In the flames of a furnace he could see, "intertwined with the gleam of steel, a maidenly figure," and in the mirroring face of machines the "sweet reflections" of a young woman's eyes glistening with spring.[159] Other worker poets created similar images of nature entering into the factory, bringing natural life to its artifice, softening its harshness.[160] Aleksei Mashirov's "Spring Visions"

---

[156] V. Aleksandrovskii, "Dve Rossii," *Kuznitsa*, no. 7 (December 1920–March 1921), 3–6.

[157] M. Gerasimov, "Vesna," *Zheleznyi put'* 1918, no. 2 (Oct. 5): 18. This poem, usually called "Vesennyi den'," was also printed, with various revisions, in *Zavod ognekrylyi*, 37–38. There the final lines read: "Where coal was, fiery furnaces / Bloom with a bloodied flower." See also M. Gerasimov, *Zavod vesennyi* and *Zheleznoe tsveten'e* (Moscow, 1923). In "Vesennee utro," in *Zarevo zavodov*, 8, spring "covers the factory in roses."

[158] M. Gerasimov, "Zavod vesennyi," *Proletarskaia kul'tura*, no. 4 (September 1918), 32 (and in many volumes of his poetry); "Zavodu" and "Liubliu," in *Zavod ognekrylyi*, 43–44; "Zarevo zavodov," in *Zarevo zavodov*, 8–10.

[159] M. Gerasimov, "Ne vyzyvaiushchei . . . ," *Proletkul't*, no. 1–2 (April–May 1919), 6–7; "Vesennee," *Zarevo zavodov*, no. 1 (January 1919), 12.

[160] See, e.g., Aleksandrovskii, "Devushke-tkachikhe," in *Zavod ognekrylyi*, 51; Nechaev, "V gute," *Rabochii zhurnal* 1924, no. 1: 34.

was typical. Going one spring day to work at the factory, which he likens to going "into combat," he carried a "lilac," which "trembled fearfully" in his hand. But the symbolic weapon had its desired effect: the shining sky, woods and fields, a summer thunderstorm (raining "diamond tears"), the returning sun, and rushing waters "bewildered the iron tongue of machines."[161]

Hesitation before purely urbanist or machine values reflected the ambivalence of these writers' aesthetic and sentimental responses to modernity as well as their symbolic intentions. Nature's compelling power was hard to ignore and its aesthetic and intellectual meanings were hard not to prefer. Sentimentally and symbolically, the natural world, as an idealized place of escape, comfort, beauty, and hope, continued to compete for workers' affections with the "fire-faced" city. More subtly, it would seem, "feminine" values (and images of self) competed with the "masculine" force of "iron-stone giants," "gigantic machines," and the "whirl of wheels and shafts." In intellectual terms, freedom and happiness remained central goals even as they were attached to ideals of revolutionary transformation and to a socialist ideology that also embraced faith in technology, rationalism, and modernization. These tensions were not easily resolved, even with the help of Marxist dialectics, and critics noted the ambiguities in workers' responses to the modern landscape. When Semen Rodov evaluated Mikhail Gerasimov's postrevolutionary writings on the themes of city, factory, and nature, he wondered aloud whether Gerasimov was expressing nostalgia for the lost village, back-to-nature populism, a mood of "mystical-perplexity," or (the correct point of view) simply the "transitional" consciousness of a worker still learning to appreciate city and factory and to cut himself off from his rural past.[162] Rodov backed away from the ambiguity he noticed by choosing one answer—the ideologically correct one. We need not choose, nor should we. Gerasimov's explorations of meanings of city, factory, and machine, like those of many worker writers, remained complex and indeterminate. Nikolai Liashko observed that "hatred of the stagnant countryside and irresistible love for it . . . exist side by side in the soul of the worker."[163] If we recognize country and city to be tropes and symbols as well as physical sites, we realize how much was at stake in this inability or unwillingness to choose.

The Pain of Ambivalence

Liashko made simple—a plain image of a "side by side" relationship—what was complex and difficult, especially at the critical level of feeling and conviction. It was also at this level that the intellectual significance of this play of metaphors becomes most clear. As worker writers struggled to reconcile their

[161] Samobytnik, "Vesennye grezy," *Griadushchee* 1918, no. 2: 14.

[162] Rodov, "Motivy tvorchestva M. Gerasimova," *Kuznitsa*, no. 1 (May 1920), 21–23.

[163] N. Liashko, "O zadachakh pisatelia-rabochego (Zametka)," *Kuznitsa*, no. 3 (July 1920), 29.

emotional, moral, aesthetic, and ideological views of the modern world—and their views of the revolution and its devotion to industrial and urban construction—we hear increasing notes of fatalistic despair intertwined with the most insistent declarations of determination and hope. Together with fervent hope that the city was indeed, as Vladimir Kirillov put it, "a great bridge to the liberation and exaltation of man," these proletarian intellectuals seem increasingly to have felt that there was no escape from the infernal machinery of industrial modernity, no dialectical transcendence. Ideological exhilaration in the face of the modern alternated with aesthetic and moral panic. Indeed, as time passed, despair increased—even during the course of the "heroic" civil war, but especially during the NEP years, when the transformative promises of the revolution remained largely unfulfilled.

These anxieties were evident in images of nature: melancholy verses about autumn and winter joined hopeful images of spring and summer.[164] But the city provided the most troubling images, even of nature. A story by a woman member of one of the proletarian clubs in Petrograd describes a working-class woman walking sorrowfully around the gloomy city streets as autumn leaves fall, surrounded by a vital and sentient nature (which understands her sadness), despairing over her lost virginity (her own "spring" now past, her "flowers" torn up) and considering suicide, though possibly saved when the wind brings to her the message of happiness through labor, struggle, and creativity.[165]

Like most of these writers, Vladimir Kirillov tried to weave together despair and hope, to deploy anguish as an expression of argument and sensibility without succumbing to its logic and weight. Also like many, he did not always succeed. As we have seen, he was so depressed by modern life that he was tempted "to beat [his] head against the stones" of the city, until he was saved by ideology in nature's form: the sun reminding him of the joy of struggle.[166] But this revolutionary epiphany did not last long. By 1920 he was again openly imagining his death and burial: dying "amidst the noise of the trams" in his "gray, stone building," and being buried amidst the "same vanities and noise on the streets of the capital," the same drunken love and drunken sorrow, and the same newspapers being hawked—only now, he added, joined by the trite and "absurd" mention of a dead poet. He admitted a slight possibility of happiness, however—not in the joy of struggle or the embrace of labor, but in the unseen and private pleasures of becoming a specter, smoking cigarettes, strolling, and, in the evening, stroking the hair of his beloved.[167]

---

[164] A. Pomorskii, "Osen'," *Revoliutsionnye vskhody*, no. 3–4 (October 1920), 7; verses by P. Oreshin and S. Obradovich in *Izvestiia*, 23 Sept. 1922; M. Gerasimov, "V dushe moei rany zazhili davno . . . ," in RGALI, f. 1374, op. 1, d. 6, l. 10 (from an unpublished collection Gerasimov was compiling in the 1920s); V. Polianskii, "Poeziia sovetskoi provintsii," *Proletarskaia kul'tura*, no. 7–8 (April–May 1919), 55.

[165] Chlen kluba im. Lunacharskogo Petrogradskogo raiona Rogneva, "Klenovye list'ia," *Revoliutsionnye vskhody*, no. 3–4 (October 1920), 8–9.

[166] V. Kirillov, "Zov zhizni," in *Stikhotvoreniia, 1914–1918*, 28–29.

[167] V. Kirillov, "Moi pokhorony," *Kuznitsa*, no. 8 (April–September 1921), 10. See also Ki-

The city generated darker and darker thoughts. Critics of Aleksandrovskii's poems of the 1920s noted with dismay that notwithstanding Aleksandrovskii's efforts to "constantly be bold" (*postoianno bodritsia*) and his insistence that his earlier anguish about city life had passed, a mood of despair was more and more "interwoven" with his deliberately bold, revolutionary songs.[168] Aleksandrovskii was not alone. Well into the 1920s, such critics as Aleksandr Voronskii found "agonizing ambivalence" (*muchitel'naia razdvoennost'*) about the city widespread among proletarian poets.[169] This mood affected even the new postrevolutionary generation of worker writers. In 1925, nineteen-year-old Nikolai Kuznetsov committed suicide. Though urban born and a member of the Communist Youth League, he hated the factory as the place where he "lost" the "country blue eyes" he inherited from his peasant mother, and where he acquired what was described as his "constant sorrow." Increasingly alienated from the people around him, from the crass cultural tastes of the masses, and from the productivist obsessions and petty everyday concerns of NEP officials (he was advised that if he wanted to be a writer he ought to write about swine feeding), he took his own life. There are many like Kuznetsov, the author of his obituary warned.[170] Indeed, there were many, he could have said, who felt that they had lost something in the city, even if it was something they had never had.

Obradovich tried to find words for the complex ideals and anxieties worker writers felt when he wrote to Aleksandrovskii: "To one born, like you, in granite / the anguish in your soul is understandable: / Whether to replace winged words / With the grassy whisper of the steppes?"[171] Others, as we have seen, spoke of the struggles of the creative imagination, of what "lies in the heart of the worker writer," of a rift between mind and heart. Ambivalence might be seen as a sign of progress beyond the simple moral categories and symbols with which most worker writers had conventionally condemned city and factory life before 1917. And a deeper awareness of contradictions, any Marxist understood, might be joined by an understanding of the dialectic of progress. No doubt some worker writers had, at least some of the time,

---

rillov's melancholy portrait of the unchanging crassness of city life ("so will it be for a thousand years") in "Byl vecher, kak vecher," *Kuznitsa*, no. 7 (December 1920–March 1921), 9. For a story focused on an urban suicide, see Liashko, "Stoiashchim na mostu: Kriki i dumy," *Kuznitsa*, no. 3 (July 1920), 25. A posthumous (though unhappy) specter, of course, features in Nikolai Gogol's famous urban critique, "The Overcoat," and Andrei Belyi's St. Petersburg teems with spectral figures.

[168] Voronskii, "O gruppe pisatelei 'Kuznitsa,'" 135–36; P. I. M., review of Aleksandrovskii's *Shagi* (Moscow, 1924) in *Rabochii zhurnal* 1925, no. 1–2: 277. This collection of poems is a good example of such deepening ambivalence.

[169] Voronskii, "O gruppe pisatelei 'Kuznitsa,'" 135–36.

[170] A. Kosterin, "Nikolai Kuznetsov," *Rabochii zhurnal* 1925, no. 1–2: 232–36. Maiakovskii's suicide in 1930, after his declaration that he had "stepped on the throat of [his] own song" and that his "love's boat" of sentiment and imagination has "crashed against the everyday [*byt*]," is comparable.

[171] S. Obradovich, "Rozhdennomu, kak ty, v granite . . ," *Kuznitsa*, no. 4 (August–September 1920), 11.

"faith that the contradictions of the city would be overcome."[172] But often ambivalence was not a way station on the road to a full embrace of urban modernity or even of its dynamic contradictions but an increasingly inescapable and discontented state of mind. Nor was this an embryonic postmodern consciousness: these proletarian intellectuals found no pleasure in indeterminacy, paradox, or irony and could not embrace "a life without truths, standards, and ideals."[173] Theirs remained a thoroughly modern anxiety about modernity.

[172] L'vov-Rogachevskii, *Ocherki*, 124.
[173] Bauman, *Intimations of Postmodernity*, ix.

6   *Feelings of the Sacred*

There are at least three points where chaos—a tumult of events
which lack not just interpretations but interpretability—threatens to
break in upon man: at the limits of his analytic capacities, at the
limits of his powers of endurance, and at the limits of his moral insight. Bafflement, suffering, and a sense of intractable moral paradox are all . . . challenges with which any religion, however
"primitive," which hopes to persist must attempt somehow to cope.
                              —CLIFFORD GEERTZ

Religious symbols which point to the structures of life reveal a more
profound, more mysterious life than that which is known through
everyday experience. They unveil the miraculous, inexplicable side
of life, and at the same time the sacramental dimensions of human
existence.

                              —MIRCEA ELIADE

Religious sensibilities suffused the creative imagination of lower-class writers in Russia on the eve of war and revolution. Even worker writers who had
embraced the secular ideology of Marxism—indeed, especially such writers,
it would seem—found in sacred symbols a way to speak of some of the most
important things: the meaning of suffering, the order and purpose of existence,
the motions of time, the ethics of life in the world. This was a discourse of the
sacred that was simultaneously interpretive, moral, and emotional. For us, in-
quiring into past experience with only texts to answer our questions, this is
the most elusive of themes. It is also among the most essential if we are to look
as deeply as possible beneath the surfaces of thought and ideas. This is not,
however, mainly an inquiry into popular religion or into the larger cultural
upsurge of spirituality and "God-seeking" in late imperial Russia, though
these histories will be noted, for they were an essential context for the religious language and imagery we find in workers' writings. In most cases, this

pervasive popular religious voice is not, properly speaking, a part of what we normally consider the history of religion. Though most of these writers were raised as Christians, when they spoke the language of religion they were not usually expressing simple Christian belief. These authors often filled their writings with Christian and other sacred terminologies, imageries, and narratives not only or even mainly for their literal meaning as a profession of Christian faith, which many had formally abandoned, but for their metaphoric and symbolic power as means of speaking in sacred terms—in a spirit of mystery, awe, and sublime power—about otherwise profane matters of everyday life and thoughts of social change. But this language was also more than metaphoric. Sacred symbols and metaphors have a special power to express deeper, more mysterious and sacramental structures of meaning in the world, and to voice, with all due multiplicity and paradox, the otherwise inexpressible.[1] Sacred symbols—like religion itself in many cases—represent neither merely theology nor merely ethics, but ways of expressing fundamentally emotional and moral ways of knowledge beyond the narrowing limits of the self-evident and rationalistic.

Religious Upheaval at the Fin de Siècle

The plebeian religious voice was an inseparable part of the revival of religion, spirituality, mysticism, and myth in Russia during the last decades of the old regime, which in turn was part of a wider challenge to positivist reason throughout the European world. The poet Aleksandr Blok wrote in 1908 of an upheaval of the "elemental," of emotion, fear, and fury breaking through the "crusted lava" of civilization. Blok considered the religious ferment of the time in Russia, especially among the lower classes, as one of its most potent signs.[2] This was, indeed, a period of great spiritual searching and crisis in Russian life—a complex time often reduced to the simple image of a "religious renaissance." Educated Russians were attracted to mystical and religious idealism, venerating charismatic moral preachers and healers, exalting the unconscious and the mythic, voicing apocalyptic premonitions, and showing widespread interest in Theosophy, Eastern religions, and other currents of spirituality, mysticism, and "occult" idealizations of imagination, feeling, and mystical correspondences, and other avenues for seeking truths beyond the merely rational. A cult of elemental feeling, a craving to transcend the limits of nature—to "fly," in the common image of the time—proliferated along with visions of both great catastrophe and redemption.[3]

[1] Mircea Eliade, "Methodological Remarks on the Study of Religious Symbolism," in *The History of Religions: Essays in Methodology,* ed. Eliade and Joseph Kitagawa (Chicago, 1959), 98–102; Clifford Geertz, "Ethos, World View, and the Analysis of Sacred Symbols," in Geertz, *The Interpretation of Cultures* (New York, 1973), 126–41.

[2] Aleksandr Blok, "Stikhiia i kul'tura" (December 1908), in *Aleksandr Blok, Andrei Belyi: Dialog poetov o Rossii i revoliutsii,* ed. M. F. Pianykh (Moscow, 1990), 396–405.

[3] Nicolas Zernov, *The Russian Religious Renaissance of the Twentieth Century* (New York,

Among the lower classes these were also times of great religious ferment. For some observers, such as Blok, this ferment seemed so immense that it appeared that an explosion, much like that of a volcano, was certainly approaching.[4] Historians of the peasantry have described the widespread interest in spiritual-ethical literature and lectures; nonconformist moral-spiritual movements; an upsurge in pilgrimages and other devotions to sacred spaces and objects (especially icons); persistent (but also changing) beliefs in the presence and power of the supernatural (apparitions, possession, walking dead, demons, spirits, miracles, and magic); renewed vitality of local "ecclesial communities" actively shaping their own ritual and spiritual lives, sometimes in the absence of clergy, and defining their own sacred places and forms of piety; and the proliferation of what the Orthodox establishment branded as "sectarianism," including both non-Orthodox Christian denominations, and various forms of deviant popular Orthodoxy and mysticism.[5]

Urban workers have been seen as relatively immune to this upheaval. Contemporaries and historians have written of a loss of faith, a decline in religious practice, and a rise of anticlericalism among urban workers, as well as among

---

1963); George L. Kline, *Religious and Anti-Religious Thought in Russia* (Chicago, 1968); Christopher Read, *Religion, Revolution and the Russian Intelligentsia, 1900–1912* (London, 1979); Bernice Glatzer Rosenthal, "Eschatology and the Appeal of Revolution: Merezhkovsky, Bely, Blok," *California Slavic Studies* 11 (1980): 105–39; Jutta Scherrer, "L'Intelligentsia russe: Sa Quête da la 'vérité religieuse du socialisme,'" *Le temps de la réflexion* 1981, no. 2: 134–51; Bernice Glatzer Rosenthal, ed., *Nietzsche in Russia* (Princeton, 1986) and *Nietzsche in Soviet Culture* (Cambridge, 1994); Maria Carlson, *"No Religion Higher Than Truth": A History of the Theosophical Movement in Russia, 1875–1922* (Princeton, 1993); Catherine Evtukhov, *The Cross and the Sickle: Sergei Bulgakov and the Fate of Russian Religious Philosophy, 1890–1920* (Ithaca, 1997); Bernice Glatzer Rosenthal, ed., *The Occult in Russian and Soviet Culture* (Ithaca, 1997); Robert C. Williams, "The Russian Revolution and the End of Time," *Jahrbücher für Geschichte Osteuropas* 43, no. 3 (1995): 364–401; Nadieszda Kizenko, *A Prodigal Saint: Father John of Kronstadt and the Russian People* (University Park, Penn., 2000).

[4] Blok, "Stikhiia i kul'tura,"400–404.

[5] Christine Worobec, "Death Ritual among Russian and Ukrainian Peasants," in *Cultures in Flux: Lower-Class Values, Practices, and Resistance in Late Imperial Russia*, ed. Stephen Frank and Mark Steinberg (Princeton, 1994); Chris Chulos, "Peasant Religion in Post-Emancipation Russia," Ph.D. diss., University of Chicago, 1994; Vera Shevzov, "Popular Orthodoxy in Late Imperial Rural Russia," Ph.D. diss., Yale University, 1994; Dave Pretty, "The Saints of the Revolution," *Slavic Review* 54 (Summer 1995): 276–304; Gregory Freeze, "Counter-reformation in Russian Orthodoxy: Popular Response to Religious Innovation, 1922–1925," *Slavic Review* 54 (Summer 1995): 305–39; Chris Chulos, "Myths of the Pious or Pagan Peasant," *Russian History*, Summer 1995; Gregory Freeze, "Subversive Piety: Religion and the Political Crisis in Late Imperial Russia," *Journal of Modern History* 68 (June 1996): 308–50; Vera Shevzov, "Chapels and the Ecclesial World of Prerevolutionary Russian Peasants," *Slavic Review* 55 (Fall 1996); Glennys Young, *Power and the Sacred in Revolutionary Russia: Religious Activists in the Village* (University Park, Pa., 1997), chap. 1; Jeffrey Burds, *Peasant Dreams and Market Politics* (Pittsburgh, 1998), chap. 7; Heather Coleman, "The Most Dangerous Sect: Baptists in Tsarist and Soviet Russia, 1905–1929," Ph.D. diss., University of Illinois, 1998; Vera Shevzov, "Miracle-Working Icons, Laity, and Authority in the Russian Orthodox Church, 1861–1917," *Russian Review* 58 (January 1999): 26–48; W. Arthur McKee, "Sobering Up the Soul of the People: The Politics of Popular Temperance in Late Imperial Russia," *Russian Review* 58 (April 1999): 212–33; Laura Engelstein, *Castration and the Heavenly Kingdom* (Ithaca, 1999); Kizenko, *A Prodigal Saint*; Christine Worobec, *Possessed: Women, Witches, and Demons in Imperial Russia* (De Kalb, Ill., 2001).

younger peasants who had worked in the city.[6] The Orthodox church recognized the growing influence of a secular mentality among the urban classes, against which it organized, in the latter years of the nineteenth century and the early years of the twentieth, a sustained public campaign of religious talks, sermons, and mission work.[7] Memoirs by workers often profess atheism.[8] This evidence notwithstanding, the decline of religion has often been misrepresented and exaggerated. Alienation from the established church—common, though far from universal—and even crises of faith often led not toward secularism and atheism but toward alternative forms of religious faith and enthusiasm. In the 1870s, for example, as Reginald Zelnik has shown, the "seductive power" that student radicals often exercised among workers who participated in their circles resulted partly from a syncretic joining of religious fervor and sacred moral purpose with social and political protest.[9] The same effect was visible in the mass influence among workers, on the eve of 1905, of Father Georgii Gapon, who similarly voiced social protest in a religious idiom and fostered a charismatic atmosphere of moral fervor and sacred mission.[10] After 1905, as among the educated—and reflecting the same dissatisfaction with an established church that often did not seem to satisfy spiritual, psychological, or moral needs—we see an impressive revival among the urban lower classes of spiritual and religious searching. Often nonconformist and functioning outside or on the margins of the established church, these movements were frequently branded by the Orthodox church hierarchy as sectarian, and the church actively tried to restore its influence among the urban population by challenging sectarians to debates, attacking them in a flurry of pamphlets, and on occasion anathematizing and excommunicating their leaders.[11] These challenges to religious orthodoxy were more complex and perhaps more troubling than secularization.

Although this popular and largely nonconformist religious revival among the urban lower classes remains little studied, the evidence of its spread is im-

---

[6] E.g., L. M. Kleinbort, "Ocherki rabochei demokratii," pt. 2, *Sovremennyi mir,* May 1913,169–70; and M. M. Persits, *Ateizm russkogo rabochego, 1870–1905 gg.* (Moscow, 1965).

[7] See, e.g., Freeze, "Counter-reformation in Russian Orthodoxy" and "Subversive Piety."

[8] For professions of lack of religious belief among worker writers, see S. Obradovich, "O sebe," *Griadushchee* 1920, no. 9–10: 1, and "Perevorot," *Kuznitsa,* no. 4 (August–September 1920), 21; Il'ia Sadof'ev on Nikolai Rybatskii, *Griadushchee* 1920, no. 12–13: 17.

[9] Reginald E. Zelnik, "'To the Unaccustomed Eye': Religion and Irreligion in the Experience of St. Petersburg Workers in the 1870s," *Russian History* 16, no. 2–4 (1989): 313–26 (quotation 315).

[10] S. I. Somov, "Iz istorii sotsialdemokraticheskogo dvizheniia v Peterburge v 1905 g.," *Byloe* 1907, no. 4: 33–34; Gerald Surh, "Petersburg's First Mass Labor Organization: The Assembly of Russian Workers and Father Gapon," *Russian Review* 40 (October 1981): 436–40.

[11] In addition to citations below, see esp. *Dumy narodnye,* no. 3 (13 Feb. 1910), 2–3; *Nash put',* no. 10 (3 Dec. 1910), 6; A. S. Pankratov, *Ishchushchie boga* (Moscow, 1911); A. S. Prugavin, *"Brattsy" i trezvenniki* (Moscow, 1912); V. Zel'tser, "Iz istorii sektantstva v rabochei srede (Sektanty v g. Nikolaeve v 1890–1900 gg. po neopublikovannym materialam)," in *Voinstvuiushchii ateizm* 1931, no. 4 (April): 29–46 (the dates in the title are misleading, since most of the evidence concerns 1902–12); A. I. Klibanov, *Istoriia religioznogo sektantstva v Rossii* (Moscow, 1965).

pressive. In Moscow, for example, diverse groups of "sectarian" workers, artisans, and petty traders regularly gathered in tearooms and taverns, especially in the famed Iama (the Pit), to discuss religious questions.[12] Large crowds comprising "mainly common people" were reported to be attending the public debates that the church sponsored in Moscow between Orthodox missionaries and sectarians (prefiguring debates that the Communist party would sponsor after 1917 to challenge the established church).[13] According to one observer, even many working-class socialists attended these meetings and some were converted by the arguments of sectarians—trading their Brownings for Bibles, retaining their "protestant spirit" but finding a new means of struggle.[14] Actual Protestants, notably Baptists and Evangelical Christians, built numerous and growing urban congregations in the years between 1905 and the revolution, mainly among lower-class Russians, as did dissident orthodox, such as the "Ioanittes," who revered Father John of Kronstadt as a prophet whose appearance marked the coming of a millennial age.[15] In addition, numerous even less conventional religious movements proliferated in urban areas, especially in working-class neighborhoods—including, according to contemporary press reports, adherents of newly established sects such as the "free Christians," "wailers," and "sons of the apocalypse," followers of individual mystics and healers, as well as older Russian groups such as the *skoptsy* (castrates) and *khlysty* (flagellants).[16] Even among trade union members, as lecture organizers for the Petersburg Union of Tailoring Workers discovered, discussions of religious themes—especially unconventional topics such as the "spiritual culture of primitive peoples"—proved the most popular and lively.[17] When Lev Tolstoy died in 1910, large numbers of workers held memorial meetings and street marches, sent telegrams to his family at Iasnaia Poliana, and sent appeals to the State Duma (the legislature established in 1906) proposing that Tolstoy's memory be honored by abolishing the immoral death penalty.[18] Such appeals make it clear that lower-class Russians tended to admire Tolstoy less as a great novelist than as a moral and spiritual leader.

The urban religious movement that most challenged the established church was the group known as the Brethren (*Brattsy*), also known as Teetotalers (*Trezvenniki*). The movement began in St. Petersburg in the mid-1890s, when the former fish and bread trader Ivan Churikov began converting the urban

[12] *Dumy narodnye*, no. 8 (20 Mar. 1910), 1; *Zvezda utrenniaia*, no. 4 (15 Feb. 1912), 6; Pankratov, *Ishchushchie boga*, 10–45; N. A. Berdiaev, *Samopoznanie* (Moscow, 1991; orig. Paris, 1916), 196–202; Klibanov, *Istoriia religioznogo sektantstva*, 266–67.

[13] *Dumy narodnye*, no. 3 (13 Feb. 1910), 3.

[14] Pankratov, *Ishchushchie boga*, 47.

[15] Coleman, "Most Dangerous Sect," chaps. 2–3; Kvadrat [Kubikov], "Vpechatlenie zhizni," *Pechatnoe delo*, no. 25 (5 Oct. 1910), 4; N. Tal'nikov, "Sektanty v Peterburge (Iz nabliudenii i vpechatlenii)," *Peterburgskii listok*, 24 Dec. 1907; Kizenko, *Prodigal Saint*, esp. chap. 6.

[16] Tal'nikov, "Sektanty v Peterburge," *Peterburgskii listok*, 7 Jan., 11 Feb., 3 and 10 Mar., 20 Oct., and 5 Nov. 1908.

[17] *Golos portnogo*, no. 1–2 (10 May 1910), 4.

[18] *Nash put'*, no. 10 (3 Dec. 1910), 8–9.

poor to a life of sober self-mastery. It spread, especially after 1905, to Moscow and other cities, as large numbers of artisans, workers in shops and factories, domestic servants, petty tradesmen, sales clerks, laborers, and the unemployed flocked to meetings of the Brethren. Followers were estimated to number between 30,000 and 100,000. In Moscow the movement was led by a former peasant, bookseller, and metalworker named Ivan Koloskov. So serious did the church consider this movement that on 7 March 1910, in selected Moscow churches, mainly in working-class neighborhoods, priests pronounced an anathema excommunicating Brother Ivan along with another popular preacher and denouncing the movement. When this anathematization failed to reduce their influence among the poor, Koloskov and several other leaders were arrested and imprisoned.[19]

The importance in popular spirituality of religious feeling joined with fervent morality is evident in the success of this movement. The ethical teachings of the Brethren were much the same as those of most sectarians (of course, the Brethren insisted that they were not sectarians) and of the missionaries and temperance advocates of the official church: stop drinking, live moral lives, keep your families together, and stop the violence between spouses and against children in order to honor God and live with a dignity befitting human beings, who carry within themselves the flame of the Holy Spirit. They went beyond the messages of the established church, however, in preaching the possibility of salvation in this life: "Hell is poverty and laziness," they preached, and heaven could be built on earth. But their appeal—by all accounts far greater than that of the established church's temperance movement—reflected the way the message was expressed, its linguistic, ritual, and performative presentation. The Brethren spoke, it was said, in simple and direct language, with real sympathy and understanding for the sufferings of the poor, and with deep spiritual passion. The worker writer Mikhail Loginov, who clearly admired this movement and was probably a participant, underscored this difference: "In the churches they instruct the common people with Orthodox teachings, which are absorbed, like any teaching, by the mind, but leave people's feelings untouched. 'Brother' Ivan knew how to set fire to the emotions: he created not a new teaching [*verouchenie*] but a faith, which, in the words of Christ, can move mountains."[20] Their meetings had the atmosphere of a revival rather than of an Orthodox service; the congregation was exultant and active, continually interrupting the preaching with shouts of agreement, repetition of the preacher's phrases, and song.[21] The Brethren believed that the common people would be inspired not by "cold preaching . . . that does not touch listeners' hearts and is soon forgotten"[22] but by a moral and spiritual vision pro-

---

[19] Pankratov, *Ishchushchie boga*, 46–85; Prugavin, "'Brattsy' i trezvenniki," *Dumy narodnye,* no. 6 (6 Mar. 1910), 1–2; McKee, "Sobering Up the Soul of the People," 212–33; Tal'nikov, "Sektanty v Peterburge," *Peterburgskii listok,* 28 Jan. and 31 Mar. 1908.

[20] *Dumy narodnye,* no. 6 ([6 Mar.] 1910), 1.

[21] Pankratov, *Ishchushchie boga*, 52–53.

[22] *Dumy narodnye,* no. 3 (13 Feb. 1910), 4.

claimed with charismatic passion and by the inward experience of personal transformation, of "rebirth" as full "human beings" amidst a community of impassioned believers. Among the growing number of lower-class adherents to Protestant and "sectarian" communities, stories of conversion and faith speak similarly of the centrality of emotion, morality, and individual rebirth.[23]

Aware of these popular movements and engaged in their own way with the philosophical and spiritual trends of their time, Russian socialists and even many Marxists shared in this turn toward the spiritual. Non-Marxist socialists, like their counterparts in Western Europe, freely drew upon Christian ethics and the symbolism of Christ, at least to strengthen and legitimize their arguments among the believing poor, but often sincerely. The suffering and self-sacrifice of Jesus and especially his moral defense of the poor were constant themes in populist socialist rhetoric.[24] Marxists too found use and value in sacred images, moods, and ideals. This was especially the case among Bolsheviks. Lenin was not acting preemptively when he fought against the corruption of the materialist worldview by religion. "God-building" (*bogostroitel'stvo*), which briefly flowered in the years after 1905, was the most prominent expression of this Marxist engagement with the sacred. Aleksandr Bogdanov, Anatoly Lunacharsky, and Maxim Gorky—the leading God-builders—recognized and shared the prevalent emotional dissatisfaction with cold philosophical rationalism. Without renouncing atheism or materialism, they revived the efforts of Joseph Dietzgen, the self-taught German tanner who proposed a "religion of social democracy" in the 1870s, to translate the spirit of religion into Marxism. In their view, deterministic materialism—Plekhanovized Marxism, as Lunacharsky contemptuously branded it, referring to the more orthodox "father of Russian Marxism"—psychologically encouraged passivity before blind fate while depriving people of the religious illusions that once gave them hope and a source of moral judgment as well as a sense of awe before the natural world. In response they argued for the importance in any collective movement of appealing to the subconscious and the emotional, of harnessing the inspiring force of myth and religion. In Lunacharsky's words, socialism needed to recapture the power of "myth," to create a "religious atheism" that placed humanity where God had been but that shared theistic religions' passion, wonderment, moral certainty, and promise of deliverance from evil and death.[25] God-building succumbed, as a formal

---

[23] Coleman, "Most Dangerous Sect," chap. 2; Engelstein, *Castration and the Heavenly Kingdom.*

[24] For some examples, see Jay Bergman, "The Image of Jesus in the Russian Revolutionary Movement: The Case of Russian Marxism," *International Review of Social History* 35 (1990): 222–26; Deborah Pearl, "Tsar and Religion in Russian Revolutionary Propoganda," *Russian History* 20, no. 1–4 (1993): 81–107.

[25] A. V. Lunacharskii, "Ateizm," in *Ocherki po filosofii marksizma: Filosofskii sbornik* (St. Petersburg, 1908), esp. 115–16, 148–57 (see also articles by other contributors to this collection); idem, *Religiia i sotsializm*, 2 vols. (St. Petersburg, 1908–11). See also Kline, *Religious and Anti-Religious Thought*, chap. 4; M. Laskovaia, *Bogoiskatel'stvo i bogostroitel'stvo prezhde i teper'* (Moscow, 1976), 62–85; Robert C. Williams, *Artists in Revolution* (Bloomington, 1977), chap. 2, and *The Other Bolsheviks: Lenin and His Critics* (Bloomington, 1986), chap. 5; Jutta Scher-

movement associated with the Bolshevik party, to Lenin's vitriolic criticism, to the Central Committee's condemnation of the doctrine in 1909, and perhaps to the God-builders' own doubts. But its spirit was broader than its direct influence and lasted longer, especially among worker intellectuals, many of whom continued to construct, with the aid of sacred stories, images, and symbols, a socialist discourse much like the one the God-builders had tried to imagine.

Worker writers shared the perception that ideas must touch the emotions to be of consequence. They filled their texts with hyperboles, metaphors, and symbols because these spoke most powerfully the language of emotion. And they found the symbolic language of the sacred especially resonant. According to Fedor Kalinin, who had been a worker student of the God-builders, worker writers were inspired by a distinctively proletarian epistemology; everyday experience had taught them that the world cannot be understood with reason alone, but required emotional intuition and knowledge.[26] Religious idioms and images were appealing partly because they were so familiar, a part of workers' worlds, especially their emotional worlds, since childhood. In autobiographies, worker writers often testified to the strong influence, especially in their youths, of religious lore, faith, and feeling. Many had deeply pious parents. As children, many heard religious stories, especially the lives of the saints and the Gospels, as well as fairy tales (*skazki*), which can be understood as mythic stories of a less Christian sort. When they learned to read, usually in rural church schools, they often read religious books (both in school, as required, and on their own) ranging from the lives of the saints and the Bible to Tolstoy and various theological writings. Religious festivals and especially the music of the liturgy often remained among their fondest memories of childhood. Some sang in church choirs, read the Psalter at funerals, and wrote religious verses. Some workers went on pilgrimages—among them to Tolstoy at Iasnaia Poliana—or even spent time in monasteries. Others recalled at least having considered becoming pilgrims or monks. Even in postrevolutionary recollections these memories retained a warmth that testified to their importance in the intellectual and personal development of these writers.[27]

rer, "'Ein gelber und ein blauer Teufel': Zur Entstehung der Begriffe 'bogostroitel'stvo' und 'bogoiskatel'stvo,'" *Forschungen zur osteuropäischen Geschichte* 25 (1978): 319–29, and "L'Intelligentsia russe."

[26] See, e.g., F. Kalinin, "Tip rabochego v literature," *Novyi zhurnal dlia vsekh* 1912, no. 9 (September): 96–97, 106.

[27] P. Ia. Zavolokin, ed., *Sovremennye raboche-krest'ianskie poety* (Ivanovo-Voznesensk, 1925), 41–42 (N. S. Tikhomirov), 62 (A. A. Sokolov), 168 (A. N. Smirnov); RGALI, f. 1068, op. 1 d. 30, ll. 3–4 (N. I. Volkov); d. 56, l. 5 (I. E. Eroshin); d. 72, l. 1 (M. A. Kiriushkin); d. 93, l. 1 (I. D. Lukashin); d. 106, l. 23 (I. A. Nazarov); d. 152, l. 2 (A. A. Sokolov); f. 1747, op. 1, l. 15 (N. N. Liashko); f. 1874, op. 1, d. 184, ll. 28–33, 53–60, 66 and d. 185, l. 36 (S. A. Obradovich); S. A. Rodov, ed., *Proletarskie pisateli: Antologiia proletarskoi literatury* (Moscow, 1924), 434 (E. E. Nechaev); S. Obradovich, "Perevorot," *Kuznitsa*, no. 4 (August–September 1920), 26–27; Vladimir Korolev, *Lazurnye prakhi: Lirika, 1909–1913* (Yalta, 1914).

When these workers turned away from the church and conventional faith in God—as most did—they typically kept hold of religious imagery, language, and sensibility. Only partly did this process involve translating familiar religious images into a secular setting: dreaming of an earthly paradise, for example, or insisting on Christ's socially subversive message. Most essentially, these writers employed religious motifs as an emotionally meaningful way to present and interpret the world and to envision change, whether or not they remained believers. They typically viewed human existence as a mythic journey through suffering toward deliverance from affliction, evil, and even death. Images of martyrdom, crucifixion, transfiguration, and resurrection remained part of their creative vocabulary, as did narrative attention to suffering, evil, and salvation. These were rarely literal expressions of religious faith, though vestiges may have been present and some remained believers. But neither were they empty literary devices. Their choice reflected ways of seeing and feeling that were as important to workers' attitudes—though more elusive—as political ideology. As Sergei Obradovich would later put it, symbolic language reflected truths that were understood best through the emotions.[28] This was ultimately a religious symbolic language—an emotionally powerful way to reveal "a structure of the world that is not evident on the level of immediate experience," to raise stories of the everyday to a more elevated, numinous sphere, to reach toward the universal.[29]

"A Chain of Suffering"

As we have seen, suffering preoccupied Russian worker writers. A vivid vocabulary of spiritual affliction pervaded their writing: *grust'* and *pechal'* (sadness), *skorb'* (sorrow), *gore* (misery, grief), *muka, muchenie* (torment, martyrdom), *stradanie* (suffering), *toska* (melancholy, anguish, longing). It was not difficult to construct narratives and images of suffering out of the raw materials of lower-class life in Russia. When workers wrote of harsh poverty, hunger, exhausting labor, physical injury, abuse, rape, and early death, these were material facts of life. As one poet writing in a trade union paper described the life of labor: "The workers' life is a chain of suffering / A river of sweat, a sea of tears."[30] When stories and images of suffering were put in writing, however, they became part of a more elevated and significant narrative of witnessing. As here, the writing was often hyperbolic, an expression of pathos. But this was also symbolic writing, an expression of meaning. In writing about the lives of the poor and subordinate, lower-class writers often spoke in symbols, for symbols by definition universalize the particular and point to deeper structures of meaning in the world, to hidden truths. Existential facts

---

[28] S. Obradovich, "Obraznoe myshlenie," *Kuznitsa,* no. 2 (June 1920), 24–25.
[29] Eliade, "Methodological Remarks."
[30] N. E. Dodaev, "Trud," *Zhizn' pekarei,* no. 1/4 (10 Mar. 1914), 2.

became, in this sense, sacramental—physical signs of a more meaningful reality. But also, like all symbols, especially sacred ones, they allowed multiple meanings, some of them ambiguous.

The stories and images of suffering in workers' writings echoed the Christian view, underscored repeatedly in the liturgy, of suffering as the necessary lot of sinful man. Thus workers repeatedly portrayed their lives as "a hard way of the cross filled with suffering" (*tiazhelyi krestnyi put' stradanii*), a "path of thorns" in which one must "bear one's heavy cross" and drink to the depths one's "overflowing chalice of suffering."[31] At the same time, worker writers were likely to reject traditional notions that they must abide suffering as an inevitable price "for the sins of the fathers." These were "priests' lies," it was said.[32] They tended instead to read suffering, as we have seen, as moral wrong, but also as bearing within itself, as the repeated allusions to Jesus' own suffering also imply, the promise of redemption and deliverance. Contrary to those who have argued for the overwhelming weight of a deep-seated Russian cultural inclination toward self-abnegation and passive acceptance of suffering—the alleged "long-suffering" essence of the Russian soul—Russian culture has long nurtured also a quite different narrative of suffering as possessing the power to transcend itself and redeem the sufferer. Orthodox Christianity, echoed in influential cultural arguments in the work of Dostoevsky and other writers, certainly placed theological and liturgical weight on the inevitability and sanctity of suffering. But this was an argument that was often understood not simply as about the fate of a sinful earthly world, but also about suffering, in kenotic emulation of Christ's passion,[33] as an elevating, empowering, and above all critical moral practice, and as a way to transcendence and salvation.

Moral Stories

Suffering, as narrative and image, was often, as we have seen, a critical moral practice. And this moral interpretation was often cast in the light of religious teachings and spiritual values. Admiration for Tolstoy as a voice of spiritual and moral criticism of the status quo was one expression of this critical Christian moral vision. Tolstoy had been excommunicated in 1901 but remained

---

[31] G. Deev-Khomiakovskii in *Drug naroda* 1915, no. 5–7: 2–3; S. Drozhzhin, ibid., 13; A-ch, "Ternistyi put'," *Samopomoshch'* 2, no. 1 (18 Dec. 1911): 6; S. Aleksandrov, "K dnei rabochego pechati," and Ivan Kolkii, "Stikhi rabochego," poems sent to *Pravda* 10 June 1914, in RGASPI, f. 364, op. 1, d. 337, l. 1, and d. 319, l. 3; S. Popov, "Pesn' goria i nuzhdy," *Chelovek*, no. 1 (13 Feb. 1911), 14–15.

[32] E. Nechaev, "Na raboty" (1881) and "Golos dushi" (first pub. 1906 in *Zhurnal dlia vsekh*), both in *Vechernie pesni: Stikhotvoreniia* (Moscow, 1914), 90–91; rpt. in *U istokov russkoi proletarskoi poezii* (Moscow and Leningrad, 1965), 41, 88.

[33] The classic accounts of Russian "kenotic Christianity" are Nadejda Gorodetzky, *The Humiliated Christ in Modern Russian Thought* (New York, 1938), and G. P. Fedotov, *The Russian Religious Mind* (Cambridge, Mass., 1946), chap. 4.

widely admired in Russia for his popular moral writings and for his sufferings. His death in 1910, during an ambiguous journey of pilgrimage, wandering, and escape from everyday life, evoked an outpouring of praise for his status as a moral prophet. "Your books became for us a Gospel," wrote one poet in the paper of the St. Petersburg metalworkers' union to the recently deceased writer, "thank you for every sacred word."[34] The waiters' union sent a telegram to Tolstoy's widow expressing "great sorrow" over the "loss of the great seeker of truth, preacher of love and equality," who, though "born in wealth and power, raised his voice for the benefit of the weak and the poor and thereby became great."[35] Numerous worker writers wrote of Tolstoy as a "sun that has set," a "prophet of labor and love" who spoke "sacred words that will remain eternal," a "titan," a "genius," and a "demigod," at whose unmarked grave pilgrims gather and even the trees bow low in honor.[36] Radical intellectuals, including Lenin,[37] nervously advised workers to embrace Tolstoy's ideals cautiously. The editors of the newspaper of the Petersburg metalworkers' union, for example, recommended that Tolstoy should be appreciated "not as a Christian teacher, but as a great artist and tireless seeker of truth and justice [*pravda*], as defender of the oppressed, opponent of inequality, and fighter for free thought."[38] Many workers, however, were attracted precisely to Tolstoy's search for deeper spiritual truth (*istina*) and his teachings of Christian love.

Mikhail Loginov, who became a writer and journalist after many years of tramping and a string of odd jobs, devoted the last years before his death from tuberculosis at the age of forty-one to promoting a socially critical Christian morality among the urban poor. The truth (*istina*) that Christ taught, Loginov insisted, has been "lost amidst human contrivances and rites," hidden from people just as the "Gospels are hidden from people behind heavy silver and golden covers and clasps." The message taught by Christ—but also by Buddha and Mohammed, Loginov added—is "love of humankind, which alone can save the world from its senseless and cruel life."[39] In the spirit of Brother Ivan Koloskov's contemporaneous teetotal movement among the Moscow poor—about which he wrote with sympathy—Loginov called on workers and

---

[34] *Nash put'*, no. 19 (3 Dec. 1910), 3.

[35] *Chelovek*, no. 1 (13 Feb. 1911), 26.

[36] *Balalaika* 1910, no. 21: 2; I. Kornev, "Velikaia mogila," *Chelovek*, no. 2 (6 Mar. 1911), 5–6.

[37] V. I. Lenin, "L. N. Tolstoi" (16 Nov. 1910) and "L. N. Tolstoi i sovremennoe rabochee dvizhenie" (28 Nov. 1910), in his *Polnoe sobranie sochinenie*, vol. 20 (Moscow, 1961), 19–24, 38–41.

[38] *Nash put'*, no. 10 (3 Dec. 1910), 1–2.

[39] *Dumy narodnye*, no. 1 (1910), 1. Until his death in 1912, Loginov edited and often published a succession of Moscow-based journals directed at lower-class readers—*Muzhitskaia pravda* (1907), *Molodaia sila* (1907–9), *Dumy narodnye* (1910–12), *Zvezda utrenniaia* (1912), and *Narodniki*. Note the similarity of the titles of *Zvezda utrenniaia* and *Utrenniaia zvezda*, I. S. Prokhanov's evangelical Baptist journal that appeared from 1906 until the early 1920s. Loginov's writings suggest that he may have sympathized with the movement, if not actually been a member of it.

the poor to awaken from their dark lives of "coarse swearing, fights, and drunken carouses" to "God's light and truth." Addressing the rich, he accused them of "sacrificing to Mammon" and quoted the scriptural threat, "He who does not work shall not eat."[40] Like Tolstoy, Loginov repeatedly insisted that the spirit of God is within each person: if you recognize this inner spirit, it will "make you free, as you were created to be."[41]

An ambivalent relation to the Orthodox church in these testimonies of moral faith is clear. Lower-class writers often agreed openly with those who criticized the church for the preponderance of religious form over feeling and thought, and especially for its neglect of true Christian ethics. This, of course, was also the message of the religious "sectarians" whose influence among urban workers grew dramatically after 1905. Worker writers typically shared this critical view of proper religiosity. "My God is not dressed in gold / Nor ornamented with diamonds / On the walls of churches and towers," wrote Sergei Gan'shin, "My God is love and light."[42] Candles should be lit, Mikhail Loginov argued, not to "illuminate the cold and dark walls of a cathedral" but on "the altar of justice" in the interests of people.[43] Were Christ to return now to the world and see the current petty state of Christianity, it was often argued, "he would be ashamed for people" and saddened. His wounds would bleed at the sight of rich cathedrals standing complacently beside prisons where men "suffering for the truth" were bound in chains.[44]

Moral anger at the ethical passivity and hypocrisy of the church led some, as we have seen, to sectarian and Protestant movements. But many strayed onto more distinctive, even individual paths. For example, the newspaper of the union of sales and clerical workers of Ekaterinodar featured the story of a young worker who had elaborated his own religious philosophy and practice. Interpreting the Gospels "in his own way," he made his workplace—a shoe store—in his imagination "like a monastery" where he would practice a godly life of humility, honest labor, and just relations to others.[45] Some were led away from religion altogether, though not from the ethical principles that made church practice appear hypocritical: "I cannot pray to one / Who cannot hear the howl of the poor / . . . Who cannot hear the cry of the oppressed / Who is alien to misery and tears. / I can pray no more / To one who is friend to the rich. / I no longer believe! I will not!"[46]

---

[40] *Dumy narodnye*, no. 1 (1910), 2; no. 5 (27 Feb. 1910), 2. See also no. 3 (13 Feb. 1910), 1–2.

[41] *Zvezda utranniaia*, no. 16 (16 May 1912), 2. Loginov's allusion is to John 8:32: "And you shall know the truth [*istina*] and the truth shall make you free."

[42] S. Gan'shin-Gremiacheskii, "Moi Bog . . . ," *Dumy narodnye*, no. 1 (1910), 5; see also editorial on 1.

[43] *Zvezda utrennaia*, no. 9 (25 Mar. 1912), 2.

[44] F. Shkulev, "Khristos," *Narodnaia mysl'*, no. 1 (January 1911), 14; *Dumy narodnye*, no. 5 (27 Feb. 1910), 1. See also E. Nechaev, "Patriot," *Ostriak* 1910, no. 70, in *U istokov*, 113–14.

[45] A-ch, "Ternistyi put'," *Samopomoshch'* 2, no. 1 (18 Dec. 1911): 6–7.

[46] Sergei Gan'shin, "Ne mogu," in RGASPI, f. 433, op. 1, d. 91, l. 3.

As here, many worker writers fashioned a critical ethics out of religious teachings, whether or not they continued to "believe." One worker, writing in 1910 to the paper of the Petersburg metalworkers' union, borrowed a familiar biblical metaphor to offer his own ironic observation that "it is easier for a camel to pass through the eye of a needle than for a working man to enter a good theater."[47] Arguments about the moral evils of inequality and definitions of desired moral goods went far deeper, of course. Egor Nechaev emphasized Christ's life of poverty and labor, his simple and honest speech, his willingness to speak truth to power, his sacrificial death in defense of love.[48] Filipp Shkulev imagined himself at Christ's resurrection, sharing in the joy and renewal, hearing the "song of great love," but also feeling his own heart "burn from pain / Seeing how everywhere the common people are suffocating, / In evil, struggle, and blood."[49] For others, such as Sergei Gan'shin, the Easter celebration of Christ's resurrection was a time for people to "disperse the darkness" by singing out, like the singing of church bells, the message of "liberty, equality, and fraternity."[50]

Pondering their own hardships, worker writers often drew on sacred moral teachings. Sergei Obradovich, as a soldier in the trenches during the First World War, writing between battles in a diary consisting of pieces of folded paper, cursed war as an evil that "makes people insolent and sour, [and] makes people forget the commandments of love and charity."[51] When Nikolai Liashko found himself again in prison in 1914 for his involvement in the Marxist underground, he started a notebook of inspirational quotations. Most were from the Bible and followed familiar lines of religiously inspired social criticism: "Land must not be sold in perpetuity, for the land belongs to me: you are strangers and guests" (Lev. 25:3). "Woe to you who add house to house and join field to field, until nothing remains for others, so that you are the sole inhabitants of the land" (Isa. 5:8); "He who does not work shall not eat" (2 Thess. 3:10). Liashko also recalled the old chant of religiously inspired peasant rebels in England: "When Adam delved and Eve span, who was then the Gentleman?"[52] By contrast, it was said that "honest labor" was a "sacred" practice.[53] Above all, as we have seen often, worker writers spoke of seeking and standing for "truth" (*pravda*) as a moral universal: for "Eternal sacred / Truth: martyr and brother."[54] And beside truth, as in the

---

[47] Odinokii, "O razvlecheniiakh dlia rabochikh," *Edinstvo*, no. 15 (12 Mar. 1910), 11–12. The reference, of course, is to Jesus' famous teaching according to Matt. 19:24, Mark 10:25, and Luke 18:25.

[48] Egor Nechaev, "Khristos," *Vechernie pesni*, 124–25.

[49] F. Shkulev, "V den' Voskreseniia," *Zvezda utrenniaia*, no. 9 (25 Mar. 1912), 3–4.

[50] S. Gan'shin, "Svetloe utro," *Zhivoe slovo* 1913, no. 15–16 (Easter): 5.

[51] RGALI, f. 1874, op. 1, d. 185, l. 26 (entry of 23 Nov. 1916).

[52] RGALI, f. 1747, op. 1, d. 145, l. 15.

[53] M. Savin, "Chestnyi trud," in *Gallereia sovremennykh poetov*, ed. A. A. Tiulenev (Moscow, 1909), 12.

[54] M. Savin, "Pravda," *Bulochnik*, no. 3 (12 Mar. 1906).

new "temple" (*khram*) that Sergei Gan'shin imagined, stood "peace, love, and beauty."[55]

Plebeian writers associated with the more populist "people's magazines" were especially likely to treat moral arguments as grounded in sacred truths and traditions. Echoing Dostoevsky, the people's magazine *Dumy narodnye* (The people's thoughts) prophesied that the Russian people were destined "to speak to the world a word that would save humanity." That word was "the feeling of love for the world" (*miroliubivoe chuvstvo*), the feeling of "honoring God in all people," a sensibility that was said to be deeper and stronger among Russians than among any other people.[56] A story that appeared during the war in the Surikov Circle's paper, *Drug naroda* (Friend of the people), made a similar argument by drawing on the critical tradition of the "holy fool" in Russian popular religion. Although actual *iurodovy,* fools for the sake of Christ, were most common in early-modern Russia, reverence for these unconventional holy men and women, a number of whom were sainted, and for the occasional latter-day holy fool remained strong into the twentieth century. Traditionally, holy fools defied everyday forms of conventional behavior and respect for authority—they lived lives of great piety, simplicity, and aestheticism but also spoke bizarrely, dared to mock the powerful openly, and might walk about wearing little or no clothing—to remind believers of simpler Christian values and of truths not visible in everyday life or expressible in everyday language. In this modern telling by a plebeian author, Aleksei the Fool (Aleksei Durak), as everyone called him, appeared daily at the house of a rich Moscow merchant to chop and carry wood, clean the yard, and help the workmen. Though he worked hard, he never asked for payment. When people gave him money, he gave it all to an aunt with whom he lived and who cared for him. When once he found three rubles that had been dropped, he "foolishly" showed them to everyone until he found the person who had lost the money and returned it. When the merchant gave him some money and suggested he buy himself something, he took the suggestion as a moral slight: "Buy something? That would be shameful!" He worked only "for love." For everyone and at all times he had "a childlike smile." And he pitied to the point of tears the most unfortunate in life. His presence transformed people around him. The merchant who employed him, disturbed by Aleksei's behavior, found something "awakened in his soul" and began to think about his own life of moneymaking and deceit. The narrator, who had been seeking truth in books and in the modern life of the city, realized that in both urban life and the thinking of the intelligentsia were to be found only "coldness, disbelief, and dissatisfaction." Only reflecting upon Aleksei the Fool revealed to him true wisdom: "his love of labor and his natural honor, great honesty, and great

---

[55] S. Gan'shin, "Postroim Khram," *Vpered!* no. 157 (14 Sept. 1917), 3. See also *Drug naroda,* no. 2 (31 Jan. 1915), 16.

[56] *Dumy narodnye,* no. 4 (20 Feb. 1910), 1–2.

humility." Only in Aleksei did he find the "pure and blessed" spirit for which he had been searching.[57]

Salvation

Even before the revolution inspired an imaginative leap toward millenarianism, secular conceptions of freedom and transformation of the world were intermixed with mythic and even mystic dreams of salvation. Although some placed their hope literally only in the "kingdom of heaven after death,"[58] more common were expectations of earthly deliverance from suffering. Often these secular dreams were constructed of transcendent and sacred materials. Like the hero of Aleksei Bibik's 1912 novel of working-class life, many saw the conscious worker as not only concerned with people but drawn to "look at the stars."[59]

To narrate suffering as part of a Christian journey was to imply the promise of deliverance. Even the Bolshevik metalworker Aleksei Mashirov (Samobytnik) was inclined to view the hell of the factory as a place of "prayer" in which he was clad in *verigi,* the heavy chains worn by religious ascetics for penance and to chasten the flesh.[60] Often, as we have noted, workers wrote of the suffering common people, and especially themselves, as living through "martyred days" upon their own hard "way of the cross."[61] And death, so often premature for workers, was a frequent subject of workers' writings. The most liminal and potentially sacred moment in human life, death was easily viewed in transcendent terms. At the end of a life of suffering, death too could be linked to Christ's passion. In a poem by Mikhail Gerasimov, this symbolic association was made literal in the portrayal of a worker killed in an accident in a foundry:

> A sudden cry. A figure lay
> Crucified on the golden sheet,
> Embraced by serpentine flames,
> Burning on a fiery cross.
>
> He died amidst mechanical sounds;
> The pig iron boiled, the steel glistened.

[57] S. Kashkarev, "Durak," *Drug naroda* 1915, no. 2 (31 Jan.): 5–9; no. 3–4 : 6–9.

[58] A-ch, "Ternistyi put'," *Samopomoshch'* 2, no. 1 (18 Dec. 1911): 7. See also Dm. Bogdanov, "Na cherdak," *Narodnaia mysl'*, no. 2 (February 1911), 130.

[59] A. Bibik, *K shirokoi doroge (Ignat iz Novoselovki)* (St. Petersburg, 1914), 40. The novel first appeared in *Sovremennyi mir* in 1912. See also Sergei Gan'shin, "Odinochestvo," *Rodnye vesti* 1912, no. 3: 1.

[60] Samobytnik, "Vesennye grezy," *Voprosy strakhovaniia*, 30 July 1916, rpt. in *Proletarskie poety,* vol. 3 (Leningrad, 1939), 26; idem, "Posle raboty," *Pravda*, 8 Nov. 1912, rpt. in *Proletarskie poety,* vol. 2 (Leningrad, 1936), 88.

[61] E. Nechaev, "K rodine" (1907), in *U istokov,* 98; Dm. Bogdanov, "Na cherdak," *Narodnaia mysl'*, no. 2 (February 1911), 130; G. Deev-Khomiakovskii in *Drug naroda*, no. 5–7 (1915), 1–2; I. K. Golikov, "Bog v pomoshch'," in RGALI, f. 1068, op. 1, d. 41, l. 15.

> But shackled to his smoky throne,
> A bloodied angel thrust forward into the distance.[62]

Occasionally faith in transcendence was grounded in literal religious faith: "No doubts are in one's soul / and with a heart at peace one believes in God."[63] But most often these were religious narratives about secular hopes. As we have seen, "optimism" and a generally "life-affirming" feeling were said to be essential qualities of the proletarian mood, especially after 1905. Poems and stories often spoke of workers' "strength of spirit," feelings of "youthful life," "faith," and certainty that all obstacles would be overcome. As one worker writer insisted, "Man was created for happiness just as a bird was for flight."[64] This faith was often cast, if only metaphorically, in religious terms. A church bell heard in the distance became the sound of "a bright divine muse," a "symbol of tears and misery" that awakened the spirit to be ready for new battles for a new future.[65] Metaphorically, this spirit was conveyed with repeated images of the inevitable physical transformation of the world, driven by cosmic forces: approaching dawn, the rising sun, the coming spring, spring rain and rebirth, and, less often, more original images such as the force of the wind and the inexorable power of streams cutting though granite.[66]

Hints of apocalyptic redemption were increasingly common. Worker writers imagined, in the familiar metaphors, an apocalyptic time of tempests, thunder, and catastrophe being followed by a new heaven and a new earth. Many wrote of a coming "golden time," of their faith in an approaching time when the "miracle of goodness" would triumph and crowds would emerge from "the depths of melancholy longing and barrenness" (*iz nedr toski i proziaban'ia*) to meet "the sacred truth" of the coming of a new world free of suffering and oppression.[67] An exiled trade unionist offered this catechism of faith from the far north: "I believe in the coming eternal happiness / I believe in the poetry of life, in goodness and love / I believe that after the storms and thunder / The burning sun will appear again."[68] As in much millenarian thinking, the coming of the new age was expected to reunite the dead with the liv-

---

[62] M. Gerasimov, "Krest," in *Sbornik proletarskikh pisatelei,* ed. M. Gor'kii, A. Serebrov, and A. Chapygin (Petrograd, [1917]), 3.

[63] M. Zakharov, "Nastroenie," *Rodnye vesti* 1911, no. 3 (4): 7.

[64] Kvadrat (Kubikov), "V. G. Korolenko i rabochaia demokratiia," *Zhivaia zhizn',* no. 1 (21 July 1913), 5.

[65] M. Tsarev, "V lesu" (1915), in *Proletarskie poety,* 3:36–37; S. Gan'shin, "Slyshite-l'?" *Vpered!* no. 115 (25 July 1917), 5.

[66] In addition to the many examples and citations in Chapter 4, see poems by Aleksei Mashirov, such as "Ruch'i," "Na rassvete vesennei zari," "Grebtsy," and "Vesennyi dozhd'," most of them first published in *Pravda* in 1912 and 1913, rpt. in *Poeziia v bol'shevistskikh izdaniiakh,* 218–19, 227, 304; P. Zaitsev, "Sapozhnik ia," *Kolotushka,* no. 4 ([Easter] 1911), 2; A. Pomorskii, "Vesennyi zvon," *Zhizn' pekarei,* no. 2 (29 June 1913), 4; Aleksandrovskii in *Novaia rabochaia gazeta,* no. 31 (13 Sept. 1913), 2.

[67] Il'ia Volodinskii, "Dumy naborshchika," *Nashe pechatnoe delo,* no. 18 (21 Feb. 1915), 5; I. K. Golikov, "Blagoslovi," in RGALI, f. 1068, op. 1, d. 41, l. 130b. See also Nechaev, "Starik," in *Vechernie pesni,* 96–97.

[68] O. R-n, "Iz ssylki," *Edinstvo,* no. 4 (23 Apr. 1909), 3.

ing. In Aleksei Bibik's autobiographical novel, the metalworker hero, Ignat Pasterniak, participates in an underground socialist study circle that reminds him "of the first days of Christianity, of the early zealots," and is led by an intellectual who even looks "a little like Christ." The circle meets at a cemetery, where Ignat feels the presence of "the spirits of those who died long ago" listening to their discussions.[69] Carrying this sort of image further, Aleksei Gastev envisioned the dead actually rising to join the struggle and even to lead the revolution: "We are coming! We cannot but come; the dark specters of fighters not long before struck down now arise; the living traditions of the past, fathers felled by wounds, stand up. We follow them."[70]

Many found it difficult to sustain such faith, however. Skepticism and even despair remained strong. The young socialist metalworker Vasilii Aleksandrovskii explored such disturbed feelings and thoughts while sitting beside a dying friend: here death appeared not as a moral symbol of an unjust social order or as a promise of deliverance, even into rest and oblivion, but as the final marker of life's grim course, of "dark, faceless dread / concealed somewhere, beyond the gloom."[71] Mikhail Gerasimov felt himself to be beyond meaningful suffering: "My soul . . . can now love no more, nor suffer / It is dead and empty."[72] Often these reflections expanded into more explicitly existential despair over life's meaning. The awakening of nature in springtime, for example, could be viewed not as a sign of hope but as only a reminder of the "melancholy, pain, and bitterness" in one's "weary soul," or of the truth that life's hardships "have no reason."[73] Many of these writers testified to shattered hopes for a "bright life," growing feelings of anguished melancholy and depression, a conviction that it was pointless to "ask for happiness," and a deepening sense of the meaninglessness of life.[74] Like so many of these proletarians, Sergei Obradovich succumbed to dark thoughts about existence:

> I thought to myself: in this world of vanities
> I am a hollow and superfluous thing,
> Nothing and unnoticed
> Beneath the weight of suffering and misfortune . . .

[69] Bibik, *K shirokoi doroge,* 41, 82–83.

[70] I. Dozorov [Gastev], "My Idem!" *Metallist* 1914, no. 1/38 (Jan. 13): 3–4.

[71] V. Aleksandrovskii, "Pered razsvetom (M. E. K.)," *Novaia rabochaia gazeta,* no. 9 (18 Aug. 1913), 2.

[72] M. Gerasimov, "V dushe rany zazhili davno," in RGALI, f. 1374, op. 1, d. 6, l. 10 (unpublished poem).

[73] S. Popov, "Vesna," *Chelovek,* no. 4 (24 Apr. 1911), 32.

[74] E.g., the many poems by V. Vegenov that were the featured literary works in *Novoe pechatnoe delo* in 1911 and 1912; Kvadrat [Kubikov], "V. G. Korolenko i rabochaia demokratiia," *Zhivaia zhizn',* no. 1 (21 July 1913), 5–6; S. Obradovich, "Zhizn'," *Sever Rossii* (Arkhangelsk), no. 1 (23 Aug. 1913), 3 (a cutting in RGALI, f. 1874, op. 1, d. 2, l. 10); S. Gan'shin, "Tiazhelo na dushe," a manuscript poem sent to Gorky, 1914, in Arkhiv A. M. Gor'kogo, RAV-PG, 37-13-1; Il'ia Volodinskii, "Dumy naborshchika," *Nashe pechatnoe delo,* no. 18 (21 Feb. 1915), 5; Vladimir Korolev, *Vsem skorbiashchim* (Iaroslavl, 1915), 5–6, 46 (Korolev was associated with the Iaroslavl printers' union, which published and distributed his poems both during the war and after the revolution).

> Loving all that the soulless world despised,
> I called upon death as if it were joy,
> And, in that indifferent darkness, in anguished doubt,
> I sought an answer to my question:
> Is there a place where life shimmers,
> Or are we fated to suffer forever?
> There was no answer.[75]

Like Obradovich, many thought to "call upon death" in the face of the silence that met their questions about meaning.

Others looked for the coming of saviors. The glassworker Egor Nechaev "prayed" to "freedom" that "in the dark of night," when his "eyes are breaking with tears" and his heart "can no longer endure the sorrow," she (not only is freedom feminine in Russian but the association of salvation with a "divine feminine" was an established cultural tradition) would come as a "savior" to "touch the sores" on his body with her "healing hand."[76] Others were more conventional in defining their savior, but as such more apocalyptic and radical. Filipp Shkulev, for example, described Christ returning to earth with a message of revolutionary deliverance from suffering: finding the people in agony—"harsh ranks of gloomy faces" and chains rattling in "gloomy prisons" framed by the golden cupolas on "rich cathedrals"—Christ, with blood seeping from his wounds, comforts a man bowed in lament and prayer: "Do not cry / A time will come, when the haughty butchers / As in an ocean seething with waves / Will be repaid in blood."[77] Many of these same writers, however, worried that no savior would ever come. Nechaev, especially in poems collected in his gloomily titled volume of 1913, *Vechernie pesni* (Evening songs), repeatedly wondered aloud, "Great God, when will you bring rest to your redeemed people?" and spoke of people (perhaps of himself) whose "prayers go without answer / Hopes perish without trace," and for whom "rays of hope and the flame of faith in God / long since burned out."[78]

Some worker writers saw *themselves* as possessing mysterious salvific powers. Ideas about the special mission and power of the writer were widespread in Russian culture. And writers from the common people, creating literature without formal education, had additional reason to see themselves as having been given a sacred "gift."[79] Many writers from among workers and peasants claimed that a "mysterious force" (*nevedomaia sila*) had compelled them to write.[80] Nechaev, for example, spoke of the appearance of a "delightful fire" that burned in his mind, calling him to a "distant unknown."

---

[75] Obradovich, "Bezsonnoiu noch'iu," *Severnoe utro* (Arkhangelsk), no. 52 (6 Mar. 1913), 2 (a cutting in RGALI, f. 1874, op. 1, d. 2, l. 8).

[76] E. Nechaev, "O svobode" (1907), in *Vechernie pesni*, 94–95.

[77] F. Shkulev, "Khristos," *Narodnaia mysl'*, no. 1 (January 1911), 14. Gan'shin has a similar poem in *Narodnaia sem'ia*, no. 3 (16 Jan, 1912), 1.

[78] E. Nechaev, "V bezsonnitsu," "Starik," "V tiurme," in *Vechernie pesni*, 96–98, 110; rpt. in *U istokov*, 93, 94, 97.

[79] *Narodniki*, no. 1 (1912), 2.

[80] M. Gor'kii, "O pisateliakh-samouchkakh" (1911), in *Sobranie sochinenii*, 24:105–8.

In hours of labor and in brief sleep,
Through the noise of machines and the talk of people,
It always, God knows from where,
Appears to me like a best friend:

Here in the tender whisper of a wave,
There in the rebirth of spring.[81]

For some, the verses and stories they created were sacred objects.[82] Ideas about the sacred value of writing and the mysterious power that inspired it were often bound up with notions that they themselves could come to the people as saviors. While some worker writers saw themselves as gentle redeemers, able to give comfort to the "sorrowing people" through "simple prayers" of catharsis and "quiet joy,"[83] others, such as Aleksandrovskii, represented themselves as coming to the people, like the Christ of the Gospels, not with peace but with a sword:

I will be there, where backs are bent
Where labor is profaned and defiled
Where cries of grief are heard
And the noise and roar of machines.
I will be there, where children perish
In the grasp of rough labor
Where unbearable need
Casts its nets.
I will instill in them indignation,
Protest and bitter vengeance against their enemies,
I will give them new thoughts
And instinctual distant desires.
Each are within me, and I am in everyone.
If you are bold enough, then together
We will penetrate the Mysteries of the World [*Tainy Mira*],
And from there take everything.[84]

Salvation often came upon wings. Human flight, of course, is a potent symbol, a dream of transcendent power and freedom, of a mystical break with the universe of everyday experience. Its roots lay equally in Christian tradition and older mythic cultures as well as, it has been argued, in the human subconscious. "Magical flight," as Mircea Eliade termed it, may be one of the most universal religious tropes, in which the boundaries of the everyday and the material world, and even of time and space, could be penetrated and transformed. Appearing in the folklore and sacred stories of many cultures—both

[81] Nechaev, "Moia pesnia," in *Vecherniia pesni*, 79–80 (also in *U istokov*, 92).

[82] S. Gan'shin, "K . . . ," manuscript poem sent to Gorky, 1914, in Arkhiv A. M. Gor'kogo, RAV-PG, 37-13-1.

[83] Korolev, *Vsem skorbiashchim*, 5–6.

[84] V. Aleksandrovskii, "Novye pesni," in *Nashi pesni*, vol. 1 (Moscow, 1913), 11.

as literal claims about the shamanistic powers of individuals and as metaphors of soaring spirits and winged ecstasy—magic flight can denote freedom from monstrous forces, a link between the profane and the sacred, a mysterious understanding and power, and transcendence above the physical bonds of the human condition.[85] Newer sources of thoughts of flight were also at hand, though the fundamental meanings remained the same. Nietzsche's influential superman was "an enemy of the spirit of gravity," who would "one day teach men to fly."[86] Gorky, too, mythologized flight as transcendent and emancipatory.[87]

Flight conveyed various meanings to worker writers. "Give me wings," cried Mariia Chernysheva,

> . . . light, swift wings
> And I would fly to the clear and all-powerful sun. . . .
> . . . toward freedom, toward the expanse.
> I would toss my chains away, the slave's shameful chains
> That shackle my body. . . .
> Give me wings! Swift, light wings. . . .
> I would revel in the freedom of flight.[88]

While Chernysheva prayed for wings and endowed them with classic powers of escape and freedom, more politicized worker poets saw them as being bestowed on those who joined the class struggle, though with much the same power. In Aleksei Bibik's 1912 novel, when the worker hero is first experiencing the awe and freedom of a strike, he declares that "wings" had appeared on his back.[89] A more collective vision was offered in a prose poem that appeared in the newspaper of the Petersburg metalworkers' union in 1913, written by Aleksei Gastev, then a leader of the union.

> Nothing frightens us: we push on through deserts and thickets! . . .
> Mountains meet us . . .
> We go to the mountaintops, we take them!
> Higher still, yet higher! In the smoke of victory, we dash from the highest rocks,
> from the most treacherous cliffs to the most distant heights!
> We have no wings?
> We will! They will be born in an explosion of burning wish.[90]

Repeatedly worker writers envisioned themselves symbolically in magical flight returning to earth as saviors. Egor Nechaev wished that he were an ea-

[85] Mircea Eliade, *Myths, Dreams, and Mysteries* (New York, 1960), 99–110.
[86] Friedrich Nietzsche, *Thus Spoke Zarathustra*, trans. Walter Kaufmann (New York, 1966), 192. *Tak govoril Zaratustra* was first published in Russia in 1898.
[87] See esp. his "Pesnia o sokole" (1895) and "Pesnia o burevestnike" (1901).
[88] M. Chernysheva, "Daite mne kryl'ia!" *Dumy narodnye,* no. 3 (13 Feb. 1910), 5.
[89] Bibik, *K shirokoi doroge,* 71.
[90] I. Dozorov [Gastev], "My Idem!" *Metallist* 1914, no. 1/38 (13 Jan.), 3–4.

gle or the sun, bringing happiness and freedom to the world.[91] Sergei Gan'shin described himself as "an eagle from the skies . . . from which my mighty voice / like a tocsin" rings out for victory "in the great and sacred struggle."[92] And Aleksei Mashirov portrayed advanced workers like himself coming to the people in inspiring flight: as birds in a black sky, as flashes of summer lightening, or as a "meteor falling into the deep abyss"—a momentary evanescence, a redeeming sacrifice, illumining the way for others.[93]

However metaphoric, winged human flight inescapably gave the ideas represented—escape, freedom, struggle—a mythic quality. By choosing this image, writers blurred the line separating secular notions of civic and social emancipation from transcendent and mystical visions of liberation. This was not a stylistic inconsistency but a reflection of perceptions and attitudes that themselves may have been unstable and ambiguous but could not avoid reaching for images that lay beyond the everyday and the profane. Even the normally cool-headed Ivan Kubikov—the Menshevik printer and literary critic—writing in the paper of the Petersburg printers' union in 1912, found compelling the fantasy of Gleb Uspenskii, born of an apparent mental illness that afflicted his last years, that he could fly and that the sight of him soaring above the world would shame the oppressors and inspire the oppressed, bringing about the reign of God's kingdom on earth.[94]

A Cult of Feeling

The emotions—which is to say, again, the self—were at the heart of much of this religious writing. When the Marxist Vasilii Aleksandrovskii declared that he felt "close to the newborn God" as Christmas approached, this was a matter not of Christian faith but of an admittedly mysterious spiritual pleasure— "a sharp knocking within my soul / from where I do not know"—at feelings evoked by glistening silver snow, winter stars, and "trembling nature."[95] In Sergei Gan'shin's metaphoric temple of truth and love, the altar was illumined "with the fire of feeling," in this case of the feelings of insult and injury felt by the people.[96] It would not be an overstatement to speak of a cult of feeling in workers' writings. This was part of the meaning of their preoccupation with the suffering and awakened self and especially with the self in the mod-

[91] Nechaev, "Pesnia nevol'nika," in *Vechernie pesni*, 151, and *U istokov*, 98–99.

[92] S. Gan'shin, "Orel," a manuscript poem sent to Gorky, 1914, in Arkhiv A. M. Gor'kogo, RAV-PG, 37-13-1; "Orlam," *Vpered!* no. 121 (1/14 Aug. 1917), 2.

[93] Samobytnik (A. Mashirov), "Zarnitsy," *Proletarskaia pravda*, 18 Sept. 1913, and "Moim sobrat'iam," *Prosnuvshaiasia zhizn'* (manuscript journal) (1913), both rpt. in *Proletarskie poety*, 2:89–90; see also in the same volume "Grebtsy" (1912), 87. Sergei Gan'shin also imagined himself as a "meteor" bringing light to "human darkness": "Ia syn stepei," *Zhivoe slovo*, no. 20 (May 1913), 6; also in *Vpered!* no. 112 (21 July 1917).

[94] *Pechatnoe delo* 1912, no. 5 (May 11): 9.

[95] V. Aleksandrovskii, "V noch' pod Rozhdestvo," *Zhivoe slovo* 1913, no. 51–52 (December): 6.

[96] S. Gan'shin, "Postroim Khram," *Vpered!* no. 157 (14 Sept. 1917), 3.

ern world. Fascinated by the feelings inspired by suffering and dreaming, which they read as holding universal meaning, they viewed strong feeling as a virtue and the voice of feeling as the ultimate measure of truth. It was also, we have seen, thought to be a marker of class difference and pride: workers were forced by their material lives to experience the world more intensely and to feel differently from other people. And feelings, of course, were thought to matter most in the search for truth.[97]

This neo-Romantic (and, in some cases, workerist) cult of feelings naturally embraced the sacred, for it was made of the same stuff. Lunacharsky and other Marxist God-builders recognized that religion's power lay in its response to people's emotional needs: their deep need to feel transcendent passion, for ethical certainty that good was knowable and that evil would be punished, and for faith that death, the most primal human fear, was not omnipotent. Worker writers used a language of the sacred for much the same reason: as a vehicle of emotional, moral, and existential meaning. It has often been observed that feeling is central to the constitution of the sacred. In the view of Rudolf Otto, whose 1917 book *Das Heilige* was the most popular book on religion in its time, the sacred was a work of emotional experience, of terror and awe before the *mysterium tremendum*. Other historians of religion have similarly underscored the essential place of emotion in defining what is sacred. Religion, it has been argued, fundamentally involves the use of symbols to evoke moods linked to transcendental interpretations of life—to see meaning in the chaos of existence, to name the good and predict its triumph, and to give form to potent feelings of mystery, awe, and the sublime. This emotional spirit is essential: there is no sacred, and hence no religion, without the play of sensibilities, passions, nostalgia, and imagination.[98]

The writing of Russian workers before 1917, in these terms, was deeply religious, even when it did not explicitly make use of religious symbols, images, and metaphors. Indeed, one might suggest that the life and work of a typical plebeian writer was much like that of a shaman. When we recall the self-narratives of worker writers' lives, we find stories of childhood and youth much like those said to typify the archetypical shaman, at least metaphorically: a stranger, growing beyond his own community, who "seeks solitude, becomes a dreamer, loves to wander in the woods or desert places, has visions, sings in his sleep." The shaman feels that he has been called to a different life. He becomes "singer, poet, musician, seer, priest," and with great "energy and self-mastery" becomes a prophet and visionary for those around him. His driving goal is "to see"—to look at the world and see truths that others cannot. And, of course, the shaman is often believed to be able to fly.[99]

---

[97] F. Kalinin, "Tip rabochego v literature," *Novyi zhurnal dlia vsekh* 1912, no. 9 (September): 96–97, 106.

[98] See esp. Clifford Geertz, "Religion as a Cultural System," in *The Interpretation of Cultures* (New York, 1973), esp. 89–103; Mircea Eliade, *The Sacred and the Profane: The Nature of Religion* (New York, 1959) and *Myths, Dreams, and Mysteries*, esp. 74, 107.

[99] Eliade, *Myths, Dreams, and Mysteries*, 66, 75–84.

When Russian worker writers wrote in an explicitly religious idiom, these writings were sometimes, we must recognize, literal professions of faith. But more often they were complex ways of speaking in universalizing terms about sacred moral right and especially of voicing the imagination, articulating things sublime and terrible, and speaking of the mythic and the mysterious—of "seeing," "flying," witnessing, and perhaps saving. This was simultaneously an interpretive and a sentimental practice. When a worker viewed the cruel and often senseless reality of his life, even if only metaphorically, as a religious journey, it may have become emotionally understandable and bearable. Suffering was ennobled and valued as a sign of moral goodness; one's tormentors were damned; and affliction was made to contain the promise of salvation. There were dark moments of doubt and despair—of hearing no answer to questions about life's meaning. And images of the apocalypse, of storms, blood, and death, did not always bring certainty of resurrection and salvation. At best, sometimes one's sufferings could become precious and powerful only as a mark of sanctifying and dignifying experience. But for most of these writers most of the time, stories and images of the sacred were positive and hopeful: impassioned, ethical, and imbued with confidence in a coming "golden time" when "truth and beauty" would be at their place in the altar. For many, the October revolution was that time. Or should be.

7 Sacred Vision in the Revolution

We want to sweep away everything that claims to be supernatural
and superhuman.
> —Friedrich Engels, 1844

[We see] some sort of admixture of Christian zealotry, Tolstoyism,
and Dostoevskyism, . . . incomprehensible pessimism, . . .
mysticism. . . . These motifs, alien to the proletariat, clearly stand
out in their contradiction to other moods.
> —P. I Lebedev-Polianskii, 1919

In September 1918, as a contribution to Lenin's plan to decorate Soviet cities
with instructive statues, bas-reliefs, and inscribed plaques and stone walls, the
cultural journal of the Moscow Soviet recommended to its readers Ivan
Shadr's idea for a "Monument to the World's Suffering," a large architectural
and sculptural ensemble conceived during the war by an artist "from the laboring classes."[1] In its function and symbolism the monument was a shrine
within which the visitor could experience a journey of spiritual awakening and
deliverance. To enter the monument, the visitor passes through a narrow gate
at the base of a massive granite wall inscribed with quotations from the Bible
about eternal life and guarded by four female colossi, heads bowed, representing Creation, Courage, Wisdom, and Eternity. Walking into a large court-
yard, the visitor comes upon a long pool—a "lake of tears," according to
Shadr. Before this pool, which is "deathly still," stands a white marble statue
representing Charity, inscribed with words from the book of Job: "Man born
of woman is short-lived and full of sorrow. Like a flower, he blossoms and

---

[1] Born Ivan Ivanov, Shadr was the son of a carpenter. As a youth he worked in a variety of
manual jobs, drawing pictures in his spare time, until the city council of his native town,
Shadrinsk, agreed to finance his studies in art school and then in Italy. See O. Voronova, ed.,
Shadr: Literaturnoe nasledie, perepiski, vospominaniia o skul'ptore (Moscow, 1978), 47–63; and
idem, *Shadr* (Moscow, 1969).

withers; he slips away like a shadow, leaving no trace."[2] On a smooth granite slab nearby lies the figure of a handsome dead youth, his face expressing "aloneness in the universe," and near him a statue of a young girl, frozen in a scream, symbolically protesting death. On the opposite side of the lake of tears she is echoed by a figure symbolizing youth and motherhood, which represent the natural striving to transcend death.

Looming over the far end of the pool is a colossal stone pyramid, representing "humanity's Golgotha with countless steps of suffering." Into the face of the pyramid is set an ancient wooden cross, a "symbol of suffering and redemption," with a granite figure of pious and suffering Job at its base. The visitor enters an opening in the pyramid and descends dark stairs toward a doorway deep in the tomb. Entering through the door, the visitor is surrounded by an "uncommon light." He is in the Chapel of Resurrection. Its walls are covered with bright mosaics and a stone floor reflects light entering the room through a "window-projector." Overhead, in a golden cupola, is a mosaic titled "Praise of Eternity," and on the walls, "written in fiery letters," are the words "Your dead will come to life, their bodies will stand again." When the visitor finally emerges from the monument, he feels "at peace, his soul one with eternity and revealed goodness, literally given sight and wisdom."[3]

Shadr's sacred vision, publicized and warmly endorsed by a government publication, was not at odds with Russia's emerging revolutionary culture. To be sure, Vladimir Friche, the Marxist cultural critic who introduced Shadr's project to Soviet readers, assured them that Shadr recognized the need to rework this "Christian variant," originally conceived in 1915–16, into a socialist work. But the required changes were not expected to alter anything of substance. The "socialist variant," even according to Friche, would still lead the visitor "through torment and sorrow, in unceasing struggle for liberation from all chains, toward a pyramid of light, perfection, and happiness." And Shadr himself insisted that he continued to believe "in the possibility of a great new art similar to the religious art of the past."[4] To become socialist art, this monument needed to be cleansed only of its literal religiosity, not of its religious feeling or its essentially religious metaphor.

Religion and the Revolution

The Soviet state and the ruling Communist party had an ambivalent relationship with religion and the sacred. On the one hand, as has often been described, the Bolsheviks embarked on a steadily escalating crusade against the church and religious faith. The campaign against established religion was an

---

[2] Job 14:1–2. This and other scriptural quotations are rendered into English from the Russian translation.

[3] *Tvorchestvo*, no. 5 (September 1918), 21–24.

[4] Ibid., 21.

essential component of their efforts to "modernize" Russia, which meant, by their definition, enabling a secular and rationalist worldview to displace the superstition, mysticism, and "fictional knowledge" (Trotsky's term) of religion. Initially this campaign was directed mainly against the church as an institution and the clergy as a social category. Almost immediately after coming to power, the Bolsheviks disestablished the Orthodox church, which had been closely linked to the monarchical state, declaring religion a "personal matter" and giving equality and full freedom to other faiths. In practice, the state ended all financial support for the church, confiscated vast amounts of property not needed directly for worship, deprived the clergy of most social rights, transferred control of many thousands of church schools to the state, and removed religious instruction from the curriculum of state schools. During the civil war, when the patriarch, Tikhon, regularly denounced the Bolsheviks (having anathematized them in the summer of 1918) and much of the higher clergy sided with the White opposition, revolutionaries frequently arrested and sometimes summarily executed priests and monks, confiscated or destroyed sacramental objects, and closed many churches and monasteries. These assaults against church and clergy were not all by central directive. These were times also of a great deal of local initiative by activists, some of it decried officially as "excesses" and "abuses," though generally tolerated: deliberate provocations by antireligious activists during religious services, violent seizures and destruction of property, and beatings, torture, and murder of clergy. Once victorious in the civil war, the government began to move still more vigorously against the church. In 1922 the government ordered the seizure of all church valuables, arrested the patriarch, and supported a pro-Soviet "renovationist" movement within the church.

Perhaps surprisingly, while the church was under sustained attack in these years, belief was initially left alone. Partly this forbearance reflected confidence that religion would quickly collapse under the weight of its own visible errors as secular education and a more modern public spirit imbued rational and scientific thinking in the population, and as the church lost its function of legitimizing state authority. But no less important—and suggesting an uncertainty about the strength of religion—the new government did not feel secure enough in its own authority, especially among the majority of rural lower-class Russians, to risk provoking open popular opposition by directly challenging deeply held religious feelings. As a result, these first years saw only modest antireligious rhetoric in public life. Religious instruction was removed from education, occasional antireligious speeches were made and pamphlets published, and a few reliquaries of venerated saints were demonstrably opened (to show the corruption of the body, which many believers assumed could not have occurred). Soon after the civil war was over and won, however, this campaign took a new turn.

Starting at the end of 1922, belief became the main target of the battle against religion. This shift followed the overall logic of the NEP period, when Soviet leaders more realistically acknowledged the obstacles they faced in transforming Russia—economic, structural, cultural—and resolved to engage in a slow struggle of institution building, education, and persuasion. Thus physical attacks on the visible church—which can be seen as having been inspired by a materialistic and utopian faith that once the material foundation was destroyed, the mental superstructure would change, but which in practice often won the church new sympathy—were largely replaced by a war of ideas, words, and rituals. The patriarch and other clergy were released from prison and direct persecutions lessened. At the same time a storm of atheist propaganda was unleashed: periodicals, pamphlets, books, posters, lectures, debates, reading circles, workplace meetings, theatrical performances, films, processions, and festivals. National organizations of the "godless" (*bezbozhniki*) played a large part in these campaigns. Befitting the more embracive and intrusive focus on belief itself, the target was now not only Orthodoxy but also dissident and sectarian belief. Local activists, unofficially though not without encouragement, often went beyond the formal scripts to insult believers, destroy religious objects, and occasionally assault and even murder priests.[5]

Alongside these official campaigns against the church and belief, the conditions of the revolution nurtured religion and a religious spirit—partly as a paradoxical effect of antireligious campaigns, partly thanks to the initial neglect of belief and the inner world of believers, partly as a result of the new legal tolerance of non-Orthodox religions, but also as a direct result of the revolutionary enthusiasms, expectations, and vision stimulated by the revolution and by Bolshevik radicalism. Attacks on the church inspired resistance and solidarity with church and clergy in many areas of the country. Even more important, the withdrawal of state financial support from the church, the secularization of the schools, and the banning of the right of clergy to charge for their services helped to stimulate lay community activism, especially in the countryside, in order to maintain church buildings, support clergy, and promote religious education. Village assemblies and even village soviets often showed great initiative and energy in working to ensure the vitality of the local ecclesial community.[6] At the same time, the disestablishment of the Orthodox Church, which meant the legal equalization and tolerance of other religions (first de facto and then in the 1918 constitution), ended discriminatory and restrictive policies that had hindered the growth of "sectarian" faiths, and so helped them to grow as well. But the religious ferment was not simply a result of the Bolsheviks' efforts to undermine the church.

The revival of faith and spirituality was also part of a much larger story of

[5] John Shelton Curtis, *The Russian Church and the Soviet State* (Boston, 1953); Dimitry V. Pospielovsky, *A History of Marxist-Leninist Atheism and Soviet Anti-Religious Policies* (New York, 1987); Richard Stites, *Revolutionary Dreams: Utopian Vision and Revolutionary Life in the Russian Revolution* (Oxford, 1989), 105–9; Glennys Young, *Power and the Sacred in Revolutionary Russia: Religious Activists in the Village* (University Park, Pa., 1997); Daniel Peris, *Storming the Heavens: The Soviet League of the Militant Godless* (Ithaca, 1998).

[6] Young, *Power and the Sacred*.

renewed spirituality and religiosity in Russia, which began before the war and was stimulated, especially among the lower classes, by the revolutions of 1917 and the civil war and the upheavals that followed. The devastations, uncertainties, possibilities, enthusiasms, and hopes of these years encouraged many Russians to turn to religion and other forms of sacred vision and spiritual culture. The editors of a Tolstoyan magazine observed in 1920 that the revolution, by "destroying all of the connections in people's lives," stimulated a "huge growth of religious and, in general, spiritual interest among the common people." The "hurricane of events" of the last few years, the editors argued, "stunned man and deprived him of the vital ability to comprehend the external world." As a result, one saw "man's inner hearing revitalized, his spiritual sight rediscovered, and the birth of a deep need to resolve the question of the indestructible, eternal meaning of human existence."[7] A participant in one of the literary circles for workers and peasants organized by the Commissariat of Enlightenment similarly described the growing interest in religion among the many people who felt "disoriented" by the revolution.[8] Many Russians perceived the revolution as an apocalyptic moment, as a time not of forward linear progress but of a sacred break in temporality, as the end of time in which unprecedented disorder would also open the possibilities of unparalleled renewal and even salvation.[9] Finally, many were drawn to religion by the positive force of the revolution—its promise of a new spirit and order, its moral vision, and its utopian enthusiasm. In varied ways, people were inclined to view revolutionary politics and culture in sacred terms.

Whatever the differing reasons and moods, these first years of revolution, civil war, and socialist construction witnessed an undeniable resurgence of religious sensibilities and practices. In Russia, as in other places and times, religious ideas and traditions offered a way of seeing and understanding revolution that could reach beyond the limits of secular ideologies, openly oppose them, mix and blend with them syncretically, or do all these things at once. Certainly large numbers of Russians, especially among the lower classes, could understand the revolutionary upheavals of 1917 in religious terms. As some historians of the revolution have observed, the language of revolution and of socialist democracy appealed to ordinary Russians precisely because it resonated so strongly with Christian ideals and vision.[10] Thus we see many

---

[7] *Istinnaia svoboda*, no. 1 (April 1920), 2.

[8] *Revoliutsionnye vskhody*, no. 3–4 (October 1920), 3–4.

[9] Robert C. Williams, "The Russian Revolution and the End of Time," *Jahrbücher für Geschichte Osteuropas* 43, no. 3 (1995): 364–401; Igal Halfin, *From Darkness to Light: Class, Consciousness, and Salvation in Revolutionary Russia* (Pittsburg, 2000).

[10] T. A. Abrosimova, "Sotsialisticheskaia ideia v massovom soznanii 1917 g.," in *Anatomiia Revoliutsii*, ed. V. Iu. Cherniaev et al. (St. Petersburg, 1994), 176–77; B. I. Kolonitskii, "Antiburzhuaznaia propaganda i 'antiburzhuaznoe' soznanie," ibid., 199–200 (a translation appeared in *Russian Review*, April 1994); Orlando Figes, "The Russian Revolution of 1917 and Its Language in the Village," *Russian Review* 56 (July 1997): 327–29, 332, 335, 344; Orlando Figes and Boris Kolonitskii, *Interpreting the Russian Revolution: The Language and Symbols of 1917* (New Haven, 1999), 75, 84, 145–46, 150–51; Mark D. Steinberg, *Voices of Revolution, 1917* (New Haven, 2001), Introduction.

lower-class Russians publicly defining the revolution as the triumph of Christian values. Soldiers, for example, when appealing in 1917 for an end to the war, often argued that it was wrong to kill men who "are not our enemies but are our brothers in the cross and in the divine commandments," and many peasants insisted that the land must belong to those who work it because "the land belongs to almighty God as his creation." For many Russians the revolution was "blessed" by God and was even God's will, a "Great Joy" for which he should be thanked.[11] Many Protestants and evangelicals, though often skeptical about the possibility of salvation in this world before Christ's return, sympathized with the revolution's drive to create a new moral order and often intermixed the language of religion and revolution: they spoke, for example, of Russia's "resurrection" and of a "revolution of the spirit" as following naturally the completed state revolution.[12] A number of educated Russians, especially those who had been seeking religious and spiritual truths beyond the conventional boundaries of the established church, similarly greeted the revolution as a moment of rare spiritual possibility: "the transfigured people, having conquered the darkness, will also conquer themselves," prophesied the journal of the Russian Theosophical Society in 1917. The new Russia "will give the world a new religious consciousness, a divine revelation . . . for a pure, virginal Spring of creativity has been revealed in the depths of the national soul."[13]

The years after 1917 experienced, contemporaries noted, "a wider and wider outpouring throughout Russia of the streams and rivers of free-religious, extra-church, and 'sectarian' movements."[14] This flood was not all outside the bounds of the Orthodox Church. Orthodox clergy often successfully attracted people to new "religious-cultural societies," public discussions (*besedy*) on religious themes, and choirs to sing sacred music. The "renovationist" movement in the church in the early 1920s, though partly a political and opportunistic accommodation to the new state, was also partly a sincere and successful effort by some clergy to build more democratic bonds between clergy and the faithful. In rural areas, many Communists continued to participate in and even organize religious ceremonies such as processions of the cross and church weddings and to venerate icons.[15] Particular dynamism was

[11] Letter to Minister of War Guchkov from soldiers of the 64th Infantry Division of the active army, 13 April 1917, in *Revoliutsionnoe dvizhenie v Rossii v aprele 1917 g.: Aprel'skii krizis* (Moscow, 1958), 497–98; letter-essay by the peasant Semyon Martynov, August 1917, in GARF, f. 1778, op. 1, d. 234, ll. 88–89ob; song by factory worker, March 1917, in GARF, f. 1244, op. 2, d. 31, l. 14; letter to *Izvestiia* from the peasant Nikolai Burakov, 30 Mar. 1917, in GARF, f. 1244, op. 2, d. 5, l. 3–30b. These texts appear in Steinberg, *Voices of Revolution, 1917*.

[12] Heather Coleman, "The Most Dangerous Sect: Baptists in Tsarist and Soviet Russia, 1905–1929," Ph.D. diss., University of Illinois, 1998, chap. 5.

[13] *Vestnik teosofii* 2 (1917): 5–6, quoted in Maria Carlson, *"No Religion Higher than Truth": A History of the Theosophical Movement in Russia, 1875–1922* (Princeton, 1993), 172.

[14] *Istinnaia svoboda*, no. 1 (April 1920), 2.

[15] Young, *Power and the Sacred*, 163–64, 198, 244–47; Edward Roslof, "The Renovationist Movement in the Russian Orthodox Church, 1922–1946," Ph. D. diss., University of North Carolina at Chapel Hill, 1994.

to be found outside Orthodox communities, however, especially before the antireligion campaigns of the mid-1920s. Among the urban educated, such organizations as the Free Philosophical Society in Petrograd, the Free Academy of Spiritual Culture in Moscow, and the Free Association of Spiritual Trends attracted thousands of visitors to their discussions on the spiritual in art and culture.[16] The number of rural and especially urban Tolstoyan groups grew steadily after 1917, and public talks by Tolstoyans—on themes such as "Love One Another" and on how to interpret war and revolution—or about Tolstoyism were increasingly popular, especially among urban workers.[17] The editors of the national journal of workers' clubs noted among its readers and authors "a gigantic interest in religious questions."[18] Evangelical Christians benefited especially from the new freedom and continuing religious searching in the country. In 1917 and after, Baptists and other evangelicals experienced a surge in conversions and an enormous expansion of organized activities, including national associations, publications, congresses, Bible schools, and missionary work, and local congregations organized thriving women's and youth groups, choirs, and religious festivals. In some places Christian evangelical agricultural communes were organized and the first steps were taken toward establishing a grand settlement to be known as the City of the Sun or Evangel'sk. Similar successes were to be found among still less orthodox believers—Adventists, Dukhobors, Molokans, Mennonites, and others—until, that is, the antireligious campaign got fully under way after 1922, though the full force of state repression came only later in the 1920s.[19]

Not all religion in the revolution was literal. As we have noted, some Marxists had earlier sought to infuse the revolutionary movement with the spirit of religion, with its moral fervor, emotional comforts, and faith in the possibilities of a renewed world and even of transcending the physical limitations of everyday life. They sought not so much a secular "godless religion" as a religion constructed consciously out of the human imagination, solely for the good of the human race, though built of the same emotional materials. One worker poet, characteristically, dreamed of a "red holiday" that could replace Easter: he knew that as a revolutionary he could no longer go to church, but he also could not forget the emotional qualities of this sacred time, when "Christ was close and simple," and his soul rediscovered depths of feeling that had been forgotten amidst everyday life and the noise of the factory.[20] Recognizing the powerful effect of ritual and sacred symbols on the emotions, the Communist state answered the needs of such workers by beginning, in the early 1920s, to develop its own set of emotionally resonant symbols and prac-

[16] Carlson, *"No Religion Higher than Truth"*, 174–76.

[17] *Istinnaia svoboda*, no. 2 (May 1920), 27–28, and no. 4 (July 1920), 31; *Sbornik Kostromskogo proletkul'ta*, no. 1 (1919), 13; A. Sh., "L. N. Tolstoi," *Revoliutsionnye vskhody*, no. 7–8 (December 1920), 10–11.

[18] *Revoliutsionnye vskhody*, no. 3–4 (October 1920), 16.

[19] Coleman, "Most Dangerous Sect," 295, 241, 365–91; Stites, *Revolutionary Dreams*, 121.

[20] I. Kustov, "Krasnyi prazdnik," in *V bure i plameni* (Iaroslavl, 1918), 49.

tices—its own "counterreligion" and "counterfaith," as it has been called. Revolutionary calendrical festivals were designed to compete with religious ones. Workers' clubs were treated as civic temples that could nurture a healthy and satisfying godless spiritual life. New ceremonies were invented to mark both personal and communal rites of passage—such as Octobering rituals (*Oktiabrina*) to replace baptism, Red weddings, and Red funerals—though they were generally unsuccessful. Public life was filled with unceasing moralistic didacticism as Communist leaders sermonized the population in word and print to work well, drink less, develop good hygiene, and avoid uncultured leisure activities. Finally, party and state activists tried to create a new socialist community through ritualized moments of common faith and emotion: through great civic festivals that marked out times and spaces apart from everyday existence and that engaged spectators in a symbolic and often mythologized vision of the world; through a visual iconography of the struggle of good against evil, often seen in both posters and festive performances, in which the opposition was portrayed as between dark and light, ugliness and beauty, heroes and monsters; through death rituals that cast fallen revolutionaries as martyrs; through marking space as new by renaming streets and other places; and especially through a growing cult of Lenin, who, even before the full-blown devotional cult inspired by his death in 1924, was eulogized as saint, apostle, and prophet, as the "light of truth" who brought to the suffering world "revealed mysteries" and who possessed an omniscient "revolutionary gaze" and a "miraculous heart."[21]

The public revolutionary discourse of these years was especially marked by a profusion of religious imagery and emotion. As a leading historian of 1917 has written, "From the Revolution was often expected not only concrete social and political changes, but a Miracle—rapid and universal purification and 'resurrection.'"[22] In appeals and letters to authority, lower-class Russians often spoke of the revolution as a time of resurrection for both Russia as a nation and Russians as free individuals. Above all, it was said repeatedly, the revolution and its goals of liberty, equality, and fraternity were sacred and holy (*sviatoi*). The revolution was often said to be a struggle for sacred "truth": for *istina*, the transcendent and essential spiritual truth, which the Scriptures defined as God's essence and as a power that can "make you free,"[23] and especially for *pravda*, the sacred moral truth, the truth of earthly justice, righ-

---

[21] Stites, *Revolutionary Dreams*, 109–23; James von Geldern, *Bolshevik Festivals, 1917–1920* (Berkeley, 1993); Victoria Bonnell, *Iconography of Power: Soviet Political Posters under Lenin and Stalin* (Berkeley, 1997); Nina Tumarkin, *Lenin Lives! The Lenin Cult in Soviet Russia* (Cambridge, Mass., 1983), esp. chap. 3; *Rabochii klub* 1924, no. 2 (February): 35. Most of the quotations are from workers' writings: Rabochii A. Rumiantsev, "V. I. Leninu," *Tvorchestvo*, no. 7 (November 1918), 22; S. Obradovich, "Truby," *Krasnoarmeets*, no. 21–22 (1920); A. Platonov, "Lenin," *Krasnaia derevnia*, 11 Apr. 1920; V. Kazin, "Da zdravstvuet V. I. Lenin," *Kuznitsa*, no. 1 (May 1920), 3; I. Filipchenko, "Lenin," *Rabochii zhurnal* 1924, no. 1: 59;

[22] Kolonitskii, "Antiburzhuaznaia propaganda," 200. See also A. M. Selishchev, *Iazyk revoliutsionnoi epokhi* (Moscow, 1928), 67–68, 126.

[23] John 8:32. See also Isa. 65:16 and John 16:13. In the Russian translations, *istina* is used for "truth" in these cases.

teousness, honesty, and goodness, but which is no less sacred (in the words of the Russian Psalter, "*pravda* comes down from the heavens" [*pravda s nebes priniche*]).[24] These terms pervaded popular appeals in 1917.[25]

The Bolshevik state and party, especially during the civil war years, deployed similar language and images. A "Proletarian Ten Commandments" was published by the government (as was a Ten Commandments for members of workers' clubs),[26] and posters often depicted workers or soldiers iconographically riding winged (and sometimes red) horses while holding sacred texts or as modern St. Georges, often dressed archaically, slaying the dragons of social and political evil. Leading writers sympathetic to the revolution—notably Andrei Belyi, Aleksandr Blok, Sergei Esenin, and Sergei Kliuev—openly linked these upheavals, perhaps symbolically or perhaps literally, to the second coming of Christ and to messianic promises of salvation. Even some Communist writers treated the revolution as an apocalyptic moment, as in Vladimir Maiakovskii's 1918 mystery play *Mystery-Bouffe,* in which the arrival of a Christ-like savior, the "Simple Man," allowed the sudden crossing of a threshold into a new time and space.[27]

Working-class writers were especially likely to view the revolution in sacred and even messianic terms. For some, this was a function of religious belief. Although many religious worker authors did not find a place (and presumably did not seek one) in the new "proletarian culture," and hence disappeared from the public record, other believing workers did. Some, such as Fedor Shkulev, joined the party and ceased to write, at least publicly, about Christ and God. Some, such as I. G. Ustinov, criticized the new regime as insufficiently communist in neglecting the teachings of Jesus Christ.[28] Others, such as Petr Oreshin, though hostile to the church, actively imagined a syncretic and millenarian Christian socialism—for which he was frequently criticized in the Communist press and marginalized (despite his working-class origins)

[24] Vladimir Dal', *Tolkovyi slovar' zhivago velikorusskago iazyka* (St. Petersburg, 1881), 2:60, 3:379. Psalm 84:12 reads, "Istina iz zemli vozsiia, i pravda s nebese priniche" (*Istina* springs forth from the earth, and *pravda* comes down from heaven). The King James Version (where this verse is 85:11) translates these terms respectively as "truth" and "righteousness" (accurately rendering the Hebrew Bible's *emes* and *tsedek*). The Revised Standard and New International Bibles translate what the Russian Bible calls *istina* as "faithfulness."

[25] For discussion and examples of this popular language of the sacred in 1917, see Steinberg, *Voices of Revolution, 1917,* esp. 30–32.

[26] Tumarkin, *Lenin Lives!,* 69; "Desiat' zapovedei dlia chlenov klubov," *Revoliutsionnue vskhody,* no. 5–6 (November 1920), 14.

[27] See, notably, Andrei Belyi, "Khristos voskres" (Christ is risen, 1918) and Aleksandr Blok, "Dvenadtsat'" (The twelve, 1918). See discussion in von Geldern, *Bolshevik Festivals,* 63–71, 79–81; Jay Bergman, "The Image of Jesus in the Russian Revolutionary Movement: The Case of Russian Marxism," *International Review of Social History* 35 (1990): 236–45; Robert C. Williams, *Artists in Revolution* (Bloomington, 1977), 138; Bernice Glatzer Rosenthal, "Eschatology and the Appeal of Revolution: Merezhkovsky, Bely, Blok," *California Slavic Studies* 11 (1980): 105–39. For a contemporary discussion, see S. Spasskii in *Zarevo zavodov,* no. 1 (January 1919), 63–67.

[28] *Gudki,* no. 5 (May 1919), 25. See also the answer of an unknown worker participant in the 1920 congress of proletarian writers who identified his "literary tendency" as "obligatory reading of Jesus Christ": RGALI, f. 1638, op. 3, d. 4.

as a "peasant writer."[29] At the very least, in these first post-October years many worker writers continued to write of religion as memory: autobiographical sketches and fictionalized stories often positively and nostalgically recalled moments such as coming upon crosses and golden cupolas while walking amidst the mint smells of the Russian forest, and portrayed workers on pilgrimage, meditating before images on an icon, reading religious texts, and praying to God to end the world's misery or their own sufferings.[30] Most often, however, as before 1917, images of religion appeared in workers' writings for their symbolic and emotional force: as a way to express knowledge and truths best understood through the emotions, to evoke a sense of the mystery and sublime power they felt in the world and in the revolution.

Moral Passion

Christian ethics continued to appeal to many workers, including party members, as they thought about the revolution. At least, many continued to present moral arguments as matters of transcendent truth and as deserving objects of passion. In the journal of the Petrograd Proletcult, Pavel Bessal'ko, a metalworker with a long career in the Social Democratic underground, argued strongly, much as Anatoly Lunacharsky had done in his book *Religiia i sotsializm,* for the subversive and empowering nature of early Christianity, identifying it even as an alternative class culture of the poor:

> In those times . . . the culture of the poor sought to free itself from the grip of the morally suffocating culture of the upper classes. To the principle of dividing people by nations they counterposed [the principle that] the poor among all peoples are brothers. Against the principle of private property they argued that it is easier for a camel to pass through the eye of a needle than for a rich man to enter the kingdom of heaven.

In time this Christian "slave culture" overwhelmed and destroyed the old order, replacing opulence and private property with Christian simplicity and "communism." Even religion was democratized in this process: in the place of the old gods was "put a man—a working man." But eventually this primitive Christianity was corrupted and made to serve wealth and power—sym-

---

[29] *Proletarskaia kul'tura,* no. 6 (February 1919), 43–44. He had defenders, however, who argued that these criticisms were narrow-minded and falsely understood communism. After all, one supporter wrote, "it is possible to be a religious-minded revolutionary and an atheist counterrevolutionary": RGALI, f. 1600, op. 1, d. 19, ll. 1–2.

[30] See memoir sources cited in Chapter 6. For some literary images, see M. Gerasimov, "Monna Liza," *Gorn,* no. 1 (1918), 11; A. Golovin, "Zhizn' (Rasskaz rabochego)," *Tvorchestvo,* no. 2 (June 1918), 9; S. Obradovich, "Otets," *Gudki,* no. 4 (May 1919), 6–16, and "Perevorot," *Kuznitsa,* no. 4 (August–September 1920), 20–21; E. Nechaev, "Po puti k 'prepodobnomu,'" *Rabochii zhurnal* 1924, no. 2–3: 61–77.

bolically expressed when "the son of a carpenter was made into a god." But the spirit of early Christianity persisted, Bessal'ko insisted, as part of the cultural inheritance of the poor.[31]

Other pro-Bolshevik worker writers similarly saw this ethical Christian tradition as belonging specially to the common people: "Were we not there in Judea / When Christ taught of love?" Gerasimov asked.[32] "He died long ago, but we are doing his work," Platonov argued in an 1920 essay titled "Christ and Us, "and he lives in us."[33] Most of these worker writers explicitly rejected literal belief in God. But even while rejecting theology as "illusion," many continued to admire the story of Christ as a compelling story of a moral prophet who knew the life of this world, for he came "not as a ruling god, alien to the turbulent green earth," but as "a Man, born to take every breath," and who taught people love for one's neighbor and disdain for property and brought to the world a love that was not "the feeble and bloodless love of the dying" but "a love-force, a love-flame, a love-hope."[34]

Even when workers' writings did not explicitly draw on Christian images and narratives to express moral argument, they were often no less inclined toward images of a sacred morality. In 1920 a member of a workers' literary circle, the daughter of a factory worker, wrote to a workers' club journal that Lev Tolstoy's ideals still appealed to many workers, for even though he failed to understand properly the need for revolutionary struggle, "his faith, his religion," revealed to him the interdependence of morality and beauty and an understanding of the evils of inequality—"luxury, debauchery, idleness on the one side and unbearable labor and physical and spiritual oppression on the other"—which made him especially "near and dear" to workers in this revolutionary age.[35] Many went much further in defining the moral spirit of the revolution. For one Proletcult writer, human progress, in which the Russian revolution was a key event, ought to be understood as nothing less than the "transition from the life of the body to the life of the spirit." In the most advanced cultures, he argued, physical egoism was already giving way to a high "spiritual state," to a path toward "perfection," where the highest and most sacred goal is simply "love."[36] Another Proletcult writer similarly declared "our God" to be a "proud, tender, and bright-eyed" deity "resurrected for love."[37] Again and again these writers returned to the ideal of "sacred love," of "love as the prime mover," of the "sun of universal love."[38] For Sergei

[31] P. Bessal'ko, "K voprosu o ponimanii proletarskoi kul'tury," *Griadushchee* 1918, no. 3 (June): 2.

[32] M. Gerasimov, "My," in *Zavod ognekrylyi* (Moscow, 1918), 19.

[33] Andrei Platonov, "Khristos i my," *Krasnaia derevnia*, 11 June 1920.

[34] Andrei Platonov, *Golubaia glubina* (Krasnodar, 1922), vi, and "Khristos i my," *Krasnaia derevnia*, 11 June 1920; Grishkin [a "peasant" member of a proletarian club], "Nechto o boge," *Revoliutsionnye vskhody*, no. 3–4 (October 1920), 3–4.

[35] A. Sh., "L. N. Tolstoi," *Revoliutsionnye vskhody*, no. 7–8 (December 1920), 10–11.

[36] N. Torba, "Neravenstvo i nasilie," *Griadushchee* 1920, no. 5–6: 16.

[37] I. Iasinskii, *Mir i chelovek* no. 1 (January 1919), 2.

[38] A. A. Sokolov, "U kazarmennogo okna," in RGALI, f. 1068, op. 1, d. 152, l. 10; A. N.

Malashkin, the proletariat's god was the "God of love."[39] And Sergei Obradovich, writing in 1920, described the journey of the revolution as like a "great way of the cross," in which the people march forward with "the inextinguishable word Love" inscribed on their red banners "with rays of light."[40] The goal of the revolution, it was said, inspired by what Platonov called "a burning anguish for impossible love" and by a burning spirit of "love and compassion," was to build a new church on the ruins of the old, "a Temple of Sacred Truth, Love, and Equality," a "Workers' Kingdom" of "Truth, Righteousness, and Love" (*istina, pravda, liubov'*).[41]

Although *pravda,* the sacred "truth" of earthly justice and righteousness, was the most common form of moral truth exalted in these writings, we also see passionate advocacy of *istina,* the universal truth of essences (of God's essence in the Judeo-Christian tradition), of what is real, authentic, and good in existence. In an essay on proletarian poetry, published in 1922 in the journal of the Kuznitsa group, Andrei Platonov philosophized about the centrality of *istina* to the emerging proletarian culture. The "path to salvation," he argued, is shaped by the knowledge that truth is eternal and derives from somewhere external to individual human beings. Salvation is to be found not in the mere pursuit of happiness (*blago,* the good that satisfies needs and gives material pleasure), which was the best ethics that capitalist civilization could offer, but in the pursuit of *istina,* of "real" truth, of "objective value."[42]

These ideals were aesthetic as much as moral—or, better, moral vision was often cast in aesthetic form, as a reflection and creation of "beauty." In the midst of bloody struggles, it was said, they were "erecting an altar to the new Beauty" and were dreaming of and fighting for a "new world" that was "clean and beautiful," "holy and pure," and filled with genuine beauty and simplicity."[43] The motto of this revolution, thought Il'ia Sadof'ev, was "Fraternity, Equality, Liberty, and Beauty."[44] In the new world being made, people would

---

Smirnov, "Blagosloven," in *V bure i plameni,* 54; A. Platonov, "Gosudarstvo—eto my," *Voronezhskaia kommuna,* 7 Nov. 1920; V. Kirillov, "Privet III Internatsionalu," *Kuznitsa,* no. 4 (August–September 1920), 3; A. Platonov, "O nauke," *Krasnaia derevnia,* 25 June 1920.

[39] S. Malashkin, "Proletariatu," *Tvorchestvo,* no. 7 (November 1918), 36.

[40] S. Obradovich, "Krestnyi put'," *Rabochaia zhizn'* 1920, no. 1–3/65–67: 20.

[41] A. Platonov, "Khristos i my," *Krasnaia derevnia,* 11 June 1920, and "V eti dni zemlia goriachee solntsa . . . ," in *Golubaia glubina,* 51; N. Rybatskii, "Ia kak-to v khrame byl," *Revoliutsionnye vskhody,* no. 5–6 (November 1920), 9–10 (quoted and discussed by Il'ia Sadof'ev in *Griadushchee* 1920, no. 12–13: 17); S. Obradovich, "Vol'nyi rabochii," *Rabochaia zhizn'* 1920, no. 5–7: 4 (cutting in RGALI, f. 1874, d. 7, l. 14). See also Samobytnik [Mashirov], "Rossiia," *Griadushchee* 1919, no. 7–8: 7.

[42] A. Platonov, "Proletarskaia poeziia," *Kuznitsa,* no. 9 (1922), 28–29. Platonov made similar arguments in "Kul'tura proletariata," *Voronezhskaia kommuna,* 20 Oct. 1920.

[43] V. Korolev, "Tvorets-Proletarii," in *V bure i plameni,* 3; I. Filipchenko, "Lenin," *Rabochii zhurnal* 1924, no. 1: 64–65; I. Sadof'ev, "Sil'nee smerti," *Griadushchee* 1921, no. 1–3: 14; Rabochii [Worker] Porokhovik, in *Griadushchaia kul'tura,* no. 3 (January 1919), 13.

[44] Aksen-Achkasov [Sadof'ev], "Iunosham," *Griadushchee* 1918, no. 1 (January): 12–13. See also V. Kirillov, "My," ibid., no. 2 (May): 4; K. Ozol'-Prednek on Sadof'ev, in *Mir i chelovek,* no. 1 (January 1919): 13–15; and A. Kraiskii, "Cherez trup," *Griadushchee* 1921, no. 1–3: 8–9.

be "perfected" in body and spirit.[45] These aesthetic and ethical ideas were sometimes strongly gendered, though in ways that complicate any simple arguments about the essentially masculine culture of the revolution. This was most explicit in the work of Andrei Platonov, who elaborated the moral idealization of beauty (and aestheticization of morality) in his reworking of the religious tradition of the divine "eternal feminine." The mystical idea of Sophia, the transfigured feminine embodiment of wisdom, was strongly developed in Russian Orthodoxy and flourished in the writings of various Russian philosophers, mystics, and poets on the eve of 1917. Sophia was an ambiguous spiritual nature that yielded the deepest wisdom by uniting in itself both chastity (hence a tendency to converge with the image of the Virgin Mary) and maternity (linked to the Russian emphasis on Mary as "mother of God" but also to older Russian myths of "moist mother earth"). Further enriching and complicating these images of a divine feminine force in the world were allusions to the apocalyptic "woman clothed with the sun," pregnant with the Savior, in Revelation.[46] Platonov's divine feminine elaborated these ideas, blending them with notions, pervasive in worker writing of his day, of suffering, morality, and redemption. Woman, he argued, who suffered to give birth and then loved what had caused her pain, is the personification of the highest ethic, love, and thus the "redemption of the mad universe." Woman "is the true embodiment of the world's consciousness of its sins and crimes. She is its repentance and sacrifice, its suffering and redemption." Adding an even stronger allusion to the Christian narrative, he concluded that "the last child of woman—her Great Son—will redeem the world and herself." The power of suffering and death, Platonov claimed, is as essential to woman's saving capacity as the force of living love and giving birth. "Woman really lives only when the desire for torment and death in her is stronger than the desire for life. For only her death breathes life into, animates, and greens the earth."[47]

The abstractness, pathos, and hyperbole of many of these representations is significant. While worker writers occasionally spoke of liberty, equality, fraternity, and beauty in concrete moral terms, they tended to be much less interested than before 1917 in everyday moral questions. They spoke often of "love," but mainly in aesthetic, intangible, and even cosmic terms. The exceptions were, tellingly, likely to be critical of the direction the revolution was

---

[45] I. Filipchenko, "Lenin," *Rabochii zhurnal* 1924, no. 1: 65.

[46] See the discussion in Joanna Hubbs, *Mother Russia: The Feminine Myth in Russian Culture* (Bloomington, 1988); and Mikhail Epstein, "Daniil Andreev and the Mysticism of Femininity," in *The Occult in Russian and Soviet Culture,* ed. Bernice Glatzer Rosenthal (Ithaca, 1997), esp. 332–35. On the discourse in Russia during the 1920s about the ideological and cultural significance of images of male and female, see Eric Naiman, *Sex in Public: The Incarnation of Early Soviet Ideology* (Princeton, 1997), and Eliot Borenstein, *Men without Women: Masculinity and Revolution in Russian Fiction, 1917–1929* (Durham, 2000), which includes (chap. 5) an insightful discussion of Platonov's ambiguous treatment of gender and his adaptations of the myth of the eternal feminine.

[47] A. Platonov, "Dusha mira," *Krasnaia derevnia,* 18 July 1920.

taking, to voice concern about the declining attention to everyday moralities. Petr Oreshin, for example, wrote a story portraying the moral self-torment of a peasant who murdered a landlord during the revolution but who could not reconcile his belief that murder is a sin with his rational knowledge that he acted to bring about a new world in which "people will be angels" and the "kingdom of God will reign on earth."[48] Even more pointedly, I. G. Ustinov— a worker poet long associated with Moscow's Surikov Circle of "writers from the people"—read a poem (a jeremiad, really) at a gathering in 1919 in the Moscow Proletcult's literature studio warning that the realization of true communism in Russia was threatened by the people's failure to remember the moral teachings of Jesus Christ. As if to underscore Ustinov's argument that Christian moral criticism had becoming unfashionable in the postrevolutionary order, his Proletcult audience soundly rejected his concerns.[49] By contrast, we see rather few morality tales promoting cultured behavior and personal respectability or even protesting the moral offenses of capitalism. Morality remained, but it was radicalized. Ideas about moral rectification became less an immediate and practical matter than part of a vision of transformation of more cosmic proportions. Empowered and emboldened by a revolution that promised a new age, even an end to traditional time, and that declared proletarians to possess the truest knowledge, worker writers who embraced these times and ideals were in a mood to imagine as they had never been before.

The Way of the Cross

The increasingly mythic vision of the world that animated worker writing after 1917 is visible in the intensity with which the long familiar theme of suffering was portrayed, interpreted, and used. As before 1917, worker writers consecrated everyday suffering and sanctified the suffering worker. The factory, though now more likely than before the revolution to be celebrated as a "cathedral where I pray to the sun of the new Lord,"[50] still often remained, at least ostensibly in memory, a site of holy suffering. The images with which this suffering was portrayed were largely familiar from earlier writings, though the subject now tended toward even greater pathos and a greater sense that this was part of a past to be overcome soon. Until the present, it was said, workers endured lives of labor "beneath the cross of poverty and suffering," their bodies "shackled / in iron *verigi*" (heavy chains worn by religious ascetics), their dreams "crucified," and "burning nails" hammered into their flesh "beside the scorching furnace."[51] The prerevolutionary image of a factory

[48] P. Oreshin, "Koriavyi," *Rabochii mir* 1918, no. 14 (Oct. 1): 4–8.

[49] *Gudki*, no. 5 (May 1919), 25.

[50] I. Eroshin, "Iz tsikla 'Pesni truda,'" in *Zavod ognekrylyi*, 48.

[51] N. Okskii, "Rabotniki," *Proletkul't* (Tver), no. 1–2 (April–May 1919), 22; M. Gerasimov, "Skovannyi," *Zavod ognekrylyi*, 39; V. Kirillov, "Proletariatu," *Griadushchee* 1918, no. 1 (January): 3; V. Aleksandrovskii, "Zavod," *Gudki*, no. 2 (April 1919), 4–5 (see also his "Mat'," *Gorn*, no. 5 [1920], 5–6).

worker literally crucified in a work accident was also echoed in post-October writing, though with greater intensity. In a story called "Iron Silence," by the former metalworker Nikolai Liashko, a worker was "crucified to the wall" by a machine. But he was not forsaken. "In the twilight," he was taken down "from his iron cross" by his comrades, who every year, in a sort of proletarian Easter ritual, honored the memory of his crucifixion with a strike and a festive holiday in the workshop.[52]

The image of the proletarian as crucified martyr, which interpreted suffering as having transcendent meaning, was especially pervasive after the October revolution and during the civil war, though now the "road to Golgotha" was seen as passing not only through the factories but also through the invariably "bloody" fields of revolutionary struggle.[53] Petr Oreshin, writing in a labor cooperative journal in 1918, portrayed the entire Russian people as "nailed to a black cross."

> Your heavy cross fell upon the whole immense land,
> Your scarlet blood flowed to all corners,
> I hear your cries of unheard-of pain,
> Cruel arrows pierce your breast.[54]

Oreshin, ideologically inclined toward populist socialism, was always the most willing to use Christian metaphor, but even avowed Marxists found this sacred construction of suffering meaningful. Vasilii Aleksandrovskii wrote of "enduring a second Golgotha . . . / Body and soul crucified / To the burning cross of our cyclone days."[55] Andrei Platonov called upon his "brothers in suffering" to "go up the mountain onto the cross." The setting Platonov imagined for this willing crucifixion, for this metaphoric act of interpreting one's shared suffering as sacred and meaningful, was beneath the "gaze of a lone star" to the sound of "white wings" beating in the silence.[56] This blend of vague mysticism and familiar Christian symbols was not unusual. Neither was the notion of willing crucifixion. "Like a bride I go up to Golgotha," wrote Makar Pasynok (Isaak Kogan, a Jewish worker author).[57] Others were similarly determined to "walk this path to Golgotha to the very end."[58] These images of crucifixion were not always mere metaphors. Iakov Berdnikov, a Petersburg metal turner, made the symbolism of the crucifixion literal in a poem in which White Guards during the civil war come to a village and threaten to nail supporters of the revolution onto a cross.[59] As readers knew, such threats

[52] N. Liashko, "Zheleznaia tishina (Nabrosok)," *Kuznitsa*, no. 2 (June 1920), 15–18.

[53] See, e.g. the collection of verse published by the Iaroslavl printers' union, *V bure i plameni*, esp. 3–4, 45, 57. 58.

[54] P. Oreshin, "Pod tiazhkim krestom," *Rabochii mir* 1918, no. 15 (Oct. 13): 3.

[55] V. Aleksandrovskii, "Vstrechi," pt. 1, *Kuznitsa*, no. 2 (June 1920), 13. See also "Glaza liubimoi ne znaiut grusti . . . ," *Griadushchee* 1920, no. 9–10: 1.

[56] A. Platonov, "Tikh pod pustyneiu zvezdnoiu . . . ," in *Golubaia glubina*, 39.

[57] M. Pasynok, "Griadushchemu," *Zheleznyi put'* 1923, no. 4: 1.

[58] I. Eroshin, "Put' golgofy," in *Zavod ognekrylyi*, 24.

[59] Ia. Berdnikov, "Mest'," *Griadushchee* 1921, no. 1–3: 7–8.

were sometimes carried out in life—this was one of the many real brutalities of the civil war.[60] As is often the case, the reality of suffering added resonance to its representation. But the full power of these images drew upon their symbolic resonance with religious tradition, for the metaphor of crucifixion signified not only exceptional suffering but also its sacralization and intrinsic promise of deliverance. Blood, pain, and wounds filled these writings as facts of life and revolution, as symbols of suffering, but especially as sacraments opening a path to salvation.

Most of these writers did not intend their images of crucifixion, even when explicitly alluding to Christ's suffering on the cross, to be taken literally. As Sergei Obradovich explained, these images were not expressions of religious faith but metaphoric revelations of the "suffering heart of the revolutionary proletarian . . . spreading his palms for rusty nails to be hammered in . . . crucified on the fiery Cross of the Great Struggle."[61] But if symbols, especially religious symbols, are meant to reveal deep structures of meaning, to speak of emotional and moral knowledge, what knowledge was this? Least of all was the message the familiar moral one, the one that predominated before 1917: a way of condemning the evils of subordination and exploitation. More often now such metaphors as crucifixion pointed to something more transcendent. For many there was something sublime here: workers were made "majestic in their sufferings," marked as special by their "aching wounds from the nails of the World Cross / The crucified martyr-proletarian."[62] Most important, the suffering and blood of the martyr-proletarian was treated as containing the promise of salvation and even the power to redeem humanity. The way of the cross and the crucifixion on Golgotha, as in the Christian narrative, were metaphorical markers on a path to resurrection and salvation. Like Shadr's monument, it was a journey "through torment and sorrow . . . toward a pyramid of light, perfection, and happiness."[63]

Resurrection and Salvation

A ceremony that took place on Red Square in Moscow during celebrations of the first anniversary of October was illustrative of the frequent imagining of the revolution as messianic deliverance. In the presence of Lenin and other Communist leaders, a large bas-relief plaque, set into the bricks of the Kremlin's Senate tower, was unveiled. The sculptor, Sergei Konenkov, later recalled that an old woman stopped by the Kremlin wall while he was installing the piece and asked the bearded sculptor, "Hey, *batiushka,* to whom are they putting up this

---

[60] See the photograph in E. Baschet, *Russland 1904–1924: Eine historische Foto-reportage* (Kehl am Rhein, 1978), 220–21.

[61] S. Obradovich, "Obraznoe myshlenie," *Kuznitsa,* no. 2 (June 1920), 24–25.

[62] V. Korolev, "Tvorets-Proletarii," in *V bure i plameni,* 3–4.

[63] *Tvorchestvo,* no. 5 (September 1918), 21. Igal Halfin also discusses Soviet discourse on proletarian suffering as salvific and the proletariat as messiah in *From Darkness to Light,* esp. 96–104.

icon?" When he answered, "Revolution," she admitted that "it's the first time I've heard of that saint."[64] Whether the old woman was being ironic or was innocently confused, the analogies are understandable. The memorial plaque, dedicated to the "fallen in the struggle for peace and the brotherhood of peoples" and glazed to match the colors of the cupolas of nearby St. Basil's Cathedral, pictured a large winged female figure, bare-breasted, with the sun rising behind her—a hybrid of the classic female personification of revolution and liberty, an angel, and the woman of the apocalypse "clothed with the sun." A palm branch (a traditional symbol of righteousness and victory and of Christ's martyrdom and resurrection) in one hand covers her breasts; in her other hand is a red banner. At her feet lie fallen swords and weapons, and behind her the rays of the rising sun spell out the words "October 1917 Revolution."[65]

Lenin, who unveiled the memorial, had doubts about the appropriateness of such imagery, especially in such an important location.[66] (Ironically, his mausoleum would later stand in front of the sculpture, until the plaque was taken down.) He had even more reason to be dubious about the cantata sung at the unveiling by a Proletcult workers' choir to lyrics written by the worker writer Mikhail Gerasimov together with the "peasant-poets" Sergei Esenin and Sergei Klychkov. Addressed to their "beloved brothers" who had fallen in battle, the cantata was filled with apocalyptic references:

> Through the haze of bloody death
> Through suffering and sorrow
> We foresee—believe, believe!
> In the golden heights and horizon. . . .
>
> The sun, with a golden seal,
> Stands guard by the gate.
>
> Sleep, dear brothers,
> Past you goes arrayed
> The people to the universal dawn.
>
> Come down from the cross, crucified people
> And be transformed. . . .
>
> In the final battle there can be no mercy,
> But beyond the boundaries of victory
> We will embrace you,
> Delivered from long years in thrall.

[64] S. T. Konenkov, *Vospominaniia, stat'i, pis'ma,* vol. 1 (Moscow, 1984), 174–75. Konenkov also created a number of works, after the revolution as before, with more explicit religious references, though until the end of the Soviet era they were not shown to the public. In 1992 a display of some of these works was opened at the Konenkov studio-museum in Moscow.

[65] A photograph appears in Mikhail Guerman, *Art of the October Revolution* (Leningrad, 1979), 7, 282. Another proposed design, by Giurdzhian, portrayed an angel (also a bare-breasted female with wings) hovering over revolutionary crowds (*Tvorchestvo,* no. 7 [November 1918], 27). Other street decorations to celebrate the first anniversary of October also included winged female figures. See Guerman, *Art of the October Revolution,* plates 179, 180, 182.

[66] A. V. Lunacharskii, *Vospominaniia o Lenine* (Moscow, 1933), quoted in *V. I. Lenin o literature i iskusstve* (Moscow, 1957), 589.

> Roar, land, with the final storm,
> Gather for battle, for the feast,
> Let a new day shine in the azure,
> The old world transfigured.[67]

These words were not exceptional, but quite typical of the images that were beginning to pervade creative visions of the revolution: the crucified people, a promise of deliverance from suffering, an apocalyptic final battle, a reunion between the living and the dead, and the coming of a new age.

Suffering was often portrayed, as in the Christian narrative of the passion, as containing the promise of salvation. "Suffering is always holy / Love is always in blood," Vasilii Aleksandrovskii wrote, for "without suffering there is no resurrection."[68]

> Set ablaze body and soul
> With the fire of suffering
> To burn out the everyday in the world
> And break the black threads.
> . . . Your Golgotha
> Has surpassed the torments of all ages.
> Soon the wings of the tempest begin to wave,
> And your red path will be illumined.[69]

Sergei Obradovich portrayed the whole Russian people, with "their bodies in rags / Painful sores on their legs / And blood in their dry cracked lungs," moving forward beneath "trembling and blazing-winged clouds," on their "Great Way of the Cross," opening a new "Book of Genesis," heralded by a dawn "crucified on the smokestacks of factories."[70] Andrei Platonov portrayed Russians as "pilgrims" on the path to God, "each person hungry and filthy / but together all pure," and walking beside them "Christ again in the world / With anguish [*toska*] in his eyes."[71] The cross repeatedly appeared as a symbol of salvation through suffering,[72] though its place could be taken, with no loss of religious allusion, by the red flag:

> Under scarlet banners—
> The emblem of our torments and suffering . . .

[67] M. Gerasimov, S. Esenin, and S. Klychkov, "Kantata," *Zarevo zavodov*, no. 1 (January 1919), 24–25.

[68] V. Aleksandrovskii, "Toboi my raspiaty, gorod . . . ," *Zvon solntsa* (Moscow, 1923), 19 (originally published in *Sever* [Moscow, 1919]); "S. K.," *Zarevo zavodov*, no. 2 (1919), 14.

[69] V. Aleksandrovskii, "Toboi my raspiaty, gorod . . . ," in *Zvon solntsa* (Moscow, 1923), 19–20.

[70] S. Obradovich, "Krestnyi put'," *Rabochaia zhizn'* 1920, no. 1–3/65–67: 20; "Gorod," *Kuznitsa*, no. 5–6 (October–November 1920): 21; "Oktiabr'," *Krasnoarmeets*, no. 28–30 (1920), in RGALI, f. 1874, op. 1, d. 7, l. 24.

[71] A. Platonov, "Bogomoltsy," in *Golubaia glubina*, 21–22. Also *Put' kommunizma*, no. 1 (January–February 1922), 54, and *Zheleznyi put'* 1923, no. 1.

[72] E.g., M. Gerasimov, "Osen' v okopakh," in *Zavod ognekrylyi*, 60–61.

> We deck the whole world in flowers,
> Flowers of incomparable suffering,
> And in agony
> We give birth to a new world.[73]

In the view of many, suffering itself opened the gate to salvation, to a "red dawn" that called each suffering "soul to set down anchor."[74]

The promise of a new world often appeared on wings. Sometimes, as in writings before the revolution, flight was a symbol of escape—of soaring away, alone, "in mute prayer," into the sky, to the sun and stars, to the unknown.[75] Even the Proletcult leader Valerian Pletnev indulged in this image in a story of a worker recalling a favorite childhood dream to grow wings and fly high into the sky.[76] In most post-October writings, flight became a more powerful symbolic magic. Some imagined gaining mystic sight: in flight above the highest mountains, "the Beauty of the Great Whole opened only a part of her Eternal Veil before me, but it was enough . . . to foresee the future."[77] Most often, flight was both less personal and more revolutionary and saving. For Platonov, we have seen, "white wings" accompanied the symbolic procession of the suffering to Golgotha, beyond which lay a new time when people themselves would fly, even to the stars and the sun.[78] Angelic or titanic winged figures often arrived to herald emancipation. Oreshin imagined figures appearing from both heaven and hell with "golden wings" in answer to his prayers for Russia's salvation from suffering.[79] The revolution itself might be portrayed as "a winged steed, of burning iron / Speeding into the Future,"[80] which brought freedom to the people to the sounds of "angelic choirs."[81] "Fire-winged" (*ognekrylyi*) was one of the favorite adjectives of the day.[82] But even as their material substance varied—fire, iron, whiteness, gold—wings appeared everywhere. The new Communist Kremlin, for example, was described as a "giant golden-winged ship," a new Noah's ark with wings from

[73] I. Molot, "Da, pobedim lish' tol'ko my (Ukhodiashchim na front)," *Molot,* no. 1 (November 1920), 3–4.

[74] M. Gerasimov, "Skovannyi," in *Zavod ognekryly,* 39–40. See also Gerasimov, "My," *Zarevo zavodov,* no. 2 (1919), 9.

[75] E.g., M. Gerasimov, "Vesna" (quoted phrase), "Vesennyi den'," "Vzlet," and "Kak v chernykh ranakh," in *Zavod vesennyi* (Moscow, 1919), 36–37, 46, 47, 59; V. Aleksandrovskii, "S. K.," *Zarevo zavodov,* no. 2 (1919), 14. See also Semen Rodov's criticism of Gerasimov in *Kuznitsa,* no. 1 (May 1920), 23.

[76] V. Pletnev, "Vesenniaia pesnia," *Gorn,* no. 5 (1920), 10.

[77] I. Ivanov, "Mashinist," *Molot,* no. 1 (November 1920), 16–17.

[78] A. Platonov, "Tikh pod pustyneiu zvezdnoiu . . . ," in *Golubaia glubina,* 39, and "K zvezdnym Tovarishcham," *Put' kommunizma,* no. 1 (Janaury–February 1922), 19.

[79] P. Oreshin, "Blagoslovi," *Rabochii mir* 1918, no. 15 (Oct. 13): 3.

[80] I. Sadof'ev, "Ritm Granita," *Griadushchee* 1919, no. 4: 3. See also Sadof'ev quoted in *Mir i chelovek,* no. 1 (January 1919), 12; V. Aleksandrovskii, "Krylia," *Gorn,* no. 5 (1920), 7–9 (read in 1919 at a Sunday meeting at the Proletcult literary studio in Moscow: *Gudki,* no. 5 [May 1919], 28); S. Obradovich, "Gorod," *Kuznitsa,* no. 5–6 (October–November 1920), 21.

[81] E. Nechaev, "Privet proletarskim ptentsam," *Tvorchestvo,* no. 7 (November 1918), 12.

[82] See, e.g., I. Sadof'ev, "Ognennyi put'," *Mir i chelovek,* no. 1 (January 1919), 4, and the collection *Zavod ognekrylyi* [Fire-winged factory] (Moscow, 1918).

which the "dove carrying the long awaited branch of salvation" had flown, and as a "Red Mecca" from which prophetic words, taking flight as meteors and rockets, soared across mountains and seas and fell to earth.[83]

Resurrection, alluded to only occasionally in prerevolutionary works, was an essential and pervasive image in this poetics of deliverance, introducing, if only metaphorically, additional elements of the miraculous into representations of life and revolution. Resurrection could be personal and individual. Dreaming at Christmastime of a meeting with a lover, Aleksandrovskii portrayed the coming tryst as a "resurrection in joy and torment."[84] But most often, resurrection had existential and political significance. These claims could be relatively modest. Il'ia Sadof'ev, in the epilogue to his poetic requiem for the dead of the civil war, wrote of the power of remembrance to return the dead to life. Through memory, he wrote, "perhaps, perhaps / You and I will be eternal / And awaken the fallen to life."[85] But most writers were less hesitant. Mikhail Gerasimov wrote, for example, of a worker's deliverance from the deadening life in the factory:

> All were stooped and cramped,
> Entombed in the factory crypt,
> When suddenly his blue-blouse shroud tore,
> And resurrected, he sped toward the sun.[86]

Resurrection signified triumph over death.[87] In a poem filled with images of the revolutionary people marching forward over the corpses and bones of the fallen, Aleksei Kraiskii, writing at the end of the civil war, imagined the dead reborn into a time of "new beauty" in which only "joyful dreams are allowed," and when a new "hymn" can comfort the lost and "awaken life in a dead corpse."[88] Dreams of overcoming death, which preoccupied many of these writers, echoing a theme to be found in a great deal of Russian literature immediately before and after 1917, may also not have been entirely symbolic. Belief in the literal possibilities of resurrection of the dead and limitless prolongation of life was one of the characteristic "scientific" fantasies of early Bolshevism, part of a widespread sense that October marked a border crossing into a new spiritual and existential environment in which every boundary and limitation, including time itself, could reasonably be questioned and even-

---

[83] V. Kirillov, "Krasnyi kreml'," *Kuznitsa,* no. 5–6 (October–November 1920), 3–4. Aleksandrovskii had somewhat earlier portrayed revolutionary Russia as an ark (*kovcheg*): ibid., no. 1 (May 1920), 5. In his 1918 play, "Mystery-Bouffe," Vladimir Maiakovskii also appropriated Noah's ark as a symbol of the revolution's messianic promise. So did Aleksandr Blok, in his 1919 essay "Krushenie gumanizma." See Rosenthal, "Eschatology and the Appeal of Revolution," 125.

[84] V. Aleksandrovskii, "Rozhdestvennskie mechty," *Sotsial-demokrat,* 30 Dec. 1917.

[85] I. Sadof'ev, "Sil'nee smerti," *Griadushchee* 1921, no. 1–3: 27.

[86] M. Gerasimov, "Letim," in *Zavod ognekrylyi,* 17.

[87] In addition to examples below, see I. Sadof'ev, "Sil'nee smerti" [Stronger than death], *Griadushchee* 1921, no. 1–3: 14.

[88] A. Kraiskii, "Cherez trup," *Griadushchee* 1921, no. 1–3: 8–9.

tually transcended.[89] For Andrei Platonov, overcoming death was the essential goal of human progress: "History is the path to salvation though the victory of man over the universe. We are coming to the immortality of humanity and its salvation from the prison of physical laws."[90]

However literal these fantasies may sometimes have been, it was the emblematic power of the sacred image of resurrection and eternal life that made it so compelling. Resurrection connoted most of all a coming new age, a millenarian rebirth of the world. The revolution, it was said, had brought the people "to the great eve of the Resurrection."[91] And this resurrection was at once a symbol of deliverance, transgression, and transformation. It was in this sense that Platonov, like many other proletarian writers, envisioned the dead rising out of graves: "resurrected" with the power of "consciousness, light, and salvation," such that all of humanity could be reborn as "a new more mighty god."[92] And, like Christ's resurrection, this was a story of bringing salvation to all humanity. "To the World," Petr Oreshin wrote in 1918, "Rus' now bestows the final Resurrection."[93] "The bell of the ancient *veche* [the communal town assembly of pre-autocratic Russia]," wrote Vladimir Kirillov, similarly blending the national and the sacred in this narrative of revolution, "prophesies to the nations that the day of Resurrection is near."[94]

Titans, Gods, and Messiahs

While a number of worker writers imagined Jesus as the deliverer—explicitly, allusively, or metaphorically (and sometimes it is hard to know which was intended)[95]—most often salvation was envisioned as the work of new and more abstract godlike human saviors, in particular of a new "proletarian messiah." Often the mythic and saving power of the proletariat as a class was represented, as in a number of posters and paintings of the time,[96] by symbolic titans (*titany*), giants (*ispoliny, bogatyry, velikany*), and lords (*vladyki*).[97] But

[89] Irene Masing-Delic, *Abolishing Death: A Salvation Myth of Russian Twentieth-Century Literature* (Stanford, 1992); Bergman, "Image of Jesus," 239–43; Tumarkin, "Origins of the Lenin Cult," pp. 43–45.

[90] A. Platonov, "Proletarskaia poeziia," *Kuznitsa*, no. 9 (1922), 28.

[91] V. Aleksandrovskii, "Pobediteli," in *Zavod ognekrylyi*, 14.

[92] A. Platonov, "Mysli," *Voronezhskaia kommuna*, 7 Oct. 1920, and "Pokhod," "Vselennoi," and "Mysl'," all in *Golubaia glubina*, 5, 6, 13.

[93] P. Oreshin, "Na prazdnik Kooperatsii," *Rabochii mir*, no. 12–13 (15 Sept. 1918), 3.

[94] V. Kirillov, "Krasnyi kreml'," *Kuznitsa*, no. 5–6 (October–November 1920), 4. See also I. Iasinskii, *Mir i chelovek*, no. 1 (January 1919), 2.

[95] Such as A. Platonov, "Khristos i my," *Krasnaia derevnia*, 11 June 1920; idem, "Bogomoltsy" and "V eti dni zemlia goriachee solntsa . . . ," in *Golubaia glubina*, 21–22, 51; V. Korolev in *V bure i plameni*, 45; S. Obradovich, "Otets," *Gudki*, no. 4 (May 1919), 12; I. Ustinov in *Gudki*, no. 5 (May 1919), 25.

[96] E.g., Ignat Nivinskii's *Krasnaia mol'niia* (1919) or Boris Kustodiev's *Bol'shevik* (1920).

[97] E.g., P. Arskii, "Pesnia o molote," *Griadushchee* 1918, no. 9, 2; V. Kirillov, "Zheleznyi mes-

most often these writers spoke of people becoming gods and of the making of a new socialist "god-man." In the first days after the October revolution, Vladimir Kirillov wrote of the old God himself looking down upon the changed world, realizing with anguish and sadness that "people themselves had become gods."[98] This humanistic conceit (and one of the most ancient human dreams) was characteristic of the times and often repeated. Workers "do not fear God," Pavel Bessal'ko wrote in 1918 in the journal of the Petrograd Proletcult, "for we are God."[99] "The mysteries of the universe are known to us," Platonov similarly wrote in 1921, "everyone can be a god today."[100]

Most important, these new gods arose as saviors. They might be imagined coming as Christ-like deliverers:

> Let blood flow in a scarlet stream from my wounds
> Dying, I will sing hymns. . . .
> I became Man, Lord of earth and beasts
> With the holy dream of eternal life.[101]

These saviors might even share the mystical parentage of Christ:

> No mother gave us birth.
> No bride's arms held us . . .
> As if we were children of another father.
> Here we are strangers and we set ablaze
> The dead world from end to end.[102]

They might come as new gods:

> Our aim was to behold the Birth of God. . . .
> Suddenly, our afflicted path of Sorrow and Worry
> Shone with unexpected light.
> Rejoice, brothers, for newborn
> Is the long awaited God![103]

---

siia," ibid., no. 4 (June): 3; M. Gerasimov, "My," *Zarevo zavodov,* no. 2 (1919), 9; V. Korolev, "Tvorets-Proletarii," in *V bure i plameni,* 3; Samobytnik, "Mashinnyi rai," *Griadushchee 1920,* no. 1–2: 1. Pavel Bessal'ko retold ancient heroic myths and legends in *Almazy vostoka* (Petrograd, 1919) and "Khromonogii Gefest [Haephestus] (Legenda)," *Griadushchee* 1918, no. 7 (October): 3–8.

[98] V. Kirillov, "Griadushchee," *Pravda,* 13 Nov. 1917; rpt. in Kirillov, *Stikhotvoreniia, 1914–1918 gg.* (Petrograd, 1918), 15–17.

[99] P. Bessal'ko, "O poezii krest'ianskoi i proletarskoi," *Griadushchee* 1918, no. 7 (October): 14.

[100] A. Platonov, "Poznany namy tainy vselennoi . . . ," *Voronezhskaia kommuna,* 29 June 1921.

[101] A. N. Smirnov, "Uragan," in *V bure i plameni,* 58. See also his "V eti dni zemlia goriachee solntsa . . . ," in *Golubaia glubina,* 51.

[102] A. Platonov, "Pokhod," in *Golubaia glubina,* 5.

[103] V. Narvskii, "25-X-17," in *Zveno* (Kharkov, 1921), 13 (a collection by worker writers from Kharkov).

Saviors often came as "iron messiahs"—figures mixing Christian, mythic, and proletarian elements. The appropriation of the Christian messianic tradition in such images was sometimes acknowledged: "For God, we represent Man; for the Mother of God, the Machine; and for Jesus the Messiah, the Conscious Socialist Hero."[104] With equal validity the formula could have been reversed and it could have been said that they represented the conscious socialist hero as Jesus the messiah. Other God images were equally common. Saviors might appear as revolutionary miracle workers causing a "red poppy" to grow at the end of frozen October.[105] One writer envisioned the proletarian in struggle to be "a God of vengeance" who "appears / With thunder and storm / Roaring like a hurricane / Over the tormented land."[106] Others preferred titanic, promethean saviors: "We are winged aspiration. / We are omnipotent and can do as we wish, / Destroy, achieve."[107]

The archetypical proletarian savior was a class messiah who emerged naturally from a world of factories. In the words of Pavel Bessal'ko, worker writers looked to the factories for the new messiah because factories are "the nerve centers of our thoughts and our feelings, the iron head of the collective, the head of the new Savior."[108] Factories were also the cathedrals to the new God: "Thrusting into the heavens / Huge smokestacks exhale incense to the new god-man."[109] The most widely known and characteristic literary portrayal of this classic proletarian savior was Vladimir Kirillov's "Iron Messiah":

> There he is—savior, master of the earth,
> Lord of titanic forces—
> In the noise of countless steel machines,
> In the gleam of electric suns.
>
> We thought he would appear in shining garments,
> In a halo of divine mystery,
> But he came to us dressed in blue smoke,
> From the factories and industrial outskirts.
>
> We thought he would appear in glimmer and glory,
> Meek, blessedly gentle,
> But he came, like burning lava,
> Multi-faced and insurgent.

[104] Knizhnik, K. Ozol'-Prednek, and A. M., "God bor'by za proletarskuiu kul'turu," *Griadu-shchee* 1918, no. 8: 17.

[105] D. Mazin, "Chudo" [Miracle], *Griadushchee* 1918, no. 8: 3. Other poems in this October anniversary issue also speak of messiahs and miracles.

[106] M. A. Kiriushkin, "Strana rodnaia," in RGALI, f. 1068, op. 1, d. 72, l. 7.

[107] I. Sadof'ev, "Chto takoe proletkul't," *Mir i chelovek* (Kolpino), no. 1 (January 1919), 12. See also "My idem," in Il'ia Sadof'ev, *Dinamo-Stikhi* (Petrograd, 1918), 5–6. A reviewer described Sadof'ev's image as that of a "Collective Prometheus, bringing a new Sun to a new humanity": K. Ozol'-Prednek in *Mir i chelovek* (Kolpino), no. 1 (January 1919), 13–15.

[108] P. Bessal'ko, "O poezii krest'ianskoi i proletarskoi," 13.

[109] V. Kirillov, "Gorodu," *Griadushchee* 1918, no. 2 (May): 6. By contrast, Andrei Belyi, who lectured at the Moscow Proletcult's literary studio, considered industrial civilization to be demonic. See Rosenthal, "Eschatology and the Appeal of Revolution," 119, 136.

He strides across the abyss of the seas,
Made of steel, undeviating and aspiring,
He scatters sparks of rebellious ideas,
And spews cleansing flames.

Wherever his powerful shout rings forth,
The depths of the earth reveal themselves,
Mountains give way in an instant before him,
The world's poles draw closer.

Wherever he goes, he leaves a trail
Of ringing iron lines,
Brings happiness and light to all,
Plants flowers in the desert.

A new sun he brings to the world,
He destroys thrones and dungeons,
The nations he calls to eternal brotherhood,
He erases boundaries and borders.

With his crimson banner—symbol of struggle—
Saving beacon of the oppressed,
We will crush the yoke of fate,
And capture enchanting paradise.[110]

The sun, and occasionally other cosmic symbols (the moon, stars, the universe as well as earthly forces such as volcanoes) also often figured as god and savior. Petr Oreshin imagined becoming one with the moon and joining it in flight above the "weeping earth," enabling him to "command the Universe."[111] Such cosmic imagery was widespread in proletarian writing in these early years, and was regularly criticized. Lunacharsky, the people's commissar of enlightenment, spoke of too much "astronomic hyperbole" in Soviet literature, while other critics mocked these tropes as reflecting an inappropriate "cosmism" and "pseudo-proletarian pantheism."[112] Almost all worker writers wrote at least occasionally in this manner, most often about the sun. They wrote of the flight of the free toward the sun, of praying to "the sun of the new Lord," and of the coming of the "sun of universal love," "the Sun of Eternity."[113] They transferred the sun's power to the proletariat, who "carried the Sun of a New Life" under its "dark work shirt" or brought its "light-stream-

[110] V. Kirillov, "Zheleznyi messiia," *Griadushchee* 1918, no. 4 (June): 3. (This is the complete text.)

[111] P. Oreshin, "Mesiatsu sinemu," *Rabochii mir* 1918, no. 8 (7 July 1918): 3.

[112] A. Lunacharskii, "Novaia poeziia," in RGALI, f. 279, op. 3, d. 7, l. 5 (an essay written for *Izvestiia*); A. Voronskii, "O gruppe pisatel'ei 'Kuznitsa': Obshchaia kharakteristika," in *Iskusstvo i zhizn': Sbornik statei* (Moscow and Petrograd, 1924), 137, 141; *Literaturnaia entsiklopediia,* vol. 5 (1931), 501.

[113] E.g., M. Gerasimov, "Vesna," in *Zavod vesennyi*, 37, and "Letim," in *Zavod ognekrylyi,* 17; I. Eroshin, "Iz tsikla 'Pesni truda,'" in *Zavod ognekrylyi,* 48, and "Zemlia i solntse," *Tvorchestvo,* no. 1 (May 1918), 17; V. Kirillov, "Privet III Internatsionalu," *Kuznitsa,* no. 4 (August–September 1920), 3; V. Korolev, in *V bure i plameni,* 45.

ing noise" to the "labor front."[114] Above all, they wrote of the sun as the symbolic power of millenarian salvation: of the sun "with a golden seal," standing at the gate leading to the "universal dawn," of the "tender Sun-Mother shining / upon the blood of the birth of love / and upon the sprouting of renewed life," or perhaps as coming with a messiah who would bring "a new sun" to the world.[115]

The spirit of myth in these writings was strong. Andrei Platonov wrote explicitly about the need to mobilize the force of mythic imagination for the revolutionary cause, to build a "temple of humanity" at the heart of a Communist Eden inspired by "great myths." For Platonov, as for many worker writers, the sun stood at the center of this mythic power. Creative people like himself must soar "to the zenith, to the very sun of freedom and knowledge." And the revolutionary people, "burning with the same force as within the sun," which was "brother" and "sister" to them, would extinguish the weary old sun and "sweep planets out of their path with fire," illumining the universe with their own light.[116] A provincial worker writer—apparently echoing Gorky's earlier flirtation with sun worship, well known from his 1905 play *Children of the Sun*—declared that "we are all now Children of the Sun," masters of "Land and Universe," able to fly like birds in the air and swim like fish in the sea.[117] Dmitrii Odintsov went even further and recalled ancient Slavic sun worship, calling on workers to relight the pagan "fires of Dazhbog," the sun god.[118] Even the normally restrained and realistic Proletcult leader Pletnev wrote an extended paean to the sun, nature, love, wisdom, and eternal life, which concluded:

People,
Oh, if you would only understand that the stern, relentless world is so full of love,
You would become a great creative force.
You would become wise and pure, like life itself.
You would become clear, like the eyes of a child.
You would become the sun.[119]

These varied images of godlike saviors and messiahs traced their roots, not only to prerevolutionary metaphysical and ethical ideas of "godmanhood" and Bolshevik "God-building," but also to a variety of older mythic traditions

[114] V. Kirillov, "Proletariatu," *Griadushchee* 1918, no. 1 (January): 3; M. Gerasimov, "Na front Truda," *Kuznitsa*, no. 1 (May 1920), 10–11 (a refrain in the poem is "*Solntse na front Truda*"). See also P. Ural'skii, "U tribuny," *Molot*, no. 1 (November 1920), 12–13.

[115] M. Gerasimov, S. Esenin, and S. Klychkov, "Kantata," *Zarevo zavodov*, no. 1 (January 1919), 24–25; I. Sadof'ev, "Sil'nee smerti," *Griadushchee* 1921, no. 1–3: 27; V. Kirillov, "Zheleznyi messiia," *Griadushchee* 1918, no. 4 (June): 3.

[116] A. Platonov in *Zheleznyi put'*, no. 9 (April 1919), 26; "Poslednii shag," *Voronezhskaia kommuna*, 15 Jan. 1921; "Pokhod" and "Vselennoi," in *Golubaia glubina*, 5–6.

[117] I. Ivanov, "Mashinist," *Molot*, no. 1 (November 1920), 16.

[118] D. Odintsov, "Iazychnitsa," in *Sbornik proletarskikh pisatelei*, ed. M. Gor'kii, A. Serebrov, and A. Chapygin (Petrograd, [1917]), 78–79.

[119] V. Pletnev, "Vesenniaia pesnia," *Gorn*, no. 5 (1920), 12.

and images: classical Titans (especially Prometheus, who stole fire for the sake of humanity from the gods' chariot of the sun) and various mighty progeny born of sexual unions between gods and humans; the biblical creation myth with its image of human beings made in God's "image and likeness" and then becoming nearly "like gods" when they dared to eat the fruit of the tree of knowledge of good and evil; and the images of the god and man Christ (including his apocalyptic second birth, according to Revelation, from the womb of the "woman clothed with the sun"). At least some writers were influenced, as many Russians were at the time, by Nietzsche's exaltation of titanic, promethean forces, of godlike supermen. Aleksei Kraiskii wrote in a Proletcult journal, "Love to you, superman (*sverkh-chelovek*) . . . / Lord of the mountains, seas and rivers / Of earth and air. Creator / Of both God and miracles!"[120] Finally, for most worker writers, the mythic mentality was reinforced by Marxism's own world-historical drama, in which the last become first, the proletariat functions as a messiah, and a reborn promethean humanity ushers in a "realm of freedom" that transcends even historical time.[121] Like so much in early Soviet culture, these ideal figures could be imbued with a masculine ethos of strong and virile men, deeply engaged in struggle, conquest, and production, and undefiled by contact with women or by traditionally feminine values; but no less evident were saviors inspired by tender love and ready for self-sacrifice. Whatever the multiple sources of these images—though the imagery and narratives of Christian myth were likely the most fundamental and powerful, for they were most familiar and emotionally rooted—it is clear that the image of godlike revolutionary saviors gave the narrative of revolution a desired quality of myth, mystery, and sublime power. Conservative Marxist critics such as Pavel Lebedev-Polianskii openly disapproved of all this "foggy, abnormal" talk about "god-man," but he could not deny its appeal.[122]

When worker writers tried to imagine the true proletarian savior—rooted in the working-class milieu, class conscious, and possessing mythic power and sight—they often saw themselves. As exceptional individuals, laboring plebeians who had mastered the power of ideas and language, especially poetic language, they often envisioned a key role for themselves in bringing about the new world. An essay in the journal of the Petrograd Proletcult appealed to the "proletarian intelligentsia" to build "new temples" and create a "new religion" to save the world.[123] Il'ia Sadof'ev similarly defined the work of the Proletcult, its efforts to stimulate proletarian creativity and spread a new proletarian culture,

---

[120] A. Kraiskii, "Liudi i solntse," *Griadushchee* 1918, no. 7 (October): 2.

[121] Robert C. Tucker, *Philosophy and Myth in Karl Marx* (Cambridge, 1961); Alasdair MacIntyre, *Marxism and Christianity* (New York, 1968); Leonard P. Wessell, Jr., *Prometheus Bound: The Mythic Structure of Karl Marx's Scientific Thinking* (Baton Rouge, 1984); Halfin, *From Darkness to Light*, chaps. 1–2.

[122] *Proletarskaia kul'tura*, no. 17–19 (August–December 1920), 93. See also V. Friche's less hostile recognition of popular attention to "the proud, free conqueror of the universe, builder of the cosmos, man-titan, man-god, son of the light-bearer Prometheus": "V poiskakh novoi krasoty," *Tvorchestvo*, no. 2 (June 1918), 6.

[123] Torskii [M. Tsarev], "K proletarskoi intelligentsii," *Griadushchee* 1918, no. 1 (January): 7.

as a "spiritual revolution . . . more terrible than any bombs of physical revolution."[124] In their literary writings, these workers often imagined themselves bringing salvation and transformation to the world through the power of words. Ivan Eroshin (in a poem written while studying in the literature studio of the Moscow Proletcult) described himself on a journey, with bloodied feet, along his own "path of suffering," his own "way of the cross," toward a "temple of joy." He knows that he will be mocked and spat upon, but the "wings" on his "dancing dreams" are light. He visits "beds infected with plague," "dark silent tombs," and places where men are blind. But in the end, he reaches the "bright city along an untraveled pathway." Arriving at the "hour of fierce storms," at the "liturgical hour," he sings a "universal psalm." The "wings" of his song, he hopes, will heal the world, "fatigued with death."[125]

This relatively gentle Christ-like image of the worker writer as savior was less common, however, than bolder and more romantic images of poet saviors as resembling rather more the Christ who came "not to bring peace but a sword,"[126] or the messiah of the cataclysmic second coming, or a conquering promethean deliverer challenging the gods themselves. Proletarian writers represented themselves as saviors who could "break chains," "transform matter" with words alone, work miracles, and themselves proclaim the new age.[127] In a parable by Ivan Tachalov published in 1922, the dark huddled masses, the "outcasts," lamenting their misery outside of the crystal palaces and cathedrals, which they had built with their own hands, hear a "prophetic song" about a savior, a "Messiah-Poet," "born of tears," who will lead them "to the temple of the gods" and "take from the altar the flame of wisdom."[128] In the writings of many worker poets were to be found similar images of poet-messiahs—of the worker writer as a "bright genius" singing the people's dreams or themselves as a "winged god" heralding or even bringing salvation.[129]

Apocalypse

The Russian revolution and the struggles and crises that followed it appeared to many at the time as an apocalyptic moment. This perception was encouraged by the growing preoccupation of intellectuals and artists, in Russia as in much of Europe, with eschatological themes, born of a hostility to the world

---

[124] I. Sadof'ev, "Chto takoe proletkul't," *Mir i chelovek,* no. 1 (January 1919), 12. See also A. Platonov, "Kul'tura proletariata," *Voronezhskaia kommuna,* 20 Oct. 1920.

[125] I. Eroshin, "Po doroge," *Tvorchestvo,* no. 5 (September 1918), 19.

[126] Matt. 10:34.

[127] P. Bessal'ko, "O poezii krest'ianskoi i proletarskoi," *Griadushchee* 1918, no. 7 (October): 13; A. Platonov, "Proletarskaia poeziia," *Kuznitsa,* no. 9 (1922), 30–31.

[128] I. Tachalov, "Dva mira (poema)," *Ponizov'e* (Samara), no. 5 (1922), 7–11.

[129] See the discussion and quotations in P. Bessal'ko, "Proletarskie poety," *Griadushchee* 1919, no. 1: 12. For a humorous version in the style of a fairy tale—in which a worker poet brings a dead man back to life by touching his gravestone—see A. Kraiskii, "Posle smerti," *Griadushchee* 1920, no. 1–2: 3–5.

as it was and of faith in the possibility of transcendence. Many Russian artists and writers had been dwelling on such themes: the radical division of the world into warring categories of good and evil, images of final battles, symbolic markers of the coming apocalypse (thunder, lightening, earthquakes, meteors, comets, purifying fire, blood, mighty angels, horsemen), and millenarian ideas about the end of all authority, the transcendence of the materialistic present ("a new heaven and a new earth") and of time itself, and the creation of a new human being.[130]

Allusions to apocalyptic final days pervade proletarian writing after 1917—echoes of the literary moods of their day, but also of their own responses, partly shaped by their knowledge of apocalyptic scriptures and lore, to the upheavals, chaos, and possibility around them. Especially during the years of civil war, economic collapse, and famine, these writings were filled with apocalyptic images of "thunder and storm / Roaring like a hurricane," of the "final storm" accompanying the "final battle" before one sees a "a new day shine in the azure / The old world transfigured."[131] Fire repeatedly appeared in these writings as an all-consuming apocalyptic inferno that would "set ablaze / The dead world from end to end," "sweeping planets out of their path with fire," and "burn out the everyday in the world."[132] Combining both images, one collection of writings by proletarian writers was fittingly titled *V bure i plamen'* (In storm and fire). Blood flowed freely in these writings, especially as blessed bearer of sacred love and the promise of redemption.[133] Evil was portrayed as a "many-headed dragon" defeated by "the legions of labor" riding upon "winged steeds."[134] And the many images of the sun as "the new Lord," as a "Sun-Mother shining / upon the blood of the birth of love," as standing at the gate leading to the "universal dawn,"[135] echo the appearance in Revelation of the "woman clothed with the sun," pregnant with the returning Christ.[136]

Millenarian visions were not limited to the devastating and utopian years of the civil war, though they were most common and intense then. They persisted to the very middle of the relatively sober and successful 1920s, when the leaders of the party and state did all they could to cool the romanticism of the civil war era, and when the economy had largely returned to its prewar

[130] Rosenthal, "Eschatology and the Appeal of Revolution," 105–39; Williams, "Russian Revolution and the End of Time;" Halfin, *From Darkness to Light.* For the biblical source of such imagery, see Revelation, esp. chaps. 6–10, 12.

[131] M. A. Kiriushkin, "Strana rodnaia," in RGALI, f. 1068, op. 1, d. 72, l. 7; I. Eroshin, "Po doroge," *Tvorchestvo,* no. 5 (September 1918), 19; M. Gerasimov, S. Esenin, and S. Klychkov, "Kantata," *Zarevo zavodov,* no. 1 (January 1919), 24–25.

[132] A. Platonov, "Pokhod," in *Golubaia glubina,* 5; V. Aleksandrovskii, "Toboi my raspiaty, gorod . . . ," in *Zvon solntsa* (Moscow, 1923), 19–20.

[133] P. Oreshin, "Blagoslovi" and "Pod tiazhkim krestom," *Rabochii mir,* 1918, no. 15 (October 13): 3; V. Aleksandrovskii, "Toboi my raspiaty, gorod . . . ," in *Zvon solntsa,* 19; A. N. Smirnov, "Uragan," in *V bure i plameni,* 58.

[134] I. Sadof'ev, "Ritm granita," *Griadushchee* 1919, no. 4: 3.

[135] I. Eroshin, "Iz tsikla 'Pesni truda,'" in *Zavod ognekrylyi,* 48; I. Sadof'ev, "Sil'nee smerti," *Griadushchee,* 1921, no. 1–3: 27; M. Gerasimov, S. Esenin, and S. Klychkov, "Kantata," *Zarevo zavodov,* no. 1 (January 1919), 24–25.

[136] Rev. 12:1, 5.

levels. Lenin's death in 1924 helped sustain apocalyptic visions by evoking a new outpouring of mystical views of politics—including those of Lenin himself as a godlike figure whose presence and power outlived his physical death.[137] Also, the unromantic compromises of NEP and the distress many Russians felt over the tolerance of so much of the old social and cultural world in "new" Russia encouraged apocalyptic prophesies of the coming of a new age—of a second coming of the revolution.

One of the most striking examples from the mid-1920s was the epic poem "Leniniada" by the young proletarian writer Grigorii Sannikov.[138] The poem was reportedly well received when it was read aloud at a gathering of proletarian writers one evening in Moscow,[139] and it was printed in installments in *Rabochii zhurnal* (The workers' journal), the new organ of the Kuznitsa literary group, with which most of the leading writers of working-class background were still associated. The poem is presented as a dream, but also as a prophetic vision—a "fata morgana," Sannikov calls it, a mirage that reveals what lies hidden beyond the horizon.

We encounter the poet-narrator sitting alone beneath the looming Kremlin walls—"as beneath heavy eternity"—not far from Lenin's mausoleum, darkly pondering the fate of the revolution: Lenin's recent death and the columns of mourners who had come to his grave; the "wine, laughter, and drunken pleasures" of the new rich of NEP; the misguided "change of course"; the forgotten battles of the October days. Dawn approached.

> Suddenly I heard noise,
> Steps,
> A disquieting knock
> (Can it be from below ground?)
> I look—
> The square was filled with the light of dawn
> In confusion,
> The Red Army guards
> Backed away from the mausoleum.
> And from the opened doors,
> From his dark prison,
> Into the dawn stepped the Leader.

The narrator stood trembling as Lenin slowly ascended the tribune on his own mausoleum and addressed the dead revolutionaries buried at the Kremlin wall: "Class heroes, it is time. / We began this together, / Arise to finish it!"

---

[137] See *Rabochii zhurnal* 1924, no. 1: 64–65, 79.

[138] Sannikov was a member of a new generation of proletarian poets and his biography reflected important differences. The son of a small-town artisan (a sled maker), he was still in his teens during the revolution (attending the Shaniavskii People's University in Moscow in 1917). Most important, unlike the older generation of worker writers, he had no real industrial career before he became a full-time party activist and writer—before 1917 he worked two years as a copy-clerk-typist. It is worth noting that as a child Sannikov sang in a church choir. See RGALI, f. 1624, op. 1, d. 193, ll. 6–7; f. 1638, op. 4, d. 6, l. 26; f. 2504, op. 1, d. 119, l. 1.

[139] *Rabochii zhurnal* 1924, no. 1: 130.

At the sound of Lenin's words, Red Square was suddenly filled with a strong wind.

> The brass chimes in the ancient tower
> Fearfully rang
> And,
> Blazing in the early dawn,
> The dead rose from their graves.

Behind the resurrected Lenin, they formed ranks and prepared for battle. But this awakening of the dead was only the opening act of Sannikov's apocalypse.

> Like the clamor of an earthquake,
> An underground rumble reached me
> And, shuddering,
> The Kremlin walls
> Fell to the ground.

"No doubt," Sannikov interprets, this was a symbol of the "state collapsing into dust." This was certainly more than the canonical communist "withering away" of the state. And it arrived with the appropriate signs.

> The sun in the sky was eclipsed
> And Red Square
> Was covered in thick darkness.
> In that dread hour
> Thunder rolled
> In the heavens, dimmed with storm clouds,
> And with a moist cleansing darkness,
> Thundering rain fell upon the earth.

Fires then blazed up all around—symbols, he explains, of eternal fighters in the struggle. And factory whistles—for this was, after all, a proletarian apocalypse—trumpeted the victory of the new time.[140] Like a good deal of proletarian writing, especially of the civil war years, "Leniniada" invoked repeatedly the symbols of biblical apocalypse: the return of the Savior, the resurrection of the dead, the end of secular government, earthquakes, thunder, fire, and trumpets heralding the final days of the old world.

Apocalypticism was properly a hopeful topos. As Vladimir Kirillov wrote in early 1918 in a poem dedicated to Aleksandr Blok, whose brilliant and influential poem of the revolution, "The Twelve,"[141] was filled with images of apocalyptic tempests, the blood of vengeance and redemption, the dying old world, and the appearance, wreathed in white roses, of Jesus Christ, prole-

---

[140] G. Sannikov, "Leniniada," *Rabochii zhurnal* 1924, no. 1: 8–12; no. 2: 76–80; 1925, no. 1–2: 126–30. Quotations are from 1924, no. 2: 76–79; 1925, no. 1–2: 128.

[141] The poem was first published in *Znamia truda,* the newspaper of the Central Committee of the Left S.R. Party, on 18 Feb. (3 Mar.) 1918.

tarian writers like himself approached the "bloody whirlwind" of the "sacred" final battle as a "bright blessed hour," with "prayers of blessing," songs, and "bright faith."[142] But not all proletarians were certain that the devastations of the times heralded redemption or salvation. This question was strongest in the thoughts of those who opposed Bolshevik power. In the newspaper of the Menshevik workers' intelligentsia, *Rabochaia mysl'* (Workers' thought), a well-known trade union activist, the metalworker Aleksandr Sharek, wrote an essay in the first days after the October revolution titled simply "Opustoshenie" (Devastation):

> "And people went to the mountains and said: mountains cover us, for it would be better to be dead than alive." These words of the Apocalypse constantly pursue me, and not only I but perhaps others, as I read the gloomy chronicles of recent days or hear the "golden-tongued" orators in the public squares. . . . Timeless values are being tossed out one after another. The people's soul is being laid waste [*opustoshaetsia*]. . . . The destruction of the people's truth is the reason for the rebirth of the words of the Apocalypse. Darkness and despair will follow in its footsteps. And people will flee to the mountains and say "cover us."[143]

Opponents of Bolshevism were not the only ones to read the revolution as a dark apocalypse, a time of terrible devastation from which deliverance and redemption were not at all certain. As we have seen, Marxist theorists of proletarian culture repeatedly insisted that the "proletarian" mood was by definition bold and optimistic.[144] Translated into images of the sacred—however "unproletarian" critics considered this language—this sensibility tended to draw upon logics of redemption and salvation. But this mood and faith did not always hold. On the contrary, critics often felt that there was too much "skepticism," "ambivalence," "melancholy," and "bourgeois pessimism" in workers' writings and an unproletarian view of life as a "mysterious sphinx."[145] Ironically, the divorce of religious language from its theological home, especially the formally atheistic symbolization of such images as crucifixion and apocalypse, may have made such symbols darker than they were for believers. In any case, a darker and less hopeful reading often seemed com-

---

[142] Poet-Proletarii [V. Kirillov], "Poetam revoliutsii (Posviashchaetsia A. Bloku), *Znamia truda*, 8/21 Feb. 1918; rpt. in Kirillov, *Stikhotvoreniia*, 11. Kirillov's poem preceded the publication of Blok's "Dvenadtsat'," in the same paper, by a week and a half. It is possible, though, that Kirillov had heard the poem and was responding to it.

[143] A. Sharek, "Opustoshenie," *Rabochaia mysl'*, no. 4–5 (12 Nov. 1917), 9. The text referred to is the significantly different Rev. 6:16–17: "And they called to the mountains and the rocks, 'Fall on us and hide us from the face of the one who sits on the throne and from the wrath of the Lamb! For the great day of His wrath has come, and who is able to stand?'"

[144] One of the most active proponents of this ideologically defined proletarian aesthetic was the increasingly powerful Pavel Lebedev-Polianskii. See his many book reviews in *Proletarskaia kul'tura*, the theoretical journal of the Proletcult.

[145] Lebedev-Polianskii, review of *V bure i plamen'*, in *Proletarskaia kul'tura*, no. 5 (November 1918), 44–45; Semen Kluben', in *Griadushchaia kul'tura* (Tambov), no. 2 (December 1918), 24; Lebedev-Polianskii, review of new writings by V. Aleksandrovskii in *Proletarskaia kul'tura*, no. 9–10 (June–July 1919), 65–66; S. Rodov, "Motivy tvorchestva M. Gerasimova," *Kuznitsa*, no. 1 (May 1920), 23; Voronskii, "O gruppe pisatelei 'Kuznitsa,'" 136.

pelling to worker writers. Shorn of the traditional hope they symbolized for the faithful, crucifixion and apocalypse could stand more starkly as images of suffering without salvation. And they often did. Thus Sergei Obradovich asked, in a 1920 lament written about the lives of workers amidst four years of revolution, "Who wears the heart of stone? / Who is nailed to the Cross? / Poisoned by anguish [*toska*], / Doubt and worry . . . / Who meets with a dark gaze / The fourth spring?"[146]

Apocalyptic images were not always signs of coming salvation. Often these writings seem to suggest the purposelessness of suffering, portraying a more existential than Christian apocalypse, lacking the hopeful teleology both of the original and of the Marxist vision of a new time. Aleksandr Smirnov's "Thoughts of a Proletarian" about the "lessons of life" dwelled above all on images of "nighttime gloom," of "clouds congealed, literally with blood / in the heavens," of "suffering, body and spirit," and of workers "drinking to the depths / the bitter cup of truth" (*istina*). The thought of a "bright future" and of the struggle "for love" were not forgotten. But the mood of the poem is more tragic than uplifting, its focus more on the pathos of suffering than on the promise of salvation. As we have seen, these writers sometimes treated the great suffering around them as signs pointing less to transcendence than to tragedy; suffering and even catastrophe were at best sublime in their enriching and ennobling power, inspiring human aspiration, though offering no escape. In this spirit, Aleksei Gastev declared "desperate torments" and death to be essential to the defining existential experience of the proletariat and hence to the emerging new ideology of the world.[147] And Andrei Platonov, in an essay titled "Life to the End," published in 1921, described "despair, torment, and death" as "the true reasons for heroic human action and the most powerful motors of history."[148] These paths of suffering and catastrophe were not necessarily seen as paths to anywhere else. Whether it was the absence of theology that made for a darker story of suffering, apocalyptic upheaval, and collapse or the only remaining logic in the face of their experiences and the values with which they judged the world, it is clear that many worker writers could not sustain the proper "proletarian" mood of fearless optimism and bold certainty in the coming of a bright new future.

Emotion, Fantasy, and Dream

Images such as crucifixion, resurrection, and apocalypse were neither empty literary devices nor (in most cases) literal signs of religious faith but signifying metaphors and symbols. This symbolic language of the sacred sought to make the hardships of their lives and the chaos of the times interpretable, as having

---

[146] S. Obradovich, "Rabochaia," *Kuznitsa*, no. 1 (May 1920), 4–5.

[147] A. Gastev, "O tendentsiiakh proletarskoi kul'tury," *Proletarskaia kul'tura*, no. 9–10 (June–July 1919), 44. See also his poem "Bashnia," first printed in *Metallist* 1917, no. 4 (Oct. 18): 4–6, and rpt. in *Griadushchee* 1918, no. 2 (May): 11–12, and in all editions of Gastev's *Poeziia rabochego udara* (1st ed. Petrograd, 1918).

[148] A. Platonov, "Zhizn' do kontsa," *Voronezhskaia kommuna*, 25 Aug. 1921.

moral and teleological meaning, even if those meanings were translated into purely earthly and social forms. At the same time, and inseparable from these interpretive and moral functions, this symbolic language of the sacred was a discourse of affect and emotion. Worker writers continued, as before 1917, to believe that ideas must touch the emotions to be of consequence. And they also often continued to believe that upper-class intellectuals, as Fedor Kalinin had argued in his often-quoted article of 1912, could not "feel" for the working class, that workers needed their own writers and artists who were proletarian not only in political ideology but, as Nikolai Liashko argued in 1920, in "life-feeling."[149] This essential "emotional side of ideology,"[150] it was believed, was conveyed best through symbols, metaphors, and illusions. Some of these worker writers explicitly argued this point. Sergei Obradovich, in an important essay on "thinking in images," and Nikolai Liashko, in a major article "on the tasks of the worker writer," both writing in the journal *Kuznitsa* in 1920, maintained that the use of "images" (*obrazy*) was preferable to mere description because images expressed truths that were best understood through the emotions.[151] In practice, most of these worker writers regularly sought images that would reflect their intuitive perceptions and emotional understandings and evoke readers' own feelings. These writers wanted to touch their readers' hearts and, perhaps most of all, to speak their own. They may have shared Aleksandr Bogdanov's view of art as a means of "organizing people's feelings."[152] But self-expression seemed still to be their greater preoccupation.

Sacred language and imagery often seemed best able to express emotions.[153] This was the symbolic language that lower-class Russians had learned as their emotions developed in childhood. But it is also in the nature of sacred discourse to voice the imagination, to articulate things sublime and terrible, to speak of the mythic and the mysterious—in other words, to speak the language of emotion, of what Platonov called "the passion of thought."[154] This was long understood in the Russian revolutionary movement. As we have noted, populists in the nineteenth century and after often deployed the language of religion in their efforts to reach the minds and hearts of lower-class Russians. Marxist God-builders in the wake of the 1905 revolution similarly recognized that even a "scientific socialist" revolutionary movement could not afford to ignore religion's power to respond to people's emotional and sentimental needs. Al-

---

[149] N. Liashko, "O zadachakh pisatelia-rabochego," *Kuznitsa*, no. 3 (July 1920): 26. See also Lebedev-Polianskii's comments—ironic given his own history as a nonworker who told workers which emotions were properly proletarian—that "nonproletarians cannot express proletarian feelings": *Kuznitsa*, no. 2 (June 1920), 28.

[150] F. Kalinin, "Tip rabochego v literature," 95.

[151] S. Obradovich, "Obraznoe myshlenie," *Kuznitsa*, no. 2 (June 1920), 24–25; N. Liashko, "O zadachakh pisatelia-rabochego," ibid., no. 3 (July 1920), 26.

[152] A. A. Bogdanov, "Proletariat i iskusstvo" (1920), in *Voprosy sotsializma: Raboty raznykh let* (Moscow, 1990), 421.

[153] In his book on language of the revolutionary epoch, A. M. Selishchev argued that the widespread use of religious language and images in the years between 1917 and 1926 was to be explained by their greater functional ability to express emotions: *Iazyk revoliutsionnoi epokhi* 126, 133.

[154] A. Platonov, "Kul'tura proletariata," *Voronezhskaia kommuna*, 20 Oct. 1920.

though the Bolsheviks formally silenced and suppressed God-building, many worker writers, including Communists, persisted in interpreting the world in sacred terms. Although regular criticism of the use of religious motifs may have discouraged them from defending their practices, they did occasionally reflect on what they were doing with such language. In his essay on thinking in images, Obradovich insisted that when a worker poet used images such as crucifixion, this was not a "naked slogan" but the "strong revelation [*vyiavlenie*] of feelings," the expression of a "suffering heart."[155] Andrei Platonov similarly asserted that "religion is the means of studying the world and relating to it by means of feelings, of passion." And though he predicted that the new revolutionary culture marked the end of religion, for it brought the triumph of "consciousness [*soznanie*] over feeling," he defined "consciousness" as "the sum of instincts, intuition, and sensation," as "a symphony of feelings."[156] Similarly, in 1924, amidst the Soviet campaign against established religion and belief, a group of writers associated with the Kuznitsa group argued that socialist art must and could replace religion in response to people's deepest needs. If the church turned out to be, as Freud and bourgeois psychiatry revealed, "a great psychiatric hospital," art must take its place as "the organizer of the subconscious—of the world of fantasy and dream [*snovidenii*]."[157]

Religious imagery and language in these writings was often emotionally uplifting, morally confident, and optimistic. With the aid of images, stories, and symbols that they had in hand or found to be useful, these workers created a view of the world much as the God-builders had tried to imagine: emotional, universalizing, and ethical, possessing a quality of mystery and destiny that was an important part of the way many Russians understood the revolution. As they wrote of workers awakening to the coming of a new age, they spoke of "deep subterranean feelings" welling up and of "vague feelings" that made people's eyes "shine with an uncommon light,"[158] and they imagined the coming new time with all the familiar images of transcendence and salvation. But these images of faith and optimism never silenced doubt and unease, feelings that continued to mark the writings of so many of these worker authors. As critics noted, plenty of melancholy, doubt, and even despair remained in these writings, and even grew. Such feelings were especially strong by the early 1920s. The NEP era seemed to some of these writers to be a time when "worker poets were crucified on the lampposts" and the crowd had turned away from them, "preferring Barabbas to Jesus."[159]

---

[155] S. Obradovich, "Obraznoe myshlenie," *Kuznitsa*, no. 2 (June 1920), 20, 24–25.

[156] A. Platonov, "Konets boga," *Prizyv* 1921, no. 3 (15 Jan.), 6, and "Proletarskaia poeziia," *Kuznitsa*, no. 9 (1922), 29.

[157] G. Iakubovskii and G. Sannikov in *Rabochii zhurnal* 1924, no. 3–4 (March–April): 133. The authors, both associated with the Kuznitsa group, wrote on behalf of "the initiative group to organize a section for the study of art under the Society of Militant Materialists."

[158] A. Platonov, "Tridtsat' krasnykh," *Krasnaia derevnia*, no. 98 (6 July 1920), 2; *Glukhar'* (Samara, 1920), 10–14.

[159] M. Gerasimov, "Chernaia pena," *Kuznitsa*, no. 9 (1922), 6–8; Sannikov in *Rabochii zhurnal* 1924, no. 3–4: 236.

Orthodox Communist critics were troubled by the frequent use of religious metaphor and symbol in proletarian writing in these first years after October, as they were by confused and alien views of the self and the modern.[160] Communist intellectuals cautioned, criticized, and even hectored proletarian authors for allowing into their writing "foggy mysticism," "feelings of romanticism," and even "an admixture of Christian zealotry, Tolstoyism, and Dostoevskyism."[161] What one needed and wanted to find in real proletarian literature, critics argued, were pictures of the everyday realities of workers' lives and struggles. Instead one found a flood of mythic and mystical images of workers and revolutionaries as "fighters for 'the great holy truth,' " as "godmen," as "builders of the cosmos," and as "titans . . . who 'can make ice crystals turn into fire,' " and too much inappropriate talk about "sacred suffering," the road to Golgotha, crucifixion, resurrection, and apocalypse.[162] In the authoritative opinion of Pavel Lebedev-Polianskii, such language and thinking were simply "alien to the proletarian revolution."[163] More generously, Aleksandr Voronskii criticized the "red prayers [*akafisty*] and red psalms" in workers' writings as simply too "abstract."[164] Worst of all, perhaps, in the view of critics, the mixing of these inappropriate moods and motifs with revolutionary commitment and fervor suggested an "ambivalence" (*razdvoeniia*) that a "worker . . . cannot and must not know."[165] But the proletarian revolution did not reduce the appeal of religious and mythic thinking or ease ambivalence and doubt. On the contrary, the upheavals, hardships, and utopian possibilities of revolution intensified both sacred vision and existential uncertainty.

[160] On the spread of Romantic and mythic ways of writing even to provincial Soviet publications, see the critique by V. Polianskii [P. Lebedev-Polianskii], "Poeziia sovetskoi provintsii," *Proletarskaia kul'tura*, no. 7–8 (April–May 1919), 4.

[161] S. Rodov, "Motivy tvorchestva Mikhaila Gerasimova," *Kuznitsa*, no. 1 (May 1920), 22–23; Lebedev-Polianskii in *Proletarskaia kul'tura*, no. 4 (September 1918), 38, and no. 9–10 (June–July 1919), 65–66.

[162] "Poeziia sovetskoi provintsii," *Proletarskaia kul'tura*, no. 7–8 (April–May 1919), 49; reviews ibid., no. 6 (February 1919), 38; no. 17–19 (August–December 1920), 93; V. Friche, "V poiskakh novoi krasoty," *Tvorchestvo*, no. 2 (June 1918), 6.

[163] Lebedev-Polianskii, review of Oreshin in *Proletarskaia kul'tura*, no. 6 (February 1919), 43–44. Although these words were used only to characterize Oreshin, in his many criticisms of religious imagery and moods in proletarian writing he essentially argues the same. See, e.g., *Proletarskaia kul'tura*, no. 9–10 (June–July 1919), 65, and no. 17–19 (August–December 1920), 93.

[164] Voronskii, "O gruppe pisatelei 'Kuznitsa,' " 135.

[165] S. Rodov, "Motivy tvorchestva M. Gerasimova," *Kuznitsa*, no. 1 (May 1920), 23.

Conclusion

The voices examined in this book arose from some of the most freighted social and cultural boundaries of modern Russian life: the borders of physical labor and intellectual creation, of popular and elite cultures, and of everyday plebeian life and the exceptional lives of wanderers and poets. When these men and women (though tellingly few of the latter) wrote about their lives and the world around them—and they wrote a great deal—they were motivated less by the wish to comment on the political and social issues of the day than by a desire to speak of deeper and more difficult questions about life's meaning and to express their own selves. Worker writers grappled with the nature of civilization and culture, the imperatives of moral and ethical truth, and the possibilities of realizing in life what they could imagine in their minds. They returned again and again to questions about existential meaning and purpose: the uncertain nature and place of the self, the promise and pain of modernity, and the qualities of the sacred in both their lives and their imaginations.

Preoccupied with the nature and significance of the human person, worker writers crafted a version of the widespread discourse in Russian and European culture about the inward self and the natural dignity of all people. These conceptions fed a fervent moral critique of the indignities and insults of subordination and exploitation, but also dreams of transcendent selves—epic heroes, winged saviors, self-perfected models of human possibility—and of a transformed society in which the individual thrived. Heroic personalities and the inward emotional and moral world of the individual preoccupied worker writers even amid the revolutionary rise of an ideology of collectivism. At the same time, these writers confronted their own unease and anxieties: they were troubled not only by socially debased selves and by people's failure to realize their full capacities as human beings but also by profound doubts about the ultimate possibility of human progress and happiness. The result was an often dark narrative of the self in the world, marked by the inescapability of alienation and suffering. At times worker writers felt the allure of solitude and even death, and a certain pleasure and sense of existential truth in the stance of the sensitive and enlightened stranger living at odds with the malevolence of the world. Difference—social, sexual, intellectual, and above all emotional—became a source of both moral outrage and self-identity.

In contemplating the modern landscape of city, factory, and machine, worker writers spoke of a symbolic terrain as well as one that was tangible and immediate. This intense and intimate relationship between physical and emblematic modernities, between social experience and cultural ideas about its meaning and value, gave particular shape and pathos to their accounts. The results were characteristically ambiguous. City, factory, and machine appeared as sources of progress, vital life, and even beauty; but they also seemed alien and hostile, filled with moral harm, aesthetic gloom, and danger. Modern life appeared to free workers from the constraints of nature and tradition, even to give pleasure, but it also engendered feelings of loss and regret and a deep sense of injury. These were most often not alternative visions but intertwined truths. From this aesthetic, emotional, and moral discordance, as from modernity itself, there was no exit.

A feeling for the sacred was essential to worker writers' understandings of modern life and the self. Although their writings were usually not religious in the literal sense of being part of organized faith and practice, worker authors wrote often in a religious idiom, making use of Christian and other sacred and mythic terminologies, imageries, and narratives. Suffering, salvation, transcendence, and redemption—often expressed through concrete images such as crucifixion and the appearance of godlike saviors—pervaded their writings. Like formal religion, such writing helped at least to give metaphoric meaning and order to the chaos of existence, as well as to lend voice to imagination and sentiment, to express deep feelings of mystery and awe before the world together with a deep sense of melancholy and even dread, and to nourish dreams of salvation.

Contemporary Marxist cultural critics were often troubled by what they heard in proletarian voices. Convinced that language is never innocent of class and ideology and believing that the proletariat represented a historically predestined force for progress naturally attracted to the forward march of secular modernity and collective identity, they struggled to teach worker writers to speak in their presumed correct voices, to purge from workers' writings "motifs alien to the proletariat."[1] These motifs were plentiful, however. Intellectual critics regularly complained, as we have seen, that worker writers paid too much attention to the sorrowing self, failed to appreciate the new aesthetic of roaring machines and vital city spaces, voiced a "foggy mysticism," and evinced an altogether unproletarian spirit of "anguish," "melancholy," and "reverie." After 1917 confused and alien views of the self and the

---

[1] P. Lebedev-Polianskii, review of recent books by V. Aleksandrovskii in *Proletarskaia kul'tura*, no. 9–10 (June–July 1919), 65.

modern and frequent use of religious metaphor and symbol were particularly disturbing, especially when they were voiced by working-class authors who had embraced the revolution and were even members of the Bolshevik party. Worker writers themselves sometimes publicly complained about the excessive "irony," "contradictory philosophy," "confusion," and "self-torment" in their fellow proletarians' writings, and about a harmful "deviation toward pessimism."[2] In the judgment of Pavel Lebedev-Polianskii, head of the Proletcult and commissar for literature and publishing in the People's Commissariat of Enlightenment, these many deviations from the proper outlook of the proletarian were simply "not our language."[3] He had to recognize, however, as did other critics, that these other languages remained a powerful presence even after the revolution. It was clear to many observers of working-class culture, as it was to another Proletcult leader, Aleksandr Bogdanov, that if one understood that there was a profound difference between the mere social fact of belonging to the proletariat and the necessary worldview that defined the conscious proletarian, it would be evident that "poetry written by workers is too often . . . not workers' poetry."[4]

Aleksandr Voronskii, the most sensitive and undogmatic of early Soviet Marxist literary critics, suggested that in proletarian writing one heard echoes of the prerevolutionary intelligentsia.[5] Indeed, many of the themes that preoccupied worker writers recalled questions that many Russian intellectuals, including some of the country's most influential writers and poets, had been struggling with for a century: the meaning and place of the human person, the interrelation between nature and culture, and the power of feeling, imagination, and the transcendent in the everyday world. Proletarian intellectuals, like educated writers and ordinary literate Russians who shared these widespread concerns with ideas and values, were deeply interested in the moral meaning of life in the world, and they found meaning (often complexly sublime meaning) in the contemplation of both human possibility and human suffering and tragedy. The vision of change they found most compelling tended, as it did for most of the intelligentsia, toward the universalistic rather than the distinctly proletarian. This was the "general democratic" ideal of human dignity, rights, and natural freedom that Bolshevik critics complained was one of the ideological shortcomings of most prerevolutionary writing by workers and seemed to persist long after.[6] No less important, worker writers often shared with many educated Russians a disturbing awareness of how often high ideals

---

[2] S. Obradovich, review of Kirillov, *Stikhotvoreniia* (Moscow, 1924), *Rabochii zhurnal* 1925, no. 4: 156–58; P. Bessal'ko, "Proletarskie poety," *Griadushchee* 1919, no. 1: 13.

[3] V. Polianskii [P. Lebedev-Polianskii], review of *Gorn* in *Proletarskaia kul'tura*, no. 5 (November 1918), 42.

[4] A. Bogdanov, "Chto takoe proletarskaia poeziia?" *Proletarskaia kul'tura*, no. 1 (July 1918), 20.

[5] A. Voronskii, "O gruppe pisatelei 'Kuznitsa': Obshchaia kharakteristika," in *Iskusstvo i zhizn': Sbornik statei* (Moscow and Petrograd, 1924), 126.

[6] See, e.g., V. Polianskii [P. Lebedev-Polianskii], "Motivy rabochei poezii," *Proletarskaia kul'tura*, no. 3 (August 1918), 7.

(beauty, morality, truth) collided with the crass realities and limited possibilities of the everyday world.

Echoes of the mentality of the intelligentsia may also be seen in the growing force of ambivalence and ambiguity in workers' writings. Marxist critics often noted the persistence and even growth in workers' writings of "agonizing ambivalence," "an inconstant mood," and an uncertain view of life as a "mysterious sphinx."[7] These observations were warnings. "Ambivalence," critics made abundantly clear, was something that a true worker "ought not to know."[8] In his opening address to the first All-Russian Conference of Proletarian Writers in May 1920, speaking for the presidium of the Proletcult, Bogdanov complained of proletarian poets who wrote in a manner so "foggy" that even some intellectuals could not understand what they meant. As illustration, Bogdanov pointed to some recent poems by Mikhail Gerasimov. Certain that the fault lay in baneful outside influences, Bogdanov advised worker writers to "beware of modernist poets" and to pay more attention to the "simplicity" (*prostota*) of such "coryphaei of literature" as Pushkin, Lermontov, Byron, Goethe, and Shakespeare.[9] Even more bluntly, a few years later, Lebedev-Polianskii warned that Soviet literature "requires clarity and precision . . . not endless indeterminacy."[10] As this chorus of warnings suggests, the opposite was too often the case. This Bolshevik version of the high-modern ideal of legibility and disciplined rationality ran afoul of a no less modern and revolutionary consciousness—the accompaniment of a modern and revolutionary reality—of pervading uncertainty and ambiguity.

The experiences of modern life and even the coming to power of communists in 1917 did not ensure the triumph of a collectivist faith, unambiguous love of the landscapes of the modern, or a scientific worldview purged of all mystery and ambiguity. The upheavals, hardships, and utopian possibilities of the modern experience and of Russian life in particular stimulated powerful but contradictory emotions. Mikhail Gerasimov subtly suggested as much, as well as something about the aesthetics of truth, when he answered Bodganov's criticisms by observing bitingly that even Pushkin was not always clear.[11]

[7] Voronskii, "O gruppe pisatelei 'Kuznitsa,'" 136; Lebedev-Polianskii's review of V. Aleksandrovskii in *Proletarskaia kul'tura*, no. 9–10 (June–July 1919), 66; review by P. I. M. in *Rabochii zhurnal* 1925, no. 1–2: 277; P. Lebedev-Polianskii, review of *V bure i plamen'* in *Proletarskaia kul'tura*, no. 5 (November 1918), 44–45.

[8] S. Rodov, "Motivy tvorchestva M. Gerasimova," *Kuznitsa*, no. 1 (May 1920), 23.

[9] "Protokoly pervogo Vserossiiskogo Soveshchaniia proletarskikh pisatelei," 10–12 May 1920, in RGALI, f. 1638, op. 3, d. 1, ll. 10b–2. Bogdanov similarly criticized Gerasimov in *Proletarskaia kul'tura*, no. 15–16 (April–July 1920), 91–92.

[10] V. Polianskii [P. Lebedev-Polianskii, then head of Glavlit, the main censorship agency], in *Rabochii zhurnal* 1925, no. 1–2: 262. See similar remarks in his review of *Gorn* in *Proletarskaia kul'tura*, no. 5 (November 1918), 42–43.

[11] "Protokoly pervogo Vserossiiskogo Soveshchaniia proletarskikh pisatelei," 10–12 May 1920, in RGALI, f. 1638, op. 3, d. 1, ll. 10b–2. One cannot help wondering whether this retort—not to mention the "foggy" writing that provoked the exchange—was used against Gerasimov when he was arrested as an enemy of the Soviet state in 1937. I did not succeed in getting access to the records of his trial. According to archivists, trial transcripts and material were destroyed after his death in 1939.

Nikolai Liashko more elaborately insisted on the inherent ambivalence of modern life: "unexpected pains and joys, vacuity and profundity, versatile coping, spiritual breakdown, tragedies of immense weight appearing at every step." In times such as these, "people sicken, go mad from exhaustion—but really live!" Worker writers, whose particular life experiences and desires made them especially sensitive to the "contradictoriness and complexity" of these times, understood this complexity most intensely.[12]

For all the ambiguity, however, this was not an embryonic postmodern consciousness. Postmodernity, it has been said, "does not seek to substitute one truth for another, one standard of beauty for another, one life ideal for another. . . . It braces itself for a life without truths, standards, ideals."[13] It is about living with ambiguity, even loving it. These proletarian intellectuals, however, could not endure a life without truths and ideals, much less find pleasure in indeterminacy, paradox, and irony. Nor could they even share the older Romantic aesthetic of pleasurable contemplation of melancholy and suffering. They were mostly socialists and Marxists, and they embraced the world-transforming idealism of the Russian revolutionary movement. Still, many found it impossible to escape from doubts and anxieties. Theirs was a sorrowful and troubled ambivalence, with no transcending harmony and pleasure. It was painful to believe so strongly in the dignity and worth of the human person, the necessity of morality and beauty, the emancipatory power of modern progress, and the possibility of a new age of happiness, and to see in both oneself and the world so much inescapable ugliness, suffering, and loss. It was painful not to be able to free oneself, even with sincere revolutionary passion, from existential doubt. At the same time, it was exhilarating to dream.

---

[12] N. Liashko, "O byte i literature perekhodnogo vremeni," *Kuznitsa*, no. 8 (April–September 1921), 29–30, 34.

[13] Zygmunt Bauman, *Intimations of Postmodernity* (London, 1992), ix.

APPENDIX

Selected Biographical Sketches

The worker writer Ivan Dement'ev (Kubikov), reviewing a new story by Maxim Gorky in 1913, commented that the strength of Gorky's account is that he portrays workers not as "an impersonal mass, but rather with all their variety of individual personalities and moods."[1] Historical accounts should be no less sensitive to these stories of individual lives, never completely reducible to other stories, which are often accounts of how social life was most tangibly experienced and thought about, how choices were made and actions begun. This appendix describes briefly the lives of some of the worker writers who began writing before 1917, while employed in working-class jobs, and continued writing into the early Soviet years. A cautionary note: As factual narratives, these stories will appear more fixed and sure than the evidence warrants. Documenting the lives of such relatively obscure individuals depends largely on their own words. We can know what they published, but not always what they did not. We have records of organizations and occasional meetings, but many small groups are poorly documented. We know what contemporaries recorded about these writers and their activities, but our main source of knowledge about their lives is their own statements, ranging from brief answers to questionnaires (typically in connection with membership in a Soviet organization) to short autobiographical essays. Like all works of memory and self-representation, these texts were shaped by forgetfulness, by values and constraints at the time of writing, by self-interest and deliberate purpose, and by other considerations of need and context. A small number of autobiographical essays were written before 1917, often as part of a deliberate presentation of a certain cultural image of themselves to others. Most of these statements were written after the October revolution, usually at the re-

[1] Kvadrat [I. N. Dement'ev], "Novaia povest' M. Gor'kogo," *Novaia rabochaia gazeta*, no. 5 (13 Aug. 1913), 2.

quest of Communist intellectuals interested in promoting proletarian creativity and recording narratives of working-class awakening. This setting affected the stories told. It also tended to leave in silence many writers who felt alienated from the new order or simply had disappeared into oblivion. Finally, it is telling that when we have much information about an individual—multiple autobiographical statements and corroborating information from other sources—we find a good deal of contradiction. Even autobiographical statements written at different times often tell slightly different stories. I have already considered these life stories as expressive (and contradictory) texts. Here I try to reconstruct the social lives implied by these stories. Although the facts of life experience may be elusive—inevitably obscured by the intentionalities and constructedness of the memories and texts that represent them—they are an essential part of the materials out of which individuals construct ideas, stories, and meanings, and they must be sought. I have tried to offer relatively coherent narratives.[2] Still, the uncertainties and instabilities, though elided here, remain part of these stories. And so do the silences—even the bare facts of marriage and parenthood are never mentioned, and we know nothing about the political and personal choices and doubts that did not seem useful or desirable to mention. In their poetry and fiction they often alluded to family, intimacy, and uncertainty, but when asked to describe their lives as pieces of history, they conventionally offered an orderly (even teleological) story of public experiences and public acts.

Vasilii Dmitrievich Aleksandrovskii (1897–1934)

Vasilii Aleksandrovskii was born on 3 (15) January 1897 (until 1918, Russia used the Julian calendar, which was twelve days behind the Gregorian in the nineteenth century and thirteen days behind in the twentieth) into a peasant family in the village of Baskakovo, in Smolensk province, in west-central Russia. To help the family survive, his father was often away in the city earning wages. His father's death when Vasilii was a child forced his mother to abandon farming and go to the city to work as a servant, leaving her children with relatives in the village. Aleksandrovskii lived with his uncle, attending a three-year zemstvo school in the winters and doing miscellaneous village work in the summer months, especially looking after children. When he was eleven years old he joined his mother in Moscow, where he spent one year in a city school and then started work in a secondhand goods store, until the owner opened a leather manufactory and sent Aleksandrovskii to work there. He was given various tasks in the workshop and office and sent on errands. He worked

---

[2] My accounts attempt to reconcile the various sources of information about their lives, cited in the footnotes to each entry. I give only brief references here; full titles can be found in the selected bibliography. In addition to the cited sources, these sketches draw on bibliographical information about their publishing careers and diverse archival data on membership and participation in various organizations in my research files.

there for six years, until 1916, when he was drafted into the army and sent to the Galician front. Wounded and released a half-year later, he returned to the leather manufactory, but he soon found better-paying work in the offices of the Moscow–Kazan Railroad.

During all these years, like other worker writers, Aleksandrovskii continued his education by reading constantly. He started to write poetry on the eve of the war. His first poems appeared in print in 1913 and 1914 in the Menshevik periodicals *Zhivoe slovo* (Living word), *Luch* (Ray), and *Novaia rabochaia gazeta* (New workers' newspaper), and in the 1913 collection of verses by worker poets, *Nashi pesni* (Our songs). After October 1917, Aleksandrovskii was able to devote himself to full-time writing and cultural work. In 1918–19 he was active in the literary studio of the Moscow Proletcult, a member of the editorial board of the Moscow Proletcult magazine *Gudki*, and a member of the author's division of the Journalists' Union. Along with other discontented Moscow Proletcultists, he was one of the founders of Kuznitsa in 1920, a member of the editorial board of the journal *Kuznitsa,* an organizer of the First All-Russian Congress of Proletarian Writers in 1920 (at which he was a member of the presidium), and a member of the board of directors of the All-Russian Association of Proletarian Writers (VAPP), and he worked in the literary department of the People's Commissariat of Enlightenment. Above all, he wrote. From early 1918 through 1925 he published prolifically (mostly poetry but also a few stories and essays) in magazines, newspapers, and anthologies and in several volumes of collected verse. He continued writing and publishing until 1932, though much less frequently—partly because his health was failing but also evidently because he was dissatisfied with the revolution's course; disillusionment is visible in many of his poems of the 1920s. It is not clear whether he ever joined the party. We know that he was sympathetic to the Mensheviks before 1917; at least he published mainly in their papers. Some Soviet sources state that he joined the Bolshevik party in 1917. In any case, we do know, from a response to a questionnaire, that he was no longer a party member (if he ever had been) by 1925.[3]

Aleksei Pavlovich Bibik (1878–1976)

Aleksei Bibik was one of a relative handful of working-class writers who wrote primarily fiction, and he was one of the most prolific.[4] Born on 5 (17) October 1878 in Kharkov, in eastern Ukraine, he was the son of a metal turner

---

[3] RGALI, f. 1638, op. 4, d. 6, l. 2 (1924–25 questionnaire); *Kratkaia literaturnaia entsiklopediia,* 1:142; *Literaturnaia entsiklopediia,* 1:93–94; *Modern Encyclopedia of Russian and Soviet Literature,* Papernyi and Shatseva, *Proletarskie poety pervykh let sovetskoi epokhi,* 498–500; Rodov, *Proletarskie pisateli,* 6–7 (1922 autobiography); *Russkie pisateli: Poety,* 1:137–55; Zavolokin, *Sovremennye raboche-krest'ianskie poety,* 105 (autobiography).

[4] Other relatively well known worker *prozaiki* include Nikolai Liashko (discussed below), Mikhail Sivachev (b. 1877), Mikhail Volkov (b. 1886), Sergei Malashkin (b. 1890), and Nikolai Kochkurov (Artem Veselyi, b. 1899).

(*tokar'*, also translatable as lathe operator). Bibik was better educated than many worker writers; perhaps that is why he turned to prose, which a number of other *samouchki* tried and abandoned as more difficult than poetry or came to later in life. Starting at the age of nine, he learned basic reading and writing at a privately owned school before enrolling in a regular city primary school in Kharkov. After completing his studies there (presumably through the fourth grade), he entered the final (fifth) year of a two-class Church parish school. Hoping to continue his education further, he enrolled in a railroad technical school. But when his father fell ill he had to return home and enter instead the Kharkov locomotive railway workshop as an apprentice metal turner (he had to claim to be a year older then he actually was in order to be allowed to work).[5] He later moved to Taganrog, on the Sea of Azov, where he found work in the railroad shops, though his real goal (he later tells us) was to enter a school for seamen in order to fulfill a dream of sailing the seas. The death of his father in 1898 forced him to return home once again to his family in Kharkov and to work as a turner on the railroad.

In the late 1890s Bibik joined an underground workers' circle and soon after joined the local Social Democratic organization in Kharkov. In 1900 he was arrested for his political activities and for organizing a strike in his workshop and exiled for three years to Viatka province, near the Ural Mountains. At the end of his exile in 1903, he was again arrested, this time for spreading propaganda among the local peasantry and for organizing a socialist circle, and was exiled again for five years to the Siberian north (Arkhangelsk province); he was freed in the 1905 amnesty. Returning to work in the Kharkov railway workshops, he joined the local Menshevik organization and in 1906 was a member of the Menshevik delegation to the Fourth (Unity) Congress of the Russian Social Democratic Workers' Party (RSDRP) in Stockholm. For many years he remained an activist in the Menshevik movement, frequently changing jobs (from 1905 to 1917 he worked variously as a turner, draftsman, machinist, carpenter, statistician, and even land surveyor) and moving from city to city (Baku, Sevastopol, Mariupol, Voronezh, Riga, and in the Don region), partly in order to avoid arrest. Still, at least twice more he spent time in tsarist prisons.

Bibik began writing during his first exile in Viatka province—"out of boredom," he later claimed.[6] His stories appeared in print starting in 1901: in provincial newspapers, in left-wing magazines, in the Menshevik press, and in a collection of his stories published in 1905. While working as a draftsman in a factory in Voronezh in 1910, he completed a novel, which he began writing in 1906, about workers' lives and struggles. Called *K shirokoi doroge* (Toward the open road), it was first published in 1912, with the help of the Marxist literary critic V. L. L'vov-Rogachevskii, in the socialist magazine *Sovremennyi mir* (Modern world) and was reissued as a book in 1914.

---

[5] For this reason, most biographical references to Bibik list his birth date as 1877.

[6] RGALI, f 1849, op. 1, d. 1, l. 8 (autobiography, evidently written after 1917).

When the Bolsheviks took power in 1917, Bibik initially stood with the socialist opposition. By 1920, however, he had abandoned Menshevism and politics altogether. He revised his first novel (several times, in fact) more in line with Communist notions about the labor movement and completed a second novel, which was published in 1922 but was viewed by Communist critics as still showing signs of "ideological confusion." For the next few years, Bibik abandoned literature and returned to work in industry and as an agronomist. He resumed writing only in 1925 and published a number of stories and plays. After 1932 he was able to quit his job and work exclusively as a writer, though from 1936 (the start of the years of Stalin's terror) until 1957 (a few years after Stalin's death) none of his works was published and we know little of his activities.[7]

Mariia Matveevna Chernysheva (b. 1873)

Mariia Chernysheva was one of a handful of female worker writers who began writing before 1917. Born in 1873, she was the daughter of a shopkeeper—her father rented a small retail store in Moscow. After a brief education in a city primary school, Chernysheva helped her father at his shop, but the business failed and she was forced to find other work. For some years she sewed clothes for a fashionable store. In 1907 Chernysheva met Maksim Leonov, a self-taught poet and one of the leaders of the Surikov Circle. He helped her get some of her verses published in newspapers, especially in the provinces. By 1910 she was editor and publisher of the Moscow people's magazine *Balalaika,* where she printed many of her own satirical feuilletons under the pseudonym Baba Mar'ia. When Leonov was exiled from Moscow in 1910 for political activities—mainly for publishing works of a populist socialist orientation—Chernysheva joined him in exile in Arkhangelsk province, where she found work selling books and other literature in the book kiosk of the local state theater. Chernysheva continued to write and to publish in local newspapers, and for a time in 1912 edited the local people's newspaper *Severnoe utro* (Northern morning). At some point in these years Leonov and Chernysheva married. Chernysheva continued to be associated with the Surikov Circle after 1917, but as she was not considered a proletarian writer ideologically, she was allowed to disappear into oblivion.[8]

Her neglect may also have been linked to her gender, especially to archetypical images of the proletarian writer as a man. Although Chernysheva was

---

[7] V. L. L'vov-Rogachevskii, Introduction to Bibik, *K shirokoi doroge* (1914); RGALI, f. 1849, op. 1, d. 1, ll. 6–8 (autobiography), and f. 341, op. 3, d. 58, ll. 1–3 (copy of above); Lindin, *Pisateli,* 31–36; L'vov-Rogachevskii, *Ocherki proletarskoi literatury,* 216–20; *Literaturnaia entsiklopediia,* 1:476–78; *Russkie Sovetskie pisateli: Prozaiki,* 1:224–34; *Kratkaia literaturnaia entsiklopediia,* 1:592; *Modern Encyclopedia of Russian and Soviet Literature,* 2:238–39; *Russkie pisateli, 1800–1917,* 1:263–64.

[8] RGALI, f. 1641, op 1, d. 38. l. 1 (autobiography of Chernysheva-Leonova); *Balalaika: Narodnyi satiricheskii i iumoristicheskii zhurnal* (Moscow, 1910–11).

arguably the most accomplished woman worker writer before 1917, she was not the only one. None, however, was paid any public attention. The two major collections of biographies and selected writings of proletarian writers compiled in the early 1920s included no women at all. At least one female author tried to be considered worthy. Ruta Isaevna Vitkovskaia, a former factory worker and Bolshevik who had fought in the civil war, had sent her autobiography and some sample poems to the editor of one of these collections, but even she was not included when the book appeared in print.[9]

Ivan Evdokimovich Eroshin (1894–1965)

Ivan Eroshin was born on 12 (24) May 1894 in the village of Novo-Aleksandrovo in Riazan province, in the central black earth region. His parents were peasants. Unlike most peasants, however, his father was literate (though his mother was not). His father died when Eroshin was not quite six years old, though he was still able to attend the village school for three years. But when Eroshin was eleven his family joined other landless peasants in resettling in Siberia. Eroshin later described this move as the beginning of his "wandering life as a starving hobo." His first employment was working the peat bogs. He then went to Moscow but often changed jobs: he worked in a bakery; served in a tearoom and as a sales clerk in a food import shop (*kolonial'naia lavka*); sold apples, cream, and bootlaces; was a newspaper boy; was employed in a pharmacy; and he even worked briefly traveling among villages selling and delivering medicines.

Constantly reading in these years, Eroshin began to write in 1914. When war broke out that year, he was drafted, and he served for three months at the front. In 1915 he moved with his wife and mother to Petrograd, where he continued to write. His first published poems appeared in the Bolshevik paper of the workers' insurance movement in 1915, though he was not active in politics and never joined the party. In 1918 he joined the Petrograd Proletcult, where he studied at the literature studio. He participated in the meeting in Moscow in May 1920 to organize a union of proletarian writers and in the First Congress of Proletarian Writers in October and served in the Red Army during the civil war. By the early 1920s he was back in Siberia, where he found work for the magazine *Sibirskie ogni* (Siberian fires) and the newspaper *Sovetskaia Sibir'*. He later lived for many years in the Altai region. Continuing to write poems, he also compiled and reworked folk songs and tales.[10]

---

[9] The two collections are Zavolokin, *Sovremennye raboche-krest'ianskie poety,* and Rodov, *Proletarskie pisateli.* Vitkovskaia's correspondence with Zavolokin is in RGALI, f. 1068, op. 1, d. 27. ll. 1–4. The fact that Vitkovskaia was Jewish may have complicated matters.

[10] RGALI, f. 1068, op. 1, d. 56, ll. 4–6, 14 (1919 autobiography and later correspondence), and f. 1638, op. 3, d. 4, l. 13–130b (1920 questionnaire); *Kratkaia literaturnaia entsiklopediia,* 9:296; *Poeziia v bol'shevistskikh izdaniiakh,* 472.

Sergei Evseevich Gan'shin (1878–1953)

Sergei Gan'shin was born in July 1878 into a peasant family in the village of Gremiachevo, in Tula province, in the central black earth region. His father worked as a carter in Moscow while his mother remained in the village with their two children. Gan'shin's father died when Sergei was only three years old. His death forced the family even deeper into poverty and dependence on the village community: the village commune, which in the Russian tradition periodically redistributed land according to family need and capacities, took away their small plot of land, since they lacked the means to farm it, and offered the family meager communal support instead.

When Gan'shin was seven, he was enrolled in the local rural school, located in a neighboring village, but he attended only a couple of weeks at most. He was unable to continue, he later recalled, because his family was too poor to afford the winter clothes he needed to make the trek to school, which was held in the winter months only, as was typical in the countryside. This is one version of his story. On another occasion he claimed that he was not allowed to attend school at all because he was abnormally short (which photographs confirm). Whatever the reason he could not attend school, that next summer he was put to work as a shepherd boy (*podpasok*), guarding calves and helping the village shepherd in the meadows. During the winter months he continued to work for the village making bast shoes, weaving baskets, or collecting brushwood from the forest. He continued this work until he was fifteen years old, when his mother decided to try her luck in Moscow.

Thus began Gan'shin's years of wandering—first with his family and then on his own. During the next fifteen years, until he settled in Moscow in 1907, Gan'shin wandered around the country working at various jobs. He worked a few years in textile factories, then headed to the Caucasus and the Don region, where he worked as a day laborer, roamed the countryside, and "got to know life and people."[11] Later, moving to Rostov-on-the-Don, he worked in teahouses and taverns and for the local newspaper. Then in 1907 he found work as a weaver in a Moscow textile factory, where he remained for several years. In Moscow he was attracted to radical politics and was arrested and jailed for distributing radical proclamations among peasants. He would later be arrested again for the content of some of his poems, and in 1916 he was sent into exile in Viatka province. Like many Russian workers and worker *intelligenty*, Gan'shin was an independent, nonparty social democrat, publishing poems in both the Bolshevik and Menshevik press.

Gan'shin began writing only in his mid-twenties, in 1904, while working at a newspaper in Rostov. Local writers encouraged him as a *samouchka* who had managed to learn to read and write almost entirely without formal schooling. When in 1908 the magazine *Iasnyi sokol* (Bright falcon, a reference to a

---

[11] Zavolokin, *Sovremennye raboche-krest'ianskie poety,* 175 (autobiography).

popular poem by Gorky) was founded in Moscow to publish the works of "writers from the people," a poem by Gan'shin appeared in print for the first time. In the following years, many magazines, newspapers, and almanacs published his poems. In 1910 he joined the Surikov Circle, which published his first book of poetry. Other collections followed; some were confiscated for political tendentiousness. In 1911 and again in 1913 he was editor of the loosely Menshevik magazine *Zhivoe slovo* (Living word), to which he was long a regular contributor, though he also often contributed poems to the Bolshevik party newspaper *Pravda* (especially in 1913–14). As he told Gorky, with whom he began a correspondence in 1911, he still hoped to find time to study, in particular at the Shaniavskii People's University in Moscow, but he never succeeded in doing so.

Although Gan'shin had long refused to get involved in what many workers saw as the petty factional struggles between Bolsheviks and Mensheviks, after the Bolsheviks came to power in October 1917, he was disturbed by their policies. As he wrote in early January 1918 to Gorky (whose columns in *Novaia zhizn'* [New life] voiced similar criticisms), he had not fought to "replace an autocracy of scoundrels and gravediggers with an autocracy of savages" who offered the people only "false socialism" and "demagogy."[12] He soon accepted the new order, but tended to emphasize what was considered then a "peasant" more than "proletarian" cultural identity. He remained a member of the Surikov Circle, serving for a time as chair of its main Moscow branch, and helped organize the first national conference of "peasant writers." In 1923 he organized a literary circle of worker poets known as Krasnyi gusliar (Red gusli player). He continued to publish in various Soviet magazines but did not succeed in becoming a professional writer. He earned a living in the early 1920s as a building manager for *Pravda*. By the late 1920s, as political toleration of the "peasant" cultural worldview receded, Gan'shin fell silent. We know little about his later years. He died in 1953.[13]

Aleksei Kapitonovich Gastev (1882–1939 or 1941)

Among men who identified themselves as workers and writers, Aleksei Gastev was among the most distinctive—in his social background, in his political and cultural career, and even in his literary style. Gastev was born on 26 September (8 October) 1882 in the town of Suzdal, in Vladimir province, in the Moscow industrial region. His father, a schoolteacher, disappeared when Aleksei was only two and was presumed dead. His mother supported the family after her husband's disappearance by sewing clothing. Gastev completed a city pri-

---

[12] Gan'shin to Gor'kii, 7 Jan. 1918, in Arkhiv A. M. Gor'kogo, KG-NP/a, 7-11-3.

[13] Arkhiv A. M. Gor'kogo, KG-NP/a 7-11-1-2; Zavolokin, *Sovremennye raboche-krest'ian-skie poety*, 174–75 (autobiography); RGALI, f. 1068, op. 1, d. 34, ll. 6–13; Eventov, *Poeziia v bol'shevistskikh izdaniiakh*, 470; *Russkie pisateli, 1800–1917*, 1:522–23; *Zhivoe slovo* (Moscow, 1911–14).

mary school (three or four years) and took technical courses in Suzdal with the hope of entering a technical institute, but he failed the entrance examinations. In 1898 or 1899 Gastev moved to Moscow and entered the Moscow Teachers' Institute, where he found it possible to pursue his technical interests by studying metalworking and carpentry while preparing to become a schoolteacher. In 1900 or 1901 he joined the RSDRP. The next year he was expelled from the institute for organizing a student demonstration marking the fortieth anniversary of the death of the radical Russian literary critic Nikolai Dobroliubov. Soon after, he was arrested for distributing socialist literature among factory workers and was exiled, first back home to Suzdal to await his sentence and then to the small towns of Ustsysolsk and Iarensk in Vologda province, in the north. It was in exile that Gastev first began writing. In 1903 he began work as a local correspondent for the Vladimir newspaper *Vladimirskaia gazeta* (Vladimir news) and published his first work of fiction, a story about life in exile, in the Iaroslavl newspaper *Severnyi krai* (Northern region) in 1904.

That year Gastev fled his exile and left Russia for Europe. On reaching Paris, he joined a large community of Russian political exiles and found work as a metal fitter (*slesar'*) in a factory, but he did not stay long. In 1905, when the revolution broke out, he returned to Russia illegally in order to work as a fulltime "professional revolutionary," closely associated with the Bolshevik wing of the RSDRP. Directing his efforts at the industrialized provinces northeast of Moscow, Gastev found industrial work and a political audience first in Iaroslavl and Ivanovo-Voznesensk and then in Kostroma, where he worked, under the party name Lavrent'ev, mainly among textile workers, organizing strikes and spreading socialist ideas. Here he also joined the local Bolshevik party committee, became well known as a speaker at workers' meetings, served as the Bolsheviks' chief spokesman in public debates with Socialist Revolutionaries, and represented the party in the Kostroma Soviet of Workers' Deputies, of which he was elected chair. By now a leading Bolshevik activist, Gastev was chosen to participate in various party conferences and congresses in 1905 and 1906, including the Fourth (Unity) Congress of the RSDRP in Stockholm (where he might have met Bibik, who was there representing the Mensheviks). After attending a regional Bolshevik conference in Moscow in 1906, he was arrested and sentenced to three years' exile in Arkhangelsk province, in the far north. Within a month he fled the country once more, returned briefly to Paris, and then went to Geneva; he was then smuggled back into Russia.

This time his destination was St. Petersburg, where he would live illegally from 1907 to 1910. But now he was no longer a loyal party activist. In these difficult years after the suppression of the 1905 revolution, Gastev, like many activists, had become disillusioned with party politics, especially the efforts by nonworkers to direct the labor movement. He now focused his efforts on the self-organization of labor and on his writing. After taking a variety of metalworking jobs, in 1908 he found work as a tram driver on the number 2 line from Novaia derevnia, on the Vyborg side, to Nevskii Prospekt. In 1907 he joined or helped organize workers' clubs, where he worked and participated in the organization and leadership of the Petersburg metalworkers' union (formed in May 1907), serving on the board of directors. Underscoring his estrangement from party politics, he quit the Bolshevik party in 1907 or 1908—at a time, perhaps not coincidentally, when various dissident groups within the party, including others favoring a more workerist orientation, were under attack.

In 1910 Gastev returned to Paris, where he lived in the Russian workers' colony and worked as a metalworker in various plants. He became secretary of the Russian Workers' Club, was active in its literary section, and joined the Russian section of the French metalworkers' union, through which he was increasingly attracted by syndicalism. He also became increasingly devoted to his work as a writer. He was attracted mainly to poetry, favoring a free style of prose poems or rhythmic prose. His poems were widely published in trade union and party papers (especially *Pravda*) and in anthologies of works by proletarian writers. In 1912 he joined the Proletarian Culture circle (also known as the League of Proletarian Culture) founded by Anatoly Lunacharsky, where he met other worker writers and had opportunities to read his poems and join in the discussions about proletarian writing. Other members of the circle included Fedor Kalinin (who succeeded Lunacharsky as its secretary), Pavel Bessal'ko, and Mikhail Gerasimov.

On returning to Russia in 1913, Gastev found work again as a metal fitter. But after only six months his illegal residence status was revealed to the police by a provocateur. He was arrested and exiled for four years to the tiny and isolated settlement of Narym, in Siberia. He escaped in 1916 and lived illegally in the Siberian city of Novo-Nikolaevsk (now Novosibirsk). He found employment in various workshops but also worked as a correspondent for the newspaper *Golos Sibiri* (Voice of Siberia), serving briefly in 1917 as editor. Responding to the amnesty that resulted from the fall of the monarchy in February 1917, he returned in the spring of 1917 to Petrograd, where he again found employment as a metalworker and became active in the union movement. He was elected to the leadership of the revived metalworkers' union and of the emerging national union.

For a few years after 1917, Gastev was active as both writer (especially poet) and cultural activist. He published several collections of his poems, many of which also appeared in various periodicals. He participated in the Proletcult and in 1918–19 was sent by the new People's Commissariat of Enlightenment (Narkompros), headed by Lunacharsky, to organize cultural and artistic life as a member of the collegium of Narkompros in Ukraine and as head of the arts department. In 1920 he abandoned literary and cultural work to focus almost entirely on the problems of the social organization of labor, production, and technical reconstruction, realized especially in the founding of the Central Institute of Labor (TsIT), which he led until 1938. He rejoined the party in 1931. He was arrested in 1938, during the terror, and died in captivity.[14]

Mikhail Prokof'evich Gerasimov (1889–1939)

Mikhail Gerasimov was born on 30 September (12 October) 1889 in the village of Petrovka, near the town of Buguruslan, in Samara province, in the Volga region. His father was a railway worker and crossing guard. His mother was a peasant of ethnic Mordvinian background. Starting at the age of nine, Gerasimov helped out around the railroad, pulling weeds near the tracks. In the winter months he attended a two-class school in the town of Kinel. After finishing school (in four or five years) while working in a variety of railroad jobs, he attended the Samara railway technical school, and after graduation became a railway technician.

During the 1905 revolution, when Gerasimov was sixteen and working on the railroad, he got involved in an armed revolutionary detachment (*druzhina*) of railway workers and became increasingly involved with the socialist underground. In 1906 he was arrested and imprisoned, but after six months he escaped through a tunnel leading to a secret Social Democratic party apartment. From there he was smuggled out of the country in the fall of 1907 by way of Finland (where he briefly met Lenin and other leading Social Democratic émigrés). For the next eight years he lived mainly in France and Belgium, where he worked variously as a loader for blast furnaces in an arms factory in Nancy, France, as a coal miner in Belgium, as a metal fitter and electrical fitter in French locomotive and automobile factories (including Renault), as a stoker on ocean liners, and in a variety of jobs in other factories. In these years in exile and labor, Gerasimov managed to explore much of Western Europe, often working in winter and wandering on foot in summer. He was arrested several times for vagrancy.

He began to write sometime before 1913. That was the year he began visiting Lunacharsky's Proletarian Culture circle in Paris, where he met other Russian émigré worker writers, including Fedor Kalinin, Aleksei Gastev, and Pavel Bessal'ko. He also began a correspondence with Gorky at this time, sending him poems for comments. Gerasimov's first poems were published in 1913 in the Bolshevik magazine *Prosveshchenie* (Enlightenment). Other poems appeared in 1914 in *Pravda*, in Ilya Ehrenburg's émigré magazine *Vechera* (Evenings), and in other publications.

[14] GARF, f. R-7927, op. 1, d. 59 [formerly d. 1], ll. 1–26; V. L'vov-Rogachevskii, *Noveishaia russkaia literatura*, 350–66; Johansson, *Aleksej Gastev*; *Kratkaia literaturnaia entsiklopediia*, 2:83–84; *Literaturnaia entsiklopediia*, 2:403–5; *Modern Encyclopedia of Russian and Soviet Literature*, 8:122–24; Eventov, *Poeziia v bol'shevistskikh izdaniiakh*, 470–71; Papernyi and Shatseva, *Proletarskie poety pervykh let sovetskoi epokhi*, 506–7; *Russkie pisateli, 1800–1917*, 1:530–31; *Russkie pisateli: Poety*, 5:344–61.

When the First World War broke out in 1914, Gerasimov volunteered to fight against the Germans in the French Foreign Legion. He saw combat at the Marne, Champagne, and the Argonne and was wounded several times but returned to battle. In the fall of 1915, for participating in antiwar agitation and for insubordination (he joined an uprising of Russian soldiers against harsh treatment by French officers), Gerasimov was deported to Russia. Returning to Samara, he was placed under the surveillance of the military authorities and the following spring was arrested and assigned under guard to a reserve military engineering battalion. Amnestied as a result of the February revolution, Gerasimov became a member of the Samara Soviet of Soldiers' Deputies and was elected chair. In June 1917 he was a delegate at the First All-Russian Congress of Soviets and chosen a member of the new national Central Executive Committee (VTsIK). In July he joined the Bolshevik party, and in October 1917 he was a delegate to the Second Congress of Soviets, which endorsed Soviet power. Returning to Samara, he became assistant chair of the Executive Committee of the Samara Provincial Soviet (*Gubispolkom*) and was named a military commissar. During the civil war he organized Red Guard detachments and commanded a unit on the Orenburg front.

While continuing to write and publish a large number of poems in a wide variety of newspapers, magazines, and collections during the years from 1918 to the mid-1930s, Gerasimov also became one of the leaders of the proletarian culture movement. In 1918 he organized and was chair of the Samara Proletcult and in 1919 edited the Samara Proletcult magazine, *Zarevo zavodov* (Glow of the factories). Later that year he moved to Moscow, where he was named head of the literary department of the Moscow Proletcult and joined the staff of the literary department of Lunacharsky's People's Commissariat of Enlightenment (LITO Narkomprosa). In 1920, at the head of a group of worker writers dissatisfied with the Proletcult, he played a central role in organizing and then leading the Kuznitsa group, helped plan the First Congress of Proletarian Writers, and was elected (along with Il'ia Sadof'ev) assistant chair of the congress and of the resulting All-Russian Association of Proletarian Writers (VAPP). In 1921, in response to the New Economic Policy, which he viewed as signaling the end of the revolution, Gerasimov quit the Bolshevik party. In the mid-1920s he became less involved in cultural organizations as well, but continued to publish—though these writings, according to Soviet critics, "diverged from the path of proletarian poetry."[15] In 1937 he was arrested. He died in prison in 1939.[16]

---

[15] *Literaturnaia entsiklopediia*, 2:470.

[16] RGALI, f. 1374, op. 7, d. 13, ll. 1–22 (fragments of autobiography, 1916); *Kratkaia literaturnaia entsiklopediia*, 2:129–30; L'vov-Rogachevskii, *Noveishaia russkaia literatura*, 350–66; *Literaturnaia entsiklopediia*, 2:468–71; *Poeziia v bol'shevistskikh izdaniiakh*, 471; Papernyi and Shatseva, *Proletarskie poety pervykh let sovetskoi epokhi*, 509–11; Rodov, *Proletarskie pisateli*, 241 (autobiography); *Russkie pisateli, 1800–1917*, 1:540–41; *Russkie pisateli: Poety*, 5:388–419; F. Levin, "Mikhail Gerasimov (1889–1939)," introduction to Gerasimov, *Stikhotvoreniia*, 7–10.

Fedor Ivanovich Kalinin (1882–1920)

Fedor Kalinin was born on 2 (14) February 1882 (1883 in some accounts), in the village of Shiklovo, in an industrial region of Vladimir province, into a family of weavers. He lived as a child in factory barracks and attended the factory primary school. Kalinin's father died when Fedor was eleven. At the age of fifteen, Kalinin entered an apprenticeship as a woodworker in a shop at a nearby railroad station. Bored and restless, he soon quit and left for Moscow, where he found work as a type compositor. After the death of his mother, Kalinin returned to Vladimir province and was hired as a weaver in a local factory. Later he moved to Iaroslavl province, where he also worked as a weaver. During these years he became associated with radical workers and students and joined a workers' self-education circle, where he showed a particular interest in philosophy.

In 1901 Kalinin was arrested for his association with a circle of radical students and workers planning to assassinate the governor of Iaroslavl province. After fifteen months in solitary confinement, he was exiled to Arkhangelsk province; in 1904 he returned to his native village under police supervision. During his exile he became associated with the RSDRP and showed an inclination toward Bolshevism. At the end of 1904, freed from the limitations of his parole, he moved to the city of Aleksandrovsk, in southern Russia, where he found work as a weaver in a textile factory and became actively involved in the socialist labor movement. During the 1905 revolution he was a leader of the insurrection in the city, which resulted in the formation of the short-lived Aleksandrovsk Republic, under the presidency of Kalinin. Arrested at the end of 1905, he spent the next two and a half years in the Butyrki prison in Moscow.

On leaving prison in March 1908, rather than accept exile to Vladimir province, he returned to Moscow on a false passport supplied by the party and worked with the Bolshevik committee there. In 1909 the party sent him to Italy to study at the new school established by the left Bolsheviks Aleksandr Bogdanov, Anatoly Lunacharsky, and Maxim Gorky at Gorky's villa in Capri, and later at the party school in Bologna. After briefly returning to Russia, where his identity was discovered and he had again to escape arrest and exile, in 1912 he left for France, where he remained until 1917. Finding work in woodworking and airplane factories in Paris, Kalinin continued to work on his own cultural self-development, encouraged by the presence of other worker *intelligenty* and the support of Lunacharsky.

Kalinin began to write in France and established a unique reputation as a worker philosopher. Over the next few years he published essays, many of them on proletarian culture, in *Novyi zhurnal dlia vsekh* (New magazine for everyone) and in the émigré party press, especially the left-Bolshevik journal *Vpered!* (Forward!). He joined and was soon named secretary of Lunacharsky's Proletarian Culture circle in Paris, where he met often with other worker writers, especially Pavel Bessal'ko, Mikhail Gerasimov, and Aleksei

Gastev. In May 1917 he returned to Russia, where he joined the leadership of the Petrograd metalworkers' union, along with Gastev.

In mid-October 1917, together with Lunacharsky, Bessal'ko, and others, Kalinin played a key role in the founding conference of the Proletcult. He was elected to the Proletcult Central Committee, served as an editor of the journal *Proletarskaia kul'tura,* and was asked by the new people's commissar of enlightenment, Lunacharsky, to head the Proletcult Department in the commissariat. During these years he wrote and published extensively on cultural ideas, literature, and art. He died of typhus in February 1920 in Moscow.[17]

Vladimir Timofeevich Kirillov (1890–1943)

Vladimir Kirillov was born on 2 (14) October 1890 (or 1889)[18] in the village of Kharino, in Smolensk province, in west-central Russia. His father worked in the city of Smolensk as a clerk in a bookshop. His mother, a descendant of German settlers, ran the household and farm. Kirillov's education was limited to one or two winters in a Smolensk primary school. The rest of the year he remained in the village. Kirillov's father died when Vladimir was young, leaving his mother to care for seven children on her own. She found work as a cook in Odessa. At the age of nine or ten, Vladimir was sent to live with relatives in Orel, in the central black earth region, and entered into an apprenticeship in a shoemaking shop, where he remained for three years. He then moved back to Odessa and entered a new apprenticeship as a sailor, working as a cabin boy on a merchant steamship, mainly on the Black Sea but also visiting Turkey, Greece, and Egypt.

During the 1905 revolution, Kirillov took part in protests by sailors. In 1906, politically inclined toward anarchism and the Socialist Revolutionary Party, he was arrested for "revolutionary-terrorist activities." Because of his youth, he avoided a sentence of hard labor or execution and was exiled for three years to Ustsysolsk, in Vologda province, in the Russian north. Joining a circle of exiled worker socialists, he became familiar with Marxist ideas, but a growing interest in literature and music led him away from politics. Exile gave him time to read not only the classic poets he knew from school (Pushkin especially) but also the newer writers, especially such Symbolists as Konstantin Bal'mont, Valerii Briusov, and Aleksandr Blok. After completing his sentence in 1910, Kirillov settled in St. Petersburg, where he earned a meager liv-

---

[17] V. Polianskii, "F. I. Kalinin," in Kalinin, *Pamiati F. I. Kalinina,* 5–16; *Proletarskaia kul'tura,* no. 20–21 (January–June 1921), 47–48; *Kratkaia literaturnaia entsiklopediia,* 3:324–25; *Literaturnaia entsiklopediia,* 5:63–66.

[18] In a 1925 autobiographical sketch Kirillov claimed to have been born in 1889 (Rodov, *Proletarskie pisateli,* 317). In a 1932 autobiography he stated his date of birth as 1890 (RGALI, f. 1372, op. 1, d. 1, l. 1). References to Kirillov give both dates, though recent accounts prefer the later one.

ing playing mandolin and *dombra* in taverns and movie houses. He joined a folk orchestra, with which he traveled to the United States in 1911, playing in New York, Chicago, San Francisco, and other cities.

Kirillov began writing poetry toward the end of his exile in 1910, though for the next few years he focused on music. Indeed, he hoped at the time to be trained as a classical pianist and become a composer, but he did not have the means. On returning from America in 1912, Kirillov began visiting the Ligovskii People's House of Countess Panina, where he met Aleksei Mashirov, Il'ia Sadof'ev, and other worker poets and joined their circle. In this new environment he was inspired to devote himself to writing. In 1913 and 1914, his first poems appeared in print, in *Narodnyi zhurnal* and *Nashi pesni,* the collection of writings by worker writers (most of whom were associated with the Ligovskii People's House). When war broke out, Kirillov was drafted and sent to the front.

The war drew him back into politics. He was elected to the soldiers' committee in his regiment. After October 1917, back in Petrograd, he was named secretary of the Moskovskii zastav (Moscow gate) district Bolshevik party committee (the same committee in which Aleksei Mashirov was active). The revolution inspired his most productive and creative period as a writer. Kirillov claimed later to have composed some of his most famous poems of 1917–18 while walking early in the morning to the party committee offices, and wrote them down late at night after meetings.[19] His poems appeared widely in the press at this time, especially in the Proletcult press, and in collections of his writings. Some of his most popular poems were set to music, recorded on phonograph records, and performed in public. He became a leading figure in the Petrograd Proletcult, led by his party comrade Mashirov, and during the civil war went to Tambov to work with the local Proletcult and to take part in "artistic-agitational" work at the front. In 1920 he moved to Moscow, where he worked with the Moscow Proletcult, served in the literary department of the Commissariat of Enlightenment (LITO Narkomprosa), helped establish the journal *Kuznitsa* (and headed the Kuznitsa group between 1920 and 1923), was chair of the organizing committee for the First Congress of Proletarian Writers in 1920 and of the conference itself, and in 1921 was elected chair of the All-Russian Association of Proletarian Writers (VAPP). During the early 1920s, like many other worker writers associated with Kuznitsa, Kirillov viewed NEP as an abandonment of the spirit of the revolution and left the party. In the mid 1920s he went in a seemingly different direction and quit both Kuznitsa and VAPP to join the All-Russian Union of Writers (VSP), a nonproletarian and noncommunist writers' organization uniting mainly "fellow travelers." His writings in this period, Soviet critics complained, became pessimistic and "decadent." He wrote very little after 1929. Toward the end of that year, he helped reorganize the Writers' Union into a more politicized but

---

[19] RGALI, f. 1372, op. 1, d. 1, l. 4.

short-lived All-Russian Union of Soviet Writers; he was named a member of the board of directors and soon its chairman. In 1937 he was arrested. He died in captivity in 1943.[20]

Ivan Nikolaevich Kubikov (Dement'ev) (1877–1944)

Ivan Kubikov, as he is usually known, was Russia's first and best-known working-class literary and cultural critic. Born on 21 February (5 March) 1877 in St. Petersburg, he worked much of his life as a compositor in printing shops. City-born and literate, he was probably educated, like other workers in his craft, in an urban two-class school.[21] He joined the RSDRP in 1902 and became a Menshevik when the party split the following year. As the trade union movement developed in the years after 1905, he became very active publishing articles on literary matters in the trade union press (especially the journal of the St. Petersburg printers' union, in which he was a regular columnist) and in the Menshevik press, and lecturing on literature to workers' groups. Before adopting the pseudonym Kubikov (from the Russian for a block of set type), he called himself Kvadrat (a *kvadrat* was a bar used by compositors to space lines of type). Very active in the Petersburg printers' union, Kubikov served as chair in 1909. In the same year he helped to reorganize and lead the Printers' Music, Drama, and Education Circle. He was arrested that November and spent several months in prison. In 1917 he was actively involved with the newspaper of the Menshevik worker intelligentsia, *Rabochaia mysl'* (Workers' thought), and in 1918 he was its editor. In November 1917 he was a candidate in the elections to the Constituent Assembly on the Menshevik-Defensist list. Soon after, he withdrew from politics and became a teacher and full-time literary critic in Moscow.[22]

Nikolai Nikolaevich Liashko (Liashchenko) (1884–1953)

Nikolai Liashko (the pseudonym under which he was generally known) was born 7 (19) November 1884 in the town of Lebedin, in eastern Kharkov province. Although he was born in Ukraine of ethnic Ukrainian parentage, he wrote his literary works in Russian. His father was a metalworker and served as a soldier at the military port of Nikolaev, by the Black Sea. His mother is

[20] Ibid., ll. 1–6 (1932 autobiography); *Kratkaia literaturnaia entsiklopediia*, 3:537–38; *Literaturnaia entsiklopediia*, 5:217–19; L'vov-Rogachevskii, *Noveishaia russkaia literatura*, 350–66; Eventov, *Poeziia v bol'shevistskikh izdaniiakh*, 474; Papernyi and Shatseva, *Proletarskie poety pervykh let sovetskoi epokhi*, 515–17; Rodov, *Proletarskie pisateli*, 317 (autobiography); *Russkie pisateli: Poety*, 10:382–405.

[21] The two-class school was a four- or five-grade elementary school with two teachers, each instructing either the lower or upper grades.

[22] *Literaturnaia entsiklopediia*, 5:698; *Kratkaia literaturnaia entsiklopediia*, 3:864; *Pechatnoe delo*, no. 16 (4 Feb. 1910), 11; *Rabochaia mysl': Rabochii zhurnal* (Petrograd, 1917–18).

identified simply as a "peasant." After three years at a local Church parish school, Liashko went to work at the age of eleven, first as a helper in a café and then as an apprentice in a confectionery factory. At fourteen he was an apprentice metal turner (*tokar'*) in a machine building factory. He completed his apprenticeship in the Kharkov Locomotive Boiler Factory. In the following years he worked as a turner in machine building and shipbuilding factories in Kharkov, Nikolaev, Sevastopol, and Rostov-on-the-Don. He continued his education by attending the Alchevskii and other Sunday schools for working-class adults in Kharkov.

Around 1901 Liashko began visiting workers' circles and by 1903 he was associated with the RSDRP, especially the Mensheviks. He began to write around 1904, favoring prose from the first, though he wrote occasional poetry and published a poem and a few stories in 1905 in local provincial newspapers. For his political associations and activities, and later for his writings and editorial work, he suffered repeated arrest between 1903 and 1914, served time in prison in half a dozen cities, and was exiled twice to the far north. Sometime during these years, most likely after he returned from his three-year exile in Olonetsk province in 1908–11, Liashko quit industrial work altogether to devote himself to full-time party work and writing. Settling in Moscow in 1912, Liashko organized an association (*tovarishchestvo*) of self-taught writers and helped to establish and edit a magazine, *Ogni*, to publish their works. The magazine was shut by the government in 1914 after only five issues and Liashko was sentenced to two years in prison. Liashko's own works appeared frequently in various newspapers and magazines, especially in *Ogni*, *Ekho* (another "people's" magazine), and the Menshevik party press.

After October 1917, Liashko initially distanced himself from Soviet institutions and publications, and published little apart from a major series of essays on urban life and labor organization published by the journal of the Moscow cooperative movement. But he began to accept the new order and become publicly active again in the early 1920s. He participated in the meeting in Moscow in May 1920 to organize a union of proletarian writers, helped organize the First Congress of Proletarian Writers held in October, and was an active contributor to the magazine *Kuznitsa* and a member of the Kuznitsa Executive Committee. His stories of the revolutionary past were widely known, and in the late 1920s much of his older work was republished. He also worked with younger writers and did some translation of Ukrainian works. In 1924 Liashko responded to the call to memorialize Lenin by applying to join the Communist party (this was the "Lenin enrollment"), but his application was rejected. A few years later he applied again and this time was evidently accepted. He continued to work as a journalist and story writer until his death in 1953.[23]

---

[23] RGALI, f. 1638, op. 2, d. 21, ll. 11–18 (1930 application for party membership); op. 4, d. 6, 16 (1924 questionnaire); *Kratkaia literaturnaia entsiklopediia*, 4:482–84; Lindin, *Pisateli*, 175–76; *Literaturnaia entsiklopediia*, 6:675–80; Rodov, *Proletarskie pisateli*, 403 (autobiography); *Russkie Sovetskie pisateli: Prozaiki*, 2:797–811.

Aleksei Ivanovich Mashirov (1884–1943)

Aleksei Mashirov, best known by his literary pseudonym, Samobytnik (unique, autonomous, self-made), was born on 5 (17) March 1884 in St. Petersburg, where his family lived on the city's industrial outskirts. His father, a goldsmith, was ruined by drunkenness and abandoned his young family when Aleksei was two and a half; reportedly he walked off into the countryside, fell ill, and died. Mashirov's mother, who took in washing and cleaned apartments, raised her three children with some help from her brother. At the age of nine, Mashirov completed a four-year city primary school. One of his teachers, impressed by the boy's love of reading and unusual ability and by his high scores on the citywide examinations, suggested that he continue his education at a technical middle school for children of artisans; the teacher would pay. His mother refused. Instead, at the age of twelve, Mashirov started an apprenticeship as a fitter in a metal products factory.

Like many Petersburg metalworkers in the late 1890s and early 1900s, Mashirov became involved in labor struggles and socialist politics, inspired partly by his encounters with "conscious workers." In 1905 he was elected to the Shidlovskii Commission when the tsarist government, after the upheavals in the wake of Bloody Sunday, asked workers in the capital to elect deputies to gather and express their needs. Illegally fired for his participation in the commission, he became increasingly politicized and found it increasingly difficult to remain employed for long in the same shop. Over the coming years he would work in a large number of metalworking enterprises, mostly small shops, as a fitter, metal stamper, laborer, harness maker, engraver, bronze-smith, and silversmith. He even briefly opened a small metal workshop in the backyard of a laundry, and there set up a secret printing press and a library of illegal political literature.

As government pressures after 1906 made open political activity increasingly difficult, Mashirov turned his energies toward cultural self-education. In 1909 he enrolled in technical classes at Countess Panina's Ligovskii People's House to advance himself professionally, but he also attended courses on literature, history, and science. Not forgetting politics, he became the leader of a Bolshevik group of worker students at the People's House. But he also joined and soon became very active in the literary circle organized sometime around 1912 among some of the workers studying at the People's House. During 1912–13 Mashirov read more than a dozen reports at gatherings of the circle on such writers as Mikhail Lomonosov, Nikolai Nekrasov, Vladimir Korolenko, Mikhail Lermontov, Semen Nadson, and Lev Tolstoy. His own poems were included in the circle's manuscript magazines and in its two print collections called *Nashi pesni*. Mashirov also became involved in a workers' theater established at the People's House in 1913 (where, to avoid arrest for his increasing political activities, Mashirov was living backstage).

Mashirov wrote his first poems while studying at the People's House—written during his hours there, but also in taverns and teashops and in the apartments of friends. His first published poems appeared in the manuscript magazines the students put out. In 1910, in the "satirical people's magazine" *Rozhok* (Horn), satirical verses by Mashirov regularly appeared under the pseudonym Prikazchik-Rasskazchik (Shop clerk–storyteller). Starting in 1912, his poems appeared in the newly legal Bolshevik press, in collections such as *Nashi pesni,* and in Gorky's 1914 anthology of workers' writings.

By 1908 Mashirov had become a member of the Bolshevik faction of the Russian Social Democratic Workers' Party and was also active in the trade union movement. His position in the party was becoming increasingly responsible. He became a member of the Moskovskii zastav (Moscow gate) district party committee in 1912 and a member of its executive committee in 1914. With the outbreak of war in 1914, Mashirov's legal situation worsened when he ignored his draft call. He was arrested in 1915 and exiled to eastern Siberia, where he remained until he was freed in the amnesty that followed the February revolution.

After returning to Petrograd, Mashirov again threw himself into political and cultural life. He continued his party work and was elected to the Petrograd City Council. And he was one of the founders and leaders of the Petrograd Proletcult, which he headed from 1917 to 1923. In 1920 he attended the First Congress of Proletarian Writers, where he was elected to the presidium. He was a member of the leadership of the All-Russian Association of Proletarian Writers (VAPP) and later also chair of the Leningrad Association of Proletarian Writers. He continued to write, and his poems, including his older works, were widely published in magazines and collections during the civil war and the 1920s. He wrote less, however, as his responsibilities as a cultural organizer grew: in 1918–20 as a member of the editorial board of the national Proletcult magazine, *Proletarskaia kul'tura;* in the late 1920s as a member of the staff of the newspaper *Krasnaia gazeta* (Red gazette), where he published regular essays on culture and art; and between 1926 and 1928, as editor of the magazine *Rabochii i teatr* (Worker and theater). During the 1930s and 1940s he worked primarily as administrator of the Leningrad Conservatory and then of the Leningrad Theatrical Institute. He died during the siege of Leningrad.[24]

Egor Efimovich Nechaev (1859–1925)

One of the oldest working-class writers still active in Russia at the time of the revolution, Egor Nechaev was, it would be said in early Soviet times, one of

[24] RGALI, f. 1821, op. 1, d. 1, ll. 1–13 (1934 autobiography), 15–16 (1933 questionnaire interview); f. 1230, op. 1, d. 669, l. 27 (Proletcult leadership); *Kratkaia literaturnaia entsiklopediia,* 6:635; Eventov, *Poeziia v bol'shevistskikh izdaniiakh,* 478–79; Papernyi and Shatseva, *Proletarskie poety pervykh let sovetskoi epokhi,* 528–29; Rodov, *Proletarskie pisateli,* 548–50 (autobiography); *Russkie pisateli: Poety,* 15:4–22; Zavolokin, *Sovremennye raboche-krest'ianskie poety,* 26–28 (autobiography; original text in RGALI, f. 1068, op. 1, d. 97).

the "founders of Russian proletarian poetry."[25] He was born 13 (25) April 1859, in the village of Kharitonovo, in Tver province, in the Moscow industrial region. Although Nechaev's grandparents were peasants (serfs until abolition in 1861), his father was, as his son would be, a skilled glassmaker. Also, unlike most peasants, who were bound to the village in many ways even after serfdom ended, Nechaev's father frequently moved his family from place to place in search of better work. As the family grew large, Egor was sent at the age of five to live with a childless aunt who could better support him. When Egor turned eight, his father insisted that he return home (now in Vladimir province) and begin to contribute to the family income by going to work in the glass factory where he worked. For the next fifty years and more, Nechaev continued to work in glass factories, much of the time in Moscow, where he worked from 1885 to 1916 (a stability uncommon among later worker writers) at the Diutfua glass and crystal works.

Growing up at a time when there were still few schools for peasant or worker youths, Nechaev learned to read and write through an unexpected conjunction of circumstances. After he was burned rather badly when molten glass was spilled on his leg only a few days after he started work as a boy of eight, his aunt took him back in. Forced to recover at home for three months, Nechaev was instructed by a local ethnic German woman, who for very little money taught local boys to read and write in Russian. In later years he advanced his literacy by reading on his own, including a great deal of poetry.

Nechaev began to write his own poetry only in his late twenties, soon after he moved to Moscow with his wife and children. A journalist he had met, A. A. Popov-Monastyrskii, encouraged Nechaev to write. In the 1890s Nechaev's work began to appear regularly in magazines and newspapers, especially the popular daily *Moskovskii listok* (Moscow sheet), in collections by members of the Surikov Circle, and in other anthologies. In 1905 he began to publish in satirical magazines and especially in *narodnye* (people's) magazines edited by other writers from lower-class backgrounds. He contributed to a banned collection of revolutionary poems titled *Pod krasnym znamenam* (Under the red flag) in 1906 and also wrote poems for children. The first collection of his verse was published by the Surikov Circle in 1911 and others followed. After 1917 his works were widely published. He began to write fiction only in the early 1920s.

Nechaev was actively involved with other "writers from the people" (*pisateli iz naroda*) and "self-taught writers" (*pisatelei-samouchki*). In the 1890s he began to visit the Moscow circle organized by Maksim Leonov, a peasant poet who worked in his father's vegetable shop. In 1902 he joined Leonov and other *samouchki* in establishing the Moscow Cooperative Circle of Writers from the People, and then in 1903, after a split in the circle, the Surikov Literature and Music Circle (Surikovskii literaturno-muzykal'nyi kruzhok). In

---

[25] *Literaturnaia entsiklopediia*, 8:31. Other critics denied this status, since his association with the Surikov Circle expressed a "nonproletarian" ideology.

1916 the Surikov Circle held a grand celebration of the twenty-fifth anniversary of Nechaev's literary activity. It was at this time as well, when Nechaev was in his late fifties, that he quit factory labor and began to work solely as a writer. After the Bolshevik Revolution, Nechaev worked for various newspapers and magazines, participated in the meeting in Moscow in May 1920 to organize a union of proletarian writers (for which he was elected to an oversight committee), attended the First Congress of Proletarian Writers in October, and joined the Kuznitsa literary group, though he was not especially active. Shortly before his death in 1925, although he had never been closely associated with the labor or socialist movement, he joined the Communist party.[26]

Sergei Aleksandrovich Obradovich (1892–1956)

Sergei Obradovich was born on 1 (13) September 1892 on the outskirts of Moscow.[27] His father, a Serb who became a Russian subject, was a watchmaker who made and sold pocket watches and keys for factory clocks. His mother was a glovemaker before her marriage; thereafter she helped her husband at his work. Sergei began helping as well when he was five years old. While working, his father often told stories or had someone read aloud from a book. But the business was not successful and the family fell into poverty. His father later took a job as a railroad switchman.

Obradovich attended a three-year city primary school, which he completed in November 1905. The following year, at the age of fourteen, he started an apprenticeship in a print shop, working as an assistant, then as a press feeder (*nakladchik*), and finally became, at the age of eighteen, a master stereotypist (a specialist who prepared stereotype plates for printing). Obradovich began writing poems soon after he started his apprenticeship—writing, he later claimed, right in the shop "amidst the machinery."[28] Typically precocious, he wrote his first autobiography at the age of sixteen, in 1908. Around 1909, Obradovich joined a group of worker friends (skilled workers in a variety of trades) in forming a circle (*kruzhok*) devoted to self-education. They subscribed jointly to several "thick" journals—mainly left-democratic magazines such as *Zavety* (Precepts), *Russkoe bogatstvo* (Russian wealth), and *Sovre-*

---

[26] I. N. Kubikov, "Egor Nechaev," introduction to Nechaev, *Guta*, 9–16; Friche, *Proletarskaia poeziia*, 58–66; Rodov, *Proletarskie pisateli*, 432–36 (1921 autobiography); RGALI, f. 1638, op 4, d. 6 (Kuznitsa questionnaire, December 1924), l. 19; Zavolokin, *Sovremennye rabochekrest'ianskie poety*, 3–5 (autobiography); *Literaturnaia entsiklopediia*, 8:31–32; Papernyi and Shatseva, *Proletarskie poety pervykh let sovetskoi epokhi*, 554–55; A. M. Bikhter, "U istokov russkoi proletarskogo poezii," in *U istokov russkoi proletarskoi poezii*, 18–21; *Kratkaia literaturnaia entsiklopediia*, 5:251–52; *Russkie pisateli: Poety (Sovetskii period)*, 16:39–62; *Russkie pisateli, 1800–1917*, 4:291–92.

[27] Although all biographical entries on Obradovich state that he was born on 2 September, in his own statements and autobiographies, Obradovich consistently gave the date as 1 September.

[28] Rodov, *Proletarskie pisateli*, 447 (autobiography).

mennyi mir (Modern world), read reports, and debated vehemently late into the night. Obradovich continued to write and began to find publishers for his verses: in 1912 his first poems were published in the Moscow people's magazines *Ekho* (Echo) and *Dolia bedniaka* (Poor man's burden) and in the Arkhangelsk people's newspaper *Severnoe utro* (Northern morning), edited by Mikhail Leonov and Mariia Chernysheva. With other members of his circle, Obradovich enrolled for the 1913–14 academic year in night classes at the Shaniavskii People's University in Moscow, where he studied math, science, writing (*diktant*), literature, political economy, Latin, French, German, history, and geography. In 1913 Obradovich also joined the Surikov Circle,[29] and became closely associated with the circle of worker writers led by Nikolai Liashko around the Moscow people's magazine *Ogni*.

When the First World War broke out, Obradovich was drafted into the infantry and sent to the front in Galicia and the Carpathians. He was several times wounded, evacuated, and returned to the front, where he remained until 1918. Although the war interfered with regular writing and publishing, he kept a reflective and often poetic diary, written mainly in the trenches, on miscellaneous sheets of paper, folded into small squares to keep in his pocket; some of its pages are stained with blood. In 1917, in the wake of the February revolution, Obradovich was elected chair of the soldiers' committee for his regiment. For fraternizing with Austrians at the front and for distributing antiwar propaganda among soldiers, court-martial proceedings were begun against him, but they were dismissed after October 1917. Returning to Moscow in early 1918, at a time of widespread unemployment, Obradovich initially survived by selling newspapers (at which he was not very good) until he found a job in a printing shop. After he fell ill, he lost this job and found work as a railroad dispatcher.

He also began to write again and published widely in a broad range of newspapers and magazines. The first collections of his work appeared in 1921. Like many other worker writers, Obradovich was also active as a cultural organizer, and this work soon allowed him to quit industrial work and become a full-time *literator* (writer, editor, and literary official). In the fall of 1918 he joined the literary studio of the Moscow Proletcult, where he attended lectures on literature and worked on his own writing. In 1919 he helped organize the Moscow Proletcult magazine *Gudki* (Factory whistles). In 1920, along with Gerasimov, Kirillov, Aleksandrovskii, and others, Obradovich left the Proletcult to establish the Kuznitsa group and its magazine, under the auspices of the literary department of the Commissariat of Enlightenment. Obradovich helped organize the First Congress of Proletarian Writers in 1920, was named secretary to the congress, and was elected secretary of the board of directors of the resulting All-Russian Association of Proletarian Writers (VAPP), a po-

[29] This is never mentioned in his later autobiographies or in Soviet biographical sketches of him, probably because the Surikov Circle was seen as ideologically nonproletarian. Obradovich's membership card is in his personal archival collection, RGALI, f. 1874, op. 1, d. 479, l. 1.

sition he retained throughout the 1920s. Starting in February 1920, Obradovich also worked in the literary department of Narkompros, responsible for editorial work on collections of proletarian writing. Between 1922 and 1927 he worked as manager of the literary section of the Communist party newspaper *Pravda,* though he was still not a party member. From the 1920s into the 1940s, he served on the editorial boards of a number of magazines and publishing houses, often holding responsible positions, while continuing to write poetry and criticism. Never very involved in politics, Obradovich became a member of the Communist party only in 1939.[30]

Petr Vasil'evich Oreshin (1887–1938)

Petr Oreshin was born on 16 (28) July 1887 in the city of Saratov, in the central Volga region. His family had recently migrated to the city from the village of Galakhovo, in Saratov province, in search of wage work. Petr's father, who also occasionally wrote poetry, worked as a shop assistant and his mother as a seamstress (*shveia*). As a small boy, since his parents both worked, Petr spent much time with his grandparents back in the village. After completing three grades of a four-year city school, he began work in a shop, like his father, but fled back to the village. He briefly studied bookkeeping but did poorly and did not complete the course. Instead, around 1903, he began a period of itinerancy, wandering for many years through the cities and villages of the Volga region and Siberia. It was during these years that he begin to write and publish poetry.

Oreshin's first published poems (along with a couple of stories) appeared in provincial newspapers, especially in Saratov, starting in 1911. In 1913, living in St. Petersburg, where he worked on the railroad, he published more widely, especially in the weekly supplement to the liberal newspaper *Sovremennoe slovo* (Modern word), in the neo-populist magazine *Zavety* (Precepts, a publication close to the Socialist Revolutionary Party), and in other periodicals. He also joined a circle of neo-populist writers in St. Petersburg, mostly writers for *Zavety,* led by Ivanov-Razumnik (R. V. Ivanov), the literature criticism editor at *Zavety.* During the First World War, Oreshin was a soldier at the front. After he returned to Petrograd in 1917, he published poems mainly in the local papers of the Socialist Revolutionary Party.

After October, Oreshin earned a living mainly as a journalist and poet, writing for newspapers and magazines. His works were widely published, though also frequently criticized for romanticizing rural life and expressing a peasant

[30] Ibid., d. 183, ll. 1–2 (1932 autobiography); d. 184, ll. 1–60 (1908 autobiography); d. 185 (wartime diaries, 1916–17); dd. 477, 478, 479, 488, 683 (miscellaneous materials); f. 1638, op. 4, d. 6, l. 20 (1924 biographical questionnaire); *Kratkaia literaturnaia entsiklopediia,* 5:363; *Literaturnaia entsiklopediia,* 8:173–75; Papernyi and Shatseva, *Proletarskie poety pervykh let sovetskoi epokhi,* 531–32; Rodov, *Proletarskie pisateli,* 446–47 (autobiography); *Russkie pisateli: Poety,* 16:63–88; Zavolokin, *Sovremennye raboche-krest'ianskie poety,* 75–77 (autobiography).

worldview. Indeed, in 1918 he was almost expelled from the journalists' union when his collection of poems, *Krasnaia Rus'* (Red Russia), was condemned by *Pravda* as "White Guardist." Though exonerated, he decided to return to Saratov. In the early 1920s, having moved to Moscow, Oreshin helped organize the section of peasant writers in the Moscow Proletcult. In 1925 he was chosen as a member of the governing board of the All-Russian Union of Poets. Later in the 1920s, as the Soviet state and the party turned against the traditional peasantry and hence against those who voiced a "peasant" perspective, Oreshin was publicly condemned and "displaced from literature." He was arrested in 1937 and shot on 15 March 1938.[31]

Andrei Platonovich Platonov (Klimentov) (1899–1951)

Andrei Platonov (the pseudonym he adopted in 1920, by which he is best known) was born on 20 August (1 September) 1899 in the settlement of Iamskaia, on the outskirts of Voronezh, in the central black earth region. His father was a metal fitter in the railroad workshops and an amateur inventor. His mother was the daughter of a watchmaker. Platonov attended a Church parish school and completed his primary education at a four-year city school. In 1914, at the age of thirteen and a half, he went to work first as an office clerk at a local insurance company, then as a smelter at a pipe factory, an assistant machinist on a private estate, a worker in a plant that produced artificial millstones, a warehouseman, and at other jobs, some of them on the railroad. He had begun writing poems by the time he turned thirteen and sent some off to papers in Moscow and elsewhere, though none were yet accepted.

In the wake of the 1917 revolutions, Platonov became very active in a variety of pursuits. He sought to advance his technical education first with preparatory courses and then at the Voronezh Polytechnic Institute, where he studied electrical technology, though he also showed great interest in philosophy. When the civil war broke out, he served on a train delivering troops and supplies and clearing snow. He may have briefly fought as a soldier. At the same time, he wrote prolifically for a variety of local periodicals, especially the paper of the local railway workers' union, *Zheleznyi put'* (Railroad), the official papers of the Voronezh provincial committee of the Communist Party, *Krasnaia derevnia* (Red countryside) and *Voronezhskaia kommuna* (Voronezh commune), *Kuznitsa,* and many others.

The range of his writings in these years was extraordinary. From 1918 through 1921, his most intensive years as a writer, he published dozens of poems, including a collection of verses in 1922, several stories, and hundreds of

[31] G. F. Samosiuk, "P. V. Oreshin," in *Russkie pisateli v Saratovskom Povolzh'e*, 222–23; RGALI, f. 1305, op. 1, d. 79 (1929 critique); f. 1600, op. 1, d. 19 (Moskovskii Soiuz Sovetskikh zhurnalistov), ll. 1–6, 12, 20, 22; f. 2222, op. 1, d. 63, ll. 1–5 (1923 critiques); *Kratkaia literaturnaia entsiklopediia*, 5:458–59; *Literaturnaia entsiklopediia*, 8:313–14; *Russkie pisateli, 1800–1917*, 4:444–45; *Russkie Sovetskie pisateli: Poety*, 17:4–61.

articles and essays. Platonov's productive energy and intellectual precocity is most visible in the remarkable range of topics he confidently wrote about: literature, art, cultural life, science, philosophy, morality, religion, education, politics, the civil war, foreign relations, economics, technology, famine, land reclamation, and more. It was not unusual, especially in 1920, to see two or three of his pieces on quite different subjects appear in the press every day for several days running. He was also involved with the local Proletcult organization, joined the Union of Communist Journalists in March 1920, worked as an editor at *Krasnaia derevnia*, was elected in August 1920 to the provisional board of directors of the newly formed Voronezh Union of Proletarian Writers, attended the First Congress of Proletarian Writers in Moscow in October 1920, and regularly read his poetry and gave critical talks at various club meetings. He joined the Communist party in the spring of 1920 and started attending the party school, but was expelled from the party in September 1921 as "unreliable" and "undisciplined." Although the specifics are vague, we know that Platonov, like many other worker writers, was dismayed about the course the party was taking with the introduction of NEP. We also know that he was deeply troubled by the terrible famine of 1921, and he openly and controversially criticized the behavior and privileges of local Communists at the time. There is also a story that he was expelled from the party when he refused to clean up other people's trash during an obligatory *subbotnik* (work Saturday). He applied for readmission in 1924 but was judged "insufficiently mature politically."

In 1922 Platonov abandoned journalism and literary work entirely to work on electrification and land reclamation projects for the Voronezh Provincial Land Administration and later for agencies of the central government. "I could no longer be occupied with a contemplative activity like literature," he recalled a few years later.[32] For the next few years he worked as an engineer and administrator, organizing the digging of ponds and wells, the draining of swamps, and the building of a hydroelectric plant; he did not write. When he did return to writing in 1926, however, he began to create works that indicated to critics and readers a major and original literary voice. Moving to Moscow in 1927, he became for the first time a professional writer. He wrote mainly fiction but also worked in the editorial departments of leading magazines. By 1931 his work came under sustained attack as anticommunist, and publication became increasingly difficult. During the Second World War he worked as a war correspondent. Platonov died in 1951 of tuberculosis, contracted from his son, who had been infected in the gulag after his arrest as a "terrorist" and "spy" in 1938, but was released during the war.[33]

[32] Autobiographical essay by Platonov, 29 Sept. 1924, rpt. in E. Inozemtseva, "Platonov v Voronezhe," *Pod"em* 1971, no. 2 (March–April): 100.

[33] Kornienko and Shubina, *Andrei Platonov*; Langerak, "Andrei Platonov v Voronezhe"; Seifrid, *Andrei Platonov*; Inozemtseva, "Platonov v Voronezhe"; Eidinova, "K tvorcheskoi biografii A. Platonova"; M. Iunger, "Predislovie," in Platonov, *Golubaia glubina*, v–viii; *Kratkaia literaturnaia entsiklopediia*, 5:790–92; *Literaturnaia entsiklopediia*, 8:688; *Russkie Sovetskie pisateli: Prozaiki*, 7 (suppl.), pt. 2: 19–56.

Il'ia Ivanovich Sadof'ev (1889–1965)

Il'ia Sadof'ev was born in St. Petersburg on 12 (24) July 1889 to migrant peasant-workers from the village of Serebrianye Prudy, in Tula province, in the central black earth region. When he was five years old, his parents returned to their native village, where Sadof'ev spent two winters at the village zemstvo school and began work as a shepherd and farmhand. At the age of thirteen, together with an uncle, he returned to St. Petersburg and found work first in a teashop, then in a vinegar factory, and then in a tin factory. He continued his education with evening courses offered by one of the Petersburg secondary schools. Beginning in 1905, he worked as a milling machine operator (*frezerovshchik*) in some of the largest metal plants in the capital. Alongside other metalworkers, Sadof'ev participated in many of the strikes and demonstrations during the 1905 revolution and was attracted to the Social Democratic movement. He continued to change jobs frequently in these years—because of persecution for his political activism, he later claimed—moving from factory to factory, but also working at times as a newspaper hawker, an office clerk, and a doorman. In 1916 he was arrested for his political activism and sentenced to six years' exile in the Siberian province of Iakutsk. He was freed in the amnesty resulting from the February revolution in 1917.

Sadof'ev had begun to write poetry at the age of ten, while he was still living with his parents in Serebrianie Prudy. But after a severe beating by his father, who considered it a "disgrace" to be a writer, Sadof'ev stopped writing for seven years. His poems first appeared in print in 1913 in the Menshevik daily *Luch* (Ray). In 1914 he faced criminal charges for his poem "V zavodc" (In the factory), published in the "peasants' and workers' paper" *Stoikaia mysl'* (Steadfast thought). He published nothing further until after the February revolution. In the years after 1917 he wrote and published widely—mainly poetry but also stories and articles. He complained, however, that time to write was limited (as it had been by labor and politics before 1917) by political and cultural organizational work: as deputy chair of the Petrograd Soviet, chair of the revolutionary tribunal, a member of the workers' directorate of the Petrograd Metal Factory, and a leading organizer of the Proletcult, of Kuznitsa, of the First Congress of Proletarian Writers in 1920 (at which he was deputy chair together with Mikhail Gerasimov), and of the All-Russian Association of Proletarian Writers (VAPP). During the civil war he also worked in the political section of the Russian Telegraph Agency (ROSTA) on the southwestern front in Ukraine. After 1921 he left many of these posts in order to devote himself to full-time writing and editorial work for various newspapers and magazines. He published many collections of poems during the 1920s and 1930s. During the Second World War he wrote agitational works.[34]

---

[34] *Kratkaia literaturnaia entsiklopediia*, 6:600–601; Eventov, *Poeziia v bol'shevistskikh izdaniiakh*, 482; Rodov, *Proletarskie pisateli*, 530–33 (autobiography); *Russkie pisateli: Poety*, 22:130–69; Zavolokin, *Sovremennye raboche-krest'ianskie poety*, 53–55 (autobiography).

Selected Bibliography

ARCHIVES

Arkhiv A. M. Gor'kogo (Maxim Gorky Archive), Institute for World Literature, Moscow, especially rubric KG-NP/a (letters to Gorky from beginning writers)

GARF   Gosudarstvennyi arkhiv Rossiiskoi Federatsii (State Archive of the Russian Federation), formerly TsGAOR (Central State Archive of the October Revolution), Moscow

f. R-5469	Central Committee of the Metalworkers' Union
f. 6860	Istprof (Committee for the History) of the Metalworkers' Union
f. 6864	Istprof of the Printers' Union
f. 6865	Istprof of the Railroad Union
f. 6868	Istprof of the Textile Workers' Union
f. 6870	Istprof of the Miners' Union
f. 6874	Istprof of the Woodworkers' Union
f. R-7911	F. I. Ozol'
f. R-7952	State publisher's "Istoriia fabrikov i zavodov" (History of factories)
f. R-7970	A. K. Gastev

RGALI   Rossiiskii gosudarstvennyi arkhiv literatury i isskustva (Russian State Archive of Literature and Art), Moscow

f. 348	E. E. Nechaev
f. 1068	P. Ia. Zavolokin (op. 1: autobiographies, questionnaires, and letters sent for the publication *Sovremennye raboche-krest'ianskie poety,* 1925)
f. 1100	V. L. L'vov-Rogachevskii
f. 1123	P. V. Oreshin
f. 1230	Central Committee of Proletarian Cultural Enlightenment Organizations (Proletcult)
f. 1307	F. S. Shkulev
f. 1346	A. A. Barkova
f. 1372	V. T. Kirillov

f. 1374   M. P. Gerasimov
f. 1381   Ia. P. Berdnikov
f. 1564   *Rabochii zhurnal*
f. 1617   A. N. Pomorskii
f. 1624   Autobiographies and questionnaires
f. 1638.   Kuznitsa All-Union Society of Proletarian Writers
f. 1641   Surikov Literature and Music Circle
f. 1703   V. F. Pletnev
f. 1747   N. N. Liashko
f. 1842   A. I. Samobytnik-Mashirov
f. 1849   A. P. Bibik
f. 1874   S. A. Obradovich
f. 2195   A. M. Gmyrev
f. 2200   M. Pasynok (I. I. Kogan-Laskin)
f. 2513   N. A. Kuznetsov

RGASPI   Rossiiskii gosudarstvennyi arkhiv sotsial'no-politicheskoi istorii (Russian
State Archive of Social and Political History), formerly TsPA IML (Central Party
Archive of the Institute of Marxism-Leninism), Moscow

f. 142   A. V. Lunacharskii
f. 259   A. A. Bogdanov
f. 364   *Pravda*, op. 1 (1912–14)
f. 433   *Zvezda* (1911–12)

PERIODICALS TO 1917

People's Magazines and Newspapers

Balagur: Iumoristichskii i satiricheskii narodnyi zhurnal. Moscow, 1910–14.
Balalaika: Narodnyi satiricheskii i iumoristicheskii zhurnal. Moscow, 1910–11.
Boi-rozhok. Moscow 1911–14 (1914 subtitled *Zhurnal zhenskogo smekha i oblicheniia muzhskogo litsemeriia*).
Dolia bedniaka: Narodnaia gazeta. Moscow, 1909–14.
Dolina: Iumoristicheskii i satiricheskii narodnyi zhurnal. Moscow, 1910–12.
Drug naroda: Literaturno-obshchestvennyi zhurnal. Moscow, 1915–16.
Dumy narodnye: Narodno-literaturnyi zhurnal. Moscow, 1910–13.
Ekho: Ezhenedel'nyi zhurnal. Moscow 1911–12.
Kolotushka: Literaturnyi, satiricheskii i iumoristicheskii zhurnal. Tver, 1911.
Letopis': Ezhednevnyi narodnyi politicheskii i literaturnyi zhurnal. Moscow, 1906–7.
Molodaia volia. Moscow, 1907.
Molodia sila. Moscow, 1907–9.
Muzhitskaia pravda. Moscow, 1907.
Narodnaia mysl': Izdanie Surikovskogo literaturno-muzykal'nogo kruzhka. Moscow, 1911.
Narodnaia sem'ia: Dvukhnedel'nyi illiustrirovanno-literaturnyi narodnyi zhurnal. Moscow 1911–12.
Narodniki: Narodnoe izdanie. Moscow, 1912.
Nashe slovo: Politicheskaia, literaturnaia i satiricheskaia gazeta. Moscow, 1910–12.
Novaia pashnia. Moscow, 1907.
Novaia volia: Literaturnaia, obshchestvennaia i politicheskaia narodnaia gazeta. Moscow, 1907.
Ogni: Ezhemesiachnyi zhurnal. Moscow, 1912–13.

Ostriak: Kopeika-zlodeika: Iumoristicheskii i satiricheskii samyi veselyi narodnyi zhurnal. Moscow, 1909–14.

Prostaia zhizn': Narodnaia politicheskaia i literaturnaia gazeta. Moscow, 1907.

Prostoe slovo: Narodnaia politicheskaia i literaturnaia gazeta. Moscow, 1912.

Rodnoe gusliar: Ezhenedel'nyi iumoristicheskii i literaturno-khudozhesvennyi narodnyi zhurnal. Moscow, 1910–11.

Rodnye vesti: Zhurnal trudiashchegosia naroda. Moscow, 1910–12.

Trudovaia rech': Ezhednevnaia gazeta. Moscow, 1906.

Veselyi skomorokh: Novyi snogosshibatel'nyi sugubo-zaviratel'nyi iumoristicheskii i satiricheskii al'manakh-khokhotun i veselyi boltun. Moscow, 1911–13.

Zaria Povolzh'ia: Obshchestvenno-politicheskii zhurnal posviashchennyi interesam rabochikh i torgovo-promyshlennykh sluzhashchikh. Samara, 1914.

Zvezda utrenniaia: Narodnyi zhurnal. Moscow, 1912. Also published as *Zvezda iasnaia* and *Zvezda iarkaia.*

Trade Union Press

Bulochnik (bakers). Moscow, 1906.

Chelovek (waiters). Moscow, 1911.

Edinstvo (metalworkers). St. Petersburg, 1909–10.

Golos bulochnika i konditora (bakers). St. Petersburg, 1910–12.

Golos pechatnogo truda (printers). Moscow, 1916–17.

Golos portnogo (tailors). St. Petersburg, 1910–11.

Golos zhizni (textile workers). Moscow, 1910–11.

Golos zolotoserebrianikov i bronzovshchikov (gold and bronze workers). St. Petersburg, 1913.

Kuznets (metalworkers). St. Petersburg, 1907–8.

Metallist (metalworkers). St. Petersburg, 1911–14.

Nadezhda (metalworkers). St. Petersburg, 1908.

Nashe pechatnoe delo (printers). St. Petersburg, 1913–16.

Nash put' (central trade union). Moscow, 1910–11.

Nash put' (metalworkers). St. Petersburg, 1910–11.

Novoe pechatnoe delo (printers). St. Petersburg, 1911–13.

Ob"edinenie (consumers). Moscow, 1916.

Pechatnoe delo (printers). St. Petersburg, 1908–12.

Professional'nyi vestnik (central trades). St. Petersburg, 1907–9.

Proletarii igly (tailors). St. Petersburg, 1914.

Rabochii po metallu (metalworkers). St. Petersburg, 1906–7.

Rabochii trud (central trades). Moscow, 1914.

Russkii pechatnik (printers). Moscow, 1909–10.

Samopomoshch' (sales clerks). Ekaterinburg, 1908–9, 1911–12, 1914.

Tekstil'nyi rabochii (textile workers). St. Petersburg, 1914.

Vestnik portnykh (tailors). St. Petersburg, 1911–14.

Vestnik prikazchika (sales clerks). St. Petersburg, 1912–14.

Zhizn' pekarei (bakers). St. Petersburg, 1913–14.

Zhizn' prikazchika (sales clerks). Moscow, 1906–7.

Zhizn' zheleznodorozhnikov (railroad workers). St. Petersburg, 1910–11.

Social Democratic Party Press

Menshevik Publications

Luch: Rabochaia gazeta. St. Petersburg, 1912–13.

Nasha rabochaia gazeta. St. Petersburg, 1914.

Nasha zaria. St. Petersburg, 1913–14.
Novaia rabochaia gazeta. St. Petersburg, 1913–14.
Severnaia rabochaia gazeta. St. Petersburg, 1914.
Vpered! Moscow, 1917.
Zhivaia zhizn': Rabochaia gazeta. St. Petersburg, 1913.

Bolshevik Publications

Pravda (Rabochaia pravda, Severnaia pravda, Pravda truda, Za pravdu, Proletarskaia pravda, Put' pravdy, Rabochii, Trudovaia pravda). St. Petersburg, 1912–14.
Prosveshchenie. St. Petersburg, 1913–14.
Rabotnitsa. St. Petersburg, 1914.
Zvezda. St. Petersburg, 1910–12.

Other Socialist Publications

Sovremennyi mir. St. Petersburg, 1906–18.
Zhivoe slovo. Moscow, 1911–14.
Zhizn' dlia vsekh. St. Petersburg, 1910–17.

PERIODICALS AFTER 1917

Proletcult Magazines

Detskii proletkul't: Organ Tul'skoi Detskoi Kommunisticheskoi Partii (bol'shevikov). Tula, 1919–21.
Gorn. Moscow, 1918–23.
Griadushchee. Petrograd, 1918–21.
Griadushchia kul'tura. Tambov, 1918–19.
Gudki. Moscow, 1919.
Mir i chelovek. Kolpino, 1919.
Molot. Orenburg, 1920.
Pereval. Petrograd, 1922.
Proletarskaia kul'tura. Moscow, 1918–21.
Proletkul't. Tver, 1919.
Proletkul't. Vladikavkaz, 1919.
Proletkul'tovets. Moscow, 1920.
Rabochii klub. Moscow, 1924–28.
Sbornik Kostromskogo proletkul'ta. Kostroma, 1919.
Tvori! Moscow, 1920–21.
Zarevo zavodov. Samara, 1919.
Zhizn' iskusstv. Kologriv, 1918.
Zori griadushchego. Kharkov, 1922.

Other Periodicals

Drug naroda. Moscow, 1918.
Gornilo. Saratov, 1918.
Istinnaia svoboda (published by Obshchestvo istinnoi svobody v pamiat' L. N. Tol'stogo i trudovoi obshchinoi-kommunoi "Trezvaia zhizn'"). Moscow, 1920.
Krasnaia derevnia (provincial party committee). Voronezh, 1920–21.
Krasnyi ogonek. Petrograd, 1918.
Kuznitsa. Moscow, 1920–22.

Metallist (metalworkers' union). Petrograd, 1917–19.
Pechatnoe delo (printers' union). Petrograd, 1917–18.
Ponizovy. Samara, 1921–22.
Prizyv (trade union cultural workers). Moscow, 1923–25.
Rabochaia mysl'. Petrograd, 1917–18.
Rabochaia zhizn'. Moscow, 1917–20.
Rabochee tvorchestvo (worker correspondents). Nizhnii Novgorod, 1923–26.
Rabochii mir (central workers' cooperative). Moscow, 1918–19.
Rabochii zhurnal (Kuznitsa group). Moscow, 1924.
Revoliutsionnye vskhody: Zhurnal proletarskikh klubov (Narkompros Clubs Department). Petrograd, 1920.
Trud (Union of Consumer Societies). Petrograd, 1916–18.
Tvorchestvo: Literatura, iskusstvo, nauka, zhizn' (published by the Moscow Soviet). Moscow, 1918–21.
Vestnik kul'tury i svobody. Petrograd, 1918–19.
Voronezhskaia kommuna (provincial soviet executive committee and provincial party committee). Voronezh, 1919–23.
Zheleznyi put' (railroad workers). Voronezh, 1918–19.
Zhizn' zheleznodorozhnikov (railroad workers). Petrograd, 1917–18.

ANTHOLOGIES AND INDIVIDUAL COLLECTIONS OF WORKER WRITING

Aleksandrovskii, Vasilii Dmitrievich. *Rabochii poselok.* Moscow, 1919.
——. *Sever.* Moscow, 1919.
——. *Shagi.* Moscow, 1924.
——. *Stikhotvoreniia i poemy.* Moscow, 1957.
——. *Veter.* Moscow, 1925.
——. *Zvon solntsa.* Moscow, 1923.
Arskii, Pavel, and Iakov Berdnikov. *Serp i molot.* Leningrad, 1925.
Artamonov, Mikhail Dmitrievich. *Kogda zvoniat kolokola.* Ivanovo-Voznesensk, 1913.
——. *Ulitsa fabrichnaia.* Ivanovo-Voznesensk, 1913.
——. *Zemlia rodnaia.* Moscow, 1919.
Berdnikov, Iakov Pavlovich. *Tsvety serdtsa.* Petrograd, 1919.
Berezovskii, Feoktist Alekseevich. *Mat'* [1923]. Novosibirsk, 1960.
Bessal'ko [also Bezsal'ko], Pavel Karpovich. *Almazy vostoka.* Petrograd, 1919.
——. *Detstvo kuz'ki.* Petrograd, 1918.
——. *Kamenshchik.* Petrograd, 1918.
——. *Katastrofa.* Petrograd, 1918. 3d ed. Petrograd, 1919.
——. *Kuz'ma darov.* Moscow, 1927.
——. *K zhizni.* Petrograd, 1919.
——. *Nesoznatel'nym put'em.* Petrograd, 1918.
Bessal'ko, Pavel Karpovich, and Fedor Ivanovich Kalinin. *Problemy proletarskoi kul'tury.* Petrograd, 1919.
Bibik, Aleksei Pavlovich. *Izbrannye.* Moscow, 1955.
——. *Kogda khochetsia tolknut' solntse.* Kharkov, 1926.
——. *K shirokoi doroge (Ignat iz Novoselovki).* St. Petersburg, 1914. First published 1912 in *Sovremennyi mir.* Rev. eds. 1922, 1926, 1935.
——. *Na chernoi polose.* Moscow, 1922. Rev. ed. 1926.
——. *Polnoe sobranie sochenie.* 6 vols. Moscow, 1928–29.
——. *Rasskazy.* Moscow, 1924.
——. *Rasskazy.* Moscow, 1927.
Chernozem. 2 vols. Moscow, 1918, 1919.

Da zdravstvuet Krasnyi Oktiabr'! Moscow, 1918.

Eroshin, Ivan Evdokimovich. *Siniaia iurta: Pervaia kniga stikhov (1918–1928).* Moscow, 1928.

Eventov, I. S., ed. *Poeziia v bol'shevistskikh izdaniiakh, 1901–1917.* Leningrad, 1967.

Ezhov, I. S., and E. I. Shamurin. *Russkaia poeziia XX veka: Antologiia russkoi liriki ot simbolizma do nashikh dnei.* Moscow, 1925. Reprinted as *Russkaia poeziia XX veka: Antologiia russkoi liriki pervoi chetverti XX veka.* Moscow, 1991.

Filipchenko, Ivan Gur'evich. *Era slavy. Stikhi i poemy, 1913–18.* Moscow, 1918.

Gallereia sovremennykh poetov. Moscow, 1909.

Gan'shin, Sergei Evseevich. *Iskra.* Moscow, 1912.

——. *Pesni grazhdanina.* Moscow, 1916.

Gastev, Aleksei Kapitonovich. *Industrial'nyi mir.* Kharkov, 1919.

——. *Kak nado rabotat'.* Odessa, 1921; Moscow, 1922.

——. *Pachka orderov.* Riga, 1921.

——. *Poeziia rabochego udara.* Petrograd, 1918. Rev. eds. Petrograd, 1919; Kharkov, 1919; Moscow, 1923, 1926.

——. *Prokliatyi vopros: Belletristicheskii rasskaz.* Geneva, 1904.

——. *Vosstanie kul'tury.* Kharkov, 1923.

Gerasimov, Mikhail Prokof'evich. *Doroga.* Moscow, 1924.

——. *Elektrifikatsiia.* Petrograd, 1922.

——. *Negasimaia sila.* Moscow, 1922.

——. *Pokos.* Moscow, 1924.

——. *Stikhotvoreniia.* Moscow, 1959.

——. *Zavod vesennii.* Moscow, 1919. 2d ed. Moscow, 1923.

——. *Zemnoe siianie.* Moscow 1927.

——. *Zhelezoe tsvetanie.* Moscow and Petrograd, 1923.

——. *Zheleznye tsvety.* Samara, 1919.

Gmyrev, Aleksei Mikhailovich. *Stikhi.* Smolensk, 1961.

Gor'kii, M., A. Serebrov, and A. Chapygin, eds. *Sbornik proletarskikh pisatelei.* Petrograd, 1917.

Gornilo: Literaturno-politicheskii sbornik. Sumy, 1921.

Kalinin, Fedor Ivanovich. *Ideologiia proizvodstva.* Moscow, 1922.

——. *Ob ideologii.* Moscow, 1922.

——. *Pamiata F. I. Kalinina: Stat'i.* Petrograd, 1920.

Kalmanovskii, E. S, ed. *I. Z. Surikov i poety-surikovtsy.* Moscow, 1966.

Kirillov, Vladimir Timofeevich. *Golubaia strana: Vtoraia kniga stikhov.* Moscow, 1927.

——. *O detstve, more i krasnom znameni.* Moscow, 1926.

——. *Stikhotvoreniia.* Moscow, 1959.

——. *Stikhotvoreniia: Kniga pervaia, 1913–23.* Moscow, 1924.

——. *Stikhotvoreniia, 1914–1918.* Petrograd, 1918.

——. *Vechernie ritmy.* Moscow, [1928].

——. *Vesennii svet: Stikhi.* Vol. 1: *1913–22.* 2d ed. Moscow, 1928.

——. *Zheleznyi messiia: Stikhi o revoliutsii, 1917–20.* Moscow, 1921.

Kirillov, Vladimir, ed. *Proletarskie poety: Antologiia.* Moscow, 1925.

Korobov, Iakov Evdokimovich. *Pesni vechernie.* Vladimir, 1910.

Korolev, Vladimir. *Vsem skorbiashchim.* Iaroslavl, 1915.

Krasnaia ulitsa: Stikhi i pesni. Ivanovo-Voznesensk, 1920.

Krasnyi khor: Sbornik stikhov raboche-krest'ianskikh poetov. Moscow, 1921.

Krasnyi zvon. Petrograd, 1918.

Krep': Stikhi. Vologda, 1921.

Kryl'ia svoboda. Ivanovo-Voznesensk, 1919.

Kuznitsa: Literaturnyi sbornik. Moscow, 1923.

K zavetnoi tseli: Literaturnyi sbornik. Moscow, 1904.

Liashko, Nikolai Nikolaevich. *Rabochie rasskazy.* Moscow, 1924.
Literaturnyi al'manakh. Petrograd, 1918.
Loginov, Ivan Stepanovich. *Nakanune.* Petrograd, 1919.
——. *Stikhi.* Kostroma, 1958.
Malashkin, Sergei. *Muskuly.* Moscow, 1919.
Mashirov [Samobytnik], Aleksei Ivanovich. *Na perevale.* Petrograd, 1921.
——. *Pervoe maia.* Petrograd, 1923.
——. *Pod krasnym znamenem.* Petrograd, 1919. Many subsequent editions.
Molot: Sbornik tul'skikh proletarskikh pisatelei i poetov. Tula, 1921.
Na perelome: Literaturno-khudozhestvennyi sbornik kruzhka proletarskikh pisatelei. Orenburg, 1920.
Nashi pesni: Pervyi sbornik stikhotvorenii. Poety-rabochie. 2 vols. Moscow, 1913, 1914.
Nechaev, Egor Efimovich. [See also *U istokov russkii proletarskii poezii.*] *Guta: Polnoe sobranie sochinenie v odnom tome.* Moscow, 1928.
——. *Gutari: Izbrannye proza.* Moscow, 1938.
——. *Izbrannoe.* Moscow, 1955.
——. *Iz pesen starogo rabochego.* Moscow, 1922.
——. *Pesni steklianshchika.* Moscow, 1922.
——. *Po puti k prepodobnomu: Iz vospominanii starogo steklianshchika.* Leningrad, 1926.
——. *Trudovye pesni.* Moscow, [1911].
——. *Vecherniia pesni.* Moscow, 1914.
Obradovich, Sergei Aleksandrovich. *Gorod: Stikhi i poemy, 1916–1922 gg.* Moscow, 1923. 2d ed. Moscow, 1929.
——. *Izbrannye stikhi.* Moscow, 1935.
——. *Miting.* Moscow, 1924.
——. *Ognennaia gavan'.* Petrograd, 1922.
——. *Oktiabr'.* Moscow, 1922.
——. *Stikhi.* Moscow, 1970.
——. *Vintovka i liubov': Stikhi, 1921–1923.* Moscow, 1924.
——. *Vzmakh.* Petrograd, 1921.
Oktiabr'skie vskhody: Rabkorovskaia poeziia. Leningrad, 1925.
Oreshin, Petr Vasil'evich. *Alyi kram: Stikhi.* Moscow, 1922.
——. *Krasnaia Rus': Stikhi.* Moscow, 1918.
——. *Zarevo: Stikhi.* Petrograd, 1918.
Osen' bagrianaia: Sbornik literaturnogo otdela zavodskogo proletkul'ta Tul'skikh oruzheinykh zavodov. Tula, 1921.
Papernyi, Z. S., and P. A. Shatseva, eds. *Proletarskie poety pervykh let sovetskoi epokhi.* Leningrad, 1959.
Pasynok, Makar [I. I. Kogan]. *Izbrannye stikhi.* Moscow, 1930.
Pervyi sbornik proletarskikh pisatelei. St. Petersburg, 1914.
Pesni russkikh rabochikh: XVIII–nachalo XX veka. Moscow, 1962.
Platonov, Andrei [Andrei Platonovich Klimentov]. *Golubaia glubina: Kniga stikhov.* Krasnodar, 1922.
Pod znamenem pravdy: Pervyi sbornik obshchestva proletarskikh iskusstv. Petrograd, 1917.
Poety iz naroda. Moscow, 1901.
Poeziia rabochikh professii. Moscow, 1924.
Poletaev, Nikolai Gavrilovich. *Rezkii svet: Stikhi, 1918–1925.* Moscow and Leningrad, 1926.
——. *Stikhotvoreniia.* Moscow, 1920.
Probuzhenie: Al'manakh pisatelei iz naroda. 5 vols. Viazniki, 1912–14.
Proletarskie poety. 3 vols. Leningrad, 1935–39.
Proletarskii sbornik. Moscow, 1918.
Rabochaia vesna. Vol. 2. Moscow, 1923.

Rabochaia vesna: Literaturnyi sbornik gruppy "Rabochaia vesna." Moscow, 1925.
Rabochaia vesna: Sbornik gruppy proletarskikh pisatelei "Rabochaia vesna." Moscow, 1922.
Rodov, Semen, ed. *Proletarskie pisateli: Antologiia proletarskoi literatury.* Moscow, 1925.
Russkie samorodki. Revel, 1916.
Rybatskii [Chirkov], Nikolai Ivanovich. *Rasskazy.* Petrograd, 1921.
Sadof'ev, Il'ia Ivanovich. *Dinamo stikhi.* Petrograd, 1918.
———. *Izbrannoe (1913–1937).* Leningrad, 1938.
———. *Stikhotvoreniia.* Leningrad, 1964.
Sanzhar', Nadezhda. *Zapiski Anny.* St. Petersburg, 1910.
Savin, Mikhail Ksenofontovich. *Novye pesni.* Moscow, 1907.
———. *Pesni rabochego.* Moscow. 1902.
Sbornik proletarskikh poezii. Samara, 1919.
Sinibluznyi mai: Literaturno-khudozestvennyi sbornik. Moscow, 1925.
Sivachev, Mikhail G. *Na sud chitatelia: Zapiski literaturnago Makara.* Moscow, 1910.
———. *Prokrustovo lozhe (Zapiski literaturnago Makara).* 2 vols. Moscow, 1911.
Tribuna Proletkul'ta: Sbornik stikhov proletarskikh poetov. Petrograd, 1921.
U istokov russkii proletarskii poezii. Moscow, 1965.
V bure i plamen'. Iaroslavl, 1918.
Vekhi Oktiabria: Literaturno-khudozhestvennyi al'manakh. Moscow, 1923.
Vzmakhi. 2 vols. Saratov, 1919, 1920.
Zaitsev, Petr Egorovich. *Rodnye pesni: Stikhotvoreniia pisatelia-sapozhnika.* 2d expanded ed. Moscow, 1902.
———. *U verstatka: Razskazy i stikhotvoreniia.* Moscow, 1924.
Zavod ognekrylyi: Sbornik stikhov. Moscow, 1918. Second edition, 1919.
Zavolokin, P. Ia., ed. *Sovremennye raboche-krest'ianskie poety v obraztsakh i avtobiografiiakh s portretami.* Ivanovo-Voznesensk, 1925.
Zveno: Sbornik stikhotvorenii Khar'kovskoi sektsii proletarskikh pisatelei. Kharkov, 1921.

STUDIES OF RUSSIAN CULTURE, SOCIETY, AND LITERATURE

Bergman, Jay. "The Image of Jesus in the Russian Revolutionary Movement: The Case of Russian Marxism." *International Review of Social History* 35 (1990): 222–26.
Bernstein, Laurie. *Sonia's Daughters: Prostitutes and Their Regulation in Imperial Russia.* Berkeley, 1995.
Bibliografiia periodicheskikh izdanii Rossii, 1901–1916 gg. Leningrad, 1958.
Bogdanov, A. A. *O proletarskoi kul'ture, 1904–1924.* Moscow, 1924.
———. "Proletariat v bor'be za sotsializm." *Vpered! Sbornik statei po ocherednym voprosam,* no. 1 (July 1910).
———. *Voprosy sotsializma: Raboty raznykh let.* Moscow, 1990.
Bonnell, Victoria. *Iconography of Power: Soviet Political Posters under Lenin and Stalin.* Berkeley, 1997.
———. *Roots of Rebellion: Workers' Politics and Organizations in St. Petersburg and Moscow, 1900–1914.* Berkeley, 1983.
Borenstein, Eliot. *Men without Women: Masculinity and Revolution in Russian Fiction, 1917–1929.* Durham, 2000.
Bradley, Joseph. *Muzhik and Muscovite: Urbanization in Late Imperial Russia.* Berkeley, 1985.
Breitburg, S., ed. *Dooktiabr'skaia pravda ob iskusstve i literature.* Moscow, 1937.
Bristol, Evelyn. *A History of Russian Poetry.* New York, 1991.
Brooks, Jeffrey. "Popular Philistinism and the Course of Russian Modernism." In *History and Literature: Theoretical Problems and Russian Case Studies,* ed. Gary Saul Morson. Stanford, 1986.

——. "Readers and Reading at the End of the Tsarist Era." In *Literature and Society in Imperial Russia, 1800–1914,* ed. William Mills Todd III. Stanford, 1978.

——. *When Russia Learned to Read: Literacy and Popular Culture, 1861–1917.* Princeton, 1985.

Brower, Daniel. *The Russian City between Tradition and Modernity, 1850–1900.* Berkeley, 1990.

Brown, Edward J. *The Proletarian Episode in Russian Literature, 1928–1932.* New York, 1953.

Burds, Jeffrey. *Peasant Dreams and Market Politics.* Pittsburgh, 1998.

Carlson, Maria. *"No Religion Higher than Truth": A History of the Theosophical Movement in Russia, 1875–1922.* Princeton, 1993.

Chulos, Chris. "Myths of the Pious or Pagan Peasant." *Russian History,* Summer 1995.

Clark, Katerina. *Petersburg, Crucible of Cultural Revolution.* Cambridge, Mass., 1995.

——. *The Soviet Novel: History as Ritual.* 2d ed. Chicago, 1985.

Clements, Barbara, Barbara Engel, and Christine Worobec, eds. *Russia's Women.* Berkeley, 1991.

Clowes, Edith, Samuel Kassow, and James West, eds. *Between Tsar and People: Educated Society and the Quest for Public Identity in Late Imperial Russia.* Princeton, 1991.

Coleman, Heather. "The Most Dangerous Sect: Baptists in Tsarist and Soviet Russia, 1905–1929." Ph.D. diss., University of Illinois, 1998.

Driagin, K. V. *Paticheskaia lirika proletarskikh poetov epokhi voennogo kommunizma.* Viatka, 1933.

Dymshchits, A. "Iz istorii proletarskoi poezii 90-kh i nachala 900-kh godov." In *Proletarskie poety,* vol. 1. Leningrad, 1935.

——. "Ocherki po istorii rannei proletarskoi poezii i rabochego fol'klora." *Uchenye zapiski Leningradskogo pedagogicheskogo instituta im A. I. Gertsen.* Leningrad, 1937.

Eidinova, V. V. "K tvorcheskoi biografii A. Platonova." *Voprosy literatury* 3 (1978): 213–28.

Eklof, Ben. *Russian Peasant Schools.* Berkeley, 1986.

Engel, Barbara Alpern. *Between the Fields and the City: Women, Work, and Family in Russia, 1861–1914.* Cambridge, 1994.

Engelstein, Laura. *Castration and the Heavenly Kingdom.* Ithaca, 1999.

——. *The Keys to Happiness: Sex and the Search for Modernity in Fin-de-Siècle Russia.* Ithaca, 1992.

Engelstein, Laura, and Stephanie Sandler, eds. *Self and Story in Russian History.* Ithaca, 2000.

Eventov, I. S. "Proletarskie poety." In *Istoriia russkoi literatury.* Moscow and Leningrad, 1954.

——, ed. *Poeziia v bol'shevistskikh izdaniiakh, 1901–1917.* Leningrad, 1967.

Evtukhov, Catherine. *The Cross and the Sickle: Sergei Bulgakov and the Fate of Russian Religious Philosophy, 1890–1920.* Ithaca, 1997.

Fedotov, G. P. *The Russian Religious Mind.* Cambridge, Mass., 1946.

Ferro, Marc, and Sheila Fitzpatrick, eds. *Culture et révolution.* Paris, 1989.

Figes, Orlando, and Boris Kolonitskii. *Interpreting the Russian Revolution: The Language and Symbols of 1917.* New Haven, 1999.

Fitzpatrick, Sheila, Alexander Rabinowitch, and Richard Stites, eds. *Russia in the Era of NEP.* Bloomington, 1991.

Frank, Stephen. *Crime, Cultural Conflict, and Justice in Rural Russia, 1856–1914.* Berkeley, 1999.

Frank, Stephen, and Mark Steinberg, eds. *Cultures in Flux: Lower-Class Values, Practices, and Resistance in Late Imperial Russia.* Princeton, 1994.

Freeze, Gregory. "Counter-reformation in Russian Orthodoxy: Popular Response to Religious Innovation, 1922–1925." *Slavic Review* 54, no. 2 (Summer 1995): 305–39.

——. "Subversive Piety: Religion and the Political Crisis in Late Imperial Russia." *Journal of Modern History* 68 (June 1996): 308–50.

Friche, V. M. *Proletarskaia poeziia.* 3d ed. Moscow, 1919.

Fueloep-Miller, René. *The Mind and Face of Bolshevism* [1927]. New York, 1965.

Goldman, Wendy Z. *Women, the State, and Revolution.* Cambridge, 1993.

Gorodetzky, Nadejda. *The Humiliated Christ in Modern Russian Thought.* New York, 1938.

Haimson, Leopold H. "The Problem of Social Identities in Early Twentieth Century Russia." *Slavic Review,* Spring 1988.

Halfin, Igal. *From Darkness to Light: Class, Consciousness, and Salvation in Revolutionary Russia.* Pittsburgh, 2000.

Hamm, Michael F., ed. *The City in Late-Imperial Russia.* Bloomington, 1986.

Hatch, John B. "The Formation of Working-Class Cultural Institutions during NEP: The Workers' Club Movement in Moscow, 1921–1923." *Carl Beck Papers in Russian and East European Studies.* Pittsburgh, 1990.

——. "The Politics of Mass Culture: Workers, Communists, and Mass Culture in the Development of Workers' Clubs, 1921–1925." *Russian History* 13, no. 2–3 (Summer–Fall 1986): 119–48.

Heldt, Barbara. *Terrible Perfection: Women and Russian Literature.* Bloomington, 1987.

Hubbs, Joanna. *Mother Russia: The Feminine Myth in Russian Culture.* Bloomington, 1988.

Inozemtseva, E. "Platonov v Voronezhe" *Pod"em* 1971, no. 2 (March–April): 91–103.

Istoriia russkoi literatury. 4 vols. Leningrad, 1980–83.

Ivanov-Razumnik [R. V. Ivanov]. *Istoriia russkoi obshchestvennoi mysli.* Vol. 1. St. Petersburg, 1914.

Johansson, Kurt. *Aleksej Gastev: Proletarian Bard of the Machine Age.* Stockholm, 1983.

Kelly, Catriona. *A History of Russian Women's Writing, 1820–1992.* Oxford, 1994.

Kelly, Catriona, and David Shepherd, eds. *Constructing Russian Culture in the Age of Revolution: 1881–1940.* Oxford, 1998.

Kernick, Barbara. "Die Lyriker der 'Kuznica' (1920–1922)." In *Von der Revolution zum Schriftstellerkongress,* ed. G. Erler et al. Berlin, 1979.

Kharkhordin, Oleg. *The Collective and the Individual in Russia: A Study of Practices.* Berkeley, 1999.

Kheisin, M. L. *Obshchestva samoobrazovaniia sredi rabochikh.* St. Petersburg, 1908.

Khrenov, K. A. *Skromnye talanty.* Moscow, 1910.

Kizenko, Nadieszda. *A Prodigal Saint: Father John of Kronstadt and the Russian People.* University Park, Penn., 2000.

Kleinbort, L. M. *Ocherki narodnoi literatury (1880–1923 gg.)* Leningrad, 1924.

——. "Ocherki rabochei demokratii." *Sovremennyi mir* 1913–14.

——. *Ocherki rabochei intelligentsii.* 2 vols. Petrograd, 1923.

——. *Ocherki rabochei zhurnalistiki.* Petrograd, 1924.

——. "Pechatnye organy intelligentsii iz naroda." *Severnye zapiski* 1915, no. 7/8: 112–28.

——. *Rabochii klass i kul'tura.* Moscow, 1925. (2d ed. of *Ocherki rabochei intelligentsii.*)

——. "Rukopisnye zhurnaly rabochikh." *Vestnik Evropy* 52, no. 7–8 (July–August 1917): 275–98.

——. *Russkii chitatel'-rabochii: Po materialam, sobrannym avtorom.* Leningrad, 1925.

Klibanov, A. I. *Istoriia religioznogo sektantstva v Rossii.* Moscow, 1965.

Kline, George L. *Religious and Anti-Religious Thought in Russia.* Chicago, 1968.

Koenker, Diane P., and William G. Rosenberg. *Strikes and Revolution in Russia, 1917.* Princeton, 1989.

Kogan, I. S. *Proletarskaia literatura.* Ivanovo-Voznesensk, 1928.

Kornienko, N. V., and E. D. Shubina, eds. *Andrei Platonov. Vospominaniia sovremennikov. Materialy k biografii. Sbornik.* Moscow, 1994.

Kosarev, V. "Partiinaia shkola na ostrove Kapri." *Sibirskie ogni,* no. 2 (May–June 1922), 63–75.

Kratkaia literaturnaia entsiklopediia. 9 vols. Moscow, 1962–78.

Kratz, Gottfried. *Die Geschichte der "Kuznica" (1920–1932).* Giessen, 1979.

Kubikov, I. N. "Proletarskaia poeziia v nelegal'nyi i profsoiuznoi pechati (Epokha 90-kh i 900-kh godov)." *Literatura i marksizm* 1931, no. 3: 78–87.

——. *Rabochii klass v russkoi literature.* Ivanovo-Voznesensk, 1926.

Langerak, Thomas. "Andrei Platonov v Voronezhe." *Russian Literature,* no. 23–24 (15 May 1988), 437–68.

Laskovaia, M. *Bogoiskatel'stvo i bogostroitel'stvo prezhde i teper'.* Moscow, 1976.

Lebedev-Polianskii, P. I. See Polianskii, Valerian.

Levin, I. D. *Rabochie kluby v dorevoliutsionnom Peterburge: Iz istorii rabochego dvizheniia, 1907–1914 gg.* Moscow, 1926.

Lindin, V. G., ed. *Pisateli: Avtobiografii i portreti sovremennykh russkikh prozaikov.* Moscow, 1926.

Literaturnaia entsiklopediia. 10 vols. (only 1–9, 11). Moscow, 1929–39.

Lunacharskii, A. V. "Chto takoe proletarskaia literatura i vozmozhna li ona." *Bor'ba,* no. 1 (1914).

——. *Meshchanstvo i individualizm: Sbornik statei.* Moscow and Petrograd, 1923.

L'vov-Rogachevskii, V. L. *Noveishaia russkaia literatura.* 7th ed. Moscow, 1927.

——. *Ocherki proletarskoi literatury.* Moscow and Leningrad, 1927.

——. "Proletarskie poety." In L'vov-Rogachevskii, *Ocherki po istorii noveishei russkoi literatury (1881–1919).* Moscow, 1920.

Mally, Lynn. *Culture of the Future: The Proletkult Movement in Russia.* Berkeley, 1990.

——. *Revolutionary Acts: Amateur Theater and the Soviet State, 1917–1938.* Ithaca, 2000.

McDaniel, Tim. *Autocracy, Capitalism, and Revolution in Russia.* Berkeley, 1988.

McKee, W. Arthur. "Sobering Up the Soul of the People: The Politics of Popular Temperance in Late Imperial Russia." *Russian Review* 58, no. 2 (April 1999): 212–33.

McReynolds, Louise. *The News under Russia's Old Regime.* Princeton, 1991.

Masing-Delic, Irene. *Abolishing Death: A Salvation Myth of Russian Twentieth-Century Literature.* Stanford, 1992.

The Modern Encyclopedia of Russian and Soviet Literature. 10 volumes. Gulf Breeze, Fla., 1977–89.

Naiman, Eric. *Sex in Public: The Incarnation of Early Soviet Ideology.* Princeton, 1997.

Neuberger, Joan. *Hooliganism: Crime, Culture, and Power in St. Petersburg, 1900–1914.* Berkeley, 1993.

Ocherki istorii russkoi sovetskoi zhurnalistiki, 1917–1932. Moscow, 1966.

Os'makov, N. V. *Russkaia proletarskaia poeziia, 1896–1917.* Moscow, 1968.

Ovsianiko-Kulikovskii, D. N., ed. *Istoriia russkoi literatury XIX v.* 5 vols. Moscow, 1908–11.

Pankratov, A. S. *Ishchushchie boga.* Moscow, 1911.

Paperno, Irina. *Suicide as a Cultural Institution in Dostoevsky's Russia.* Ithaca, 1997.

Patrick, George, ed. *Popular Poetry in Soviet Russia.* Berkeley, 1929.

Peris, Daniel. *Storming the Heavens: The Soviet League of the Militant Godless.* Ithaca, 1998.

Pletnev, V. F. *Prav li t. Trotskii?* Moscow, 1924.

——. *Rabochii klub: Printsipy i metody raboty.* Moscow, 1923.

Poggioli, Renato. *The Poets of Russia, 1890–1930.* Cambridge, Mass., 1960.

Polianskii, Valerian (P. I. Lebedev). *Na literaturnom fronte.* Moscow, 1924.

Pretty, Dave. "The Saints of the Revolution." *Slavic Review* 54, no. 2 (Summer 1995): 276–304.

Priamkov, A. *Pisateli iz naroda.* Iaroslavl, 1958.

Prugavin, A. S. *"Brattsy" i trezvenniki.* Moscow, 1912.

Rabochii klass Rossii ot zarozhdeniia do nachala XX v. 2d ed. Moscow, 1989.

Read, Christopher. *Religion, Revolution and the Russian Intelligentsia, 1900–1912.* London, 1979.

Rosenberg, William G., ed. *Bolshevik Visions: First Phase of the Cultural Revolution in Russia.* 2d ed. Ann Arbor, 1990.

Rosenthal, Bernice Glatzer. "Eschatology and the Appeal of Revolution: Merezhkovsky, Bely, Blok." *California Slavic Studies* 11 (1980): 105–39.

——, ed. *Nietzsche and Soviet Culture.* Cambridge, 1994.

——, ed. *Nietzsche in Russia.* Princeton, 1986.

——, ed. *The Occult in Russian and Soviet Culture.* Ithaca, 1997.

Rubakin, N. A. *Chistaia publika i intelligentsiia iz naroda.* 2d ed. St. Petersburg, 1906.

——. *Etiudy o russkoi chitaiushchei publike.* St. Petersburg, 1895.

Russkie pisateli: Poety (Sovetskii period): Biobibliograficheskii ukazatel'. (Until 1992 titled *Russkie sovetskie pisateli: Poety. Biobibliograficheskii ukazatel'.*) 22 vols. to date. Moscow, 1977–92; St. Petersburg, 1994–.

Russkie pisateli, 1800–1917: Biograficheskii slovar'. 4 vols. to date. Moscow, 1992–.

Russkie pisateli v Saratovskom Povolzh'e. Saratov, 1964.

Russkie sovetskie pisateli: Prozaiki. Biobibliograficheskii ukazatel'. 7 vols. Leningrad, 1959–72.

Scherrer, Jutta. "Les Ecoles du parti de Capri et de Bologne: La Formation de l'intelligentsia du parti." *Cahiers du monde russe et soviétique* 19, no. 3 (1978): 259–84.

——. "'Ein Gelber und ein blauer Teufel': Zur Entstehung der Begriffe 'bogostroitel'stvo' und 'bogoiskatel'stvo.'" *Forschungen zur osteuropäischen Geschichte* 25 (1978): 319–29.

——. "L'Intelligentsia russe: Sa Quête da la 'vérité religieuse du socialisme.'" *Le Temps de la réflexion* 1981, no. 2: 134–51.

Seifrid, Thomas. *Andrei Platonov: Uncertainties of Spirit.* Cambridge, 1992.

Selishchev, A. M. *Iazyk revoliutsionnoi epokhi.* Moscow, 1928.

Shevzov, Vera. "Chapels and the Ecclesial World of Prerevolutionary Russian Peasants." *Slavic Review* 55, no. 3 (Fall 1996).

——. "Miracle-Working Icons, Laity, and Authority in the Russian Orthodox Church, 1861–1917." *Russian Review* 58, no. 1 (January 1999): 26–48.

——. "Popular Orthodoxy in Late Imperial Rural Russia." Ph.D. diss., Yale University, 1994.

Shishkin, V. F. *Tak skladyvalas' revolutsionnaia moral': Istoricheskii ocherk.* Moscow, 1967.

Siegelbaum, Lewis H., and Ronald Grigor Suny, eds. *Making Workers Soviet: Power, Class, and Identity.* Ithaca, 1994.

Sochor, Zenovia. *Revolution and Culture: The Bogdanov-Lenin Controversy.* Ithaca, 1988.

Steinberg, Mark. Introduction to Maxim Gorky, *Untimely Thoughts: Essays on Revolution, Culture, and the Bolsheviks, 1917–1918,* trans. Herman Ermolaev. New Haven, 1995.

——. *Moral Communities: The Culture of Class Relations in the Russian Printing Industry, 1867–1907.* Berkeley, 1992.

——. *Voices of Revolution, 1917.* New Haven, 2001.

Stites, Richard. *Revolutionary Dreams: Utopian Vision and Revolutionary Life in the Russian Revolution.* Oxford, 1989.

Sylvester, Roshanna. "Crime, Masquerade, and Anxiety: The Public Creation of Middle-Class Identity in Pre-revolutionary Odessa, 1912–1916." Ph.D. diss., Yale University, 1998.

Terras, Victor, ed. *Handbook of Russian Literature.* New Haven, 1985.

Thurston, Gary. "The Impact of Russian Popular Theater, 1886–1915." *Journal of Modern History* 55 (June 1983): 237–67.

Trudy pervogo vserossiiskogo s"ezda deiatelei obshchestv narodnykh universitetov i drugikh prosvetitel'nykh uchrezhdenii chastnoi initsiativy (S-Peterburg 3–7 ianvaria 1908 g.). St. Petersburg, 1908.

Tumarkin, Nina. *Lenin Lives! The Lenin Cult in Soviet Russia.* Cambridge, Mass., 1983.

Vengerov, S. A., ed. *Russkaia literatura XX veka.* 3 vols. Moscow, 1914–16.

Volkov, A. A. "Proletarskaia poeziia." In *Russkaia literatura XX veka: Dooktiabr'skii period,* 3d ed. Moscow, 1964.

——. "Ranniaia proletarskaia literatura." In *Ocherki russkoi literatury kontsa XIX i nachala XX vekov,* 2d ed. Moscow, 1955.

Von Geldern, James. *Bolshevik Festivals, 1917–1920.* Berkeley, 1993.

Voprosy byta: Epokha "kul'turnichestvo" i ee zadachi. 2d ed. Moscow, 1923.

Voronskii, Aleksandr. "O gruppe pisatelei 'Kuznitsa': Obshchaia kharakteristika." In *Iskusstvo i zhizn': Sbornik statei.* Moscow and Petrograd, 1924.

Wagner, William G. *Marriage, Property, and Law in Late Imperial Russia.* Oxford, 1994.

Wildman, Allan K. *The Making of a Workers' Revolution: Russian Social Democracy, 1891–1903.* Chicago, 1967.

Williams, Robert C. *Artists in Revolution.* Bloomington, 1977.

——. "Collective Immortality: The Syndicalist Origins of Proletarian Culture, 1905–1910." *Slavic Review* 39, no. 3 (September 1980): 389–402.

——. *The Other Bolsheviks: Lenin and His Critics, 1904–1914.* Bloomington, 1986.

——. "The Russian Revolution and the End of Time." *Jahrbücher für Geschichte Osteuropas* 43, no. 3 (1995): 364–401.

Worobec, Christine. *Peasant Russia: Family and Community in the Post-Emancipation Period.* Princeton, 1991.

——. *Possessed: Women, Witches, and Demons in Imperial Russia.* De Kalb, Ill., 2001.

Young, Glennys. *Power and the Sacred in Revolutionary Russia: Religious Activists in the Village.* University Park, Pa., 1997.

Zelnik, Reginald, "Russian Bebels." *Russian Review,* July and October 1976.

——, ed. *A Radical Worker in Tsarist Russia: The Autobiography of Semen Ivanovich Kanatchikov.* Stanford, 1986.

——, ed. *Workers and Intelligentsia in Late Imperial Russia.* Berkeley, 1999.

Zel'tser, V. "Iz istorii sektantstva v rabochei srede (Sektanty v g. Nikolaeve v 1890–1900 gg. po neopublikovannym materialam)." *Voinstvuiushchii ateizm* 1931, no. 4 (April): 29–46.

Zernov, Nicholas. *The Russian Religious Renaissance of the Twentieth Century.* New York, 1963.

Index

Akhmatova, Anna, 128
Akselrod, Liubov', 142
Aleksandrovskii, Vasilii, 55, 91, 98, 132,
133–35, 136, 140, 156–57, 162, 173, 182
(photo), 190, 196, 200, 204–5, 218–19,
222, 240, 242, 244, 261, 264, 266, 288–
89 (biography)
Alienation and estrangement, 14, 31–34, 89–
93, 91, 97–101, 122–24, 128–29, 154,
157–58, 178–79, 222–23. *See also* Ambivalence and ambiguity
All-Russian Association of Proletarian Writers (VAPP), 56, 289, 301, 305, 308, 312
All-Russian Circle of Writers from the People,
45
Ambivalence and ambiguity, 5–6, 17–20,
144–46; concerning the nature of the self,
65–66, 99–101; concerning work, 71–73;
concerning collectivism, 105–6, 112–13;
of modernity as expressed by worker writers, 147–69, 190, 197–203, 209–13, 218–
23, 277–78, 281, 285–86; in revolutionary
project of remaking the world, 184–223.
See also Alienation and estrangement
Andreev, Leonid, 67, 75
Anthologies, 44–45, 52
Anti-Semitism, 86, 137, 150. *See also* Jews
Apocalypse, 146, 239–40, 246, 251, 263,
273–78, 281
Arskii, Pavel, 110
Artamonov, Mikhail, 157–58
Art and architecture, 126, 186, 247–48,
262–63
Artsybashev, Mikhail, 69
Atheism, 227, 230, 250

Baba Mar'ia. *See* Chernysheva, Mariia
Bakhtin, Mikhail, 199
Balalaika (people's magazine), 34, 49, 291

Bal'mont, Konstantin, 144, 300
Baudelaire, Charles, 6, 18, 147, 204n
Bauman, Zygmunt, 6–7, 187
Beauty, 4, 6, 71, 84, 124, 132, 144, 246,
265–66, 286; of the city and the modern,
150, 152–60, 180, 193–95, 199–201;
moral idealization of, 258–59; of nature,
169–73, 177
Belinskii, Vissarion, 63–64, 67–68, 142
Belousov, Ivan, 44–45
Belyi, Andrei, 52, 148–49, 207n, 255
Berdnikov, Iakov, 261
Berman, Marshall, 6, 152
Bessal'ko, Pavel, 51, 115–16, 191, 215–16,
256–57, 268–69, 296
Bibik, Aleksei, 71, 72, 87, 93, 155–56, 166–
67, 170–71, 176, 214, 238, 240, 243,
289–91 (biography), 295
Bible, 71, 126, 231, 236, 264
"Black Foam" (Gerasimov), 140
Blok, Aleksandr, 97, 140, 144, 207, 225–26,
255, 276, 300
Bogdanov, Aleksandr, 41, 55–56, 58, 60–61,
65, 103, 105, 107–8, 130, 141–42, 205,
207, 213, 230, 279, 284–85
Bolshevik revolution (October 1917): as
apocalypse, 246, 273–78; and the city,
162–63, 185, 190, 192, 216, 221; and religion, 248–56, 262–64, 267; and rise of
collectivism, 102–4, 106, 108–11, 118–
20, 141, 143
Bolshevism and Bolsheviks, 27n, 42, 46, 50–
51, 53, 55, 56n, 58, 116, 129, 135, 151,
173, 238; adaptation of religious symbols
and rituals, 230–31, 247–48, 253–55; antireligion campaign, 248–50, 253, 280;
criticism of worker writers' understanding
of socialism, 141–43, 193, 197–98, 205,
270, 272, 277–78, 281, 283–85; left Bol-

327